SCHOOL PSYCHOLOGY:

Past,
Present,
and Future

Second Edition

Thomas K. Fagan
The University of Memphis

Paula Sachs Wise
Western Illinois University

Published by National Association of School Psychologists

Copies may be ordered from
NASP Publications
4340 East West Highway, Suite 402
Bethesda, MD 20814
(301) 657-0270
(301) 657-0275, fax
e-mail: *publications@naspweb.org*
www.nasponline.org

ISBN 0-932955-90-8

Printed in the United States of America

Fourth Printing, 2002

10 9 8 7 6 5 4

From the NASP Publications Board Operations Manual
The content of this document reflects the ideas and positions of the authors. The responsibility lies solely with the authors and does not necessarily reflect the position or ideas of the National Association of School Psychologists.

NATIONAL ASSOCIATION OF SCHOOL PSYCHOLOGISTS

To

Ruth and Paul Fagan	Bella and Milton Sachs
Susan Fagan	Dan Wise
Shannon, Lance, and Colleen	Ben

and to past, present, and future generations
of school psychology students

Contents

CHAPTER 10 INTERNATIONAL SCHOOL PSYCHOLOGY 355

Thomas Oakland, University of Florida

Preface

For several years prior to the publication of the first edition of this book, each of us had searched for an appropriate textbook for graduate students starting out in the field of school psychology. We, and our students, had been particularly unhappy with the so-called "introductory texts" of the recent past which were actually edited books of in-depth chapters that seemed more suitable for specific advanced courses or seminars rather than for a general introductory course. Other available texts for an introductory course seemed more concerned with conveying the author's particular theoretical viewpoint than with providing a realistic overview of the past, present, and future of the profession of school psychology. The first edition of this text, then, was an effort to find a book that each of us could use in our own Introduction to School Psychology classes.

When we first discussed co-authoring an alternative to the books available on the market, we found that we were in strong agreement about the type of book each of us was searching for. Such a book would provide general information about the many facets of school psychology without overwhelming readers with details and references that are mandatory for more advanced students but less important and often confusing at this introductory level. Such a book would also provide an overview of some of the most important issues and challenges facing psychologists currently working in the schools. Such a book would be readable and thought-provoking, challenging excellent students to look forward to continuing their studies in school psychology while portraying the profession in an honest and realistic manner. We wanted a book that represented a "Best lectures in school psychology" philosophy. We were reasonably satisfied that the first edition of *School Psychology: Past, Present, and Future* was the type of book we had sought. Judging from the reactions we received from book reviewers, from our colleagues, and, most important, from our students, the first edition was a success.

We now offer you this revised and updated version of the book. We continue to address what we consider to be the most important topics and issues relevant to the history, the current status, and the future of the profession of school psychology. We are delighted that the National Association of School Psychologists has agreed to publish this second edition.

The book was developed around certain assumptions. First, we assume that the book will be used primarily as a text in courses designed to be the students' first examination of the profession of school psychology. Second, we assume that readers have had some undergraduate psychology coursework. Third, we assume that readers have come to school psychology training from a variety of backgrounds. Some students will have had limited experience in grade schools and high schools aside from their own 12 or so years as students and perhaps as parents of school children. Others have had experience in a variety of capacities within the school system. Our fourth assumption in our writing is that this book is only a small part of a student's total professional preparation. The information included will be discussed, expanded upon, and perhaps demonstrated through other classes and field experiences. Finally, we assume that those reading the book are bright and capable students, interested in the subject matter of school psychology.

Some readers may be wondering if school psychology is the "right" profession for them to pursue. Our experiences as trainers of school psychologists and as advisors to undergraduate psychology majors have taught us that some students are sure they want to become school psychologists, occasionally even as entering freshmen. They seem convinced from the start that school psychology is the best possible career option for them. They like children; they are interested, and have done well, in the subject matter of psychology; and they see school psychology as a logical way to combine these two interests.

Other students remain skeptical, sometimes throughout their graduate training and beyond. They debate between clinical psychology and school psychology or between school counseling and school psychology. Many are concerned about the amount of time they will spend testing relative to the amount of time they will spend counseling children.

Although both of us are strong proponents of school psychology, we recognize that it is not the ideal profession for everyone. Each student must make a personal decision, carefully weighing the advantages and disadvantages of the profession before making a final selection. Although career decisions are in no way irreversible, spending three years or more in training to gain knowledge and to acquire skills you may never use is neither efficient nor advisable.

We hope, among other things, that this book will help in the decision-making process for those of you struggling to determine whether school psychology is an appropriate professional identity for you. Our intention is to present a candid view of the past and present of school psychology while offering some educated hunches as to what school psychology may become in the future. We have attempted throughout the book to link the history of school psychology with current developments and with future professional directions.

Keep in mind as you read this book and throughout your studies that school psychology does not operate in a vacuum. When schools are under attack, when laws change, when new legislation is adopted, when societal changes occur—the impact of each of these developments is felt within school systems in general and within the profession of school psychology specifically. Changes from within the field of school psychology influence us also. When leading school psychologists support changes in professional roles and functions, when new intervention techniques are presented in the literature, when new and revised tests are published, all of these developments change the practice of school psychology.

We have attempted to provide a balance of "formal" information which we believe students need in their training with "less formal" information that students want. Throughout the book we have attempted to speak directly to our readers, to draw them into the discussion, and to get them actively involved as trainees within the profession of school psychology. We recognize that many of the readers of this book will be our colleagues of the future. With that thought in mind, we have provided some hints or guidelines to expedite the passage from student to professional.

Throughout this book we will be examining fundamental questions and dimensions regarding the nature and delivery of psychological services within the public schools. In this manner, Chapter 1 is organized around 14 basic questions often asked by beginning and prospective school psychologists. The intent of Chapter 1 is to provide critical information immediately that will be more fully treated throughout the book and likely throughout your training.

Chapter 2 presents an overview of the history of school psychology. The chapter relates the development of psychological services to schools in the context of the development of psychology and education and the changing treatment and status of children in America. A major premise of the chapter is that the history of school psychology can be divided logically into two eras: the Hybrid years (1890-1969) and the Thoroughbred years (1970-present).

Chapter 3 examines the unique opportunities and challenges available to those who choose to practice psychology within the educational context. Included is a discussion of the goals and purposes of education, the structure of regular education, special education, administration, and special services, arrangements for the delivery of psychological services, and the significance of power and authority relationships in the system. The chapter also addresses the issue of clientage: who is the client of the school psychologist? The child? Parents? Teachers? Administrators? School Board? The notion of the school psychologist as a "guest in the house of education" is first presented in Chapter 3. In addition to the traditional public school setting for the school psychologist, Chapter 3 contains a discussion of the employment context of the school psychologist employed in alternative settings (e.g., clinics, hospitals).

Chapter 4 examines the various roles and functions of school psychologists, including a discussion of which of the roles are most common and most appropriate. The roles and functions of school psychologists are presented within the context of the ultimate goal of school psychology; that is, helping children. The variables that influence the roles and functions of individual psychologists are addressed as well. References are suggested that should enable readers to learn more about many of the topics presented briefly in Chapter 4.

Chapter 5 focuses on the topics of professional evaluation and accountability. The chapter examines the ways in which school psychological services are planned and evaluated and suggests methods for improving not only the effectiveness of school psychology, but also the methods by which school psychology is judged. The importance of professional accountability and evaluation for the school psychologist is emphasized.

Chapter 6 examines such topics as the training of school psychologists, professional standards, issues of accreditation, and the need for continuing professional development. Various models of training are presented, and readers are introduced to the types and levels of training which coexist in school psychology. Opportunities for continuing professional development are also discussed.

Chapter 7 focuses upon the symbols and definitions of professions. An effort has been made to answer the question, *To what extent is school psychology a profession?* The chapter addresses the notions of regulation and control of the profession of school psychology through accreditation, credentialing, and practice regulations. Practice regulations includes a discussion of the legal and ethical aspects of school psychological services. Factors controlling the profession of school psychology and suggestions for role and function change are also put forth.

Chapter 8 presents information about field experiences in school psychology including practicum placements and internship settings, as well as post-internship employment in traditional and non-traditional settings. Chapter 8 also addresses some of the factors involved in selecting and obtaining an internship and eventually a more permanent employment setting. A discussion of internship guidelines and provider standards is given that expands upon earlier discussions of credentialing and training guidelines. The problems of professional stress and burnout are also discussed.

Chapter 9 provides a discussion of the past, present, and future of school psychology in Canada. Topics such as roles and functions, training, and regulation are discussed. Chapter 9 is a new addition to the book and one which we hope provides Canadian readers with some information of particular interest to them.

Chapter 10, another new addition to the second edition of this book, expands the scope of the book to the practice of school psychology around the world. This international perspective should provide an interesting view for all readers in the United States, Canada, and elsewhere. As with the Canadian chapter, topics discussed include roles and functions, training, and regulation.

Chapter 11 presents some ideas as to what the future of school psychology may be and what it could be. The authors' personal predictions are given in the context of those of other authors. Ideas and suggestions to facilitate a positive future for school psychology are also presented.

One particularly unique feature of this book is the attention we have paid to the information our students want to know. From the 14 questions posed in Chapter 1, to the exercises following many chapters, to Appendix A, which allows readers to gather and organize material regarding national and state organizations, as well as rules and regulations that govern the practice of school psychology, in all of these we have tried to remain cognizant of who our readers are and what they want and need to know to become successful professionals.

As noted above we designed the text to be read within the context of a total school psychology curriculum or program. Readers will notice frequent references in the book to other courses and areas of study (e.g., consultation, interventions, and assessment). In writing an introductory book in a field, it is necessary in the interest of time and space to discuss many vital issues quite briefly. Although we have emphasized particular areas (e.g., demographics, history, and role and function), we have also attempted to be as inclusive of other important ideas as possible even though some are only briefly treated. We are confident that readers will learn more about these concepts and issues throughout their training.

ACKNOWLEDGMENTS

Special thanks go to the following individuals who have contributed their time and talents:

Jason Craggs, University of Memphis
Marilyn Brazier, National Assocation of School Psychologists
Gina Grieb, National Association of School Psychologists
Joshua Magelby, University of Memphis
Paul Mendez, National Assocation of School Psychologists
Linda Morgan, National Assocation of School Psychologists
Jack A. Naglieri, Ohio State University
Jerry Oliver, Western Illinois University
Nancy Sherer, Western Illinois University
Perri Dawn Wells, University of Memphis

Introduction to the Field of School Psychology

It is often difficult for individuals immersed in a profession to describe that profession to others not similarly immersed. In an effort to circumvent this difficulty, our introduction to the field of school psychology begins with responses to several questions about the field frequently asked by prospective and new students and by others seeking basic information about school psychology. The questions and responses provide a quick synopsis of the major aspects of professional school psychology. Much of this information is explored in greater detail in other parts of the book. The questions include:

1. What is a school psychologist?
2. What are the most common services provided?
3. What are the most common settings in which school psychologists are employed?
4. At what levels are school psychologists trained?
5. How do school psychologists differ from other psychologists?
6. How are practitioners credentialed for practice?
7. How many school psychologists are there?
8. How are school psychologists dispersed geographically?
9. What is the typical service ratio of school psychologists to school-age children?
10. To what professional associations do school psychologists belong?
11. What are the major journals in the field of school psychology?
12. Do school psychologists have standards for professional practice?
13. What contract and salary arrangements are most common?
14. How attractive are job prospects for trainees?

The questions, and this entire book, are about the who, what, when, where, and why of school psychology. The questions are not about *how to do* school psychology. In several instances we provide data from surveys, often employing the membership of the National Association of School Psychologists (NASP) or its National Certification System. We believe the databases of these studies are among the best available and that the results provide the most representative and reliable demographic and practice information. In some analyses we combine data from more than one source. Data like those reported in this book have been used for the preparation of national-level career profiles about psychologists and school psychologists that appear in *Mental Health, United States, 1996* (Manderscheid & Sonnenschein, 1996) for example.

Following responses to the 14 questions, we present a position on the primary role and function of the school psychologist. In contrast to some authors, it is our opinion that the assessment role is among the primary roles of the school psychologist. This role is broadly construed to consider assessment of children, systems, programs, and families. It clearly is not limited to testing. It is our opinion that all roles and functions of the school psychologist necessarily involve assessment and that the school psychologist is among the most expert assessment specialists in the educational setting.

RESPONSES TO COMMON QUESTIONS ABOUT SCHOOL PSYCHOLOGY

What Is a School Psychologist?

Most professions elude precise definition. This is because such definitions are difficult to write and achieve consensus on and because, by defining a profession (e.g., who they are and what they do), professionals fear giving the impression that the rest of the field of practice belongs to someone else. Such so-called turf issues are at the core of the position of the American Psychological Association (APA) to treat training and credentialing issues generically; even the APA "Specialty Guidelines for the Delivery of Services By School Psychologists" were couched in complicated policies of training, titles, and broad areas of function (APA, 1981). Though less concerned with generic issues, the National Association of School Psychologists (NASP) also has defined the school psychologist in terms of its own policies and standards (NASP, 1997b). At its website *(www.nasponline.org)*, NASP answers the question "Who are school psychologists?" as follows:

> School psychologists have specialized training in both psychology and education. They use their training and skills to team with educators, parents, and other mental health professionals to

ensure that every child learns in a safe, healthy, and supportive environment. School psychologists understand school systems, effective teaching and successful learning.... School psychologists can provide solutions for tomorrow's problems through thoughtful and positive actions today.

The NASP description then mentions levels of training and the major types of services provided and the settings in which school psychologists work.

In 1998, APA's Commission for the Recognition of Specialties and Proficiencies in Professional Psychology (CRSPPP) approved the "Petition for Reaffirmation of the Specialty of School Psychology" (Petition for Reaffirmation, 1997). The lengthy document provides an abundance of viewpoints about the field. Its shorter archival description defines school psychology as follows:

School Psychology is a general practice and health service provider specialty of professional psychology that is concerned with the science and practice of psychology with children, youth, families; learners of all ages; and the schooling process. The basic education and training of school psychologists prepares them to provide a range of psychological assessment, intervention, prevention, health promotion, and program development and evaluation services with a special focus on the developmental processes of children and youth within the context of schools, families, and other systems.... School psychologists are prepared to intervene at the individual and system level, and develop, implement, and evaluate preventive programs. In these efforts, they conduct ecologically valid assessments and intervene to promote positive learning environments within which children and youth from diverse backgrounds have equal access to effective educational and psychological services to promote healthy development (Archival Description of the Specialty, 1998, p. 8).

The petition is perhaps the most complete description of the specialty of school psychology available, although it is slanted toward doctoral professional psychologists (but without actually stating such).

Another comprehensive description appears in *School Psychology: A Blueprint for Training and Practice II* (Ysseldyke, Dawson, Lehr, Reschly, Reynolds, & Telzrow, 1997). To the extent the document serves as a definition of school psychology, it does so by describing the functions of school psychologists in 10 domains: data-based decision making and accountability; interpersonal communication, collaboration, and consultation; effective instruction and development of cognitive/academic skills; socialization and development of life competencies; student diversity in development and learning; school structure, organization, and climate; prevention, wellness promotion, and crisis intervention; home/school/community collaboration; research and program evaluation; and legal, ethical practice, and professional development. It is a description of what the school psychologist should strive to be in the future rather than a description of the contemporary school psychologist. The authors do not present a concise definition of the field of school psychology.

Other definitions tend to be brief and general. For example, an early description by Walter (1925) simply referred to the purpose of the school psychologist as "to bring to bear upon educational problems the knowledge and technique which have been developed by the science of psychology" (p. 167). A similar viewpoint was expressed by Bardon and Bennett (1974): "School psychology differs from other psychological specialties in that it brings psychological knowledge, skills, and techniques to bear on the problems presented by the school as a total, unique place in which people live and work and on the problems of the people living in the school" (p. 8). Magary (1966) identified more than a dozen brief statements attempting to define the school psychologist that were published in the early 1960s. Each of them would be, in part at least, true today. The International School Psychology Association (ISPA) published a set of guidelines that help to define school psychology (Oakland & Cunningham, 1997). These guidelines are described in Chapter 10.

For the purposes of this book, the school psychologist is defined as follows:

A school psychologist is a professional psychological practitioner whose general purpose is to bring a psychological perspective to bear on the problems of educators and the clients educators serve. This perspective is derived from a broad base of training in educational and psychological foundations as well as specialty preparation, resulting in the provision of comprehensive psychological services of a direct and indirect nature.

Our definition draws upon existing viewpoints, links the field to training in educational and psychological foundations as well as specialty training, and also indicates the importance of comprehensive service provision. The overarching identity of school psychology is in terms of the perspective and the setting in which it is brought to bear. The definition is not specifically linked to issues of credentialing and levels of training, which guide the definitions of the APA and NASP, nor is the specialty confined to school settings. We also speak in terms of the provision of comprehensive services of both a direct and indirect nature. No specific roles and functions are stated or implied. Other definitions and descriptions of the school psychologist often exist in state-level credentialing and practice regulations, and in published training program descriptions.

School psychology also can be defined by demographic descriptions of persons in the field. Various sources provide data about gender, ethnicity, degrees, level of experience, and so on. The following figures are from the NASP membership renewal survey of November 1999.

Gender. (*N* = 14,949) Female: 72.30% Male: 27.70%
Median Years of School Psychology Experience: 11-15 years

Ethnicity (*N* = 14,489)	%
White	92.04
African-American	2.14
Other Hispanic	1.46
Other (Unspecified)	1.36
Asian American/Pacific Islander	0.93
Chicano/Mexican American	.91
Puerto Rican	.76
American Indian/Alaskan Native	.40

The female representation has increased by at least 5% in comparison to the figure cited in the first edition of this book (Fagan & Wise, 1994, p. 3). Departing from the format of other surveys, Reschly and Wilson (1992) reported that 62% of practitioners were married, 24% were divorced, and 14% were unmarried. Sixty-eight percent reported having children, with 20% saying their children were of preschool age and 40% that their children were of school age. The studies provide a fairly consistent picture of school psychology in the United States as a field that is highly feminized, and whose practitioners have more than a decade of experience, are usually married, and have children. The field has a persistently small representation of minorities in disproportion to the school population served. The median and mean ages of practitioners reported in Reschly & Wilson (1992) were 40.3 years and 41.4 years, respectively. Curtis, Hunley, Walker, and Baker (1999) reported a median age category of 41 to 45. An international perspective is provided by data from 54 countries and indicates that "school psychologists are typically between ages 31 and 39, and female (62%)," with 10 years of experience (Oakland and Cunningham 1992, p. 109).

What Are the Most Common Services Provided by School Psychologists?

Several surveys on the role and function of the school psychologist were reported in the first edition of this book (e.g., Smith, 1984; Smith & Mealy, 1988;

Reschly & Wilson, 1992; and the database of NASP). Overall, they found that school psychology practitioners reported spending 52–55% of their time in psychoeducational assessment, 21–26% in interventions (e.g., counseling and remediation), 19–22% in consultation, and 1–2% in research and evaluation. Few national surveys have been conducted since then, and their results are not as easily compared. For example, Reschly and Wilson (1995) studied role change from 1986 to 1991-1992. Based on a 40-hour work week, they concluded that, "over one-half of the time [was] devoted to psychoeducational assessment, about 20% to direct interventions, 16% to problem-solving consultation, and 5% or less to systems-organizational consultation and research-evaluation" (p. 69). A subsequent analysis by Reschly (1998) comparing 1997 data to that of 1992 found virtually the same percentage of time allocations. That is, slightly more than half of practitioners' time was spent on psychoeducational assessment, 20% of time continued to be in direct interventions, 17% devoted to problem-solving consultation, 7% to systems/organizational consultation, and 2% to research/evaluation. However, during the period 1986–1997 there was an 8% reduction in the amount of time spent on special education eligibility services. In 1997 it was 59.9%.

The results reported by Curtis, Hunley, Walker, and Baker (1999), based on data from the 1994-1995 school year, do not lend themselves to overall percentage allocations. However, school psychologists reported spending considerable time on special education evaluations with 59.1% spending more than 70% of their time on such evaluations, and only 2.7% reporting they did not complete such evaluations at all. More than three-fourths of respondents also reported doing evaluations for purposes other than special education. They concluded that "school psychologists continue to spend the majority of their time conducting psychoeducational evaluations related to special education" and "relatively little time conducting psychoeducational evaluations for purposes other than special education" (p. 113). Although not reporting time spent in such activities, they also found that most respondents reported being engaged in consultation (97.4%), individual counseling (86.4%), in-service education programs (77.8%), and student group counseling or other group sessions (53.5%). These studies are also consistent with 1992 and 1993 surveys by Bontrager and Wilczenski (1997) and a time study analysis of practitioners in San Diego (McDaid & Reifman, 1996). Collectively, the research findings reveal a consistent pattern of school psychologist activities over at least a 15-year period. As the reliabilities of the measures employed are unknown, the small differences among some categories probably are not significant. It is clear that school psychologists spend the largest amount of their time in assessment-related duties, and less of their time involved in direct interventions and consultation. Research and evaluation functions have consistently carried the least weight across surveys of school psychologists reported in the literature. Thus, even though school psychologists may be active consumers of research and evaluation through journals and conferences, their active involvement in research and evaluation is infrequent. The pattern of these role and function studies has been replicated in a survey of services to charter schools, a relative newcomer to the education industry (Nelson, Peterson, & Strader, 1997).

What Are the Most Common Settings in Which School Psychologists Are Employed?

The 1999 NASP membership renewal survey reported the following distribution of employment settings (N = 13,462):

Setting	%
Public school	76.58
Private school sectarian	1.11
Private school nonsectarian	1.27
Residential institution	1.15
Private practice	4.54
State department of education	.45
Mental health agency	1.41
Preschool	1.18
College/university	6.92
Other	5.40

School settings of all types (except colleges and universities) appear to comprise about 80% of the employment setting data. Reschly (1998) reported data over three time periods, 1986, 1992, and 1997, as follows:

Year	Public School	College Univ.	Private Practice	Institution Residential	Clinic/Hosp. Other
1997	89.0	2.9	3.6	0.5	3.9
1992	86.0	1.3	4.2	1.0	7.5
1986	88.0	0.0	2.8	2.0	7.1

Curtis, Hunley, Walker, and Baker (1999) reported that 11.9% of school psychologists were engaged in some private practice, but only 2.8% worked in private practice full time (40 or more hours per week). An earlier sample of Nationally Certified School Psychologists (NASP, 1989) indicated that school psychologists most often worked in elementary and secondary school settings with both regular and special education programs. A division along lines of school and non-school settings suggested that non-school settings comprised about 10% of the respondents' (N = 647) settings. Thus, over the past two decades, the school continues to be the dominant employment setting (80–90% of respondents) with private practice consistently in the 3–5% range, and other settings making up the difference.

The most common employment setting for school psychologists is the single school district. Here the school psychologist serves the entire elementary or secondary school system or both, including regular and special educational programs. The next most common setting appears to be the cooperative agreement district, sometimes called a special education cooperative. Cooperatives have the advantage of combining the services and personnel of several districts to maximize service options at less overall cost than each district attempting to do the same individually. Such options are especially useful to small rural and suburban districts. Another service option is where the same school psychologist serves multiple school districts, perhaps under more than one contract. These three service options have been the traditional settings for school psychologists for most of the twentieth century.

As the surveys reveal, school psychologists also work in nontraditional settings such as public and private community or state agencies, including community mental health centers, developmental disability centers, or rehabilitation centers; independent and church-related private schools; and private practice either individually or in groups of service providers. Even within school settings differentiation occurs, with some practitioners serving elementary schools and others serving secondary schools, or some performing specific tasks (e.g., working with sensory-impaired children) and some working as generalists. Although traditional school settings dominate the field, the number (not necessarily the percentage) of school psychologists in nontraditional settings continues to grow (D'Amato & Dean, 1989). Practice settings are discussed in Chapters 3, 4, and 8.

At What Levels Are School Psychologists Trained?

Training of school psychologists has been available at the master's, specialist, and doctoral degree levels, corresponding roughly to 36, 60, and 90 semester hour minima. The average number of semester hours required of programs has been reported to be 40, 68, and 106, respectively (Thomas, 1998). Compared to the master's and doctoral degrees, the specialist degree is a relative newcomer to higher education (American Association of State Colleges and Universities, undated). These degrees are granted most often by colleges of education, although several psychology departments in colleges of arts and sciences now also grant specialist degrees. The hourly requirements for the specialist degree are about midway between the traditional master's and doctoral degree requirements and usually include credits for practicum and internship experiences. There may be a thesis or research report, or other culminating experience near the end of the degree, but the internship often substitutes for this requirement. The specialist degree is considered the equivalent of the master's degree plus 30 hours and fits conveniently into school district salary schedules that often include an M.A. plus 30 level. The degree is usually abbreviated as Ed.S. Doctoral degrees include the doctor of philosophy (Ph.D.), doctor of education (Ed.D.), and doctor of psychology (Psy.D.). The availability of Psy.D. programs has increased in recent years, and the degree is now available from free-standing professional schools of psychology (e.g., The California School of Professional Psychology initiated its program in 1999).

Information on school psychologists in training is provided in a comprehensive survey by Thomas (1998), which reports data for 1996-1997. This survey found at least 218 institutions in 46 states (including the District of Columbia) offering some type of school psychology training program. The survey report provides brief descriptions for 218 different institutions offering 294 programs. For responding institutions, there were 8,587 students enrolled in training, and there were 1,897 students who were graduated or recommended for certification in 1996-1997. Almost all programs required field experiences including both a practicum and an internship.

Sub-specialty training in several areas (e.g., neuropsychology, preschool, and vocational) is available at many institutions, though typically at the doctoral level only. Chapter 6 provides a list of the sub-specialization areas of U.S. and Canadian doctoral programs responding to a 1998-1999 survey. There is a discernible trend for students increasingly to seek post-master's-level education; the specialist level is rapidly becoming the entry-level expectation, and increasingly students are seeking doctoral training.

It is NASP policy that the educational specialist degree level is appropriate for entry into the profession. APA policy contends that the doctoral degree is appropriate for entry as a professional psychologist, but APA has made some concessions in its policy for school psychologists trained at the specialist level. Most state education agencies allow entry with the master's or specialist degree whereas entry into non-school and private independent practice is most often limited to persons holding the doctoral degree. The 1999 NASP membership renewal survey ($N = 14,650$) found that 54% held the specialist degree or equivalent training and 26% held a doctoral degree. Curtis, Hunley, Walker, and Baker (1999) reported that almost 79% of school psychologists were prepared at the specialist level or higher. Earlier studies of practitioners (Smith, 1984) found that 17% held the master's degree, 45% the master's plus 30 hours, 22% the specialist degree, and 16% the doctoral degree. Reschly and Wilson's (1992) data follow: 23% master's, 56% specialist, and 21% doctoral. Graden and Curtis (1991) found 28% doctoral representation in a sample that included university faculty as well as practitioners. Overall these studies support the national consensus that at least two-thirds of school psychologists continue to hold a specialist degree or its equivalent or a higher degree.

School psychology training programs exist in most states but their geographical distribution is based largely on historical patterns of program development of earlier decades. In the NASP *Directory of Graduate Training*

Programs (Thomas, 1998), which acknowledges the existence of 218 program institutions, eight states (California, Illinois, New Jersey, New York, Ohio, Pennsylvania, Texas, and Wisconsin) accounted for 47% of all training institutions with New York having 20 and California having 21 such institutions. Several states have no formal training programs (e.g., Alaska, Hawaii, New Hampshire, Vermont, and Wyoming).

How Do School Psychologists Differ from Other Psychologists?

There are many types of psychologists differentiated along lines of research and application. The most visible types of psychologists are those referred to as professional psychologists including school, clinical, and counseling psychologists. Industrial/organizational psychologists are also visible among applied psychologists but are less identified with the health services-provider conceptualization of professional psychology. Industrial/organizational psychologists work with the applications of psychology concerning problems of business and industry including organizational development, systems analysis, personnel selection, program evaluation, and human factors applications.

There are few clear-cut dividing lines among school, clinical, and counseling psychologists, and overlap in training and practice is common for some, though not all, practitioners. Bardon and Bennett (1974) identified the unique feature of school psychology as its focus on the school setting and the problems of those who live and work in the school. In contrast, clinical psychologists "assess and treat mental, emotional, and behavioral disorders. These range from short-term crises, such as difficulties resulting from adolescent rebellion, to more severe, chronic conditions such as schizophrenia" (APA, 1996, p. 6). Clinical psychologists usually are employed in medical facilities, clinics, and private practice. "Counseling psychologists help people to accommodate to change or to make changes in their lifestyle. For example, they provide vocational and career assessment and guidance or help someone come to terms with the death of a loved one. They help students adjust to college, and people to stop smoking or overeating" (APA, 1996, p. 6). Counseling psychologists usually work in settings similar to those of clinical psychologists. School psychologists are also distinguished from other professional psychologists by their background and training in educational foundations and applications, their concern for the individual learning and behavioral problems of students, their school-age clientele, and the educational settings in which they are most often employed. However, clinical and counseling psychologists occasionally work in school settings, and school psychologists may work in traditionally identified clinical or counseling settings. Of course, many clinical, counseling, and school psychologists are involved in teaching and research in higher education.

Because many school psychologists are trained in academic departments of educational psychology, they are sometimes confused with educational psychologists. The confusion is understandable, and in some locales the term "educational psychologist" is synonymous with "school psychologist." Generally, however, educational psychologists are trained as research psychologists and not as professional psychologists. They study the learning process generally rather than how individual children or groups of children adjust to that process. Thus, educational psychologists share much with other psychologists in the study of motivation, learning and cognition, and human development and how these can be applied to the improvement of education. School psychologists, obviously interested in such matters as well, concentrate on the study of those individuals and groups of children and youth (sometimes adults) who have difficulty with the process of education, including both its learning and mental health aspects. Educational psychologists often conduct research and evaluation on matters of school curriculum and are directly involved in teacher preparation programs in academic settings. Historically, school psychologists have shared kinship with both educational and clinical psychologists. For further information on the many types of psychologists, request a copy of *Psychology/Careers for the Twenty-First Century* from the APA (1996).

Persons also inquire as to the differences between a school psychologist and a guidance counselor. Although the boundaries between these two groups are sometimes blurred, significant differences in training and practice exist. School counselors historically have worked primarily with secondary school students providing academic and vocational guidance. In recent years there has been a trend for counselors to implement comprehensive developmental guidance programs throughout all school grades. In this role, counselors provide a total program that includes individual, group, and crisis counseling; developmentally appropriate classroom presentations; and teacher and parent consultation. School counselors are usually required to possess a teaching certificate, and often teaching experience, in order to be credentialed for school-based practice. They are usually hired to provide services to only one or two school buildings. Their training programs are nearly always housed in education colleges or departments. Trainees typically take few, if any, courses in departments of psychology, and there is much less emphasis on working with children having disabilities. Some of the guidance counselor's functions overlap with those of the school psychologist, including group testing, testing of student achievement, individual and group counseling, and teacher and parent consultation. In some districts, a secondary school may have building-based school psychologists and guidance counselors working together and their functions may overlap considerably. Many states now require school districts to have elementary counselors, and they too may be building-based. Generally, school psychologists work for entire districts or sets of schools and are not building-based. A few school systems have taken a broader pupil personnel services approach, employing persons trained in both guidance counseling and school psychology (e.g., Charlotte-Mecklinburg Schools in North Carolina).

There is also some overlap of school psychologist services with those of school social workers. School social workers provide services directly to children and their parents and consultation with teachers, and intervention services with students and parents, individually and in groups. School social workers and school psychologists often have similar training in counseling, interviewing, and psychotherapy, are assigned to several buildings or district-wide services, and do not need a teaching credential to acquire a school social work credential (Constable, McDonald, & Flynn, 1999).

How Are Practitioners Credentialed for Practice?

School psychology practice is regulated in school and non-school settings by different agencies, typically a state department of education (SDE) and a state board of examiners in psychology (SBEP), respectively. Each of these agencies grants a paper credential, and the SDE issues a certificate (the trend is to call this a license), whereas the board of examiners in psychology issues a license (sometimes called a certificate). There are often major differences in the criteria for obtaining a practice credential from these agencies. The most recent type of school psychology credential is that issued by the NASP National School Psychology Certification System. Although the Nationally Certified School Psychologist (NCSP) is not a practice credential, it serves to recognize the appropriateness of one's training and experiences, and thereby may facilitate the acquisition of state certification and licensing.

A candidate applies for the respective credential after completion of training, including field experiences such as practicum and internship. Requirements vary from state to state, and NASP's *Credentialing Requirements for School Psychologists* (Curtis, Hunley, & Prus, 1998) is a valuable source of information on certification and licensing. In some states school psychologists are eligible to apply for credentials as mental health counselors, certified professional counselors, and so on. Each state is different in its credentialing practices and requirements. As discussed in Chapter 7, credentialing is a complex but very important aspect of professional psychology.

Types of credentials tend to follow degree levels. Although almost all basic SDE credentials are available to persons holding master's or specialist-level training, non-school-setting licensing is most commonly available only to those holding doctoral degrees. The state-to-state variation is observable in the NASP credentialing book. Curtis, Hunley, Walker, and Baker (1999) found that among practitioners, 94.1% held state education agency certification as a school psychologist, 11.3% held a separate doctoral-level license as a psychologist or school psychologist, and 17.4% held a separate non-doctoral license (e.g., school psychologist, psychometrist, and psychological associate). Sixty-two percent held the NCSP, a considerably lower figure from the 76% reported by Reschly and Wilson (1992). The figure for NCSPs is currently about 50% of NASP members.

How Many School Psychologists Are There?

Highly reliable national estimates of the number of persons in the field of school psychology in the United States have never existed and are seldom available even at the state level. However, reasonable estimates have been made from surveys taken in several states, or by NASP and APA, and even from studies of the international school psychology community. For several years it was believed that there were about 40,000–45,000 school psychologists in the world (Catterall, 1979b). A more recent study based on 54 reporting countries (including the United States) estimated 87,000 school psychologists (Oakland & Cunningham, 1992). A consensus figure of 25,000 school psychologists in the United States has been estimated in recent years. Table 1.1 provides state and regional figures for June 1999, based on a NASP membership of 21,408. The figures provide the best available estimates of the state-by-state distribution of school psychologists. Assuming that perhaps 70% of all school psychologists belong to NASP, the 25,000 figure seems reasonable, and perhaps conservative.

How Are School Psychologists Dispersed Geographically?

Table 1.1 presents a regional and state distribution of school psychologists

TABLE 1.1 State/Regional NASP Membership Data (June 1999)		
REGION	**MEMBERS/%**	**STATES**
Northeast	7,166/33.35%	CT (692), DC (50), DE (89), MD (506), ME (145), MA (793), NH (137), NJ (861), NY (2391), PA (1190), PR (78), RI (169), VT (65)
Southeast	4,570/21.27%	AL (118), AR (93), FL (874) GA (468), KY (272), LA (202), MS (73), NC (476), SC (301), TN (339), TX (740), VA (532), WV (82)
Central	5,205/24.22%	IL (1150), IN (414), IA (249) KS (248), MI (549), MO (131), MN (358), ND (47), NE (245) OH (960), OK (123), SD (92) WI (639)
West	4,265/19.85%	AK (75), AZ (488), CA (1828), CO (412), HI (25), ID (118) MT (89), NV (166), NM (96), OR (266), UT (169), WA (482), WY (51).
Other (International)	282/1.31%	
Total Membership	21,408/100%	

based on NASP membership data for June 1999 (June data represent the largest membership for the year). The NASP regional structure, established in the early 1970s, was revised in the late 1990s. The shift from five to four regions make regional membership comparisons with earlier data difficult. Where previously the northeast and north central regions contained more than half the entire NASP membership, there is greater balance among the regions now. As with the previous structure, however, the five largest membership states [California (1,828), Illinois (1,150), New York (2,391), Ohio (960), and Pennsylvania (1,190)] continue to have 35% of the entire membership (N = 7,519 of NASP's total membership of 21,408). A much earlier study of APA Division of School Psychology members (Hyman, Bilker, Freidman, Marino, & Roessner, 1973) revealed these same states accounted for 51% of the total, suggesting the relative professional influence of these states (and New Jersey) in the development of school psychology in the past several decades. Another measure of dispersion is provided by Reschly and Wilson (1992) and Reschly (1998), whose survey respondents were employed in settings as follows: largely urban (27-28%), largely suburban (33-38%), largely rural (21%), and combination settings (14-17%). Another survey indicated 30.3% urban, 44.8% suburban, and 24.9% rural (Curtis, Hunley, Walker, and Baker, 1999). The data, however, do not necessarily represent the situation in a particular state. For example, in Ohio, which might be considered by some to be a fairly urban and populous state, the dispersion was identified as approximately 29% urban, 39% suburban, and 32% rural (Mcloughlin, Leless, & Thomas, 1998). How school psychologists are dispersed geographically can influence practice and professional organization, especially at the state level.

In Canada, school psychologists are available in all the provinces and territories, but their distribution tends to cluster in the southern portions of the provinces and in major population centers. From an international perspective, school psychologists are dispersed predominantly in North America, Europe, the Mediterranean, and in some historically British colonies of Africa and the Far East. The availability of school psychological services tends to correspond to the availability of educational and special educational services (Catterall, 1979b) and to a country's level of economic development (Oakland & Cunningham, 1992). For greater detail on Canadian and international distributions see Chapters 9 and 10, respectively.

What Is the Typical Service Ratio of School Psychologists to School-Age Children?

The ratio of practitioners to children served is a popular concept in our literature and frequently used to judge quantitatively the acceptability of services. The ratio of school psychologists to school-age children has continued to improve throughout the century (Fagan, 1988b; Curtis, Hunley, Walker, & Baker, 1999). Wide variation within and among states exists. The range may be as high (favorable) as one school psychologist to 500 school children or as low (unfavorable) as 1:7,000 in some settings. For example, in 1994, California reported a statewide ratio of 1:2,030 (up from 1:1,793 in 1991), and for its counties the ratios ranged from 1:1,199–3,357 (Per Your Request, 1995). The NASP (1999) Membership Renewal Survey reported that 56% of 13,441 respondents worked with a ratio of 1:1,000 or less, and only 15% reported a ratio greater than 3,000. A survey based on the 1994-1995 school year (Curtis et al., 1999) with 1,430 respondents, reported approximately 49% working with a ratio of 1:1,500 or less, and approximately 12% reported a ratio greater than 3,000. This estimate is consistent with an earlier survey finding of 1:1,875 that suggested the ratio had remained the same between 1989 and 1993 (Lund, Reschly, & Connolly Martin, 1998). The Lund et al. publication also reports regional estimates and a discussion of factors influencing the ratio (e.g., per pupil expenditures by state). The most recent national survey (Thomas, 1999b) estimates the average ratio to be 1:1,816.

Ideal ratios have been recommended by professional associations. NASP (1997b) recommends 1:1,000 while APA (1981) recommends 1:2,000. NASP has recommended a ratio of 1:1,000 since 1984 (NASP, 1984b). NASP qualifies its ratio by also recommending a maximum of four schools served by a school psychologist. Given the number of public school buildings in the country (i.e., about 86,000) we already have approximately one school psychologist for every four school buildings but only on a nationwide basis. At the local district level, many school psychologists serve more than four buildings even though some serve only one. By comparison, the recommended ratio for school counselors is 1:250 and for school social workers is 1:800 (Allensworth, Lawson, Nicholson, & Wyche, 1997).

Rural and urban setting ratios have been studied by Reschly and Connolly (1990), and historical comparisons of urban ratios have been studied by Fagan and Schicke (1994). These studies suggest that the best ratios are in suburban settings, and that rural and urban ratios do not differ significantly from each other or from the overall national ratio. However, in the previously cited report of California ratios, the 20 largest school districts ranged from 1:1,296 to 1:5,822.

Internationally, the median ratio is reported as 1:11,000 (Oakland & Cunningham, 1992; see Chapter 10 for more details). Practitioner-to-children ratios serve only as rough indicators of the quality of service provision. Nevertheless, they have been an important index of services for several decades.

To What Professional Associations Do School Psychologists Belong?

School psychologists belong to associations at the international, national and state levels. The International School Psychology Association (ISPA) is the best source of information about school psychology in other countries. The NASP and the Division of School Psychology in the APA (APA, Division 16) are the primary national organizations in the United States, with approximately

22,000 and 2,500 members, respectively. The Division of School Psychology is one of 52 active divisions in the 159,000 member APA. The Canadian Association of School Psychologists (CASP) is the primary association for school psychologists in Canada, although many belong to the Canadian Psychological Association in addition to CASP. Secondary organizations to which school psychologists belong are numerous (e.g., American Counseling Association and Council for Exceptional Children). Each state also has an organization of school psychologists that is usually an affiliate of the NASP. In most instances, the state organization for school psychologists is independent of the state psychological association, though in a few states school psychologists are organized as part of the state psychology group.

School psychologists are seldom organized on a regional basis across several states, but within states it is common for there to be regional and local groups affiliated with the state organization. For a discussion of professional associations and their development see Fagan (1993, 1996a), Fagan, Hensley, and Delugach (1986), and Oakland (1993). Several state associations have descriptive and historical publications. The cost of association membership varies considerably. Although national association annual dues are typically in excess of $100, state association dues range from $15 to $100 (Smith, 1997). Most organizations have special student membership rates allowing students the opportunity to become involved without dipping too deeply into already strained student budgets.

What Are the Major Journals and Newsletters in the Field of School Psychology?

School psychology journals are available as a function of association membership or on a subscription basis. Journals received as part of membership include NASP's *School Psychology Review*, Division-16's *School Psychology Quarterly* (APA members also receive the *American Psychologist*), and CASP's *Canadian Journal of School Psychology*. The ISPA has as its official journal *School Psychology International*, which is provided to members at a reduced subscription rate. Unaffiliated school psychology journals available by subscription include the *Journal of School Psychology* and *Psychology in the Schools*. The content of school psychology journals is similar though editorial policies vary (Wilczenski, Phelps, & Lawler, 1992). There are many other related journals that may be of interest to school psychologists. Some deal with broad issues and practices in professional psychology (e.g., *Journal of Consulting and Clinical Psychology, Professional Psychology: Research and Practice*), some with foundational research (e.g., *Developmental Psychology, Journal of Educational Research*), and some with specific orientations or practices (e.g., *Behavior Therapy, Exceptional Children, Journal of Learning Disabilities, Journal of Educational and Psychological Consultation, Journal of Psychoeducational Assessment, Mental Retardation*, and *Special Services in the Schools*). Only rarely has a state association published a journal, though newsletters have been commonplace (Fagan, 1986a).

National and international groups publish newsletters several times each year. These include the APA's *Monitor* and its Division of School Psychology's *The School Psychologist*, NASP's *Communiqué*, the *Trainers' Forum* from the Trainers of School Psychologists, and the *CDSPP Press* from the Council of Directors of School Psychology Programs. An independent newspaper, *The National Psychologist*, is a useful source of information especially for psychologists in private practice. Other sources on the literature of school psychology may be found in Fagan, Delugach, Mellon, and Schlitt (1985), Fagan and Warden (1996), French (1986), and Whelan and Carlson (1986).

Do School Psychologists Have Standards for Professional Practice?

Two codes of ethics are employed by school psychologists in the United States: that of the APA (APA, 1992; see Appendix C) and that of the NASP (NASP, 1997a; see Appendix D). In some instances, a state association of school psychologists will adopt one or both of these codes or may prepare a code for its own use. There are also ethics codes developed or adopted by the CASP (see Chapter 9) and by the ISPA (see Chapter 10). Standards also exist for the provision of school psychological services (APA, 1981; NASP, 1997b). Unlike ethics, provider standards attempt to specify acceptable levels at which services should be provided. These standards are expressed in terms of service ratios, employment conditions, breadth of services, agency relationships, and so on. Ethics and standards are discussed in Chapter 7.

What Contract and Salary Arrangements Are Most Common?

The 1999 NASP membership renewal survey produced the following salary information ($N = 13,813$):

Salary in Dollars	% Responding	Cumulative %
Under $10,000	5.94	5.94
10,000-14,999	3.20	9.14
15,000-19,999	2.50	11.64
20,000-24,999	2.78	14.42
25,000-29,999	3.24	17.66
30,000-34,999	7.65	25.31
35,000-39,999	10.55	35.86
40,000-44,999	12.26	48.12
45,000-49,999	11.15	59.27
50,000-54,999	12.77	72.04
55,000-59,999	8.09	80.13
60,000-69,999	11.26	91.39
70,000 and more	8.62	100.01

The low-end salaries probably reflect student members including interns and part-time employees. On the basis of the 1999 NASP data, Thomas (1999a) reported median and average practitioner salaries of $48,000 and $49,089, respectively. In 1994 the average salary was reported to be $43,000 (Dawson, Mendez, & Hyman, 1994). Earlier, Reschly and Wilson (1992) reported a median salary for practitioners of $35,800 and an average salary of $37,587. It appears that salaries have grown by about 30% in the past decade.

Thomas (1999b) presented salary data in combination with years of experience and education, revealing that salaries rose as a function of both. Dawson, Mendez, and Hyman (1994) provided data for a full-time practitioner's salary by age, gender, degree, and NCSP status, but not in combination (it is still a useful source of earlier data). Thomas and Witte (1996) made similar comparisons from a sampling of 10 states. Salaries appear to range widely as a function of length of contract, experience, teacher versus non-teacher pay schedules, and degree level. Gender differences, if any, are confounded by indications that males and females differ in the distribution of their experience and degrees (Thomas & Witte, 1996). Differences often are not large between specialist- (Ed.S) and doctoral-level salary schedules. Of course, the principles of supply and demand operate as well with some areas willing to pay considerably higher salaries owing to the relative scarcity of practitioners. A starting salary for a fully trained and credentialed beginning school psychologist in a school setting could range from $25,000 to $45,000. In most instances, an administrative position would provide higher pay partly because such positions involve 12-month contracts.

Some school psychologists belong to unions or other collective bargaining groups, which may also affect salaries. Collective bargaining arrangements exist mainly in urban areas where the school psychologists often may belong to the teachers' association and/or bargaining unit or may have their own bargaining unit. Curtis, Hunley, Walker, and Baker (1999) reported that 38.4% of respondents belonged to a union.

Full-time employment of 40 hours a week has been the most common employment arrangement. Reschly and Wilson (1992) reported that the average number of days in the school psychologist's contract was 202 and the median was 192. Curtis et al. (1999) reported similar data based on the 1994-1995 school year. The 1999 NASP Membership Renewal Survey reported that 55% had contracted for 180-199 days and 20% for 200-219 days. Since a "school year" is typically about 180–185 days, the survey data translate into a school year plus 2–4 weeks. These data are consistent with earlier data (Graden & Curtis, 1991) and suggest that the trend has been toward increased numbers of 10–month contracts and corresponding decreases in 9–month and 12–month contracts.

The relationship of salary and setting is not clear, though salaries in non-traditional settings may be higher. The additional salary, however, may be attenuated by the costs of liability insurance, equipment, travel, and the length of the contract. This is especially true of private practice settings. Some school psychologists choose to work part-time, a phenomenon that may become more popular as a larger number of practitioners retire but seek continued employment. Reschly and Wilson (1992) reported that part-time employment was typically a personal preference rather than a necessity. They also reported that 35% of school psychologists were engaged in some amount of outside secondary employment, averaging about $6,800 additional income. However, as was mentioned earlier (see employment settings), only a small percentage of school psychologists engage in private practice and even fewer engage in private practice on a full-time basis.

How Attractive Are Job Prospects for Trainees?

Despite occasional downturns related to economic recessions, the employment opportunities for school psychologists have been consistently favorable throughout the history of the field. In the Reschly and Wilson (1992) survey, among the 23% reporting they had not worked for 1 or more years since being certified as a school psychologist, only 15% (of the 23%) indicated "job not available" as the reason. The three more prevalent reasons were other professional work (32%), family responsibilities (20%), and graduate school (16%). The employment market in the 1990s was especially favorable, with a serious shortage of available personnel predicted to continue for several years. The best employment opportunities are in rural and developing states, school systems under pressure to increase personnel and services, major urban, and geographically isolated areas. The employment picture is favorable for doctoral as well as non-doctoral personnel. Having unique expertise such as a sub-specialization or fluency in a second language also will be helpful. Students not restricted to seeking a position in a specific geographic or service setting should have numerous employment options available. Earlier surveys suggested a favorable job market for school psychologists over the next two decades. For example, substantial vacancies existed for the 1987-1988 school year, and an updated report for 1989-1990 by Connolly and Reschly (1990) identified more than 500 vacancies for that year. Although the recessionary times of the early 1990s tightened school district budgets, the job market continued to be characterized by greater demand than supply, but the personnel shortage may have lessened (Lund, Reschly, & Connolly Martin, 1998). The shortages exist in practitioner and in academic settings and the employment market continues to look favorable.

PRIMARY ROLES OF THE SCHOOL PSYCHOLOGIST

Since early in the history of school psychology, practitioners and their trainers have been concerned about the roles school psychologists could and should play in the educational setting. For the past 80 years there has been concern that school psychologists should do more than merely administer and score psychoeducational tests facilitating the educational bureaucracy's efforts to remove children from the educational mainstream and place them in special educational programs. A corresponding theme of this literature is that the schools, not to mention the school psychologists themselves, would be better served through non-testing roles such as interventions including individual and group therapy, consultation, research and evaluation, and in-service education. Unfortunately, over time we began to see the issue as black and white: Either you supported the traditional assessment role or you supported a nontraditional, anti-assessment role. The roles were treated as though they were mutually exclusive. University trainers often espoused the nontraditional model (sometimes called the alternative services delivery model). Interns and first-year practitioners were apt to experience shock when they realized that the many roles for which they had been prepared were viewed as secondary to the psychoeducational evaluations and reevaluations they were expected to complete on the job.

The earlier predominance of the assessment role has continued across the century but has yielded to two other major roles for school psychologists: interventions and consultation. These three roles account for most of the school psychologist's time. However all roles of the school psychologist are based on assessment. The primary criticism of the assessment or child study role is not that it involves testing and other assessment-related tasks, but, rather the criticism lies in the fact that too often the assessment ends with the presentation of assessment data but without providing interventions for resolving the presenting problem. We take it for granted that educational placement decisions require assessment data. On the other hand, effective case consultations also require assessment of the relevant characteristics of the context and parties involved. Effective family therapy requires assessment of the family members individually and as a group. Effective staff or system development requires assessment of the strengths and weaknesses of the individuals in the system. Thus, all roles have underlying assessment functions.

We contend that it is the school psychologist's assessment expertise, viewed in its broadest context, that has been the basis of the growth and success of school psychology. Thus, whether our roles and functions are conceptualized in terms of traditional versus nontraditional roles or direct versus indirect services, our legacy has been one of assessment contributions prior to interventions. The field's shortcoming has been the unfortunate trap of finding it difficult to go beyond assessment to being integrally involved in the next phases of intervention at individual, group, family, and system levels.

In the delivery of school psychological services there is no such thing as services without prior assessment. The California Association of School Psychologists (CASP, 1991) approved a formal position on assessment, stating in part:

Assessment is the cornerstone of educational and psychological services delivery. Assessment is required to define pupil needs, guide children's education, and to provide data which may be used to evaluate educational outcomes. Educational research shows that assessment is necessary because individualized interventions and educational programs conducted without ongoing assessment may be detrimental to children, because (a) programs not based on empirical data are often based on flawed assumptions regarding the nature and causes of problems; (b) programs often raise unrealistic expectations, which impair future intervention efforts; and (c) programs without data are unaccountable, and cannot be adequately evaluated to determine whether resources are appropriately allocated (p. 4).

The CASP position embraces traditional school psychologist functions, including psychoeducational testing, but it is much more encompassing of assessment as being important to all levels of functioning, from individuals to groups to systems.

Our espousal of the assessment model as a basic aspect of school psychological services embraces the most comprehensive conceptualization of assessment in its quantitative and qualitative dimensions (Newland, 1980). Some professionals believe that assessment is counterproductive and opposed to other roles and functions. In contrast, we believe that assessment is complementary to all roles and functions of the school psychologist. It appeared less complementary in much earlier times because school psychologists were not being trained to have skills beyond basic assessment. Contemporary training includes both assessment and interventions of a wide variety, from consultation to therapy. The future success of school psychology does not rest in the abandonment of its assessment legacy but in the joining of that legacy to the arena of interventions, consultation, and other roles. School psychologists currently are being trained in very broad areas and have the appropriate school climate in which to involve themselves in interventions to a greater extent. Alternative delivery systems in school psychology are not simply alternatives to assessment but an alternative to an era when most school psychologists were trained largely for assessment and when most consumers wanted little else from them.

In summary, we do not espouse a refer-test-report model (which is not truly assessment in our estimation). In fact, we abhor assessment models that are primarily test-based. Rather, we endorse a complementary model combining assessment and interventions in agreement with ideas expressed in *School Psychology: A Blueprint for Training and Practice* (National School Psychology In-service Training Network, 1984) and its 1997 revision; the helping process put forth by Maier (1969); the positions of Susan Gray (1963b) and of Roger Reger (1965), who viewed the school psychologist as a "data-oriented problem solver" and as an "educational programmer," respectively, and which is also consistent with the viewpoint of a widely respected source book on alternative delivery systems (see Ysseldyke & Christenson, 1988). The future, therefore, is heavily related to being able to overcome the images of our past, but we must not lose sight of the fact that the school psychologist has been, and will continue to be, the best trained person in assessment in most educational communities. If our future is bright, then we will be perceived as among the best trained persons for interventions as well.

PRACTICAL EXERCISES

1. Throughout the book we have attempted to personalize your reading by encouraging you to gather information about school psychology. Information related to the material in this chapter can be gathered to complete the data sheet in Appendix A. The data sheet provides a convenient source of information from national and state levels for use during your training and practice. It will provide up-to-date information about national and state organizations, training, and credentialing, as well as an overview of the practice of school psychology in your state and local area.
2. How are school psychologists defined in your state and training program?
3. Several state-level surveys have been conducted of school psychologists' services. Can you locate results for school psychologists in your state or local area?
4. Try to determine how school psychologists in your state are dispersed and what impact this has on practice and state association activity.
5. What is the service ratio of school psychologists to children in your community and state?
6. How do job prospects appear in your state?
7. What code of ethics is employed by your state and local groups?
8. Why are memberships in professional associations important?
9. What school psychology and related journals are available in your college or university library?
10. Conduct a class discussion on the authors' assertion that assessment is the primary role of the school psychologist.

CHAPTER 2

Historical Development of School Psychology[1]

Historical study reminds us of where modern school psychology fits in the overall evolution of U.S. society and schooling. In the opening segment of the respected Public Broadcasting System series, *Cosmos*, Carl Sagan described the evolution of the universe in a single-year cosmic calendar in which each month represented 1.25 billion years, each minute 30,000 years, and each second 500 years. Sagan noted that not until 10:30 p.m. of the last day of the cosmic calendar year do we observe the first humans, and the emergence of cities did not occur until 11:59:35! Extrapolating from Sagan's analogy, we can state that everything important to the history of school psychological services and the structure of schooling as we know it in U.S. society has occurred in the past 100–150 years, or in the last milliseconds of Sagan's calendar. No significant aspect of contemporary school psychology, including its practitioners, was present before the 1890s. Thus, although the history of school psychology and education is fairly long in some respects, it is quite short in the broader development of society. Such a perspective reminds us that the ways in which we arrange schooling and psychological services are far from proven or permanent; rather, they are quite recent, generally untested, and constantly in search of improvement.

The advent of the centennial celebration of the American Psychological Association (APA) in 1991-1992 served as a stimulus for the historical study of psychology. Several investigations have clarified origins, trends, events, and persons significant to the development of school psychology. Although considerable research has been done, numerous areas of research continue to be worthy of attention (Fagan, 1990c). This chapter is a synopsis of that research and the development of school psychology in the United States. The discussion only touches upon the concurrent social, economic, and political history, and the historical development of related professional fields. A chronological discussion of major developments is provided, organized into several decades within the periods referred to as the hybrid years and the thoroughbred years. This chapter focuses on the development and growth of school psychology in several areas. We consider the discussion as prerequisite to the remaining chapters, which build upon this material.

THE HYBRID YEARS AND THOROUGHBRED YEARS DEFINED

School psychology's period of historical development can be divided into the hybrid years (1890-1969) and the thoroughbred years (1970-present). These are arbitrary timelines between two overlapping but different historical periods. The first was a period when "school" psychology often was a blend of many educational and psychological practitioners loosely mobilized around a dominant role of psychoeducational assessment for special class placement. Even in the latter decades of the hybrid years, school psychology was a mix of practitioners certified in various fields, many from teacher education or guidance and counseling who entered school psychology as an "add on" to their existing education credentials. The thoroughbred years, though certainly not rid of the earlier theme, differ from the hybrid years because of the growth in the number of training programs, practitioners, state and national associations, and the expansion of literature and regulations, all of which have contributed to a stabilized professional entity called "school psychology." Since 1970, school psychologists have been employed in positions titled "school psychologist"; in states offering school psychology credentials; and for persons who have completed training programs titled as school psychology, operated by school psychologists, and accredited as school psychology programs. Although exceptions existed with some states having more established professional identity for school psychology, the identity was not consistently present across the entire United States during the hybrid years. The more developed states (e.g., California, Illinois, Ohio, New Jersey, New York, and Pennsylvania) provided leadership and direction for other states to follow into the thoroughbred years. Even in developed states, however, the professional identity and development were more noticeable in urban and suburban locales (Mullen, 1967).

Table 2.1 provides a chronology of school psychology's historical events and landmarks. Each chronological period is labeled according to its most salient characteristics and not necessarily the accomplishments of that decade. In this format, the activities of a particular decade can be linked to the accomplishments seen in later decades. For example, the decade of the 1950s was an era of strong effort toward professional identity, even though that identity was not generally accomplished across most of the United States until the 1970s. The table provides an outline for the historical discussion that follows.

TABLE 2.1 A chronology of events and landmarks in the history of school psychology

I. THE HYBRID YEARS (1890-1969)

1890-1909 Origins of Practice

1890 Cattell publishes article on mental tests
1892 Founding of the first U.S. organization for psychologists, American Psychological Association
1896 First psychological clinic established by Lightner Witmer at the University of Pennsylvania
1899 First school-based psychological clinic founded in Chicago public schools
1905 First version of the Binet-Simon Scales published
1907 First practitioner journal, *The Psychological Clinic* founded and published
1908 First internships in clinical psychology at the Vineland Training School in New Jersey
1909 Rochester, New York, public schools appoint a Binet examiner

1910-1929 Expansion and Acceptance

1910 Cincinnati public schools starts Vocational Bureau
1910 First literary usage of term, "school psychologist" appears in the German language literature
1911 Term "school psychologist" first appears in English language literature
1912 First psychoeducational clinic (University of Pittsburgh)
1913 First survey of practitioners/examiners (Wallin)
1915 Gesell is first person appointed with title "school psychologist" and serves in Connecticut until 1919
1916 Terman publishes Stanford revision of the Binet-Simon Scales (Terman, 1916)
1917 Founding of the first organization for clinical psychologists (American Association of Clinical Psychologists)
1919 APA Section of Clinical Psychology founded
1923 First journal article with "school psychologist" title published (Hutt, 1923)
1925 New York City schools established first psychologist licensing exam
1928 New York University offers first training program in school psychology

1930-1939 Emerging Regulation

1930 First book on school psychology published (Hildreth, 1930)
1932 Association of Consulting Psychologists founded
1935 New York establishes first state department of education certification standards
1937 Pennsylvania establishes state department of education certification standards
1937 First applied psychology association with subdivisions founded (American Association of Applied Psychologists)
1938 Pennsylvania State University initiates Ph.D. in school psychology

1940-1949 Organizational Identity

1942 Special issue of *Journal of Consulting Psychology* on school psychology published
1943 First state association founded (Ohio School Psychologists Association)
1945 APA reorganizes into divisional structure and provides first organizational identity for school psychologists (Division 16, APA)
1945 Connecticut enacts first psychologist licensure
1947 First accreditation of clinical psychology programs by APA
1948 Boulder Conference on clinical psychology

Table 2.1 continued on page 26

Table 2.1 continued

1950-1959 Professional Identity
1952 APA accreditation extended to counseling psychology
1953 University of Illinois starts first recognized/organized doctoral program in school psychology
1953 APA publishes its first code of ethics
1954 National Council for Accreditation of Teacher Education established
1954 Ohio State Department of Education establishes first state-approved internships
1954 Thayer Conference in West Point, New York, is first national conference on school psychology

1960-1969 Training and Practitioner Growth
1962 First school psychology journal founded (*Journal of School Psychology*)
1962 First NCATE reference to school psychology programs
1963 *Psychology in the Schools* journal founded
1963 Peabody Conference on the school psychology internship held
1968 Ohio hosts invitational conference on school psychology
1969 Organizational meeting to form a national group held in St. Louis
1969 First national organization for school psychologists founded (National Association of School Psychologists)

II. THE THOROUGHBRED YEARS (1970-Present)
1970-1979 Trainer and Practitioner Regulation; Association Identity and Growth; Professional Division
1971 First APA accreditation of a school psychology program at University of Texas-Austin
1972 NASP publishes *School Psychology Digest*
1974 Public Law 94-142 enacted
1976 NASP affiliates with NCATE
1977 First training and certification directories published by NASP
1978 APA/NASP Task Force established
1979 *School Psychology International* journal founded

1980-1989 Professional Reorganization
1980 Spring Hill Symposium held in Wayzata, Minnesota
1981 Olympia Conference held in Oconomowoc, Wisconsin
1981 APA publishes specialty guidelines
1983 First joint APA/NCATE accreditation of a school psychology program (University of Cincinnati)
1985 Canadian Association of School Psychologists founded
1985 *Canadian Journal of School Psychology* founded
1985 *Professional School Psychology* journal founded by APA-Division 16
1988 NASP initiates folio review system for training program approval and approves first programs
1988 American Psychological Society founded
1988 NASP initiates National Certification System
1988 First National School Psychology Examination administered
1989 First National Certification in School Psychology granted

1990-1999 Stable Growth, Reform, Identity Reconsidered
1991 Concern for Personnel Shortages
1991 First APA accredited school district internship in the Dallas, Texas, public schools
1993 Founding of the American Board of School Psychology
1994 Founding of the Society for the Study of School Psychology
1994 NASP revises standards documents
1996 Division 16 reconsiders its name and the definition of school psychology
1997 Official specialty recognition to school psychology granted by APA
1998 Implementation of NASP governance changes

THE HYBRID YEARS (1890-1969)

Origins of Practice (1890-1920)

Changing Status of Children and Youth

The origins of school psychological services can be traced to an era of social reform in the late nineteenth and early twentieth centuries. Several reform movements were related to the emergence of school psychological services. Among these movements were compulsory schooling, juvenile courts, child labor laws, mental health, vocational guidance, the growth of institutions serving children, and an array of other child-saving efforts (Cohen, 1985; Cravens, 1985; Siegel & White, 1982). In contrast to earlier generations, which viewed the father as savior of the child (the child as redeemable), there was at the turn of the century strong sensitivity to the proposition that in children lay the salvation of society (the child as redeemer) (Wishy, 1968). Thus by improving the conditions of children's lives, particularly through systematic education, society hoped to overcome many of the problems of the urban United States and stem the fearful erosion of U.S. moral and economic values in the wake of immigration, urban growth, and industrialization (Cohen, 1985; Cravens, 1985; Cremin, 1988; Cubberley, 1909).

The "child-savers" operated from the assumption that "children constituted a special, vulnerable group in the population whose members should be protected through public policies" (Cravens, 1987, p. 159). According to Hoag and Terman (cited in Cubberley, 1920): "The children of today must be viewed as the raw material of a new State; the schools as the nursery of the Nation. To conserve this raw material is as logical a function of the State as to conserve the natural resources of coal, iron, and water power" (p. 683). This viewpoint toward children evolved over a long period during which attitudes and practices about schooling shifted from the home to community agencies outside the home, and when the model of the family shifted from primarily patriarchal to separate spheres for father and mother. More recently there was another shift to a contemporary family model characterized by individuation and children's rights. Children have become important, and childhood has emerged along with adolescence as distinct and separate stages in the life cycle, different from infancy and adulthood. The meaning of children and childhood changed from an economic source of labor to a psychological source of love and affection (Zelizer, 1985). Children were important not just for their potential labor asset but also for their psychological meaning as representatives of the next generation of American adults. The notion that by properly educating children society could rise above its problems has been a pervasive theme in twentieth-century U.S. education. At least in theory, even when problems were known not to be intrinsic to children, it would be the proper instruction of children that would remove the problems of society

---

(e.g., delinquency, unemployment, poverty). Because children held the key to the future, and the schools were places in which all children congregated for several years, the school curriculum came to represent a major opportunity for societal intervention. The contemporary school curriculum continues to reflect this philosophy with programs on drug and sex education, in addition to the traditional school offerings. Thus to some extent these "tack-on" curriculum programs actually represent conservative efforts to maintain the proper character of society as well as liberal attempts to adapt the curriculum to meet society's needs. In recent decades, some "tack-on" curricula have become politically unpopular, considered as interfering with the basic academic curriculum (e.g., bilingual education) or as attached to narrow constituent groups (e.g., AIDS, gay and lesbian education). Discussing the political and business interests in recent school reform efforts, Nelson (1998) reemphasizes the external influences on the purposes of schooling:

> We come to the end of the second millennium in a political/ cultural environment remarkably similar to that of the previous turn of the century. Accountability is the byword for politicians infatuated with control. Authority is more and more the dominant social infrastructure. The "progress" of technology echoes the "progress" of industry in the previous age. Business interests dominate the social policy debate. At stake in many areas of life is nothing less than the very conception of the principles of democracy. As our largest public institution, public education is the epicenter of the struggle for the control of the hearts and minds of the next generation (p. 684).

Compulsory Schooling

The preeminent force behind the need for school psychological services, and which reciprocally influenced child study and clinical psychology, was compulsory schooling. Field (1976) suggests two interacting explanations for the growth of compulsory schooling: (a) a "human capital" explanation contending that compulsory schooling emerged in response to the need for a more educated labor force to coincide with increasing industrialization and (b) a "structural reinforcement" explanation contending that compulsory schooling emerged in response to issues of social order and the need to maintain the character and social structure of society. Related to the human capital explanation is the possibility of organized labor's resistance to children in the workplace: Labor unions may have encouraged compulsory schooling. Also, a humanistic motive must be considered as well as the needs for social control and an educated labor force (Cohen, 1985). Tyack (1976) divided the compulsory schooling movement into a "symbolic" stage (1850–1890) and a "bureaucratic" stage (after 1890). In the latter stage,

---

"school systems grew in size and complexity, new techniques of bureaucratic control emerged, ideological conflict over compulsion diminished, strong laws were passed, and school officials developed sophisticated techniques to bring truants into schools" (Tyack, 1976, p. 359). It was an era when scientific and bureaucratic experts were on the rise as specialists and administrators worked in increasingly segmented school systems including divisions for "elementary, junior high, and high schools; vocational programs of several kinds; classes for the handicapped; counseling services; research and testing bureaus" (Tyack, 1976, p. 374). The first state to enact a compulsory attendance law was Massachusetts in 1852, and the last was Mississippi in 1918.

The increasing enactment and enforcement of compulsory attendance laws between 1870 and 1930 dramatically changed public education. Table 2.2 reveals the unprecedented enrollment growth and financial commitment the nation made to public education during this period. The condition of U.S. education in that era of heavy immigration, compulsory education, and child labor laws created the need for specialized school services to work in conjunction with the small but growing services in remedial and special education. School enrollment increased dramatically and included many children who had not been in school previously or had been unsuccessful in school, and yet whose attendance was now required. Enrollment comparisons for this period (Table 2.2) demonstrate the rapid growth of elementary and secondary education.

For the origins of school psychology, the change in the scope of schooling was even more important than the change in its size. The combination of compulsory attendance, large numbers of immigrant children, and poor child health and hygiene forced upon the schools a large segment of the population that heretofore had been only occasionally, if ever, in regular attendance. Not only were there more children of more diverse backgrounds for longer periods of attendance, but many had little or no prior record of schooling and age was not a reliable estimate of proper grade placement (Thorndike, 1912). A single classroom might have children with an age range of 6 years!

TABLE 2.2 Comparison of Attendance and Enrollment Data for 1890 and 1930		
	1890	**1930**
Average Days in School Year	135	173
Average Days Attended Per Pupil	86	143
Public School Enrollment	12,723,000	25,678,000
Public Secondary School Enrollment	203,000	4,399,000
Total Expenditures	$140,507,000	$2,316,790,000

Source: *Digest of Educational Statistics 1997* (Table 39) by T. D. Snyder, C. M. Hoffman, and C. M. Geddes, 1997, Washington, DC: USDE, Office of Educational Research and Improvement.

Prevalence of Physical and Mental Defects

Compulsory schooling quickly necessitated adjustments of the educational system. Among these were mandatory medical examinations, or "inspections." A survey by Wallin (1914) provided a vivid description of the poor general health of the school population. Wallin contended that "physical defects in children are not restricted to any clime, race, environment or social condition" (p. 5). Summarizing his nationwide surveys he stated:

> ...the percentage of pupils of various defects are as follows: defective teeth (one or more cavities, serious malocclusion), from 50-95%; defective vision and adenoids and nasal obstruction, from 5 to 20%; seriously enlarged or diseased tonsils, 5 to 15%; curvature of the spine, 2 to 7%; malnutrition, 1 to 6%; weak or tubercular lungs and defective hearing, 1 to 2%. It is estimated that 12,000,000 of the pupils in the public schools of the country are to some extent handicapped by one or more physical defects (pp. 5-6).

The attention to physical defects is understandable in an era of much poorer medical knowledge and practice. It was widely regarded that defects of physical health could be symptomatic of defects in ability, school achievement, and behavior as well. In addition to physical defects, Wallin (1914) noted that mental defects and related educational problems necessitated the provision of psychological inspections. Because good physical hygiene was considered a precursor to mental hygiene and educational attainment, both medical and psychological inspections were important. Thus medical and psychological inspections were among the early adjustments to compulsory schooling made by school districts. According to Wallin (1914), failing students should be given a physical examination to detect

> defects of the eyes, ears, nose, throat, teeth, glandular system, lungs, heart, nutrition, nervous disorders, etc.; and a psychological examination... for the detection of intellectual retardation and anomalies of sensation, movement, memory, imagination, association, attention, imitation, color perception, speech, number sense, fatigue, and for the determination of indices of stature, weight, vitality and dynamometry, etc. (p. 17).

Wallin's data also provided a basis for extending the logic of compulsory schooling to the provision of services for the exceptional child: If the child was to be compelled to attend school, "is it not his right, under a parity of reasoning, to demand that the state put him in such condition that he can assimilate those contents demanded of him by a compulsory attendance law?" (Wallin, 1914, pp.

17-18). Here was the ideology for why there should be special treatment of those children having physical and mental handicaps. Thus compulsory schooling necessitated the management of children with varied mental and physical conditions, and demanded that ways be found to cope with such conditions for a longer period of time, typically ages 7–14. During this same period, concerns for the general health of all children encouraged the rise of pediatric medicine (King, 1993).

Emergence of Special Education

Compulsory attendance was only gradually enforced for "normal" schoolchildren, and many states failed to provide comprehensive services for the handicapped until legislative initiatives of the post-World War II era. By comparison to modern times, when special education enrollment represents at least 10% of the school population, Dunn's (1973) figures (below) suggest less than 1% representation in the early years. Nevertheless, the schools were inundated with unanticipated children with disorders and forced to cope by using unproven interventions. These conditions were particularly acute in the school systems of major cities, which enrolled large percentages of students with "mental, physical, and moral" impairments, the three primary categories of exceptionality used at that time. During this period special education programs emerged, and although they were small in number by current comparisons, they were available in many urban and some rural school systems by 1910 (Van Sickle, Witmer, & Ayers, 1911; Wallin, 1914). These sources do not provide figures about the total number of children then served in special education. However, the Van Sickle et al. (1911) study concluded that the top and bottom 4% of the school population were gifted and feebleminded, respectively, and that there were large numbers of students who were normal intellectually but "for whom the present school curriculum and regime are ill adapted" (p. 18). This last group was mostly boys who made slow progress in school, and in the average city the group constituted one-third of the student population. Later statistics (Dunn, 1973) for special education enrollment showed the following pattern of growth: 26,163 (1922), 162,116 (1932), 310,467 (1940), 356,903 (1948), 837,291 (1958), 2,857,551 (1971-1972); current enrollment is more than 5 million. Dunn (1973) reported national special education enrollment of more than 26,000 children in 1922, which mostly included children with mental retardation. The studies suggest that the number of children in need of services and those enrolled were vastly discrepant. Dunn's figures are therefore conservative and based only on the numbers being served. The studies suggest that approximately the same percentage of the school population (10-12%) were in need of special services throughout the twentieth century. However, the make-up of the exceptional child population and the related problems of these children would change considerably. As medical and public health technology improved, fewer children would be handicapped due to physical health conditions. An example of this change is the decline in the use of open air classes for children having respiratory distress and the virtual disappearance of school physicians by mid-century.

The early categories of special education and their nomenclature were considerably different from those of recent times. In addition to the common categories now in existence, special classes were provided for truant, delinquent, backward, adult education, and other categories that today are outside the legislated scope of special education and that reflected the "human capital" and the "structural reinforcement" explanations of compulsory schooling. That is, special educational arrangements were offered by the schools for adults and children to enhance both their employability (human capital) and their adjustment to U.S. society (structural reinforcement).

Corresponding to the segregation ideology of the period, seriously atypical children most often were "educated" in facilities apart from the regular school, and most school psychologists were hindered from making contributions to regular education programs owing to heavy caseloads with referrals for special class placement. Hall (1911) put the segregationist position quite bluntly, stating, "habits of stupidity and inertness are often more contagious than are the examples of the best workers. This is why the elimination of the stupids is so urgent and so often effected today by segregating them in various ways" (p. 607). Wallin (1914) believed the psychological clinic should serve as an educational clearing house for the segregation of feebleminded and backward pupils from average and bright pupils—some to be segregated temporarily, others permanently, often through institutionalization. Such segregationist practices have been observed throughout the twentieth century, although they declined as the ideology shifted toward mainstreaming of handicapped children, and their placement in what is now called the least restrictive environment, both of which were required by the Education for All the Handicapped Children Act of 1975 (Public Law 94-142) and subsequent reauthorizations of this law. The trend also is reflected in a gradual shift in practices in several sectors including mental health, education, public health, medicine, and corrections (Pfeiffer & Reddy, 1999).

Emergence of School Psychological Services

Compulsory schooling was potent among those forces creating the circumstances for the emergence of special educational services and the subsequent need for "experts" to assist in the process of child selection, their educational segregation, and the increasing bureaucratic segmentation of the public schools. However, it was the resulting need for and growth of special education that provided the fertile ground for the emergence of pupil personnel services (attendance officers, guidance counselors, school nurses and physicians, school psychologists, school social workers, speech and language clinicians, and vocational counselors). In the limited extent to which school psychological services existed, they were directly or indirectly delivered to children from agencies inside and outside the school, were based upon the available methodologies of child study and clinical psychology, and were provided by the pioneers in these new fields. It is reasonable, therefore, to hypothesize that among the primary reasons for securing and employing school psychologists was the specific notion of having them help educators sort children reliably into segregated educational settings where they might be more successful individually and where their absence would help the system itself function better for the masses of "average" children. In plain language, pupil personnel services including school psychologists were not central to the system of schooling; rather, they were employed to facilitate the system's goals of educating the masses more efficiently while dealing with the problems such goals presented (see, e.g., Kaplan & Kaplan, 1985). The concept of the school psychologist, therefore, as an ancillary member of the system, and as a "gatekeeper" for special education, has a long historical precedent. These images of the school psychologist are reflected in the analogy of school psychologists as "guests" in the house of education (Elliott & Witt, 1986b), and there are many historical and current accounts of discrepancies between school psychologists' perceptions of role and function and those held by school administrators (e.g., Hughes, 1979; Moss & Wilson, 1998; Symonds, 1933). The "guest" analogy is discussed in chapter three. A similar impact of compulsory schooling at the international level can be observed in Turkey in their recent increase in compulsory attendance laws from 5 to 8 years of elementary education (Albayrak-Kaymak & Dolek, 1997).

Psychological services in the United States emerged from the activities of Lightner Witmer at the psychological clinic that he founded at the University of Pennsylvania in 1896 (the first in the United States). Considered by many to be the father of both clinical and school psychology, Witmer advocated the training of a "psychological expert who is capable of treating the many difficult cases that resist the ordinary methods of the school room" (Witmer, 1897, p. 117). Witmer also is credited with coining the term "clinical psychology" and founding *The Psychological Clinic,* an early journal related to clinical services and handicapped children (Brotemarkle, 1931). This journal served as an outlet for disseminating Witmer's ideas of practice, the work of the first psychological clinic, and the work of other significant psychologists. It was read by many of the relatively small number of practitioners early in the twentieth century. The journal is considered to have been a major publication for clinical psychologists until the time it ceased publication in 1935. It was widely circulated to practitioners and college or university libraries. Witmer (1907) stressed an individualized approach to children that would use psychological knowledge to solve their problems, especially problems related to schooling. A comprehensive account of Witmer's life and contributions appears in McReynolds (1997).

Another major early figure was G. Stanley Hall who founded the American Psychological Association (APA) in 1892, as well as several journals including *American Journal of Psychology*, and *Pedagogical Seminary* (now the *Journal of Genetic Psychology*). Hall was the father of the child study movement, which influenced the establishment and functions of the Department of Scientific Pedagogy and Child Study in the Chicago Public Schools in 1899, the first clinic facility operated within the public schools (Slater, 1980). Wallin and Ferguson (1967) described the mix of normative and clinical casework conducted in the early years of this facility. Initiated with a research orientation, the Chicago clinic evolved quickly into a major school service agency. In contrast to Witmer's idiographic clinical method, Hall espoused a nomothetic approach that also was observed in the later work of his Clark University students Goddard, Gesell, and Terman. English and English (1958) define nomothetic as "characterizing procedures and methods designed to discover general laws" and idiographic as "attempts to understand a particular event or individual" (p. 347). Slater (1980) contended that the relationship between psychology and education at that time was essentially symbiotic, with each needing the other to advance. He surmised that Hall was the stimulus for education's response and that Witmer was a response to the stimulus provided by education. Both were important influences in establishing the twentieth century as the first century in which the scientific study of children and adolescents occurred. Witmer and Hall were the bellwethers of early school psychology (Fagan, 1992). It was the intellectual descendants of Witmer and Hall who bridged their different concepts and practices and thus influenced the wider acceptance of school psychological services. A comprehensive account of Hall's life and contributions appears in Ross (1972).

Lightner Witmer
Source: Reprinted by permission of the Archives of the History of American Psychology, University of Akron, Akron, Ohio

Granville Stanley Hall
Source: Reprinted by permission
of the Archives of the History
of American Psychology,
University of Akron, Akron, Ohio

Thus, early models of school psychological services evolved primarily from two orientations: idiographic clinical psychology and nomothetic educational psychology. Even though not derived solely from Witmer and Hall, these orientations can be seen in the variety of practices of the emerging clinics in the United States. Some of these clinics provided individualized services organized around case studies, whereas others were at least in part organized around research emphases, studying individuals in terms of normative characteristics. At least in the early years of operation, the idiographic model could be observed in the practices of the clinic at the University of Pennsylvania and the nomothetic model in the Chicago Public Schools' Department of Scientific Pedagogy and Child Study. These two orientations, singly or in combination, are observed throughout our history of training and practice. For example, school psychologists have continued to provide individualized psychological services while making categorical decisions for special education along normative lines of deviance. Thus the individual child study model, employing idiographic and nomothetic data, has been the primary identity of school psychologists and often has served to distinguish the field from related fields. School psychology's knowledge base and practice continue to be heavily influenced by developments in education and psychology and the research in these fields (Fry, 1986), and the dual influences are reflected in the recently revised document, *School Psychology: A Blueprint for Training and Practice II* (Ysseldyke et al., 1997).

Rise of Clinics and Psychoeducational Testing

Following the efforts of Witmer, Hall, and others, school- and non-school-based clinics (sometimes called research bureaus or child study departments) spread quickly between 1900 and 1930, with most large-city school systems having access to some form of what was most often called "clinical psychology." Child study services also were provided to children by clinics located in juvenile institutes, courts, universities, hospitals, vocational guidance bureaus, and other settings. These services were a mixture of educational and clinical psychology more akin to modern-day school psychology than to either current educational or clinical psychology. Developments of the late nineteenth century in measurement and psychological science had laid the groundwork for the study of individual differences and test standardization. These concepts fit well with the need to segment the school population into different instructional groups including special education. The spread of psychological services was spurred by the development of psychological and educational tests and the interest of school systems in segmenting their student population, especially according to "intelligence."

Wallin's (1914) survey described the availability of services; the backgrounds, tests, and inspection methods employed; and financial resources of the providers of early psychological inspections. His study identified clinics in several settings under various names. He identified 19 school-based clinic facilities and their dates of establishment between 1899 in Chicago and 1914 in Detroit. He concluded that there were 26 clinics in institutions of higher learning; that more than 20 clinics were affiliated with correctional facilities, mental health institutions, vocational centers, and so on; and that 84 city school systems of 103 responding to the survey "report that psychological tests are given either by employees of the school boards or by outside agencies" (Wallin, 1914, p. 393). The clinic often was nothing more than a small room and a single examiner, and the psychological examination usually involved only the use of the Binet-Simon intelligence scale, a precursor of Goddard's Binet and Terman's Stanford-Binet, or form board tests (Fagan, 1985). After reviewing the backgrounds of the 115 examiners identified as working in school-based clinics, Wallin concluded that only about one-fourth were qualified and the rest were nothing but amateur Binet testers (e.g., special class teachers, supervisors, or administrators including school superintendents). Wallin's study revealed the variable conditions of psychological services during the period. However, he predicted the following:

> Psychology is destined to have not only a pedagogic but a clinical value for education. Eventually we shall have an independent science of clinical psychology or clinical education, instruction in which will be afforded in all of the large progressive normal schools and colleges of education. And we shall also have psychological or psycho-educational clinics in the large school systems, manned by psychological and educational experts, for the purpose of classifying the educational misfits (Wallin, 1914, pp. 20-21).

The early years of the testing movement demonstrated the advantage of ability and achievement tests in segregating individuals for specialized treatment. Although school personnel had been familiar with nineteenth-century work in phrenological and anthropometric measurement, it was the work of Binet and Simon in France, and the many adaptations of their tests in the United States, that truly spurred the individual testing movement to new conceptualizations. Phrenology had been the study of character and mental capacity from the conformation of the skull; certain brain segments were thought to control various characteristics and protrusions were thought to represent strengths associated with that area. Phrenology was popular in the late eighteenth and much of nineteenth century, but then lost credibility. Anthropometry was the study and technique of human body measurement for use in anthropological classification and comparison. It included such measures as a cephalic index (ratio of length to width of head), lung capacity, grip, and ratio of upper limb to lower limb. Anthropometric measurement was very popular in early school psychological assessment and could still be observed in practices of the 1920s.

World War I had a major influence on the development of standardized tests and their public acceptance. The Army Alpha and Beta tests demonstrated the utility of group devices in screening large numbers of army inductees in a short period of time, and the success of this effort brought public attention and acceptance of tests. Several versions of the Binet-Simon scales were available between 1910 and 1920, but it was Terman's Stanford Revision (Terman, 1916) that captured the attention of educators and psychologists for several decades. Much later, the Wechsler scales would successfully compete for this attention, and in present times we observe several other tests with sizable shares of the ability-testing market. School achievement and aptitude tests also developed rapidly with the growth of educational psychology after 1910.

School Psychologist Roles and Functions

The development of group and individual ability and achievement tests in the early decades of the twentieth century facilitated the needs of educators for student differentiation. They also became the forte of psychologists serving educational settings. Although dissenters certainly existed, there was widespread acceptance of these tests and their use by educators and psychologists. Thus, psychological and educational tests quickly became the major identifying characteristic of psychologists employed in school settings, and the administration and interpretation of these tests became the primary role and function of early school psychologists (see, e.g., Kehle, Clark, & Jenson, 1993).

Interventions were influenced by many ideas including Thorndike's learning principles and educational psychology, the educational philosophies of Dewey and James, Freudian therapeutic conceptualizations, and Watsonian behaviorism.

However, prior to World War II, interventions were a modest aspect of many psychologists' roles, in or out of school settings, though some psychologists even then were engaged in intervention and consulting activities. Overall, testing had given applied psychologists including school psychologists a respectable methodology for practice, in part because many tests developed out of earlier laboratory procedures that connected practitioners to academics. As applied psychology evolved, testing procedures developed along more pragmatic lines and were influenced by the interaction of applied psychologists and their clients (van Strein, 1998). That is, school psychologists' tools were developed and selected to answer specific questions of predictive validity needed by school districts rather than to simply provide a descriptive report of children's strengths or weaknesses. In this early period, therapeutic activities were not well accepted by the scientific psychology community, and therapy functions of psychologists often were thwarted by the psychiatric community. Behaviorism, linked to experimental psychology, was more readily accepted and was quite popular with educators early in the century. Educational literature of this period suggests an acceptance of learning and behavioral principles decades in advance of the widespread influence of Skinnerian applications familiar to contemporary school psychologists.

Individual and group counseling functions of the contemporary school psychologist have early origins in vocational guidance and Freudian conceptualizations, and more recent origins in Rogerian conceptualizations and the conceptualizations of several other significant persons (e.g., Adler, Ellis, Maslow, Perls, Sullivan, and Wolpe). These and other orientations have influenced school psychological services for several decades (Sandoval, 1993). However, throughout the hybrid years the dominant ideology was diagnostic services for special education placement, which encouraged a dominant school psychology role model of psychological assessment. Following the introduction of Binet's scales in 1905 and especially the adaptations by Goddard and Terman, psychological testing was widespread by the 1920s. This encouraged Hollingworth (1933) to comment that the situation "within the past 25 years has transformed Binet's name into a verb (nearly all teachers now know what it is to 'binet' a pupil)" (p. 371).

The term "school psychologist" in the English literature emanated from Stern's (1911) article translated from the German literature and was not in widespread usage for many years. The term "clinical psychologist" was in greater usage, reflecting the generic orientation of Witmer's conceptualizations in which clinical psychology was considered to be a methodology employed by psychologists in many settings with a variety of clients as opposed to a separate specialization per se (Witmer, 1907). The development of distinct specialties occurred after the 1920s (Fagan, 1993).

Leta Stetter Hollingworth
Source: Reprinted by permission
of the Archives of the History of
American Psychology, University
of Akron, Akron, Ohio

Early Organizations and Training

Table 2.1 indicates that the period from 1890 to 1920 provided a framework for many later developments. In addition to the origination of services, the period also included the founding of several journals (e.g., *Journal of Educational Psychology*, Witmer's *The Psychological Clinic*, and Hall's *American Journal of Psychology* and *Pedagogical Seminary*), the establishment of organizations for applied/clinical psychologists, individual and group tests, and special education classes. Other literary benchmarks included the first appearance of the term "school psychologist" in U.S. literature and several early articles and manuals that described the state of services (Fagan & Delugach, 1984). Wallin (1914) and Van Sickle et al. (1911) provide the most comprehensive descriptions of school conditions, availability of special classes, psychological services, and the nature of service providers. Working for Connecticut, Arnold Gesell wrote several manuals which were prototypical of materials produced by current state consultants for school psychological services. Many test manuals and compendia of tests appear to have enjoyed widespread popularity (e.g., Stern, 1914; Whipple, 1914, 1915).

Organizational developments also were important. Throughout the APA's first several decades, scientific rather than professional or applied orientations dominated its political structure and policy (Napoli, 1981). The APA, founded in 1892, failed to respond to the interests of applied psychologists for standards and assistance, and provoked the founding of the American Association of Clinical Psychologists (AACP) in 1917. Responding to overtures from the APA, the AACP disbanded and became the Clinical Section of the APA in 1919. For a variety of reasons most school psychologists were not affiliated with the APA or any other national group during the early decades of the twentieth century. Further, there were few if any state or local associations for professional affiliation. The organizational developments of the period served to point out the problems of applied psychologists within the APA and the significant role that splinter groups, such as AACP, would play in the history of psychology, including school psychology (Fagan, 1993).

During the period 1890–1920 the relatively small number of practitioners of psychology in school settings gained their preparation from a variety of backgrounds. Informal training efforts, including field experiences, existed at a few institutions, but there were no formal training programs specifically for school psychologists (Fagan, 1999). Witmer had provided instruction in connection with his clinic, and Wallin and Hall also offered instruction along the lines of exceptional children and child study, respectively. Goddard and Gesell provided early training classes on testing and special education in New York City, and Goddard is credited with organizing the earliest internships at the Vineland Training School in New Jersey (Morrow, 1946). One of his assistants, Norma Cutts, was at Vineland in 1913-1914 and with Goddard's help found employment as a psychological examiner with Gesell. That position provided the stage for her own eminent career in school psychology and special education in New Haven, Connecticut (Fagan, 1989a).

Important Contributors

Well-known "school" psychologists of the period included Arnold Gesell, Henry Goddard, Gertrude Hildreth, Leta Stetter Hollingworth, Bertha Luckey, Clara Schmitt, Lewis Terman, John Edward Wallace Wallin, Margaret Washburn, Lightner Witmer, and Helen Thompson Wooley. The early representation of women in school psychology practice, and applied psychology generally, can be attributed to discrimination in higher education settings, lack of career options for women outside of education, and the feminization of elementary and secondary school teaching, which spread in the nineteenth century and provided the base from which many would later seek positions in guidance and psychology. Describing the circumstances of "career-minded women in male-dominated America before World War I," Schwarz (1986) states:

> For all their intelligence and ability, these women were expected to forget their ambitions and years of schooling as they reached their twenties. Society's dictates on what was a normal and acceptable life for American women narrowed to marrying a man, raising a family, and settling down to an existence lived mainly as an adjunct to other's lives once they left college (p. 56).

There were, of course, numerous examples of educated women who resisted society's dictates and chose other paths (Rosenberg, 1982). In this regard, the psychological career of Leta Stetter Hollingworth has gained considerable attention (Benjamin & Shields, 1990; Fagan, 1990b). Other notable examples include Norma Cutts (Fagan, 1989a) and Gertrude Hildreth (Fagan, 1988a). Despite society's dictates, many women considered careers in teaching and psychology to be fulfilling and natural extensions of their traditional child-rearing role. Women often held administrative positions in school psychological clinics and contributed widely to the spread of school services (French, 1988). The increasing acceptability of the employment of married women, including those with school-age children, has radically altered the gender structure of the U.S. workplace. In comparison to other psychology fields, women have held strong proportional representation throughout the history of school psychology, perhaps never less than 30% and currently about 70%. A discussion of recent contributions of women in school psychology appears in Hagin (1993).

Among the most prominent examples of school psychology practitioners in this period was Arnold Lucius Gesell (1880-1961). Gesell is believed to have held the first position titled "school psychologist," serving the Connecticut State Board of Education from 1915 to 1919. His position was a mix of direct and indirect services, and archival records vividly describe the conditions of his employment and practice. His experiences were similar in many ways to those of current practitioners: His caseload was often too large, his administrative superiors preferred diagnostic services to others, he traveled considerably from one service setting to another, and he mixed school and non-school practice (Fagan, 1987a).

Arnold L. Gesell
Source: Studio portrait by Crosby, New Haven, Connecticut. Reprinted by permission of the State Historical Society of Wisconsin.

Though some rural services existed, the growth of psychological and special educational services was confined mainly to urban schools. Surveys by Van Sickle et al. (1911) and Wallin (1914) revealed that special education and psychological services were most prevalent in the northeast and Great Lakes regions and in large urban and city school districts. The urban settings, having the most schoolchildren, were most pressed for adjustments to meet district and children's needs. Many rural settings lagged behind in the provision of services for several decades. Not until the latter decade of the hybrid years and the era of Public Law 94-142 were widespread rural services observed.

1920-1940

Though 1890–1920 was a formative period, school psychology lacked many of the primary characteristics of a profession: practitioner autonomy and professional regulation of training, credentialing, and practice. Because psychological practice was largely unregulated and titles such as clinical or consulting psychologist, psycho-clinicist, or psychological examiner were employed generically, it is fair to say that all of professional psychology was without much professional status and symbolism at this time. Psychologists in school settings may not have had as much professional status as those in other settings even though they had acquired more in terms of professional symbols. This lesser status was attributable to the prevalence of non-doctoral practitioners and the fact that many school practitioners were women. Later, in the post-World War II era, clinical psychology as a separate specialty would outstrip other specialties including school and counseling psychology in the acquisition of professional symbols and status, and initiate a state of catch-up for other practice groups that would last throughout the remainder of the century.

Training and Credentialing

To a limited extent the professional symbols of autonomy and regulation of training, credentialing, and practice were discernible for school psychology in the period 1920–1940. Whereas psychologists previously had been trained in conjunction with certain university clinics, it was recognized that psychologists serving schoolchildren were in need of more formal preparation (Fagan, 1999). Witmer had established a training program in clinical psychology at the University of Pennsylvania, and though several of his graduates worked in school systems, the program was not designated school psychology. The first training programs identified as school psychology were at New York University (NYU) in the mid-1920s, where programs existed at the undergraduate and graduate levels. By the late 1930s, Pennsylvania State University was offering doctoral training in school psychology. Other institutions, including Ohio State University, recommended specific courses for persons seeking preparation for school practice. Thus there were relevant training courses at some institutions and formal programs at NYU and Penn State during this period (Fagan, 1986b).

That New York and Pennsylvania were pioneers in training was no accident. In the mid-1920s an examination for employment as a school psychological examiner was in use in New York City schools. To be eligible for the examination, applicants had to have completed a master's degree in psychology from a "university recognized by the Regents of the University of the State of New York" and had to have "one year's experience in mental measurement satisfactory to the Board of Examiners" (Examination for License as Psychologist, 1925). It seems plausible that the NYU program may have been developed in response to the availability of such employment and this examination. State Department of Education certification occurred in Pennsylvania and New York in the mid-1930s. French (1984) provides a detailed description of developments in Pennsylvania, which was among the few states actively developing statewide school psychology services even in its rural counties.

By 1940 at least two states, Pennsylvania and New York, were credentialing school psychological practitioners through their state departments of education, and at least New York City conducted a formal examination of its prospective psychologists. As yet no states offered credentials to psychologists in the non-school and private sectors. Another aspect of professional regulation was the initiation of a short-lived national certification program available to APA members from 1921 to 1927 (Sokal, 1982). The program, though unsuccessful, was an early example of recognition by means of a national-level credential that would reappear in the 1940s in APA's American Board of Examiners in Professional Psychology and in the 1980s as NASP's National Certification in School Psychology. Thus, two primary symbols of professional development, training and credentialing, emerged in the period 1920–1940. More rapid and widespread growth in training and regulation emerged in future periods, especially following World War II.

Literature

The literature available to school psychologists continued to appear in a variety of sources. With no journals specifically devoted to school psychology, most of the field's literature continued to appear in related psychology and education journals, particularly *The Psychological Clinic, School and Society, Journal of Educational Psychology*, and *Journal of Consulting Psychology*. This literature was devoted to professional and organizational issues, psychoeducational assessment, the problems of children, and the accompanying need for psychological services. There were also numerous books on similar topics. A major literary accomplishment of this period was the first text specifically about school psychology, *Psychological Service for School Problems* (Hildreth, 1930).

Gertrude H. Hildreth
Source: From the Gertrude Hildreth Papers.
Reprinted by permission of the Educational
Testing Service Archives.

Role and Function and Employment Opportunities

In the early 1920s, Gertrude Hildreth worked briefly as a school psychologist in Okmulgee, Oklahoma, before leaving for Columbia University, where she received her doctoral degree and became a faculty member (Fagan, 1988a). Her pioneer book described the historical development of services and vividly portrayed the school psychologist's role and function. Box 2.1 is taken from her text and demonstrates the typical practice of the period as well as a remarkable similarity to current practice. The comparatively strong involvement in group testing reflects the mixture of guidance and school psychology services less often observed in contemporary descriptions of role and function. The variety of activities Hildreth portrayed reminds us that diversity in role and function existed throughout our history and that Leta Hollingworth's earlier cited concerns for Binet testing were not uniformly applicable. Hildreth's book put forth more of an ideal than real model, and her listing was far more diverse than her previous practice had been in Oklahoma. The book portrayed the possibilities for broader services even though the assessment model, often narrowly construed as ability testing, was dominant. For the first half of the twentieth century, most school psychologists were enmeshed in a refer-test-report model with other functions consuming much less of their time

Psychological testing continued to be the dominant characteristic of role and function for school psychologists throughout this period. Numerous group and individual ability, aptitude, and achievement tests were now available, and the technical adequacy of instrumentation and the variety of tests available were increasing. Among the most prominent was the Stanford Revision of the Binet-Simon Scales introduced in 1916, which was revised in 1937 to include both a Form L and a Form M (the initials stood for the authors' first names, Louis Terman and Maude Merrill).

BOX 2.1　　　　Hildreth's Illustration of a School Psychologists' Day

The following outline illustrates the daily activities on an ordinarily busy day of one psychologist employed in a progressive school:

Morning

Examination with the Binet test of a child applying for admission.
The administration of group tests to a small group of absentees who missed the test during the recent testing survey.
Conference on a problem child in the high school.
Conference on a problem child in the elementary school.
Answering correspondence and making requisitions for the tests to be used in the next survey.

Afternoon

Completion, for the principal, of reports of a group of seventh-grade children whose achievement was found to be deficient on recent tests.
Further work on the construction of reading and arithmetic readiness tests for the primary grades.
Instructions to an assistant for making a set of flash cards for diagnostic work in reading.
Partial diagnosis of the reading difficulties of an upper elementary grade pupil.
Study of the reading progress of a French child who had recently entered the school.
Conference with a high school teacher.
This day began at 8:30 and closed at 5:45, with a half an hour's recess at noon.

The rank order of activities engaged in by the same psychologist, arranged according to the amount of time consumed in their performance during the year, is approximately as follows:

1. Conferences with school staff members, parents, visitors, psychologists in training.
2. Individual testing of pupils.
3. Group testing.
4. Test scoring.
5. Tabulation of results and the construction of graphs and charts.
6. Diagnostic work with individual pupils.
7. Research including test construction and conferences with staff members conducting research.

SOURCE: *Psychological Service for School Problems* (pp. 246-248) by G.H. Hildreth, 1930, Yonkers, NY: World Book Co.

Adequate employment positions had been available throughout the early decades of practice, but the depression years of the 1930s had a substantial impact on employment opportunities for psychologists. Large urban districts such as Chicago and New York City lost several positions and were forced to make adjustments in staffing, including the hiring of Works Progress Administration psychologists to weather this difficult period (City of New York, 1938; Mullen, 1981). Despite the loss of positions in several settings and limited employment opportunities for applied psychologists, the field continued to grow (Napoli, 1981). Services continued to be concentrated in urban areas, but by 1940 school psychology had been accepted nationwide, and the number of practitioners had grown from only a few hundred to probably 500 practitioners employed in schools under various titles.

The earlier clinic system model was now widespread, with some rural areas gaining services through traveling clinics. In Massachusetts, the traveling clinics included psychologists, social workers, and psychiatrists operating as a team from a regional mental health facility (Martens, 1939). In Ohio, services were provided from a research bureau affiliated with the College of Education at Ohio State University (Rosebrook, 1942). Although helpful, the traveling clinics were unable to provide the intensity and array of services available to districts employing their own psychologists. Articulating services with local districts was a widespread problem for such clinics in rural areas. The problem can still be observed in areas where services continue to be provided on an indirect basis even when organized within a larger educational agency (e.g., special education cooperative). The growth in school district-based special education increased the demand for district-based psychological examiners. The growing acceptance of school psychology was reflected in an increasing number of districts that found the resources to employ their own school psychologists. By the end of this period the clinic model was being complemented by the single-district model, and services were expanding beyond the urban centers to smaller cities and rural areas.

The following list identifies the range of service delivery models available during the history of school psychology, many of which were operating in this period. The first 10 service arrangements differ from the latter by not typically employing a "school" psychologist. The range is still observed in practice but the dominant model has shifted to joint-agreement and district-based provisions (options 14 and 15). The clinic-based and traveling models faded quickly after World War II. Despite this expansion of service delivery models and growth of employment opportunities between 1920 and 1940, services continued to be provided by persons with a variety of training and titles, and a well-defined professional specialty of school psychology was not yet discernible.

These are the systems for the delivery of school psychological services.

1. Psychological clinics in institutions of higher learning (university/college, medical school, normal school), or institutional facility
2. School district-based clinic, research bureau
3. Community-based clinic, guidance center
4. State department of education employee serving entire state or region of the state
5. State department of education supervision of regional/county employees
6. School-district contracts with psychologist from nearby city
7. University-based comprehensive clinic serving several districts in its region
8. Regional services or traveling clinics provided by institutional facility
9. Psychologists and examiners in independent practice contracted to provide services to schools
10. Psychologists and examiners employed by community mental health center to serve districts in its region
11. School psychologist in independent practice contracted to provide services to schools
12. School psychologist employed by community mental health center to serve school districts in its region
13. School psychologists employed by several school districts concurrently (with or without formal inter-district contract)
14. School psychologist employed by special education agreement district (e.g., cooperative, Bureau of Cooperative Educational Services (BOCES), Area Education Agency (AEA))
15. School psychologist employed by single school district

Organizational Development

There was considerable activity during this period related to professional organizations. Following the establishment of the APA Division of Clinical Psychologists in 1919, splinter groups continued to develop. Many consulting psychologists, especially in New York State, continued to maintain a separate association that led to the founding of the Association of Consulting Psychologists (ACP) in 1930 and then to the American Association of Applied Psychologists (AAAP) in 1937. The fact that the AAAP was subdivided into four broadly defined specialties—clinical, consulting, educational, and business and industrial psychology—was a significant symbol of professionalization (English, 1938). School psychological practitioners typically belonged to AAAP's Clinical or

Educational Sections, but most school practitioners, and probably most applied psychologists, did not hold membership in either the APA or the AAAP. These organizations typically granted full membership privileges only to those who held the doctoral degree, with lesser status accorded to non-doctoral practitioners. Owing to the growth in the number of school practitioners and their certification, some concessions appear to have been made for them in the AAAP membership requirements (Fagan, 1993). The orientations of these groups also reflected the long-standing differences between academic and applied psychologists. However, relationships between the APA and the AAAP generally were cordial, with many shared memberships and annual meetings. The two groups remained separate until developments prior to World War II encouraged the unification of psychology groups into one organization. There were several AAAP state-level affiliates, which typically held similar names (e.g., Ohio Association of Applied Psychologists). There do not appear to have been separate school psychology state associations in this period though there may have been a New York City association of school psychologists.

1940-1969

The final three decades of the hybrid years are noteworthy for role confusion, shaping organizational identity, and the quantitative growth of training programs and practitioners. Education had grown enormously as a result of the post-World War II "baby boom." Once again, the schools were expanding in size and were in need of additional psychological services. Special education was serving more than 2 million children in 1968, up dramatically from 310,000 in 1940 and 837,000 in 1958 (Dunn, 1973). From 1940 to 1970, the number of school psychologists grew from about 500 to 5,000, and the number of institutions with formal training programs grew from as few as 2 to more than 100, enrolling a total of perhaps 3,000 students. The ratio of practitioners to schoolchildren improved from 1:36,000 in 1950 to 1:10,500 in 1966 (Fagan, 1988b). Credentialing accomplishments included the growth of school certification from 13 states in 1946, to 23 states in 1960, to perhaps 40 states by 1970 and the initiation of licensure for psychologists in 1945, with licensure in all states by 1977. The rapid growth and change in school psychology during the period 1940–1970 can be gleaned from Cutts (1955), Farling and Hoedt (1971), and Symonds (1942).

Literature

The school psychology literature continued to be scattered though some concentration was provided by the *Journal of Consulting Psychology* (now the *Journal of Consulting and Clinical Psychology*) and the newly founded APA journal, *American Psychologist*. Until the 1960s, the Division 16 newsletter was the only national publication devoted exclusively to school psychology. The 1960s was the most productive literary decade of the hybrid years and included the founding of the *Journal of School Psychology, Psychology in the Schools*, and *Professional Psychology* (now *Professional Psychology: Research and Practice*), and the publication of 14 books on school psychology (Fagan, 1986a). Even though the literature reflected problems of role confusion and professional identity, it was the first period in which school psychologists were writing books on topics of their own interest and publishing journals for their own audience. Unique among these books were those presenting philosophies on the training and practice of school psychologists. Gray's (1963b) "data-oriented problem solver" and Reger's (1965) "educational programmer" are orientations with continuing relevance. The Gottsegens' three edited volumes on *Professional School Psychology*, were without peer until the *Advances in School Psychology* series of the 1980s (these appear in Appendix B). The frequency of authored, in contrast to edited, texts is another trademark of the 1960s. Only in recent years have unedited texts of significance returned to our literature. In comparison to the period 1940–1969, the many edited volumes since 1970 reflect the complexity of the field, whereas the return of a few unedited books reflects a welcome return of philosophical orientations, some espousing certain practice models (e.g., Phillips, 1990a; Plas, 1986; Reynolds, Gutkin, Elliott, & Witt, 1984). Valett's (1963) *The Practice of School Psychology: Professional Problems* served as a guidebook for professional and ethical dilemmas at a time when only generic codes of ethics were available from APA.

Conferences

Among the most cited accomplishments of the period 1940–1970 is the Thayer Conference, conducted in 1954 (Cutts, 1955). The conference helped to shape ideas for several decades regarding levels of training, credentialing, and practice. The Thayer Conference proceedings is one of only a few comprehensive surveys of school psychological services undertaken in the first half-century of school psychology, and it is clearly the most comprehensive picture available of the circumstances of school psychology circa 1950. During the 1950s and 1960s, other professional school psychology conferences were conducted in several states. For example, the Peabody Conference (Gray, 1963a), held by the Southern Regional Education Board, was part of a series of meetings that drew attention to the need for training programs and internships. State and regional conferences brought practitioners together, which often led to the founding of state organizations. California provides an excellent example of how coordinated efforts of the state department of education and university staff led to substantial development in a short period of time. It is difficult to determine whether this flurry of meetings was stimulated by the Thayer conference and Division 16, but there appears to have been some connection. These conferences served to facilitate the development of a consensus on role and function and training even though such a consensus was not actually achieved during this period.

Professional Development

Although the impact of the Thayer Conference on school psychology is difficult to judge, it seems to have been less than the impact of the 1949 Boulder Conference on clinical psychology. Clinical psychology shared a closer kinship nourished by an APA Division of Clinical Psychology dating to 1919, numerous state affiliates, a training and internship system supported by APA accreditation and the Veterans' Administration, struggles with organized medicine and psychiatry, and a rapidly growing network of state licensing boards. Despite organizational strength in a few states, school psychology lacked a national kinship at the time of the Thayer Conference and throughout the hybrid years. Thus when APA reorganized, school psychology was off to a slower start than the other professional specialties (i.e., clinical and counseling psychology).

With the reorganization of APA, an upward spiral of development in adult clinical psychology was launched. The full effects of that spiral are observed in contemporary licensing, accrediting, reimbursement policies, and other aspects of clinical psychology, some of which Albee (1998) has criticized as a sell-out to the medical model. Clinical psychology's focus on adults was so strong that only in the past few decades have we observed the reemergence of a strong child-clinical subspecialty. Where World War I had demonstrated the value of tests, World War II launched therapeutic interventions as another service domain for psychologists. Prior to this time, clinical psychology services frequently were delivered to children and adults. The state hospital system was largely controlled by psychiatry, and psychologists' services to adults frequently were restricted or supervised by psychiatrists. State department of education certification for school practice antedated licensure by at least a decade and freed school psychologists from supervision by medical personnel (French, 1990). Psychologists had been unsuccessful in gaining legislative recognition for practice in other settings. The first licensure occurred in Connecticut in 1945 when almost a dozen states already had certification for psychologists practicing in schools. Licensure laws were aimed directly at legitimizing practice by doctoral and to a lesser extent non-doctoral psychologists. No doubt the intent was to free psychological practice from the reins of medical practitioners. The focus was decidedly upon clinical psychologists and, to a lesser degree, counseling and consulting psychologists.

School psychologists were less involved in licensure because they were largely free of medical supervision in the schools and already were being credentialed by several state departments of education. Because many school psychologists were trained in clinical or educational psychology programs, those seeking non-school practice already had preparation in a related field and could quickly identify with that field (e.g., clinical psychology). School psychology was perceived as highly setting-specific. For all practical purposes, it was conducted almost entirely in school settings, usually public schools. Not until the late 1960s was the title of school psychology's APA division changed from school psycho*gists* to school psycho*logy*. The change reflected the quest for a broader identity than practice confined to school settings and an identity distinct from educational and clinical psychology.

School psychologists gained only indirect benefits from the postwar government sponsorship of clinical psychology. Instead, much of school psychology's growth was tied to developments in education. Nevertheless, the postwar period of the hybrid years was important to school psychology even though the profession's growth lagged significantly behind that of clinical psychology. It was the first era in which different groups of professional psychologists became recognized and considered to be professional specialties. Although official recognition of specialties would not occur until the late 1990s (by way of APA's Commission for the Recognition of Specialties and Proficiencies in Professional Psychology), the distinctions would have much to do with the struggles and growth of school psychology in the thoroughbred years. To a large extent, the initial distinctions of specialties were drawn as a result of inter-professional conflicts between clinical psychology and psychiatry, the side effects of which created conflicts between clinical psychology and other psychology specialties. The role expansion in clinical psychology toward therapy was less noticeable in school psychology. Psychological testing continued to dominate the school psychologist's role and function, and broad expansion was thwarted by school administrative restrictions and overlapping claims to intervention functions by guidance and special education personnel (Napoli, 1981). Numerous role perception surveys were conducted in the 1960s along with studies of real versus ideal functions of school psychologists. The studies revealed dissatisfactions with the dominant traditional testing role and preferences for greater involvement in consultation and intervention (Roberts & Solomons, 1970). A national survey by Farling and Hoedt (1971) found that the dominant activities were individual psychoeducational evaluations, report writing, and parent-teacher conferences, and ideal role preferences typically were in favor of reductions in the dominant testing activities with corresponding increases in other areas then receiving lesser attention (e.g., consultation, program evaluation, behavior management).

Role dissatisfactions and preferences evolved from several factors:

1. The professional organization of practitioners provided opportunities to discuss such issues and to propose alternative service systems.
2. The rapid growth of training programs after 1960 put forth a broader philosophy of school psychological services and began to emphasize

non-test functions, and thus a new wave of school psychologists was being produced to replace those leaving the field. The new wave not only was larger, and more broadly oriented to services, but held higher degrees from programs in school psychology, which fostered greater professional identity.

3. Federal education funds were available to sponsor innovative training practices and school services.

4. The special education arena had taken a major expansion when it officially recognized learning disability (LD) as a categorical condition in the late 1960s. While the traditional testing model was spurred by this recognition, there was a flurry of activity in the remediation of LD, and some school psychologists perceived this as an opportunity to shift toward intervention roles (e.g., Valett, 1967).

5. Society's concerns for problems in education were reflected in viewpoints of the schools as systems and organizations. Toward the end of the hybrid years and for much of the next decade there was intense effort to describe school psychologist functions along these lines (e.g., Schmuck & Miles, 1971).

6. The 1960s was a decade of emphasis on prevention and mental health. The Community Mental Health Centers Act and other federal initiatives of the 1960s sensitized the public to mental health, poverty, and social issues requiring intervention. The rapid establishment of mental health centers, community mental health associations, and Head Start programs was reminiscent of an earlier era of clinics and child study clubs.

7. The latter part of the hybrid years was characterized by a shifting intervention orientation from Freudian and dynamic conceptualizations to nondirective Rogerian counseling, brief psychotherapies, sensitivity training, and behavioral therapies. The new approaches were perceived as more compatible with practice in school settings.

8. Finally, there was frustration with the status quo of requiring students to fit into diagnostic categories, ethical concerns about labeling children, and an anti-testing mentality surfacing in the 1960s.

The period also was historically significant for the struggles in civil rights along lines of race, ethnicity, gender and sexual preference. The unprecedented increase of federal involvement in education was observed in events surrounding the space race, school desegregation, and federally funded educational programs (including Head Start). These were significant departures from the past. Public education for many decades had been viewed as an appropriate arena within which to seek major changes in the social fabric. Now, however, it was federal, instead of state and local, agendas that would be encouraged. With the acceptance of federal assistance by schools, though seen by some as an intrusion, the schools could be urged by the federal government to accomplish goals that state and local authorities had failed or refused to accomplish previously.

Organizational Development

The merger of the AAAP into a reorganized APA in 1945 gave school psychologists their first national organizational identity in the form of the Division of School Psychologists (Division 16). As a separate division, school psychology was a distinct organizational entity from clinical psychology (Division 12) and educational psychology (Division 15). Reflecting APA membership generally, membership in Division 16 grew from 133 in 1948, to 601 in 1956, to 1,229 in 1968. Though the division struggled for many years to gain stability, it provided an organizational identity for a growing number of trainers and practitioners, established a loose network of communication among school psychologists in the existing state psychological associations, and drafted guidelines for training and credentialing (see Magary, 1967a, pp. 722-726, for a copy of Division 16's 1962 certification standards). The division also initiated efforts at program accreditation in 1963 and gained approval for the awarding of a school psychology diplomate from APA's American Board of Examiners in Professional Psychology in 1968 (Bent, Packard, & Goldberg, 1999). The annual institutes within the division's APA Convention programs were initiated and widely respected. Though the division failed to capture the membership of most school psychology practitioners nationwide, throughout much of this period it served as a beacon of identity and represented the field to the broader political arena of U.S. psychology and education. During the latter part of the hybrid years, the Division of School Psychology (APA) was an important factor in giving school psychology national recognition and in shaping the sensitivity of state departments of education to the need for improved credential and practice standards.

Though state and local associations for psychologists dated to the 1920s, those for school psychologists were more recent. Ohio appears to have had the first separate state association for school psychologists, founded in 1943, and it was probably among no more than three state groups in the 1940s. Five more associations were founded in the 1950s, and by 1969 there were 17 state school psychology associations (Fagan et al., 1986). The literature of the 1960s helped disseminate the proceedings of several invitational school psychology conferences to a loose network of state and local association members and piqued the interest of school psychologists in Ohio to call an invitational meeting in Columbus in 1968 to consider establishing a rival national group. That meeting led to the historic St. Louis convention, at which the National Association of School Psychologists was officially formed in March 1969. The complex circumstances surrounding this event are described in Fagan (1993).

The trends and accomplishments of the postwar period created an atmosphere of identity for school psychologists, even if it seemed confused in the philosophies of textbook authors and the perplexing mix of training, credentialing, and practice titles. It was under these conditions, and the perceived need to bring practitioners nationwide together in a more stable and strengthened identity, that the National Association of School Psychologists (NASP) was established. The founding of NASP extended the quest for professionalization not only beyond the traditional struggle of academic and applied psychology but also beyond the traditional confines of organized psychology itself, the APA. The event marked the end of the hybrid years and served as the first in a series of events that would characterize the thoroughbred years.

THE THOROUGHBRED YEARS (1970 to PRESENT)

By the end of the hybrid years, school psychology was at least a potentially significant political and professional entity in psychology and education, though potent already in some locales. Most of the symbols of professionalism already had appeared in some form. For example, in the 1930s state education agencies informally identified universities that offered classes appropriate for school psychologists, but formal recognition via accreditation did not appear until the 1960s from the National Council for Accreditation of Teacher Education (NCATE) and in 1971 from APA. The use of standards specifically for school psychology did not occur until the 1980s within the NCATE/NASP relationship (Fagan & Wells, 2000). Thus during the hybrid years training program recognition emerged, but the accreditation model observed today is considerably more formal. The earliest model was a prototype of modern-day state department of education (SDE) program approval. In many states today, both SDE program approval and national accreditation models exist, often interdependently. Similarly, certification procedures today are more sophisticated than at much earlier times when some school psychologists sought certification by going to their state education agency and demonstrating their skill in giving the Binet. Since World War II, state departments of education increasingly have relied upon procedures of transcript review, formal program approvals, and reciprocity in their credentialing practices. Examples for other symbols of professionalism could be given. The point is that much of what has been accomplished in accreditation, association growth, credentials, levels of training, literature, loci of practice, or role and function was discernible by the end of the hybrid years. The existence and impact of these facts (i.e., school psychology's identity), however, were not equally distributed across the country. Many states and most rural areas still lacked viable psychological services in their schools. Variability in services, especially along rural-urban lines, has persisted throughout the history of school psychology.

Regular and Special Education

Table 2.1 identifies the decades of the thoroughbred years as characterized by regulation, association growth, and professional division and reorganization. A number of factors since 1970 have strengthened school psychology's identity and promoted more widespread services. One of these factors was a series of legal challenges to special education. Perhaps best known is *Larry P.* v. *Riles* (1984), which focused on minority assessment and placement issues. These challenges, and subsequent court decisions, brought into sharp focus the need for more sensitive multicultural assessment, improved technical adequacy of tests, broader conceptualizations of assessment, and more responsible caseloads. Perhaps the most significant event was the enactment in 1975 of landmark civil rights legislation, The Education for All Handicapped Children Act (Public Law 94-142), which sensitized every school district to the need for the availability and implementation of special education, including psychological services for all handicapped children. The legislated right to an appropriate education regardless of the nature of handicap followed a long historical struggle of guaranteeing education to women and to minorities, including Native Americans, Hispanics, and African-Americans. The implementation of this legislation, and later that of Public Law 99-457 (1986), extended the educational rights of the handicapped to birth! A third event, 1974 legislation regarding the handling and confidentiality of school records (Public Law 93-380), drew attention to service issues in special and regular education.

These laws had widespread effects on the delivery of psychological services. Prior to this time it was common practice to conduct psychological assessments and recommend special class placements without parent permission. The litigation and federal/state legislation broadened the rights of individuals with disabilities to a free and appropriate public education and reasserted parental and family rights to privacy. Although the legislation and related litigation affected education generally, such laws also served to draw attention (albeit not always favorable) to psychological services, and this attention served as a catalyst for improved practice guidelines. The guidelines emanated from local, state, and national levels. As in the hybrid years, many of these guidelines were externally produced by state education agencies, or other non-psychologist groups. One impact of the new guidelines and regulations was the necessity for gathering and maintaining extensive case documentation related to assessment, conferences, educational plans, placement, reevaluations, and due process hearings. This impact was burdensome for school administrative, instructional, and assessment staff members.

Another factor in the thoroughbred years was the decline in regular education enrollments from 1970 to 1990 and modest increases thereafter. During the same period, special education enrollments increased to 4.5 million children by the late 1980s and to more than 5.5 million by the late 1990s. The large jump in the handicapped student population was an outgrowth of Public Law 94-142 and its subsequent reauthorizations (e.g., Public Law 105-17 in 1997). Within a few years following the implementation of Public Law 94-142 in 1975, special educational services were spreading into previously unserved and underserved regions of the country, and emphasis also was placed on serving children for whom many school districts had not previously assumed responsibility. In the decade preceding this law, the field of learning disabilities had gained official recognition, and its rapid growth in the 1970s contributed to the overall impact of Public Law 94-142. Reminiscent of a much earlier period, education was again experiencing problems in serving the needs of selected groups of students, and school psychologists were called upon for assistance. The impact was observed in the growth in the number of school psychology practitioners and in national and state association activity. The number of practitioners grew from 5,000 in 1970 to at least 10,000 by 1980, 20,000 by 1988, and perhaps 22,000 by the mid 1990s; and the ratio of practitioners to schoolchildren improved to approximately 1:2,000 (Fagan, 1988b) where it has remained (Lund, Reschly, & Connolley Martin, 1998).

Services were available nationwide despite continued variability in delivery systems and practitioner qualifications. However, the resurgence and growth of special education made the distinction between special and regular education even greater. By 1980 most districts had two largely separate systems of instruction: regular education and special education. Comprehensive remedial services, long a part of the regular education arena, all but disappeared in the wake of the enormous growth in services for learning-disabled children in the special education arena. The "Regular Education Initiative" and the inclusion movement of the 1980s and 1990s (a trend toward serving children with disabilities in regular educational settings) may be responses to problems perceived by the dual systems of schooling created since the 1960s. School psychology was now mature enough to be a part of the changing initiatives.

Organizational Developments

By the onset of the thoroughbred years, most states had enough practitioners to organize state associations for school psychologists. In concert with a rapidly growing NASP, the state associations fostered the development and implementation of guidelines for improved practice. One fundamental difference between this and the earlier historical period was a shift from reactive to proactive modes of operation of school psychology association leadership. School psychology was no longer simply responding to what other agencies decided. Instead, school psychology was working proactively to influence the types of decisions other agencies might make. Thus professional regulation was shifting from external to internal influence. This was most clearly seen after 1980 but originated in association activities of the 1970s.

APA also took reactive and proactive positions on legislation throughout this period. Its Division of School Psychology was influential in these positions but lacked the resources to have a significant impact on the field beyond input to its parent organization. The successful growth of NASP drew attention and membership away from Division 16, which before 1969 had been the only national-level school psychology group. Division 16 membership remained stable during this period at between 2,000 and 2,500. Still, APA and Division 16 made important contributions in recent decades. After 8 years of planning by Division 16, APA accredited its first school psychology doctoral program in 1971. APA accreditation grew from three programs in 1972 to 20 in 1980 and, spurred by growing interest in doctoral training and non-school credentials, the number grew to 42 in 1990 and 59 in 1998, including 9 combined specialty programs (APA-Accredited Doctoral Programs in Professional Psychology, 1998; Fagan & Wells, 2000). The approval of school psychology program accreditation was a major symbol of professionalization that helped to establish the field on a closer par with clinical and counseling psychology. Perhaps the only remaining discrepant symbol was the fact that school psychology continued to be practiced primarily by non-doctoral personnel in school settings.

A 1977 APA Council resolution declaring the doctoral degree as required for the title "professional psychologist," and the growing tension between NASP and APA over entry-level and title issues, led to the creation of an APA/NASP Task Force in 1978, currently called the Interorganizational Committee. The organizational tension between APA and NASP reflected state-level tension between state psychology and school psychology associations over matters of credentialing for non-school practice. The task force influenced several interorganizational events and facilitated the possibility for joint accreditation at the doctoral level. The task force also worked with Division 16, NASP, and the University of Minnesota's National School Psychology Inservice Training Network to plan the Spring Hill symposium in 1980 and the Olympia conference in 1981. NASP and Division 16 jointly published the proceedings of the conferences in *School Psychology Review* (see Vol. 10, No. 2, and Vol. 11, No. 2). These conferences helped focus attention on the practice of school psychology. In 1981, APA published its *Specialty Guidelines for the Delivery of Services*, which included separate guidelines for school psychology (APA, 1981). In 1997, APA's Commission for the Recognition of Specialties and Proficiencies in Professional Psychology approved a specialty definition for school psychology prepared from the input of several key school psychology groups including Division 16 and NASP.

In contrast to its first half-century, the second half-century of APA history was increasingly practice-oriented and accompanied by a dramatic shift in practitioner membership. Long-standing tensions between academic and applied psychologists resurfaced. The scientist-practitioner model of the post-World War II APA served as an acceptable compromise between these forces for decades. By the 1980s, however, that perception had changed. The scales appeared to have tipped heavily in favor of the practice side. Professional issues such as licensure, practice privileges, liability insurance, managed care, and third-party payments seemed to consume the energy and financial resources of the APA. Internal political issues led to several unsuccessful attempts to reorganize APA along lines more acceptable to members with scientific interests, and in 1988 the American Psychological Society (APS) was founded as an alternative organization for more academic/scientific psychologists. Whereas practitioners had historically established associations as alternatives to academic-scientific dominance within the APA, the academic-scientific constituency now established an association in response to perceived professional dominance. By 1990 APS boasted 7,500 members, a newsletter (*APS Observer*), a journal (*Psychological Science*), an employment bulletin, and a separate convention. Of historical significance was the formation of the American Association of Applied and Preventive Psychology (AAAPP), which by 1991 was offering its own newsletter (*The Scientist Practitioner*), a journal (*Applied and Preventive Psychology: Current Scientific Perspectives*), a convention in tandem with the APS convention, and a program of liability insurance. By 1999, the membership of the APS was more than 16,000 and that of the AAAPP was more than 800. APS had also added a second journal, *Current Directions*. The APA-APS struggles are analogous to those of the APA and AAAP in the late 1930s. The current struggle, however, pits psychologists against psychologists along presumed lines of scientific interests and pits applied psychologists against one another along presumed lines of clinically based practice versus scientifically based practice. The longevity of these recent organizational life-forms, and their impact on school psychology, remain to be seen. At present their impact has been negligible. At the very least, the national representation of psychologists is now divided more than it has been for nearly a half-century. Should the trend continue, and include the creation of separate state affiliate associations with APS/AAAPP, it could disrupt the political relationships of professional psychologists at the state level. On the other hand, it may renew state-level academic memberships that waned as state associations took on increasingly professional characteristics. Curiously, the APA-APS-AAAPP struggle has gone almost unnoticed in the official discussions of NASP.

From the standpoint of national representation for school psychologists, the thoroughbred years have been dominated by NASP, whose membership grew from 856 in 1969, to 5,000 in 1979, to 14,000 in 1989, and to more than 21,000 by 1999. NASP began accepting state affiliate associations in the early 1970s. Soon the existing associations were affiliating with NASP, while NASP, in turn, was fostering the establishment of new associations that would later become NASP affiliates. By 1980 there were 43 state associations, 33 of which were NASP affiliates, and by 1998 the number had grown to 52 affiliates representing all 50 states, the District of Columbia, and Puerto Rico. The relationship of state associations and NASP was symbiotic. State associations' affiliation with NASP provided a reciprocal network for action that was not possible through Division 16. An example of the utility of the NASP-state relationship came from the 1980 Spring Hill symposium and its follow-up Olympia conference in 1981. The main impact of Division 16 had to be made at the conference because it lacked a network for further action. In contrast, NASP and its affiliates took the framework established at those conferences and carried it back to the state associations for further implementation. This network disseminated and promoted NASP policy implementation and ideas throughout the states. The policies and ideas of Division 16 and APA had to be promoted via the state psychological association network, which represented few school psychologists. Almost every new state school psychology association was established apart from the existing state psychological association. Thus the growth of differently affiliated associations served to extend the NASP-APA differences from the national level to the state level. Reviews of NASP history appear in *School Psychology Digest* (Vol. 8, No. 2), *School Psychology Review* (Vol. 18, No. 2), Fagan (1993, 1994), and Fagan, Gorin, and Tharinger (in press).

Professional Regulation

APA-NASP differences were greatest over policies on the appropriate entry-level and title for school psychologists. At the state level, differences were reflected in conflicts over credentialing. In several states, school psychologists challenged the authority of state-level credentialing agencies to restrict their practice and title to school settings on the basis of not holding the doctoral degree. Where the struggles of clinical psychologists to obtain practice privileges had involved battles with psychiatry and medicine, the battles for non-school practice by school psychologists were almost exclusively between school and clinical psychology groups. The efforts of state associations were assisted by NASP, but this was not a nationally coordinated effort, nor was APA's general opposition coordinated. Primarily these were state-level skirmishes bolstered by national-level technical and financial assistance. Several successes for school psychology were gained, though less so since the mid-1980s. The struggles and successes did much to spur the identity and morale of the profession. In most states, these struggles could not have occurred before the thoroughbred years. By the early 1990s much of the tension had dissipated. The relative calm could be related to several factors: The APA Practice Directorate, with a full-time school psychologist employee, was better able to communicate with NASP; there were more school psychologists obtaining doctoral degrees than earlier in the period (the percent holding the doctorate had jumped from 3% to 20%), making the issue of non-doctoral practice less important; for many non-doctoral school psychologists, non-school and private practice was not a high priority; the NASP National Certification System conferred a new status on many, and that perhaps allayed the need for greater recognition; and in several states credentialing concerns were shifting to the state education agency, where potential credentialing changes threatened long-established school-based practices.

In the school credentialing arena, much of the activity was directed at maintaining high standards in states threatening to downgrade requirements and at raising state requirements to the NASP expectation in states undergoing long-needed revisions. In this latter regard, the NCATE partnership agreements with state education agencies for program accreditation have fostered higher credentialing standards as well. A good bit of the success in improving certification can be attributed to the efforts of the members of the National Association of State Consultants for School Psychological Services. Even though state consultant positions date to the time of Gesell's practice, only about half the states have a state consultant. Little has been written to recognize the efforts of the persons in these state government positions, and perhaps they are among the endangered species in our future. Where they served in a highly administrative role in the hybrid years, in recent times they have also served as liaisons among SDEs, local school psychologists, university training programs, and state associations. The relationship has been important to the reciprocal conveyance of perceived needs of children from school psychological and SDE perspectives. In contrast to the hybrid years, every state has some form of SDE credentialing for school psychology personnel, and many now have non-school practice privileges as well, often by way of specialized licensure (Curtis, Hunley, & Prus, 1998).

Where Division 16 had carried the national banner for school psychology from 1945 to 1970, NASP increasingly has carried it since. Both groups helped to enhance the regulation of the profession and to shift such regulation from strictly external to largely internal mechanisms. The two systems of school psychology operating in the United States—one controlled by education and the other by psychology—will continue to influence training and practice (Fagan, 1986c). Conflicts between APA and NASP dissipated in the past decade, although the process of achieving agreement on the official specialty definition of school psychology revealed long-standing differences in policies and orientations. Division 16 has renewed efforts to raise its practitioner membership and to support practitioners through revising its journal format, focusing on broad educational issues, and producing a series of videotaped interviews on practitioner issues. Perhaps in the coming decades the stage will be set for a consolidation of organizational efforts in school psychology, although formal efforts at unification are not observable. At the very least, continued positive collaboration between APA and NASP and education and psychology could lead to the long-awaited single control system of the profession.

For many years there had been a work force of school psychologists ready to respond to a call for professional organization. NASP and its affiliates provided the call with guidelines and activities that went beyond reactive responses to legislative and litigious events of the period. Almost from the start, NASP initiated training guidelines and accreditation inquiries to NCATE. By the end of its first decade, NASP had approved standards for training, field placements, credentialing, and practice, in addition to a code of ethics and several position statements on important issues (Batsche, Knoff, & Peterson, 1989; Curtis & Zins, 1989). The NASP's standards documents were revised in 1984, 1994, and 1997, and those for training were promulgated through a revised NCATE unit accreditation process that allowed NASP to perform program evaluations through folio review and to list the programs it approved. This followed upon NASP's formal relationships with NCATE, including affiliation in 1976 and constituent member status in 1978. The revised credentialing standards were prominent in the National Certification System in School Psychology (NCSP) initiated in 1988-1989, which included the National School Psychology Examination developed by the Educational Testing Service. The involvement of NASP in the creation of this exam is an excellent example of the reactive-proactive involvement of the 1980s. The NCSP, another symbol of professionalization, enjoyed considerable success, enrolling more than 15,000 school psychologists by 1991 before declining to about 11,000 in 1998. It improved the identity of the field before state credentialing bodies, some of whom quickly adopted the examination, the credential, or both as part of their own credentialing requirements. NASP's training and credentialing requirements were being considered for revision again in 2000, and NASP is exploring the development of an advanced practice credential in addition to the NCSP. The latter is a response to related efforts at national certification for teachers.

Literature

The period 1970–2000 was an extension of the literary accomplishments of the 1960s. NASP established a newsletter in 1969 (now the *Communiqué*), the *School Psychology Digest* in 1972 (now *School Psychology Review*), and published the first directories of training programs and credentialing requirements. The second decade of NASP witnessed a shift toward also publishing books and products for profit, the most successful being *Best Practices in School Psychology* and its revisions (Thomas & Grimes, 1985, 1990, 1995). For its part, Division 16 published a monograph series between 1973 and 1980, and in 1986 began publishing *Professional School Psychology* (now *School Psychology Quarterly*).

In addition to the literary accomplishments of Division 16 and NASP, this period included the founding of *School Psychology International, Journal of Psychoeducational Assessment, Special Services in the Schools*, and more than 30 books on school psychology. The *Handbook of School Psychology* and its revisions

(Reynolds & Gutkin, 1982; Gutkin & Reynolds, 1990; Reynolds & Gutkin, 1999) reflected the combination of diversity and specialization and provides a resource for the field along lines of an earlier handbook by Magary (1967b). Content analyses of this literary period suggested emphasis on testing and assessment and role and function (Fagan, 1986b) and legal issues and future perspectives (Kraus & Mcloughlin, 1997). Other literary shifts are discernible: (a) the proportion of edited books reflected the increased diversity of the field, (b) the sub-specializations were emerging in training and practice, and (c) the school psychologists were not only writing for themselves but for other educational and psychological audiences. Influences beyond school psychology are observable in the areas of test construction, child neuropsychology, special education, and preschool assessment. In the earlier literary period, school psychology had finally produced its own literature, but in the thoroughbred years, this literature spread to other fields. Over a 50-year period school psychologists had shifted from learning about their field from others to teaching others about school psychology and contributing to the literature of other fields. The shift lends further emphasis to the field's maturity and professionalization as a result of the purification process of the thoroughbred years. However, this conclusion is challenged by Frisby (1998) who found that school psychology journals tended to store citations from other (non-school psychology) journals to a greater extent than they fed citations to other journals.

Training

During this period the number of institutions offering training programs grew from an estimated 100 to more than 200. Program enrollment increased to 7,450 in 1977 but decreased to 5,634 in 1987 and then rose to 8,587 by 1997. However, the number of graduates per program has been stable since 1987 (8.4 to 8.9; Thomas (1998)). Over the past 30 years, program and enrollment growth were most notable at the specialist and doctoral levels, corresponding to a sharp decline in master's level programs (Thomas, 1998). Program accreditation became increasingly desirable, benefiting both NCATE and APA. Through its relationship with NCATE, NASP began formal program folio reviews that resulted in programs being designated as NASP approved, in addition to or independent of, the institution's NCATE accreditation status. This development allowed NASP a stronger role in school psychology program recognition even though NASP itself held no accrediting authority. In contrast to the hybrid years, in 1997 all school psychology programs were assumed to hold SDE approval, and 57% of the 294 programs held some form of national accreditation (Thomas, 1998).

Role and Function

The dominance of the assessment role of school psychological services evident in earlier periods has persisted throughout the thoroughbred years (Reschly, 1998).

The 1970s began with a surge of interest in school consultation and organization/systems development but seemed to regress to traditional assessment models as a function of Public Law 94-142. The 1970s was a period of intense special education placement and litigation although their impact on the role and function of most school psychologists seemed more to contract than to expand activities. One study designed to assess the impact of Public Law 94-142 found that though the school psychologist's role had not changed it continued to be constricted, "with heavy emphasis on assessment, rather than prevention, consultation, or intervention," and that too much time was spent with bureaucratic paperwork and with children suspected of having handicapping conditions (Goldwasser, Meyers, Christenson, & Graden, 1983, p. 163). School psychologists reported spending about 70% of their time in assessment activities, 20% in consultation, and 10% in direct intervention to children, and 71% of their time was spent with handicapped children. These activity percentages were supported by Smith (1984). Smith also found that school psychologists desired less time on assessment activities and preferred more time on interventions, consultation, and research. Several of the actual-time versus desired-time discrepancies achieved statistical significance, supporting our contention that role dissatisfaction of the 1960s continued into the 1980s. The trend also was observed in the Reschly and Wilson (1992) and Reschly (1998) studies. It is worth noting that in all of the real-ideal or actual-desired type role and function studies, assessment functions consistently have been the strongest function, whether real or ideal. Thus there is not only an historical tradition of the assessment role but also a strong preference for the role, albeit within limits. The Reschly (1998) data revealed that while the assessment role remained dominant, the specific functions within this role (e.g., assessment techniques) were shifting and that the use of nontraditional assessment approaches were no more nor less time consuming than traditional techniques.

By the late 1980s, forces internal and external to the profession were raising concerns regarding the expansion of special education, especially the more than 100% increase in the number of learning disabled children served. In opposition to the traditional refer-test-report (and placement) delivery model, reformers, including school psychologists, rallied around the banners of alternative services, the *Regular Education Initiative* and varying amounts of inclusion (a modernized, expanded version of an earlier term, mainstreaming). The Regular Education Initiative and its opposition reflected the political instability of traditional special education service models in the wake of persistent efforts to implement the least restrictive environment provisions of Public Law 94-142 and its reauthorizations. Discussions of earlier decades about non-categorical services in special education were shifting (at least for the mildly handicapped, and perhaps for others) to discussions of services outside of special education, the possible reduction of special education enrollments, and the use of funds to prevent children from eventually needing to be placed in special education. Pre-referral assessment and intervention models rapidly gained attention. No doubt rising costs of education at a time when government spending was under scrutiny spurred efforts to reduce special education enrollments since the per pupil cost of special education was more than twice that of regular education (Moore, Strang, Schwartz, & Braddock, 1988).

Changes in the American family since the 1960s gained widespread recognition by the 1980s. The model of the two-parent family, where the father worked out of the home and the mother remained at home to focus upon child rearing and other homemaking duties, became increasingly diminished. Instead, the family of the late twentieth century was often single-parent as the result of divorce, forcing mothers into the workplace for economic survival. The rising cost of living also created hardship for married couples and remarried couples, requiring in many cases both spouses to work outside the home in order to secure and maintain a decent standard of living. A widespread effect of these changes was that many children were being raised in comparatively unsupervised circumstances. The subsequent problems of these and other circumstances were eventually observed in the schools, which prompted national studies and their implications for school psychologists (Fournier & Perry, 1998). By the late 1980s, the intense focus on special education was shifting to another target group: "children at risk." These were not traditional special education children under a new catch phrase. Instead the new, broad category, "children at risk" (Barona & Garcia, 1990) included children of divorce, "latchkey" kids, substance abusers and their children, suicide prone children, pregnant teens, potential "drop outs," and other students who required academic and psychological assistance but probably not traditional special education. These were not necessarily children whose "traits" were consistently impaired but rather whose "states" were temporarily problematic and who were at risk of becoming chronically problematic. Such youngsters required assistance somewhere on a continuum between regular education and special education. In the 1990s, school violence also has captured public attention. Several major incidents in which guns led to the killing of children on school grounds drew school psychologists into another social and educational arena. The U.S. Secretary of Education asked NASP to develop a guidebook for districts, a major achievement in the governmental and professional relations arena for NASP (United States Department of Education, 1998).

Because most at-risk children were not at risk for special education, the potential for consultation-intervention models, in regular education and special education settings, seemed greater than prior to Public Law 94-142. The at-risk population also required assessments and interventions conducted in the regular educational arena. An Office of Special Education and Rehabilitative Services (OSERS/USDE) statement, "The Role of School Psychology in Providing Services to All Children," was a further impetus for positive change (Will, 1989). The recent clamor of direct and curriculum-based assessment may set the stage for the return of widespread remedial services between regular and special education, and the emergence of more effective teacher-assistance services. Where the first decade of the Public Law 94-142 era was assessment and placement intensive, the second decade seemed to shift toward instruction and related services, and more recently toward functional assessments. The shifts toward pre-referral assessment, interventions, and at least secondary prevention for at-risk groups are potential indicators of changes in role and function. There has been a resurgence of activity and interest in consultation and a systems approach to family assessment and intervention, including home-school collaboration (Christenson & Conoley, 1992). However, less resurgent interest in organizational consultation and development seems to have occurred. The future will help determine whether the field is truly emerging from the retrenchment of the 1970s and making its first enduring major role and function change or if Reschly's (1998) data for the period 1985–1996 predict persistent role stability.

One potential barrier to lasting role change is the shortage of practitioners over the past decade. The supply-demand gap is a significant training and service issue. With students facing higher levels of required training, and practitioners entering employment in more diverse settings, the supply problems are anticipated to persist. Though the majority of practitioners continue to be employed in school settings, many have found other employment. Training requirements have increased as a function of higher expectations for program accreditation and for practitioner credentialing at both the doctoral and non-doctoral levels. Other potential barriers to role and function changes are well known: high caseloads, modest salaries, inadequate school budgets, role perceptions held by school administrators, and narrow conceptualizations of the nature of psychological services in schools. Other factors influencing roles and functions are discussed in Chapters 4 and 7. It is not yet clear what impact technological advancements such as computers will have on this process of change. Not surprisingly, this technology has appended itself to the traditional roles of the school psychologist. The advent of computer-generated scoring and report writing services has been received with mixed reviews. However, the expanding availability of information and assistance via internet services may also foster change.

The events of the thoroughbred years have helped the profession of school psychology realize its potential to be a significant entity in education and psychology. The first decade of the thoroughbred years was characterized by association growth and division, professional identity, and increasing regulation of training and practice. It remained for the second and third decades to seek the means to implement such regulation effectively and to consolidate the forces in school psychology. Half or more of the number of training programs, accredited programs, practitioners, available credentials, state associations, and professional literature have developed in the thoroughbred years.

CONCLUSION

The history of school psychology is interwoven with the development of education and psychology in the latter part of the nineteenth century and in the twentieth century. Many of the structural characteristics of contemporary education and psychology were present by 1920, and most structural characteristics of school psychology emerged by that time. This is the first century, however, in which education, psychological science, and school psychology have coexisted and in which formal schooling was widely accepted and required. Over the course of our profession's history we observe a chronology including perceived need for services and then an emergence of services and then training and then credentialing, and all this is followed by rapid growth in all former areas and then accreditation and then, finally, external and internal regulation. The process can be followed in Table 2.3.

Historical study in school psychology suggests the existence of different models of training, credentialing, and practice as opposed to direct extrapolations or expansions of earlier models. For example, in the practice area we still observe many school psychologists functioning similarly to practitioners in the 1920s, but the dominant form today is much different in terms of employer expectations, available technology, referrals, and practitioner preferences. Although testing has persisted as the dominant model, its conceptualizations have changed. In the nineteenth century, phrenology had many advocates, but that method predated the appearance of school psychology. By the late 1800s, Cattell had proposed a battery of "mental tests" (Cattell, 1890) reflecting anthropometric and other ideas that failed to achieve broad acceptance owing largely to problems of external validity and the rival testing methods. It was the application of Binet's work in the early 1900s that brought "mental testing" to the study of higher processes and then gained widespread acceptability. Stern added the notion of the ratio intelligence quotient, and Terman and Merrill made the Binet a household word. Much later

---

TABLE 2.3 Growth of practitioners, training Program institutions, journals, SDE licensure, and state associations in school psychology*

Area	1890	1920	1940	1970	1990	2000
Practitioners	0	200	500	5,000	22,000	25,000
Training Institutions	0	0	2	100	230	218
Certification by SDE	0	0	3	40	50	50
State Associations	0	0	3	17	52	52
Journals	0	0	0	2	7	7

* The figures are approximations based on data available for dates closest in time to the divisions presented. The number of journals includes the *Canadian Journal of School Psychology* and *School Psychology International*.

---

the concept of ratio IQ was replaced by the deviation IQ concept so familiar the Wechsler Scales, and eventually to all major intelligence tests. More recent we observe the growing influence of less inferential assessment forms in adaptive behavior scales, behavior rating scales, curriculum-based assessment, and process-oriented cognitive assessment (Anastasi, 1992). Still, some of the items on contemporary intelligence tests are identical to items 70 years ago, and certain subtests are similar to Cattell's 1890 list (e.g., Number of Letters Repeated on Once Hearing). The case records of Witmer's clinic also reveal direct practical approaches to the assessment of academic problems similar to approaches advocated today. These developments serve to remind us of our roots and that earlier forms of practice may continue to influence present practice. Despite some similarities to earlier practitioners, the dominant ideology of earlier decades was directed at limited ability testing and direct services, with practically no preventive or accountability functions. Current ideology, espousing consultation, therapy, prevention, and accountability, could be observed in limited ways at earlier times, but the testing ideology was dominant in the preferences of employers *and* school psychologists. The roles and functions of the school psychologist have evolved from roles of necessity, to role possibilities, to role preferences and dissatisfactions, to role expansion opportunities. The traditional assessment role itself has broadened in scope as additional personal and environmental factors have gained recognition for contributing to the problems of schoolchildren and their schooling (Fagan, 1995). The focus of psychoeducational assessment is no longer exclusively on the person referred.

The historical study of school psychology reveals that service origins, innovations, or reforms never occur with universal agreement, that change is better appreciated as a well-intended effort at improvement, and that change never occurs uniformly across settings. Our history should be viewed as a period of evolution and transition from various available ideologies and practice models, with one ideology or another and model being dominant in different periods. We must also acknowledge that ideology and practice are not always synonymous. Current professional standards espouse an ideology of training, credentialing, and practice that is far from widespread. Even today, in an era of ideological transition to treatment and prevention in educational settings, we continue to see some educators and practitioners insist on traditional testing functions. What school psychology has sought for many years is a consensus of its ideology with that of its employers that would lead to practice along lines of prevention, consultation, and accountability (research and evaluation), in addition to necessary assessment and therapeutic functions. The advancements of the thoroughbred years have placed such consensus within reach for the first time. For more than a century, our society has looked to its schools and its children as the potential long-range solution to its problems. In that process, society has increasingly turned to various professionals to assist its long-term goals. The historic model of school psychology served well the limited arena of special education placement. That model, and its arena, are ready for change, and already may be in transition. The future of school psychology depends largely on the profession being able to learn from, and improve upon, the ideologies and models of its past.

Many events have helped shape the present condition of school psychology. However simple it may seem, the fact that long ago some psychological practitioners chose to provide services as employees *of* boards of education, as opposed to being external service providers *to* boards of education, may be the most significant trend in school psychology in the twentieth century. This single factor set into motion a field of practice that would increasingly be influenced and regulated by the forces that shape public education and its employees. School psychologists would thereafter struggle to survive and prosper in the two worlds of education and psychology.

In the remaining chapters of this book contemporary issues and practices are discussed that relate to the historical development of school psychology. As you study the following chapters, consider the historical periods and origins discussed in this chapter. Everything discussed has been built upon our history and will at some future point be a part of that history.

NOTE

1.   Portions of this chapter are excerpted from a chapter by Fagan (1990a) and cited here with the permission of the National Association of School Psychologists; from a chapter by Fagan (1990b) and cited here with permission of Lawrence Erlbaum Associates, Inc.; and from an article by Fagan (1992) and cited here with the permission of the American Psychological Association.

CHAPTER 3

The Employment Context of School Psychologists

Where do school psychologists fit into their employment settings? This chapter focuses on U.S. public education, the relationship between its structure and school psychology, and several organizational issues related to practice. Although it touches on educational administration, policy, and finance, this is not a chapter about such matters. Rather it is an introduction to selected topics of schooling relevant to the preparation and practice of school psychologists and serves as an introduction to the educational foundations courses in your preparation. If you have a better understanding of the school psychologist's position in employment settings, your studies of other aspects of education and psychology should be more meaningful.

Society's needs for regulation and governance, protection, recreation, health, and education are served by a complex interplay of public and private agencies at the federal, state, and local level. Although some school psychologists work in federal- and state-level agencies, the majority work at the local community level and almost exclusively with health and educational agencies. Their employment is most often in public educational institutions including county and city school systems, cooperative educational agreements, and related public agencies with educational programs (e.g., developmental disabilities centers, universities). Less frequently, school psychologists are employed in private educational facilities, mental health agencies, medical facilities, and independent private practice. Regardless of their employment setting, school psychologists will be serving children with school-related problems and need to have an understanding of the school setting. Thus, because school psychologists are at some time involved with public schools, we focus our attention first on that institution. Non-school- setting issues are interwoven into the discussion and are discussed separately near the end of the chapter.

PURPOSES OF SCHOOLING

The absence of widespread compulsory schooling prior to the twentieth century does not mean that this has been the first century in which Americans have taken their education seriously. On the contrary, the concept of education and the presence of schools were observable in the early settlements of colonial North America and during every subsequent historical period. The evolution of U.S. society over several centuries reached a point where various forces came together to create a fertile environment in which compulsory education emerged and grew as the dominant model of schooling. The factors involved in creating these conditions included industrialization, urbanization, child labor laws, the changing structure and function of the family, changes in the meaning and status of childhood, the changing status of women, and increased European immigration. As observed in Chapter 2, in combination these forces provided the bases for compulsory education while the subsequent problems of schooling were met by other developments including the rise of psychological science and the availability of "experts."

Whether dominated by religious influences or by the three "R's," U.S. schools have served the dual purposes of transmitting both the basic academic content necessary for individual economic survival and the cultural values considered necessary to ensure the survival of the nation. Goslin (1965) describes the principal functions of schooling as the maintenance and transmission of culture, the encouragement and implementation of change and the discovery of new knowledge, and the allocation of individuals to positions in society. Similar purposes are discussed by Spring (1989) in his description of political, social, and economic purposes of education. Other purposes the schools serve include child care, delinquency prevention, courtship and mate selection, cultural and subgroup identity and stability, and effecting social reforms (Goslin, 1965; Spring, 1989). The purposes of schooling reflect the previously discussed human capital and structural reinforcement interpretations of compulsory schooling (Chapter 2). The U.S. schools are concerned with transmitting knowledge and inculcating proper moral character for citizenship. Recent crises in U.S. education are related to the perception of declining scores on nationally standardized tests (content) and to societal concerns about substance abuse, crime, teen pregnancy, and other "at-risk" conditions that suggest a deterioration of our national character (values).

The broad purposes of schooling are generally consistent across school settings, public or private, serving child populations with or without special needs. However, their interpretation into specific curricular objectives and activities may vary considerably among school settings. Developing character and citizenship may lead to a much different curriculum in a parochial school than in a public school. The public school may offer elementary guidance activities on values clarification whereas the parochial school may prefer religious education stressing obedience to parental authority. In rare instances psychological services may be perceived as counterproductive, as in the case where counseling might encourage the child to behave against parental wishes. In general, however, psychological services are well received in public, private, and parochial school settings.

Varied interpretations of purposes also may occur within a school system. For example, all structural elements of a school system may be in general agreement regarding the system's goal of developing good citizenship. However, when this is interpreted by the school board to mean the provision of sex education, parental and other dissent are often expressed. On the other hand the goal of providing basic educational skills may be interpreted as requiring segregated remedial education programs instead of grouping within the regular classroom. Even though districts have fairly high consensus on goals, the means to the ends for their goals vary, and it is in this variation of means and their outcomes that we observe most sources of controversy.

What does this mean for the school psychologist? School psychologists are employed to help schools develop and achieve their goals. They are aware of the important relationship between academic learning and positive mental health. For school psychologists, personal and social learning as well as academic learning of students are considered important goals for the schools. Thus, through a variety of services, school psychologists seek to improve both the academic and the mental health environments of the school. One frequently encountered conflict is the narrow interpretation of school psychological services by some school administrators and teachers. For example, the goal of developing student character, which could capitalize on consultation and intervention skills, may instead simply employ a school psychologist's testing skills to help the district sort those children judged to have lesser character into special classes which presumably develop greater character. Surveys of school psychologists consistently find the dominance of the assessment role, which raises serious questions regarding the perceptions held by administrators about the match of psychological services to the goals of education. It is an unfortunate fact that in some school districts school psychologists might not be employed if it were not for federal and state legislation requiring those psychologists to perform these assessment functions. School psychologists should be concerned with where they fit into the structure and purposes of education and with what can be done to broaden others' recognition of the school psychologist's training and potential contributions.

The conflicts of goals and their implementation have implications for training as well. Should we train school psychologists strictly for assessment roles and functions since that is what the schools typically employ them to do? For as long as training issues have been discussed, the ideology has been to train school psychologists to perform functions not only within typical employment roles, but also as much or more so for what the role of school psychologists ideally might be. Accredited programs offer comprehensive training for assessment, intervention, consultation, research and evaluation, and other roles. By so doing, training should equip the school psychologist to provide services that go beyond the status quo and to provide role diversity for the present and leadership for the future.

In an ideal world, there would be harmonious congruence among the goals of all parties to education and among the means to implementing these goals. That is, the goals of training programs for school psychologists would be consistent with the goals of school boards and administrators and also would be consistent with those of parents and teachers. Although congruence, or at least similarity of goals, is fairly common, the reality of implementation is often problematic. The constituencies that make up education come from different training orientations and backgrounds that influence their choices of methods for selecting and achieving goals. Sarason's (1971) work discusses conflicts in the perspective of the culture of the school. Even though his book was not directed to school psychologists, it is relevant to their situation. Differences of opinion on the implementation of goals and the use of psychological services are a fact of life. They are even a healthy fact of life, offering alternative viewpoints from among which we may choose goals and the methods for implementing them. In an arena where the training and backgrounds of the constituencies merge to create policy and practice, all parties must be prepared to negotiate preferences to create as harmonious an implementation as possible. Because the school psychologist is in a position of power rather than authority (see later discussion in this chapter), the school psychologist's viewpoint may be given less attention than the viewpoints of groups with more powerful or authoritative influence. This reinforces the importance of the public relations and collaborative consultation roles of the school psychologist.

We should not take for granted that our system of education will survive indefinitely in its current form or that it will always employ school psychologists to facilitate the accomplishment of its goals as it presently does. For most of the history of U.S education, the schools have been without the services of experts such as school psychologists. We must be concerned with the conditions of schooling that make the availability of psychological services important. We have previously identified several historical reasons for the emergence and growth of school psychological services in the twentieth century. It is unlikely that the historical roles (the "sorting" and "repairing" of individual children) alone can effectively and efficiently continue to serve the changing structure and needs of U.S. education. It is important for every prospective school psychologist to ponder why our society has schools, and why those schools employ school psychologists. Consider being asked by a potential employer, "What do you think our district is trying to do in this community, and what can you do to help us achieve those goals?" These are difficult questions to answer if you have been narrowly trained for a basic special education testing model and have little understanding of the overall goals and structure of that school system. If you are not asked such questions during a job interview, we suggest that *you* ask them instead. The answers provide you with a better understanding of what your employer perceives as the needs of the local schools and where you are going to be expected to fit into that perception. Such employer perceptions are crucial to the local determination of the school psychologist's role and function (see Chapters 4 and 7).

SOME BASIC CHARACTERISTICS OF U.S. SCHOOLING

In earlier years, the U.S. public schools consisted primarily of children, teachers, and administrators. Practically no other professional employees, such as supervisors, counselors, or school psychologists were available. Today, there are approximately 5 million school employees, including 2.6 million teachers, 348,000 administrative personnel, 51,000 librarians, 87,000 guidance counselors, and 23,000 school psychologists. They are educating more than 45 million children in more than 16,000 regular and special school districts with more than 87,000 school buildings (Snyder, Hoffman, & Geddes, 1997). The magnitude continues to reflect the opinion of Orlosky, McCleary, Shapiro, and Webb (1984) that "one fifth of the total population of the United States is involved in the education industry, either as students or as employees" (p. 209). Including the private schools would add another 5 million students, 331,000 teachers, 23,600 administrators, 8,900 librarians, 8,600 guidance counselors, serving 26,000 school buildings. Data on the presence of school psychologists in U.S. private education are not available. Virtually every public school district in the country has the availability of specialized services including those of school psychologists, and there are thousands of mental health workers including counselors, psychologists, psychometrists, family therapists, social workers, and other school psychologists practicing outside the schools. The sheer magnitude of the education and mental health industries draws attention to the complexity of schooling and the significance of finding ways to improve services to children through educator/mental health worker collaboration. Despite this magnitude and diversity, considerable structural commonality exists among the local school districts. Before discussing the basic structure, a few points deserve attention.

Responsibility of the States

Federal interest in education has grown in importance throughout the twentieth century corresponding to the changing status of children and the growing interest in them shown by the federal government. Although the future of federal government interest and involvement are unclear, there has never been a period in U.S. history when children were more important or had greater legal status. Despite federal education agencies, legislation, regulations, and funding, and all the national political rhetoric about the value of education, our system of education is the constitutional responsibility of state government and is regulated at the state and local level. There is no national school system. Pressure in various forms is brought to bear from the federal level, but the schools are regulated by the states, according to laws enacted by each state legislature and regulations established by each state board of education and implemented through the state department of education (SDE). The relationship between state and federal governments is one where states voluntarily agree to respond to federal incentives, usually financial incentives, through grants and other funds available to those states that demonstrate compliance with federal regulations for education. The widespread growth of special education since the passage of Public Law 94-142 in the mid-1970s has been an outgrowth of state and local educational agencies responding to federal agency initiatives and regulations. Although this is a voluntary arrangement, it may not be perceived as voluntary because funding is directly linked to compliance, and compliance is viewed as essential to the civil rights of persons with disabilities. Because all states participate in these federal programs, every local district must demonstrate to its SDE that it, too, is in compliance with the federal regulations as interpreted and enforced at the state level.

Diversity and Commonality of Practices

Although states hold the responsibility for education, they differ in the means by which they provide for the education of their citizens. The structure and practices in one state, no matter how effective, may not appear in other states. Some states, such as Nevada, have large county-based school systems resulting in few districts, whereas others, such as Texas and Illinois, are highly decentralized with more than 1,000 districts each. Most states have a mixture of county and local systems resulting in a nationwide total of more than 16,000 school districts. Even within states, the structure and provision of schooling differ greatly. More affluent school districts may offer regular and special educational programs of greater quality than poorer districts. Urban and rural schools may have greater financial problems than suburban schools. Agencies other than the public schools may provide special programs that supplement those offered by the district. The result is a labyrinth of diverse systems and practices of schooling. By leaving education to the states, we have in effect created 50 or more ongoing state-level experiments in regulation and more than 16,000 systems of local implementation.

Despite this diversity, states share several commonalities: They comply with federal regulations in order to secure additional funds; they have an SDE whose staff oversees the delivery of schooling in the state; they are responsible for ensuring that educational opportunities are available to all children in the state; and they establish funding mechanisms, regulations, and procedures for that purpose. However, with the exception of Hawaii and the District of Columbia, no state has a system of schooling that is directed only from the state government level. Instead each state provides for schooling by overseeing the activities of local school districts. It is worth noting, however, that the recent crises in education have led several states to consider statewide curricula, objectives, and testing programs. Despite these efforts to provide greater statewide uniformity of curricula and funding, the delivery of schooling remains at the county and local community levels.

Political Influences and Funding

The schools are intensely political places. There is some truth to the cliché that almost everything that goes on in the school has been voted on at some time, by someone, at some level of government. In an era of increasing accountability, we are witnessing legislative enactment of competency testing with statewide curricula and increased local pressure for student performance linked to increased local government funding. State school boards and many employees of a state's department of education may be politically appointed by the governor. Local school board members are elected by their constituent citizens, some of whom may be parents of children attending the local schools. These locally elected school boards have the final vote on many activities including disciplinary procedures, curricula, special programs, textbooks, and employment. The schools may employ thousands of professional educators, but the enterprise is intensely influenced by a political process managed by nonprofessionals and non-educators. Professionals such as school psychologists, employed to work with or for the public schools, must understand that this political influence is considerably different from employment in non-public school settings. Although such influence is not consistently favorable, it exists in law and holds significant authoritative influence on education and those employed therein.

A closely related aspect of this political influence is the complex process by which public education is financed. School districts obtain their funds from federal, state, and local sources. The interplay of federal, state, and local funding is complex. In comparison to state and local funds, federal funds account for a small portion of a district's overall budget. Since 1919-1920, the percentage of total school revenues from federal sources has increased from .3% to 6.8% in 1994-1995. For the same period, state funding increased from 16.5% to 46.8%, and local funding decreased from 83.2% to 46.4% (Snyder, Hoffman, & Geddes, 1997). The 1994-1995 operating budget for kindergarten through twelfth grade in the United States was approximately 275 billion dollars.

Funds come mainly from state and local sources. These sources include legislative appropriations based on state revenues from a variety of taxes, primarily sales and income taxes, and from city and county sources, primarily local property taxes and secondarily local sales taxes. Thus most school-district financing is closely related to the wealth of its residents and their property, and to the district's ability to attract retail businesses. These tax bases are established and regulated by state and local governments. The allocation side of school finance has its political aspects as well. The portion of local property taxes that will go to the schools is politically regulated by local governments, and the state government usually has rules by which its funds are allocated to districts. Finally, the school district's budget is reviewed and approved by the school board and often by city or county governing boards. Thus all the major sources of funding and the allocation of funds are politically driven. It is easy to understand public sensitivity to education issues considering the extent to which education is supported by taxation and that the only major sources of increased funds for education are through new taxes, increased taxes, or both. This sensitivity is heightened by the fact that citizens may or may not have a direct vote on these tax sources or rates.

State funding may be allocated according to minimum funding formulas that guarantee a minimum per pupil or per classroom expenditure to all districts, or funds may follow a more complicated pattern of differential allocations based on specific employee or educational categories (e.g., different categories of special education). These methods have resulted in a statewide mixture of minimally funded districts with other districts of moderate and more substantial funding. A common benchmark for comparison has been the per pupil expenditure of districts and states. In 1994-1995 the average per pupil expenditure for the United States was $5,988. The range was from a low of $3,656 in Utah to a high of $9,774 in New Jersey (Snyder, Hoffman, & Geddes, 1997). A 1999 newspaper account cited the average per pupil expenditure for the United States at $6,300 (Byrd, Goldsworthy, & Robertson, 1999). Because of various factors, the per pupil expenditure is only a rough index of educational quality, and a large range of such expenditures usually exists in every state (Biddle, 1997).

Achieving greater equity in school district funding among poor and wealthy districts, and often among rural and urban districts, has become a major political issue. The struggle appears to be between the child's right to an equal educational opportunity and the state's responsibility to guarantee at least a minimally adequate education for every child. An obvious and noticeable difference exists between an adequate education and the *most* adequate education one could receive. Although widespread radical reform of school financing seems unlikely, the debate over greater equalization continues. The political controversies and funding schemes have a strong impact on the quantity and quality of educational services available including those delivered by school psychologists. The impact may be observed in available program options; the number of school psychologists employed; and their roles and functions, salaries, and benefits.

A state's foundation program also may guarantee certain levels of funding for various local employee categories. Thus a certain amount of funding may be provided for each teacher in the district (e.g., $8,000). The remainder of the teachers' salaries and benefits are provided through local funds. In several states, foundation categories include pupil personnel workers. Having school psychology as part of the state's minimum foundation program can spur both increased employment and the adequacy of salaries. It is important to note that in most instances the minimum foundation program applies only to employees credentialed through the SDE. Consequently, psychologists who are licensed for private practice but who are not otherwise credentialed by the SDE may cost the district more local funds to employ. Therefore, most school districts employ school psychologists who hold the proper credential from the state department of education. SDE credentials may also determine the availability of tenure within the school setting (Tenure...Questions & Answers, 1997). The distinctions in psychologist credentials will be discussed in Chapter 7. An analysis of school funding in the United States appears in Jordan and Lyons (1992).

Finally, the political nature of public education has its legal side as well. The intermingling of politics and law can be observed in the range of issues, topics, and constituencies the public schools must attempt to manage. For example, the schools must be sensitive to the multicultural character of society. This sensitivity is expressed in its hiring practices, home-school communications, assessment techniques, curricula, and programs. Schools must address gender equality issues in the same areas, as well as in their sports programs. In dealing with children with disabilities, school districts must provide a range of programs and related services including interpreters for the hearing impaired. Physical changes to school buildings must be made to ensure proper access for the disabled or to ensure a more healthy environment by asbestos removal. The necessity to manage so many different perspectives has emerged mainly from legislation and litigation in the past three decades. The greatly increased rights of children to a free and appropriate education have not occurred without subsequent financial woes to most districts. The management of these political-legal aspects in the context of uncertain and changing sources of school funding is a major challenge to the future of public education.

Professional and Business Perspectives

In recent years, attention has been directed at the schools from a private business or corporate perspective in contrast to the professional educational perspective. Some school administrative reform proposals have been drawn from the practices of corporate America. Hence we observe recent practices of school-based decision making and total quality management, with their emphases on local-level input, and business concepts about raw materials, motivation, and productivity (Glasser, 1990; Bender, 1991; Valesky, Forsythe, & Hall, 1992). There is no question that U.S. education is a big business and that business concepts and practices may be successful in improving some aspects of schooling. After all, according to one source (Pipho, 1999) "the K-12 market is a $318 billion market, or 48% of total education expenditures. It is projected to grow 38%, to $440 billion, by 2007" (p. 422). However, the business analogy does not apply in toto to the schools. The schools must strike a balance between business and professional practices and school reform via top-down or bottom-up decision-making practices (Clinchy, 1998). There must be a recognition that children will never enter the business with equal "inputs" and that the environment of the school does not have as much control as the typical business environment has over the "raw material" with which it will choose to work. We must be wary of a competitive spirit which makes gains in academic achievement the "bottom line" for decisions. No doubt several aspects of schooling can be improved by such applications. It is important that school psychologists have participatory involvement in these local-level efforts to improve school management. Such involvement is consistent with the school psychologist's goal of bringing a psychological perspective to bear on the problems of education. The trend of applying a business perspective to the schools is closely related to accountability issues for the school psychologist (discussed in Chapter 5).

SCHOOL PSYCHOLOGISTS IN THE EDUCATIONAL SYSTEM

Power and Authority

To understand the relationship of schooling and school psychology better in the complexities of this political environment, we must understand the relationships of power and authority. For purposes of this discussion, "power" means the individual or collective capacity to hold influence over other people and/or situations. Power may include the use of aggressive, even hostile, physical force, but it is not authorized in law or regulation. A child may have influence over the teacher's methods of instruction or discipline, but the child has no authority to dictate such matters. Parents have the power to resist having their child placed in special education but lack the authority to make the final determination. For a comprehensive discussion of power in school consultation, see Erchul and Raven (1997).

"Authority" means the legal or regulatory capacity to make decisions and have the responsibility for decision-making. In the typical school system, administrative employees have decision-making authority over a limited sphere of activity. The superintendent is responsible for activities within the entire system, principals are responsible for all that goes on in their buildings, and teachers are responsible for the activities of their classrooms. Professional pupil personnel employees (e.g., guidance counselors, school social workers, school psychologists) have practically no decision-making capacity unless it is delegated to them by others in authority. Authority may be direct, as in the case of the relationship between the school board and the superintendent or the superintendent and the school psychologist, or it may be indirect, as in the case of citizens using their elected school board members to carry out their wishes authoritatively.

The relationships of power and authority in a typical school system are depicted in Figure 3.1 and include the following scenarios:

1. Authority, which is greatest at the top, lessens with each level from the top downward; power, which is greatest at the bottom, lessens with each level from the bottom upward.
2. Typically there are fewer people in authority than are in power.
3. The consumers of the system, including parents and children, have little authority despite considerable power.
4. Power-authority conflicts in the school system are the basis of most interprofessional problems.
5. Professional psychologists employed by the schools never make decisions for others in any authoritative manner except when such authority has been delegated to them by someone in the system who has such authority.
6. Power and authority may vary as a function of the situation. For school psychologists this simply means their power (influence) will be greater or lesser in some situations. For example, the school psychologist may be perceived as having greater influence in team decisions related to children with mental retardation than in decisions related to children with physical disabilities.
7. Perceived authority exists in situations where an employee having no real authority is believed by others to have authority. Occasionally parents and teachers will ascribe to school psychologists authoritative roles that school psychologists do not possess. For example, parents may behave toward school psychologists as though the latter have the decision-making authority for placing their children in special education. Although perceived authority may appear to be an advantage for the practitioner in some situations, the limits of one's authority always should be made clear to the client(s).

School psychologists operate from a base of power, but they generally have no authority to make decisions that affect others in their sphere of activity. For example, the school psychologist individually does not have the authority to make a final decision regarding a child's eligibility for special education services. Such decision-making authority rests with a multidisciplinary team to which the school psychologist should belong. Of course, school psychologists influence these decisions by exercising their professional judgment of the child's circumstances based on psychological observations and interpretations. It is important to note that school psychologists only provide opinions based on their professional expertise. They do not make decisions for others. As legal guardians of their children, parents are free to contest the opinions of the psychologist and may seek second opinions or redress through due process hearing provisions of the special education regulations. Although the school psychologist may be displeased with or threatened by such prospects, that is the nature of the professional-client relationship. Before jumping to conclusions, place yourself in the role of parent and ask what parental authority you would like to retain in the event that your child were referred to a psychologist. More about this relationship is discussed later in this chapter.

FIGURE 3.1 Power and authority relationships in school settings. Although the number of persons increases with each lower level, the relative sizes presented are not intended to convey specific proportions. School psychologists are included in special services.

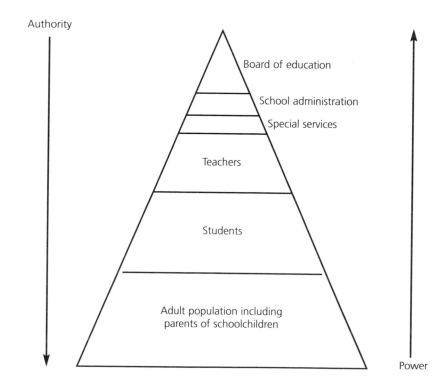

In recent years, opportunities have improved for school psychologists to advance to administrative positions in school districts. Thus the former school psychologist, operating from a base of power, may now hold an administrative position such as school principal, pupil personnel director, director of special education, or perhaps even district superintendent. In such instances, the trained school psychologist has been allocated a position of considerable authority. However, the person is now serving the district as an administrator and not as a school psychologist. Nevertheless, the new position could bring about an effective blend of authority and power. The change of position may sensitize other administrators to the value of school psychological services. Perhaps with increased numbers of school psychologists aspiring to such positions, greater opportunities for broadening the role of psychological services will be achieved (see e.g., Blagg, Durbin, Kelly, McHugh, & Safranski, 1997).

School psychologists customarily operate from bases of power that include "referent power" and "expert power" (Martin, 1978). Referent power exists when school psychologists are perceived to be helpful persons with values and goals similar to those of their clients. Referent power is a process of identification that usually develops over a long period of time in a working relationship between school psychologists and their clients. Expert power exists when the school psychologist is perceived to have valuable information regardless of the level of referent power. Expert power may be developed on a short-term basis and related more to credentials and perceived professional knowledge than to the extent to which the professional's goals seem similar to those of the client. Developing a balance of referent and expert power is important to overall success in the day-to-day practice of the school psychologist. The concepts of power and authority are important in developing an understanding of the school psychologist's position in the structure of schooling, as well as in the state and national arenas of credentialing and accreditation (see Chapter 7).

Structure and Location of Services

Let us now look at the organizational location of psychological services within the basic structure of schooling at the state and local levels. Figure 3.2 represents the flow of power and authority in the structural arrangement of education in the state. The principal agencies include the legislature; SDE; subordinate educational agencies including city, county, urban, and cooperative educational systems; and the subparts of those systems from governing board to individual pupil. In the examples provided, authority flows from the legislature's constitutional responsibility for the education of the state's citizens to the state board of education and its state department of education, which prepare and implement regulations to carry out the legislature's decisions, to the local board of education responsible for implementing the state's regulations, while also representing the desires of its constituent

FIGURE 3.2 Flow chart of responsibility for education

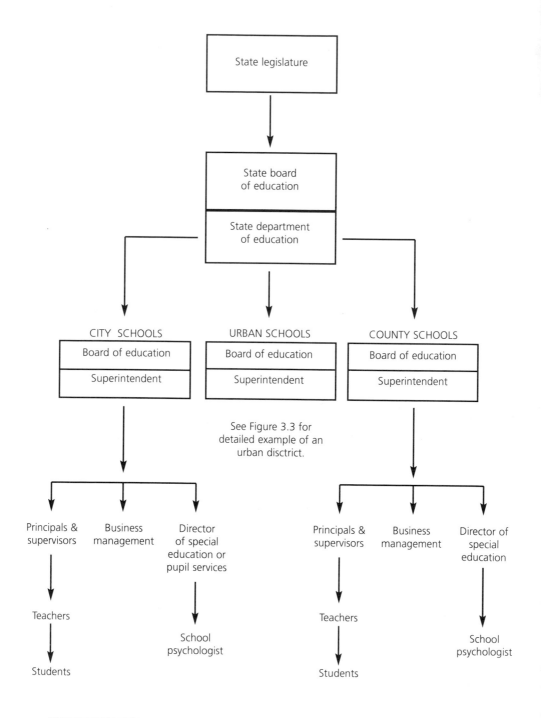

See Figure 3.3 for detailed example of an urban disctrict.

populace regarding the style of local schooling, to the superintendent and administrative structure responsible for carrying out the local board's decisions and to the principals responsible to the superintendent for the implementation of policies in their buildings and then to teachers responsible for the classroom interpretation and curricular delivery of the many state and local decisions. Undergirding the entire structure is the power of parents and guardians, whose children are the recipients of all of the above.

Figure 3.2 shows the usual position of school psychologists in this structure for city and county school systems. The model is representative of most smaller school systems including those in rural areas. The school psychologist usually is directly responsible to the school superintendent or to a director of special education or pupil personnel services. In the small city and county system, the school psychologist often is linked directly with special education, may be immediately responsible to the director of special education, and may even have an office in physical proximity to the district's top administrators.

Another structural arrangement is represented in Figures 3.3 and 3.4, which identify the position of school psychologists in a large urban school system with a vast array of special services. The figures depict the structural arrangements for the Memphis City Schools, a district that in 1995 had 109,000 students and ranked 21st in size among districts in the United States. In contrast to Figure 3.2, the urban school psychologist is one of many service providers within an administrative structure for psychological services. The structure may be within a larger administrative unit for special education, mental health, or pupil personnel services. The school psychologist may be in relative proximity to other mental health and pupil service professionals but not be very close to administrative lines of authoritative influence. The example locates school psychologists in the Memphis City Schools Mental Health Center (MCSMHC), which is administered by the Division of Mental Health and Student Support (Figure 3.3). The array of psychological, social work, and other mental health services provided by the center is depicted in Figure 3.4. School psychologists may be assigned to traditional assessment and consultation roles, as well as to alcohol and drug abuse, sex abuse, or other special assignments. The MCSMHC has an overall director, with two center administrators over services to different geographic areas of the district, a third administrator for the Center for Safe and Drug Free Schools, and a Guidance Program coordinator (Figure 3.4). The division of Mental Health and Student Support is structurally related to the Division for Exceptional Children, with both under the Department of Student Programs and Services. The organizational relationship of both of these divisions is authoritatively separated from the Division for Pupil Services. This may have considerable impact on the overall orientation of services. School psychologists are not linked solely to special education to act as gatekeepers for special educational eligibility even though they provide

FIGURE 3.3 Example chart of responsibilities and administrative relationships in urban school settings. Reproduced by permission of the Memphis City Schools, Memphis, TN.

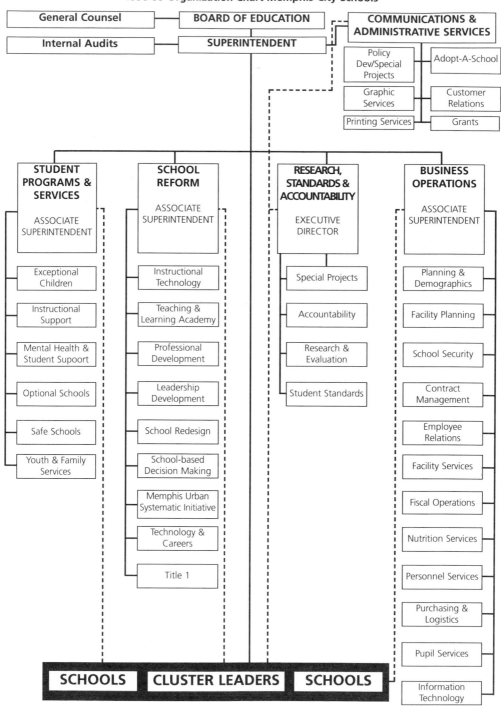

1998-99 Organization Chart Memphis City Schools

several diagnostic and other services for the special education division. In this district's structure, the Division of Pupil Services does not include the services of school psychologists, counselors, and social workers but is instead linked to attendance and management information services. Furthermore, the services of school psychologists are structurally disconnected from research and evaluation and several school reform efforts under other departments. Nevertheless, the title of the psychological services unit as a mental health center signals the breadth of its orientation and services as well as its availability to the regular education sector. As noted in Figure 3.4, each subdivision of the center has broad role expectations for prevention, intervention, assessment, treatment, and training. The Memphis City schools' organization of school psychological services is supported by local, state, and federal education funds and by other federal and state funds related to mental health. The MCSMHC was started in the early 1970s and it serves as one of several centers in the local county's overall mental health plan. It is a full-fledged mental health center and provides a comprehensive range of mental health services including crisis intervention, family counseling, drug and alcohol abuse counseling, and sex abuse counseling. All school psychological services for the Memphis City Schools are delivered through this center, which employs appropriately credentialed school, counseling, and clinical psychologists in addition to social workers, guidance counselors, and substance abuse counselors. Although the overall organizational structure of the Memphis City Schools is typical of large urban districts, the mental health center concept is a unique service delivery scheme. Other issues related to school psychologists' organizational position are discussed later.

Additional organizational structure arrangements are represented in Figure 3.5, which depicts three alternative types of service delivery to one or more school settings, public or private. The first is where the local educational agency is a "cooperative agreement district." Several arrangements of joint or cooperative agreements are in operation in the United States (Benson, 1985). For example, in rural areas several school districts may combine resources to provide services for children with disabilities. Even in suburban areas districts may combine resources to provide more efficient services for children with low-incidence disabilities (e.g., blindness). Cooperative arrangements typically are found in rural areas but may be distributed throughout the entire state to serve special populations of children. These arrangements attempt to maximize the provision of services while minimizing the costs of service provision through sharing. In most instances, these agreements are created among local and county school districts, and the overall agreement is managed by one or more member districts. The special educational services typically are provided in the existing facilities of participating districts. The joint agreement will have its own board and director and will employ a variety of special teachers and pupil service workers including school psychologists. The cooperative may contract for, or employ, specialized services such as physical therapists.

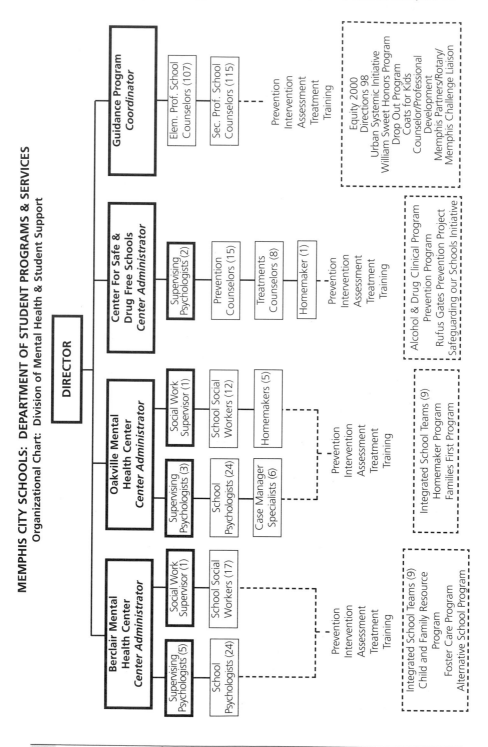

MEMPHIS CITY SCHOOLS: DEPARTMENT OF STUDENT PROGRAMS & SERVICES
Organizational Chart: Division of Mental Health & Student Support

FIGURE 3.4 Example chart of responsibility and relationships in urban school psychological services. Reproduced by permission of the Memphis City Schools, Memphis, TN.

A second arrangement is where the school psychologist is hired by a "non-educational agency," such as a rural mental health center, specifically to serve the needs of several school settings that have agreed to share the cost of such services. In this instance, the school psychologist will usually be an employee of the mental health agency and not of the participating school districts. Services could be delivered from the center to the school settings with the school psychologist's office located at the mental health center. In other arrangements, the services are provided at the center with children being brought to the center by parents. In this arrangement, the school psychologist often works side by side with clinical or counseling psychologists who are not serving the schools, and perhaps with social workers, and a psychiatrist who is on-call to the mental health center. The size and diversity of the staff often are a function of the center's location, funding, and the availability of other service agencies. In rural areas, the staff may be small, and the mental health center may be linked to an adult rehabilitation center.

A third arrangement is where the school psychologist is "self-employed" and working with several school settings concurrently, serving perhaps one day per week in each. This practice, often referred to as "contractual services," generally is frowned upon by district-based school psychologists because duties tend to be limited narrowly to testing services. In addition, the local district can be perceived as shirking its responsibility to provide comprehensive psychological services. Nevertheless, contractual services are common in some rural settings particularly

FIGURE 3.5 Other organizational arrangements for delivering school psychological services

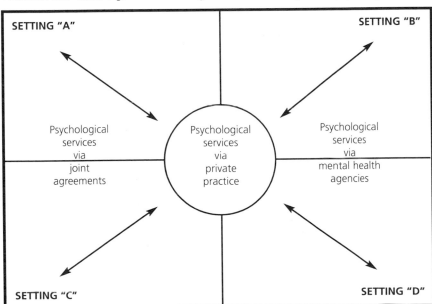

when a full-time school psychologist cannot be recruited, and this arrangement may be used for selected services such as reevaluations in combination with other services provided by district-based school psychologists. Examples exist that provide the favorable aspects of contractual services (Allen, 1993; Wonderly & Mcloughlin, 1984). In response to some contractual practices, associations have tended to provide guidelines for such services rather than shun them entirely (American Psychological Association, 1995; NASP, 1997b). In Tennessee, for example, the SDE has a chapter on contractual services in its *Student Evaluation Manual* (Tennessee Department of Education, 1993). The chapter discusses the concept of contractual services, the importance of comprehensive services to all schoolchildren, the credentials to be sought in contractual employees, and a sample contractual agreement. It is stressed that contractual services are not intended to be a less expensive substitute for offering more comprehensive services via district-employed school psychologists. Although the dominant model of service delivery is depicted in Figure 3.2, the examples in Figure 3.5 suggest the diversity of delivery options that may be appropriate in some circumstances. It is our opinion that the future of school psychology will witness increasing diversity in the options available for the delivery of school psychological services (see Chapter 11). Among these will be comprehensive school-based health clinics (Pfeiffer & Reddy, 1998; Tyson, 1999; Vance & Pumariega, 1999).

FIGURE 3.6 Relationship of pupil personnel services to regular and special education

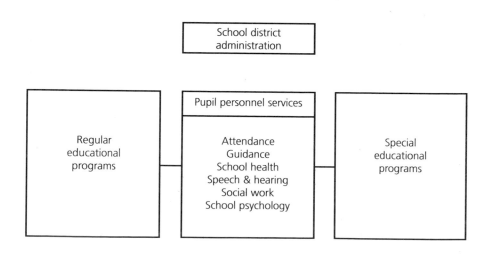

Importance of Administrative Location

At the local level, public education is composed of two major instructional sectors: regular education serving approximately 90% of the school population and special education serving about 10%, which includes children identified as disabled according to federal guidelines (e.g., mentally retarded, learning disabled) and additional categories according to state or local guidelines (e.g., gifted, teen pregnancies). The rapid growth of special education since the 1960s has been accompanied by a decline in generally available academic remedial services in regular education. In effect, public education has become divided into students within the regular educational sector and those within the special educational sector. For too many students this means special assistance is unavailable unless their circumstances are serious enough to warrant placement in special education. One exception to this decline has been the widespread availability of "Chapter 1" instructional services for millions of disadvantaged children (Stringfield, 1991). Yet many districts continue to have a very limited number of remedial services available to students in the domain of regular education who are not qualified for Chapter 1 services. The recent interest in direct assessment and intervention for pupils' academic and behavioral problems is an outgrowth of the realization that many students in need of assistance are not now eligible, nor are they likely to be eligible later, for placement in special education. Pupil personnel service workers are involved in the referral to and delivery of available remedial services in much the same way that they serve the arena of special education.

School psychologists are part of a concept of "pupil personnel services" (PPS) situated between regular and special education. These services may be administered from different district departments or contracts and are depicted together in Figure 3.6 only for convenience of illustration. The concept of PPS historically has included persons in the fields of school psychology, school social work, guidance and counseling, speech and hearing, school health, and attendance (Ferguson, 1963; Hummel & Humes, 1984). The PPS staff may be large and diverse as in urban districts (see Figures 3.3 and 3.4) or very small by comparison as in many rural districts (e.g., see Devore & Fagan, 1979).

Pupil personnel services, though available for the educational improvement of students in regular and special educational sectors, often help to regulate the flow of students from one sector to the other, or within sectors. It is this relationship that has led to the term "gatekeeper" being assigned to school psychologists and others involved in this activity. Different combinations of pupil personnel workers spend varying amounts of time working on behalf of each sector. The flow between regular education and special educational services often involves school psychologists, speech and language clinicians, and social workers. These professionals also spend time working with children in the regular sector but traditionally have been more heavily involved with special education. School health, guidance and counseling, and attendance workers spend most of their time on behalf of children and programs in the regular sector.

Within the special education sector a variety of service options exist. The general model for these options was presented by Deno (1970) and discussed in Dunn (1973) and often is referred to as the "cascade plan of services." Regardless of the categorical nature of the child's disability, the options serve as a guide for intervention and placement decisions, and the options are related to the concepts of mainstreaming, normalization, inclusion, and the least restrictive environment provisions of federal and state regulations. Many of the options overlap the regular and special education sectors. A detailed discussion of these services and options will be given in your courses on childhood exceptionalities and interventions.

Within the special education sector, the school psychologist often is administratively responsible to a director of special education (most often a trained special educator with administrative certification). Almost the entire business of referral management—assessment, placement decisions, interventions, follow-up, and reevaluations—routinely flows through this administrator's department. At the local school-building level, school-based support teams review requests for service, conduct pre-referral assessments, and engage school psychologists in various roles. There are also multidisciplinary assessment teams and teams that develop individual educational plans and/or family service plans including an array of instructional and related services for eligible children. The school psychologist should be organizationally positioned to work on behalf of children in the regular and the special education sectors and to be involved with the entire array of these service options.

When administratively located within a department of pupil personnel services, school psychologists may have a greater identity with the entire school system and not just with special education. In this arrangement, psychological services on behalf of children suspected of having disabilities are coordinated through the pupil personnel services and the special education units. A natural tension often exists between these units as their respective administrators strive to serve the needs of the regular and special educational sectors of the district. When the respective directors have parity in administrative authority and influence with upper level administrators, comprehensive service delivery should result. When parity is lacking, school psychological services may be drawn too heavily toward or away from regular or special education. In some instances, special education and pupil personnel services may be under one another's administrative authority, as when PPS is organizationally subservient to a department of special education and its director. In this arrangement school psychological services are likely to be drawn more toward the needs of children suspected of having disabilities than to the needs of other at-risk children in the regular setting. The trend toward serving eligible special education students in regular educational settings (sometimes referred to as "mainstreaming," the "regular education initiative," or "inclusion") may be more difficult when organizational location of school psychologists is inconsistent with the desired practices. It also is unclear what impact the movement toward inclusion will have on the organizational location of special education and psychological services.

It is important to note that in the above organizational arrangements (Figures 3.1 to 3.5), school psychologists consistently are disconnected from the line of authority extending from administrators to students and are instead organizationally appended to the lines of powerful influence. The physical proximity of the school psychologist to the school administration is an important consideration in these arrangements. There are trade-offs involved. Whereas the school psychologist has the advantage of professional psychologist supervision in the larger school settings, considerable distance may exist between the practitioner and the central administration, and it is doubtful the school psychologist obtains a working knowledge of the entire district. In smaller districts, closer access to administration exists. The school psychologist often serves every school in the district but may be provided administrative supervision by a non-psychologist. These trade-offs have implications for the power-authority issues in practice. That is, the organizational placement of school psychologists affects how much influence, or power, school psychologists may be able to exert on system policies and programs.

A related issue is whether the school psychologist's office should be in the local school building or in a more centralized office. The advantages and disadvantages of the central administration location has already been mentioned. Although an office in the local building would have the advantages of proximity to teachers and students, especially for consultation and crises, and encourage the school psychologist to feel more like one of the building's professional employees, there are disadvantages, too. For example, few school psychologists have the luxury of serving only one building. Consequently, teachers and administrators in other buildings, where the school psychologist is not housed, might feel slighted. Being in a local building might also lead to an overload of referrals and complaints that the school psychologist is not spending enough time on assessments. Much of the school psychologist's time can be devoted to consultation and administrative tasks that are not as visible to others in the building. Objectivity may be an issue as well. Among the services a school psychologist brings to the schools is a professional viewpoint from beyond the building-level context and perhaps its biases. Nevertheless, where availability of school psychologists is sufficient to support services on a single-building basis, we believe the advantages would outweigh the disadvantages as long as school psychologists continue to have opportunities to provide input on district-wide policies and concerns.

The local organizational arrangements often have counterparts in the state department of education. For example, school psychological services usually are coordinated at the state level by the SDE (see Figure 3.2) through a department of special education, special services, or pupil personnel services. The state-level department has the dual role of developing as well as disseminating credentialing requirements, training and employment opportunities, and practice guidelines. The person responsible for coordinating this may have little or no school psychology training. In almost half the states, there is no credentialed school psychologist working for the state education agency to whom districts and school psychologists may turn for assistance. Thus power-authority and organizational issues and conflicts observable at the local district level may pervade the delivery of services statewide.

Administrative Versus Professional Supervision

The issue of administrative versus professional supervision is very important. "Administrative supervision" refers to supervision regarding specific interpretation and implementation of district policies and regulations to school psychologists in their capacity as employees (Strein, 1996a). For example, the superintendent approves school psychologists' requests for reimbursement for expenses at professional meetings according to a specific per diem schedule of payment. Professional supervision" refers to specific interpretation and implementation of actions taken by school psychologists in their capacity as professional psychologists (Strein, 1996b). For instance, the director of psychological services assists school psychologists in their interpretation of case study information and intervention recommendations. In many instances, school psychologists are organizationally subordinate to non-psychologists (e.g., director of special education, principal, or superintendent). In an earlier survey, the most frequently identified backgrounds for the practitioners' supervisors were special education (35%), school psychology (37%), clinical psychology (4%), and regular education (16%) (Smith et al. 1992). Persons without background in school psychology accounted for more than 60% of the supervisors. School psychologists have the responsibility for choosing their methods of assessment and intervention, though in some unfortunate instances this is usurped by persons in administrative authority without such expertise. Psychologists must retain the capacity to make choices within their domain of expertise (e.g., selection of tests, counseling strategies, and program evaluation methodologies) when administratively supervised by non-psychological personnel. In larger school systems, professional and administrative supervision are more often available from persons trained in psychology or a closely related field. This arrangement better assures that administrative supervision will be sensitive to the issues of psychologists and that professional supervision will be available from another trained psychologist. Such arrangements are in closer conformity with the standards of national organizations for school psychologists (APA, 1981; NASP 1997b). A recent survey of practicing school psychologists indicated that clinical (professional) supervision fell below the levels recommended by the APA and the NASP. Only 10% of responding practitioners were involved in clinical supervision, although most school psychologists desired to be involved in such supervision (Fischetti & Crespi, 1999). A study of school psychologists in West Virginia suggests that the supervisor's level and area of training are related to the overall job satisfaction of school psychologists (Solly & Hohenshil, 1986). In the Fischetti & Crespi (1999) study, the practitioners involved in supervision were generally being supervised by qualified personnel.

Systemic Influences

Where the school psychologist is positioned in the organizational structure also influences service delivery. System factors have been discussed in many sources, and conflicts with school administrators and organizational policies have been discussed throughout our history (Symonds, 1933; Wallin, 1920). Organizational influences on school psychology practice are described by Curtis and Zins (1986), Illback, (1992), and Maher, Illback, and Zins (1984). Organizational factors and the topic of school reform appear in a *School Psychology Review* miniseries (1996, Vol. 25, No. 4). These discussions view the school system and other employment settings from a dynamic systems perspective in which changes in one aspect of the system influence greater or lesser changes in other parts. Thus aspects of the system's goals, administrative structure, policies, funding, or collegial relationships influence the manner in which psychological services will be organized and delivered within the system. Curtis and Zins (1986) also discuss the factors influencing the delivery of services within the school psychology administrative unit (e.g., orientation and philosophy, supervision). Little is known empirically about the impact of these different factors on the effectiveness of services. The available discussions, however, provide informative and practical investigations of the intuitive relationships that exist. This topic will be discussed again in Chapters 4, 7, and 8.

Employee Benefits

In addition to the factors that influence practice, employee benefits deserve consideration. There are distinct advantages to public school district or agency employment that often are not available with other arrangements. These include the possibilities for tenure, collective bargaining, employment and salary stability, travel expenses and mileage, continuing education, sick leave and insurance programs, retirement programs, credit unions, office space, secretarial assistance, equipment, phones, and mail. Further, districts and agencies often provide their own assessment policies and procedures, testing equipment, intervention materials, and supplies at no cost to the employee. Few of these benefits are available to school psychologists in independent private practice and some (e.g., tenure) are not available to those employed in non-public school settings.

Collective Bargaining

The issue of collective bargaining is perhaps of greater significance to teachers than to most school psychologists. However, because teachers constitute the largest employee group in a public school district, their bargaining unit often seeks to represent and bargain on behalf of many other employee groups, including school psychologists. The implications of this include power-authority conflicts that can affect services to children and families. School psychologists, especially those in urban settings, became concerned with such matters in the 1960s and 1970s, when greater militancy on the part of teachers often placed school psychologists between the administration and teachers in the event of strikes. Some associations of school psychologists adopted the position that school psychologists were neither administrators nor teachers and that they should not be forced "to support actively one side or the other" or be assigned "to duties other than those regularly pursued by the psychologist in normal circumstances" (NASP Adopts Position on Testing and Strikes, 1973, p. 1). More recent policy statements make references to relationships with other professionals but do not directly discuss collective bargaining and work stoppages (APA, 1981; NASP, 1997b). In some larger districts, school psychologists have established their own bargaining unit, whereas in others, typically small and rural settings, school psychologists negotiate individually with the administration. An earlier survey of NASP membership indicated that 37% belonged to the National Education Association (NEA), 9% to the American Federation of Teachers (AFT), and 35% to a local teacher union (Graden & Curtis, 1991). Local membership in a teacher union may be contingent on belonging to its state and national affiliate. In the previous example of the Memphis City Schools, the school psychologists have a representative to the teacher union, the Memphis Education Association, which bargains for them. Local membership fees include dues for state and national membership.

Collective bargaining is related to the "guest" analogy (see later discussion) and the question of whether school psychologists also should hold teacher licensure (see Chapter 6). In some states, the school psychology credential issued by the SDE is considered a teaching credential with simply an endorsement in school psychology as though it were a teaching field. In others, the SDE may issue a separate credential for pupil personnel services specialists or a similar title. The regulations and policies in education typically are oriented to SDE credentialed instructional personnel. Persons not so credentialed may not be included in some benefits of the school setting. Recent legislation in Arizona has created conditions where SDE-credentialed school psychologists may not continue to enjoy the same contract and due process rights held by teachers (Sanders, 1992). In other instances, school psychologists who hold teacher certification have been concerned that during teaching strikes they might be pressed into classroom service. The issues involved reflect the long history of psychological personnel seeking parity and status with others in the school setting while also seeking a separate identity as psychologists. For a discussion of the issues and positions surrounding collective bargaining in school psychology see Agin (1979) and Hyman, Friel, and Parsons (1975). For a brief discussion of collective bargaining via the NEA and the AFT see Spring (1989).

Job Satisfaction

Job satisfaction is a frequently surveyed aspect of the employment setting. Studies of job satisfaction have shown that school psychologists, especially those with several years of experience, are generally satisfied with their employment and that they have a positive outlook on the future of school psychology (Smith, 1984; Smith et al., 1992; Brown, Hohenshil, & Brown, 1998). A related study suggested that the percentage of practitioners planning to remain in the field until retirement had increased from 31% to 41% since the mid-1980s, and 77% said they would choose school psychology again as a career (Reschly & Wilson, 1992). Affiliation with professional school psychology associations seems positively related to satisfaction (Levinson, Fetchkan, & Hohenshil, 1988). The ratio of school psychologists to students seems related to satisfaction as well (Anderson, Hohenshil, & Brown, 1984; Fagan, 1988b), and this relationship may be partially explained by the broader functioning of school psychologists who serve with better ratios (Smith, 1984; Smith et al., 1992). There is also some evidence that job satisfaction may be related to gender issues in the workplace (Conoley & Henning-Stout, 1990; Henning-Stout, 1992). As indicated earlier, a study of school psychologists in West Virginia suggested that the supervisor's level and area of training were related to overall job satisfaction of school psychologists (Solly & Hohenshil, 1986). Satisfaction seemed greater when the supervisor's training and expertise approximated that of the school psychologist. Two factors appear most closely related to dissatisfaction: (a) school system policies and practices and (b) perceived lack of opportunities for advancement (Anderson, et al., 1984; Levinson et al., 1988). No doubt, the perception of dissatisfaction caused by policies and practices is related to supervisory and organizational issues. Finally, job dissatisfaction including employment conditions related to caseloads, supervision, and desire to leave the profession appears to be implicated in practitioner burnout. The extent of burnout has been judged to be a "serious concern" (Huebner, 1992), and several aspects of school psychologist employment have been identified as stressful (Wise, 1985). We return to such issues in our discussion of seeking employment in Chapter 8.

The limitations to career advancement within the school system are inherent in the nature of school psychologist preparation. As shown in the next section, the school psychologist is to some extent treated as a "guest" in the public school system. Because school psychologists' credentials are unlike those of other members of the system (i.e., they typically lack a teaching credential and experience), there are few avenues for advancement within the schools. The most typical avenues of advancement for school psychologists are administrative positions in psychology or pupil services (e.g., director of psychological services). For school psychologists who hold a teaching certificate and sufficient experience, advancement to other administrative positions is available (e.g., director of special education, principal). In several states, school psychologists have gained approval to use years of experience as a school psychologist as a substitute for the teaching experience requirement for administrative credentials.

The "Guest" in the School

The house of education is populated primarily by teachers and others trained in education and historically has been perceived as devoted primarily to the teaching of children. It is perceived by many members of the school and the broader community as a place for the delivery of instructional services and not necessarily psychological services. With all the previously discussed factors influencing the schools and the character of its organizational structure, it is easy to understand how non-instructional and non-administrative personnel such as school psychologists are perceived as outsiders or as "guests" in the house of education (Elliott & Witt, 1986b). In a recent survey of school personnel, more than half viewed the school psychologist as a guest in the building rather than a member of the school staff (Hagemeier, Bischoff, Jacobs, & Osmon, 1998). School psychologists may lament these perceptions but they are part of the reality of many school systems. Even staff members in maintenance, cafeteria, and office positions may be perceived as more important to the operation of the school than is the school psychologist. We expand upon the guest analogy by positing several ways in which school psychologists are perceived due to the attributions and expectations generally held of guests. All pupil personnel workers share these problems of perception to greater or lesser degrees.

1. Each house has its own rules. Every school building, and to some extent each of its classrooms, has its own written and unwritten rules for many things including dress, conduct, communication, scheduling, or protocol. Because school psychologists are neither instructional nor building-based personnel, they may not be perceived as fitting easily into the established rules of the local building or classroom. Instead school psychologists often are perceived as belonging to a different house with a different set of rules. Thus the school psychologist's general orientation may be more akin to the issues and values of psychologists than to those of classroom teachers. The situation is

reminiscent of Sarason's (1971) descriptions of the conflicting orientations of math supervisors and math teachers regarding the process of curricular change.

2. Guests typically are invited to one's house. Frequently school psychologists are invited to the school building by way of referrals from teachers. The referral process ordinarily involves a third party, such as the director of special education, who assigns the teacher's referral to an assessment team including a school psychologist. That is, the referral does not pass directly from the teacher to the school psychologist. Nevertheless, the teacher initiates the "invitation." Sometimes, however, the school psychologist may be an uninvited guest who appears at the classroom door unannounced on the referral of someone other than the teacher. Further, in most school districts teachers have no participation in the decision regarding who will be their school psychologist. In many joint agreement districts, even school administrators may have little or no input in such decisions.

3. Guests in one's house typically are not perceived as members of the family. School psychologists may not be perceived as members of the education family. They do not have an office, nor do they have to dine in the school building. Many school psychologists have no prior teacher preparation, and about half of them have no formal teaching experience (Graden & Curtis, 1991; Smith et al., 1992). Regardless of studies demonstrating that teaching experience is not essential to the practice of school psychology, the perception of many educators is that such experience is important (see Chapter 6). Another disadvantage is that some educators do not perceive special education as an indispensable aspect of the school district. Hence school psychologists, perceived as closely related to special education, may not be perceived as indispensable to the district either. This is less of a problem for guidance counselors, who typically are required to be credentialed teachers with a few years of teaching experience and who are less identified with the special education sector of the school district. In some instances, a school psychologist with a proper teaching credential may teach or be otherwise involved in the high school-level psychology course in addition to working as a school psychologist. Few school psychologists appear to have such involvement due to the comparatively smaller number of school psychologists serving secondary schools, the lack of necessary teaching credentials, the difficulties of finding the time for such involvement, and the potential conflict of interest from serving as an instructor to students who may now or later be receiving psychological services from the same school psychologist (Pickover,

Barbrack & Glat, 1982). For discussions of secondary-level school psychological services see Nagle and Medway (1982) and Steil (1994).

4. Guests are perceived as temporary. School psychologists often are available in buildings only for short periods. In most instances they are not building-based employees but are rather district-based employees. Hence they fit the guest perception well, which may work against their being seen as members of the family in the buildings they serve. This is especially true for psychologists who come to the school building from non-district agencies such as mental health centers or intermediate units.

5. Guests usually have similar background and status to those of house members. That is, guests are usually people with whom we have much in common. Despite similarities in gender and age, in many cases school psychologists are seen as different, perhaps even as "shrinks," and as having little in common with other educators. With more formal education, especially in psychology, school psychologists may be perceived as having specialized knowledge, greater privileges, and higher salary (even in those settings where they are paid the same as teachers at the same degree level). Such perceived inequality works against school psychologists being perceived as members of education's house.

Thus the guest analogy serves to alert school psychologists to the potential of being perceived, and treated as, outsiders in the house of education. It does not mean that school psychologists are peripheral to the family of education or that they share little in common with educators, but rather that the effective school psychologist must work to overcome such perceptions and to be perceived as integral to the schooling of children. Although being perceived as an outsider may be detrimental, the fact that most school psychologists are not building-based may be a strength. The school psychologist may be the only member of the building-based team who brings an alternative objective perspective to that shared by the insiders.

Among pupil personnel workers themselves, there is less of a sense of guest status. That is, school psychologists are less likely to be perceived as guests in their relationships with guidance counselors or social workers, and vice versa. It is probable, however, that school psychologists often perceive teachers and administrators as guests in the domain of psychological services.

The guest analogies are important to the issues of role and function and changing one's role and function. This is especially so in problems of implementing consultation services where the services are perceived as indirect, at least in terms of applications to pupils. The delivery of school psychological services is embedded in the cultural milieu of the school and the community (Sarason, 1971). Even the traditional role of psychological testing is delivered in the context of assumptions about the importance of certain types of ability and achievement to the process of schooling and the outcomes of schooling in that society. Consultation is equally, if not more, enmeshed in context. Its success depends heavily upon the relationships among the individuals involved and the cultural expectations about these relationships. The guest status may be less problematic to conceptualizations of consultation where the relationship is one of "expert" to teacher. However, in the more recent collaborative consultation conceptualization, the guest analogies present serious barriers to consultation especially in its entry stage (see the discussion of consultation in Chapter 4).

The collaborative consultation approach, which views teachers and school psychologists as professional peers and partners (Curtis & Meyers, 1985; Graden, 1989; Gutkin & Curtis, 1990; Zins & Ponti, 1990), would not have been widely supported in earlier times when the expected relationship was perceived to be one between teachers and outside experts. We are witnessing an important shift in the delivery of services that also recognizes the teacher as an expert in certain diagnostic and intervention aspects of child study. The success of this relationship could lead to a healthy erosion of the guest analogy and provide the long sought after family member status for school psychologists in the house of education.

The guest analogies posited for educational settings apply to some extent in other settings as well. With few exceptions, most of the non-school settings in which school psychologists are employed were not designed primarily or exclusively for the provision of psychological services. Medical centers, developmental disability centers, rehabilitation centers, comprehensive mental health centers, and universities serve a variety of other purposes. Thus school psychologists are often employed in someone else's "house." It is important for school psychologists to have a broad understanding of their employment settings and a proper perspective of their role in these settings. Sarason's (1971) perceptive account of the process of change in the schools, or the lack of such change, is important to the understanding of key factors in all employment settings.

Who Is the Client?

In every profession, services are rendered on behalf of clients. Given several available employment settings and constituencies served by school psychologists, it is worth considering who is the school psychologist's client. There are no simple answers. The answer may vary as a function of employment setting and/or service request. The term "client" may refer to the person in need of professional help, the person who employs a professional, the person paying for the help, the person who is under the protection of another, the person receiving the services of a professional, or the person benefiting from such services. Consequently in the work of the school psychologist, the client may include one or more of the following: child, parent(s), teacher, principal, special education director, school superintendent, school board, or an agency administrator or governing board.

In perhaps the simplest employment context, independent private practice, parents of a dependent, minor-age child request psychological services directly from the school psychologist. As the child's legal guardians, the parents have considerable legal influence in the case study and can be logically considered the psychologist's client. But what about the child, who not only receives the services but also will ultimately benefit from the services and who has the individual power to refuse to participate cooperatively in such services? It is for these often conflicting circumstances that school psychologists commonly view the child *and* the parents as their most immediate clients. This attitude is held by school psychologists in most settings although often school psychologists see the child as the most important client.

Despite emphasis on the parent(s) and child, a case can be made for considering others as clients. For example, school administrators are responsible for the school psychologist's employment, they pay for such services, and they may be held legally responsible for the outcomes of the services delivered. Teachers have direct influence on children and usually will be involved in the referral and the intervention process. From a power standpoint, providers of school psychological services would be seriously hampered if teachers were to choose to protest psychological services by simply not making referrals. Finally, other professionals with whom school psychologists work may perceive themselves as indirect clients since they, too, are involved in the case study and may have served as a conduit for the referral (e.g., a pediatrician).

In some circumstances, the school psychologist may provide services of direct benefit to employees that have only indirect benefits to parents and children. For example, the school psychologist may seek to improve referral procedures through in-service education of teachers. Another example would be when a school district or community agency employs a school psychologist to conduct stress management sessions for its employees. The client issue is complicated in any employment setting because of the legitimate interests of parents, teachers, and others in authority and the importance of the child as a direct or indirect service recipient. Even though parents and children are near the bottom of the power-authority pyramid (Figure 3.1), school psychologists most often work at the request and approval of parents and children and provide services for their benefit.

The power-authority context of client issues is sometimes referred to as a dilemma of divided or mixed loyalties. The dilemma pits the school psychologist's loyalty to one client against loyalty to another client. The dilemma is relevant to all professional psychologists who work with children. Discussions of client-professional relationships as a function of employment parameters and roles are provided by May (1976) and Stewart (1986). These discussions help school psychologists understand the frustrations of their circumstances as well as those of their employer and consumer clients. The divided loyalties issue is most acute in circumstances where one or more of the potential clients behave as though they are the school psychologist's exclusive client. This may occur, for example, when administrators demand that the psychologist makes case study recommendations from their perspective but the psychologist prefers taking a position advocating for the child, when parents remind the psychologist that their taxes pay the psychologist's salary and they vehemently disagree with the psychologist's judgment that their child does or does not qualify for a particular program, when teachers question the psychologist's value to the school district because the psychologist fails to recommend that a problem child be removed from their class, or when a director of special education demands that the psychologist tests more children per week than the psychologist feels is ethically responsible to the children being served.

With experience, the school psychologist comes to understand that almost all referrals of children involve several clients. To minimize client conflicts, the school psychologist persists in keeping the interests of the child as the most important focus of the assessment and intervention process. Each of the potential clients presumably is most concerned with doing what will have the greatest benefit for the child. If school psychologists can keep that as the focus and reasonably assure all clients that they have only the best interests of the child as the focus of their work, serious conflicts should be avoided. Minimizing conflict also involves preventive groundwork where the school psychologist strives to involve all relevant parties and treat them as valued significant collaborators throughout the entire referral process. As persons of powerful, and not authoritative, influence, school psychologists assure all clients that their job is not to make decisions for the clients or the child but rather to provide objective professional judgments on behalf of the welfare of the child, who theoretically is the focus of everyone's concern. School psychologists, and other professionals, should recognize that clients are not dependent on us, we are dependent on them; that clients are not an interruption of our work but are the purpose of our work; and that clients are doing us a favor by letting us serve their needs and are an important part of the business of school psychology (*Our Voice*, 1983).

The traditional practice of focusing services on the individual child with assistance from the parents has been changing in the direction of focusing on the entire family. The shift is seen not only in school psychology but in several professional fields, and it is commonplace to hear phrases such as "family assessment" or "family therapy." The family service plan of federal legislation for the handicapped is an expression of this shift in focus. It seems reasonable, therefore, to consider the family as an emerging client of the school psychologist, which embraces the above aspects of the child and parents as client. In recent years, several publications have focused on services to families of exceptional children (Barbarin, 1992; Christenson & Conoley, 1992; Fine, 1991; Gallagher & Vietze, 1986; Gargiulo, 1985; Seligman, 1991; Seligman & Darling, 1997), and family systems assessment and intervention was the theme of a 1987 issue of the *School Psychology Review* (Vol. 16, No. 4). As noted in that issue, although school psychological practice continued to be focused on the individual child, growing interest in a family perspective was anticipated (Carlson & Sincavage, 1987).

SCHOOL PSYCHOLOGISTS IN THE COMMUNITY

All school psychologists work in and with the community, including a community's families, public and private schools, service agencies, and government. As such workers, they are strategically located in social ecology service delivery models (Bronfenbrenner, 1979; Elliott & Witt, 1986a; Seligman & Darling, 1997; Woody, LaVoie, & Epps, 1992). Although most school psychologists work in the public schools, a growing number have taken employment in other settings, including denominational and independent schools, non-school agencies, and independent private practice (D'Amato & Dean, 1989; Graden & Curtis, 1991; Reschly & Wilson, 1992; Reschly, 1998). These settings are indirectly linked to the public schools because they often work with children for whom the public schools are responsible. Thus we now see the phrases "school-based" and "school-linked" services to represent these two sectors of practice (Reeder et al., 1997). School psychologists in community settings (school-linked) may be employed for similar reasons as those in public-school (school-based) settings but under different contractual agreements, role and function expectations, and supervision. In denominational and independent schools, psychological personnel are often employed on a part-time basis and are more likely to be administratively responsible to the principal or director of the facility. Because the student population usually is smaller and more select, the school psychologist may be asked to provide a narrower range of services such as learning disability evaluations and individual and group counseling. Some community facilities serve only those children with disabilities and employ school psychologists to provide specific services (D'Amato & Dean, 1989; Mordock, 1988). If the psychologist is a full-time employee, then conditions of employment and benefits similar to public-school settings may exist.

School psychologists also may be employed in community and regional mental health centers. In the structure of these agencies, the school psychologist may be part of the psychological services department, serving under a director or a supervising psychologist who in turn is responsible to the director of the mental health center and the center's governing board. Here, administrative and professional supervision are typically from mental-health–trained employees, though the supervisor usually will not be another trained school psychologist. In non-public school settings, school psychologists still are under the authority of others and must continue to operate from a base of power. Referrals for service typically are directed to the school psychologist from others in the agency following a contact with the agency made by a parent or other professional. In independent or group private practice, the school psychologist often acquires referrals directly from parents on behalf of their minor age children. Resources to assist in gathering information about independent private practice include the state association resources and guidelines document by the Iowa School Psychologists Association (1983), an annotated bibliography by Rosenberg and McNamara (1988), and Rosenberg (1995). Though directed more to clinical and counseling psychology, considerably more recent information is available from APA Books, the journal *Professional Psychology: Research and Practice*, or the newsletters *APA Monitor* and *The National Psychologist* (for the latter contact 6100 Channingway Blvd., Suite 303, Columbus, OH 43232). The APA also has a division for psychologists in independent practice (Division 42).

Employment in non-public school settings may increase psychologists' proximity to children and families while decreasing their proximity to public school settings and services. Because most community services for children with disabilities are provided through the public schools, the power-authority trade-offs of service settings are an important consideration. For example, case study recommendations from an outside psychologist may be given less credibility (or occasionally more) by the district administration than those provided by a district-employed psychologist. For example, parents may seek the advice of a non-district school psychologist (school-linked) because they perceive the district school psychologist (school-based) as aligned with the school administration. In any employment setting, however, psychologists do not make decisions for clients; rather they act as resources for a comprehensive array of psychological services when called upon to provide such by their clients. The school psychologist is an important source of professional opinion but is not a decision-making authority.

In school settings the school psychologist is a recognized member of a team that makes important decisions about the education of children. The teams in which the school psychologist participates may be called school-based assessment or support teams, pupil services, placement teams, or multidisciplinary teams. By law, decisions regarding special educational placements and services are the responsibility of school-based teams and not the responsibility of individual practitioners whether they be school-based or school-linked. School psychologists in non-school settings must recognize that their efforts are but one piece of the complex puzzle of child assessment and intervention. This can be a serious source of conflict between school-based and school-linked practitioners based in the community. Whereas a practitioner in private practice may choose to diagnose a child as having a learning disability, the school district may disagree based on its multidisciplinary team's assessment and comprehensive case review. Issues of power and authority, and the setting from which the school psychologist enters teamwork, are important to team functioning. It is readily apparent that school psychologists, regardless of employment setting, need to understand the dynamics of the school system, its policies and procedures, and the place of school psychology in the context of teamwork. Several studies of team functioning have been conducted that demonstrate the varying power of the school psychologist in team decisions (Butler & Maher, 1981; Crossland, Fox, & Baker, 1982; Pfeiffer, 1980; Yoshida, Fenton, Maxwell, & Kaufman, 1978). Also helpful is a special issue of the *School Psychology Review* devoted to the topic of multidisciplinary teams (1983, Vol. 12, No. 2), and a chapter by Rosenfield & Gravois (1999). The *School Psychology Review* miniseries on mental health programming in schools and communities (1998, Vol. 27, No. 2) is also pertinent to this topic. We return to the discussion of school psychology in nontraditional settings in several chapters of this book. The issue of settings is relevant to role and function, preparation, credentialing, and seeking employment.

COMMUNITY RESOURCES

Whether school psychological services are provided from within the public schools or from other settings, it is unlikely that the setting is able to serve the needs of its clients completely. School psychologists should be highly familiar with resources available to assist certain client needs. These resources may be available in the local community, through county and state offices, and through national-level associations and government agencies. A discussion of such agencies is available in Happe (1990), which includes a procedure for acquiring information on community resources and a convenient listing of many state and national agencies and associations.

In your own preparation in school psychology, perhaps you will develop a format for gathering resource information. Several of your courses and field experiences may include requirements for developing a community resource file of agencies contacted or visited. A format for creating such a file also appears in Happe (1990).

The importance of the school psychologist's involvement with community resources often is overlooked in role and function discussions that usually emphasize assessment and consultation. The school psychologist's role as a "liaison agent" between the school and other agencies is important. The school psychologist often "provides the best link among the schools, the family, and various agencies because of his or her association with the institution in which the child spends several hours a day and because of his or her training and experience in human relations, professional jargon, and educational matters" (Plas and Williams, 1985, p. 332). As part of the interdependent network of helping services and agencies, school psychologists serve as community resources to others while serving as liaisons for their own clients.

Now that you have a better understanding of the settings in which school psychologists are employed, we turn our attention to the practice of school psychology in those settings by discussing various roles and functions.

PRACTICAL EXERCISES

1. Ask a local school administrator to visit your class and discuss the goals of the district and where psychological services fit into such goals.
2. How are school psychological services represented in your state department of education? Are they a part of pupil services or special education? Under whose authority are psychological services in your local district?
3. Discuss issues of power and authority, administrative organization, and clientage with a school psychologist in private practice.
4. Diagram the organizational relationship of psychologists, including a school psychologist if employed, in a local or regional mental health center serving your community.
5. See how many reasons you can generate for the legitimate claim to clientage by children, parents, teachers, and administrators. Conduct an in-class debate on the topic.
6. Create a file of community resources in a school district/community of your choosing. Note the commonality of resources to those gathered by others in your class.
7. Attend a meeting of the local school board, and report to your class on the issues discussed and their relevance to psychological services.
8. Diagram the administrative structure of education in your state and local district. Place the names of key administrators on your chart. Describe where school psychologists are located in this structure.
9. Conduct a panel discussion on the structure of service delivery with school psychologists from public school, private school, mental health agency, and independent practice settings.
10. How are public schools financed in your state? What portions of local district financing are from federal, state, and local sources?
11. How has your district or agency complied with federal and state regulations regarding services for children with disabilities?
12. Develop a list of the federal and state regulations with which your employment setting is expected to be in compliance.
13. What is the official policy position of school psychologists in your state or local district regarding collective bargaining and work stoppages?

CHAPTER 4

Roles and Functions of School Psychologists

Thus far in this book we have described what a school psychologist *is*. In Chapter 1 a definition of a school psychologist was provided. In Chapter 2 the evolution of the profession was outlined. In Chapter 3 the educational environment in which school psychologists typically work was examined.

In this chapter, we describe what a school psychologist *does*. You learn about the roles most common for school psychologists as well as the specific day-to-day functions of the psychologist in the schools. The notions of roles and functions from an indirect or direct service delivery model also are presented and discussed.

As stated throughout this book, the information provided is designed to be one part of an overall school psychology training program curriculum. We expect that much of the information in this chapter will be discussed and elaborated upon in other classes (e.g., assessment, consultation, and intervention) as well as in practica and/or internships. An effort has been made to include up-to-date and relevant readings for persons wishing to follow up on specific topics of interest.

HISTORICAL BACKGROUND

The roles and functions of school psychologists are described and understood much better currently than they were in the early part of the twentieth century. Now almost every year new data become available describing the typical practice of school psychologists. The earliest such study appears to have been a survey of the training and testing practices of practitioners conducted by Wallin (1914). Wallin found that most practitioners were not particularly well trained nor were they providing a broad range of services. The role of psychometrician was considered not only appropriate but also essential, and practice often was limited to the administration of the few ability and achievement techniques available at that time. In this role, the school psychologist facilitated the "sorting" of children into different educational programs.

Soon the role expanded to include interventions, often remedial instruction and/or some counseling, as reflected in the description by Hildreth (1930) appearing in Chapter 2. Role expansion also was observed in the discussions of school psychology in a special issue of the *Journal of Consulting Psychology* (Symonds, 1942). Nevertheless, the "sorter" role persisted as the primary role, whereas other roles and functions could be considered to fall within the framework of "repairer." There also were lesser roles in research, consultation with teachers and parents, administration, and teaching.

Thayer conference discussions focused heavily on roles and functions especially as related to doctoral and non-doctoral training and credentialing (Cutts, 1955). Reporting results of surveys of the early 1950s, the proceedings indicated that testing and assessment functions continued to account for more than two-thirds of the practitioners' time. Cutts also reported on administrators' and others' perceptions of the work of the school psychologist.

The literature of the 1960s and 1970s was replete with opinions and surveys regarding the most appropriate roles and functions of the school psychologist (see e.g., Fagan et al., 1985). The era was characterized by a persistent dissatisfaction with the psychometric testing role (sorter) and the accompanying limited testing functions. Preference was given for interventions, especially counseling and consultation (repairer) roles, during an era of training program growth and curricular expansion. For example, in her 1963 book, Gray suggested two roles for the psychologist in the schools: (a) the data-oriented problem solver, who brings research competencies to bear on the problems of the schools, and (b) the transmitter of psychological knowledge and skill, who helps to disseminate current research into the applied setting of the school. Unfortunately from our perspective, the traditional sorter role has been resistant to change, with practitioners continuing to report that more than half of their professional time is spent in such activities although they would prefer devoting more time to other activities (Reschly, 1998; Reschly & Wilson, 1995).

CURRENT PRACTICE

In general, the portrayal of comprehensive roles and functions put forth by the National School Psychology Inservice Training Network in 1984 and refined in 1997 (Ysseldyke et al.) has yet to be achieved on a wide scale. Thus, although several roles have been available throughout the history of our profession, the sorter and repairer roles have been dominant. Roles and functions have been shaped by many forces throughout our history, and these forces continue to shape new roles and functions while preserving traditional ones. In addition, just as children are influenced by many factors in their environments, the current roles and functions of individual school psychologists are influenced by numerous personal, professional, and external variables. In Chapter 1, data were provided regarding the average percentages of time school psychologists engage in various professional activities. Although such data are helpful as summaries, they do not describe the activities of any one practicing school psychologist. In fact, it is probably safe to say that currently no two school psychologists spend their time in exactly the same way.

DETERMINANTS OF ROLES AND FUNCTIONS

As seen in Figure 4.1, the role of each individual school psychologist can be viewed as a combination of *what the person brings to the job* (e.g., personal characteristics and professional skills), *job-site characteristics* (e.g., job descriptions and school system expectations), and *various external forces* (e.g., legislative developments, social changes, and research findings).

What You Bring to the Job
Personal Factors
Consider how you first learned of school psychology as a career option. You may have taken an undergraduate course taught by a school psychology faculty member. The professor may have mentioned school psychology, and because you were looking for something to do after graduation the idea clicked. You may have worked with a school psychologist at some time during your own childhood or adolescence. Perhaps you have a child or a sibling who required the services of a school psychologist. Perhaps you are a teacher who worked with a particularly effective school psychologist. You may have stumbled across school psychology by accident or you may have had a school psychologist as a family member or neighbor. Whichever of these possibilities applies to you—and this list is by no means exhaustive—the reason you were attracted to school psychology training may influence your eventual on-the-job performance. (Additional comments on student characteristics and desires appear in Chapter 6.) Variables such as age, gender, race, marital status, socioeconomic status, the type of community in which you were raised (e.g., urban, suburban, or rural), and the type of schooling you received (e.g., public versus private schooling, enrichment programs versus special education) also may influence your professional role.

Personality characteristics likewise exert an influence on your professional role (Itkin, 1966). For example, outgoing, assertive and gregarious individuals may be more apt to enjoy consultation, staff development, and public speaking activities. School psychologists perceived to be warm, friendly, and nonjudgmental may be more sought after by teachers for advice about classroom management, crisis intervention, or other work-related problems.

Professional Training Factors

Certainly, professional training has a major impact upon the way you function on the job. Even when two school psychologists possess identical academic transcripts, there may be vast differences in orientation based upon the period of time in which their training occurred, the theoretical orientation of the faculty with whom they studied, and the experiences they had at the particular schools they attended. For example, someone attending certain graduate schools on the east coast during the more psychoanalytic era of the 1960s had far different training than someone trained in the Midwest in the behavioristic 1970s. In addition, even within a given training program, the faculty members you have for classes and practica may move on, go on sabbatical, or retire, creating a quite different program for the next group of students.

In the same way, the other students going through school with you may influence your thoughts and feelings. A group with several slightly older students who have taught and/or have children of their own creates a different learning atmosphere than does a group of students all of whom are 22 years old and right out of college. Likewise, the diversity of students in terms of gender, professional experience, and cultural background provides a unique blend with a strong impact on the individuals in the program.

FIGURE 4.1 Variables influencing school psychologists' professional roles and functions

What you bring to the job
Personal characteristics
Personal background
Professional training
Reasons for choosing school psychology
Professional interests

What you find on the job
Job-site characteristics
Expectations
Job description
Needs
Available resources

External forces
Legal and legislative changes
Societal problems
Research findings
World events

The type of graduate degree you obtain also may influence your professional functioning. As has been mentioned previously and as is described in greater detail in Chapter 6, currently the "specialist" level of training (a minimum of 60 graduate semester hours spread over a 3-year period and including practicum and internship experiences) is nationally acknowledged as the appropriate minimum entry level for school psychologists. Beyond that entry level, practicing school psychologists are expected to continue to upgrade their knowledge and skills through a variety of continuing education options and opportunities.

School psychology training programs, particularly doctoral programs, often emphasize one particular area of specialization over others (e.g., behavioral consultation, individual and group counseling, or psychoeducational assessment). Graduates of such programs are well prepared for positions emphasizing these specialized skills in addition to possessing basic practitioner competencies. Other programs (including most specialist-level programs) attempt to provide more generalized training so that students can adapt to a variety of professional environments. Chapter 6 provides an in-depth look into differences between doctoral and specialist-level training.

The state in which you receive your training, the practicum and internship requirements you fulfill, the research interests of faculty members during your training, even (or perhaps especially) the interpersonal dynamics of the faculty members with whom you work likewise may contribute to your role. The administrative issue of whether your program is in a department or college of education, a department of psychology within a college of arts and sciences, or a department of educational psychology administered jointly by education and psychology may influence the type of training you receive and your eventual role as a school psychologist (see Chapter 6 for a discussion of this topic). Do you take mostly psychology courses or education courses? Who are the other students in your classes? Are they students in other psychology graduate programs or students in education-related areas including special education and/or school counseling?

Some graduate programs, particularly those in larger metropolitan areas, may attract a large number of part-time students who work on their school psychology degrees while concurrently holding jobs or taking care of families. Other programs are composed primarily of full-time students who complete all academic requirements in 2 years and go immediately into internship positions.

Many training-related issues are settled more by chance than by plan. Students choose to apply to specific graduate programs for a variety of reasons, not necessarily because of the quality or reputation of the program. For example:

1. "My spouse was also accepted to a graduate program there."
2. "I can live with my parents and keep my expenses down."
3. "Since I went there as an undergraduate, I already know my way around."

Other students may not have much choice as to the program they attend. "Place-bound" students, for example (those students who, for a variety of reasons usually related to family and/or financial status, are unable to move somewhere to attend graduate school), must sometimes choose between either attending a local program or not attending graduate school at all.

The availability of financial assistance is another important determinant. All other factors being equal (e.g., quality, length, and reputation of the program), it is our experience that most students will choose the program that offers them the best deal financially in terms of tuition waivers, additional stipends, and duties or hours of work required to earn assistantship funding.

Typically, the decision-making process about graduate schools is different for students contemplating masters or specialist-level training than for those contemplating doctoral training. Doctoral training traditionally is more specialized than pre-doctoral training, and prospective students (particularly those who have already completed masters or specialist training programs) generally are more aware of the need to find a match between their own professional interests and the emphasis of a given doctoral program (Erchul et al., 1989). Although geographical, financial, and personal variables still may influence the prospective student's choices of doctoral institutions, other factors such as reputation of the program, the research interests of the individual faculty at an institution, and the accreditation status of the program take on added importance for many candidates. Doctoral programs generally have more stringent entrance requirements than pre-doctoral programs. Therefore, a prospective student's choice of a doctoral-level institution may be dictated more by whether or not the student is accepted into a particular program.

Job-site Characteristics
Number of Pupils Served

In Chapter 1, reference was made to the notion of a psychologist-to-student ratio. In general, the more students you are expected to serve, the greater the number of children with disabilities and the more time you will need to spend in assessment activities surrounding the identification, diagnosis, and placement of these children. Some school psychologists find it difficult simply meeting the demands of assessing children with disabilities and participating in decisions on appropriate educational interventions for these children. School psychologists working with fewer children may choose to, and may indeed be expected to, expand their roles to those of teacher consultant, individual or group counselor, staff development planner, group testing coordinator, and/or educational researcher.

Other Job-Related Factors

Many other job-related factors influence a school psychologist's professional practice. Some school psychologists work only in elementary schools, some only in secondary schools, and others in a combination of elementary and secondary schools. Secondary schools differ from elementary schools not only in the age of the students but also in structure (e.g., different teachers for each subject, standardized instructional periods). The role of the school psychologist in each setting reflects these age and structural differences.

Role and function also may vary depending upon whether you work in an urban, a suburban, or a rural district. Some of these differences were discussed in Chapter 3. How many students do you serve? How much of your time is spent driving between schools? Where is your office located: in an administrative building or in one of your schools? Who is your immediate supervisor, and what is that person's professional training? A supervisor with training in school psychology or in special education may have different expectations than a supervisor without a school psychology or special education background.

Sometimes it seems that a school psychologist's job is largely related to what one's predecessor's role was. If the predecessor was perceived as competent and was well-liked, then the newly hired school psychologist will be expected to function in much the same way. If the predecessor was perceived as incompetent, unpopular, or both, the newly hired school psychologist may be able to do almost anything as long as it represents an improvement.

Oakland and Cunningham (1999) conceptualize the forces that have an impact on the role of the school psychologist depending upon the amount of control school psychology has. For example, variables such as licensure and certification, professional associations, and training are controlled largely by those in the field of school psychology. Variables such as financial support for the schools, state and federal statutes, and technology are controlled or influenced at least to some extent by school psychology. Other variables such as the political climate, the changes in society, and the history of certain situations are out of the control of the field of school psychology. Oakland and Cunningham (1999) suggest further that sources of tension exist that may need resolution for the profession of school psychology to move forward. The tensions discussed include unity versus plurality in school psychology, brevity versus completeness of professional preparation, thoroughness versus economy, services needed versus ability to deliver them, remediation versus prevention programs, special education versus general education, and traditional versus emerging assessment practices.

The Presence of Related Personnel

School psychologists' day-to-day functions may be influenced by the presence or absence of other related professionals. Some school districts, for example, hire school social workers who are responsible for obtaining social and developmental information about children from parents and/or conducting individual and group counseling in the schools. Some school districts employ paraprofessionals or other personnel to perform some of the assessment duties often expected of school psychologists. Paraprofessionals are individuals who are not actually members of a given profession (in this case school psychology) but who receive sufficient training to be able to assist professionals with some tasks. Still other districts may employ school counselors, speech and language clinicians, occupational and physical therapists, psychiatrists, and other psychologists. The presence or absence of such professionals in the schools may dramatically modify the role of the school psychologist.

External Forces
Societal Changes

As noted in Chapter 2 and in the beginning of this chapter, the school psychologist in the year 2000 and beyond does not operate in the same way as the school psychologist of the 1990s, 1980s, or before. Society has changed, and these changes have had a dramatic impact on children in the schools and consequently on the professional role of the school psychologist.

In most classrooms nationwide, the children who live in intact two-parent homes are in the minority. More than 70% of mothers of school-age children work outside the home. Most of these women are employed at least partly out of economic necessity. Because few households have stay-at-home parents, many children, even elementary school-age children, are at home unsupervised for long periods. These so-called latchkey kids are of great concern to educators as well as to parents who feel that there are no available or affordable alternatives. Parents of junior high and high school age children often worry about leaving their teenagers home without supervision in an era of substance abuse and sexual experimentation.

Most children entering school today have been enrolled in preschool or day care programs. This in itself represents a vast change from children starting school 20 or 30 years ago. In addition, critical events such as unemployment, poverty, or substance abuse may influence your professional practice. The societal context of schooling has changed, and this, in turn, has influenced the need for and type of services required of school psychologists in the changing educational system. Recent publications aimed at school psychologists reflect this change in services: *Student Aggression: Prevention, Management, and Replacement Training* (Goldstein, Harootunian, & Conoley, 1994), *Adolescent Substance Abuse* (Kaminer, 1994), and *The Scared Child: Helping Kids Overcome Traumatic Events* (Brooks & Seigel, 1996).

Legal and Ethical Issues

When we consider the factors that have shaped school psychology over the years, two of the most influential factors have certainly been legal and ethical issues. In terms of legal issues, school psychologists often are involved in many facets of the legal system, particularly in court cases surrounding assessment-related issues. For the sake of convenience we can divide such legal issues most relevant to school psychologists into two major categories:

1. Legal cases resulting from the application of psychological assessment (i.e., cases in which assessment practices themselves are being challenged)
2. Legal cases introducing psychological assessment as evidence or support (i.e., cases in which psychological assessment results are used to substantiate or refute a claim)

The court cases that have focused upon the relationship between educational tests and cultural biases (the first group above) have been most influential in affecting the roles and functions of school psychologists (Bersoff, 1981). The fundamental question posed by legal challenges in such cases is, *Are traditional psychological tests in educational settings fair for all students regardless of race, ethnic background, and gender?* A second and more subtle question is, *What happens to children as a result of testing in the schools?* (Reschly, 1979).

The first such case was *Hobson* v. *Hansen* (1967), in which a disproportionate number of black children in the Washington, D.C., public schools was placed in lower-level classes on the basis of scores on group-administered tests. The primary issue in *Hobson* v. *Hansen* revolved around the question of whether the results of such group tests actually reflect a student's "innate abilities." In *Hobson* v. *Hansen,* the court found that the group tests used were not sufficient to justify placement in low-ability level classes.

Since *Hobson* v. *Hansen,* a number of other cases have been adjudicated focusing upon individual intelligence testing and the resulting overrepresentation of minority group members in special education classes, especially classes for the mildly or "educably" mentally retarded. Such cases include *Diana* v. *California State Board of Education* (1970); *Guadalupe Organization, Inc.* v. *Tempe Elementary School District* (1972); *Larry P.* v. *Riles* (1984); and *P.A.S.E.* v. *Hannon* (1980). (Additional information on specific cases can be found in Bersoff, 1982a, 1982b; Jacob-Timm & Hartshorne, 1998; Reschly, 1983; and Reschly, Kicklighter, & McKee, 1988a, 1988b, 1988c). One difficulty that has transcended all of these court cases involves defining and measuring the construct "intelligence." Much of what we have traditionally included in our definitions of intelligence may in reality be more closely related to one's ability to function within a predominantly white, middle-class, public-school system and less related to any innate general cognitive ability that we may think of as intelligence. Reschly (1979) suggested that every time IQ test results are included in a report or in a student's file, such results should be accompanied by a warning such as the surgeon general's warning for cigarettes:

IQ tests measure only a portion of the competencies involved with human intelligence. The IQ results are best seen as predicting performance in school, and reflecting the degree to which children have mastered middle class cultural symbols and values. This is useful information, but it is also limited. Further cautions: IQ tests do not measure innate-genetic capacity and the scores are not fixed. Some persons do exhibit significant increases or decreases in their measured IQ (p. 224).

More recent legal cases under the first group have switched the focus from the ambiguous notion of a student's innate intelligence to the more straightforward evidence of a student's actual level of achievement in the classroom setting (Reschly et al., 1988c). In one such case cited by Reschly et al. (*Marshall* v. *Georgia*, 1984, 1985), students had been divided into instructional groups not based upon an IQ score but based upon their mastery of specific skills within an established curriculum. The students' progress was closely monitored in each subject. Students were not simply placed into a certain level and left there without regard to their successes or failures. Even though a disproportionate number of black students was in the lowest classroom group in the *Marshall* case, the judge found in favor of the schools. As noted by Reschly et al. this probably was because the type of curricular-relevant assessment used, often called "curriculum-based assessment" (CBA) or "curriculum-based measurement" (CBM) in the literature, was found to be directly related to positive learning outcomes. (For more information about curriculum-based assessment and curriculum-based measurement see Gickling & Rosenfield, 1995; Shinn, 1995.) Such cases have a direct impact upon the everyday assessment and intervention practices of school psychologist.

The second group of legal cases, as defined above, includes cases in which psychological tests have been introduced as evidence to substantiate or refute a claim. Although individual cases in this group have not received the attention given to the cases cited in the first group, many school psychologists over the years have been summoned to testify about psychological tests. Some of the more controversial cases are those involving special education versus regular education placement decisions. For example, based upon a child's test scores, classroom performance, and other data, would that child be better off in a residential program or in a regular classroom than with the services decided upon at the multidisciplinary staffing? Child custody decisions concerning children who have been evaluated by a school psychologist are also controversial.

School psychologists also may become involved in other types of legal issues or cases. They may be asked to work with students who have been victims of or witnesses to crimes. Likewise, they may be asked to work with students who have committed crimes. As addressed later in this chapter, in the discussion of crisis consultation, school psychologists may be asked to perform a more indirect role in some of these instances by working with teachers whose students are facing crises.

Moving from legal cases to legislation and its influences on school psychology, the clearest examples are surely Public Law (P.L.) 94-142, the Education for All Handicapped Children Act of 1975, the Education of the Handicapped Act Amendments of 1990 (P.L. 101-476) which became known as the Individuals with Disabilities Education Act (IDEA), and the Individuals with Disabilities Education Act Amendments of 1997 (P.L. 105-117). As noted in Chapters 2 and 7, P.L. 94-142 mandated that all children regardless of handicapping condition are entitled to a free and appropriate public education in the least restrictive environment. In other words, *all* children are entitled to an education at public expense and in the most "normal" program possible. P.L. 94-142 specified that all handicapped children must be identified, diagnosed, and placed in the least restrictive educational environment. Although school psychologists often are involved in the identification, diagnosis, and placement of handicapped children, the diagnostic responsibilities set out in P.L. 94-142 are often the most time-consuming for the psychologist in the schools. P.L. 101-476 and P.L. 105-117 have reinforced and expanded upon P.L. 94-142 by extending the principles to infants and young children, including more provisions for assistive technology, and emphasizing the need for family involvement in educational planning.

What about ethical issues facing school psychologists? As described in some detail in Chapter 7, school psychologists operate under a variety of ethical guidelines (e.g., national organizations, state associations). The APA and NASP ethical codes appear in Appendices C and D. Although many ethical issues are clear-cut, others are more ambiguous and can only be decided after careful consideration of all of the facts in a given situation. Throughout this chapter, information about legal and ethical issues will be provided as such information applies to the various roles and functions of the school psychologist. (Jacob-Timm & Hartshorne, 1998, provide a comprehensive discussion of legal, legislative, and ethical issues that have an impact on school psychologists.)

BASIC SKILLS USED BY SCHOOL PSYCHOLOGISTS

Although many factors influence the precise roles and functions of individual school psychologists, there are commonalities of training and practice. Most school psychologists have been trained in certain basic skills that they will use to greater and lesser extents depending upon the factors described above. The remaining pages of this chapter present information about these basic skills. We begin with descriptions of some of the most common functions of psychologists in the schools (depicted in Figure 4.2). After these descriptions, three scenarios are presented to demonstrate how school psychologists may combine these functions into a typical day's schedule.

A school psychologist's ultimate professional goal is to help children. There are many ways to attain this goal but not all ways are appropriate in all situations with all children. Figure 4.2 shows some of the ways in which the roles and functions of school psychologists achieve the goal of helping children. Each of the roles and functions depicted in Figure 4.2 is described more fully below.

Other authors (e.g., Elliott & Witt, 1986) have conceptualized the roles and functions of school psychologists in terms of the services school psychologists possess in their professional repertoires and the ways in which these services are delivered. In this "service delivery" model, roles are viewed as helping students directly (e.g., counseling) or indirectly (e.g., consultation with teachers) or as falling somewhere in the middle on a continuum from direct to indirect (e.g., assessment of an individual student, designing interventions that teachers or parents will implement).

The roles and functions described below are not necessarily unique to the practicing school psychologist working within a public school system. In Chapter 8 we discuss the ways in which these roles may be applied to non-traditional settings. Some of the roles and functions of school psychologists are similar to the activities of clinical and counseling psychologists (e.g., counseling, some types of assessment) whereas other roles and functions of the school psychologist seem more unique to our profession (e.g., planning school-based interventions, participating in multidisciplinary staffings).

Overall, in order to help children, school psychologists must be able to conceptualize problems, support their ideas with data about the problems, work with others to help solve the problems, and evaluate outcomes. Presented below are the primary roles of the school psychologist with descriptions for each role of the skills and knowledge which school psychologists must possess in order to function effectively in each role.

Assessment of Individual Children
Description

As previously noted, the traditional role of the psychologist in the schools revolves around the assessment of individual children. This so-called *child study* role remains a major one for the school psychologist. A brief review of the assessment process is presented here as an introduction to later in-depth discussions in your assessment and practicum (field experience) courses.

It is important to note the difference between the terms *assessment* and *testing*. These terms should not be used interchangeably. As defined by Cohen, Swerdlik, and Phillips (1996, p. 6) psychological assessment can be seen as "the gathering and integration of psychology-related data for the purpose of making a psychological evaluation, accomplished through the use of tools such as tests, interviews, case studies, behavioral observation, and specially designed apparatuses and measurement procedures." Psychological testing according to the same

FIGURE 4.2 Roles and functions of school psychologists relevant to helping children

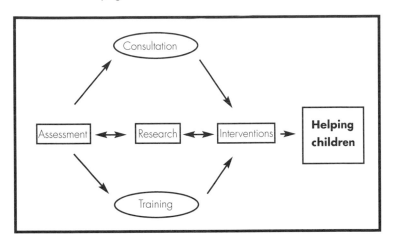

authors refers to "the process of measuring psychology-related variables by means of devices or procedures designed to obtain a sample of behavior."

In this book, when we talk about assessment, we are using the term to refer to a complex problem-solving or information-gathering process. The reason that school psychologists assess individual students is to understand the difficulties a child is experiencing in order to intervene and ultimately help the child. Although administering psychological tests may be a part of this assessment process, such tests should be administered only when necessary to understanding a child's difficulties and should not be automatically administered in every case to every child.

Assessment occurs in the context of a *referral process.* The assessment of an individual child begins with a referral form usually completed by the child's teacher and signed by a parent or guardian. A sample referral form is shown in Figure 4.3. What types of children and their difficulties are most commonly referred for school psychological services? Data from a national survey of school psychologists serving elementary as well as secondary school settings (Harris, Gray, Rees-McGee, Carroll, & Zaremba, 1987) appear in Table 4.1. Referrals most often were the result of a teacher's concerns, although sometimes referrals from parents or even self referrals are made; males were 3.5 times more likely to be referred for services than females; elementary school students (i.e., kindergarten through fifth graders) were more likely to be referred than older students; and students with poor academic performance or with social/emotional difficulties constituted more than 80% of the referrals. Racial differences have also been found in referrals by teachers (Andrews, Wisniewski, & Mulick, 1997). The nature of referrals suggests that children in schools often need instructional as well as psychological assistance. A Canadian study (Cole, 1992) produced similar findings. One recent study examined differences between high referring and low referring teachers (Waldron, McLeskey, Skiba, Jancaus, & Schulmeyer, 1998). Results indicate that low referring teachers tend to use referral to the school psychologist as a last resort after trying a large number of interventions. High referring teachers on the other hand use referral to the school psychologist as a first step in solving a problem a student is experiencing. Lately there has been increased emphasis on a process known as *pre-referral assessment.* Pre-referral assessment arose from a desire to reduce or at least to focus the large number of referrals received by school psychologists. The process involves a team problem-solv-

TABLE 4.1 Characteristics of referrals to school psychologists

Grades from Which Referrals Were Received	Percent
Kindergarten -2	37
3-5	25
6-8	19
9-12	15
Ungraded	3
Sex of Those Referred	
Male	70
Female	30
Ethnic Origin	
White	71
Black	13
Hispanic	10
Asian or Pacific Islanders	2
Other	5
Referral Agents	
Classroom teachers	57
Parents	15
Other pupil personnel workers	8
Administrators	4
Resource teachers	3
Outside agencies	2
Self-referrals	2
Two or more referral agents	6
School staff members combined	75
Reasons for Referral	
Poor academic performance	52
Social/emotional difficulties (deficits)	13
Social/emotional difficulties (excesses)	17
Bizarre or unusual behavior	1
Other reasons	17

SOURCE: Adapted from "Referrals to School Psychologists: A National Survey" by J.D. Harris, B. A. Gray, S. Rees-McGee, J. L. Carroll, and E. T. Zaremba, 1987, *Journal of School Psychology, 25,* pp. 343-354. Reprinted by permission of Pergamon Press.

FIGURE 4.3 Sample referral form

I. Personal Information

Name of child _____ Date of request _____

Home address _____ Date of birth _____

Home telephone _____ Age _____ Grade _____

II. Family Information

Name _____ Education _____ Occupation _____

Father _____

Mother _____

Ages of Siblings _____ _____

Is this child ___adopted or stepchild?   ___foster child?

___living with only one parent?   ___living with both parents?

Primary language of home: ___English ___Other (specify) _____

III. School Information

Name of school _____

Address _____ Phone _____

Principal's name _____ Teacher's name _____

Grades repeated _____ Years in present school _____

Services presently offered to the child _____

Attendance record _____

Previous schools attended _____

IV. Health Information

Date of last physical examination _____

Doctor's name _____

Results of last physical examination _____

Is the child on medication? _____ If so, what? _____

Date and results of last vision screening _____

Date and results of last hearing screening _____

General physical health _____

During the last two years has the child experienced any medical problems? _____

If yes, please explain. _____

V. Reason for Referral

Why are you referring this child for psychological evaluation at this time? _____

_____

What questions would you like to have answered? _____

_____

Is there anything about the child's home or family environment that you believe might have a bearing on the child's attitude and behavior? If so, please explain. _____

_____

What types of interventions have already been tried to address the child's difficulties?

_____

_____

ing approach to diagnose difficulties occurring in the classroom and to intervene early on, if possible, bypassing the more traditional referral process (Brandt, 1996).

Informed Consent

Once a referral is initiated, parents or guardians must give signed consent for an assessment. In fact, P.L. 94-142 and its reauthorizations take parental consent a step further and address the issue of *informed consent*. Not only must parents be given the opportunity to consent to assessment, but also a reasonable effort must be made to ensure that parents are notified that an assessment is being recommended and that they understand what an assessment is, why it is being suggested, and what might result from the assessment. Most of the time this requirement is fairly straightforward. Occasionally, securing informed consent takes the form of finding an interpreter, when the parents' primary language is not English, or tailoring an explanation to parents with limited education or ability so that they understand it.

Referral Questions

When the referral form has been completed and informed parental consent has been obtained, school psychologists often translate the request for assessment into one or more referral questions. What does the teacher, parent, or student want to know? What is the nature of the "problem"? The clarification of referral questions is also an important part of the pre-referral assessment process. Keep in mind at this step and at subsequent steps of the assessment process the first assumption that Elliott and Witt (1986, p. 21) make with regard to school psychological delivery systems: "Behavior and learning problems of children are functionally related to the setting in which they are manifest." In other words, be aware that the child exists within particular school and home contexts. What one teacher or parent perceives as a problem may not necessarily be perceived as a problem by another teacher or parent. Also, conditions in certain classrooms or homes may cause or intensify a child's "problem behavior." Such environmental factors deserve careful consideration throughout the assessment process.

Data Collection Procedures

To address referral questions, a number of data collection or assessment procedures are conducted, often but not automatically including testing. School psychologists use a *multifactored* approach to assessment. No single source of data addresses all aspects of a referral question so multiple sources must be used.

Keep in mind that school psychologists do not simply assess for assessment's sake; assessment should be done with a purpose in mind. Salvia and Ysseldyke (2001) suggest that within school settings, assessments are conducted to help make four types of decisions about students:

1. Pre-Referral Classroom Decisions: Is there something that can be done by the teacher within the classroom to help the student? Can other teachers in the building help (i.e., through the building-wide intervention assistance team)?

2. Entitlement Decisions: Are the student's problems serious enough to warrant a referral to the school psychologist and other child study team members? Assessment procedures enhance the abilities of school personnel to identify students who are significantly above or below average in general abilities, in academic achievement, and/or in social or behavioral skills. In addition, assessment results are used by multi-disciplinary teams in deciding whether an individual child qualifies for and might benefit from special instructional services.

3. Post-Entitlement Classroom Decisions: Assessments are conducted to provide information about an individual child's or a group of children's academic strengths and weaknesses. Such information should be applied within the classroom environment and be helpful in developing an individualized instructional plan for a child or in making classroom-wide, building-wide, or district-wide curricular modifications.

4. Accountability/Outcome Decisions: Assessments provide additional information to teachers, parents, and children themselves regarding how much benefit individual children are deriving from their class-room placements. On a broader scale, assessments can help provide information as to how well educational programs in general are achieving their goals.

As mentioned above, the school psychologist's first step in the assessment process often involves meeting with the individual who made the referral to determine specific referral questions. Even at this early stage, the psychologist begins to formulate initial hypotheses about the child's difficulties. This process of hypothesis formation is one of the most difficult steps for school psychology students because such hypotheses tend to be hunches based upon professional experience and training.

Although the teacher most often is the person responsible for filling out the referral form, it is critical to meet with the parents as well as the teacher to gain an understanding of the problems the child is experiencing. The parents may have additional concerns or insights to share prior to testing. The parents also have information about the child's health history, educational progress, and developmental milestones that may not be available from other sources.

On the other hand, if the parents have made the referral, meeting with the teacher provides much additional information about the child's academic, social, and behavioral progress. Teachers also have the advantage of seeing how the child compares with others of the same age within the classroom. If the parents initiate a referral and the school psychologist is working outside of the school setting (e.g., private practice, mental health center), then parental permission is needed before the teacher or anyone else may be contacted concerning the child.

Classroom Observations

Following discussions with teachers and parents regarding the clarification of the referral question, many school psychologists begin to gather first-hand information about the referred child by completing one or more direct observations. Several standardized systems exist (e.g., Sattler, 1992) for completing such observations, although some school psychologists report that their classroom observations center around a number of rather specific questions:

1. What was the child doing? What were other children doing?
2. What was the child supposed to be doing?
3. Where did the observation occur: classroom, playground, or elsewhere?
4. When and for how long did you observe?

According to Sattler (1992), classroom observations give the examiner the opportunity to observe and to record systematically the child's behavior in a natural setting. Data collected from observations can be compared with reports from the child's teachers and parents. Data from naturalistic observations (i.e., observations in settings familiar to the child) also can be helpful when compared with observations of the child's behavior during the more structured and less familiar standardized testing setting if such testing is conducted. Along the same lines, Elliott and Witt (1986, p. 21) note that "a primary goal of psychoeducational assessment is to determine what a child does and does not know, and how the child learns best so successful interventions can be designed." Seeing the child in the natural habitat of the classroom can provide a perspective on the child that would not be gained in the one-to-one setting in which most psychological testing occurs. In addition, Hintze and Shapiro (1995, p. 651) state that in cases of problematic classroom behavior, systematic classroom observations allow us to observe "the behavior of interest in the settings where the problem actually has been happening. As such, the data are empirically verifiable and do not require inferences from observations of other behaviors."

Increasingly, school psychologists are trained not to limit their observations to the individual child in question but also to observe and assess instructional environments. As Ysseldyke and Elliott (1999) note, there has long been an interest in instructional environments but only recently has technology advanced to the point that such environments can be described using standardized measurement procedures. Examples of the variables considered in assessments of instructional environments include use of classroom time, motivation techniques, and opportunities provided for practice of skills.

Examination of School Records

A great deal of information can be gleaned from school records. For example, the school psychologist will want to determine the child's current grade placement, previous schools attended, school history (i.e., has the child ever been retained, accelerated, or received any kind of special services), group test results, attendance record, and whether a previous assessment has been conducted. Information about health history and results of vision and hearing screenings also may be found in school records. Such information is critical in understanding the difficulties the child is experiencing. Checking the child's date of birth and age is often advisable as well because individuals filling out referral forms have been known to make mistakes and because results of testing are often based on the child's chronological age.

Testing

Throughout the interviews with teachers and parents, the classroom observations, and the examination of school records, the school psychologist attempts to gain a clearer picture of the child and his or her difficulties. The use of a variety of test instruments is often helpful at this point to gather more information about the child. Testing, sometimes portrayed as the albatross around the neck of the school psychologist, actually has many direct and indirect benefits. Not only do tests provide us with quantifiable data about an individual child, but also they afford us the opportunity to work with the child on a one-to-one basis. Skilled examiners often learn as much or more about a child through their observations during testing as they do through the actual administration of the tests and computation of test scores. In addition, children often enjoy the opportunity to work one-to-one with an adult at school. In keeping with the notion of a multifactored assessment, some or all of the following types of tests may be administered as part of a test battery:

1. Cognitive ability tests: Tests that traditionally have been called intelligence tests or aptitude tests.
2. Academic achievement measures: Tests that assess a child's performance in one or more academic areas (e.g., reading comprehension, spelling, or math).
3. Perceptual tests (visual, auditory): Tests that examine a child's perceptual abilities (e.g., hearing differences between words with similar sounds or seeing hidden figures).
4. Tests of fine and gross motor abilities: Tests that look at a child's coordination including everything from drawing and handwriting (fine motor abilities) to tossing a bean bag or walking a balance beam (gross motor abilities).
5. Behavioral/personality/adaptive behavior measures: Such measures

typically are outside the realm of academic tasks. Instead they address children's behavior in various settings, their overall level of adjustment, and their non-school related skills (often called "self-help skills").

6. Curriculum-based assessment techniques: As mentioned earlier with respect to recent legal cases, curriculum-based assessment (CBA) is specifically geared to the academic tasks the child is expected to master. Such assessments usually look at tasks the child has already mastered, tasks the child is on the verge of mastering, and tasks which are beyond mastery at a given time.

Interviews

Parents, teachers, and others (e.g., physicians, reading specialists, speech and language therapists, social workers, extended family members) often are quite aware of the difficulties a child is experiencing. Talking to these individuals early in the assessment process helps to provide a more complete picture of the child. In many cases, children themselves are quite aware of their own difficulties, and even young children can be fairly candid about the reasons for these difficulties. Be aware, however, of the ethical considerations involved in maintaining confidentiality under such circumstances. For those looking for assistance in this important area, Sattler (1998) has devoted an entire book of more than 1000 pages to interviewing children and families.

Once all of the assessment procedures have been completed, it is time to pull the results together, relate the results to the referral question(s), and share the results with others. Sharing the results usually takes two forms: (a) a written report designed to be read by school personnel and placed in the student's permanent record and (b) an oral recounting of the results in conferences with parents or teachers, and/or in multidisciplinary staffing sessions.

Report Writing

There are many formats for psychological or psychoeducational reports (e.g., Ross-Reynolds, 1990; Sattler, 1992; Tallent, 1993). Ideally the psychological report should take the reader through the process of assessment in a logical and chronological style. Reports should be written clearly and as free of technical jargon as possible. Keep in mind as you write who the consumers of the report will be and what information would be most helpful to them. In some instances, explaining the test results so someone with little background in psychological assessment will understand them is necessary as well as vital to the assessment process. Every effort should be made to relate the information in the report to the referral questions. There is no need to include in the report everything that is known about the youngster. All of the data accumulated during the assessment process cannot possibly be contained in a single report. Rather, the psychologist must find the most effective ways to synthesize all of the data and to communicate effectively the most important points and how they lead to recommendations for intervention. Ownby (1991) emphasizes that the psychologist's report should shape the thinking and the beliefs of those reading the report and perhaps even modify the behavior of the reader.

If a test battery has been administered to the child, then the report should describe the individual test results as well as integrate the results. How do the results of the various tests and subtests relate to each other? Look for threads of consistency as well as any apparent inconsistencies in the child's performance.

Although quantitative test results bear reporting, the qualitative or behavioral aspects should also be addressed. Did the child initiate conversation or merely answer questions? How did the child respond to praise and/or frustration? Were there particular behaviors exhibited on all of the tests that seemed to indicate low self esteem? Talk about the child's behavior and give specific examples. Do not say "Leta was very anxious during the testing" but, rather, "Leta seemed anxious during testing. She bit her nails throughout, rarely made eye contact with the examiner, and never initiated conversation." The report should, as precisely as possible, describe the behavior that led to this conclusion.

There is a growing controversy about computer-generated psychological report writing. Although most school psychologists of our acquaintance gratefully use computer programs to score results of psychological tests, they are usually less comfortable or confident in allowing computer programs to interpret the test results and write reports. Cohen, Swerdlik, and Phillips (1996) note that there are several different types of computer reports available. *Simple scoring reports* provide test scores. *Extended scoring reports* expand the data by providing more complex statistical analyses. For example, are there significant differences between subtest scores? Neither of these scoring report programs, however, attempt to interpret test scores.

According to Cohen et al. interpretive reports can be broken down further into *descriptive reports, screening reports,* and *consultative reports.* Descriptive reports provide brief comments about the various test scales. Screening reports highlight certain more unusual test results bringing them to the attention of clinicians as areas on which to follow up. Consultative reports are designed to provide technical information to be shared among professionals. Finally, and of most concern to professionals, are *integrative reports.* As their name implies, integrative reports attempt to integrate information about the person being assessed, pulling together information from a wide variety of instruments and observations, summarizing that information, drawing conclusions, and even suggesting interventions or strategies.

Although there are many advantages to using computer-assisted software with testing instruments, readers need to keep in mind that test scoring of instruments used by school psychologists and test interpretation of just about any psychoeducational assessment instrument are, in part, subjective processes for which extensive training is needed. The interpretation of assessment data by a program designed by an individual is no better or worse than the interpretation done by any other individual. Those just starting out in the field may choose to view computer-generated reports and to select portions of the reports that seem accurate and valuable. One should never assume, however, that the report is accurate just because of its appearance or because it is marketed. Tallent (1993, p. 206) notes that "computerized testing is a still-emerging technology... with the potential to have influence on many lives" and cites the *Guidelines for Computer-Based Tests and Interpretations* (American Psychological Association, 1986) as establishing critical rules for those using such report-writing systems.

Parent Conferences

The best approach to take in parent conferences is to put oneself in the position of the parent and imagine how parents would want to be informed of their children's results and what they would want to know (Wise, 1986, 1995). Most parents identify strongly with their children. They want to hear strengths as well as weaknesses. They want to know that anyone working with their child thinks of their child as an individual not as just another case study. Even parents who are quite aware of their children's limitations may become emotional in the course of parent conferences. Tears as well as denial are not uncommon reactions of parents.

Parents of children with disabilities may experience feelings of guilt and grief (Murray, 1985). The guilt may arise from the notion, founded or unfounded, that something the parents did caused the disability. The feelings of grief may arise from the knowledge that certain dreams parents have for their children may not come true with this particular child. It is sad for parents to realize that a child with limited intelligence may not go to college or that a child with a physical disability may never become a great athlete. Parents of children without disabilities often take for granted the unlimited options open to their children. Parents of children with disabilities may learn to accept more limited options.

Many resources exist on the topic of parent conferences. Some of those most relevant to school psychologists include Featherstone (1980), Fine (1991), Gallagher (1980), Gargiulo (1985), Murray (1985), Seligman and Darling (1997), and Wise (1986, 1995).

Teacher Conferences

Teacher conferences present their own unique challenges. Some experienced teachers can be particularly intimidating to new school psychologists. Teachers and school psychologists sometimes seem to think of themselves as adversaries, each knowing what is best for a child. Teachers may be suspicious of a school psychologist who has never been a teacher and "wants to tell me what to do," whereas school psychologists may view teachers as being intolerant of children who are different from the norm in any way. Of course, both positions are counterproductive to helping the child. As described below, the "consultation" role for school psychologists encourages collaborative problem solving between teachers and psychologists and is probably the best strategy in meeting the needs of children.

Multidisciplinary Staffings

Since the passage of P.L. 94-142 in 1975, school psychologists and school systems generally have moved away from individual parent and teacher confer- ences in favor of sharing assessment results with all involved parties at the same time. The advantages of such staffings are that ideally each person in attendance will be able to hear all of the information presented and then will be able to participate as an equal partner in the decision-making process. The recent concep- tualization of multidisciplinary staffings evolved as an effort to limit any one individual's influence and to protect against decisions that may be biased against minority children (Huebner & Hahn, 1990). The disadvantages of such staffings include the notions that parents may find it intimidating to face so many educators at once, that parents and others may be reluctant to disagree with recommendations supported by several trained professionals, and that parents may need time to absorb the results of testing before they are ready to think about what is best for the child (Wise, 1995).

Much of the work that school psychologists do takes place within teams of other professionals. As mentioned earlier, school psychologists were often considered the gatekeepers of special education; that is, the data that the school psychologist presented decided whether or not a student qualified for certain programs. Now most of these decisions are made by a group, each member of which holds a particular piece of the puzzle that, when put together correctly, should reveal the best educational placement for that student. Of course, anyone who has worked on a group project of any sort knows that sometimes groups work together in productive ways and sometimes they don't. Shaw and Swerdlik (1995) provide a discussion of topics related to team functioning.

General Issues

To fulfill the responsibilities of the child study role, a number of issues must be addressed. Some of these issues are listed below in question form.

1. What is the established referral process?
   a. Who decides on the referral form to be used?
   b. Who completes the referral form?
   c. Who secures parental consent?
   d. What if parents refuse consent?
   e. Should students be given a chance to refuse testing?

f. Who decides which children should be seen first?

g. Where are completed referral forms kept?

2. Who should be referred?

   a. Are the school psychologist's services limited to children who may qualify for special education services?

   b. Are the school psychologist's services available to any child experiencing difficulty at school or at home?

   c. Are the school psychologist's services available to children who may be gifted or talented?

3. What are the alternatives to the "refer-assess" cycle?

   a. Is pre-referral intervention available?

   b. Are other services available through the school (e.g., counselor, social worker)?

   c. What community services could be used (e.g., mental health center)?

4. Should a classroom observation be conducted?

   a. When should the observation be done?

   b. How long should the observation last?

   c. What observational method(s) should be used?

   d. What might be learned from an observation?

   e. How might the school psychologist's presence influence the observation?

5. Where and how are school records maintained?

   a. Are records kept for life or disposed of periodically?

   b. Who has access to student files?

6. What testing procedures should be used?

   a. What are the reasons for testing this child?

   b. Which tests are most appropriate based upon the child's age, race, sex, native language, and presenting problem?

   c. Are these tests readily available to the school psychologist?

   d. What qualifications are needed to administer, score, and interpret the tests?

   e. Will the tests help to answer the referral question(s)?

7. Who should be interviewed about the child's difficulties?

   a. The classroom teacher?

   b. The parent(s) or other family members?

   c. The child?

   d. Other school personnel (reading teachers, speech and language therapists, counselors, social workers)?

   e. Non-school personnel (e.g., physicians)?

8. What is the purpose of these interviews?

   a. To gain information about the child's strengths and weaknesses?

   b. To obtain a social-developmental-medical history?

    c. To find out more about the people in the child's environment?

    d. To share information and findings?

9. When should these individuals be interviewed?

    a. Before testing?

    b. After testing?

    c. Instead of testing?

    d. Before and after testing?

10. How should these individuals be interviewed?

    a. Separately or collectively?

    b. At school or at the child's home?

    c. In person or over the phone?

11. How should the assessment results be conveyed?

    a. Orally in a parent conference?

    b. Orally in a multidisciplinary staffing?

    c. In the form of a written report?

    d. Orally as well as in written form?

Legal and Ethical Issues

As noted, specific legal and ethical issues are relevant to each of the roles and functions of school psychologists. For the child study role, the most relevant issues tend to involve students' and parents' rights throughout the process.

1. Parents and older students have a right to allow or deny consent for the assessment process based upon the information they have been provided.

2. Parents, students, and school personnel have the right to assume confidentiality in all of their dealings with the school psychologist except in situations involving danger to one or more individuals. The limits of confidentiality should be explained clearly in initial interviews with all parties.

3. Children and parents have a right to their privacy and a right not to have their privacy invaded.

4. Children and parents have the right to expect competent and current assessments. School psychologists are expected to keep up with developments in the field and to provide appropriate services to their clients. At the same time, school psychologists should recognize their limitations (in terms of professional training, professional experience, and time management).

5. Children and parents have the right to expect assessments that do not discriminate on the basis of race, religion, nationality, primary language, cultural background, gender, or socioeconomic status.

Training Needs

To be prepared for the child study role, the school psychologist needs training and practice in techniques of behavioral observations, interviewing techniques, a variety of assessment skills (e.g., skills for selecting, administering, scoring, and interpreting results of individually administered tests, skills for assessing classroom environments), skills in conducting conferences and meetings, and report-writing skills. It also is imperative for the school psychologist to be aware of the administration and organization of schools, normal versus exceptional child development, and general psychological testing and measurements principles. Likewise, training in legal and ethical issues is mandatory to ensure adherence to the highest professional standards. Finally, the school psychologist needs good critical thinking skills to be able to pull all of this information together and understand all of the forces responsible for creating the existing problem.

Advantages and Disadvantages

The advantages of the child study role are that it can be useful in many circumstances in helping to understand the behavior of a particular child, that it provides direct contact with the student that it is traditional and comfortable, and that it is mandated in legislation. Many people choose the profession of school psychology because they like the idea of working on a one-to-one basis with children. Assessment provides opportunities to do so.

In addition, the assessments performed as part of the child study role are data-based. In *norm-referenced* assessment, each child's performance is compared to that of other children.

> "Commercially prepared norm-referenced tests are standardized on groups representative of all children, and typical performances for students of certain ages or in certain grades are obtained. The *raw score* that an individual student earns on a test, which is the number of questions answered correctly, is compared with the raw scores earned by other students. A *transformed score*, such as a percentile rank, is used to express the given student's standing in the group of all children of that age or grade"(Salvia & Ysseldyke, 1998, p. 34).

In *criterion-referenced* assessments a child's progress can be monitored. Criterion-referenced tests allow us to "measure a person's mastery of particular information and skills in terms of absolute standards" (Salvia & Ysseldyke, 1998, p. 35). Criterion-referenced tests provide answers to questions such as *How many lowercase letters of the alphabet can Tracy identify?* Ideally, criterion-referenced assessments and norm-referenced assessments complement one another by providing two important measures of a child's progress. In addition, data gathered from both types of assessments can lead directly to research, a role too often viewed as the lowest priority for school psychology practitioners. The data-based nature of the assessment role can lead to increased accountability among school psychologists.

The disadvantages include the notion that there are many children with problems and that spending several hours with each of them will hardly make a dent in the needs of a school system. A recent study by Lichtenstein and Fischetti (1998) found that time spent on evaluations ranged from just under 4 hours to more than 24 hours with a median of nearly 12 hours per case. Therefore, conducting lengthy evaluations is probably not the best way to have a major impact on the schools. Also, functioning in the child study role day after day may be the quickest road to professional burnout. Every time a school psychologist finishes with one child two more referrals appear.

Finally, now that the data have been collected and interpreted, so what? The child still has not been helped. In fact, when the child study role involves labeling children there may even be negative consequences for the child. A discussion by Hynd, Cannon, and Haussmann (1983) summarizes arguments for and against labeling children. The most critical negative factors appear to be that labeling a child disabled may prejudice the way others respond to that child, that many may focus upon the negative facets of the child, and that the label may lower everyone's expectations for the child. On the other hand, labeling a child as disabled may be the only way the child is able to receive special services because of various state and federal regulations.

Planning and Implementing Interventions
Description

The logical next step after the child study model is the planning and implementing of intervention strategies. The diagnostic work is complete, and it is time to work with others involved in the case and come up with some remedial techniques that will solve the problem and help the child. This is, after all, the reason the diagnostic case study was conducted. Keep in mind, however, that although helping children through interventions is the ultimate goal of assessment, a comprehensive assessment as described above does not automatically precede intervention. In fact, many school psychologists currently advocate and indeed many states now require a pre-referral intervention or intervention assistance approach in which intervention assistance teams (often called teacher assistance teams, or TATs) meet with teachers individually or in small groups to discuss youngsters experiencing a variety of difficulties. Such teams plan strategies collaboratively which in turn may eliminate the need for a formal comprehensive case study evaluation. The *pre-referral intervention* or *intervention assistance* approach is described in Graden, Casey, and Bonstrom (1985), Graden, Casey and Christenson (1985), Zins, Curtis, Graden, and Ponti (1988) and Ross (1995).

When a child is having difficulty in school, some steps need to be taken to alleviate or correct the difficulty. Making recommendations and developing interventions involve creativity and common sense, as well as familiarity with current research. Witt and Elliott (1985) provide guidelines to employ when considering various interventions. They suggest examining the effectiveness of the intervention (i.e., how well it works) along with the acceptability of the intervention (i.e., how positively it is perceived by consumers). Some factors to consider in determining the effectiveness and the acceptability of an intervention strategy include the duration from implementation to results, the type of intervention (e.g., is it something that easily fits into the daily routine?), the time and other resources needed for the intervention to be successful, the theoretical orientation of the intervention (e.g., behavioral), and the person(s) responsible for implementing the intervention (e.g., teacher, parent). Witt and Elliott suggest that the child's perceptions of the acceptability of the intervention strategy also be considered.

Acceptable intervention strategies are those that consider the available resources as well as the dynamics of the individual situation. Phillips and McCullough (1990) present a list of eight "feasibility considerations" to take under advisement when deciding upon interventions to implement. Their list includes:

1. How disruptive the intervention will be for the teacher, the classroom, and the school.
2. How various individuals and systems will be affected (e.g., student, teacher, family).
3. The availability of required support services.
4. The degree of competence of the person(s) expected to carry out the intervention.
5. The chance of the intervention's success.
6. The length of time before results are obtained.
7. The probable prognosis if the intervention is not implemented.
8. The chance that the intervention will lead to a permanent change in the student's behavior.

It is the authors' experience that students and interns often wonder how to come up with interventions to consider. To begin, students need to think about those courses or practica in which interventions were or are to be discussed. What ideas were provided in those classes? There are also some books available linking particular problem areas with intervention ideas (e.g., Akron, Ohio Public Schools, 1991; McCarney, Wunderlich, & Bauer, 1993). Time should be spent researching interventions in journals, in books, and over the Internet. What ideas have been tried out with children and how well did they work? Teachers, parents, and

FIGURE 4.4 Catterall's model of strategies for prescriptive interventions

	Indirect Approach	**Direct Approach**
Environmental	Environmental "around the student"	Installed "to the student"
Personal	Assigned "by the student"	Transactional "with the student"

co-workers often will have ideas that can be used or adapted. For behavioral difficulties, try behavior modification plans. For children having difficulty dealing with a particular problem or situation, suggest counseling, bibliotherapy on the topic, and so forth. Be aware of resources and referral sources available nearby. Network! Are there tutoring services provided for youngsters meeting certain qualifications? What alternative methods of reading instruction are employed by other teachers in the child's grade? Keep a notebook of good ideas you learn of to address particular problems. Go to workshops and conferences to help expand your own resourcefulness in these areas. Each issue of the *Communiqué*, the NASP newsletter, contains pull-out pages on particular issues suitable for handing out to parents and teachers. Canter and Carroll (1998) compiled many of these pull-out pages and added others in a book entitled *Helping Children at Home and School: Handouts From Your School Psychologist.*

Interventions include all of the suggestions directed toward a particular difficulty. To organize the array of interventions available, Catterall (1967) suggested a four-part model of intervention activities. He categorized intervention techniques according to two dimensions: First, is the activity direct or indirect in its focus, and, second, is the intervention technique focused on the environment of the student or on the student himself or herself? Figure 4.4 shows Catterall's model of intervention activities.

Catterall described *environmental interventions* as those activities implemented *around* the student (e.g., pre-selecting a particular classroom, establishing classroom rules). *Installed interventions* are strategies in which something is done *to* the student (e.g., positive reinforcements, punishments, peer tutoring). *Assigned interventions* are activities done *by* the student (e.g., honors assignments, homework). *Transactional interventions* are those activities done *with* the student (e.g., individual or group counseling, classroom contracts). Catterall's model may be especially useful in ensuring that all possible types of intervention strategies are considered.

Maher and Zins (1987) presented a different approach to the organization of school-based intervention strategies. They identified six intervention *domains*: cognitive development, affective functioning, socialization, academic achievement, physical fitness, and vocational preparation. They also identified three intervention *modes*: one to one, group, and consultation. For example, if we wanted to suggest something to help a child improve his or her academic achievement, then we might try individual tutoring (one to one), small-group remedial reading (group), or working with the classroom teacher to enhance the child's learning within the classroom (consultation).

Keep in mind that procedures for recommending intervention strategies for children identified as having disabilities are different from procedures for recommending intervention strategies for non-disabled students. Since the passage of P.L. 94-142 in 1975, decisions made concerning children with disabilities (particularly decisions involving part-time or full-time special education class placement) must be joint decisions agreed upon in multidisciplinary conferences with documentation placed in the child's individualized educational plan (IEP). Prior to the passage of P.L. 94-142, school psychologists often decided single-handedly which students qualified for special education services, which students did not qualify, and which students, if any, should be taken out of special education placements. Currently, though school psychologists often wield a fair amount of influence in placement decisions, the final decision is made by a team composed of professionals and the child's parent(s) or guardian(s).

Notice that individual and group counseling are mentioned in Catterall's model above as examples of transactional interventions; that is, interventions done with students. The amount of time a school psychologist spends in individual and/or group counseling is greatly influenced by the setting in which the school psychologist works; the training, experience, and interest in counseling possessed by the school psychologist; the time and flexibility of scheduling the school psychologist has; and the presence or absence of other qualified professionals within the school and the community. Some school districts employ school counselors, school social workers, or other professionals specifically to perform counseling services for students in all grades. Other districts employ counselors who are available only in the high schools and who may spend much of their time coordinating class schedules, arranging group testing, and providing vocational and college advising for students.

Some school districts expect school psychologists to perform crisis intervention activities, a type of counseling that is short term in nature and addresses a student's immediate needs to talk to someone about a particular problem (e.g., death of a family member or a parental divorce). Other school c expect the school psychologist to counsel secondary school students on others may encourage school psychologists to refer nearly all potential cases to local mental health centers or other facilities and individuals in vicinity. In such cases, when the psychologist is involved in referring students for counseling outside of the school district, the psychologist functions as a liaison with human service providers in the community.

Depending upon the state in which you practice, a school district may be required to provide all necessary psychological services, including counseling, to students with disabilities or even to all students. In some cases, school psychologists may be expected to spend a large amount of time providing individual and group counseling to these students. In fact, school psychologists may be the professionals most qualified to provide counseling to students with disabilities. Most school psychologists are prepared to provide some individual and group counseling services, and many enjoy this role. Examples of group interventions in which school psychologists may be involved include work with children of divorce, children having difficulties with anger management, and children dealing with grief along with more general groups helping students improve their social and problem-solving skills.

Training Needs

School psychologists involved in planning and implementing recommendations need to possess competencies in a number of areas including interpersonal skills (e.g., establishing and maintaining rapport, listening, working collaboratively), skills in generating realistic solutions to problems (e.g., knowledge of intervention research, knowledge of available resources, knowledge of and access to the Internet), and skills in evaluating outcomes (e.g., skills in research, program evaluation, and deciding what changes need to be made for an intervention to be successful, as well as computer skills). Patience is also needed if, as found by Waguespack, Stewart, and Dupre (1992), teachers recall fewer than half of the steps involved in an intervention after a week even when provided with written instructions for implementation. Some of these skills are acquired during training (e.g., research skills) while others are acquired over time during the internship and later on the job. Students should not expect to have all of the answers when they complete their training. Instead, we hope that students acquire an interest in continuing their education throughout their professional lives so that they continue to keep up with research-based trends and innovations.

Legal and Ethical Considerations

The major legal and ethical considerations associated with the intervention concern the appropriateness of particular interventions. Two of the most controversial intervention techniques in the schools have been the use of corporal punishment (i.e., spanking or paddling) and the use of "time-out" procedures in which an individual student is in some way removed from classroom activities and isolated from peers for a period of time. Each of these is discussed at length in Jacob-Timm and Hartshorne (1998). Another body of literature surrounding legal and ethical issues in the use of intervention techniques addresses problems unique to counseling. If a student during counseling suggests that the student is going to harm someone else, that the student is going to kill himself or herself, that the student is being abused by his or her parents, that the student is pregnant, or that the student is taking or selling drugs, is the psychologist obligated, legally and/or ethically, to reveal this information to someone? Again, school psychologists must be aware of current ethical and legal thinking on such dilemmas. Becoming familiar with the ethical principles of NASP, APA, and any state associations to which the school psychologist belongs is the place to start. Jacob-Timm and Hartshorne's (1998) book is an excellent source of down-to-earth discussion of these issues. Training programs are also urged to provide students and interns with the opportunity to consider all aspects of these matters.

A final ethical question with respect to interventions is more general and examines the right of any professional to change another person's behavior without that person's expressed permission. It is one thing for someone who wishes to quit smoking to make an appointment with a psychologist or counselor to learn behavior modification techniques to reach that goal. It is another matter for a teacher to ask a school psychologist for help in modifying the behavior of a child who has difficulty completing assignments, who asks questions without raising his or her hand first, or who talks too frequently to classmates. Jacob-Timm and Hartshorne (1998) advise that the school psychologist has a responsibility to set reasonable goals that will be in the best interest of the child over the long run. Be aware, however, that it would be nearly impossible to ascertain whether, for example, teaching a 6-year-old child to raise his or her hand before asking a question is a reasonable goal that is in the child's own lifelong best interest.

Advantages and Disadvantages

The intervention role affords the school psychologist the opportunity to help children by making suggestions to teachers, parents, and others. When your suggestions work, the intervention role provides feelings of professional accomplishment and success. Something *you* did or suggested may have made a difference in one child's life. These are the kinds of rewards most school psychologists are hoping for; that is, having a positive impact on the lives of children.

Some of the disadvantages of the intervention role are similar to the disadvantages of the assessment role. Even if one child is helped there are still a lot of other needy children out there who are not being helped. Working with one child at a time is rewarding, but is there something that could be done that would help more teachers to help more children in the same amount of time? Some of the intervention activities (e.g., behavior modification plans or social skills training) require the expenditure of large amounts of time, often by the school psychologist who explains the program, sets it up, and evaluates its effectiveness. Unlike the well-established reliability and validity of many instruments employed in assessment activities, many if not most intervention ideas have little research to support their validity, although efforts are underway to remedy this problem by authors such as Elliott, Witt, and Kratochwill (1991). In addition, often the interventionist hears only of those strategies that did not work. ("I tried that behavior modification plan like you said for one day but Billy still wouldn't listen, so I gave up. Any other ideas?") When this happens the school psychologist may end up in a losing battle to combat the "yes-but" response discussed by Berne (1964) ("Yes, but that won't work because he doesn't do any of his work." "Yes, but his parents won't go along with that." "Yes, but I have 30 other students who will want rewards, too.")

Consultation

Description

To avoid the "yes-but" response and to have an impact upon a greater number of students, many school psychologists have embraced a consultation role. Whereas the assessment role allows us to determine the nature of services needed by a student, consultation strengthens the chances that the appropriate services will be delivered. The term *consultation* is used to mean a great many things. More than a dozen types of consultation are discussed in Fagan and Warden (1996). At times consultation has been used synonymously with, for example, advise, counsel, suggest, and solve problems. When used by school psychologists, consultation generally refers to a mutual problem-solving process between two or more professionals. One of the professionals, the consultant, is viewed as an expert in some area. The other professional, the consultee, is experiencing a work-related problem and seeks out the consultant for help in solving the problem. This definition comes from the mental health literature, most notably the work of Caplan (1970).

Other issues that arise in discussions of consultation include the notion of consultation as an *indirect role*. That is, school psychologists work with consultees, often teachers, to solve work-related problems the teachers are having, usually with their students. School psychologists, then, are helping students indirectly by working directly with teachers. The consultee actually has direct responsibility for the client and may choose to accept or reject the consultant's assistance. Martin (1983) also emphasizes the idea of consultation as being focused upon "prevention" rather than "intervention."

Consultation must be voluntary; that is, no one should be forced to consult about a work-related problem. Rather they should seek out the consultant. When people come to a consultant for help because they have been told they must (e.g., a parent is told, "If you and your child don't cooperate with the school psychologist, your child will be suspended from school") the chances of establishing a positive working relationship conducive to mutual problem solving are just about nil.

Consultation differs from counseling. First, in consultation the focus is on a work-related problem rather than a personal problem. A teacher having difficulty controlling her class is an example of a work-related problem appropriate for consultation. Parents wishing to discuss their marital situation is not a work-related problem. In addition, the consultant is expected to function more as a resource person or facilitator than as an expert, an advice giver, or a psychotherapist.

It is particularly important for school psychologists to view consultation as a collaborative relationship between two or more professionals. Curtis and Meyers (1985) note that "one of the most fundamental principles underlying (consultation) is that a genuinely collaborative professional relationship among those engaged in the problem solving process is essential to success" (p.81). Zins and Ponti (1990, p. 675) are more specific about the collaborative nature of consultation. "Consultants and consultees work together to solve problems, and it is highly desirable for them to do so in the context of a partnership that emphasizes trust, openness, and cooperation."

Consultation encompasses many different skills. To be an effective consultant, you must possess a strong knowledge base as well as good interpersonal skills. In other words, you must know what you are talking about and be able to communicate that know-how effectively without turning people off. In addition, the effective consultant develops the consultee's ability to use inner resources. The consultant will not always be present when a problem arises. Therefore, the consultee should not be encouraged to depend upon the presence and advice of the consultant. Conoley and Conoley (1992), among others, provide an elaborated version of this consultation model.

Certain steps or stages are characteristic of consultative relationships. These steps can be summarized as:

1. Entering into the consultation relationship
2. Diagnosing the nature of the work problem
3. Collecting data
4. Creating and maintaining a workable relationship
5. Defining boundaries of the consultation relationship
6. Identifying and developing possible resources
7. Making decisions
8. Terminating the consultation relationship

Consultation can involve working with individuals or with whole groups or systems. The most common forms of consultation practiced by school psychologists are *mental health consultation, behavioral consultation, crisis consultation,* and *organizational consultation.* Other types of consultation relevant to school psychologists include advocacy consultation, case consultation, collaborative consultation, ecological consultation, parent consultation, and problem-solving consultation. Readers are referred to Fagan and Warden (1996) for descriptions of these additional types of consultation.

Mental Health Consultation

Mental health consultation has been described as the "prototypic consultation approach" (Conoley & Conoley, 1992, p. 6). Caplan's (1970) volume, *The Theory and Practice of Mental Health Consultation,* was a milestone work in defining the nature of consultation particularly as it applied to the mental health field. Meyers, Alpert, and Fleisher (1983) define mental health consultation as being based upon the notion that for problem solving to occur, the feelings of the consultee must be addressed. The reasoning is as follows: When a teacher consults with a school psychologist regarding a student in the teacher's classroom, the teacher's relationship with, and feelings toward, the student should be considered; if the consultant can alter the teacher's feelings about the student, then the teacher's behavior toward the student might change; and, if the teacher's behavior toward the student changes, then it will likely cause a change in the student's behavior. It is further believed that if the teacher is aware that a change in his or her behavior toward the student has brought about a change in the student, then the teacher will generalize what she or he has learned to similar situations in the future. If we extend a bit the definition of mental health consultation, it seems logical that school psychologists might consult with other school personnel in promoting positive mental health in the schools and preventing or addressing mental health-related difficulties. Johnson, Malone, and Hightower (1997, p. 81) cite research "which demonstrates that competence, mental health, and achievement are inseparable in schools." Building on the work of previous researchers, they suggest further that school psychologists use their consultation skills in working with teachers to improve the climate of the schools in order to facilitate the positive mental health of large numbers of students.

Behavioral Consultation

Behavioral consultation involves applying behavior modification and social learning theory principles and procedures to the work-related problems of the consultee. Typically a teacher comes to the school psychologist with a specific child or group of children who are exhibiting some type of unacceptable behavior.

Assume a teacher mentions to you his/her concern about a child who picks fights with other children on the playground. You have now, with this teacher contact, entered into the consultative relationship. The next step would be to get the teacher to clarify the problem. You might ask some questions: Does the child fight only on the playground? How about in the classroom? Does the child fight only with one particular child or with several children? How often do these fights occur? How long has this fighting behavior been going on? Is the child experiencing any other kind of difficulty in the classroom or at home? Does the child have any friends in the classroom? Do the fights only occur during a specific type of activity (e.g., competitive games)? Notice that considerable similarity exists between the initial stage of the behavioral consultation role and the pre-referral aspects of a comprehensive assessment, discussed earlier in this chapter.

In the data-gathering step, you would observe on the playground and perhaps in other settings as well. You would want to keep track of the number of fighting episodes as well as the antecedents and the consequences of the fighting.

Note that in consultation (behavioral and other types) overlap exists with the "assessment of individual children" role of the school psychologist. In fact, a great deal of overlap occurs among the various roles of school psychologists. It is quite common for school psychologists to perform several roles on a day-to-day basis. Note also the importance of assessment techniques in the role of the behavioral consultant.

When you define an inappropriate or problem behavior (e.g., fighting or pushing) you also should look for an incompatible appropriate behavior; that is, an acceptable behavior that cannot be done at the same time as fighting. Running laps around the playground, for example, or taking turns would be incompatible with pushing or fighting.

During your observations of the antecedents, and consequences of the inappropriate and appropriate behavior, look for teacher behaviors, peer behaviors, classroom or playground events, and the child's own behaviors that might be maintaining the inappropriate behavior. Throughout this process you should be monitoring your working relationship with the teacher. Check in when you are in the vicinity and ask how things are going. Make certain the teacher knows what steps you are taking and what to expect next. The teacher also should have realistic notions of the boundaries of the working relationship. You might say, "I'll be observing Jennie on the playground, in the cafeteria, and in the classroom on several occasions this week. Then I'll get back to you when I'm here next week so we can set up a plan for you to use with Jennie to decrease her pushing behavior and increase her cooperative behavior."

During your meeting the next week you would share the information you have gathered and work with the teacher on setting up a system that reinforces Jennie's efforts at cooperation and decreases her aggressive behavior. Perhaps

Jennie could earn points for running a certain number of laps per week and lose a given number of points for every fight in which she is involved. The important part of this is that the teacher should be at least an equal partner if not a greater partner in suggesting the possible resources, deciding which program to follow, and implementing the program. Remember that Jennie is the teacher's responsibility, and, therefore, the teacher can accept or reject your assistance. Common sense suggests that the more involved the teacher is in setting up a program, the stronger his or her commitment will be and, therefore, the greater the chances that the program will succeed.

The step in consultation involving termination of the consultation relationship is different for school psychologists than for consultants in other fields. School psychologists often are viewed as not exactly insiders in a given school but not exactly outsiders either. As discussed in Chapter 3, school psychologists may be viewed as guests who make frequent visits to the schools. After Jennie's teacher has a plan in place, you will still in all likelihood want to maintain a working or collaborative relationship with her in case other problems develop or other children in her classroom need direct or indirect services from you in the future. The notion of follow-up is particularly important for school psychologists for this reason. As mentioned above, you should check in with teachers who have consulted with you to find out whether your mutually-arrived-at plan is succeeding. Such checking in may be brief and informal—often it occurs in the hallway or in the teachers' lounge—but it lets the teacher know you are thinking about Jennie and it provides her with an opportunity to let you know whether the plan is working. Keep in mind that consultation involves a relationship-building process. It is not merely a task to be completed by the school psychologist. Rather, it is a way of functioning as a partner with teachers, parents, and others that transcends many if not all of the other roles and functions of the psychologist in the schools.

Crisis Consultation

Crisis consultation takes an indirect approach to the idea of crisis intervention (mentioned above under the intervention role) by helping teachers or others in the school to deal with students undergoing crises. The school psychologist discusses strategies with the teacher so that the teacher can work more effectively with one or more students facing a particular crisis. Students who have not worked previously with the school psychologist may be uncomfortable talking to a stranger about a private issue. They may be more comfortable talking to a favorite teacher. This teacher, however, may be uncertain as to how to deal with the student and may request some suggestions or ideas from the school psychologist.

In one study (Wise, Smead, & Huebner, 1987), school psychologists were given a list of 32 critical events and asked to mark those that they had been approached about during the previous semester. More than half of the psychologists were asked to deal either directly (crisis intervention) or indirectly (crisis consultation) when students were failing a subject, when students were being abused, when students' parents were divorcing or separating, and when students were experiencing problems with one or more teachers, repeating a grade, having difficulty with parents, and moving.

The valuable contributions that school psychologists make in helping school personnel respond to crises were emphasized during the 1997-1998 school year after a series of unfortunate incidents in which students were involved in in-school shootings. Scott Poland, a leader in the area of responding to school crises and co-author of *Crisis Intervention in the Schools* (Pitcher & Poland, 1992), serves as a team leader of the National Organization for Victim Assistance (NOVA) and is a member of the National Emergency Assistance Teams (NEAT). Poland's NEAT team, consisting of two school psychologists and five other helping professionals, was invited to Jonesboro, Arkansas, after two students shot and killed a teacher and four students at a middle school. The team's role was to identify those most in need of services, to provide professional support and training to the caregivers already in the community, and to conduct a public forum to facilitate the processing of emotions within the community. (Poland's account of his team's work in Jonesboro appears in the NASP *Communiqué*, June 1998, *26* (8), pp 4-5.) As an outgrowth of the attention focused on school-based violence during the 1997-1998 school year, NASP played an active role in developing *Early Warning, Timely Response: A Guide to Safe Schools* (Dwyer et al., 1998) published by the U.S. Department of Education and disseminated to more than 100,000 public and private schools in September, 1998.

Organizational Consultation

Organizational consultation applies the principles and practices of consultation to the larger framework of a school building or an entire school system in an attempt to improve the functioning and/or implement planned changes within the entire organization. Any skilled observer who spends time in the schools, and in most other organizations as well, can see areas in need of change.

Centra and Potter (1980) developed a model of school-related variables, any or all of which may have an impact on student learning. These variables include:

1. School or school-district conditions
2. Within-school conditions
3. Teacher characteristics
4. Teaching behavior
5. Student characteristics
6. Student behavior
7. Student learning outcomes

Usually when we talk about organizational consultation in the schools, we are talking about making changes relating to some or all of these seven variables. Harrington (1985) suggests that organizational problems within schools typically concern ambiguous, changing, or unmeasurable goals; poor communication within the system; or attempting to implement changes without enough forethought. Harrington (1985) further suggests that school psychologists interested in organizational development and consultation adopt one or more of the following four roles:

1. Planning leader: Helping to organize and coordinate change.
2. Information and communications link: Collecting organizational data, clarifying, synthesizing, and interpreting the data to others.
3. Learning specialist: Applying knowledge about learning and educational theory to the problems at hand.
4. Consultant to management: Clarifying the problems and solutions for administration and acting as a liaison among the various groups involved.

School psychologists may be in ideal positions to engage in organizational consultation for a variety of reasons. First, the school psychologist is neither an insider nor an outsider in the school. Usually school psychologists are somewhere between being a guest and being a family member in the house of education as described in Chapter 3. Because school psychologists rarely work in just one school they are not considered regular staff members in a given building, yet over time they usually work with sufficient numbers of individuals within a given school such that they are not strangers either. Consider also an advantage that many school psychologists have when they work in a number of different schools: They have the opportunity to observe what works in one school and what does not work in another school. Finally, school psychologists' backgrounds in research design, consultation, and assessment skills should prove useful for the practice of organizational consultation.

Illback, Zins, and Maher (1999, p. 922) suggest that "viewing schools from a systems perspective enables the evaluator to gain a broader understanding of factors that potentially influence the operation of the school." They note that systems are made up of subsystems. In schools, such subsystems may be the individual school buildings, the school administration, the board of education, the special education personnel, or even the school psychologists. Subsystems are all interconnected, and a change in one subsystem causes changes in the other subsystems. Illback et al. note that one important organizational role for school psychologists relates to evaluation of programs. As schools move toward more of an outcome-based assessment of students for purposes of accountability, the program evaluation role may escalate in importance.

Training Needs

As noted above, to consult effectively individuals need good interpersonal skills, an awareness of the parameters of consultation, and knowledge about the subject under consideration. Conoley and Conoley (1992) label the skills needed for consultation "relationship-enhancing skills," skills in "problem formulation and resolution," and "personal and group process skills." School psychologists new to the profession or even new to a particular school may not be immediately sought out as consultants. They may have to prove themselves first as competent professionals in more traditional roles (e.g., child study and intervention). At the same time, newly trained school psychologists may not possess the knowledge and experience needed for effective consultation. They may have effective interpersonal skills and feel comfortable with brainstorming and problem-solving strategies, but they lack the wealth of resources and techniques that teachers or parents may be looking for. A great deal has been written about consultation in the school psychology literature. For more information, see Conoley and Conoley (1992), Gutkin and Curtis (1999), and Zins and Erchul (1995). One thought-provoking article about training needs suggests that not only do school psychologists need to be trained as consultants but that teachers should be trained as consultees. Such training would enable teachers to formulate better questions and to become more active participants in the consultative relationship (Duis, Rothlisberg, & Hargrove, 1995).

Legal and Ethical Issues

Hughes (1986) suggests that certain ethical issues apply to all types or models of consultation. For example, regardless of the type of consultation, school psychologists need to be concerned with students' rights, parents' rights, the rights of consultees, and the rights of the school system that employs them. With regard to students' rights, Hughes notes that school psychologists' actions "should (a) not abridge children's rights and (b) promote values of human dignity and respect for individuals' rights" (p. 490). If school psychologists become aware, through consultation or other roles, of practices that are unethical or that go against a child's rights, they have a responsibility to the child to work to change these practices.

Parents have a right to privacy and confidentiality and a right to give or withhold informed consent to any plan or program in which "a child is singled out for special treatment in a manner that permits classmates to perceive the child as different in a negative way" (Hughes, 1986, p. 492). Consultees have a right to privacy, confidentiality, and informed consent as well (Hughes, 1986).

As mentioned earlier, the consultative relationship is a voluntary one, and consultees have a right to accept or reject any suggestions or advice that evolves from the consultation.

What rights do employing school districts have? Hughes (1986) suggests that school districts have the right to know how successful their school psychologists have been in achieving the objectives of consultation. In other words, as discussed in Chapter 5, school districts have a right to accountability data from the school psychologist; that is, they should be told how the school psychologist spends his or her time and how effective the school psychologist is.

Jacob-Timm and Hartshorne (1998, p. 196) raise similar ethical issues regarding the consultation role for school psychologists. They note that "In providing school-based consultative services, the school psychologist is working within a network of relationships. Consistent with the broad ethical principle of integrity in professional relationships, the practitioner strives to be honest, accurate, and straightforward about the nature and scope of the services he or she has to offer." As with all professional roles, school psychologists acting as consultants have a responsibility to students, parents, and school personnel to carry out all duties in a professional, competent, fair, and confidential manner.

Advantages and Disadvantages

Consultation in all of its various forms can be an extremely valuable and satisfying role for the school psychologist. Consultation activities provide school psychologists with the opportunity to have an indirect impact on a large number of students. Consultation may be viewed by school personnel as a particularly valuable resource when difficult problems arise. In addition, consultation may be a valuable tool in preventing problems. Consulting with a new teacher about behavioral strategies, for example, may help that teacher develop the confidence and skills needed to face subsequent problems as they arise.

Many school psychologists enjoy one-to-one contact with children. Since the consultation role is indirect with respect to students, the psychologist acting as consultant may spend more time with adults and less time with children. The idea that the consultee, usually the teacher, is free to accept or reject the suggestions of the consultant can be another frustrating aspect of consultation. A great deal of time and energy may be spent in collaborative problem solving only to have the results ignored completely or inconsistently applied.

Additional Roles and Functions

Most school psychologists working in school systems spend the majority of their days involved in helping students through the activities described:

1. Assessment of individual children
2. Interventions (including individual and group counseling)
3. Consultation (mental health, behavioral, crisis, and organizational)

On the other hand, many school psychologists are involved in one or more less traditional roles and functions to some degree. Usually these roles, (e.g., research, training, and administration) do not help students in a direct manner but rather help students through providing data, training, supervision, and support to others who do work directly with students. A few less traditional roles, however, do benefit children directly but expand services to somewhat less traditional clients or are offered in less traditional settings (e.g., providing support for post-secondary students, expanding services to infants, providing services to those in charter schools).

Some school psychologists become involved in *short-term* or *long-term research projects*. Examples of the kinds of research projects include:

1. Evaluating the effectiveness of a behavior modification plan for an aggressive fifth-grade boy
2. Developing local norms for an achievement test
3. Examining past records to determine sex differences in the reason-for-referral section of the referral form
4. Evaluating the effectiveness of special class placement versus mainstreaming for junior high students with learning disabilities

School psychologists' involvement in research endeavors traditionally has been conducted in large part by university-based trainers of school psychologists. As described in Chapter 6, trainers typically acquire additional skills in research and statistics in pursuit of their doctoral degrees. Some trainers may have become trainers because they enjoy the research aspect of the job. In addition, universities generally expect faculty to conduct and publish research in order to be promoted and tenured, the so-called *publish-or-perish* syndrome. Finally, university settings generally have facilities that support research efforts (e.g., computers, libraries, and even graduate students to serve as research assistants).

School psychologists employed by the public schools usually are not encouraged to conduct research. Those wishing to conduct research may have to make time for such projects in addition to all of their other job demands. Some school psychologists have ideas for research projects they would like to undertake, but they lack the technical expertise to do so on their own. In recent years, efforts have been made to link practitioners in the field interested in certain areas of research with individuals at universities who have the resources to assist in relevant projects. Such "professional matchmaking" efforts should be encouraged on a larger scale. There is a similar practice evolving in teacher training in which professional development schools are established with close collaborative relationships between education faculty and school-based teachers and administrators. Such a practice provides better field experiences for students, cooperative teaching arrangements on- and off-campus, and increased opportunities for education research projects.

Occasionally school psychologists become involved in research projects somewhat involuntarily. Because school psychologists may be the members of the school staff with the most background in research design and statistics, they may be sought out by administrators, teachers, or school board members to plan studies, gather data, and disseminate the results.

Phillips (1999) proposes a view in which research is incorporated more effectively and less painfully during training (e.g., faculty need to be models of research skills, students should be included in research projects early in their training) and in which research is viewed more broadly in practice. In other words, research should be seen as a problem-solving process, a means of defining important issues in the profession, and as a way of keeping in touch with professional literature. He makes a distinction between school psychologists who are "knowledge brokers," that is the evaluators and disseminators of research, and school psychologists who are "melders," those who are actually conducting research projects.

An additional task undertaken by many school psychologists involves *staff development* or *in-service training*. As they travel from school to school and consult with teachers and other school personnel, school psychologists may be able to identify training needs common to a school or even an entire district. For example, as more students with disabilities are included within regular classrooms, school psychologists may hear from teachers who want help in integrating such youngsters into their classrooms without disrupting other students. Such requests may provide excellent opportunities for teacher in-service workshops in which information about inclusion is provided, various types of disabilities are defined, and suggestions are shared. In many ways the planning of in-service workshops can be viewed as a sort of grand-scale consultation. At times the school psychologist may be the presenter at such in-service workshops. At other times, the school psychologist may be involved in planning the workshops and locating speakers from outside the district.

Some students may view *public speaking* either at in-service workshops or in other forums (e.g., PTA meetings or groups such as Parents Without Partners) as opportunities to be avoided. Keep in mind, though, that through public speaking you may be able to reach a large audience and to have an impact on children's lives.

Those readers currently enrolled in school psychology graduate programs may have already realized that a large number of school psychologists are involved in *training prospective school psychologists.* Some trainers work for universities and spend all or most of their time in teaching, research, and professional service activities. Other school psychologists are employed as practitioners in the schools but spend some amount of time supervising practicum students and school psychology interns, and/or teaching university classes sometimes as part-time adjuncts to training programs.

Along the same lines, some large school districts or special education cooperatives hire one school psychologist to *supervise* the other school psychologists and to *perform the various administrative functions* necessary to the running of a psychological services unit. Such an individual usually possesses a doctoral degree in school psychology, educational administration, or a related field. A school psychologist functioning in such a supervisory capacity usually has a reduced caseload relative to other school psychologists on staff to compensate for time spent in administrative and supervisory duties. Although every school psychologist has some administrative responsibilities (e.g., paperwork, organizing meetings), supervising school psychologists may spend the majority of their time involved in these and other administrative activities.

PROFESSIONAL ROLES AND FUNCTIONS: RESEARCH

There is a substantial body of professional literature regarding what school psychologists do on the job (actual role), what school psychologists would like to do (preferred role), and what others (e.g., parents, teachers, students) think school psychologists actually do or wish they would do (perceived role). Other studies have focused on the training needs of school psychologists in order to be prepared to function effectively on the job.

Studies of actual roles (e.g., Lacayo, Sherwood, & Morris, 1981; Smith, 1984) generally have asked school psychologists to maintain logs of their activities for a certain period of time or to estimate how much of their time is spent engaged in particular roles and functions. Occasionally these studies are focused on one particular activity. For example, Fish and Massey (1991) were interested in how much time school psychologists spend with the various systems in students' lives (i.e., family, school, and community members). They asked their subjects to record the contacts they had with family members, school personnel, and various members of the community. Their findings suggest that school psychologists spend an average of 18% of the day in contact with school personnel, 8% of the day in contact with family members, and 2% of the day in contact with other members of the community. (Presumably the remainder of their time was spent with students or engaged in other activities such as completing paper work, reading professional literature, or driving between schools.)

Another study (Watkins, Tipton, Manus, & Hunton-Shoup, 1991, p. 328) examined the *role relevance* and *role engagement* of various professional activities to school psychologists. Role relevance was defined as "the degree to which various roles are seen as relevant to (or important defining features of)" the field of school psychology. Role engagement includes the roles in which school psychologists are involved in their professional practice. The study found common ground between role relevance and role engagement. School psychologists responding to the study were engaged in assessment, consultation, counseling, and interventions and also considered these roles relevant to the practice of school psychology. In addition to the more traditional roles, school psychologists in the study were engaged in several other activities that they considered relevant to the profession, namely, program development and accountability, continuing education, training and supervision, and educational/vocational counseling.

Reschly (1998, p. 4) discovered that school psychologists continue to spend more than 50% of their work time in tasks related to psychoeducational assessment, most often in determining eligibility, new or continued, for special education programs and services. He found that between 1992 and 1997 "there have been no discernible changes in either current or preferred roles." In the 5 year period, school psychologists continued to express preferences for a combination of the traditional roles of assessment, intervention, and consultation. Few of the practitioners expressed interest in expanding their roles in the direction of systems/organizational consultation or research/evaluation. Bahr (1996) presents data supporting Reschly's (1998) work. Bahr's study suggests that school psychologists support some role changes (e.g., increased use of curriculum-based assessment, increased consultant follow-up with teachers) but that generally school psychologists are unwilling to overhaul completely their traditional roles.

Still other studies have examined others' perceptions of the role of the school psychologist. Roberts (1970) found some similarities between school psychologists' own perceptions of their actual and desired roles and teachers' perceptions of the actual and desired roles of school psychologists. In Roberts' study the area of greatest difference involved teachers' desire for school psychologists to be more involved in counseling individual students. Hughes (1979) asked school psychologists, pupil personnel directors, and school superintendents for their actual and ideal perceptions of the role of the school psychologist. All three groups supported a move away from the traditional diagnostic assessment role. However, the three groups differed in the direction they wanted to see school psychologists go. School psychologists in the sample wanted to expand their roles in consultation (mental health and organizational development) and research. Pupil personnel directors wanted the time saved from the assessment role to be evenly distributed to all of the other roles (e.g., counseling, parent education, consultation). The superintendents in the study wanted school psychologists to spend their time doing more counseling. More recently, Peterson, Waldron, and Paulson (1998) asked a group of midwestern teachers about their interactions with school psychologists. Results indicated that while most of the teachers (89%) had at least talked to a school psychologist, the majority had few contacts because the school psychologists were rarely around. The teachers in the study preferred the psychometrician and the problem-solver roles for school psychologists and they believed that school psychologists could offer valuable suggestions about teaching practices. Unfortunately, the teachers believed that the school psychologists were unavailable because of heavy caseloads and multiple building or district assignments.

In an effort to determine what students would like from school psychologists, Culbertson (1975, p. 192) asked a group of college undergraduates two questions:

1. If you were to plan an ideal elementary, middle or junior high, or high school, would you include a psychologist as a member of the school team?
2. If "yes" to the above, what would you like the role and duties of the psychologist to be? Please describe.

Ninety-two percent of the students indicated that they would include a psychologist as a team member. As to what such an individual would do, the top five responses in order were a helper (i.e., someone to talk to), an assessor of students' abilities, a counseling advisor, an ombudsman, and an information communicator.

BALANCING THE ROLES AND FUNCTIONS

Most school psychologists perform a combination of the roles and functions discussed above. Although in a text such as this we talk of assessment, intervention, and consultation as though they are mutually exclusive activities, in practice the distinctions among them become blurred. Interviewing a teacher about a particular child, for instance, may be part assessment, part intervention, and part consultation. Chapter 1 provides survey information about the relative portion of time school psychologists spend on these roles.

The scenarios in Boxes 4.1, 4.2, and 4.3 portray the overlap among the roles in the practice of school psychology to future practitioners. As you read the three daily logs, note the variety of activities in which the school psychologists are involved, the differences in activities depending upon the ages of children served, and the differences in activities depending upon the setting.

BOX 4.1   School Psychologist 1: Daily Log

Background: School Psychologist 1 is employed by a fairly large suburban school district. She works in three elementary schools and a junior high with students in grades 1–8. The total number of students she serves is 1,800. She spends 1 day per week in each of her four schools. Fridays are spent at her office catching up with phone calls, messages, and report writing. Fridays are also the one day in the week that all four of the psychologists employed by the district try to go out to lunch together to stay in touch with each other, to share what is going on in the various schools, and to discuss professional issues.

Monday, October 2

7:45 AM	Stopped at office for messages and supplies.
8:15	Arrived at Grace School.
8:15-8:45	Sat in teachers' lounge; arranged with two teachers to observe children in their rooms this morning (at 9 and 10); checked with a teacher about how a behavior management program was progressing (we decided to change the daily reward and send parents a note).
8:45-9:00	Checked with principal regarding new referrals.
9:00-9:45	Observed third-grade boy who gets into fights.
9:45-10:00	Paperwork.
10:00-10:30	Observed first-grade boy with attention problems.
10:30-10:45	Talked to first-grade teacher about my observations; teacher decided to move child to front of room and to check with parents about whether he needs glasses.
10:50-11:50	Administered individual intelligence test to fourth-grade girl whose teacher suspects a learning disability.
11:50-1:00	Teachers' lounge: had lunch and talked with teachers about their needs for in-service programs; topics suggested included working with LD children in the regular classroom, working with children of low average intelligence who cannot keep up in regular classrooms, and working with children experiencing crises (parental divorce, sexual abuse, death of sibling); no decision yet. A more formal "needs assessment" will be developed.
1:00-1:30	Counseled a sixth-grade student who has just moved into the district and is having trouble adjusting.

Box 4.1 continued on page 154

Box 4.1 continued

1:30-2:20	Administered achievement tests and sentence completion test to fifth-grade boy referred for academic difficulties and low self-esteem.
2:30-3:30	Met with district-wide group testing committee to establish a district testing plan.
3:30-4:30	Returned phone calls; wrote drafts of two reports.

BOX 4.2 School Psychologist 2: Daily Log

Background: School Psychologist 2 is one of two school psychologists assigned full-time to work in a large urban high school. His office is in the building and he spends all of his time there. The school has 3,000 students grades 9–12.

Monday, October 2

8:00 AM	Arrived at Hillcrest High School.
8:00-9:00	Met with ninth-grade teachers concerned about students' attitudes toward school and poor study habits. Planned a PTA program for later in the month on the topic of how parents can help students succeed; also, discussed the possibility of a peer counseling program.
9:00-10:00	Group counseling session with six tenth-grade girls identified as having low self-esteem and poor social skills. In the session last week, four of the six admitted having been abused by their boyfriends and most had been either abused or neglected by family members.
10:00-10:30	Phoned leader of a community task force aimed at stopping gang activities. Discussed ways in which school and community personnel could work as a team.
10:30-11:30	Administered achievement tests and talked with an eleventh-grade boy who is failing all of his courses and is thinking about dropping out.
11:30-12:30	Had lunch in the teachers' lounge. Two teachers voiced concern about a twelfth-grade girl whom they suspect is pregnant. Another teacher asked for help with a hearing impaired student who has been mainstreamed into her class but does not seem to be keeping up with assignments.
12:30-1:30	Individual counseling with a ninth-grade boy who referred himself for help in dealing with serious family problems.
1:30-2:15	Met with two school psychology graduate students; gave

Box 4.2 continued

them a tour of the building; discussed the role of the school psychologist in the secondary school; answered some of their questions.

2:15-3:15 Observed in a cross-categorical resource room at teacher's request. Students are not getting along with each other and these problems are interfering with getting work completed.

3:15-4:00 Paperwork, phone calls, etc.

7:00-9:30 PM Attended class at local university on vocational assessment for high school students with disabilities.

BOX 4.3 School Psychologist 3: Daily Log

Background: School Psychologist 3 works for three small rural school districts. In each district, there is one elementary school and one combined junior and senior high school. The total number of students served by School Psychologist 3 is 1,200. She spends more job time driving than School Psychologists 1 and 2 combined, often covering 100 miles per day from the time she leaves her home in the morning until the time she returns home in the evening.

Monday, October 2

8:00 AM Arrived at Fairland School (considered "main office").

8:00-9:00 Sat in teachers' lounge catching up on latest news; arranged to test a kindergarten child and to observe a first-grader later in the day; talked to principal about setting up a volunteer program to help with reading; heard about a child who has just moved into the district (fourth grade) and can't read, his mother is coming in after school to talk to his teacher about having me do some testing (I'll try to attend for a while to introduce myself and ask some questions about previous schooling).

9:00-10:00 Observed kindergarten boy in regular classroom and in music—very distractible! He was on task only 4 minutes!

10:00-10:15 Talked to kindergarten teacher about my observations; she would like me to test him formally but she also wanted some ideas for helping him pay attention in the meantime. I suggested placing him somewhere in the room (front row? back corner?) with the fewest distractions.

10:15- 11:00 Began some testing of the kindergarten child. He needs frequent breaks and has great difficulty sitting

Box 4.3 continued on page 156

Box 4.3 continued

	still. When he is paying attention, he seems to be of at least average ability.
11:00-12:00	Went to junior-senior high to meet with eighth grade teacher team concerned with the large number of students who cannot read or write beyond the most basic level. We considered an after-school remedial program 2 days a week. The program would be voluntary but "strongly recommended" to some students if they want to pass their courses this year. Discussed writing a grant proposal for next year for the same type of program.
12:00-12:45	Lunch in junior high teachers' lounge. Continued discussing the problems with the current group of eighth graders.
12:45-1:30	Counseled an eighth-grade girl who is upset because her parents are getting divorced.
1:30-2:30	Group counseling with eight tenth graders considered at risk for dropping out of school.
2:30-3:15	Counseled a twelfth-grade boy who has a history of fighting and other problems with controlling his anger.
3:30-5:00	Met with the group-testing committee to develop a less expensive but still informative district testing plan.

The Trainers' Dilemma

University professors engaged in training students to enter the field of school psychology are in a unique and sometimes uncomfortable position. Most of us have worked in the schools as practicing school psychologists at some point in our careers and we recognize the realities of the field (e.g., too many students, too much paperwork, pressures to place students in special education classrooms). On the other hand, we know that school psychologists have the training and skills to do more than serve as the gatekeepers to special education. Further, we recognize the needs schools have for additional services that the well-trained school psychologist is able to provide. We know that if we do not train our students in the traditional skills of assessment these students may not be employable, but if we do train our students in the traditional assessment skills, they may not make adequate use of the whole repertoire of other skills they possess. Therefore, most of us try to achieve a balance. We teach students a variety of skills including assessment, consultation, and interventions and we hope that each graduate is not only employable but also will work as a change agent in expanding the role of the school psychologist.

CONCLUSION

The role of the school psychologist is truly multifaceted. School psychologists are engaged in numerous activities all ultimately aimed at helping children. Although each role demands unique training and skills, all of the roles, from child study to intervention and from consultation to research are based upon assessment. Without assessment to identify a child's strengths and weaknesses, to determine whether our intervention strategies work, to support the efficacy of our consultative skills, and to support or refute our research hypotheses, we are at best do-gooders; that is, individuals with good intentions but without empirical substantiation for our work. In Chapter 5 we continue in this same vein to emphasize the importance of accountability; that is, the assessment of the effectiveness of school psychologists on the job.

Professional Evaluation and Accountability

So far in this book we have described the history of school psychology, examined the relationship of school psychology to education, and elaborated upon the actual and ideal roles and functions of school psychologists. The present chapter addresses the various processes involved in the evaluation and accountability of school psychologists as a group and as individuals. Few issues are as important to the profession of school psychology as a whole, or as potentially anxiety-producing for individual school psychologists, as the issues of professional evaluation and accountability. In fact, in a study of stressful events in the professional lives of school psychologists (discussed in greater detail in Chapter 8), "notification of unsatisfactory job performance" was ranked as the most stressful event, more stressful even than "potential suicide cases," "threat of a due process hearing," or "working in physically dangerous situations" (Wise, 1985).

Although most of us agree with the general principle that the overall practice of school psychology should be examined periodically to determine its effectiveness and its relevance, when it comes to evaluating individual members of the profession to determine their professional effectiveness, we become a bit more cautious and a good deal less enthusiastic. After all, school psychologists are only human! Yet, by agreeing that the evaluation of others is useful, as most school psychologists seem to do on a daily basis, we commit ourselves to being evaluated also.

HISTORICAL BACKGROUND

Evaluation and accountability are continuing phenomena rather than new ones to the profession of school psychology. Lightner Witmer had to make his case for the clinic at the University of Pennsylvania and maintain records of cases and services delivered (Brotemarkle, 1931). Gesell frequently was held accountable to the State of Connecticut for his caseload and practice (Fagan, 1987a). The notion of an annual report was quite popular in large urban schools. Readers are referred, for example, to the *Bureau of Child Guidance Five Year Report 1932-1937* (City of New York, 1938), a hardbound book of more than 150 pages, including descriptions of services, enumerative data, and results of treatment. *The Bureau of Child Study and the Chicago Adjustment Service Plan* (City of Chicago, 1941) is another example of an annual report containing similar accountability data.

The founding of some urban school clinics was accomplished with private funds in all likelihood because the administration was unwilling to risk public funds for such ventures prior to substantiation of the clinics' value or outcomes. This was the case for the Vocational Bureau of the Cincinnati Public Schools founded in 1910 (Veatch, 1978). Veatch's dissertation provides a historical account of the development of the bureau into its current psychological services and of its accountability struggles over several decades. Annual reports were also filed that were part of the Cincinnati district's annual report to the board of education. The reports include considerable details about services (e.g., Cincinnati Public Schools, 1912).

Although most of these historical annual reports are largely enumerative (e.g., accountings of how many students were seen), some outcome data (i.e., the outcomes or results of the school psychologists' activities) are present also. From examining documents such as those mentioned above, we can see that although accountability has become more prevalent during the past 25 years, it has been an important concept within school psychology throughout the history of the profession. Undoubtedly records such as those cited above helped to convince school personnel and school boards to maintain such services even during the depression of the 1930s (Mullen, 1981).

CURRENT PRACTICES

Think for a moment about the ways in which prospective school psychologists and practicing school psychologists are evaluated at various points in their careers. To be admitted to a school psychology training program, prospective school psychologists must meet or exceed certain criteria. These criteria usually include an examination of a student's undergraduate academic record, scores on the Graduate Record Examination or another standardized test (e.g., Miller Analogies Test), three or more letters of recommendation, and perhaps an autobiographical sketch and/or a personal interview. Such criteria provide university trainers with the opportunity to accept applicants into their programs who have a reasonable chance of completing the training program successfully and becoming competent and productive school psychologists. At the same time, an effort is made to screen out applicants who for one reason or another appear to be unacceptable candidates for training and practice.

Once a student has been admitted to a graduate program, certain standard academic evaluation requirements (e.g., term papers, course exams, and research projects) help faculty members to monitor the student's progress. At the non-doctoral level, students often are required to complete master's theses and/or comprehensive examinations before receiving their degrees. Students in doctoral programs must meet additional entrance and exit requirements (e.g., qualifying examinations, dissertation completion, and dissertation defenses).

In tandem with academic requirements, most school psychology trainers attempt to evaluate in some way the students' personal and professional characteristics. As discussed in Chapter 6, several authors have identified desirable personal characteristics for school psychology students and practitioners to possess (Bardon, 1986; Bardon & Bennett, 1974; Fireoved & Cancerelli, 1985; Magary, 1967a). The most recent edition of the credentialing standards of NASP (NASP, 1994a) includes a list of such professional work characteristics as well. Characteristics listed in the standards include "communication skills, effective interpersonal relations, ethical responsibility, flexibility, initiative and dependability, personal stability, and respect for human diversity" (p. 29-30). Ysseldyke et al. (1997) suggest that school psychologists "be prepared to listen, adapt, deal with ambiguity, and be patient in difficult situations" (p. 11). Certainly these are characteristics that school psychology students must possess as well.

Although most school psychology faculty members acknowledge the importance of such characteristics or attributes in professional success, the challenge for training programs is to define the characteristics in sufficiently specific and meaningful terms such that they are measurable as well as discriminatory. (In this sense the term "discriminatory" refers to the ability of a measure to differentiate between those students who possess the particular skill and those students who do not.) Although it is difficult to reach a consensus regarding these issues among school psychology faculty members and/or practitioners, it is likely that during the course of training, and particularly in practicum courses, students may be evaluated in some or all of the following areas:

1. Listening skills
2. Oral expression skills
3. Writing skills
4. Ability to accept constructive criticism
5. Overall emotional maturity
6. Ability to work with children
7. Ability to work with parents and school personnel in a positive, non-threatening manner

8. Willingness to go "beyond course requirements"
9. Flexibility in adapting to change
10. Observance of school protocol and school rules (e.g., checking in at office, dressing appropriately, securing parental permission)
11. Observance of professional ethics (e.g., maintains confidentiality, does not overstep boundaries of training, presents data honestly)

Once a characteristic is defined in specific and measurable terms, program faculty members also must decide whether an individual who is deemed deficient in that characteristic is willing and able to remediate the deficiency and also whether an enduring deficiency in that characteristic is sufficient grounds to terminate a student from a training program or an internship. As noted by Ysseldyke et al. (1997, p. 12), "Absence of prerequisite interpersonal and social skills may be an insurmountable barrier to development of a high level of expertise" in such areas as consultation and collaboration.

Upon completion of graduate studies and prior to state certification, students may be required to take a state-mandated minimum competency examination. Such a test may assess basic skills (i.e., language and math) as well as knowledge of the field of school psychology. Since 1988, school psychologists interested in national certification have been required to submit to a national board evidence of their professional training, knowledge, and experience including their scores on a national certification test. The national certification exam also may be taken independently of the national certification process and is, in fact, used for certification by some states.

As described in Chapter 8, the internship year is designed to be a time of careful evaluation as well. For many school psychologists, the internship year is the last time that they will be so closely and totally supervised by a practicing school psychologist, someone who, through training and experience, is qualified to comment on the intern's technical expertise as well as on general progress and skills. Upon completion of an internship, trainees move from student status to professional status, and evaluations by appropriately trained and knowledgeable supervisors may no longer be possible. Therefore, during the internship, university trainers as well as field supervisors want to make certain that their students meet the highest professional standards before those students receive an official seal of approval. It should be noted that for new school psychologists the NASP credentialing standards (1994a) call for 1 year of supervision as practicing school psychologists following initial certification before permanent certification is granted. Practical considerations, however, render this requirement difficult in many settings particularly for those employed in rural and small school districts.

Once the internship and any additional training program and state-mandated credentialing requirements are completed, the graduate's first test of professional competence is in being able to find a job. Of course, finding a job often depends upon factors other than professional competence such as the status of the job market, the applicant's ability to relocate, and how well the applicant's skills and interests match those in existing job openings. (These factors are discussed in Chapter 8.)

Upon obtaining employment, school psychologists undoubtedly will be subjected to periodic professional evaluations. School systems generally require evaluation of members of their professional staffs on an annual basis, particularly before granting tenure to those persons. Such evaluations are conducted in order to help individuals improve their skills as well as to weed out the occasional staff member who is not performing adequately. Educators often speak of "formative" and "summative" evaluation procedures. Formative evaluations are those carried out during the course of an intervention or program. Summative evaluations are those carried out at the conclusion of a program. In the case of a first-year school psychologist, a formative evaluation might include on-the-job observations during assessments or multidisciplinary staffings, progress reports, feedback from those who have had direct experience working with the school psychologist, and so forth. A summative evaluation for a first year school psychologist likely would be an end-of-year report detailing activities and accomplishments. Strengths and weaknesses may be noted as well.

In his book, *Handbook of Teacher Evaluation*, Millman (1981) distinguishes between the formative and summative roles of evaluation as such evaluations apply to teachers, in a more pragmatic way. "Formative teacher evaluation helps teachers improve their performance by providing data, judgments, and suggestions that have implications for what to teach and how. On the other hand, summative teacher evaluation serves administrative decision making with respect to hiring and firing, promotion and tenure, assignments, and salary" (p.13).

Although most school psychologists probably would agree that evaluations can be beneficial, many would be less than agreeable to such evaluations if their salaries, their assignments, or even their jobs themselves were riding on the results of evaluations. In reality, however, jobs often do depend on the results of evaluations.

As mentioned above, a difficulty that often arises for school psychologists, particularly those employed in small school districts and/or in rural areas, is one of finding someone qualified to conduct an evaluation of their skills. There may not be anyone in the school system, including the school psychologist's immediate supervisor, with training or background in school psychology. Thus an evaluation of professional skills may pose something of a dilemma. Tennessee initiated a career-ladder program to address this dilemma. In recent years the state department of education employed school psychologist evaluators from around the state to conduct evaluations of school psychologists. Local districts in other states could address this issue as well by hiring external reviewers to conduct periodic evaluations. The problem of having school psychologists evaluated by non-psychologists again raises the issue of administrative versus professional supervision discussed in Chapter 3.

EVALUATION OF SCHOOL PSYCHOLOGY TRAINING PROGRAMS

University training programs also undergo formative and summative evaluation procedures. Universities generally have offices of institutional research and planning that are responsible for maintaining data regarding the number of students enrolled in each program on campus, the number graduating from each program, student demographic data (e.g., age, gender, and race), the number of faculty members assigned to each program, and so forth. In tough economic times, these numbers may be carefully scrutinized by administrators and by the various boards that govern the university (and to whom the university as a whole is accountable) to determine a program's cost-effectiveness relative to the number of graduates "produced."

In addition to completing university-maintained records, school psychology program directors may be asked to complete annual reports focusing upon the number of program inquiries and applicants, the number of students admitted to the program, the quantity and quality of students currently enrolled, the major accomplishments for the year, job placement record of graduates, and so on. Such reports may be read by the department chairperson, the college dean, the university provost and academic vice president, the president, and perhaps even the higher board that oversees the governance of the university.

Depending upon a program's state and national approval status, periodic reviews by state departments of education, by regional accreditors, by NASP in conjunction with NCATE, and by APA are conducted as well. Such reviews generally are conducted on a multiyear cycle (e.g., every 5, 7, or 10 years) and serve to examine whether the training program is continuing to maintain high professional standards. Many readers who are students currently enrolled in school psychology training programs may be asked to participate in such reviews. Usually such participation entails an individual or group meeting with one or more reviewers from off campus. For the most part, meetings by evaluation or accreditation teams with students are intended to determine if the information about the program prepared by the faculty is accurate. For example, if the written information states that faculty members hold monthly meetings for all program faculty, students, and staff, students may be asked about the frequency and content of these meetings. Students may also be asked for information about the skills they have acquired in order to determine if the training is producing desired outcomes.

PROFESSIONAL ACCOUNTABILITY AND SCHOOL PSYCHOLOGY

For practicing school psychologists, the notion of evaluation has been closely related to, if not synonymous with, the concept of "professional accountability." Professional accountability concerns the documentation or accounting of one's professional activities. Those who work for others, particularly those who receive local, state, or federal monies, are answerable to their employers and to the public. Trainers are responsible for demonstrating how they spend their time and earn their salaries. Indeed, Ysseldyke et al. (1997) note that data-based decision making and accountability should be the "organizing theme" of school psychology.

Accountability is important for a number of reasons in addition to this basic idea of responsibility to the public. First, accountability may help psychologists to help children more effectively (Zins, 1990)—generally considered the major goal of school psychology as discussed in Chapter 4. By maintaining records and also by evaluating what is done, what works well, and what does not work well, increasingly accurate and beneficial decisions to meet children's needs should be possible. If, for instance, records indicate that children with disabilities who are included in regular classes make greater academic gains than students who remain in self-contained special education classes, the school psychologist probably would be more likely to suggest including children with disabilities in regular classrooms in future cases. On the other hand, if records indicate that children with disabilities who remain in self-contained classrooms do about as well academically as those who are included but have higher self-esteem than those who are in regular classes there may be more of a tendency to favor self-contained classrooms when the assessment data warrant such placement decisions.

Canter (1991b) describes the ways in which an accountability system implemented by the school psychologists in the Minneapolis public schools had direct and indirect influences on professional practice:

> For example, when data over 10 years consistently indicated that boys are referred two to three times as often as girls, discussion and reviews of the research literature generated concerns regarding the underreferral of girls for problems such as anxiety and depression. Further literature review, internal staff development, inservice programs for schools, and consultation with community professionals helped heighten awareness of less visible problems that could be addressed by early prevention and intervention activities (p. 61).

A second and related reason for accountability relates to the improvement of our own professional effectiveness (Zins, 1990). Assume that a school psychologist develops a survey to evaluate his conference skills and distributes the survey to teachers and parents with whom he has worked. The completed surveys indicate that although the conferences were positive overall, a few of the parents believed the school psychologist used too much technical jargon to explain their children's strengths and weaknesses and a few of the teachers noted that the psychologist seemed to talk down to them. The psychologist might be willing and able to use that feedback to make changes in the ways in which he relates to parents and teachers in conference settings. Of course, improving one's own professional effectiveness will simultaneously be improving services to children. The more effective a person's conferencing skills, for example, the more likely that s/he will be able to influence decisions made by others.

Feedback about effectiveness can lead to professional renewal. A school psychologist may decide that certain practices need to be modified and others should remain the same. Many school psychologists voice feelings of frustration at not receiving sufficient feedback when their efforts have been successful. As the only school psychologist in one or more schools, the only feedback received from teachers may be when things go wrong; that is, when an intervention plan fails to work. When an intervention succeeds few people make a special effort to seek out the school psychologist. Accountability efforts can provide occasional pats on the back for a job well done.

On a district-wide basis, accountability efforts may indicate that changes are needed (Zins, 1990). A school administrator keeping track of a district's school psychologists' daily activities may find that the school psychologists spend an average of 15% of their time driving from various schools back to their main office. When asked why so much time is spent on the road, several school psychologists indicate that they share test kits with one another and therefore must pick up the test kits they need every morning and drop them off every afternoon. The administrator might then decide to purchase additional test kits, or at least find a more efficient way of sharing materials, thus cutting back on driving time and increasing time spent productively.

A fourth reason for accountability relates to the repercussions of accountability data for the profession of school psychology as a whole (Zins, 1990). We might term this, at least in part, a public relations, a consumer-based (Medway, 1996) or a marketing (Tharinger, 1996) view of accountability. School psychologists need to evaluate and keep records of their work to show that they are productive and essential members of a school staff. Rosenfield (1996) provides one example of accountability data leading directly to a school board's expansion of psychological services. Particularly in the face of gloomy economic conditions for education, school boards may be looking for ways to trim their budgets without cutting academic programs or increasing class size. School psychologists and other non-instructional personnel in the schools (e.g., counselors, social workers, and speech and language therapists among others) may be viewed as frills, nice to have around when money is plentiful but not essential when schools are faced with cutbacks.

As Trachtman (1996, p. 9) notes, if he were a school administrator who "had a few additional dollars to spend, I'm not really sure how I would choose between maintaining a gym, a science lab, a library, a music or art room, a uniformed marching band or a school nurse, guidance counselor, or psychologist." Fortunately, up until now Public Law 94-142 and its successors have protected school psychologists by mandating that federal monies are contingent upon the identification, diagnosis, and placement of all children with disabilities. If these laws were to be rescinded or significantly modified, however, school psychologists would need extensive documentation of their effectiveness merely to justify their presence in the schools. Along the same lines, accountability data can reinforce school psychologists' efforts at role changes by showing the impact of certain functions or by getting consumers to respond to the district advocating desired services. Phillips (1990b) suggested that in an effort to explore their day to day functions, it might be useful to have a group of school psychologists carry beepers. Each time the beeper went off, the school psychologists could note what they were doing, who they were with, and so forth. Relevant to this discussion, an awareness of school psychologists' activities is critical for training programs in determining what to emphasize and for accrediting bodies in determining what to require (Williams & Williams, 1992).

A fifth reason for accountability is important albeit less concrete and less frequently mentioned than the other reasons. Accountability is simply the proper and the ethical thing to do. Trachtman (1981, p. 153) differentiated between two types of accountability: "accountability-imposed" and "accountability-offered." Accountability-imposed refers to the accounting of our professional activities at the request of someone with authority over us (e.g., a supervisor or a district superintendent). Accountability-offered refers to efforts to document professional activities not because the documentation is required but because the school psychologist feels a professional and ethical responsibility to do so. School psychologists who contribute to so many critical decisions about young people based upon assessment data would be hypocritical to neglect the assessment of themselves and their own activities. It borders on unethical behavior for a school psychologist to practice his or her skills day after day and year after year without examining those practices periodically to determine their effectiveness.

With all of these reasons in mind, readers may ask why any school psychologist would *not* be involved in accountability efforts. Arguments against accountability tend to be based upon a short-range view of the profession rather than a long-range view. We have heard some colleagues argue that accountability efforts are too time-consuming, taking time away from activities that are more important. We also have heard colleagues complain that "no one ever reads our annual reports anyway, so why bother?" and that "collecting accountability data is an exercise in futility." It is our experience that, for the reasons stated earlier in this section, accountability provides school psychologists with a somewhat rare opportunity to reflect upon their professional activities and to consider changes that might improve the ways in which they function. We maintain that accountability is a much needed and often underrated function of school psychologists. Particularly if education is viewed from an outcome-based perspective, accountability is a critical process for demonstrating professional outcomes. Accountability data can also have advantages for an individual who is seeking employment or undergoing a professional evaluation. What better way to prove one's capabilities than to present data from consumers documenting successful efforts and programs? In addition, data collected for 1 year are useful as a comparison with data from other years to illustrate changes in services over time.

Reflecting upon these arguments for and against professional accountability efforts, we propose three assumptions regarding professional accountability:

1. Professional accountability is possible.
2. Professional accountability is desirable.
3. No single system of accountability can properly evaluate the variety of roles and functions of school psychologists.

With all of the reasons for accountability and with our three assumptions in mind, we turn our attention to the questions of how professional accountability can be accomplished. We will discuss various types of accountability and sources of accountability data, as well as examine actual efforts toward accountability from the school psychology literature.

Types of Accountability

Imagine for a few moments that you, the reader, are the director of school psychological services in a large school district. You are informed on May 1 that your annual administrative report is due in the superintendent's office on June 30. In that report you are asked to include the following sections:

1. Goals set during previous school year for current year
2. Budget for current school year
3. Staff activities for current school year

The first section, "Goals Set During Previous School Year For Current Year," involves a discussion of those goals listed last year. In your report you probably would include a few statements about how the goals were met. If some of the goals were not met, you would discuss impediments to the meeting of the goals (e.g., insufficient money, staff shortages, or excessive numbers of referrals). You also would be likely to describe other accomplishments that were not included in the original goal statement but that were carried out during the time period in question.

The budget section for the previous year is also fairly straightforward. You, as Director, were allocated a certain amount of money. The largest single expenditure typically was assigned to personal services or salaries. Your salary, the salaries of the school psychologists who work in your unit, and the salaries of the secretaries employed to work for your staff were the expenditures in this category along with employee benefits (e.g., health insurance, dental insurance, and retirement plan). Other items in the budget for school psychological services included computers and relevant software, assessment instruments (new, replacement, or additional copies), test protocols, travel expenses (mileage between schools; conference registration fees, transportation, and hotel costs for professional meetings), books and journals, photocopying, telecommunication, and miscellaneous office supplies.

Related to the issue of budget, a 1983 NASP filmstrip entitled *Improving School Psychology through Accountability* (Fairchild, Zins, & Grimes, 1983) answers the question *What does it cost to employ one school psychologist today?* in the following manner:

> A typical annual salary is over $24,000. Support costs such as insurance, retirement, and other fringe benefits add another $6,800 and indirect program costs including such items as the district business manager, secretarial and janitorial services average approximately $6,400. Added together the total cost for one school psychologist unit comes to over $37,000. This is an average of over $186 per day or over $23 per hour (p. 9).

In recent years, a typical starting salary for a full-time school psychologist is more than $30,000, bringing the total annual cost for a first year school psychologist (including benefits and other expenses) to at least $50,000.

When you consider inflation and some of the other costs mentioned above (e.g., mileage, equipment, photocopying, and telecommunication) the cost of employing school psychologists is an expensive endeavor. With this much money at stake, accountability takes on added importance. In fact, you probably can see why administrators might be tempted to compute the cost of school psychologists on a per case basis and why they see the caseload as a useful criterion to measure costs per accomplishments.

Now we arrive at the staff activities section of your report. You have a general idea of what the individual school psychologists in your administrative unit have been involved in, but how do you summarize their activities over the past year in a brief but meaningful way? Several different types of accountability are listed in Figure 5.1.

Monroe (1979) distinguished between *descriptive* and *evaluative* approaches to accountability. A descriptive approach merely describes what took place whereas an evaluative approach studies the impact of the events that occurred. Usually when considering a report like the one in our example, the first approach to be

FIGURE 5.1 Sources and types of accountability data

| | SOURCES | | | | |
Types	School Psychologists	Teachers	Administrators	Parents	Students
Descriptive					
Activity log	*				
Enumerative	*		*		
Evaluative					
Process	*	*		*	*
Outcome	*	*		*	*

considered is a descriptive one involving what might be termed an *activity log*, or a listing of the various activities in which staff members were engaged. Thus, in our exercise, you, the author of the report, might write:

> During the current school year school psychologists on our staff were able to complete, in a timely fashion, all assessments referred to them. In addition, the psychologists were engaged in the following activities:
>
> 1. Introducing the concept of "inclusion" to district personnel through a series of in-service workshops.
> 2. Co-founding (with high school counselors) a counseling group for high school students with children.
> 3. Applying for and receiving a grant of $10,000 to study new ways of teaching social studies and science to students with reading disabilities.
> 4. Acting as liaisons to local health professionals in identifying and treating children with Attention Deficit Hyperactivity Disorder (AD/HD).
> 5. Starting a group for parents of children with low-incidence handicaps.

The second type of descriptive approach to accountability is termed an enumerative one. Such an approach entails a listing and frequency count for each of several activities. To prepare an enumerative report, you would ask each school psychologist on your staff to complete a number of tables similar to Figure 5.2.

From these tables you might compile a set of master tables listing:

1. The number of children assessed in your district this year.
2. The number of children referred for assessment who have not yet

FIGURE 5.2 Sample yearly activity sheet for school psychologists

Directions: Mark the number of hours you spent engaged in each of the activities during the current school year.				
	Grade Level of Youngster			
Activity	**Preschoolers**	**K-6**	**7-9**	**10-12**
Classroom Observation				
Review of School Records				
Teacher Interview				
Parent Interview				
Intellectual Assessment				
Assessment of Achievement				
Social/Behavioral Assessment				
Personality Assessment				
Parent Conferences				
Multidisciplinary Staffings				
Psychological Reports				
Individual Counseling				
Teacher Consultation				
Staff Development				
In-service Workshops				
Contact with Outside Agency				
Continuing/Professional Development of the School Psychologist				

been assessed.
3. The number of children assessed who have been placed in various types of special classes.
4. The number of children assessed according to various age groups.
5. The number of teacher consultations in which school psychologists have participated.
6. The number of children counseled on an individual basis by school psychologists.
7. The number of children worked with in group counseling settings by school psychologists.
8. The number of parent conferences held.
9. The number of multidisciplinary staffings in which school psychologists have participated.
10. The number of research and evaluation activities engaged in by staff members.

Enumerative data also may include information regarding the average amount of time spent in professional activities. Thus it would not be unusual for school psychologists to be asked how much time, or what percentage of their time, they spend per week in teacher consultations, in parent conferences, or in assessment activities. For example, LaCayo et al. (1981) asked a national sample of 750 randomly selected school psychologists to record their daily activities. They found that school psychologists in their sample spent 39% of their time in assessment, 33% in consultation, 6% in counseling, and the remainder in other activities. A more recent study (Reschly, 1998, p. 4) found that school psychologists in 1997 "devote slightly over half of their time to psychoeducational assessment, about 20% of their time to direct intervention, about 17% to problem solving consultation, and 7% to systems/organizational consultation, and 2% to research evaluation."

Counting the number of case studies completed or the number of children placed in special education programs, or estimating the amount of time spent in teacher consultation is relatively easy albeit somewhat bothersome to complete. It is not nearly so easy to evaluate the effectiveness of the school psychologist's job. How may a school psychologist's skills as a consultant be measured? Was counseling successful? Did special class placement help? How satisfied are parents and teachers with the psychologist's conferencing or report-writing skills? How much has a child's life in school improved because of the school psychologist's expertise? Is the amount of time spent engaged in certain activities warranted? To answer these questions we need to collect evaluative information, often broken down into two components: *process* data and *outcome* data.

The difference between descriptive data (i.e., activity log or enumerative) and evaluative data (i.e., process or outcome) as seen in Figure 5.1 can be thought of as a difference between *accounting* and *true accountability*. Accounting, though important for purposes of record keeping, does not examine the quality or effectiveness of services provided. Process and outcome accountability, on the other hand, focus on the non-quantitative aspects of service delivery such as the quality of the services, the satisfaction of the parents and teachers, and the benefits to the child served.

The collection of process data involves the gathering of information regarding others' perceptions of our effectiveness in reaching objectives and delivering services. For example, Cornwall (1990) conducted a study in which teachers, parents, and physicians were asked to rate psychoeducational reports in terms of their clarity, whether or not they addressed and answered the referral questions, how well they described the youngster's difficulties, and how useful the recommendations were. Knoff, McKenna, and Riser (1991) conducted an exploratory study of school psychologists and trainers of school psychologists as a first step in the development of a *Consultant Effectiveness Scale*. Their scale lists factors most important to effective consultation (i.e., knowledge of the consultation process, expert skill, personal characteristics, interpersonal skills, and professional respect).

Process data are important in order to provide school psychologists with useful information about the ways in which they function. For example, a school psychologist who works primarily with junior high and high school students, wants to know how the students perceive her role and her competence in that role. She develops a form (Figure 5.3) which she then distributes to all of the students she has worked with during the current school year. The form is mailed to all of the students at their homes. They are asked to complete the form anonymously and drop it off in Ms. Carver's mailbox at school by the end of the week. Results are then tabulated. Ms. Carver learns that of the 20 students who completed the form, all agreed that the time spent with her was worthwhile. Most of the students agreed that she listened to them and that she cared about them. All of them said they would send their friends to her if they had problems in school or at home.

Keep in mind that the collection and the interpretation of process data may be more complicated than it appears at first glance. A form such as the one in Figure 5.3 is far from perfect in terms of technical adequacy (e.g., reliability). In Ms. Carver's case, most of the students had voluntarily sought out the school psychologist for help with a particular problem they were having. Those students who did not think Ms. Carver would be helpful probably did not ask for her assistance in the first place. In addition, the students may have been equally positive in rating anyone willing to listen to their problems and to act in a caring manner. What about the students who did not return the survey? Can we assume that they had equally positive feelings about the counseling? Of course not!

A related example with which most if not all readers of this book are familiar is that of the evaluation of college and university faculty members. Universities as a whole or departments or colleges within universities often have policies regarding teacher evaluations. Students may be asked to complete evaluations of their professors in some or all of their classes each semester. Faculty members have found these evaluations to be helpful and informative in many cases. However, complicating factors may exist. For example, do professors who give higher grades receive higher marks themselves than professors who are tough graders? If so, what does this say about the validity of teacher ratings as a measure of teacher effectiveness? Do professors of elective courses receive higher marks than professors of required courses? Do professors of graduate courses with small numbers of students receive higher marks than professors of large, undergraduate survey courses? Such questions make it difficult if not impossible to compare professors' ratings in determining the best teacher in an academic department or area.

Similar questions arise in the collection of process data for accountability among school psychologists. Do parents who hear bad news (e.g., your child is in the educable mentally retarded range of intelligence) or criticisms (e.g., your child's problems seem most influenced by factors in the home) rate the school psychologist as highly as parents who hear good news (e.g., your child has done so well in the learning disabilities resource room this year that we are suggesting she be placed in the regular classroom full-time for next year)? Does a teacher who wants a troublesome child out of his classroom give the school psychologist high ratings when the intervention plan involves leaving the child in his class? What kind of ratings will you get from a principal who views retention as an ideal remedial strategy for immature youngsters if you oppose retention?

Returning to our example in which you, as the director of psychological services, have been asked to turn in an annual evaluation, by this time you have filled out tables of enumerative data based upon the information furnished to you by the school psychologists on your staff. Perhaps you also have glanced at evaluation forms completed by parents and teachers in an attempt to assess the psychologists' consultation skills. Now is the time to start collecting outcome data. Outcome data collection involves taking a look at intervention strategies and asking the questions: How many intervention strategies have been implemented as agreed to in meetings between school psychologists and teachers or school psychologist and parents? How

FIGURE 5.3 Sample evaluation process form

Directions: Please answer the questions below as they apply to your work with Ms. Carver during the current school year.

1. How many times during this school year have you worked with Ms. Carver?_____

2. What have you done during your time with Ms. Carver? (check all that apply)
   ___a. taken tests   ___d. talked about my family
   ___b. talked about school   ___e. talked about a specific problem
   ___c. talked about relationships with others   ___f. talked about my goals

3. Do you think that the time you spent with Ms. Carver was worthwhile?
   ___Yes   ___Sometimes   ___ No

4. Check all of the following statements that you agree with.
   ___a Ms. Carver helped me to understand my school problems better.
   ___b. Ms. Carver helped me to understand my own strengths and weaknesses.
   ___c. Ms. Carver taught me problem solving techniques.
   ___d. Ms. Carver listened to me.
   ___e. Ms. Carver cares about me.
   ___f. Ms. Carver helped me to do better at school.
   ___g. I would recommend that other kids see Ms. Carver if they're having trouble with. _____
   _____

5. I wish Ms. Carver had spent more time _____
   _____

6. I think Ms. Carver is (check all that apply)
   ___nice   ___mean   ___friendly   ___a good listener   ___dumb   ___helpful

7. I will probably come back to see Ms. Carver if _____
   _____

---

many of the intervention strategies that were implemented have been effective? To what extent was the child's referral problem resolved or alleviated?

Sources of Accountability Data

Implicit in discussions regarding types of accountability is the assumption that someone must be responsible for keeping track of the school psychologist's professional activities and/or evaluating the process and outcome of the services. Usually in the case of descriptive data such as activity logs or enumerative data, school psychologists are asked to maintain records of their professional activities and turn in the records periodically to a school administrator (e.g., director of psychological services or special education director). Forms such as those in Figure 5.2 may be furnished to the school psychologists at the beginning of the year to improve the chances of accurate record keeping. (Imagine the difficulties that would arise if, on May 1, a totally unexpected memo was distributed to school psychologists asking them to fill out the form in Figure 5.2 for the entire past year. Looking through one's appointment calendar for the past year and counting up the number of manila folders on one's desk may be the only method some would have of recalling 9 or 10 months of professional activities.)

The evaluative data types of accountability described above (i.e., process and outcome) rely on consumers of psychological services as sources of information. Certainly with process data, students, parents, teachers, and administrators are the most likely parties to evaluate the level of satisfaction with the school psychological services provided. Although all of these people also are sources of outcome data, there is another source as well. Paraprofessionals, graduate students, or other impartial individuals may gather outcome data in a much more scientific manner. For example, if a behavior modification plan is introduced as an intervention, a trained student or paraprofessional could observe the child and record data during all phases of the project. One way of seeing whether a social skills training program is working is to have someone observing the children in the program in a naturalistic (i.e., real life, non-laboratory) setting either on the playground, in the lunchroom, in the hallways, or in the classroom.

OBSTACLES TO ACCOUNTABILITY EFFORTS

What are the obstacles to the practices of professional evaluation and accountability? Many have already been mentioned or at least alluded to above.

1. Accountability efforts take time away from other activities.
2. Accountability efforts can be perceived as burdensome. Busy people, asked to keep track of the time spent on each activity in which they were engaged for an entire month, are required to have either extraordinary

organizational skills to keep continuous records or extraordinary memories to mark down all that they did at the end of a week or a month. Fairchild and Seeley (1996, p. 46) note that accountability efforts "become unmanageable when efforts are made to evaluate all services and involve all consumers without adequate resources to accomplish such a task."

3. Accountability efforts are often expected but rarely rewarded.

In addition to these three obstacles to all types of accountability efforts, there are often additional obstacles specific to the collection of evaluative accountability data. For instance, how much time should you allow for an intervention to take effect before evaluating its success? Should you look at short-term effects, long-term effects, or both? What constitutes success? If a third grader was reading at the early first-grade level in October and had progressed to the late first-grade level by March, was the intervention successful? If a seventh grader was involved in 10 fights during the first 2 months of the school year and was involved in only 5 fights in January through March, is the group counseling strategy effective? If an intervention strategy was not implemented as designed is it appropriate to count that against the school psychologist? Difficulties such as those described above in defining successful outcomes and in eliminating extraneous variables are among the obstacles inherent in the process of accountability. These issues often perplex those involved in data collection and interpretation.

Another obstacle to the collection of outcome data relates back to our earlier discussion of clientage. As described in Chapter 3, the client of the school psychologist may at times be a child, a parent, a teacher, a school administrator, an entire school board, and/or an agency administrator or entire board. Ambiguity with regard to clientage complicates the issue of accountability to the extent that one person's perception of the outcome may be different from another person's perception of the same outcome. For example, a school psychologist consults with a first-grade teacher about a child who has difficulty paying attention in class, sitting still, and completing work independently. The teacher and principal believe that the child is immature and would benefit from another year in first grade. The parents are not in favor of retention believing the child will grow out of it and succeed in second grade next year. After talking to the teacher and the parents and observing the child in the classroom, the psychologist's recommendation is to place the child in second grade. It is further recommended that the child be placed in the most structured second-grade classroom available. Finally, it is suggested that the child's behavior be carefully monitored to determine whether a full case study would be appropriate sometime during the coming year if difficulties continue. If the principal, the teacher, and the parents are questioned regarding their level of satisfaction with the outcome of the school psychologist's decision, opinions obviously will vary.

Professional Competence Versus Professional Excellence

Are there other obstacles to the processes of professional accountability and evaluation? Emphatically yes! For example, even if successful outcomes could be defined, there is still the problem of defining competence and excellence in the practice of school psychology. How is competence defined within our profession? What constitutes professional excellence? Consider other professions. We might think of a competent medical doctor as one who is cautious, makes few mistakes in diagnosis or treatment, and treats patients with respect. We might think of an excellent medical doctor as one who saves the most lives, makes the fewest mistakes, faces the fewest malpractice suits, is consulted most frequently by his or her medical colleagues, or perfects a particular operation. A competent attorney is one who is familiar with the laws and does a good job representing her clients. An excellent attorney may be one who wins the most cases, brings in the highest settlements, or sways the greatest number of jurors. It is reasonable to think of doctors and lawyers in terms of products (e.g., people cured and cases won).

What qualities define a teacher as competent or as excellent? Again we might think in terms of products. A competent teacher is one whose students progress at an appropriate pace. An excellent teacher may have students who make great gains academically. Perhaps one teacher's students score higher on standardized tests than do other students in the school. Perhaps a particular teacher seems to inspire students to produce excellent reports, artwork, or musical compositions. Perhaps the teachers in the next grade report that students who had one particular teacher are better prepared to continue their studies. Perhaps parents report that their children are more enthusiastic about learning and have made greater gains than they had in previous years.

What are the products of the competent school psychologist compared to the excellent school psychologist? The answers are much more difficult to pinpoint. Doctors, lawyers, and teachers all work directly with individuals or groups for extended periods of time. In Chapter 4 we noted that school psychologists often take a more indirect role with children. They may work with children mainly through their parents or teachers. Trachtman (1981) suggests that school psychologists often work as "enablers" (through our efforts we enable parents or teachers to help children). How do you separate the efforts of the enabler (i.e., the school psychologist) from the efforts of the enactor (i.e., the parents or teachers)?

School psychologists rarely save children's lives, fix children's difficulties single-handedly, or consistently sway participants at multidisciplinary staffings. The changes brought about usually are more difficult to define and more dependent upon the efforts of others in the child's environment. Yet, is it reasonable to hold school psychologists accountable for interventions that other people are responsible for implementing? If an intervention is successful, can a school psychologist take credit for the success? If an intervention does not succeed, is the school psychologist to blame?

Another difficulty in evaluating school psychologists relates to the physical context of much of our work. The functions of assessment, counseling, parent conferencing, and teacher consultations are generally conducted in one-to-one settings behind closed doors, with no one except the client around to watch and evaluate the psychologist's performance. Can a child evaluate assessment or counseling skills objectively? Can parents be objective in evaluating conferencing skills when they are emotionally involved in the process of sharing information? Can psychologists be at all objective in evaluating their own activities and skills?

School psychologists might wish to consider what has been termed a "collaborative model of professional evaluation" in which teams of psychologists help each other set annual goals, discuss how the achievement of the goals might be attained, collect data to support the attainment of goals, periodically meet to discuss progress towards goal attainment, and share documentation of goal attainment. This is adapted from a model for teachers set forth by McLaughlin, Vogt, Anderson, DuMez, Peter, and Hunter (1998). One member of the team might examine her skills in working with parents of preschoolers, a second member might examine his counseling skills with middle school students, and a third team member might examine her skills in classroom environmental analysis. Each individual would establish unique goals for the year. Within the team, however, ideas for skill development, evaluation, and documentation could be shared and discussed at the start of the year. Progress towards goal attainment could be discussed at mid-year and ideas to overcome barriers to goal attainment could be generated. At the end of the year, the team could share the data collected by members and consider goals for the following year. Advantages of such a model include the support and suggestions received from other team members, the notion that evaluation does not have to include every part of the job every year, and the presentation of a finished evaluation product without a tremendous expenditure of time.

These questions, dilemmas, and possibilities are presented not to frustrate readers, but rather to challenge readers to come up with solutions or at least to consider alternative methods of dealing with the issues involved in professional evaluation and accountability. For those readers just beginning training in school psychology, we want to emphasize the importance of accountability in all professional endeavors. When planning interventions, engaging in assessment activities, consulting with teachers or parents, or counseling children, consider how the effectiveness of the activity might be measured. If school psychologists enter the profession with accountability etched in their minds, then accountability becomes an integral part of all professional activities rather than one more professional burden to be endured.

Current Practices in Accountability

With all of the information gained thus far about accountability and with the advantages of and the obstacles to accountability in mind, readers might be curious as to how many school psychologists are actually involved in accountability efforts? A study by Fairchild and Zins (1992) attempted to answer this and other questions by polling a random sample of NASP members. More than half (57.8%) of Fairchild's and Zins's respondents reported that they were involved in the collection of accountability data. Of those collecting accountability data, almost all (96.8%) were involved in collecting enumerative data. More than one-third (36.6%) collected process data while 44.1% reported collecting outcome data. More than half of the respondents (52.7%) who were involved in the collection of accountability data reported collecting two or more types of accountability data.

In an earlier article, Fairchild (1975) described six accountability tools that he thought might be beneficial to school psychologists. The six tools included the following:

1. The daily log: Fairchild identified five activities in which school psychologists were involved (assessment, intervention, evaluation, consultation, and administration). He then developed a coding system to facilitate the recording of this information into a daily log format. From these he tallied weekly, then monthly, and finally yearly summaries of his activities.
2. Time-elapsed information: In this technique, a log is kept of the date a child was referred for services, the initial contact date, and the date of the conference with the individual referring the child.
3. Accountability interview: Fairchild viewed this technique as a means of enabling the school psychologist to obtain feedback and to prevent potential problems. In the article, Fairchild notes that he elicited teacher feedback indirectly through building principals.
4. Follow-up questionnaire: Teachers and parents whose children were seen by the school psychologist completed anonymous surveys containing three questions:
   a. "Did you have a better understanding of the child as a result of your discussion with the school psychologist?
   b. Were recommendations realistic and/or practical?

c. Were the recommendations of the psychologist effective?" (p. 157).

5. Telephone follow-up: Fairchild made at least one phone call to parents of all children he had evaluated.

6. Behavioral consultation: When a referral was received from a teacher, the school psychologist met with the teacher to identify a particular target behavior. The teacher and psychologist then decided upon a criterion of success (e.g., Andy remains in his seat 90% of each 50-minute class period). Baseline behavior is measured as is behavior throughout and following the implementation of the intervention plan. Success can thus be plotted.

Fairchild's (1975) description of the six tools for school psychologists to consider in their efforts to be accountable was proposed as an early effort to show school psychologists how they could document their professional activities.

Other accountability efforts can also be found in the school psychology literature. A NASP publication, *Accountability for School Psychologists: Developing Trends* (Zins, 1982) is a compilation of accountability instruments developed by school psychologists across the country. The first part of the publication is divided into three sections corresponding to the three types of accountability: enumerative data ("Descriptive Approaches"), process data ("Effectiveness as Perceived by Others"), and outcome data ("Measures of Behavior Change"). Following these three sections, an annotated bibliography is provided, organized by topics. The six topics include: program documentation, quality assurance, personnel evaluation, program planning, program dissemination, and self-monitoring and self-change.

In the first few pages of this chapter we discussed the general reasons for professional accountability among school psychologists. Readers should note that the whole question of accountability has become much more vital within the past decade or two. Reschly (1983) noted that accountability is gaining momentum throughout the field of education partly because of legal decisions:

> The due-process procedures and other legal guidelines establish the potential for close scrutiny of nearly all aspects of the work of the school psychologist. Psychological reports, regarded a decade ago as confidential documents which were not shown to parents, are now among the educational records which parents can examine. Information in the reports can be challenged by parents through their submission of additional information or by requesting a hearing. Classification decisions, interpretations of behavior, and recommendations are now open to question. The validity and fairness of tests and other assessment devices can be challenged on the basis of due-process protections and on other legal grounds (p. 87).

Note that school psychologists in a variety of settings are also involved in accountability efforts. As mentioned, trainers are particularly apt to find themselves immersed in evaluations of their programs. Information such as credit-hour production, program enrollment, graduation rates, and success and placement of graduates is frequently requested within the university by department chairs and deans who must write their own annual evaluations to submit to those individuals or groups assigned to oversee them (e.g., higher administration, state boards of higher education). In addition, training program faculty must prepare periodic reports of the program's activities and accomplishments to remain in compliance with state and national accreditation agencies as discussed in Chapter 7.

Even professional organizations are accountable to their members and at times to other governing bodies as well. Officers of such associations may be asked to furnish information regarding membership, money spent, publications produced, and other activities in order to prepare an annual report to the membership.

Aside from the evaluation of their own work as school psychologists, in the schools and in other settings, there are additional ways in which school psychologists may be involved in accountability. Armed with graduate-level training in psychological research methods and statistics, the school psychologist may be asked to become involved in district-wide accountability efforts. Such efforts may involve anything and everything from teacher evaluation to curriculum evaluation. In fact, with the current "outcomes oriented" movement within education, many school districts nationally are attempting to identify learning objectives and assess whether those objectives are being met. As assessment specialists, school psychologists may be involved in identifying these learning objectives, developing or selecting assessment instruments to measure the level of attainment of the objectives, and interpreting and evaluating the results of the assessment efforts.

CONCLUDING REMARKS

Accountability is a vital part of the school psychologist's professional role. In the short run, it provides feedback about professional performance and suggests ways in which we may improve. In the long run, accountability may be the most important part of our jobs, for it may justify our reason for being in the schools and thus ensure our continued existence.

PRACTICAL EXERCISES

I. Consider each of the statements marked 1-6 below.
    A. Rank order each of the statements in terms of its importance to the practice of school psychology. Which one is most important? Which one is least important?

B. Are there items that you would like to have added or omitted?

C. How could you define each statement sufficiently in order to measure a given individual's level of expertise?

1. An excellent school psychologist administers tests quickly and accurately.

2. An excellent school psychologist has superb interpersonal skills: people talk freely and listen to you, people cooperate with you.

3. An excellent school psychologist is committed to helping children.

4. An excellent school psychologist writes excellent reports.

5. An excellent school psychologist performs in an exemplary manner even under less than perfect circumstances (e.g., outdated test kits, unreasonable number of students to serve, less than excellent team members).

6. An excellent school psychologist performs in an exemplary manner in all professional settings (e.g., preschool through high school; assessment, counseling, and consultation).

II. Identify the characteristics of an excellent school psychology graduate student. How does an "excellent student" differ from an "adequate student"? Write a brief description evaluating your own strengths and weaknesses as a student in a school psychology program. Are you an excellent student? What evidence do you have to support your excellence? If you were asked to document your skills in the form of a personal portfolio, what materials would you include?

III. If you asked your family members, your friends, your professors, and your classmates whether or not you are an excellent student, would their answers agree with each other? Why or why not?

IV. In your state or national newsletters, locate the most recent recipient of the School Psychologist of the Year awards. What characteristics set the winner apart from other school psychologists?

C H A P T E R 6

The Preparation of
School Psychologists[1]

Most texts on school psychology limit the discussion of how school psychologists are trained or treat the topic briefly in conjunction with discussions of credentialing. We choose to discuss credentialing in the context of professional regulation (see Chapter 7) and training in a separate chapter. An understanding of how school psychologists are prepared for practice is as important to students in preparation as it is to undergraduates who might choose to enter school psychology or to faculty who prepare them. In Chapter 1, we introduced the most common levels of training obtained by persons seeking to be credentialed as school psychologists. This chapter provides greater detail about the preparation of school psychologists, some issues important to preparation, how preparation relates to standards for program accreditation and credentialing, and our expectations for the continued professional development of future school psychologists. This information will help you understand the potential training and credentialing problems encountered when moving from one state to another, and the relationship between basic and advanced graduate preparation in school psychology. Readers also should be able to make some comparisons between national-level trends and guidelines for preparation and the program in which they enrolled.

GROWTH OF TRAINING PROGRAMS

As discussed in Chapter 2, early practitioners functioned as generalists responding to a variety of referrals and problems. Practice largely involved individual psychometric evaluation of children and adolescents suspected of being mentally, physically, or morally defective. The purpose of psychological services in most settings was to assist school personnel in sorting children into more appropriate classroom placements, including the relatively small but increasing number of special education classes. Most practitioners had only limited involvement with direct interventions, often along the lines of academic remediation, counseling, and parent-teacher consultation.

Reflecting the limited role and function, early training of practitioners was a mix of concepts from Hallian child study and Witmerian clinical psychology. The Hallian orientation evolved into developmental and educational psychology whereas the Witmerian orientation evolved into several clinical fields. It has been posited that the training and practice of school psychologists have been influenced by these two orientations and their transformations in practice brought about by disciples of Hall and Witmer (Fagan, 1992). Training usually was in a psychology or philosophy department, often in the education college, and emphasized experimental studies with few applied courses, except for those in clinical psychology (Fagan, 1999). The lack of available training meant the demand for school psychological personnel was met by persons with training in a variety of education- and psychology-related fields. Training emphasized the use of newly developed tests of intelligence, school achievement, and motor skill. Early practitioners held various titles and degrees: some held the bachelor's degree, more held the master's degree, and a few held the doctoral degree. University course sequences appropriate for students planning to work in the schools were available in the 1920s. However, the first preparation programs labeled "school psychology" were in the undergraduate and graduate program offerings at New York University in the late 1920s (Fagan, 1999). Graduates of training programs specifically in school psychology were rare. Until the 1930s there were no state education agency certification requirements, nor were there national training standards espoused by APA or other national groups to influence the direction of training. In some instances, practitioner training was simply teacher training augmented by a crash course in intelligence testing.

With the development of associations for applied psychologists, the study of school psychology training gained importance. A committee report on training in New York State put forth recommendations for professional courses, field experiences, length of program, and desirable personal characteristics of students (New York State Association for Applied Psychology, 1943). The similarity of the committee's recommendations to contemporary program descriptions is notable (e.g., two and a half years of graduate study, practica, and a minimum of a half-year of internship). Broader and more school psychology-specific preparation was increasingly available after 1935. The Pennsylvania State University doctoral program was founded in the late 1930s and the program at the University of Illinois in 1953.

Although the Illinois program established by T. E. Newland was not the first doctoral program in school psychology, it was among the first well-organized programs (Cutts, 1955). Early descriptions of the Illinois program reveal its sensitivity to educational as well as psychological foundations; the need for broad, generalist preparation; and other aspects still included in professional training standards.

By the time of the Thayer Conference in 1954, only 28 institutions offered programs specifically in school psychology with 10 granting the doctoral degree (Fagan, 1986b). The institutions were not well distributed geographically. Leadership roles in training were taken by New York University, Pennsylvania State University, Columbia University, the University of Michigan, and the University of Illinois. Many persons contributed to the early training of school psychological workers and later to actual program development: Charles Benson, H. H. Goddard, Gertrude Hildreth, Leta Hollingworth, Francis Maxfield, T. E. Newland, Percival Symonds, J. E. W. Wallin, Lightner Witmer and countless more recent figures. Contemporary trainers owe much to the planning and thinking of these persons.

The Thayer Conference was the first comprehensive national meeting to deal with issues of training in school psychology. The proceedings of the conference (Cutts, 1955) were distributed widely for several years following the conference and identified the need for more master's and doctoral programs (Fagan, 1993). By the 1960s, training programs offered courses in foundations of psychology and education, special education, intelligence and personality testing, academic remediation, and psychological interventions (e.g., counseling, psychotherapy, and consultation). Nevertheless, traditional experimental psychology requirements continued to be evidenced in most programs. Several factors served to broaden the range of preparation after 1940: increased demand for practitioners, greater acceptance of non-testing roles for psychologists, increasing numbers of states having state department of education certification requirements, training guidelines developed by APA's Division 16, improved testing technology, widespread interest in school and community mental health, and the level of theory development during this period (e.g., psychodynamic, behavioral, Gestalt, non-directive).

The historical growth of training programs, most dramatic between 1960 and 1980, has been the subject of several studies summarized in Fagan (1986b). At present, there are about seven times as many training institutions as existed in 1960. The 1998 NASP *Directory of Graduate Programs* identified 218 institutions that provided information on their programs (Thomas, 1998). The number of institutions offering training in school psychology appears to have stabilized throughout the 1990s. Greater similarity in the content of programs also has developed along with discernible distinctions between doctoral and non-doctoral preparation (Brown et al., 1998; Reschly & Wilson, 1997).

STUDENT AND PRACTITIONER CHARACTERISTICS

Motivations and Academic and Employment Backgrounds

School psychology attracts students for many reasons and from many backgrounds. Excellent job opportunities and stability, employee benefits, interest in education, desire to work with children, and a generally strong humanitarian attitude are among reasons given for entering the field. Because many of these motivations overlap with those for entering other helping fields, it is common to find that some school psychology trainees have had previous experience in teaching, guidance and counseling, or mental health. In addition, students may have varied undergraduate backgrounds including sociology and social work, elementary and secondary education, special education, and psychology. Psychology and education fields account for most of the students' backgrounds, and a diversity of undergraduate teaching majors is often observed. For example, the authors have had students enter their training programs from art education, counselor education, educational administration, physical education, social studies, and special education.

Desirable Personal Characteristics

In addition to the varied motivations to enter the field, there are several personal characteristics that are desirable among trainees and practitioners. Perhaps foremost is the academic ability and aptitude to complete graduate-level education successfully. We also believe a strong sense of personal responsibility and an appreciation of moral and ethical responsibilities to the profession and its clients are important. An early statement of desired characteristics included "maturity in manner and outlook, ease in inter-professional relationships, responsiveness to the effects of rapidly changing educational and social conditions, and above all emotional security and objectivity" (New York State Association for Applied Psychology, 1943, p. 239). Discussing the importance of learning to think like a psychologist in real-life situations, Bardon and Bennett (1974) state that the school psychologist

> must care about what happens to people. He must be capable of genuine identification with different kinds of people and their modes of behavior, including those whose cultural backgrounds, ethnic origins, and basic beliefs may be different from his. He must have a sincere and positive attitude toward humanity that will enable him to try new approaches and to persist even in the face of discouragement, lack of results, and frustration (p. 176).

More recently, Bardon (1986) summarized several others' opinions of successful attributes in addition to those cited in 1974. These include interpersonal warmth, flexibility, sensitivity, stress resistance, circumspection, eagerness to learn, dedication, reflective judgment, and "an attitude of positive skepticism" (p. 65-66). Bardon's thinking is consistent with the characteristics specified in the Rutgers University program where he taught in the 1960s (see, Magary, 1967a, pp. 741-742). Also important are desirable employee characteristics of being well-organized, prompt, adaptable, able to profit from supervision, and able to get along with parents, educators, and students. One survey of school psychology supervisors indicated that after basic competency, the supervisors were most interested in the candidate's ability to work closely with others, "facility in verbal and written communication, diplomacy, consideration for others' viewpoints, empathy for the client, and a dedication or commitment to the field of school psychology" (Fireoved & Cancelleri, 1985, p. 4). Magary (1967a) identified desirable characteristics based on training program and state department brochures and the thinking of Carl Rogers. Magary noted that "the school psychologist should be characterized first and foremost by an interest in wishing to help children" (p. 740). Being able to work effectively with a variety of teachers, having desirable personality characteristics, and having sensitivity and communication skills were also identified.

There is no list of such characteristics that has achieved consensus among trainers and employers. However, national-level sanction is implied in the list of characteristics that appears among the first set of criteria in NASP's credentialing standards (NASP, 1994a). This list includes: communication skills, effective interpersonal relations, ethical responsibility, flexibility, initiative and dependability, personal stability, and respect for human diversity. The credentialing standards will be revised in 2000 but the same characteristics appeared in the March 1999 draft proposal. The 1994 edition appears to be a condensed and revised version of the 1985 edition which lists adaptability, communication skills, conscientiousness, cooperation, independence, motivation, personal stability, productivity, professional ethics, and professional image. Although definitions of these characteristics are absent, the list at least ensures that these characteristics were reviewed by many groups and the NASP school psychology leadership prior to being adopted. Even in the absence of definition or consensus, personal characteristics are considered to be important. Throughout training, students are closely observed for evidence of appropriate personal characteristics, especially during their field experiences. Trainers of school psychologists have been as concerned about their students' personal characteristics as they have been about their academic progress. Bardon (1986) properly acknowledges that "it is possible the effectiveness of school psychologists is determined as much, if not more, by the way they function and interact than by what they know and what duties they perform" (p. 65).

Diversity Representation

For a variety of reasons, professional fields of psychology lack proportionally representative diversity. School psychology as a field includes less than 6% minorities (see Chapter 1; Curtis, Hunley, Walker, & Baker, 1999), far below percentages of minorities in the general population; minority representation in the field may be declining (Hunley & Curtis, 1998; Sleek, 1998). More encouraging levels of ethnic diversity are observed among graduate students (17%) and program faculty (15%; Thomas, 1998). A national *Directory of Bilingual School Psychologists* (NASP, Multicultural Affairs Committee, 1998) includes only about 400 listings across 35 language proficiency types (including sign language and visual impairment). Since 45% of the entries were for Spanish and some entries were from persons outside the United States, the directory further reflects school psychology's need for greater diversity. The lack of preparation for school psychologists in conducting assessments with Hispanic students was observed in a study by Ochoa, Rivera, and Ford (1997). The continued improvement of minority representation in school psychology requires a long-term professional effort that will not be easily accomplished (Fagan, 1988b; Jackson, 1992; Zins and Halsell, 1986). The NASP Education and Research Trust offers minority scholarships but they are limited to ethnic minorities.

The disproportionate representation is observed across all American psychology fields. Training programs, especially through field experiences, should assure exposure to diverse populations (Sleek, 1998). A few training programs have grants or special expertise for the training of school psychologists to work with diverse populations. Some of these are identified in the subspecialty listings for doctoral programs in this chapter. A framework for diversity training is presented by Gopaul-McNicol (1997) and the Division 16 (APA) newsletter, *The School Psychologist*, which published two series on the topic of multicultural training and specific programs (1994, Vol. 49, No. 4, and 1995, Vol. 50, No. 1).

In contrast to minority representation, gender representation has increased considerably. Females comprise about 80% of the school psychology graduate student population, 46% of program faculty, and at least 70% of practitioners. The female representation has increased consistently in the past three decades and can be expected to continue to increase (see e.g., APA, Committee on Employment and Human Resources, 1986). In the most recent NASP training directory (Thomas, 1998), 17% of school psychology students were classified as minority and 80% of them were females. Consistent with the pattern of increased female representation is the publication patterns for females in school psychology journals (Skinner, Robinson, Brown, & Cates, 1999).

As persons with disabilities continue to enter the workforce with the assistance of the Americans With Disabilities Act (Public Law 101-336), we can anticipate greater numbers of such persons entering school psychology. Little is known of the representation of persons with disabilities among school psychology practitioners or of efforts to include such persons in training and practice. Some programs (e.g., Gallaudet University) are obviously involved in such training but little is known about training specifically for persons with disabilities. The authors have trained several students with self-acknowledged learning disabilities, and making reasonable accommodations for them in their training and practice was usually uncomplicated. Training persons with more severe disabilities however, could present challenges not surmountable with present technology for accommodations matched with employer expectations for on-the-job performance. To maintain an atmosphere of fairness and encourage appropriate representation of persons with disabilities in the field, training programs with the assistance of professional associations, should develop a list of critical job skills and behaviors that applicants must have, or be reasonably expected to develop, in order later to perform effectively as practitioners.

Teacher Certification and Experience

As long as training issues have been discussed, the question has arisen whether school psychologists should have prior certification and/or experience as teachers. Although discussions generally consider such preparation desirable, empirical studies have not found a significant relationship between teaching experience and a school psychologist's success (Gerner, 1981, 1983). From 1940 to 1980, the number of state departments of education requiring teacher certification and/or experience for credentialing in school psychology fell dramatically. At present very few states require teacher certification without providing some alternative avenues for those lacking such certification (for specific state requirements see Curtis, Hunley, & Prus, (1998). Still, as noted in Chapter 3, many school psychologists hold teaching credentials and have prior teaching experience, perhaps reflecting the ongoing recruitment of school psychologists from the ranks of experienced teachers and persons in undergraduate teacher education programs. None of the state psychology licensing boards require teaching credentials for the title "school psychologist," and to our knowledge none has ever required it. This distinction further demonstrates the relative influence of psychology or education in the dual controlling system in the field of school psychology (see Chapter 7). The important consideration is to ensure through training and field experiences that future school psychologists gain a comprehensive understanding of the educational system in which they will be directly or indirectly employed as well as an appreciation for the role of the classroom teacher. Finally, as school psychologists expand their range of practice settings, it will be important for such individuals to gain an understanding and appreciation of relevant non-school settings as well. Supervised field experiences and continuing education may be the most constructive avenues for such preparation.

Most Common Degree Levels of Preparation

In Chapter 1 we provided a synopsis of school psychologists' typical level of training including data from Smith (1984), Wilson and Reschly (1995), and recent NASP membership data. Table 6.1 summarizes the levels of training held by respondents to these and an earlier survey. The Smith (1984) and the Reschly and Wilson (1995) data emphasize practitioners although the latter includes trainers. Despite the different methodologies in these surveys, it is obvious that most school psychologists hold non-doctoral degrees. Approximately two-thirds of school psychologists hold the specialist degree or at least a two-year master's degree level of training, and one-fifth to one-fourth hold the doctoral degree in school psychology or a closely related field; not surprisingly, the percentage holding the doctorate is higher when trainers are included in the sample (Graden & Curtis, 1991), and this is observed in the NASP data. Over the past 30 years there has been a distinct trend toward increasing practitioner training at the specialist and doctoral levels with declines in the master's degree level and the virtual disappearance of bachelor's level training.

Enrollment patterns provide another means of judging the typical training of school psychologists. The survey data of Brown and Minke (1984), McMaster, Reschly, and Peters (1989), and Thomas (1998) suggest that total enrollment in school psychology programs decreased in the 1980s (from 7,293 to 5,634), and then increased to 8,587. The increases were only at the specialist and doctoral levels with a substantial decrease at the master's level. Between 1984 and 1998 the proportion of graduate students changed as follows: at the master's level it declined

TABLE 6.1 Summary of studies of training levels (percentage distribution of training in school psychology)

	NASP Member Data[a]	Reschly and Wilson[b]	Smith[c]	Farling and Hoedt[d]
Bachelors	-	-	0	1
Master's (1 yr)	-	-	17	28
Master's (2 yr)	18	23	45	63
Master's (3 yr) or Specialist	56	56	22	1
Doctorate	26	21	16	3

[a] Based on membership data for the National Association of School Psychologists as of November, 1998, $N = 13,356$. BA and BS degree data not included since they almost exclusively represent students and not practitioners.

[b] "School Psychology Practitioners and Faculty: 1986 to 1991-92 Trends in Demographics, Roles, Satisfaction, and System Reform" by D. J. Reschly and M. S. Wilson, 1995, *School Psychology Review*, 24(1), 62-80. This study employed only three categories: master's (30-59 semester hours), specialist (60 or more semester hours), and doctoral.

[c] "Practicing School Psychologists: Their Characteristics, Activities, and Populations Served" by D. K. Smith, 1984, *Professional Psychology: Research and Practice*, 15, 798-810.

[d] *National Survey of School Psychologists* by W. H. Farling and K. C. Hoedt, 1971, Washington, DC: National Association of School Psychologists.

from 20.1% to 2.6%, at the specialist level it increased from 48.3% to 68.5%, and at the doctoral level there was a slight decline from 31.6% to 28.9%. A comparison of the McMaster, Reschly, and Peters (1989) survey with that of Thomas (1998) reveals a decline in the number of master's level programs from 42 to 13, a gain in specialist level programs from 164 to 193, and a gain in doctoral level programs from 67 to 82. These data and the analyses by Reschly and McMaster-Beyer (1991) and Reschly and Wilson (1997) suggest that the specialist degree level is gaining in popularity and that growth at the doctoral level may be less pronounced than the predictions of Brown and Minke (1986) and Fagan (1986c). The directories during the period 1977-1998 reveal that the number of institutions offering training has been fairly stable (mean = 209, range 203-218 of reporting institutions), but the average number of graduates per program declined from 1975-1976 to 1981-1982 (12.2 to 11.1) and has been stable from 1986-1987 to 1996-1997 (8.4 to 8.9). The total number of graduates declined about 20 percent from 2,350 in 1981-1982 to 1,897 in 1996-1997 (Thomas, 1998).

We continue to predict increased proportions of specialist and doctoral programs, fewer two-year programs, and the elimination of one-year master's programs. Surveys of practitioners will increasingly reveal sixth-year, specialist, or doctoral training, with lesser trained personnel fading entirely within the next two decades.

The length of training programs provides another perspective on the typical training of school psychologists. The 1989 NASP *Directory of Graduate Programs* (McMaster, Reschly, and Peters, 1989) indicates that the average number of semester hours required for Master's, Specialist, and Doctoral Degrees in 1986-87 were 42, 66, and 100 respectively. The 1998 directory (Thomas, 1998) reports 40, 66, and 103.5, respectively. Information about typical course requirements by degree level is discussed later in this chapter.

What Level of Training Will Students Need?

School psychologists are competent to provide a broad range of services when trained at the specialist degree level (Brown et al., 1998; Reschly & Wilson, 1997; Woody & Davenport, 1998) even though specialist level preparation for non-school settings has been questioned (Reschly & McMaster-Beyer, 1991). Although doctoral level training is becoming more common, specialist level preparation will continue to be most common for the foreseeable future. Persons seeking training in school psychology should pursue nothing less than a specialist degree or equivalent level of preparation with a minimum of 60 graduate semester hours, in a training program approved through NASP or a state education agency that acknowledges NASP standards (perhaps through an NCATE partnership). Such program approvals enhance the student's later eligibility for the NASP National Certification System (NCS).

Various arrangements may be used in order to meet the NASP guidelines for training and for national certification. Many programs offer the master's degree and the educational specialist degree (Ed.S.) in tandem for a total minimum of 60 semester hours. In some instances, the hourly requirements are met through a lengthy master's degree or through the Ed.S. degree only. The content of the program and its accreditation status are more important than the title of the degree offered. However, in some states the educational specialist degree is required for credentialing.

Students often inquire about the necessity of earning the doctoral degree. The issue of whether a practitioner should hold the doctoral degree has existed throughout the history of school psychology and has been of increasing interest since the reorganization of the American Psychological Association (APA) in 1945. For independent practice, every national organization from which school psychologists have sought professional identity has considered the doctorate as the proper level of training with the exception of NASP (Fagan, 1993). The intensity of the issue for school psychologists grew and intensified with the APA Council of Representatives decision (in 1977) to recognize only the doctoral level for the title "professional psychologist." The doctoral-non-doctoral issue is too complex for in-depth coverage in this book; summary viewpoints are available in Fagan (1986c, 1993), and *School Psychology Review* (Vol. 16, No. 1, and Vol. 18, No. 1). It is worth noting that the percentage of school psychologist practitioners holding doctoral degrees has climbed from about 3% in 1970 to more than 20% in the 1990s. Even though the majority of school psychologists have been trained at the non-doctoral level, the demand for doctoral level personnel can be seen in the growth of doctoral programs in the past 20 years. This trend will continue with gradual increases in the doctoral force relative to the non-doctoral force. The trend also can be observed in the growth of APA-accredited doctoral programs since 1971 (Fagan & Wells, 2000).

Since the doctoral degree is seldom required for practice in the schools, and since the schools will continue to be the primary employment setting, one important consideration is the relative cost of doctoral study compared to the income that could be gained from continued employment. In 1996-1997, the average tuition for resident school psychology students was $4,308 per year and the average cost per credit hour was $219 (Thomas, 1998). These figures are more than double those reported for 1986-1987 (McMaster et al., 1989). Assuming one already holds the specialist degree and is credentialed for school practice, pursuing doctoral work on a full-time basis would involve giving up one's salary for perhaps 3 years before returning to employment. For example, the salary loss for 3 years might total $85,000 to $120,000 and tuition would cost at least $12,000. The conservative estimated cost ($97,000) could not be matched by graduate student stipends, tuition waivers, and a paid internship, the total of which might be only around $45,000. Add the costs of living expenses, transportation, out-of-state tuition, books, and materials, and it becomes obvious that under any circumstances doctoral preparation is a long-term investment and not a short-term financial advantage. Unless the practitioner anticipates returning to a significantly greater salary level in his or her former employment and/or additional sources of revenue such as from private practice or an administrative position, there may be no financial advantage to pursuing a doctoral degree. Nor does pursuing the doctorate in order to enter a university position guarantee a financial advantage; some academic positions do not pay as well as doctoral- or even specialist-level practitioner positions. Reschly and Wilson (1995) reported an average primary employer income of $37,587 for practitioners and $46,657 for faculty, but the faculty had an average age 6.5 years greater than that of practitioners (47.9 versus 41.4). Although income growth has occurred in the 1990s, it is unlikely this gap has been greatly reduced.

From a financial standpoint, it may be better for the student to pursue a doctoral program immediately after completion of the specialist degree than to return for such training after a period of employment. The length of additional academic preparation is at least one year, plus an additional doctoral-level internship usually has to be completed. Lifestyle considerations are also involved and various matters such as family responsibilities and expenses or availability of employment leave can make returning to graduate work more difficult than pursuing it originally. Prospective doctoral students should weigh the advantages and disadvantages of advanced training against their long-term career goals. Although doctoral programs often prefer full-time students, many offer part-time studies in order that students can maintain employment and defray the cost of their education. Graduate student stipends and tuition waivers, however, are seldom available to part-time students.

Money may not be the most important issue involved in a decision, however. Foremost may be the opportunities to obtain greater knowledge, competence, and status and to expand one's professional options. Some contend that the doctoral degree is not necessary for school-based practice, and that advanced preparation affords little or no additional competence necessary for school practice. As discussed later, there appear to be reliable differences between doctoral and non-doctoral preparation. Even though the specialist level appears to be sufficient for school practice, additional competencies are surely afforded by doctoral training and may be more significant to effective practice in non-school settings (Phillips, 1985; Reschly & McMaster-Beyer, 1991). The doctoral degree may be an advantage to school psychologists. Breadth of training, opportunities for advancement in school settings, and employment in the private sector with full professional privileges are worthy incentives for one's long-term career choices. In a field where an increasing percentage of practitioners hold the doctoral degree, seeking the doctorate for its own sake will also be an incentive. Finally, regardless of whether a student seeks doctoral or non-doctoral preparation, one should apply only to those programs holding appropriate state and national approval or accreditation.

PROGRAM CHARACTERISTICS

Even though the reader may already be enrolled in a school psychology training program, the following questions should be considered in exploring one's preparation:

1. Do you desire to work with school-age children and with many children who have disabilities?
2. Do you desire to work primarily in public school settings?
3. Will you be comfortable as an employee in a public school environment?
4. Do you desire a non-doctoral or doctoral degree?
5. Do you desire generalist or specialized training?
6. Are your long-term interests in a practice or academic setting?
7. In what state, or region, do you intend to seek employment?

Because answers to these questions may assist in the selection of a training program, you have already made some decisions along these lines. The questions may also help you choose among program electives, and to assist you in a decision about seeking doctoral preparation.

Resources for Selecting a Program

The NASP publishes a *Directory of School Psychology Graduate Programs* (Thomas, 1998) that can be used to gather information on institutions students are considering for graduate and advanced graduate preparation. The directory provides curriculum and semester-hour requirements for each training institution and other specific program information useful in selecting a program and judging its content. An annual publication by the APA, *Graduate Programs in Psychology*, provides similar information about school psychology and other psychology programs and complements the NASP directory. Students also find useful information on the internet at web sites for specific institutions and graduate programs. Because doctoral and non-doctoral programs are increasingly complying with the standards promulgated by NASP and APA, the published program standards also are useful references (APA, 1996b; NASP, 1994b, 1994c). The NASP standards are scheduled for revision in the year 2000. We further suggest that prospective and incoming students make an on-the-job visit with one or more practicing school psychologists to observe firsthand what school psychology is about.

In considering any particular program, it is best for students to seek answers to their questions from the program administrator. Inquiries to these institutions will provide sufficient program data to allow students to make more informed decisions regarding the appropriateness of the program for their needs and interests. Students also will want to determine what prerequisite course work is desired or required. The program administrator is the most reliable source of information. With rapid growth in training, even recently published directories and university bulletin descriptions may not keep pace with changes. When possible, visit the program and talk directly with faculty and currently enrolled students. Information on the historical development and philosophy of certain doctoral programs can be found in former issues of *Professional School Psychology* (now *School Psychology Quarterly*). Some programs have an unpublished written history available for distribution. Many programs also have descriptive information as part of their institution's website.

In addition to the NASP and APA program standards and directories, certain other documents are helpful. Still a useful guide is Gerner and Genshaft (1981) which provides a guide to selecting a program by addressing such issues as degrees, field experiences, credentialing requirements, program orientations, and interviewing questions. They also refer to the relationship between a training program and the credentialing requirements of the state in which the program is located. This is a major consideration at the non-doctoral level. Because most programs are organized to meet requirements of a particular state department of education (SDE) or state board of examiners in psychology (SBEP), non-doctoral programs often conform closely to state agency requirements. Thus NASP's *Credentialing Requirements for School Psychologists* (Curtis, Hunley, & Prus, 1998) is helpful in the process of choosing a program and includes summary tables for school-based and independent credentialing requirements. Additional resources for use in internship selection are discussed later in this chapter and in Chapter 8. Another useful guide was recently prepared by Morgan (1998). Students interested in research-oriented programs might find Little's (1997) survey helpful.

Administrative Location of Preparation Programs

Compared to some areas of psychology, school psychology has had a confusing history of training, credentialing, and accreditation. Throughout this history, training programs have been located in psychology and non-psychology departments in colleges of education and colleges of arts and sciences. If readers review the entries in the NASP training directory, they will be surprised by the diversity of department and college titles in which school psychology preparation occurs. The diversity has resulted from historical trends in the development of school psychology, including graduate admission of students from diverse backgrounds in education and psychology, conflicts between psychology and education departments, accreditation influences from different agencies, and, until recent years, lack of clear professional identity. Departmental diversity is the norm, not the exception, in school psychology training and will probably continue. There are more than a dozen different departmental titles in which school psychology programs are located in the United States. An analysis of data in the NASP directory (Thomas, 1998) and from the Council of Directors of School Psychology Programs (CDSPP) resulted in the distributions shown in Table 6.2.

It is clear that approximately two-thirds of specialist level and three-fourths of doctoral level programs are in education units (e.g., colleges of education). The distributions in Table 6.2 are consistent with earlier analyses (Brown and Lindstrom, 1977; Goh, 1977). The diversity also can be observed in the numerous degree titles granted, with the most common being M.S., M.A., Ed.S., Ph.D., and Ed.D. The diversity reflects the essence of the Hybrid Years discussed in Chapter 2. In some states, programs tend to be in education units (which sometimes includes the psychology department) while in others they tend to be located in psychology departments in colleges of arts and sciences.

Being housed in a unit other than a psychology department does not necessarily mean the program is not psychological. Frequently programs are in a department of educational psychology, counseling and guidance, or other academic unit which is clearly psychological in nature. The content of the program is more important than its administrative location or the title of the degree it may confer. This principle is reflected in the diversity of administrative units observed for program accreditation. Programs in education and in psychology departments are accredited at the doctoral and non-doctoral level. As of December, 1998, 75% of the 59 APA accredited doctoral programs in school psychology (including 9 combined programs) were in education unit departments. Non-doctoral accreditation is well dispersed across education and psychology units.

Does academic location of the program make a difference in the quality of preparation? We are not aware of any studies of the job effectiveness of school psychologists related to the location of their academic preparation. An earlier analysis based on data from the 1989 NASP directory found no significant

TABLE 6.2 Location of school psychology training programs by academic unit

Academic Unit	Number	Percent
Doctoral Degree Programs (N = 87)		
Education	64	74
Psychology	21	24
Unable to Determine	2	2
Specialist Level Programs (N = 196)		
Education	126	64
Psychology	55	28
Unable to Determine	15	8

differences in programs based on academic location or accreditation (Reschly & McMaster-Beyer, 1991). A much earlier study suggested that the importance of content areas did not differ significantly as a function of academic administrative unit (Goh, 1977). Ross, Holzman, Handal, and Gilner (1991) cautiously suggest that, at least among APA-accredited doctoral programs, academic unit may be related to performance on the Examination for the Professional Practice of Psychology (EPPP) employed by state licensing boards.

Location could help prepare school psychologists to work more effectively with teams made up of other educators and psychologists. For example, location in an education unit could lead to training pupil personnel services students to learn and work together as teams. Or a psychology department location could lead to training health services provider students to learn and work together as teams. Even with many school psychology programs strategically located in education units and in accredited combined psychology programs, the authors know of no program that specifically purports to train school psychologists concurrently with other specialists in a team format. Greater efforts may occur once the student begins an internship or is employed. Florida recently conducted a joint student services conference for interns from the fields of school counseling, nursing, social work, and school psychology (Luellen & Avant, 1998). Although annual intern conferences have been around for a long time in some states, the interdisciplinary nature of the Florida conference is noteworthy. There is also a growing number of APA accredited combined professional psychology programs, a trend that may continue. Combinations are with clinical (including child-clinical) and counseling psychology (Beutler & Fisher, 1994; Minke & Brown, 1996). While some may believe that psychology department-based programs are superior, among the 1995 *U.S. News and World Report* rankings of the six best school psychology programs five were identified as being in education units. In summary, it is our opinion that there is no reason to judge programs in one academic unit, education or psychology, as inherently superior to others regardless of degree level.

There are pragmatic concerns that encourage persons to seek one academic unit or another. Programs located within education units are often more flexible in admissions criteria and scheduling of classes. In an education-based program a student may be more likely to be admitted on a part-time basis, with a selection of daytime and evening courses. Some psychology-based school psychology programs are located in colleges of education where a "spread effect" may have influenced greater flexibility than is the case in psychology units in arts and sciences. Because of student employment opportunities and the influence of adult education, urban programs may also be more flexible in these respects than rural programs.

In addition, your state board of examiners in psychology (SBEP) may only recognize courses completed in a psychology unit and may prefer the Ph.D. and Psy.D. over the Ed.D. for licensure as a psychologist. State departments of education (SDE) usually grant approvals through mechanisms coordinated with colleges of education (see Chapter 7) and may prefer that training be completed in an education unit. Problems with degrees and units are more common when applying for private practice licensure than when applying for a school psychology credential through the SDE. Thus, although students should feel confident that training programs administered from within either education or psychology units will provide appropriate preparation, they should be aware of potential credentialing implications. Graduating from a program that has proper accreditation in school psychology, especially at the doctoral level, minimizes difficulties that may be encountered with any credentialing authority.

In recent years, professional degrees such as the doctor of psychology (Psy.D.) have emerged and offered advanced training in nontraditional formats available to school psychologists. Among academic school psychologists in the early 1990s, 3% held the Psy.D. 76% held the Ph.D., 17% the Ed.D./D.Ed. and 3% other degrees (Daniel Reschly, personal communication, 1999). However, in 1998-1999, Wells and Fagan (1999) found that among a sample of new doctoral graduates in school psychology (faculty and practitioners) 24% held the Psy.D., 70% the Ph.D., and 6% the Ed.D. An earlier study of the acceptability of the Psy.D. suggests it is not as widely accepted for academic employment as the traditional Ph.D. or Ed.D. though greater acceptability may occur in the future (Prout, Meyers, & Greggo, 1989). Such problems seem less prevalent among recipients of the Psy.D. in clinical psychology (Hershey, Kopplin, & Cornell, 1991). The Psy.D. seems to have greatest appeal to persons seeking practitioner positions, and training programs seeking doctoral status, which are unable to get authorization for the Ph.D., may seek to confer the Psy.D instead. The 1989 NASP directory of training programs identified only four programs offering the Psy.D., but the 1998 directory identified nine such programs. Holding the Psy.D. degree does not appear to be a hindrance in seeking SDE or SBEP credentialing. In the future we anticipate an increasing number of free-standing professional schools with doctoral degrees in school psychology. It is not clear how these programs will be received by the broader school psychology training and credentialing groups.

Relationship of Training to Accreditation and Credentialing

Levels of training and types of degrees have complex relationships to accreditation and credentialing. The relationships dictate the type of professional title and practice one is eventually permitted. The complexity of these relationships is discussed in Chapter 7 and suggested by Figure 7.1. Persons understanding the organizations, committees, agencies, and programs represented in Figure 7.1 should have little difficulty in recognizing the complex nature of accrediting and credentialing in school psychology (see also Fagan, 1986c; 1990a). In selecting a training program, close attention should be paid to national professional standards for accreditation and credentialing and to the requirements of the SDE and the SBEP for the state in which the program is offered and/or the trainee desires to practice.

Models of Training

The term "model" has several meanings when used in discussions of training, practice, credentialing, and accreditation. For example, we hear about the behavioral model of training, the consultation model of practice, the NASP model of credentialing, or the APA model of accreditation. In these contexts, model may connote a preference, an ideal to emulate, a theoretical orientation, or an exemplary practice. The outcome of the different usages has resulted in a litany of so-called training models. We read of a consultation model, a scientist-practitioner model, an ecological model, a behavioral model, or a medical model (see, for example, Conoley & Gutkin, 1986). The term gets more confusing when we observe the blending of meanings, such as in a "behavioral consultation model." Although such blends lend precision to the orientation of a particular model, every example can be considered a miniature of some larger model. That is, each training program may be viewed as a reflection of some larger standard or ideal. The precision afforded by defining training models in this way lacks recognition of the many other forces that combine to create the specific program of preparation encountered by a student. For this reason, the authors choose to use the term model to simply represent the salient characteristics of a particular program of preparation. Although program commonalities certainly exist, every program is unique and has its own specific model, though it may reflect one or more of the master models identified below. Programs are like fingerprints that provide individual identification while conforming to general principals of anatomical design. To our way of thinking, therefore, the University of Memphis or the Western Illinois University models of preparation are more descriptive than some broader connotation of the term model.

Master Models: Scientist-Practitioner, Professional, and Pragmatic

Despite our preference for a program-specific approach, the authors recognize that various forms of three broad training models permeate thought about the preparation of school psychologists. Referring to these as master models, we provide the following explanation for the purpose of better understanding Figure 6.1. and Table 6.3. Professional psychology training programs often identify themselves with either the scientist-practitioner (S-P) or the professional (P) model. This is especially true of doctoral programs in the development of their rationale and curricula within the parameters of national-level accreditation.

Scientist-Practitioner (S-P)

The S-P model was adopted in the context of clinical psychology training at the Boulder Conference, held in Boulder, Colorado in 1949 (Raimy, 1950).

The model has been applied generally to the training of all professional psychologists and linked to the process of accreditation in clinical, counseling, and school psychology. The S-P model advocated that preparation "should be grounded *on* and *in* research in general and experimental psychology" and that professional psychologists should be expected to *do* research (Frank, 1984, p. 427). Training should include a blend of psychology's research and practice orientations such that trainees are prepared to conduct and understand research, as well as practice effectively with clients. In this respect, the school psychologist would be expected to be first of all a psychologist in the traditional sense of the term, and secondly a practitioner. As the model evolved in practice, programs identified themselves along a continuum such that some could purport to emphasize training in the direction of science and research and others in the direction of practice. The proper positioning of a program's rationale, and the demonstration of its implementation, became important to its accreditation. Programs slanted toward the scientist end of the continuum presumably emphasize more statistics, research design and experience, theses and dissertations, and generally appear to view training as preparation for conducting school psychology research. On the practitioner end, requirements are greater in the areas of assessment and intervention, ethics, professional development issues, supervised practica and other field experiences.

FIGURE 6.1 Program-specific model of preparation

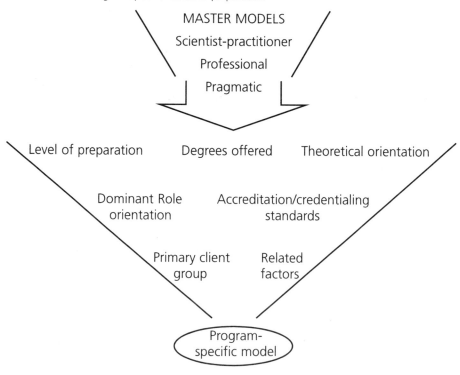

TABLE 6.3 Factors influencing specific training program models

Level of Preparation	Degrees Offered	Theoretical Orientation
Paraprofessional	B.A./B.S.	Psychodynamic
Entry-Level	M.A./M.S.	Behavioral
	Ed.S.	Ecological
Advanced	Psy.D.	Social Learning
	Ed.D.	Eclectic
	Ph.D.	Empirical

Accreditation/Credentialing Standards	Related Factors
APA, NCATE/NASP	Faculty Characteristics
State Department of Education	Available Courses
Regional Accreditation	Institutional Support
State Psychology Licensing Board	Physical Facilities
NASP National Certification	Student Characteristics

Dominant Role Orientation	Primary Client Group
Assessment	Infant/Toddler/Preschool
Consultation	Elementary
Research and Evaluation	Middle/Junior High
Prevention	Secondary
Interventions	Post-Secondary
Systems/Organizational Development	Parents
Mixed	Teachers
Other	Administration/System
	Non-School
	Urban/Suburban/Rural
	Mixed
	Other

Of course, most programs position themselves between the end points of the continuum. There is also the notion that a continuum was not intended by the model; rather all professional psychology programs should adhere to some balance of research and practice preparation within the S-P concept. Knoff, Curtis, and Batsche (1997) believe the scientist-practitioner model should be extended to specialist and doctoral level preparation.

The S-P model has been criticized on the grounds that professional psychologists need not be trained to perform research, that few persons trained under the model later engage in research, that research and clinical skills may even be incompatible, and that scientists and practitioners differ along several personal dimensions (Frank, 1984). Despite such criticisms, the model has survived. A historical discussion of the model appears in Lambert (1993).

Professional (P)

With the growth of professional psychology other models were put forth, including the professional model emerging from the Vail Conference in 1973.

The Vail Conference deliberated a broad range of issues including admissions; minority and female representation; faculty involvement in practice; understanding of social, political, and community ramifications of practice; understanding of employment settings and the range of clients served; and the need for continuing professional development (Korman, 1974). In the P model, training to conduct research is de-emphasized in favor of training for program evaluation and understanding of research. In addition, greater emphasis is placed upon preparation for practice emphasizing the professional identity of the psychologist and the world of practice. As described by Korman (1974), the original intent of the model was not to abandon comprehensive psychological science or to depreciate the value of the S-P type training program. Instead it was to provide "one type of heuristic model to guide those programs defining themselves by a basic service orientation" (p. 442). The model is more than just an emphasis on the practitioner end of the S-P model's continuum, though overlaps are apparent. The acceptance of the P model is associated with the rapid growth of free-standing (not university affiliated) schools of professional psychology granting the doctor of psychology degree (Psy.D.) and preparing a large percentage of recent graduates in clinical psychology. These schools are represented by the National Council of Schools and Programs of Professional Psychology. For a discussion of the group's educational model see Peterson, Peterson, Abrams, and Stricker, (1997). The Doctor of Psychology degree was proposed as far back as 1918 (Hollingworth, 1918), well before accreditation of programs or credentialing of practitioners existed.

Variations of the S-P model dominate school psychology doctoral programs. The strong presence of this model in school psychology training may be related to several factors: (a) the presence of few free standing professional schools offering the Psy.D. in school psychology, (b) the historic influence of educational psychology and its research orientation, (c) the comparatively slower professional development of our field compared to clinical psychology, (d) the importance of evaluation and accountability to successful practice in school settings, (e) the diversity of academic units in which school psychology programs are housed, and (f) the influence of empirical orientations to the practice of school psychology such as Gray's (1963b) data-oriented problem solver. The research aspect of the S-P model applied to school psychology has several benefits for conceptualizations of practice, service delivery and its evaluation (Bardon, 1987; Martens & Keller, 1987; Stoner & Green, 1992). Widespread doctoral training is a relative newcomer to school psychology and the attendant training ideologies have been promulgated by persons who have long-term association with the S-P model. For example, the model fits appropriately into Phillip's (1985) distinctions between the terms "training" and "education" and into Bardon and Bennett's (1974) discussion of learning to think like a psychologist. As school psychology continues to gain in professional stature, it may adopt alternative models for practitioner preparation as already observed in clinical and counseling psychology. In considering a shift of models, we should acknowledge Cook's cautionary statement that "difficult as it may be to train the scientist-professional and then to enable him to maintain this role in his work, it offers our best hope of avoiding a commonplace profession and a disembodied science" (Cook, 1958, cited in Gray, 1963b, p. 394).

Because doctoral programs in school psychology often are intermingled with non-doctoral programs at the same institutions, there is a tendency to consider the S-P model as permeating all levels of preparation. Although we advocate a scientific approach to training at all levels, we believe that the S-P and P models should be applied only to doctoral programs. This is because lesser training cannot be expected to fulfill the assumptions of these models for comprehensive preparation. Consequently, though one's M.S. or Ed.S. degree may be part of a doctoral program identified as scientist-practitioner, the S-P model refers only to the entire preparation sequence culminating in the doctoral degree. The typical semester hours devoted to various aspects of study at each degree level support this position (see Table 6.4).

Pragmatic (Pg)

To what model, therefore, do non-doctoral degree programs adhere? We proffer a third model, also relevant to the accreditation process, that we call the pragmatic model. In this orientation, the preparation of school psychologists is directed primarily toward the credentialing requirements of the state in which the program is located. The Pg model, which influences most non-doctoral programs, may be highly prescriptive with courses required in direct correspondence to courses and competencies specified in state education agency regulations. Because credentialing is important to psychologists at all levels of preparation, there is some prescriptiveness in every program. The Pg model overlaps both the S-P and P models and suggests that all professional preparation programs experience some external control. However, non-doctoral programs, limited by university hourly requirements that must be aligned with state credentialing expectations, can become almost entirely prescriptive. The prescriptiveness can result in a high degree of similarity among programs. Such similarity is an unavoidable tradeoff with prescriptiveness in state regulations. Accreditation standards, which also have

TABLE 6.4 Average number of semester hours by areas and degree

Areas	Master's	Specialist	Doctorate
Core Psychology	15	18	31
Assessment	10	12	13
Intervention	9	12	13
Educational Foundations	6	8	8
Professional School Psychology	9	16	20
Average Total Hours	42	66	100

a prescriptive influence, may encourage similarity at the entry level while encouraging advanced generalist training or subspecializations at the doctoral level. As NASP accreditation guidelines specify competencies in many areas that also apply to non-doctoral programs, they are more prescriptive in comparison to the guidelines of APA.

We consider the Pg model appropriate and necessary for ensuring the later entry-level credentialing of trainees. There is nothing intended in its pragmatic orientation that precludes students from being educated as opposed to trained or from becoming professionals as opposed to mere technicians (Ysseldyke, 1986). The technician level of preparation is more likely in states where the non-doctoral credentialing standards are directed at only practice issues and prescribe virtually all of a program's coursework, and where the curriculum is oriented toward narrow traditional psychometric tasks. We believe such inflexibility is diminishing among state regulations and programs. A guideline document for improving circumstances is *School Psychology: A Blueprint For Training And Practice: II* (Ysseldyke, et al. 1997), an updated version of the 1984 publication of the same name.

Influences on Program Models

The three master models influence a program's broad conceptualization of training and its subsequent development of a specific program model. The specific model of a preparation program is influenced by factors identified in the seven categories of Table 6.3: level of preparation, degrees offered, theoretical orientation, accreditation and credentialing standards, related factors, dominant role orientation, and primary client group. Several alternatives are given for each category but the items included are only examples and are not inclusive. The interaction of these factors culminates in the model of training observed in a specific program, and the model may be different for each program (e.g., Ed.S. or Ph.D.), at the same institution. For example, one program's model might be characterized as offering the specialist degree for entry-level preparation, to provide services primarily in elementary school settings, employing a behavioral orientation, in a pragmatic curriculum developed to meet state certification. Another program could be characterized as being at the advanced level culminating in the Ph.D., to prepare school psychology academicians, employing an ecological orientation, in a curriculum slanted toward the scientific aspects of APA's scientist-practitioner model.

With so many possible combinations, it is not surprising that analyses of training models have failed to discern any single dominant or generally accepted model or the effectiveness of one specific model of training over another (see, for example, Pfeiffer & Marmo, 1981). Bardon and Bennett's (1974) comment, "Characteristic of school psychology training programs is their lack of a single, identifiable model" (p. 177), is still appropriate. Nevertheless the diversity of program models has been judged a healthy trend that has existed for decades (Bardon, 1986; Bardon & Bennett,

1974). Perhaps research on models of training would be more fruitful if the methodology accounted for the variety of factors influencing preparation in addition to broad theoretical orientations. Thus research on ecological models of training should match the so-called ecological-model programs on other variables. Even though we will continue to see training programs identified with the scientist-practitioner, professional, or pragmatic master models, we should be aware that an interaction of several factors provides a more specific overall description of a program's training model.

Content of Programs

The following is a discussion of program content for entry-level (specialist degree) and doctoral programs, with the latter including a discussion and listing of available subspecializations. Despite increased course offerings, growth in the number of training programs and their diverse administrative locations, the content of entry-level programs has considerable uniformity. This uniformity reflects the influences of professional and political forces, perceptions of the realities of daily practice, and enforcement of accreditation standards at the entry level. Table 6.4 presents a summary of content-area emphases at each degree level based on the 1989 NASP directory (McMaster, Reschly, & Peters, 1989; the 1998 directory has no comparable analysis). On average, entry-level training consists of a balanced menu of core psychology, assessment, intervention, and professional course work. Doctoral training on average appears to add emphasis to the core psychology and professional areas while retaining almost the same emphases in assessment, intervention, and educational foundations. The differing emphases at the doctoral and non-doctoral levels reflect long-standing analyses of program data (Goh, 1977; Pfeiffer & Marmo, 1981; Reschly & McMaster-Beyer, 1991). In Goh's (1977) study, nine areas of emphasis were found to account for 73% of the total variance: (a) school-based consultation, (b) educational assessment and remediation, (c) behavior modification technology, (d) psychological evaluation, (e) psychotherapeutic procedures, (f) quantitative methods, (g) community involvement and consultation, (h) professional roles and issues, and (i) psychological foundations including child development and learning. These factors were present in both doctoral and non-doctoral programs, with factors a, b, and c accounting for 49% of the variance at all levels.

Entry-Level Programs

From surveys of course content and an earlier NASP training directory (Brown & Lindstrom, 1977) the following courses/experiences have been found to be most often present in non-doctoral, entry-level programs:

1. Advanced Statistics
2. Research Methods/Design
3. Child and Adolescent Development

4. Psychology of Learning
5. Intellectual Assessment
6. Personality Assessment
7. Educational Assessment
8. Educational Foundations (e.g., administration, curriculum)
9. Child Study Practicum
10. Seminar on School Psychology
11. Counseling/Psychotherapy
12. Consultation
13. Educational Remediation
14. Characteristics of Exceptional Children
15. Behavior Management
16. Practicum
17. Internship

A 1983 survey of school psychology trainers by Knoff (1986) provides information about the content, objectives, and texts of courses in the areas of professional issues and foundations, assessment, consultation, and field experiences. The survey summarizes the emphases of content within courses, and thus can serve as an earlier normative resource for organizing courses in these areas. More recent directories of training programs have not included specific curricular content analyses. However, the specificity of SDE credentialing requirements and the non-doctoral training standards of NASP appear to have influenced a commonly observed set of non-doctoral program courses and experiences. A survey of training for projective assessment appears in Hermann and Kush (1995). Supervisory practices appear in Romans, Boswell, Carlozzi, and Ferguson (1995).

The current NASP training program standards (NASP, 1994c) are considerably more rigorous than those first published by NASP (NASP, 1972). Even though APA Division 16 promoted training standards well before those of NASP, they were not widely adopted by education groups. The NASP standards, promoted by way of its relationship with the National Council for Accreditation of Teacher Education (NCATE), gained increasing acceptance by SDEs during the 1980s. Because of their widespread acceptance, the NASP standards provide one of the best means of anticipating entry-level program content. Accreditable programs are expected to demonstrate in both policy and practice that they have 60 or more semester hours of academic credit in didactic and field experiences. The curriculum guidelines of the NASP standards indicate areas of competency rather than specific course requirements, and are divided into the following areas:

Psychological foundations.
1. Biological bases of behavior
2. Human learning

3. Social and cultural bases of behavior
4. Child and adolescent development
5. Individual differences

Educational foundations.
1. Education of exceptional learners
2. Instruction and remedial techniques
3. Organization and operation of schools

Interventions/problem-solving.
1. Assessment (diverse models and methods linked to direct and indirect interventions)
2. Direct interventions, both individual and group
3. Indirect interventions (including consultation, systems and organizational change)

Statistics and research methodologies.
1. Research and evaluation methods
2. Statistics
3. Measurement

Professional school psychology.
1. History and foundations of school psychology
2. Legal and ethical issues
3. Professional issues and standards
4. Alternative models for the delivery of school psychological services
5. Emergent technologies
6. Roles and functions of the school psychologist

The NASP standards include expectations for field experiences including practica and internship, with practica occurring prior to the school year-long supervised internship. The internship must include a minimum of 1,200 clock hours, at least half of which must be in a public school setting. Related internship standards define the nature of supervision, setting, and other experiences desired of a quality internship. The internship may be completed on a full-time basis for one academic year or part-time over 2 years. For additional information on internships see Chapter 8.

The NASP standards are built around an expectation that trainees will receive a minimum of 60 graduate semester hours of preparation (as many as 6 of which may be granted for the internship) that meets all competency and field experiences, as well as other desirable characteristics of a school psychology program. The preparation should culminate in the granting of the specialist degree or its equivalent. As mentioned earlier, this level of preparation is usually achieved by offering the master's degree in tandem with the specialist degree (e.g., 36 and 30 hours, respectively), the specialist degree only (minimum of 60 hours), or a lengthy master's degree of 60 hours. The terms "specialist" and "sixth-year" programs represent similar levels of training, (i.e., 4 years of undergraduate and 2 years of graduate training not including internship). The specialist program culminates in the awarding of the specialist degree, whereas the sixth-year program usually does not terminate with a degree, though a certificate of completion may be awarded (a sixth-year certificate or certificate of advanced graduate study). Specialist degree programs often have more terminal requirements (e.g., written and oral exams, research papers) than sixth-year programs. The specialist degree often requires a "culminating experience" in addition to an internship. A 1997 survey of NASP-approved non-doctoral programs revealed that the most frequent required culminating experiences were oral examination (28%), written comprehensive examination (59%), research thesis (43%), and major paper but not a thesis (21%). The most frequent other required culminating experiences included student portfolios and internship. Programs typically had more than one required culminating experience (Fagan, 1997).

The curriculum and degree configuration employed to achieve compliance with NASP standards varies as a function of what graduate degrees an institution is authorized to confer. State higher education governing boards allow only certain institutions to offer post-master's degrees including the specialist degree. With proper planning, appropriate preparation of entry-level school psychologists can be accomplished by each of the above examples (lengthy master's degree or master's plus specialist degree). The NASP reference to specialist level can be met by any of these approaches. Students pursuing specialist-level training on a full-time basis should expect it to require a minimum of 3 years of full-time study, including the internship. By pursuing studies in the summer, this may be reduced somewhat depending upon the frequency and sequencing of required coursework. Part-time students should expect their training to last at least 4 years. Part-time students also should be aware that institutions maintain time limits on degrees such that after a set number of years (e.g., 6) earlier work may have to be revalidated or repeated. Every academic degree has a window within which it must be completed.

Doctoral Programs

Many doctoral programs are offered in academic departments also offering non-doctoral school psychology programs. In some departments, a career ladder approach may be available in which students might progress from one degree to another without loss of credits. However, in most instances the doctoral degree is more than an extension of the non-doctoral level, and the doctoral track may have little overlap with the non-doctoral track. In the first few years of training, doctoral students may pursue a different curriculum than non-doctoral students. In some instances, the differences are minimal in the first few years, and doctoral students may even be drawn from applicants already in the non-doctoral track or from among graduates already credentialed or practicing as school psychologists. Students considering doctoral training should explore these differences because considerably more time may be required to complete a doctoral degree when a non-doctoral track has been pursued in one's early years of graduate study. As a general rule, full-time students pursuing doctoral degrees can expect a minimum of 4 years of study, which usually does not include the pre-doctoral internship year. Part-time study, which would take considerably longer, is available in some doctoral programs though financial assistance is seldom available to part-time students. Part-time students again should be aware that institutions maintain time limits on degrees such that after a set number of years (e.g., 10) earlier work may have to be revalidated or repeated.

The curriculum portion of the NASP training standards does not differentiate between the doctoral and non-doctoral levels. The entry-level competency areas required by NASP (listed earlier), apply as well to the content of doctoral programs. This tends to make the standards highly prescriptive for non-doctoral programs but ensures that both entry-level and doctoral school psychologists have a comprehensive level of preparation for the world of practice. Differences between the two levels are mainly in the extent of emphasis placed on research and subspecializations, structural aspects of the program, and the internship. For example, the 1994 NASP standards require a minimum of 90 graduate semester hours and a 1,500 hour internship, at least half of which must be in a school setting (unless a previous school based internship has been completed). The NASP standards have outcome-based expectations in addition to the traditional process-based training standards. The outcome orientation had been called for earlier by Curtis and Batsche (1991). An outcome orientation is expected to dominate the next revision of the NASP training standards. The changes should be finalized and in effect by 2002 and will be reflected in the NCSP requirements in 2005. The draft revision disseminated in early 1999 linked the content expectations for programs to the *Blueprint for Training and Practice* (Ysseldyke et al., 1997) and represented a potentially substantial departure from previous NASP training standards.

In contrast to NASP, APA considers the doctoral degree as the appropriate entry level for the title "school psychologist" and for independent practice in any employment setting. The APA's training expectations are directed only to the doctoral level. The APA specialty guidelines for school psychology (APA, 1981) provide a statement about the curriculum expected in the preparation of professional school psychologists:

> The education of school psychologists encompasses the equivalent of at least 3 years of full-time graduate academic study. While instructional formats and course titles may vary from program to program, each program

has didactic and experiential instruction (a) in scientific and professional areas common to all professional psychology programs, such as ethics and standards, research design and methodology, statistics, and psychometric methods, and (b) in such substantive areas as the biological bases of behavior, the cognitive and affective bases of behavior, the social, cultural, ethnic, and sex role bases of behavior, and individual differences. Course work includes social and philosophical bases of education, curriculum theory and practice, etiology of learning and behavior disorders, exceptional children, and special education. Organization theory and administrative practice should also be included in the program (p. 43).

The *Guidelines* also identify the field placement expectations, which are virtually identical to those stipulated before for NASP. These expectations are reflected in the specialty definition document for school psychology (Petition for Reaffirmation of the Specialty of School Psychology, 1997). The APA's accreditation Domain B: Program Philosophy, Objectives, and Curriculum Plan stipulates the following curriculum areas and topics: biological aspects of behavior, cognitive and affective aspects of behavior, social aspects of behavior, history and systems of psychology, psychological measurement, research methodology, techniques of data analysis, individual differences in behavior, human development, dysfunctional behavior or psychopathology, professional standards and ethics, theories and methods of assessment and diagnosis, effective intervention, consultation and supervision, evaluating the efficacy of interventions. Relevant to all areas of training are cultural and individual diversity and attitudes essential for life-long learning, scholarly inquiry, and professional problem-solving as psychologists in the context of an evolving body of scientific and professional knowledge. Field experiences including practica and internship are also expected (APA, 1996b). APA accreditation guidelines are applied to programs in the United States and Canada.

As indicated earlier, Goh (1977) reported factor results on combined doctoral-sub-doctoral programs and analyzed emphases that trainers rated significant to the doctoral level. The only areas consistently cited at the doctoral level were "school-based consultation" and "quantitative methods." These results were supported by Brown and Minke (1986) who found that advanced graduate training in school psychology differs most from specialist training by providing areas of subspecialization and additional research information/skills and by Reschly and Wilson (1997) and Woody and Davenport (1998). Such differences reflect traditional conceptualizations of the doctoral degree and the significance placed on the scientist-practitioner model in professional psychology (Martens and Keller, 1987). As a general rule, the doctoral student can expect to encounter additional statistics and research courses, a major research requirement such as a dissertation, related requirements such as a major area paper, additional written and oral examinations, and an internship experience. Some institutions accept previous internships completed at the entry level. The analyses of entry-level and doctoral programs by Reschly and McMaster-Beyer (1991) found that "the broader scope of doctoral training provides better preparation for practice in diverse settings such as private practice, mental health clinics, and medical settings and may, as well, establish a better background for understanding learning and behavior problems in school settings" (p. 373). They concluded that the different emphases in program levels support the distinction of credentials for school and non-school practice. Their analyses are judged to be in support of the long-standing APA policies on credentialing, and not in support of the NASP policy that considers the specialist level as sufficient for credentialing for school and non-school practice.

The *International School Psychology Association (ISPA) Guidelines for the Preparation of School Psychologists* are useful because they are cross-cultural in nature and reflect the guidelines of several countries (Cunningham & Oakland, 1998). The guidelines emphasize core knowledge in psychology; professional practice preparation; professional skills in decision-making, reflection, and enquiry; interpersonal skills; and research and statistical skills; and knowledge of ethics and establishment of professional values. Although the ISPA guidelines do not specify degree level expectations, the general model curriculum overlaps heavily with the expectations of APA, NASP, and no doubt several other countries. At present, these standards appear to have little bearing on the organization of programs in the United States and Canada. However, they will likely increase the awareness of trainees to international issues and practices. They could also have an impact on the development of programs in other countries, especially where programs do not already exist. The ISPA training guidelines and other international perspectives are discussed in Chapter 10.

The Internship as a Training Experience

Considerable information about the internship is provided in Chapter 8. Keep in mind that the internship, like other field experiences, is essentially a training experience. It is a direct extension of the training program and affords supervised opportunities within which to demonstrate acquired knowledge and skills from already completed didactic experiences, and to acquire new knowledge and skills in the field. Standards, therefore, require close supervision of the internship through the cooperation of the training program, the intern, and the field supervisor.

Several resources will assist students in seeking an internship and understanding accreditation of doctoral level internships. A book by Dana and May (1987) provides information on professional psychology internships and a conceptual grasp of the ways in which school psychology training deals with field experience requirements. For a concise discussion of internships and their accreditation see Pryzwansky and Wendt (1987). The annual December issue of the *American*

Psychologist lists APA-approved doctoral internship centers but does not identify them by specialization. The magnitude of this enterprise is reflected in the December 1998, listing of 433 internship sites in 47 states and the District of Columbia (Accredited Internship and Postdoctoral Programs for Training in Psychology: 1998, 1998). The Association of Psychology Postdoctoral and Internship Programs (APPIC) publishes an annual directory of its members who meet specific doctoral internship criteria, and APA-accredited internships are automatically included. Each of the internship entries identifies which psychology specialties (clinical, counseling, and school) are sought and whether only APA-accredited program applicants are selected or if they are "preferred" or "acceptable." Non-APA accredited applicants are rated accordingly. In the 1997-1998 APPIC directory there were 521 sites accepting one or more specialties (Association of Psychology Postdoctoral and Internship Centers, 1997). The directory included 124 North American sites (121 from 47 of the United States and 3 from Alberta, Nova Scotia, and Newfoundland in Canada) that will entertain school psychology applicants. The preference is strongly for those from APA-accredited programs. Of the 31 states with APPIC sites, 7 states have five or more and account for 59% of the 121 sites (California, Illinois, Michigan, New Jersey, New York, Tennessee, and Texas). The APPIC initiated a computer matching program for internships and applicants in 1998-1999. The rationale and matching program are described in Keilin (1998). There is also an annual guide to full-time and half-time internship sites that either specifically seek, or will accept, school psychology trainees. The 1999 internship listings (Joint Committee on Internships, 1999) identifies 113 internship sites in 27 states and one in Alberta, Canada.

The relative scarcity of school psychology doctoral level internship sites and their limited geographic distribution are serious barriers to the development of school psychology at the doctoral level. Another barrier is that certain APPIC requirements to be listed in its directory are perceived as incompatible with the delivery of school psychological services in many settings (e.g., availability of additional professional psychologists and interns). As a result, few of the internships listed are in school districts, and most are in medical facilities, mental health centers, or residential schools. The Council of Directors of School Psychology Programs (CDSPP), a doctoral program faculty group, is an advocate for the creation of additional school-based and school-psychology related internships and approved internship guidelines (CDSPP Doctoral Level Internship Guidelines, 1998). Because NASP internship requirements are part of its training standards, and because those standards are directed at entry-level school practice, it is not surprising that the NASP standards are inconsistent with those of APPIC. With increased student interest in obtaining doctoral degrees, there is a strong need for NASP to develop separate doctoral standards for training and to assist in developing a greater number of nationally accredited doctoral internship sites. The selection and evaluation of doctoral-level internships typically are controlled by the program, the student, and the internship site.

At the non-doctoral level, there are many internships but there is no national directory of sites. Some states have well-organized internship systems coordinated among the training programs, state departments of education, and the internship sites which are usually local school districts. Ohio and Illinois are excellent examples of this level of organization and each state may offer as many as 100 sites each year. Unfortunately, most states are not well organized, and internships are found or created on an ad hoc basis and controlled only by the training program and the internship site. We speculate that the majority of all internships are of the latter variety, and they often are simply informal arrangements between the training program and selected local school districts.

Subspecializations[2]

The prescriptive nature of most specialist-level programs precludes allowing students to concentrate studies in a particular area of expertise. In contrast, the doctoral level usually provides elective course opportunities for subspecialization or for more in-depth coverage of several topics. Because many school psychology doctoral programs combine courses from academic units in psychology and education, a variety of advanced generalist and subspecialty concentrations are available. In some programs, the subspecialization permeates several aspects of the program including its field experiences. For example, a doctoral program may be recognized as preparing school psychologists with subspecialization in neuropsychology. Its students may be expected to complete a dissertation on a neuropsychological topic and to seek an internship in a medical facility with supervised neuropsychological training. The following lists provide a summary of doctoral programs and their associated areas of subspecialization as reported for the 1998-1999 year.

Subspecializations in Doctoral School Psychology Programs[3]

Code No.	Name of Institution	Subspecialty Code
United States School Psychology Doctoral Programs		
1.	Alfred University	2, 11, 12, 18, 22, 30
2.	Andrews University	12, 19b
3.	Arizona State University	5, 19a
4.	Auburn University	12, 27
5.	Ball State University	12, 19b, 25
6.	Bryn Mawr College	19a
7.	Central Michigan University	2, 6, 11, 19b
8.	Columbia University-Teachers College	19b, 25, 27, 32
9.	City University of New York (CUNY)- Graduate College	19a
10.	Florida State University	12, 35
11.	Fordham University	5, 15, 27, 33
12.	Georgia State University	13, 18, 25, 30

13.	Hofstra University	19b
14.	Howard University	19a
15.	Illinois State University	19b
16.	Indiana State University	19b
17.	Indiana University	19a
18.	Indiana University of Pennsylvania	17, 25
19.	James Madison University	19a
20.	Kent State University	11, 19b, 27, 32
21.	Lehigh University	12, 26, 32
22.	Louisiana State University	19a
23.	Loyola University of Chicago	9, 11, 31, 33
24.	Michigan State University	19b
25.	Mississippi State University	1, 2, 3
26.	National Louis University	13, 19b, 22, 25
27.	New York University	8, 12, 13, 19b, 25
28.	North Carolina State University	19b
29.	Northeastern University (Boston)	19a
30.	Northern Arizona University	27
31.	Northern Illinois University	19b
32.	Ohio State University	19a
33.	Oklahoma State University	19b
34.	Pace University (New York City)	19a, 27
35.	Pennsylvania State University	19b
36.	Rutgers University, Graduate School of Applied Psychology	2, 24, 28, 29
37.	St. Johns University	5, 19b
38.	Seattle Pacific University	19a
39.	State University of New York (SUNY)-Albany	19b
40.	State University of New York (SUNY)-Buffalo	3, 6, 12, 26, 28
41.	Syracuse University	1, 11, 19b, 22, 25
42.	Temple University	1, 27
43.	Tennessee State University	19b
44.	Texas A. & M. University	5, 8, 21, 33
45.	Texas Woman's University	12, 19b, 25
46.	Tulane University	6, 13, 26, 34
47.	University of Alabama	19a
48.	University of Arizona	25, 30, 31, 32, 36
49.	University of California-Berkeley	19a
50.	University of California-Davis	5, 19b, 28

51.	University of California-Riverside	1, 2, 3, 32
52.	University of California-Santa Barbara	19b
53.	University of Cincinnati	11, 19b, 24
54.	University of Connecticut	19b
55.	University of Delaware	19b
56.	University of Denver	19b
57.	University of Florida	2, 19b, 25, 27, 30
58.	University of Georgia	12, 18, 23, 25
59.	University of Iowa	2, 6, 19b, 25
60.	University of Kansas	19b
61.	University of Kentucky	19a
62.	University of Maryland	19a
63.	University of Massachusetts	1, 2, 30
64.	University of Memphis	19b
65.	University of Minnesota	11, 13, 17, 28, 31
66.	University of Missouri	19b
67.	University of Nebraska-Lincoln	2, 11, 17, 31, 33
68.	University of North Carolina-Chapel Hill	19a
69.	University of Northern Colorado	12, 19b, 25, 33, 34
70.	University of Oregon	1, 2, 3, 22, 27, 33
71.	University of the Pacific	19a
72.	University of Pennsylvania	2, 3, 7, 8, 9, 11, 17, 19b, 22, 23, 27, 28, 29, 30, 31, 34
73.	University of Rhode Island	9, 11, 19b, 25, 27, 28
74.	University of South Carolina	19b
75.	University of South Dakota	7, 10, 12, 13, 18, 19b
76.	University of South Florida	2, 11, 19b, 23, 24, 30
77.	University of Southern Mississippi	1, 2, 3, 34
78.	University of Tennessee	3, 28, 30
79.	University of Texas-Austin	19b
80.	University of Toledo	12, 18
81.	University of Utah	19b, 25, 33
82.	University of Virginia	8
83.	University of Washington	2, 19b, 22, 25, 28
84.	University of Wisconsin-Madison	3, 7, 19b, 28
85.	University of Wisconsin-Milwaukee	19a
86.	Utah State University	2, 8
87.	Wayne State University	19a
88.	Western Michigan University	1, 2, 3, 19b, 22
89.	Yeshiva University	5, 13, 17, 27

Canadian School Psychology Doctoral Programs

90.	Dalhousie University (Halifax)	19a
91.	McGill University	19b
92.	Ontario Institute for Studies in Education at the University of Toronto	8, 32
93.	University of Alberta-Edmonton	12, 15, 23, 32
94.	University of British Columbia-Vancouver	19a
95.	University of Calgary	19a
96.	University of Manitoba	19a
97.	University of Montreal	19a
98.	University of New Brunswick	19a
99.	University of Quebec at Montreal	19a
100.	University of Saskatchewan-Saskatoon	19a
101.	University of Victoria (British Columbia)	19a

It is not clear if all the above Canadian institutions have doctoral programs that are dedicated to school psychology. Most did not respond to the survey and were, therefore, identified as generalist in orientation. Some appear to overlap more with educational and clinical psychology, or school counseling and special education. Other Canadian institutions believed to be involved in the non-doctoral training of school psychologists are Acadia University, University of Western Ontario, University of Prince Edward Island, University of Newfoundland, and Mount St. Vincent University (Halifax). It appears that there may be as many as 12 doctoral program institutions in Canada and an additional 5 institutions offering non-doctoral training.

Subspecialization Areas[4]	*Institution Codes*
1. Applied Behavior Analysis	25, 41, 42, 51, 63, 70, 77, 88
2. Behavioral Assessment/Intervention	1, 7, 25, 36, 51, 57, 59, 63, 67, 70, 72, 76, 77, 83, 86, 88
3. Behavioral Consultation	25, 40, 51, 70, 72, 77, 78, 84, 88
4. Behavioral Medicine	None Reported
5. Bilingual/Multicultural	3, 11, 37, 44, 50, 89
6. Child Pediatric	7, 40, 46, 59
7. Childhood Psychopathology	72, 75, 84
8. Clinical and Clinical Child Psychology	27, 44, 72, 82, 86, 92
9. Cognition/Instructional Psychology	23, 72, 73
10. Computers in Education	75
11. Consultation, School Based Consultation	1, 7, 20, 23, 41, 53, 65, 67, 72, 73, 76

12.	Counseling	12, 26, 27, 46, 65, 75, 89, 93
13.	Developmental Psychology	12, 26, 27, 46, 65, 75, 89
14.	Discipline	None Reported
15.	Educational Psychology	11, 93
16.	Experimental	None Reported
17.	Family-School Relations	18, 65, 67, 72, 89
18.	Family Systems/Therapy	1, 12, 58, 75, 80
19.	Generalist Orientation	
	a. generalist orientation without subspecialties	3, 6, 9, 14, 17, 19, 22, 29, 32, 34, 38, 47, 49, 61, 62, 68, 71, 85, 87, 90, 94, 95, 96, 97, 98, 99, 100, 101
	b. generalist orientation but subspecialty area may be developed by student; program is not identified with one or more subspecialties	2, 5, 7, 8, 13, 15, 16, 20, 24, 26, 27, 28, 31, 33, 35, 37, 39, 41, 43, 45, 50, 52, 53, 54, 55, 56, 57, 59, 60, 64, 66, 69, 72, 73, 74, 75, 76, 79, 81, 83, 84, 88, 91
20.	Gifted	None Reported
21.	Hispanic Handicapped	44
22.	Learning Assessment/Intervention	1, 26, 41, 70, 72, 83, 88
23.	Measurement/Statistics	58, 72, 76, 93
24.	Organizational Development	36, 53, 76
25.	Neuropsychology	5, 8, 12, 18, 26, 27, 41, 45, 48, 57, 58, 59, 69, 73, 81, 83
26.	Pediatric Psychology	21, 40, 46
27.	Preschool/Early Childhood	4, 8, 11, 20, 30, 34, 42, 57, 70, 72, 73, 89
28.	Prevention	36, 40, 50, 65, 72, 73, 78, 83, 84
29.	Program Evaluation	36, 72
30.	Psychoeducational Assessment	1, 12, 48, 57, 63, 72, 76, 78
31.	Research/Field Experimental	23, 48, 65, 67, 72
32.	Special Education	8, 20, 21, 48, 51, 92, 93
33.	Therapeutic Intervention	11, 23, 44, 67, 69, 70, 81
34.	University Teaching/Training	46, 69, 72, 77
35.	Vocational School Psychology	10
36.	Other: Law and Psychology	48

Almost two-thirds of U.S. doctoral programs identify with the advanced generalist orientation, with most of these allowing the student to develop a subspecialty (47%). The more popular subspecialties appear to be behavioral assessment/intervention, consultation, neuropsychology, and preschool/early childhood. In comparison to the survey 10 years earlier (see Fagan & Wise, 1994, pp. 183-186), the data reflect a stability of subspecialty designations over time. The listings indicate a growth in the number of doctoral programs in the United States from 72 to 89 or about 24% growth in the past decade.

In rare instances, subspecialization is provided at the entry-level. For example, Gallaudet College and Rochester Institute of Technology offer non-doctoral subspecialization with the hearing impaired. Such instances are infrequent and therefore no listings are provided for non-doctoral programs. Because many subspecializations are related as much or more to faculty expertise as to a commitment of the administrative unit, subspecializations may wax or wane as a function of faculty mobility and interests. For instance, rural subspecialization is not always related to the geographic location of the program (Cummings, Huebner, & McLeskey, 1985). Some students attend urban universities but obtain rural subspecialization as a function of selected courses, faculty expertise, and field experiences. In short, when the faculty leave, the subspecialization often goes with them.

Generalists and Specialists

Throughout the history of school psychology, most practitioners have performed a variety of functions while adapting to the range of problems presented them. The necessity for practitioners to have broad training to meet these conditions has long been recognized. Thus most entry-level training programs embraced a generalist orientation that drew upon knowledge and skills from educational foundations, experimental and clinical psychology, special education, and related fields. The generalist model has prevailed in training despite the common reference to school psychologists as "specialists," members of "specialized services teams," or holding a specialist degree.

The issue of whether practitioners should be trained as generalists or specialists has been discussed frequently although little has been published on the subject. With rapid professional development since the 1970s, the issue gained increasing attention. Studies suggested that rural or urban practitioners benefit from specialized training experiences related to the socio-cultural characteristics of their settings; that subspecialty training is more likely to occur in doctoral programs than in non-doctoral programs; and that there is a need for, and growing interest in, several areas of subspecialization, including consultation, early childhood, family services, bilingual/bicultural services, neuropsychology, and vocational school psychology.

We believe several factors will interact to encourage greater subspecialization. These include an increasing number of students selecting doctoral programs, the

continuing education requirements of the NASP National Certification System, a strong employment market for doctoral generalists and subspecialists both in and out of school settings, and the implementation of state and federal regulations. For example, Public Law 99-457 may have heightened job opportunities for school psychologists with subspecialization at the infant-toddler and preschool levels. The potential impact of the "highest qualified provider" standard in the personnel requirements of that law could hasten advanced training and subspecialization generally. Although those requirements could be interpreted in some states to mean that only doctoral providers can be involved in unsupervised service provision to young children, this has yet to be a problem. In the aftermath of the growth in special education as a result of Public Law 94-142, we can expect an increased need for practitioners specializing in vocational school psychology, secondary, transition, and post-secondary services.

In the past, most psychologists with areas of subspecialization were clinical psychologists. It was fairly common for referrals to be exchanged between school psychologists in school settings and clinical psychologists in non-school agencies or private practice. An offshoot of the increased number of doctoral practitioners and those with subspecializations is a trend in the direction of school psychologists moving into non-school practice in hospitals, clinics, professional groups, and self-employment (D'Amato & Dean, 1989). Although the trend is observable it has not been strong nor has it significantly affected the size of the school-based workforce. With school psychologists increasingly entering agency and private practice, competition will build between them and clinical or counseling psychologists. Constraints imposed by managed care and an oversupply of clinical and counseling psychologists may encourage them to seek the schools as an additional marketplace.

It will be more common in the future to see an exchange of referrals between school-based and non-school-based school psychologists. It also is likely that the schools will commonly employ generalists and that school psychologists in the non-school sector will compete with one another for referrals from the schools. Some of that competition will be along lines of subspecializations such that school psychologists with recognized subspecializations may be more competitive in the non-school sector.

Finally, from observations of developments in clinical and counseling psychology, we anticipate that school psychologists in non-school settings initially will be most commonly self-employed or employed in community agencies, and later will seek collective employment with other health services providers. Such collective employment should also encourage greater subspecialization.

Persons considering doctoral-level preparation should consider their desire and need for either advanced generalist or subspecialty training. Making a choice along those lines facilitates the selection of a doctoral program because the number of programs offering subspecialization and the range of subspecialties available are not great (see the lists above). As described earlier, there is greater similarity of training emphases at the non-doctoral level with areas of subspecialization generally occurring at the doctoral level. Due in part to prescriptive regulations that apply only to the non-doctoral level of preparation, doctoral programs in the same state often have different areas of subspecialization despite commonalities in their non-doctoral programs.

Of course, through experience, continuing education, and personal interests, many school psychologists specialize without obtaining a doctoral degree. For example, recognizing a need in their employment settings, school psychologists may obtain additional expertise in the assessment of low-incidence handicaps, preschool assessment, or parent training. As practitioners become more experienced, areas of special expertise commonly develop. Many school psychologists, practitioners and trainers alike, find their interests have changed after several years of employment and they choose to specialize in a particular topic. Such subspecialization does not always involve returning to graduate school for formal preparation. Frequently the necessary expertise is gained through conventions, workshops, in-depth reading, and supervised apprenticeships. In some instances, a concentration of graduate courses in a subspecialty area is completed but not as part of a doctoral degree program.

The interest in subspecializations can be observed in the popularity and growth of special interest groups in NASP. Initiated in the late 1970s, these groups are a vehicle for promoting communication among persons sharing expertise in selected areas. In 1992 there were 14 NASP interest groups. In 1998-1999, there were 10: *Autism/Pervasive Developmental Disorders, *Behavioral School Psychology, Computers and Technological Applications in School Psychology, *Crises in the Schools, *Early Childhood Education, Neuropsychology in the Schools, Prevention, School Psychologists for the Deaf, *State School Psychology Consultants, and Supervision. Those marked with asterisks (*) were not in the 1992 NASP list, and, for whatever reasons, the following interest groups are no longer listed: Families, International Relations, Post-secondary Services, Preschool, Rural, Social and Emotional Assessment, System/Indirect Services, Urban, and Vocational School Psychology. The changes probably reflect shifting interests and leadership over time, although all of the interest group topics continue to be important. School psychologists with subspecializations are active in policy development and in preparing manuscripts for topical issues of journals. In retrospect, although the subspecialties in training have remained fairly constant, the special interest groups of NASP have not.

CONTINUING PROFESSIONAL DEVELOPMENT

It is generally conceded that formal preparation should provide the basic skills, theories, concepts, and supervised experiences to initiate one's professional career successfully. Regardless of one's entry level of preparation, there is an expectation for continued professional development (CPD). The range of settings, clients, presenting problems, and professional issues are simply too great to be accounted for in one's formal academic preparation. This has been characteristic of professional training throughout its history. Even if formal professional psychologist preparation were expanded to the postdoctoral level, this need would still exist. Formal preparation attempts to bring the future professional to a broad understanding of psychology and education, and to inculcate a sense of professional responsibility that includes recognizing when one's skills and professional judgments are insufficient to deal with certain situations. Throughout the history of school psychology there have been various informal means for CPD such as journals and convention programs. More formal opportunities have developed in the past few decades, especially following the initiation of professional institutes for school psychologists by Division 16 in the 1950s (Fagan, 1993). With the unprecedented growth of state school psychology associations since 1970, there are CPD opportunities available in varying degrees in every state. Workshops and special skill development programs have become a very popular means of improving one's skills. The annual conventions of the APA and NASP provide excellent CPD opportunities. The Division of School Psychology (Division 16-APA) offers school psychology presentations in the context of the broader arena of the APA convention. Sometimes tapes of convention presentations are available for purchase during and after a convention. Several associations and publishers offer audiotapes and videotapes for rental or sale on numerous topics. In recent years, both NASP and APA's Division 16 have developed CPD tapes specifically for school psychology. Tapes are a very popular means of acquiring CPD and will likely increase in popularity. The internet offers another strong potential outlet for CPD. Websites and computer technology relevant to school psychologists are regularly identified in professional newsletters.

National Certification Requirement for CPD

The most organized CPD effort in school psychology is that included in the NASP National School Psychology Certification System. In addition to its membership requirements, the system requires that the school psychologist complete at least 75 contact hours of CPD within each three-year renewal period. Certificate holders are expected to obtain CPD in a variety of job-related activity areas. The activities that can be used are flexible and include nine categories, each with credit allowances, ceiling limits, and required documentation: workshops, conferences, and in-service training; college/university courses; teaching and training activities; research and publications; supervision of interns; post-graduate supervised experiences; program planning/evaluation; self-study; and professional organization leadership. Some state departments of education, psychology licensing boards, and state associations for school psychologists also have CPD requirements. Though not specific to school psychology, APA-sanctioned continuing education programs are frequently listed in its newsletter, the *APA Monitor*.

Respecialization

A related issue to continuing professional development is that of respecialization at the doctoral level. Students occasionally wish to know what is expected should they choose to switch from one professional psychology specialty to another (e.g., from school to clinical psychology) or to "retread" from a nonprofessional to a professional field (e.g., from developmental psychology to school psychology). Few institutions offer formal retread programs; however, some will admit students who have already completed a doctoral degree in a psychology field. The retraining process involves the completion of all requirements, often including an internship, or a second internship, for the new field of specialization. Although allowances will usually be made for some common requirements (e.g., certain courses and research experiences), retraining can be expected to require at least 1 year of academic preparation and an additional year of internship.

Postdoctoral Study

Postdoctoral study is another means of gaining continuing education while furthering one's doctoral specialization. Postdoctoral study has been available in psychology for many decades but has only recently been considered by doctoral recipients in school psychology. Its general absence is a function of the lack of postdoctoral opportunities specifically in school psychology and the strong employment market for doctoral recipients. In some fields of psychology, the employment market has been less attractive and doctoral recipients have sought postdoctoral studies as a means of making themselves more competitive for future positions, usually academic positions. With increased subspecialization in school psychology doctoral programs, postdoctoral study will be a natural extension of graduate work. It is also possible that the increasing professionalization of the field will eventually require post-doctoral study for full practice privileges in the private sector, especially in medical-related facilities. Several states already require a year of post-doctoral supervised experience for psychology licensure by the SBEP. Further, there is ongoing discussion of guidelines for post-doctoral education and training in school psychology and APA accreditation of post-doctoral residency study (Pryzwansky, 1998). As of January, 1999, APA accredited only 2 postdoctoral sites, neither of which were for school psychology.

NONCURRICULAR CHARACTERISTICS AND ACCREDITATION

Many aspects of a program's overall quality are not necessarily obvious from an inspection of its curriculum. Gerner and Genshaft (1981) advise students to examine several factors when making program selections and even include hints for interviewing in the application process to programs and internships. Their suggestions help you to judge a program's orientation, its involvement with students, balance of content, and relationships with other academic units. Accreditation guidelines of APA and NCATE/NASP also specify many areas in addition to program content.

National Accreditation

School psychology program accreditation is conducted by both APA and by the National Council for Accreditation of Teacher Education (NCATE). Within the NCATE process, programs are evaluated against the standards of NASP; hence, the acronym NCATE/NASP is employed in school psychology accreditation discussions. It is important to note, however, that NASP is not an accrediting body, but an affiliate of NCATE. In the NCATE process, programs are evaluated by NASP through a review process in which a program must document that in policy and practice it meets each of the NASP standards. The program review process was introduced with the revised NCATE accreditation process of the mid-1980s. A program's folio is reviewed by NASP and its recommendations forwarded to NCATE as part of its broader accreditation review. The NCATE accreditation process performs a similar but broader review of the institution's education unit (e.g., the college of education) of which the school psychology program is a part. The NASP standards employed in the NCATE process include the areas of program values; knowledge base, training philosophy, goals and objectives; practica; internship; performance-based program accountability; and program level and structural characteristics.

The APA accreditation standards apply to professional psychology generally and are not specific to school psychology programs. As of 1999, APA offered accreditation only to programs in clinical, counseling, and school psychology and combinations of these specialties. Other specialties or subspecialities were not recognized for accreditation. The APA process focuses on a program's identity with psychology regardless of its institutional location. APA accreditation reviews several domains including a program's general eligibility; philosophy, objectives and curriculum plan; program resources; cultural and individual differences and diversity; student-faculty relations; program self-assessment and quality enhancement; public disclosure; and relationship with the accrediting body (APA, 1996b). A noticeable difference between the standards of APA and those of NCATE/NASP is APA's focus upon the psychological character of the program and its clear curricular and noncurricular identity with professional psychology and either the scientist-practitioner or professional model.

Despite favorable evaluation of a joint accreditation pilot project in 1982-1983, a joint APA-NCATE accreditation process has never been implemented (Fagan & Wells, 2000). At present, parallel reviews may be conducted by both agencies but a truly joint process, which blends the standards of each agency, does not exist. It is possible that NASP will attain greater autonomy for program reviews through the NCATE process which could open avenues for further collaboration with APA at least at the doctoral level.

The NASP *Directory of School Psychology Graduate Programs* (Thomas, 1998) indicated that NASP/NCATE accredited 180 (61%) of the 294 reporting programs including 102 (53%) of the 194 specialist-level programs. At the doctoral level, NASP/NCATE or NASP/NCATE & APA accredited 78 (90%) of the 87 programs; APA only accredited programs accounted for 44 (51%). In the same analysis, virtually all programs held state department of education approval. However, 128 of the 294 programs (44%) are identified as having only SDE approval, suggesting that only about 56% of all programs hold some form of national accreditation.

The decisions of the NCATE and APA accrediting bodies provide an excellent source of information about school psychology programs. The APA annually publishes a list of accredited doctoral programs in the December issue of its *American Psychologist*. NCATE publishes its *Annual List*, which includes programs in school psychology at the doctoral and non-doctoral levels in the accredited education units. Because NCATE officially accredits the education unit and not specific programs within the unit, a school psychology program's listing in NCATE's *Annual List* does not in itself guarantee that the program met NASP guidelines. A list of those granted conditional or full approval by NASP in its review process is available from NASP and periodically published in the *Communiqué*. Listings of accredited programs and copies of the accreditation standards may be obtained by writing to the following organizations:

1. American Psychological Association, Education Directorate, Office of Program Consultation and Accreditation, 750 First St. NE, Washington, DC 20002-4242 (*www.apa.org/ed/accred.html*).
2. NCATE, 2010 Massachusetts Ave. NW, Suite 500, Washington, DC 20036-1023 (*ncate@ncate.org*).
3. NASP, 4340 East West Highway, Suite 402, Bethesda, MD 20814-9457 (*www.nasponline.org*).

State and Regional Accreditation

Several states have their own process of program approval whereby the SDE reviews school psychology programs either independently or concurrently with others' reviews (e.g., through NCATE partnerships). For a list of states employing program approval or partnership agreements contact NCATE, or the National

Association of State Consultants for School Psychological Services (contact NASP for the current address of the State School Psychology Consultants interest group). In almost all instances, the institution in which a school psychology program is located participates in regional accreditation. National accreditation is predicated on the institution holding proper regional accreditation. The names and addresses of the six regional accrediting bodies are available through most libraries or from NCATE. A historical overview of school psychology accreditation appears in Fagan and Wells (2000).

Paraprofessional Training

Issues of training and accreditation are directed only at sanctioned levels of preparation in school psychology. For the most part, these include the master's, specialist, and doctoral levels. The question has been raised occasionally as to whether or not there is a role for lesser-prepared school psychological personnel, often referred to as paraprofessionals. The paraprofessional "undergoes training involving certain limited aspects of a discipline and works alongside the professional under direction and supervision" (McManus, 1986, p. 10). Paraprofessionals perform a range of very specific skill-oriented tasks and may be trained at the bachelor's-degree level or less; in some instances school psychologists may even solicit students at the local district level. Gerken (1981) notes the early interest of NASP in paraprofessionals through its Competency Continuum of seven levels (NASP, 1973). She also notes that the practice has failed to gain widespread acceptability because of fears that paraprofessionals would reduce potential positions for better qualified school psychologists and perhaps erode the quality of services. McManus (1986) describes the use of student paraprofessionals in the areas of peer tutoring and counseling, record keeping, and assessment and reviews literature suggesting the benefits for consumers while expanding the role of the school psychologist to other activities. The paraprofessional concept attracted more attention in the early 1980s than in recent years. The reviews of Gerken (1981) and McManus (1986) are the most comprehensive available in the school psychology literature. Together they provide strong support for the concept and use of paraprofessionals to bolster and improve the delivery of school psychological services. They provide examples of successful models in several settings and guidelines for the use of paraprofessionals for those interested in establishing such practices in their own settings. Additional opinions are expressed in the NASP *Communiqué* (Vol. 9, No. 6, and Vol. 10, No. 6).

Tips for Students for Completing Their Program

Every program in every academic department exists in a bureaucratic institution of higher education. The experienced graduate student can tell the entering graduate student that there is more to graduating than just completing the courses and field experiences. The program's regimen of courses and experiences is the content of one's training, but there are many rules and regulations for actually completing the degree. These very important requirements are usually spelled out in the institution's graduate bulletin and/or in a departmental graduate student handbook. These official publications are the student's guide to degree completion. Read them carefully. The faculty is not responsible for making sure you have reviewed and/or followed them. For example, it is the student's responsibility to know how and when the thesis or dissertation is to be filed with the graduate school. It is important to know the requirements and procedures for the following:

1. Selecting an advisor and major professor
2. Preparing a degree plan
3. Registering for courses including changes of program
4. Taking leaves of absences
5. Being able to transfer credit, take experiential credit, and get credit by examination
6. Getting annual student evaluations
7. Securing financial support
8. Fulfilling expectations for students granted fellowships, research or graduate assistantships
9. Choosing a thesis and dissertation committee
10. Conducting and defending one's research, including clearance from departmental and institutional research review committees
11. Taking specialty examinations
12. Filing for graduation

In addition to graduation requirements, there are hurdles in the filing of one's materials for credentialing. Early in their training, new students should inquire about the process of filing for certification and licensure. This will avoid considerable difficulty at the end of the formal training period. This process is discussed in Chapter 7.

PRACTICAL EXERCISES

1. Prepare a summary of the history of the training program in which you are enrolled.
2. Would you describe your program's model of preparation as Scientist-Practitioner, Professional, or Pragmatic?
3. What is the nature of the accreditation held by your program?
4. What are the characteristics and backgrounds of students in your program?
5. By sampling school psychologists in your area, develop a list of desirable personal characteristics of the school psychologist. What characteristics are considered critical by the faculty in your training program and how are you judged on such characteristics?

6. By using the factors identified in Figure 6.1 and Table 6.3, provide a brief statement of the model employed by your training program.
7. How does your program ensure that students gain familiarity and understanding of the settings in which they will be employed and exposure to multicultural influences on education?
8. What resources are available in your program for selecting advanced training programs and for reviewing SDE and SBEP licensing requirements?
9. How do the emphases in content areas in your program compare to those of Table 6.4?
10. Are paraprofessionals used in your local school districts? If so, how are they trained, what tasks do they perform, and what has been the impact on the supervising school psychologist?
11. In districts with both doctoral and non-doctoral practitioners, can you identify differences in their respective roles and functions?

NOTES

1. Portions of this chapter appeared previously in a chapter by Fagan (1990a) and are reproduced here by permission of the National Association of School Psychologists.

2. The term subspecialty refers to an area of special proficiency or competency within the specialty of school psychology. The term "specialty" refers to the professional fields of clinical, counseling, school psychology, and others approved by the APA Commission for the Recognition of Specialties and Proficiencies in Professional Psychology (CRSPPP; Murray, 1995). In February, 1998, school psychology was among the first specialties to receive reapproval (Petition for Reaffirmation of the Specialty of School Psychology, 1997; Phelps, 1998).

3. Responses are based on a survey of 90 school psychology programs in the United States identified by the mailing list of the Council of Directors of School Psychology Programs (CDSPP) and/or Thomas (1998). The survey was conducted from October 1998 to February 1999. One program was discovered no longer to have a doctoral program in school psychology (Iowa State University), and returns were obtained from 84 of the remaining 89 known doctoral programs (94%). Programs that failed to respond were assigned to category 19a. The Canadian listings are based on a survey of the 17 programs identified in Brown and Lindstrom (1977) and information from personal communications.

4. All subspecialty areas identified in earlier surveys (1984 and 1989) are herein listed even though some were not reported by institutions in the 1989 and 1998 surveys. In contrast to the earlier surveys, an institution could specify a

"generalist orientation" with or without subspecialty areas. Some of these institutions offer concentrations or minors in certain areas but not subspecializations. Institutions were not required to provide documentation of the subspecializations they listed. Persons inquiring about training at any institution should request specific information about subspecializations.

The Regulation
of School Psychology[1]

The professional control and regulation of school psychology can be conceptualized in three spheres: accreditation, credentialing, and practice. In Chapter 6, we discussed the nature of training and identified its relationships with accreditation and credentialing. This chapter reviews the many factors that influence and regulate the field of school psychology including the preparation of students, how school psychologists are credentialed for practice, and the factors that influence their day-to-day roles and functions. The variables involved in the three spheres are interrelated but there is also considerable independence.

Unlike most other books about school psychology, this book does not have a separate chapter on legal/ethical aspects of the field. Legal/ethical issues are best understood in the context of regulation and daily practice. We have chosen to include such material in this chapter discussing overall professional regulation, and at other points in the book relevant to practice. We believe this provides a more integrated and comprehensible treatment of school psychology's regulation and brings such matters to bear on important issues of practice such as those discussed in Chapters 3 and 4. We recognize that all school psychologists will encounter legal and ethical aspects of their practice but that few will be involved in practice litigation. In contrast, all school psychologists face training and credentialing controls and are confronted by a complex array of variables, including legal/ethical variables, that influence their practice. We believe this integrated approach provides a more realistic picture of the circumstances readers will encounter. Further, comprehensive treatments of legal/ethical considerations are more readily available than in the past. These resources will be identified for further investigation.

Before we discuss the factors involved, consider what factors you believe influence or control (a) the programs by which you are prepared to become a school psychologist, (b) the requirements according to which you receive a credential to practice, and (c) roles and functions you will undertake on the job. On a piece of paper, list several factors for each of these three areas. After reading this chapter, compare your list to the factors discussed.

BACKGROUND AND INTRODUCTION

Professionalization

The twentieth century has witnessed the growth of several professions and their search for status through the achievement of various symbols (Hatch, 1988). Despite confusion over the meaning of the term profession, it is typically defined along lines of specialized knowledge, advanced training, practitioner independence and autonomy, and moral commitment. The professional "does not work in order to be paid, but is paid in order to work" (Hatch, 1988, p. 2). That psychology is a profession is no longer a matter of debate (Bevan, 1981; Fox, Barclay, & Rodgers, 1982; Petersen, 1976). Achieving professional status for psychology overall has included some unique features such as academic origins and field experiences and has involved the acquisition of the major symbols of professionalization, including (a) the organization of the members of the profession into an association, (b) an identifiable body of knowledge unique to the profession, (c) restricted access to this body of knowledge, (d) a code of professional conduct and ethics, (e) specialized training, (f) credentialing, (g) regulation of training practices, (h) professional autonomy in practice, (i) employment opportunities for professionals, and (j) a literature specific to the profession. School psychology, as a specialty area within psychology, also has acquired most of the major symbols of professionalization, and some even contend that it should be considered a separate profession. However, the same could be said of other specialty areas of psychology. It is generally accepted that the major professional psychology specialties (e.g., clinical, counseling, and school psychology) have long shared considerable knowledge and practice (Bardon, 1979; McKinley & Hayes, 1987) and, therefore, are not separate professions. Thus we customarily speak of the profession of psychology and the specialty of school psychology.

Increased professionalization is accompanied by increased regulation. Such regulation usually accords the profession greater prestige and respect because regulation implies that the field has advanced to a point where the public and the profession require protection from unqualified practitioners. The forms of professional regulation may be internal, like a code of ethics, as well as external to the field, like legislation and licensing laws. Even though the concept of professional regulation may have negative connotations such as increased regimentation and decreased flexibility, none of the established professions are without regulation. According to Schudson (1980), "What is distinctive about the professions is nothing intrinsic to the work of professionals but is simply the status-honor they somehow accrue....Social recognition is the crucial feature in defining a profession" (p. 218). In this chapter we discuss several factors that help to define school psychology as a major professional specialty of psychology while at the same time controlling the field in various ways.

Emergence of Regulation

The present structure of factors influencing regulation of school psychology evolved over several decades. As observed in Chapter 2, the earliest national credential for psychologists was that granted through the short-lived APA certification program of the 1920s. State-level regulation of school psychology originated in the 1930s with state department of education (SDE) certification standards in New York and Pennsylvania. These were the earliest state-level attempts to regulate the manner by which one became credentialed to practice school psychology. The certification standards were no doubt influenced by existing training in those states and laws regulating the examination of children for the provision of special educational programs for the mentally retarded. The SDE certification standards were intended for, and limited to, psychological service providers within the jurisdiction of the SDE, typically the public schools. Following World War II, psychologists began to be licensed for private practice by a separate state-level board of examiners in psychology (SBEP), whose jurisdiction was statewide with broad practice exemptions for government agencies including the public schools. The separate credentialing models by SDE and SBEP were employed in other states, and by the late 1970s both avenues of credentialing were available in almost every state. Each model was aligned with state and national education or psychology groups creating two separate networks of credentialing standards and practices for school psychologists.

Somewhat later, primarily in the 1960s and 1970s, the regulation of school psychology training programs through national accreditation was initiated. In some states, official SDE program approval linked to its own certification regulations preceded national level accreditation. For example, the SDE would review a training program for school psychological examiners/school psychologists and officially designate the program as having met its requirements for certification. Graduates of an approved program would thereby be "entitled" to certification for practice in the settings under the jurisdiction of the SDE. Because public education was regulated and represented through state-level organizations and agencies that were aligned with national-level groups, national accreditation of training programs in the arena of education, including school psychology, was brought under the jurisdiction of education accreditors. Currently the major education accreditor is the National Council for Accreditation of Teacher Education

(NCATE), which was formed from a merger of other education groups in 1954, and began reviewing school psychology programs in the 1960s (Fagan & Wells, 2000).

The psychology arena developed as a separate entity with its own state-level regulatory and representative groups and agencies. These state-level groups and agencies also had national level counterparts (e.g., APA) that developed a system of accreditation for professional psychology. The major psychology sector accreditor is the American Psychological Association (APA), which has held exclusive authority to accredit doctoral programs in professional psychology since the late 1940s. To our knowledge, state-level program approval by the SBEP (like that of the SDE) has never existed in the psychology sector. That is, state psychology boards have never been in the business of reviewing training programs and formally approving them. Instead, state psychology boards have relied on the accreditation and recognition processes of APA, regional accreditors, or other groups. The accreditation of programs specifically in school psychology by NCATE or APA became better defined during the 1970s. The APA accredited its first school psychology program in 1971. Although the NCATE-NASP relationship dates to the early 1970s, NCATE's accreditation of school psychology programs employing NASP standards did not occur until the early 1980s. Today almost all school psychology training programs hold SDE program approval and/or national level accreditation (Thomas, 1998). Discussions of historical aspects of credentialing and accreditation appear in Fagan and Wells (2000) and Pryzwansky (1993).

The regulation of day-to-day practice is less clear in our history. Although guidelines for school psychology practice have been in existence for just the past few decades, the American Psychological Association published its first statement of professional ethics in 1953 (APA, 1953). Several revisions have been published, and the 1992 edition appears in Appendix C. The National Association of School Psychologists ethical principles were first published in 1974 (NASP, 1974), revised in 1984 (NASP, 1984a) and 1992 (NASP, 1992), and the most recent 1997 revision (NASP, 1997a) appears in Appendix D. Many other factors influence day-to-day practice including local employment circumstances, legislation, litigation, and funding.

In summary, the regulation of school psychology is a mixture of factors in the arenas of education and psychology for credentialing, accreditation, and practice. In the historical evolution of regulation, we observe the duality of control evident in so many aspects of the field of school psychology that have created "two worlds" of school psychology, education and psychology.

Structure of Accreditation and Credentialing

The complexity of these historical relationships is observed in Figure 7.1. As mentioned in Chapter 6, persons understanding the relationships among the organizations, committees, agencies, and programs represented here should have little difficulty recognizing the complex nature of accrediting and credentialing in school psychology (Fagan, 1986c). The structure of these relationships can be understood by reviewing the summary analysis in Figure 7.2. Imagine that Figure 7.2 is superimposed on Figure 7.1. What emerges are two major areas of quality control in the profession: (a) accreditation, the procedure for evaluating the preparation of persons desiring to function as, and refer to themselves as, school psychologists; and (b) credentialing, the procedure for granting titles and functions to persons following the completion of their professional preparation. In recent years, SDEs have further confused the credentialing arena by increasingly using the term "license" instead of "certification" as the credential it grants. For purposes of simplification, throughout our discussion we shall use the term "SDE license" to refer to practice credentials granted by the state department of education and the term "SBEP license" to refer to practice credentials granted by the state board of examiners in psychology. In some states the SDE or the SBEP credential is still referred to as a certificate. The range of titles employed by the SDE or SBEP appears in Curtis, Hunley, and Prus (1998).

A few guidelines will assist in understanding the relationships described by these two figures.

1. Recall our discussion of power and authority in Chapter 3. In Figure 7.1 dotted lines represent power relationships and solid lines represent authority relationships regardless of the extent of power that may coexist. Inspection of Figure 7.1 reveals a considerably greater number of power than authority relationships involved in accreditation and credentialing. Although it often seems to be a necessity, decisions to get involved in accreditation or credentialing are in fact strictly voluntary for training programs, agencies, associations, and individuals. There may be serious consequences for nonparticipation but the process is voluntary.

2. North-South Relationships: Organization, committee, and agency relationships in the top portion of the chart (north) relate to accreditation; those in the bottom portion of the chart (south) relate to credentialing. Relationships in the north portion of the chart are typically conducted at the national level whereas those in the south portion are typically conducted at the state level. Note that there is no authoritative link between the north and the south. That is, the regulation of credentialing is largely independent of the regulation of training. Nevertheless considerable powerful and influential relationships exist between the sectors. These relationships appear in Figure 2.

3. East-West Relationships: Organization, committee, and agency relationships in the left portion (west) of the chart relate to established structures and policies of education. Those on the right portion (east)

of the chart relate to psychology. Note that there is little authoritative link between the east and the west. That is, the regulation of psychology is largely independent of the regulation of education. Within both the education and the psychology sectors, there are much stronger cross-regional relationships running north and south than east and west. That is, state-level education and psychology groups tend to have closest ties to national level education and psychology groups, and generally weak east-west relationships exist at both levels.

4. Mediating Forces: Few agencies are positioned to mediate effectively across education and psychology arenas either for accreditation or credentialing. At the national level, the Association of Specialized and Professional Accreditors (ASPA, founded in 1993) can serve this purpose for accreditation. At the state level, the legislature may serve a mediating function for matters of credentialing. For example, conflicts between SDE and SBEP licensing laws or regulations may have to be mediated by legislative action or by the efforts of other government agencies.

Let us now look at the three main areas of professional regulation: accreditation, credentialing, and practice.

ACCREDITATION

It is through the process of accreditation that doctoral and non-doctoral programs of preparation achieve recognition as having met national standards of program quality. The common characteristics of programs and their areas of evaluation were identified in Chapter 6. As observed in Figure 7.1, With the exception of the training programs themselves, the major forces influencing accreditation operate at the national level (see northern portion). At present, the main national-level forces involved in the accreditation of school psychology programs include ASPA, NCATE, APA, and the APA/NASP Interorganizational Committee (IOC).

ASPA

Originally founded in 1949 as the National Commission on Accrediting, a Council on Postsecondary Accreditation (COPA) was founded in 1975 to identify qualified accreditors in numerous fields. COPA recognized and monitored "dozens of organizations across the country that, in turn, set standards for colleges and universities or prescribe criteria for programs in a wide range of disciplines" (Jacobsen, 1980, p. 10). Generally, COPA designated one organization to have exclusive accrediting authority within a field, and through periodic review ensured

FIGURE 7.1 Power and authority for accreditation and credentialing in school psychology

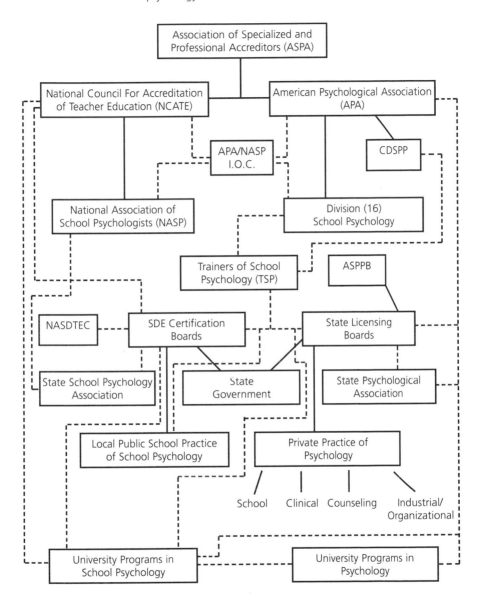

SOURCE: "School Psychology's Dilemma: Reappraising Solutions and Directing Attention to the Future" by T.K. Fagan, 1986, *American Psychologist, 41. pp.*851-861. Copyright 1986 by the American Psychological Association. Reprinted by permission.

FIGURE 7.2 Power and authority relationships among the four major areas of control in the accreditation and credentialing process

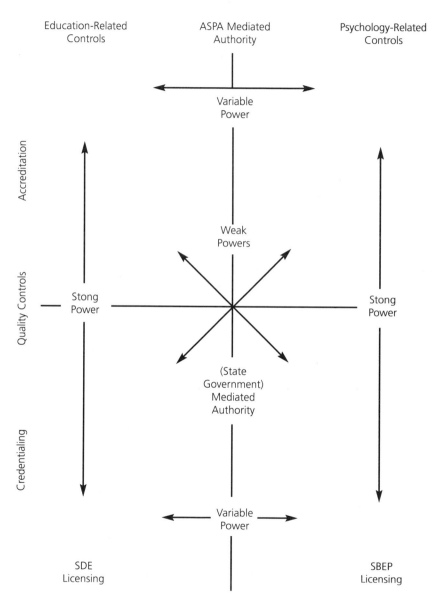

Education-Related Controls

ASPA Mediated Authority

Psychology-Related Controls

Variable Power

Accreditation

Weak Powers

Quality Controls

Stong Power

Stong Power

(State Government) Mediated Authority

Credentialing

Variable Power

SDE Licensing

SBEP Licensing

SOURCE: "School Psychology's Dilemma: Reappraising Solutions and Directing Attention to the Future" by T.K. Fagan, 1986, *American Psychologist, 41. pp.*851-861. Copyright 1986 by the American Psychological Association. Reprinted by permission.

that the accreditor was performing appropriately. COPA was dissolved in 1993 and a new group, the Association of Specialized and Professional Accreditors (ASPA), was formed to continue these accrediting responsibilities. For their part, accreditors require institutions or programs to conduct self-studies and be reviewed by the accreditor at regular intervals. This includes the submission of detailed reports for review and on-site review by a team of evaluators representing the accrediting organization. Recognition by ASPA means the accreditor has developed quality standards, broadly represents the professionals in that field, has the resources and motivation to conduct accreditation activities, and its accreditation does not seriously conflict with any existing accreditor recognized by ASPA. Although the accrediting agencies are part of a voluntary, nongovernmental process, their decisions influence government funding agencies, scholarship commissions, employers, and potential students. "Accrediting bodies have, therefore, come to be viewed as quasi-public entities with certain responsibilities to the many groups which interact with the educational community" (Chernay, n.d., p. 1).

Overlapping Authority of APA and NCATE

Some fields appear to lend themselves to rather simple designation of exclusive accrediting authority. Psychology is more complex. While APA has exclusive authority to accredit in the professional fields of clinical, counseling, and school psychology, other organizations have authority to accredit practitioners in related areas of practice. For example, the Council For Accreditation of Counseling and Related Educational Programs (CACREP) (in part related to the American Counseling Association (ACA)) accredits in the field of counseling, and the Council on Rehabilitation Education (CRE) accredits rehabilitation counselors. Thus overlaps exist in accreditation for fields related to counseling.

The NCATE/NASP accreditation relationship is an example of accrediting authority which overlaps with that of the APA in the field of school psychology. APA's authority to accredit clinical and counseling psychology programs has existed since the late 1940s. NCATE was formed in 1954 and granted authority to accredit in all fields of teacher education. Conflicts arose in the late 1960s when NCATE was already reviewing programs in school psychology and when APA was seeking to extend its authority to school psychology. NCATE was broadening its authority to include all programs leading to SDE credentials (in both instructional and non-instructional fields) regardless of the administrative location of the program on campus. Thus its reviews were no longer confined to colleges of education but included school psychology programs regardless of their academic location, and all programs were either in a college of education or a psychology department in a separate college. The intensity of the conflicting authority for accreditation in school psychology heightened in the late 1970s leading to the formation of the APA-NASP Task Force in 1978 (the name was changed several years later to the APA/NASP-Interorganizational Committee, or IOC). It was the task of this group to seek an acceptable means of managing the conflicts in doctoral level accreditation. As indicated in Chapter 6, the conflict though presently unresolved, is far less intense. The IOC serves an important function of mediating differences between NASP and APA on matters of credentialing as well as accreditation standards. It has no accreditation authority nor does it directly regulate such matters. The type of conflict experienced between APA and NCATE/NASP has not been as problematic between APA and CACREP or CRE because they are not purporting to accredit in a field whose professional programs and titles include the term "psychologist." Historical information about the IOC may be found in Fagan (1993), and Fagan and Wells (2000).

Diversity of Influence and Representation

Other groups that may influence the process of accreditation include the Division of School Psychology-APA, NASP, and organizations of trainers including the Council of Directors of School Psychology Programs (CDSPP), and Trainers of School Psychologists (TSP). The means by which these groups influence the accreditation process are many and varied. Typically they influence the development and revision of accreditation standards, and the policies and procedures for their implementation and enforcement. In our opinion, the most important indirect groups are Division 16 and NASP, which have direct power relationships to APA and NCATE, respectively. However, it must be understood that the authority to accredit rests exclusively with APA and NCATE; all others in the arena, excluding ASPA, have only power relationships to these accreditors. The CDSPP, representing doctoral programs only, has close power alliances with APA and Division 16, and supports APA policies regarding the doctoral degree as the appropriate entry-level for credentialing with the title "professional psychologist." TSP, representing both doctoral and non-doctoral programs, is an unaligned organization. Where CDSPP has direct access into Division 16 and APA accreditation networks, TSP does not, nor does it have access into the networks of NCATE/NASP. For the most part, TSP has had only minor influence on accreditation. For historical discussion of CDSPP and TSP see Phillips (1993).

Where accreditation is concerned, there are relatively few organizations directly involved in either the education sector (northwest) or psychology sector (northeast). Presumably, of course, those involved represent a broad constituency in school psychology. However, the major accreditors themselves (APA and NCATE), representing a wide variety of psychologists and educator groups, afford those groups substantial influence on school psychology accreditation. For example, APA accreditation criteria and procedures are determined by APA's governing body upon recommendation of the APA Committee on Accreditation and the Office of

Program Consultation and Accreditation in the APA Education Directorate. The Committee's membership represents five domains (with number of members in parentheses): graduate departments of psychology (4), professional schools and training programs (10), professional practice (4), the general public (2), and consumers of education and training (1) (APA, 1996b). All NCATE criteria and procedures (NCATE, 1997) are approved by the NCATE Council representing teacher education organizations, teacher organizations, policymaker organizations, subject-specific organizations, child-centered organizations, technology organizations, specialist organizations (e.g., NASP), administrator organizations, and others (e.g., National Board for Professional Teaching Standards). Despite considerable compatibility of the APA and NASP accreditation standards at the doctoral level, significant differences between the APA and NCATE are the controlling influence of non-psychologists on the enforcement of NASP standards via NCATE, and the lack of educator influence on school psychology accreditation via the APA. School psychology's direct influence is limited to CDSPP representation to APA's Committee on Accreditation, and one NASP representative to the NCATE Council.

Accreditation Conflicts and Issues

The following aspects of school psychology accreditation help to clarify the nature of conflicts and issues involved.

1. APA develops its accreditation standards for professional psychology generically (APA, 1996b). It does not have specific school psychology standards, but rather applies its generic standards to specific specialties of professional psychology through on-site program reviews. A three-member team reviews program materials, makes an on-site visit, and reports its findings/recommendations to APA's Committee on Accreditation for final action. APA accredits in the fields of clinical, counseling, and school psychology only at the doctoral level; and it has no authority to accredit programs at subdoctoral levels. Thus accreditation conflicts between APA and NCATE/NASP apply only to the doctoral level. APA also has authority for separately accrediting psychology internship centers (APA, 1996b). APA does not accredit nonprofessional programs such as those in experimental psychology. In recent years, there has been growth in the number of accredited combined specialty programs (e.g., counseling and school) and encouragement for more growth (Beutler & Fisher, 1994; Minke & Brown, 1996). Finally, APA is a multipurpose professional association of which accreditation is but one activity.

2. In contrast to APA, NCATE is a single-purpose organization which exists exclusively to conduct accrediting activities on behalf of the many

groups represented on its governing council. NCATE holds ASPA recognition to accredit teacher education institutions and programs at both the undergraduate and graduate levels including doctoral preparation. NCATE standards are applicable to an entire education unit (e.g., college of education) while employing the guidelines of several specialty groups or state partnerships to review specific program areas. Although NASP has both doctoral and specialist school psychology training standards (NASP, 1994c), NASP has no authority to independently accredit school psychology programs. As a constituent member of NCATE, NASP is permitted to have its training guidelines promoted and enforced via the authority of the NCATE accreditation process. As mentioned in Chapter 6, NASP employs a review process for approval of school psychology programs. Although this process is an important part of NCATE's overall accreditation review of an institution, in most instances this process does not include a specific on-site review of the school psychology program by trained NASP evaluators. However, through NCATE partnerships with states, specific program reviews may be conducted by a team of state-level evaluators selected by the SDE and this team would be more likely to include a school psychologist. The pros and cons of these reviews are discussed in Fagan and Wells (2000). There are trade-offs in being reviewed for accreditation by APA and NCATE/NASP. APA employs generic standards and a site review, whereas NCATE/NASP employs specific standards but a site review is not required. At the non-doctoral level, NCATE/NASP is the only accreditation available in school psychology. It remains, however, that NASP's official designation represents primarily a "paper review."

3. An agreement between NCATE and NASP allows NASP separately to approve programs at institutions that do not participate in the NCATE accreditation process, or which have been denied NCATE unit accreditation. With the large number of non-doctoral specialist-level programs in school psychology, NASP's approval from NCATE to identify NASP approved programs separately marked an important shift in the recognition of NASP standards. This was an approval and not an accrediting agreement, and NASP has no authority to accredit. It is uncertain if additional changes allowing NASP greater influence, and perhaps even authority in the accreditation of programs, will occur in the future.

4. In 1991 NCATE/NASP agreed that if a program already held APA accreditation, it could receive a streamlined process of NASP review within the NCATE process. If the APA accredited program is graduat-

ing students whose internships meet NASP standards for school experience, NCATE/NASP approval is reasonably assured. However, APA does not offer reciprocal approval for NCATE/NASP accredited doctoral programs.

5. Although APA accredits internship sites, NASP does not. NASP internship standards are incorporated into the training standards that are promoted via NCATE. Training programs are responsible for ensuring that the internships of its students meet NASP internship standards. Separate approval of internships is not part of the NCATE/NASP accreditation process.

Acquiring Accreditation

A simplified chronological sequence of obtaining accreditation follows. First, a program is established with identifiable philosophy and goals, curriculum, faculty, facilities, policies, and student body. After graduating several students, the program voluntarily applies for accreditation. Sometimes a pre-review visit is made by a consultant to determine the feasibility of going forward with accreditation at that time. If considered ready for formal review, a period of self-study leads to the preparation of a program report which is submitted to the accreditor (APA or NCATE/NASP). In the APA process, the program's materials are evaluated and a site visit is made. Following the visit, the visiting team makes recommendations to the APA. After further review, including opportunities for the program to rejoin the accreditor's report, the program is granted or denied accreditation. In the NCATE process, NASP program approval is only one part of the overall education unit accreditation process of NCATE. The program folio is submitted directly to NASP for review. The results of the review are conveyed to NCATE and the program. The program will have an opportunity to respond to NASP's decisions regarding program weaknesses before a final decision is reached about the program's approval status. In both processes, the length of time from initial request to a final decision could be 2–3 years. Reaccreditation reviews, including site visits, are conducted periodically (e.g., 5–10 years).

Pros and Cons of Accreditation

Programs that identify themselves as APA and/or NCATE/NASP accredited have passed a rigorous review and by supposition can be relied upon to provide quality preparation. Accreditation allows the institution and program to advertise itself accordingly, and its students to boast that they have graduated from an accredited program. Of course, such a stamp of approval is no guarantee that accredited programs prepare better school psychologists than those prepared through unaccredited programs. Nevertheless, on average, such assurance seems logical and does guarantee that a required pattern of studies is provided. The achievement of accreditation is a clear indication that a field has progressed to a point where its practitioners require various forms of regulation. Accreditation is among the more powerful symbols of professionalization.

Although accreditation affords training programs several privileges, the sacrifice is sometimes considered too great. Program accreditation can be financially expensive, require extensive faculty time in preparation and review, and necessitate arranging the curriculum to others' expectations. For these reasons, some institutions have chosen not to participate in national accreditation. The penalties for nonparticipation vary. Some students may be deterred from applying to the program because the absence of accreditation suggests lower quality or because of concern that it will make more difficult their later efforts to get credentialed. There is also a potential loss of prestige for the program and its institution. The program might also not qualify for SDE approval and/or its graduates might not be acceptable for state certification and/or licensure. For these and other reasons, most school psychology programs hold some form of national accreditation, and virtually all hold SDE approval. A study by Wells and Fagan (1999) compared recent APA accredited and non-APA accredited doctoral program graduates. The findings raise questions about the value of accreditation for doctoral program graduates. For example, there were no statistically significant differences observed for obtaining APA accredited internship sites, practice credentials obtained, employment settings and salaries. With accreditors shifting to require outcome data on graduates, these results suggest that at least some outcomes have unclear relationships to the training process.

Other Influences

Formal accreditation is not the only aspect of control or regulation over training. A less formal review process is that of "designation" (Pryzwansky & Wendt, 1987). Conducted jointly by the Association of State and Provincial Psychology Boards (ASPPB) and the Council for the National Register of Health Service Providers in Psychology (National Register), doctoral programs in professional psychology are voluntarily reviewed for inclusion in an annual publication, *Doctoral Psychology Programs Meeting Designation Criteria*. The National Register employs several criteria for designation, many of which correspond closely to those for APA accreditation. The purpose of designation is to provide assurance that a doctoral program is basically psychological in nature, a concept that corresponds closely to the language of many state licensing laws. Designation facilitates the work of state licensing boards, all of whom are members of the ASPPB.

Of course, other factors also influence the manner in which students are prepared. The internship experience is very important (see Chapter 8). The nature of this influence is expressed in the accreditation or approval criteria for internships promoted by APA (1996b), Association of Psychology Postdoctoral and Internship Centers (1997), and NASP (1994c). However, among the direct controlling variables of preparation for employment, national accreditation, designation, and SDE program approval are paramount. Another important direct factor is the orientation of the student's training program and its faculty (this aspect was discussed in Chapter 6). Among the indirect factors influencing preparation for employment are SDE credentialing requirements; the position statements, policies, and standards of APA, NASP, ASPPB and state associations of school psychologists; the SDE rules and regulations for the approval of training programs; and the regulation of practice. In combination, these forces strongly influence, and in some instances dictate, the type of curriculum, faculty, facilities, and policies of graduate training in school psychology. The influence can result in a highly prescriptive training program (recall the Pragmatic Model) designed to meet the non-doctoral accreditation criteria of NCATE/NASP and the approval criteria of the SDE. Accreditation and approval are important because of their close relationship to another major area of regulation, credentialing.

CREDENTIALING

The importance of credentialing to the status of a profession cannot be overstated. The current widespread practice of SDE and SBEP licensure in school psychology is a clear recognition of the professional accomplishments of our field. Three types of credentials are available to school psychologists: practice credentials for the school sector via SDE licensure, practice credentials for the non-school sector via SBEP licensure, and non-practice credentials including the diploma from the American Board of School Psychology (ABSP) and National Certification in School Psychology (NCSP). Practice credentials legally authorize an individual to use particular titles and/or to render particular services; thus the credentialing agencies control titles and practice. For discussions of the variety of credentials offered in school psychology see Prasse (1988), Pryzwansky (1993, 1999), and Pryzwansky and Wendt (1987).

Practice Credentials

Almost all states offer an SDE credential to practice school psychological services. The requirements for SDE licensure vary, with titles and practice responsibilities often aligned with degree and field experiences. Though many states license at one title and degree level only (e.g., "school psychologist": master's or specialist degree), several have multiple levels and titles. A few states provide SDE licensing in conjunction with, or dependent upon, SBEP licensing. Most SDE overall rules and regulations for the schools include comprehensive descriptions of services to be provided by school psychological personnel (e.g., assessment, consultation, counseling). In states with multiple levels of licensing, the lower levels may correspond to limited service provision (e.g., assessment only). A few states operate a career ladder approach with different levels of licensing related to peer reviews and experience though still employing one title. For example, in the past decade Tennessee school psychologists, licensed by the SDE at the non-doctoral level, participated in the SDE's career ladder of three levels, with master school psychologist at Level III. Levels II and III were attained by passing peer review evaluations, and were accompanied by higher salaries. The title "school psychologist" and the functions permitted were the same at each level. The future of Tennessee's career ladder program is in doubt due to funding cuts.

SBEP licensing is generally at 1 level, psychologist, or 2 levels, psychologist, and psychological examiner or associate, aligned with the doctoral and master's degrees, respectively. Some states also license with specialty designations (e.g., clinical, or school psychologist) at one or more levels. The influence of managed medical care has accompanied the increasing use of the designation, "health service provider" (HSP) for qualified professional psychologists. In general, the HSP holds the doctoral level license from the SBEP and any additional qualifications to be granted that title (Pryzwansky, 1999). An HSP designation may be necessary for insurance program reimbursement as a professional psychologist.

As a general rule, single level licensure, such as doctoral level with the title "psychologist," is accompanied by broad definitions of practice, even when specialty designations are included in the license. In theory, professional psychologists are expected to confine their practice to their areas of competency in accord with their professional ethics. In effect, the credential brings together the psychologist's individual training and competencies with the profession's code of behavior. In states having more than one level of licensure, the limits of practice for psychological examiners or associates are typically spelled out in the law or in its regulations. In some states, there are also practice descriptions and/or limitations for the doctoral level. A few states have specialty licenses for school psychologists at non-doctoral levels to practice in the non-school sector, and limits of practice are often included. A detailed analysis of licensing as it pertains to school psychology appears in Prasse (1988), and state-by-state requirements appear in Curtis, Hunley, and Prus (1998). Because most school psychologists hold non-doctoral degrees, an SDE practice credential is most common (see Chapter 1). Among non-practice credentials, the NCSP is the most widely held. Though rare exceptions can be found, generally speaking, none of the available credentials require postdoctoral academic training, and paraprofessional credentials are unavailable. However, a postdoctoral year of supervised experience is often required for SBEP licensing.

Conflicting Positions of APA and NASP

Despite numerous variations in state-level certification and licensing, the basic controversy surrounding school psychology credentialing is related to the title and practice accorded the doctoral and non-doctoral levels, positions that are aligned with the APA and NASP, respectively. The APA reserves the title "school psychologist" for persons holding the doctoral degree and meeting the licensing requirements of the SBEP. The APA's position is intended to apply to the school sector as well; that is, APA advocates the doctoral level for the title school psychologist via SDE licensing. Non-doctoral persons should be allowed to practice only with other titles (e.g., school psychological examiner) and under the supervision of doctoral level psychologists. On the other hand, NASP advocates that for the entry-level credential, the title "school psychologist" be granted in both the school and non-school sectors to persons holding the specialist degree or its equivalent (60 semester hours) including an internship. To attain the independent practice level, the entry-level school psychologist should be supervised for 1 year of post-degree practice and complete continuing professional development consistent with NASP credentialing standards (NASP, 1994a).

The standards of APA and NASP represent more their ideologies than the state of the art. Few states credential according to the NASP positions, although the non-doctoral level is practically universal for school practice and is recognized for non-school practice in several states. In the SBEP licensing arena, APA guidelines are followed in most states though variations are common. The close alignment of APA standards and state psychology licensing laws demonstrates the importance of power relationships between the national and state levels for both accreditation and credentialing. Eventually NASP would like to command similar influence in the SDE and the SBEP credentialing arenas. However, such influence in the SDE arena has been gradual, and in the SBEP arena it continues to be a long way off. The APA-SBEP accreditation and credentialing relationship has led to efforts to alleviate inconsistencies between changing accreditation and licensing requirements. In the past 40 years, changes in these areas have occurred which make it difficult for licensing boards to evaluate the preparation of persons who obtained their degrees many years before. In 1992, the APA Council of Representatives approved guidelines for the evaluation of persons prepared prior to 1979 (APA Education Directorate, personal communication, 1992). The guidelines emphasize the importance of regional accreditation of the training institution, a dissertation that is primarily psychological in nature, and the equivalent of a one-year supervised internship experience.

The controversy between NASP and APA, often referred to as the "doctoral issue," is as related to professional titles as to degrees. Titles appear in laws and regulations related to third-party insurance reimbursements for services. In most states, such privileges are reserved for those with the title "psychologist." When the term "psychologist" appears in the titles of practitioners with different levels of preparation, debates over service provision and privileges gain in intensity. Also involved are issues of status and identity as a professional psychologist. These conflicts in credentialing "may be the most emotionally laden aspect of APA's position on non-doctoral school psychologists" (Engin, 1983, pp. 38-39). Discussions of the doctoral issue appear in Bardon (1983), Fagan (1986c; 1993), Trachtman (1981), and *School Psychology Review*, (Vol. 16, No. 1, 1987 and Vol. 18, No. 1, 1989). For background discussions of the training and credentialing perspectives of the APA see Pryzwansky (1982), and for NASP see Engin and Johnson (1983).

The overlapping authority observed between education and psychology agencies in the accreditation arena is observed in the credentialing arena as well (see bottom half of Figure 7.1). Unlike accreditation entanglements, the overlap in credentialing has been managed in most states by restricting credentials to certain locales of practice. Thus the SDE credential applies only to the jurisdiction of the SDE, usually public school agencies. Recognition of the SDE's authority to credential its own personnel is observed by the presence of exemptions for SDE credentialed school psychologists and counselors in state SBEP licensing laws and in the APA's model licensure act (APA, 1987a). The exemptions allow school psychological personnel to use their titles and perform their functions so long as such are confined to the jurisdiction of the SDE. In some states, the SDE's authority also extends to private schools.

The differing SDE and SBEP credentialing requirements have created conflicts for school psychologists in most states. Although exemptions allow them to practice in the schools, many desire to extend their practice to the non-school sector without having to attain a doctoral degree. This has led to several confrontations among state psychology and school psychology associations, state departments of education, and state licensing boards. One of the most combative credentialing controversies in recent years occurred in Texas in 1995-1996. The Texas controversy involved issues of titles and degrees as well as jurisdictional authority of different boards and at different times. Published discussions of this case are instructive on the complicated issue of credentialing (Clay, 1996; Curtis, Batsche, and Tanous, 1996; Hughes, 1996). This and other confrontations have resulted in amended SDE and SBEP credentialing laws, broader exemptions, and other "creative credentialing" pursuits to allow limited non-school practice privileges. Although such efforts have resulted in the desired practice extensions in several states, these practitioners have not been accorded the same privileges as those granted to doctoral licensed psychologists (e.g., third-party insurance reimbursement).

Another avenue to non-school practice has been through credentials created for non-doctoral practitioners in fields related to school psychology, notably mental health and counseling. For example the North American Association of Masters in Psychology (NAMP, founded in 1994) offers its Nationally Certified Psychologist credential. The American Counseling Association (ACA) has supported the creation of non-doctoral credentials such as the Licensed Professional Counselor and the Licensed Marriage and

Family Therapist. The ACA and its state affiliates have been successful in their efforts in many states. The American Mental Health Counselors Association (AMHCA) advocates on behalf of non-doctoral counselors but does not offer a specific credential. These alternative avenues may allow school-based school psychologists to offer some of their services (e.g., counseling) beyond the school sector, but only within the limits of the regulations for these credentials, the personal competence of the practitioner, and without the use of the title "school psychologist." The NAMP certificate, initiated in 1998, is not a practice credential but rather a recognition credential similar to NASP's NCSP. The options for counselor licensure among school psychologists is discussed by Crespi and Fischetti (1997).

Linking Training with Credentialing

The relationships between training and credentialing can virtually dictate the type of professional title and practice one will have. It is as important to understand these relationships as it is to grasp other aspects of professional preparation. Students should be knowledgeable about the state(s) in which they plan to practice because most of the relationships in the education sector lead to SDE credentialing while those in the psychology sector lead to non-school-based and private credentialing, and because these credentialing mechanisms are authoritatively regulated at the state level. Although commonalities exist among SDE and SBEP credentialing authorities, reciprocity of credentials and/or equivalence of credentialing requirements in school psychology is the exception, not the norm. Two examples demonstrate the importance of the decisions involved and the relationships in Figure 7.1.

In the first example, student "A" is interested in employment as a school psychologist in his home state, has no interest in non-school setting practice, and is not committed at this time to pursuing a lengthy program of graduate preparation leading to a doctoral degree. Familiar with the non-doctoral nature of SDE credentialing in his home state and the fact that the SDE closely scrutinizes the programs of preparation, "A" selects an institution that holds both NCATE/NASP accreditation at the specialist level and SDE program approval, a state-level mechanism of quality control available in several states. Upon completion of the program, "A" is automatically endorsed for SDE credentialing by his institution and the SDE subsequently grants him its practice credential. "A" is now authorized to practice as a school psychologist in the public school systems of that state. Depending on the similarity of the home state's requirements to those of other states, "A" may or may not be eligible to obtain similar credentials elsewhere. Nor is "A" authorized, or eligible, for non-school practice as a school psychologist because SBEP credentialing requirements in his state do not specify a non-doctoral credential. Should "A" move to another state with different credentialing requirements, no reciprocity with his current SDE, and a doctoral-level-only SBEP licensure requirement, "A" could be without any credential to continue independently delivering psychological services.

In the second example, student "B" is interested in maximizing flexibility in the marketplace and seeks preparation for school and non-school based practice, while retaining the title "school psychologist" in both sectors. "B" wants to practice in the same state as "A" but is interested in subspecializing in a particular area of school psychology. "B" selects an out-of-state institution that holds NCATE accreditation at the doctoral and non-doctoral levels, APA accreditation in school psychology at the doctoral level, and an advanced graduate concentration in the desired subspecialty. "B" also notes that the program requirements readily match those for credentialing of her home state's SDE. Upon completion of the doctoral degree which included an approved one-year internship, "B" returns to her home state and makes application for both SDE and SBEP credentialing. After completing additional written and oral examination requirements of the SBEP, "B" is credentialed to practice independently as a school psychologist in school and non-school settings, and privately. Should "B" choose to move to another state, it is very likely that additional credentials for both school and non-school practice could be obtained with a minimum of additional examination or other requirements. However, a year of postdoctoral supervised practice might be required for an SBEP credential. Credentialing to practice in the schools would be virtually guaranteed in every state.

The examples demonstrate the manner in which two persons, defining their goals differently, achieve appropriate training. Many variations of these patterns could be employed to show the intricate relationships among training, accreditation, and credentialing. For instance, had the home state provided non-doctoral credentialing for school psychologists to practice in the non-school sector, or had all credentialing of school psychologists been under the control of the State Board of Examiners in Psychology, each person may have made different choices for training. Thus it is important for prospective entry-level and advanced students to consider the credentialing requirements of their chosen state(s) and the accreditation status of the training program. Even before entering training, students should consider the state(s) in which they will later seek practice, and whether they desire to work primarily in the school or non-school sector.

Acquiring Credentials

The procedure for securing one's credential is straightforward. In the case of the SDE credential, two routes are most common. In states without SDE program approval, or for persons entering from out-of-state, one may submit an application, including transcripts, evidence of internship, and program completion statement, directly to the credentialing office in the SDE. This process, sometimes called transcript review, matches your application materials to the SDE's requirements and a credential is issued, or deferred pending clarifications, or denied. In states with program approval, applicants submit materials through the credentialing office of the college of education at the institution in which they completed their approved training program. Out-of-state applicants may have to do the same through one of the approved programs in the state to which they have moved. In these instances, one's application materials are matched against the requirements of the approved program through which one seeks certification. The dean of the college of education or designated representative serves as the institution's credentialing officer to the SDE. The college of education gathers the applicant's materials and, after its review, forwards them with a recommendation for credentialing to the SDE. According to the approved program concept, the applicant's materials are not forwarded to the SDE until every requirement of the approved program appears to have been met. The SDE works out any problems directly with the college of education, which in turn works them out with the applicant. Our experience has been that securing SDE credentialing can take 1–3 months after the completion of one's training. Students are encouraged to contact the college of education about its procedures well in advance of completing the program. In either process, transcript review or program approval, out-of-state applicants often encounter some deficiencies in their training compared with the new SDE's requirements. In some cases, additional coursework must be completed prior to being approved for credentialing in the new state. To the extent possible, it is important for students to match their training program to the SDE requirements of the state(s) in which they desire employment. The SDE credential is periodically renewed according to state requirements. Since the mid-1990s several states have required new applicants to undergo a criminal history check through the state's bureau of investigation.

Securing a credential by way of the state board of examiners in psychology (SBEP) is almost always a completely separate procedure from that for securing a credential from the SDE. Application materials are sent directly to the SBEP, usually located in the state capital. Requirements for SBEP credentialing involve specific degrees, field experiences, letters of recommendation, and a passing score on the Examination for Professional Practice in Psychology (EPPP). For the initial credential, the SBEP reviews the person's degree and field experiences and makes a determination about eligibility to take the EPPP. The EPPP is given only twice per year in each state. The SBEP may also require an oral examination of each candidate who has passed the EPPP. Once these hurdles are achieved, a credential is issued which must be renewed on a regular basis. Generally speaking, SBEP credentialing fees are much higher than SDE credentialing fees. Cutoff scores for the EPPP vary by state and one can usually acquire reciprocity in another state so long as he or she already has an acceptable EPPP score and a valid credential. The Association of State and Provincial Psychology Boards (ASPPB) is working to smooth the process of interstate reciprocity for credentials; one effort is the offering of a Certificate of Professional Qualification in Psychology (CPQ, McGuire, 1998). Several publications related to SBEP credentialing and the EPPP are available from ASPPB including, *Certificate of Professional Qualification in Psychology, Entry Requirements for the Professional Practice of Psychology, The Handbook of Licensing and Certification Requirements for Psychologists in the United States and Canada, Items from Previous Examinations* (for the EPPP). Other publications are related to past performance of doctoral candidates on the EPPP and information about the examination's construction, content, and administration. ASPPB offers a practice version of the EPPP via the internet. There also is an effort to devise a national model for the oral licensing examination. ASPPB is the most important source of SBEP licensing across the United States and Canada (contact: ASPPB, P.O. Box 4389, Montgomery, AL 36103 or www.asppb.org). The organization's previous name was American Association of State Psychology Boards and its early history is discussed in Carlson (1978).

Pros and Cons of Credentialing

Credentialing is a major symbol of professional status. One's credentials virtually assure the right to use certain titles and practices. Needless to say, there are advantages for the agencies and consumers who employ psychologists. However, though the growth and contributions of credentialing are well known, they are not uniformly appreciated. As with accreditation, there are sacrifices involved in the legalization of the credentialing process. Discussing the history of the effectiveness of licensing, Hogan (1983) indicated that licensing practices had the following shortcomings because: (a) they did not necessarily protect the public from incompetent practitioners; (b) they may exacerbate shortages in the supply of practitioners and in their distribution; (c) they may increase the cost of professional services; (d) they may prevent the use of paraprofessionals; (e) they may inhibit the change of training processes; and (f) they may discriminate against minorities, women, the aged, and the poor. Despite these apparent downsides to credentialing, the certification and licensing of psychologists continues to become more stringent and popular. Recent data on credentialing indicate that SDE credentials are held by at least 90% of school psychologists, and SBEP or other agency credentials by about one-third with almost two-thirds of faculty holding a SBEP license (Graden & Curtis, 1991; Hyman, Flynn, Kowalcyk, & Marcus, 1998).

Non-Practice Credentials

A third type of credential is a national-level recognition certificate. These credentials include the diploma from the American Board of Professional Psychology (ABPP) and the certificate from the NASP National Certification System. Both credentials are recognitions of quality preparation or practice, but they are not credentials which authorize one to render services. That is, they are not substitutes for SDE or SBEP practice credentials. The diploma in psychology was initiated by APA in 1947 for clinical psychology and extended to school psychology in the late 1960s (Fagan, 1993; Pryzwansky & Wendt, 1987). Those holding the diploma are called diplomates or Board-certified psychologists. As with all credentialing procedures, in order to obtain this recognition, one voluntarily agrees to be rigorously examined. The process, limited to doctoral level psychologists, involves interviews and extensive evaluation of one's practice. The credential is awarded only once and need not be renewed. In 1992, the American Board of Professional Psychology expanded its influence by forming a federation of specialty boards including an American Board of School Psychology (ABSP). The ABSP provides the only competency-based doctoral level school psychology credential. Board-certified school psychologists are fellows in the American Academy of School Psychology (Pryzwansky, 1999). Relatively few doctoral level school psychologists are ABPP diplomates. A survey of trainers (Hyman, Flynn, Kowalcyk, & Marcus, 1998), found that only 7% (nine trainers) of respondents held a diplomate (five in school, three in clinical, one other). Though not published in the final report, Reschly and Wilson (1995), found that about 1% of the field overall held the diplomate in a 1992 survey. Wells and Fagan (1999) found that of recent doctoral recipients, 2% held the diplomate, 2% were in the process of getting it, and 10% planned to pursue it. This suggests that even among newer doctoral members of the field, only a small proportion are pursuing the diplomate. A history of the ABPP appears in Bent, Packard, & Goldberg (1999).

Another option is to be listed with the National Register of Health Service Providers in Psychology, a widely recognized registry of more than 16,000 doctoral psychologists that may influence one's private practice especially in the arena of managed care. The credentialing options related to the register are described in its *Register Report* (June 1997, Vol. 23, No. 2 pp. 12-13).

In 1988, NASP initiated its National Certificate in School Psychology (NCSP), a program of national certification premised on its standards for training and credentialing. The requirements for the national certificate include a degree in school psychology from a program that meets NASP training standards, including those for the internship, a certificate or license to practice school psychology, and a passing score (using the cutoff established by the National School Psychology Certification Board) on the school psychology exam, a specialty test of the National Teacher Examination (NTE). One does not apply for national certification until the completion of training including the internship. Students should take the NTE school psychology exam at or near the completion of the internship. The school psychology examination is geared to the training and practice standards of NASP and in our opinion is much more applied in scope than the EPPP. The EPPP is geared to the generic standards for psychology credentialing and includes broad coverage of both experimental and professional psychology. Preparatory courses for the EPPP are offered at different locations throughout the year. There are no counterpart courses or materials geared specifically to the NTE school psychology exam. A recently published study guide is not geared to the current content of the exam (National Learning Corporation, 1997). NCSP renewal occurs every 3 years and requires the completion of 75 contact hours of continuing professional development (CPD). The CPD requirement is both stringent and unique among credentials in school psychology. The entire NCSP program and CPD requirements are outlined in a brochure available from NASP. In the early years of the certification program, at least three-fourths of school psychologists had obtained national certification. As of 1999, about 50% of the field held the NCSP credential.

One of the long-term objectives of the national certification program is improved state-to-state credentialing reciprocity. Among the requirements for their credential, several states have initiated school psychology examinations with a cutoff score. The national school psychology examination has already been adopted by several states as part of their credentialing requirements. Because the NTE area exam is a part of the NASP National Certification System (NCS), one should be able to use the same test results in any state. However, cutoffs may vary. Ideally, reciprocity would improve to a point where holding a NASP certificate would be sufficient to reestablish automatically one's credentials when moving. The NCS provides the framework within which NASP guidelines for training and credentialing, APA and NCATE/NASP accrediting guidelines, and the diverse state credentialing requirements could evolve into greater homogeneity. In that instance, the NCS could emerge as the major mediating factor between the national and state levels for school psychology credentialing at least in the education arena of Figure 7.1. For a discussion of the development of the NCSP and its requirements, see Batsche (1996).

Credentialing Summary

Two practice credentials exist in almost every state—SDE and SBEP licenses—and two national-level, non-practice credentials are also available; that is, ABPP(ABSP) and NCSP. The credentials are closely aligned with the organizations and policies that influence school psychology from both the education and the psychology arenas. Students progressing through their training from the non-doctoral to the doctoral levels and beyond could secure all these credentials. However, few will ever need to attain all the available credentials. Most school psychologists will attain an SDE credential and the NCSP.

The primary agencies influencing credentialing are the SDE and the SBEP whose authority is mediated by the state legislature. SDE and SBEP laws and regulations have direct influence on credentialing. Indirect influences emanate from other documents (e.g., NASP and APA standards). The accreditation standards of NASP and APA are often closely aligned with the credentialing standards by the SDE and SBEP, respectively. Other indirect influences on credentialing standards and procedures include official position statements of APA, NASP or the state associations (e.g., statements of comprehensive services), the policies of the Association of State and Provincial Psychology Boards (ASPPB) or the National Association of State Directors of Teacher Certification; and the orientation of the state's training programs and faculty. The primary organizational documents influencing credentialing include the *Specialty Guidelines for the Practice of School Psychology* (APA, 1981), APA's model licensure act (APA, 1987a), and the *Standards for the Credentialing of School Psychologists* (NASP, 1994a). The ASPPB also approved a model licensing act that could further enhance reciprocity in licensing (Association of State and Provincial Psychology Boards, 1998).

Multiple Credentials

It is common to find school psychologists who hold more than their SDE credential for school psychology practice. Some may also be licensed as psychological examiners or psychological associates. At the doctoral level the school psychologist may be SDE credentialed and separately credentialed in school, clinical, or counseling psychology for non-school practice. As mentioned earlier, the school psychologist may be eligible for a certified professional counselor or marriage and family therapist license through a board separate from the SBEP. Finally, some may be credentialed in several areas by the SDE. For example, they may be credentialed as teachers, guidance counselors, or educational diagnosticians, as well as school psychologists. A small number also hold school administrator credentials.

Academic Credentials

What credentials are needed to be considered for a position as an academic school psychologist or employed as a faculty member in a school psychology training program? The expected entry-level credentials for such positions include the doctoral degree in school psychology, including an appropriate internship experience, letters of recommendation, and a resumé describing one's education and experience. Depending on the type of academic position desired, the Ph.D. may be preferred over the Ed.D. or the Psy.D. degree. While school-based experience as a school psychologist is very desirable (see e.g., NASP, 1994c), the reality is that research experience and publications will likely be more heavily weighted in one's application because of the need for such to later achieve tenure. In non-doctoral granting institutions, and programs offering the Psy.D. degree, field experience as a school psychologist may be preferred. For purposes of program accreditation, holding practice credentials or being eligible for practice credentialing is often necessary. Although not appearing in the published version of the research, Reschly and Wilson (1995) found that among program faculty the following degrees were represented: Ph.D. (76%), Ed.D./D.Ed. (17%), Psy.D. (3%), and other (3%). Graden and Curtis (1991) suggest that faculty comprise only about 4.6% of the membership in school psychology. Prorated against a figure of 22,000 at that time, this suggests a total of about 1000 academic school psychologists in the United States. The proportion has probably not changed in the past decade. The proportion of women in academic positions has increased from about 33% in 1989, to 46% in 1998. Minority representation in faculty positions has increased from 11% in 1989 to 15% in 1998, about equally balanced among male and female minorities. Overall, non-minorities comprised 85% of the faculty in school psychology programs. Seventy percent of the 874 faculty were identified as SDE certified and 58% were licensed as psychologists or school psychologists (Thomas, 1998). A useful guide for women and minority faculty is produced by the American Psychological Association (1998). In a survey by Hyman et al. (1998), 65% of responding trainers indicated they were licensed as psychologists in their states and 38% believed the license enhanced their academic standing. Among credentialing concerns of trainers is the widespread requirement for postdoctoral supervised experience to be licensed. It is difficult to acquire this experience in the context of academia where tenure is judged on research, teaching, and service, and supervised experience could detract from those pursuits. Relatedly, Crespi (1998) has discussed the types of credentials that supervisors should possess for post-doctoral to school-based specialist level supervision (see also, Fischetti & Crespi, 1997).

Other Credentials

Considered broadly, credentials include almost any evidence of accomplishments relevant to one's career as a school psychologist. Credentials are obviously enhanced by higher degrees, more experience, and recognitions such as the ABPP or the NCSP. Other recognitions exist in school psychology that also add to one's credentials. Among these are awards from state associations such as School Psychologist of the Year, continuing professional development certificates, and distinguished service awards from professional organizations. Awards and citations from local groups (e.g., PTA, CEC chapters) are also important. These recognitions add to one's credentials when seeking to establish and document the quality of one's efforts.

PRACTICE

In Chapter 3, we identified several systemic influences on the delivery of psychological services in school settings (Curtis & Zins, 1986; Maher et al., 1984). In Chapter 4, we identified several factors that influence the role and function of the school psychologist. In an early consideration of such factors, Tindall (1964) identified six variables influencing role development:

1. School administrative leadership and needs
2. The psychologist's self-concept as a clinician or as a tester
3. The stature of psychology in the schools among other professional psychologists
4. Comparative development of other school specialists
5. SDE certification requirements
6. APA-Division 16's proposed training standards

In addition to those already mentioned, Monroe (1979) identified the potential influence of the psychologist-pupil ratio, litigation and legislation, and ethics. Even though we have ethics and standards for practice from APA and NASP, and SDE regulations for the delivery of services, to a large extent practice is regulated by very local factors enmeshed in the employment context. Drawing upon earlier work and our own considerations, we believe the following direct factors hold the greatest influence over what school psychologists do on a daily basis.

Direct Influences
District Demands and Expectations

What school administrators, especially directors of special education and superintendents, perceive the role and function of the school psychologist to be is a major determinant of what the school psychologist will do. In too many settings, administrators know only of the school psychologist's traditional role of administering and interpreting tests and conducting case studies of children suspected of being eligible for special education. Because school administrators have authority over the school psychologist, this is perhaps the strongest direct influence on the psychologist's role and function. It follows from our discussions of power and authority, that as professionals, school psychologists may have competence in a broad range of services, but lack the authority to determine what services they shall provide for their consumers, or when and where they will provide them. These decisions emanate from those in authority. It is the rare school psychologist who can say without exaggeration that he or she totally defines his or her role and function and the parameters of service delivery. In their roles as consultants, school psychologists should employ public relations and information-giving skills which better inform consumers of the entire range of possible services and how they match the needs of the district. Effective use of such public relations strategies improves the employment conditions of school psychologists. Ineffective use (not necessarily the fault of the school psychologist) results in role and function restrictions. School districts could facilitate such efforts by having a readily available job description for its school psychologist employees. Aspiring school psychologists should ask to see a job description when seeking employment. If one is not available, he or she should prepare one.

The School District's Perceptions of its Needs

Ordinarily the district's demands would be expected to follow closely from the district's perceptions of its needs. However, frequently a district has not adequately assessed its needs in areas that relate to the deployment of psychological services, or, regardless of its needs assessment, the district continues to relate its needs to its psychological services in a traditional way (recall the discussion of goal conflicts in Chapter 3). For decades role and function research has shown that school psychologists spend 60 to 70% of their time in activities that make up only about 25% of their training. That is, much of their training is underused in areas such as consultation, interventions, research, and evaluation. For all the change that U.S. education has undertaken, it is surprising that the traditional role and function of school psychologists has persisted. Because school psychologists are assessment specialists, they need to be involved in the process of assessing district needs, and should improve their efforts at articulating how more diverse roles and functions can better meet district needs. For example, a school psychologist's needs assessment might determine that many children in the school district are in need of assistance in dealing with their anger and developing more appropriate social skills. Instead of providing traditional one-to-one assessment and intervention services, the school psychologist could establish group services, perhaps with the assistance of the school-based guidance counselor or social worker. The important point is that need perceptions influence district demands. A district should involve as many constituencies as necessary to assess its needs properly and to consider more broadly the ways in which school psychologists can help to meet them.

Consumer Response to Services

The kind of feedback a district receives about its psychological services, or about the services that other districts' psychologists are providing, can also shape the role and function of the school psychologist. Feedback, positive or negative, may emanate from parents, educators, or students. Consumer satisfaction with services is very important to the maintenance of services, and their dissatisfaction can be a significant source of change. Feedback is necessarily after the fact (reactive), and thus consumers' feedback about services presume that such services were able to be offered. The accountability strategies of Chapter 5 are helpful in conveying to the school administration the importance of broadly conceived psychological services. Consumer response can also be proactive. Consumers may pressure the administration to offer psychological services of a different type that they have learned of elsewhere or to increase certain existing district services with which they have been highly satisfied. School psychologists can even nurture this process by advocating with consumer groups for improved psychological services, changes in special education, the referral process, and so on. Consumer response can be an effective reactive and proactive influence for change. Although this fact is widely recognized, this role and function determinant is not widely used to improve school psychological services. Publications that may be useful to practitioners are *Making Psychologists in Schools Indispensable* (Talley, Kubiszyn, Brassard, & Short, 1996), the *Professional Advocacy Resource Manual* (Canter & Crandall, 1994), and the NASP handouts series (Canter & Carroll, 1998).

School psychologists need also to offer concrete expectations for outcomes (i.e., reinforcers) for attitude and behavior changes on the part of administrators. This highlights the importance of using existing outcome studies (e.g., consultation and pre-referral assessment procedures reduce formal referrals and costs) to entice attitude and behavior change. The variable of consumer response can be among the most influential because it can influence change based on the potential pressure of the consumer at either the ballot box or in the media. School administrators listen to consumers because they perceive the consequences of failing to do so. Consumers can also emphasize the importance of practices observed elsewhere without appearing to be self-serving in seeking role changes among school psychologists. Thus a combination of information, expectations, and contingencies may be more effective in changing district demands for school psychological services. Too often, the primary contingency is the lack of funds from noncompliance, and thus the dominant demand is for more traditional case work to achieve compliance. We need to alter demands by demonstrating that compliance can be more effectively achieved in the long run through reduced formal referrals premised on broader service delivery and presumably stronger consumer satisfaction. In short, simply informing school authorities of our broad training and potential services falls short of effective change strategies. In our scheme of influence on daily practice, the determinants of district demands and needs would still be ahead of consumer response, but this determinant can have an important impact on perceptions of needs and subsequent district demands.

Desired Functions of the School Psychologist

This determinant refers to the kinds of roles and functions the individual school psychologist wishes to perform. Studies of school psychologists' actual and preferred services have consistently shown discrepancies and attest to the distinction between this determinant and that of district expectations and demands (see e.g., Curtis, Graden & Reschly, 1992; Smith, 1984; Smith et al., 1992). A survey of Ohio school administrators suggested that some services valued highly by practitioners may not be so valued by administrators (Thomas & Pinciotti, 1992). Perhaps these discrepancies relate to accounts of job-related burnout among school psychologists (Huebner, 1992; Miller, Witt, & Finley, 1981; Wise, 1985). A direct determinant of moderate strength, what school psychologists desire to do, probably has less influence in the system than what others in authority expect them to do. This determinant is closely related to the next two determinants (personal competencies and orientation of the training program).

Personal Competencies of the School Psychologist

Every school psychologist brings to the workplace a body of knowledge and skills acquired through formal training, experience, and continuing education. This body of knowledge and skills comprises the ethical limits of the individual school psychologist's practice. In theory, at least, school psychologists confine their activities to the skills in which they are competent. Role and function discrepancy can easily result when the district's expectations and demands call for services that the school psychologist is not competent to provide. Role and function discrepancy can occur in two ways. The usual way is where the available skills of the school psychologist are underused by restrictive expectations, or when the expectations call for services beyond the available skills of the school psychologist. It is important for school psychologists to assess the service needs of their consumers and strive to acquire the necessary skills through additional formal education, supervised experience, and continuing education. The broader the skills of the school psychologist, the greater the potential for comprehensive service delivery.

Indirect Influences

Several indirect factors also help to determine the role and function of the school psychologist in daily practice. These include the following factors:

Orientation of the Training Program

Each training program is organized around some type of model, with both didactic and experiential training. The orientation of the training program, which is partially dependent upon the competencies and orientations of its faculty, influences the day-to-day practice of the school psychologist. If the faculty holds strong behavioral psychology orientations, such strategies are likely to be expressed in their students' approach to problems. Thus orientation of the training program, personal competencies, and desired functions are closely related determinants of role and function. Because the program's orientation does not guarantee personal competencies, and because that orientation and set of competencies may not be in accord with consumer or district perceptions of their needs, role and function expectations and demands are not directly influenced. A related aspect to this influence is that the internship is usually considered a training experience, and a part of the overall training program. The orientations of the supervisor(s) and colleagues involved in the internship experience may differ from that of the academic faculty. It is frequently acknowledged by trainers that the orientation they imparted to their students is modified or enhanced, but often eroded by internships where the students were encouraged to practice differently. It is also likely that as school psychologists gain experience, they alter their orientations. Thus a program's orientation may not be a consistent predictor of its students' short-term or long-term orientations.

Credentialing Requirements for School Psychologists

The nature of a state's SDE and SBEP credentialing requirements indirectly influences one's day-to-day practice. They do this by defining the areas in which one is to be trained and/or judged competent. This determinant is closely related to the orientation of the training program determinant, and we observed earlier the significant relationships among accreditation, training, and credentialing. Changes in credentialing standards might not be observed in practice for several years. That is, such changes are seldom retroactive to those already credentialed. Nevertheless, changes in credentialing requirements can have long-term impact on role and function. The most immediate impact of changes in credentialing requirements would be observed in training program requirements, especially those of non-doctoral programs that tend to follow the pragmatic model. The influence of credentialing requirements on the strongest direct determinants of role and function (district demands and expectations, district's perceptions of its needs) is considered weak and therefore indirect.

State Laws and Regulations

Most states have statutes or SDE rules and regulations for the approval of schools that generally describe the role and function of school psychologists. However, such statements are typically guidelines about service provision and not enforceable statements about what the school psychologist must be doing. For example, they might stipulate that assessment, consultation, and in-service education are important services, but fail to prioritize them or to stipulate what portion of a school psychologist's time should be applied to each area. In fact, the rules and regulations might only require the district to have the availability of psychological services and not its own school psychologist. More definitive statements appear in federal legislation for the disabled and the SDE rules and regulations for their implementation. In some states, these statements may be so specific as to indicate what tests the school psychologist is expected to administer for certain types of referrals. However, all SDEs have statements about the expectations for assessment and related services, due process procedures, confidentiality, team meetings, and so on that directly influence the school psychologist's daily practice. Unlike credentialing requirements, laws and rules and regulations are often immediately enforceable, and apply to all those in practice regardless of when they were credentialed. We consider this to be an indirect determinant because seldom do laws and regulations address school psychologists specifically (i.e., in name), and they do not stipulate priorities. Nevertheless, because such influences have authoritative backing, with proper wording such laws and regulations could have a direct and dramatic impact on role and function. Imagine an SDE description of services that required school psychologists to spend no less than 30% of their time in consultation activities or that stipulated a caseload of no more than 75 per year based on an average of no more than 2 case studies per week. Of course, local district guidelines or collective bargaining agreements that stipulate such expectations would have direct impact but we consider these to be included in the first two determinants (i.e., district demands and expectations; district's perception of its needs).

State and Local Professional Associations

Though strictly power groups with no authority for making changes, state and local professional groups can be effective indirect determinants of school psychologists' daily practice. Perhaps their strongest indirect influence is upon training programs, credentialing requirements, and SDE rules and regulations. Through SDE and legislative lobbying efforts, influence can also be brought to bear on the state laws, rules and regulations, and their implementation. To the extent such associations could have direct impact on daily practice, it would most likely be via changing the response of consumers, the perceptions of the district's needs, and subsequently the expectations and demands for services.

NASP and APA Positions

More removed from the sphere of daily practice than state associations, the efforts of national groups are also indirect influences. The training, credentialing, and practice standards of the APA and NASP are actually formal position statements of these groups. Especially related to daily practice, or role and function, are *General Guidelines for Providers of Psychological Services* (APA, 1987b), *Specialty Guidelines for the Delivery of Services by School Psychologists* (APA, 1981) and, *Standards for the Provision of School Psychological Services* (NASP, 1997b). The latter two documents identify the proper role of the school psychologist in accordance with training and ethical guidelines, and specify a preferred service ratio. NASP position statements on such topics as mental health services in the schools, school violence, early childhood care and education, grade retention, reevaluations, or corporal punishment may also influence practice. Many of the chapters in *Best Practices in School Psychology* (Thomas & Grimes, 1985, 1990, 1995), though not formal position statements, reflect the interests of NASP. The series of videotapes on consultation and current issues produced by Division 16-APA also reflect the interests of this national group. These unofficial, yet obviously sanctioned, books and products may indirectly influence daily practice. Certainly the national organizations would like to think they have some influence. Finally, there are organization-sponsored standards or guidelines that do not get the visibility that those above have received but are nonetheless very important. These include *Standards For Educational and Psychological Testing* (APA, 1985, a revision is under consideration) and the *Guidelines for Computer-based Tests and Interpretations* (APA, 1986).

Although the influence of formal standards documents can be observed in accreditation and credentialing practices, the mechanisms for national level influence on daily practice is complicated and unclear. In a few instances, NASP and Division 16-APA have become involved in local practice and professional issues such as the *Larry P.* case in California, and the *Muriel Forrest* case in New York. There also have been incidents in which NASP made direct contact with a district superintendent expressing concern for the problems identified by that district's school psychologists. The expression of national organization support for the school psychologists in these cases has been more noteworthy than the outcomes. The cases help the national group to scrutinize its policies and their impact and to articulate its positions to the field better. However, the authors can think of few if any instances where the national groups' intervention led to direct changes in daily practice. In those instances where subsequent change has occurred, it has been the result of local forces employing the guidelines or positions of the national or state associations to influence changes. The improvements were more a result of changes in district perceptions and expectations than from national group intervention. Often the uninvited intervention of a national group is not appreciated by the school district and can heighten tensions between administrators and psychologists. Nevertheless, important changes can be made by proper coordination of national and state group intervention with the influence of local determinants.

Changing Roles and Functions

What do the direct and indirect determinants suggest about the process of role change? The strongest mechanisms for role and function change are local. The primary determinants of the school psychologist's daily practice are in the school district and its community. The traditional assessment role of the school psychologist is strongly allied with the growth of special education and its reliance on assessment procedures for determining student eligibility. With 3% to 5% of the school population being referred each year for assessment, 92% of that group being formally tested, and about 73% of that group being placed in special education (Algozzine, Christenson, & Ysseldyke, 1982, cited in Salvia & Ysseldyke, 1998), the schools continue to be some distance from removing or seriously reducing the assessment expectations for their school psychologists. At the same time, school psychologists are being bombarded with professional ideology on role and function that seems contradictory to the expectations of districts for school psychology practice. The ideology stresses role expansion beyond testing to assessment, beyond normative assessment to criterion assessment, beyond assessment to consultation, and so on. Ideology represents the ideals of the profession, the conditions which it hopes to create, and not necessarily the conditions as they exist. Should practice stray too far from expectations, practitioners face alienation. Perhaps even worse, were the ideology to be adopted by those in control of the first three determinants (district demands and expectations, district's perception of its needs, and consumer response to services) before practitioners were prepared to deliver alternative services, a demand-supply gap could conceivably result in the need to replace many school psychologists. Surveys of school psychologists have consistently revealed that many school psychologists and their respective training programs are not yet prepared to contend with ideology as reality. Thus we need to synchronize our training efforts carefully with our ideologies about role and function.

In our scheme, efforts to change school psychologists' roles and functions will be ineffective without changing the first three determinants, which in order of importance are district demands and expectations, district need perceptions, and consumer responses. An APA effort may positively influence the direct determinants of role and function (see e.g., Task Force on Psychology in the Schools, 1993). Less direct efforts such as changing training and credentialing requirements, improving legislative recognition of school psychological services, taking formal positions on practice, or revising standards and ethics are important but less influential. Many of these indirect efforts have been employed for decades. Witness the continued concern for restrictive role and function even after doubling the training requirements of school psychologists, changing credentialing practices, and presumably delivering a far more competent school psychologist to the district than ever before! Meaningful role and function change necessitates shifts in the three most direct determinants, concurrent with shifts in desired functions and personal competencies, that have presumably been influenced by the indirect variables in Table 7.1. (e.g., training, credentialing). In our analysis, role and function change requires coordinated efforts at the local, state, and national levels by practitioners, trainers, and the leadership of power and authority groups in school psychology. It also requires the acceptance of lasting change as a gradual process rather than the result of revolution or school reform delivered from the state or national levels.

Ethical and Legal Influences

A few of the above determinants deserve extra comment. These include professional ethics, legal matters related to federal legislation, and litigation.

Ethics

Each of us has ideas about what constitutes ethical behavior, what is right, or what one ought to do in certain circumstances. That is, each of us has a personal code of behavior. When we choose to join a profession, we voluntarily modify or expand our personal beliefs by accepting the code of practice of that profession. It is this allegiance to a prescribed set of professional behavior guidelines that symbolizes the profession's ideal of placing the client's interests before all others. It is this aspect of professionalism that is sometimes referred to as a calling to one's profession. When we join a professional association, we agree to adhere to its code of ethics and can expect to be held accountable accordingly by the association. Thus in making professional decisions, school psychologists modify their "intuitive level" of decision making in favor of a "critical-evaluative level" (Jacob-Timm & Hartshorne, 1998). We make decisions based upon the observations and research findings related to our practice. This is the essence of Gray's (1963b) concept of the data-oriented problem solver and of the scientist-practitioner model. We also make decisions based upon current legal decisions and ethical considerations.

General Concepts

The practice of school psychology does not require frequent review of the APA or NASP codes (see Appendices C and D, respectively). School psychologists have had instruction in ethics, including reviews of the codes, during their academic preparation and have demonstrated an appropriate sense of professional responsibility during training and internship. Nevertheless, situations arise that require practitioners and academic school psychologists to review what course of action would be most proper. In so doing, school psychologists are guided by general concepts embraced by ethical codes.

1. Codes of ethics refer to the overt behavior of the professional. They relate to what the professional ought to do, rather than feel or think, about situations. Thus codes guide overt behaviors.
2. Client welfare, and the welfare of the community, are paramount considerations in guiding professional behavior. This general concept is related to those ethical principles dealing with competence, the rights, dignity, and welfare of others, and responsibility to the broader community. These propositions are identified in the APA code's preamble and general principles, and in the NASP code's sections II ("Professional Competency") and III ("Professional relationships And Responsibilities"). The APA code preamble specifically indicates that its primary goal is "the welfare and protection of the individuals and groups with whom psychologists work" (see Appendix C).
3. Behaving as you would reasonably be expected to behave by your peers is a highly useful guide. This presumes that professionals keep abreast of developments in their field and have a reasonable sense of what their peers do or would do in similar situations. One important

aspect of continuing professional development (CPD) is to facilitate ethical knowledge and practice. Peer review is encouraged in difficult situations. If you are unclear about how to resolve a situation, discuss it with other school psychologists before reaching conclusions and taking action.

4. Regardless of the profession, its titles or limitations, in any credentialing process the use of ethics to guide professional behavior is central to the regulation of practice. While the "let your conscience be your guide" approach would seem to lend itself to abuse, review mechanisms exist in each SBEP for handling suspected violations of the credentialing law including violations of the profession's code of ethics. Similar mechanisms exist within SDE credentialing processes. Violations of ethics may also be reviewed by the state psychology and school psychology associations and/or by the APA and NASP, and ethical codes may be used by the courts as guidelines for determining proper behavior.

5. Professionals respect the work of their colleagues and that of practitioners in other professions. The school psychologist avoids belittling the work of other school psychologists or making recommendations only to certain other professionals in the community. For example, suppose that elementary teachers in your district tell you that they are opening a tutoring service in the community and would appreciate your steering referrals their way. Should you engage in this activity? To do so would suggest that you are capable, knowledgeable, or sanctioned to evaluate their work as more competent than the tutorial work of others or that you can competently evaluate the work of practitioners in professions about which you may know very little. Dealing with such situations is not always easy. Practitioners often avoid these dilemmas by maintaining lists of available referral resources in several service categories. The lists can be provided to persons seeking specific services such as tutoring, and *they* can choose among the available resources. No doubt, with experience school psychologists come to appreciate the work of certain professionals in the community more than others. Nevertheless professionals should avoid showing preferences for the services of certain other professionals. If they believe that the practices of some practitioners are improper, the alleged violations should be handled in the same manner as other ethical violations; and not by systematically steering referrals to favored colleagues in school psychology, or in other fields.

6. In the management of alleged ethical violations, the overriding goals are to correct the present situation and prevent its recurrence. The process is less punitive than corrective and educative, though in some instances punitive actions may result including dismissal from graduate training

or expulsion from association membership. Of course, in court proceedings, the process can be far more adversarial with very serious punitive consequences in cases of malpractice. In most instances, professionals seek to resolve suspected ethical violations privately and informally with the parties involved. Procedures have been developed by APA and NASP for the adjudication of ethical complaints and guidelines are available from these organizations. Because one is expected to report and properly adjudicate such complaints, failure to do so may in itself constitute a violation of the codes (see, e.g., APA code, section 8, "Resolving Ethical Issues"). Jacob-Timm and Hartshorne (1998) discuss an eight-step problem-solving model for considering ethical complaints based on the work of Keith-Spiegel and Koocher (1985). The model emphasizes identifying the problem and ethical issues involved, and considering various options for action and their implications.

The above serves as general considerations with which to review codes of ethics. Other configurations exist. Jacob-Timm and Hartshorne (1998) consolidate their considerations about ethical codes around four broad principles: "(1) Respect for the Dignity of Persons (Welfare of the Client), (2) Responsible Caring (Professional Competence and Responsibility), (3) Integrity in Professional Relationships, and (4) Responsibility to Community and Society" (p. 10). Their configuration captures the essence of the guiding principles of both the APA and NASP codes.

APA and NASP Codes

The APA *Ethical Principles of Psychologists and Code of Conduct* consists of a preamble, six General Principles (A through F), and specific ethical standards (1.01 thru 8.07) which are not considered exhaustive but are broad enough to apply to psychologists in varied professional and scientific roles (APA, 1992). The code is applicable to psychologists in all practice settings. However, because they apply to clinical and counseling psychologists who typically do not work in school settings, the APA code may be especially relevant to school psychologists practicing outside the schools. For example, the code more specifically addresses therapy than the NASP code, and SBEP credentialing examinations assume familiarity with the APA code. Both codes address assessment, relationships including sexual misconduct, consent, and confidentiality. The 1992 APA code was a substantial revision of the 1989 ethical principles which were developed around a preamble and 10 principles (APA, 1989). Still the most recent version, the 1992 edition gained in comprehensiveness and in specificity and appears in Appendix C. The APA code is under review for a revision that may be available in 2002 (Martin, 1999).

The 1997 edition of the NASP *Principles For Professional Ethics* is specific to the specialty of school psychology and applies to all school psychologists regardless of setting. Thus the code is applicable to school-based and non-school-based practitioners as well as university trainers, state consultants, administrators, or supervisors in their respective roles and places of employment. The principles are organized around several broad areas: Professional competency, professional relationships and responsibilities, professional practices-public and private settings, professional practices-private settings. The NASP code is especially helpful to school-based practitioners and addresses conflicts that may occur in the context of school practice and in the relationship to non-school practitioners and to the private practice of school psychology. The 1997 edition appears in Appendix D. The ethics complement NASP's *Standards for the Provision of School Psychological Services* (NASP, 1997b) and reinforce them in several appropriate ways. For example, both documents provide guidelines for school psychologists in private practice and specifically forbid private practice by district school psychologists with clients for whom they are responsible in their school setting. This is an important issue since an increasing number of school psychologists are seeking dual employment, which may give rise to conflicts of interest. Familiarity with both documents is assumed in the examination process for the NCSP. The distinctions between the intent of the NASP code and that of the providers standards are addressed by Reinhardt and Martin (1991).

Examples of Ethical Problems

In the previous edition of this book we reported that there had been no reliable, nationally representative study of the ethical dilemmas of school psychologists. This has been partially rectified by a survey of NASP members (Jacob-Timm, 1999) in which 226 respondents identified 222 ethically challenging incidents that were assigned to 19 categories. The more prevalent categories were administrative pressure to act unethically (49 dilemmas), especially incidents related to special education eligibility, placement, and services; assessment (32 dilemmas), such as questionable findings and diagnoses, inadequate interpretations, and poor quality reports; confidentiality (30 dilemmas), like duty to protect child from harm, breach of confidentiality; and unsound educational practices (28 dilemmas), for example, detrimental teaching practices, ineffective programs, discipline. Other categories included failure to address student needs, job competence and job performance, psychologist-parent dilemmas, psychological records, conflictual relationships, client self-determination and informed consent, therapeutic interventions, academic settings, supervision, sexual issues, payment, taking credit for other's work, confronting unethical conduct, credentials, research and publishing, and a twentieth category, miscellaneous (e.g., psychologist was a poor role model). Despite not achieving a nationally representative sample of respondents, the identification of specific incidents encountered by many school psychologists makes this research useful for instruction.

An earlier national survey of APA members and fellows identified 23 categories of 703 "ethically troubling incidents" with the top three categories related to confidentiality, conflictual relationships, and methods of collecting fees (Pope & Vetter, 1992). Fifteen incidents (2% of the total) were mentioned in the category "school psychology," and the examples given suggest administrator-practitioner conflicts in role and function. Examples included, "My school district administrator would like me to distort test data to show improvement" and "As a school psychologist there is often pressure from administrators to place children in programs based on the availability of services rather than the needs of the individual student" (Pope & Vetter, 1992, p. 406). Despite a lack of representativeness in sampling, the problems cited by the school psychologists in this study suggest serious ethical conflicts related to some employer-employee relationships. It is our opinion that the problems often attending the supervisory relationship of school psychologists by non-school psychologists (recall discussion in Chapter 3) contribute to these dilemmas, and that they may be more widespread than we recognize. Survey data reported in Jann (1991) suggest that supervisory pressures are fairly common, though less problematic, when the supervisor is a school psychologist. However, regardless of the circumstances, the alteration of assessment information and/or the placement of children in programs on bases other than their needs constitute serious ethical and legal misconduct.

A related ethical dilemma occurs when school psychologists' supervisors ask them to perform services for which they are not competently prepared. This issue is relevant to the need for continuing education and to ethical principles dealing with practitioner competency and client welfare. This particular dilemma was addressed in a *Communiqué* article as part of a series on ethical issues (Grossman, 1992). Needless to say, performing outside one's competence was not advocated. In other instances, school psychologists may engage in activities for which they think they are competent but are not. For example, the SDE's comprehensive job description for school psychologists may not apply to all persons so credentialed. Some practitioners may not be adequately prepared in some areas (e.g., consultation or group counseling) and should not provide such services until preparation has been acquired. A more blatant ethical violation is practice outside the bounds of what is typically considered the field of school psychology. For example, making diagnoses and/or recommendations about sensory functioning and physical health are considered to be within the domain of other professionals. Information relevant to the domain of school psychology training and practice is provided in *Petition for Reaffirmation of the Specialty of School Psychology* (1997) and in Ysseldyke et al. (1997). Among the more egregious examples of practitioner incompetence was the case of "Dr. Gestalt." "When a school board member asked his school psychologist about the nature of the Bender-Gestalt test used in his practice, the psychologist, with incredible and undeniable naiveté, replied, 'Oh, that's a test made up by Dr. Bender and Dr. Gestalt'"(Rosenfeld & Blanco, 1974, p. 263).

Services to special categories of children and expanding psychologist practice privileges raise additional dilemmas. For example, in some states school psychologists may be prohibited from providing services to children identified as having traumatic brain injury (TBI) until additional training has been acquired. Efforts at the national level to secure prescription privileges for professional psychologists could also be problematic. Division 16-APA has issued a report on the implications of prescription privileges in school psychology (Kubiszyn, Brown, Landau, DeMers, & Reynolds, 1992). Prescription privileges and other special practice applications will probably have different implications for doctoral and non-doctoral practitioners. Continuing professional development will be essential to role and function expansion and to ethical practice in the future (Fowler & Harrison, 1995).

Respecting the client's right to privacy is a paramount ethical and legal aspect of practice. Working in a public school setting with colleagues who have varying interest in your work, can create problems of confidentiality. These concerns are closely related to the dilemmas of clientage discussed in Chapter 3 where parents, teachers, administrators, and others may desire involvement in your work and access to information which you and your client consider confidential. The accessibility of assessment records and reports, conversations about your work, written communications, phone conversations, and so on all pose threats to confidentiality that are less probable in the isolation of one's private practice. As seen in some litigation, maintaining confidentiality is not itself a simple matter when the client is a minor aged child, and the school psychologist does not have the security of "privileged communication." That is, under certain and not necessarily rare circumstances, school psychologists and other pupil personnel workers can be forced, perhaps even expected, to divulge information that the child may have thought was being discussed confidentially. The concepts of confidentiality, privileged communication, and respect for the privacy of others are essential to the ethical practice of psychologists.

Although specific to students in clinical and counseling psychology, the findings of Fly, van Bark, Weinman, Kitchener, and Lang (1997) provide a perspective on the ethical transgressions of students in training. Using a critical incident technique employed by previous studies, they found that the categorical proportion of transgressions were confidentiality (25%), professional boundaries, sexual and nonsexual (20%), plagiarism or falsification of data (15%), welfare (10%), procedural breach with ethical implications (10%), competency (9%), integrity-dishonesty (8%), and misrepresentation of credentials (3%). Outcomes of the transgressions included remedial action in 44% and dismissal from the program in 22% of cases. The study pointed to the importance of managing ethical incidents in professional training even though 54% of the students involved had taken an ethics course.

School psychologists also should be familiar with the concept of "defamation of character" including "libel" (written defamation) and "slander" (spoken defamation). A complicated area of confidentiality is the accessibility of test protocols to persons having legitimate interest in their contents versus the need to protect the copyright privileges of test publishers (see e.g., APA, 1996a; Canter, 1990b; Woody, 1998). The arena of confidentiality probably poses the most intense dilemmas for pupil personnel workers.

In some instances, ethical behavior becomes enmeshed with law. For example, issues of confidentiality have both ethical and legal ramifications. Jacob-Timm and Hartshorne (1998) discuss the conflicting ethical and legal aspects of *Pesce* v. *J. Sterling Morton High School District* (1986) a case in which the school psychologist's decision to maintain confidentiality was judged to be inconsistent with the state's child abuse reporting laws (see pp. 178-180). The school psychologist's claim to confidentiality was insufficient to ignore the reporting requirements of abuse laws. It is generally conceded that legal requirements supercede ethical considerations.

Although sexual harassment and gender issues in employment have been openly discussed, almost nothing is known about the frequency of sexual misconduct and abuse between school psychologists and their clients. Occasionally such matters make their way into the local paper and the authors are aware of a few isolated incidents in which practitioners had engaged in such misconduct. Such behavior is most reprehensible and almost certainly results in the revocation of all practice privileges and credentials of the practitioners involved.

With increasing interest in private practice and the availability of "third-party reimbursement" for school psychological services, school psychologists must be familiar with the ethical issues and legal aspects of private practice. For example, fraudulent practices in billing for services have attended the recent expansion of professional psychology into the private sector (Pope & Vetter, 1992). The issues surrounding third-party insurer payments for school psychological services are discussed by Canter (1990a, 1991a). For discussions of areas in which ethics and law overlap and often conflict see Cardon, Kuriloff, and Phillips (1975), Jacob-Timm and Hartshorne (1998), Phillips (1990a), Prasse (1995), Reschly and Bersoff (1999), and Sales, Krauss, Sacken, and Overcast (1999).

Other Resources

The Canadian Psychological Association has a code of ethics (CPA, 1991), which with slight modification has been adopted by the Canadian Association of School Psychologists (CASP). The CASP also provides *Standards for Professional*

Practice in School Psychology (CASP, n.d.). The International School Psychology Association has a code of ethics that corresponds closely to the main provisions of the APA and NASP codes (Oakland, Goldman, & Bischoff, 1997). A related set of ethical standards is that of the American Counseling Association (ACA, 1995). Though not directly applicable to school psychologists who are not ACA members, these standards are unique in providing sections specifically on counseling relationships, consulting, and private practice. The ASPPB publishes its own *Code of Conduct* and a related instructional videotape, *Ethical Dilemmas Facing Psychologists.*

Few texts are available on ethics and law specifically addressed to school psychologists (Gredler, 1972; Jacob-Timm and Hartshorne, 1998; Valett, 1963). The Jacob-Timm and Hartshorne text draws together legal decisions and ethical codes to assist in clarifying professional actions in most situations. The book is a comprehensive treatment of legal and ethical issues in school psychology and includes numerous case study examples illustrating specific principles. An earlier work by Valett (1963) is also relevant to contemporary school psychological practice. The Valett text is an interesting discussion of professional issues and dilemmas related to several areas of practice. The book discusses many aspects of the field of school psychology and within each chapter poses practical problems for discussion. The following example is related to administrative problems:

> A group of parents have questioned the continued use of personality tests in the counseling and school psychology program. They have requested that the school psychologist make a presentation at the next PTA meeting of all tests presently used and the way in which they contribute to the educational program and work with individual students (Valett, 1963, p. 269).

The many vignettes in the book provide practice problems relevant to ethical, legal, and just plain practical concerns. Technological advancements have raised additional ethical concerns including the use of computer-generated report writing and test scoring programs (Carlson & Martin, 1997; Sutkiewicz, 1997), FAX machines (Batts & Grossman, 1997), and pagers (DiVerde-Nushawg & Walls, 1998; Tracy, 1998). The APA will address the matter of delivering services by telephone, teleconferencing, and the internet in future revisions of its code. An interim statement however was issued in November, 1997 (see Ethics Committee Issues Statement, 1998). A recent survey of the use of technology and related ethical concerns by practitioners in private practice supports the need for additional guidelines (McMinn, Buchanan, Ellens, & Ryan, 1999).

Finally, it is important to rely on recent research and opinion related to ethical behavior. Although earlier reviews provide perspectives on professional behavior, expectations of professionals change over the years, reflecting the broader societal context in which services are delivered. Some state association newsletters carry regular columns on ethics, and a series of ethics articles have appeared in the Division 16 newsletter, *The School Psychologist*, and in the NASP *Communiqué* (see e.g., the index in Volume 19, No. 7). Case studies occasionally appear in the *American Psychologist*. Reviews of ethical issues in training and practice have also appeared in the journal, *Professional Psychology: Research and Practice*. Since ethics and best practices guidelines are closely related, *Best Practices in School Psychology* (Thomas & Grimes, 1985, 1990, 1995) is a very useful guide to practice. Issues in the graduate education of ethical principles are discussed in a special section of *Professional Psychology: Research and Practice* (Vol. 23, No. 3, 1992), and the nature of school psychology program training in ethics is discussed in Daley, Nagle, and Onwuegbuzie (1998) and Swenson (1998). Additional information on legal/ethical issues is provided by the school psychology literature related to child maltreatment and children's rights. Historical perspective is provided by Hart (1991), and comprehensive discussions appear in special issues of the *School Psychology Review* (see Vol. 16, No. 2, 1987, on psychological maltreatment of children; Vol. 20, No. 3, 1991, on children's rights; and Vol. 25, No. 2, 1996, on children, research, and public policy). In addition to the ethical aspects of conducting research, the issue of publication authorship has recently been addressed (Murray, 1998), as have concerns for copyright laws in the use of test and instructional materials (Woody, 1998).

Liability Insurance

The complex relationships of ethics, legislation, and litigation underscore the importance of carrying professional liability insurance. Only a few agencies and major carriers offer professional liability insurance plans. Typically school psychologists purchase liability insurance through their membership in NASP or APA. Student insurance coverage is also available in some plans. Rates vary as a function of coverage and practice setting. For example, the cost of coverage through NASP in 1999 (with limits of liability equal to $1,000,000/$1,000,000, i.e., each wrongful act or series of continuous, repeated or interrelated wrongful acts or occurrence/aggregate) ranged from $23 per year for students, to $121 per year for employed school psychologists, and to $304 for self-employed school psychologists. A mental health counselors' plan available from the same agency that handles NASP insurance, for the same liability limits, quoted rates of $136 for school counselors, $121 for employed counselors, $304 for self-employed counselors-certified hypnotists, and $815 for psychologists-sex counselors. The plan also quoted agency rates and cost variations that existed for certain states. Higher costs might be anticipated from other carriers including plans available for doctoral psychologists from The Trust affiliated with the American Psychological Association. Rates are influenced by several factors including employment setting, clientele, nature of practice, and risk of being sued.

Liability insurance protects practitioners from excessive costs of defending themselves in litigation brought by clients, and protects clients by providing compensation in instances where harm is shown to have been done by practitioners. Other organizations offering insurance programs include the American Counseling Association and the American Mental Health Counselors Association. A useful booklet is *Shopping the Market: Finding the Malpractice Insurance Policy That Fits Your Needs* (Bogie, 1997).

Legislation and Litigation

As mentioned in Chapter 3, public education is an intensely regulated business. Part of that regulation is related to legislation, constitutional provisions, and court rulings delineating the scope of the state's responsibility to educate its citizens, the rights of students, the needs of exceptional students, the provision of professional services, professional malpractice, and research. In-depth discussions of the background and implications of these influences appear in Fischer & Sorenson (1991), Jacob-Timm and Hartshorne (1998), Phillips (1990a), Reschly and Bersoff (1999), Reynolds et al. (1984), and Sales et al. (1999). Among the most important legislation for the daily practice of school psychologists were 2 laws passed in the 1970s. The first was the Family Educational Rights and Privacy Act of 1974 (FERPA, Public Law 93-380). Influenced by the Russell Sage Foundation Conference Guidelines (Goslin, 1969), Public Law 93-380 clarified the rights of parents and of students age 18 and over to inspect, challenge, and correct records and required written permission for the gathering and dissemination of records. The second was the Education For All Handicapped Children Act of 1975 (Public Law 94-142), influenced by Section 504 of the Rehabilitation Act of 1973, and most recently reauthorized in 1997 as the Individuals with Disabilities Education Act (IDEA, Public Law 105-17). This legislation was virtually a civil rights act for the disabled, entitling them to a free and appropriate public education (FAPE), nondiscriminatory assessment practices, due process procedures, and an individualized educational plan (IEP) for services to be delivered under the least restrictive environment (LRE) concept. An extension of Public Law 94-142 was made in 1986 to grant aspects of the previous law to infants and toddlers employing an individualized family service plan (IFSP) (Public Law 99-457). These laws virtually ended an era in which student records were liberally shared among school personnel and community agencies, when students were evaluated for special educational placement without parental permission, and when special education was often delivered in highly segregated facilities. The laws established what have become routine requirements for providing special educational programs for all eligible children regardless of the nature of their disabilities, and providing related services including psychological services. Parental consent is now an integral part of the assessment process, as well as in the gathering and dissemination of child study information. Among the more controversial aspects of the legislation for the handicapped have been the provisions for nonbiased assessment, due process and informed consent, and educational placement in the least restrictive environment, sometimes implemented by such practices as mainstreaming and inclusion. The impact of the legislation on school psychology was the topic of a special issue of the *Journal of School Psychology* in 1975 (see Vol. 13, No. 4). The issue includes articles on school psychologists as witnesses in due process hearings, legal-ethical conflicts, and training. The literature of the mid-1970s was replete with discussion of Public Law 93-380 and Public Law 94-142. That literature and more recent discussions are highly relevant to practice. For example, Telzrow (1999) questions the extent to which schools and professionals are prepared to implement the major provisions of the 1997 amendments to IDEA and offers suggestions for better implementation. Havey (1999) found that 38% of reporting school psychologists had been involved in one or more due process hearings and on average spent 1 hour testifying and 7.5 hours in preparation. The most common issues in their hearings were assessment and appropriateness of placement. For useful tips on serving in due process hearings and/or as an expert witness, see Elias, 1999; Kimball and Bansilal (1998) and Stumme (1995).

Recent discussions have also centered on inclusion (see e.g., Pfeiffer & Reddy, 1999). Recent trends toward greater inclusion of special education students within regular education programs, and the provision of services to at-risk children, have drawn attention to the differences between the provisions of Section 504 and those of the IDEA. The former is more inclusive and requires services for some children who are not eligible according to the IDEA (e.g., children with attention deficit disorder). It seems probable that in the future more families will turn to the provisions of Section 504 to justify special instructional and related services for their children. This could speed up a shift in special education toward more non-categorical services and a greater emphasis upon interventions and outcomes. Both Section 504 and IDEA have overlapping protections for children and families related to due process, assessment, educational plans, and so on.

There are also important differences. Comparisons of the laws are published in a *Communiqué* series initiated in September, 1992, and a resource manual on which the series was based is available from the Council of Administrators of Special Education, Inc., 615 16th St. NW, Albuquerque, NM 87104. The diagnostic decisions of school psychologists are heavily influenced by the disability classification definitions of these laws and their regulations. Most school districts adhere to these definitions in the implementation of special education programs.

Another classification system is that of the American Psychiatric Association published in its *Diagnostic and Statistical Manual of Mental Disorders: 4th Edition* (DSM-IV, American Psychiatric Association, 1994). Together these classification systems virtually drive the diagnostic categorization of the practice of school psychology. The application of DSM-IV to school psychology was discussed in a special issue of the *School Psychology Review* (Vol. 25, No. 3, 1996).

Related to federal legislation have been a series of major court decisions that have influenced the delivery of special education and the practice of school psychology, especially in the area of assessment (Reschly & Bersoff, 1999; Salvia & Ysseldyke, 1998). Some of these decisions preceded and influenced the wording and enactment of Public Law 93-380 and Public Law 94-142. The rulings have affected the rights of disabled children to a free and appropriate education (*Mills* v. *Board of Education for the District of Columbia*, 1972; *PARC* v. *Commonwealth of Pennsylvania*, 1971, 1972); the assessment of minority children (*Hobsen* v. *Hansen*, 1967; *Guadalupe Organizations, Inc.* v. *Tempe Elementary School District No. 3*, 1972; *Larry P.* v. *Riles*, 1984; *P.A.S.E.* v. *Hannon*, 1980); the confidentiality of professional-client communications (*Pesce* v. *J. Morton Sterling High School District*, 1986; *Tarasoff* v. *Regents of California*, 1974, 1976; Zirkel, 1992); the importance of professional ethics in practice (Forrest v. Ambach, 1980, 1983); and the necessity to follow the provisions of special education laws (*Mattie T.* v. *Holladay*, 1979). Many other cases also have influenced the practice of school psychology and special education. These are often discussed in graduate courses related to special education, psychoeducational assessment, and legal/ethical aspects of practice. The work of Reschly, Kicklighter, and McKee (1988a, 1988b, 1988c) describe the impact of selected cases on school psychology practice. Assistance in conducting research on litigation is available in Knapp, Vandecreek, and Zirkel (1985).

School psychologists have become much more active in the legislative process at the state and national levels. The activity is both reactive (responding to legislative efforts already in progress) and proactive (initiating legislative efforts) on issues of import to children and families, education, psychology, and school psychology. Several state associations have active legislative networks or lobbyists. The NASP has been highly visible in its School Psychologists Action Network (SPAN). In this process, school psychologists often provide testimony to legislative bodies. The importance of such efforts was learned in the 1970s when school psychology struggled with the mandates of Public Laws 93-380 and 94-142. Although NASP and APA had input into the legislative process at that time, it was very modest compared to their present positions. A guide to providing psychological testimony appears in Sorenson, Masson, Clark, and Morin (1998), and in materials available from the NASP and APA.

Advocate or Adversary

The widespread regulation of practice in the past 30 years has created potentially uncomfortable circumstances in several areas of service delivery. Parental and guardian permission to initiate services is now routine, sharing records among professionals and agencies is more cumbersome, and clients ineligible for traditional special education categorical services are often eligible under Section 504. All of these conditions are well known to practicing school psychologists. In the 1990s two additional areas of concern emerged. First was the necessity of a diagnosis for families to receive supplemental security income (SSI) from the government through its Social Security Program. This is different from school districts receiving Medicaid reimbursements for school psychologists' related services. The SSI compensation is paid directly to the person or parent or guardian and not to the school district. "To be eligible for SSI, a person must be age 65 or older or disabled or blind, have limited resources and income and meet certain other requirements" (Social Security Administration, 1998, p. 8). The SSI program applies to adults and children with physical or mental impairments. The monthly compensation to a family may approach $500 for each disabled child in the family. School psychologists have been approved in many states to assess children for SSI income benefits. Some school psychologists feel under pressure by parents to identify their child as disabled in order to receive these funds. It is not known how widespread a legal-ethical problem this has become but the controversial program has come under scrutiny (Stanhope, 1995). Little has been published regarding abuse of the assessment process in the school psychology literature although many school psychologists have privately acknowledged that parents of some indigent children have pressured them to label their children in order for them to receive SSI.

A second concern is the rapid growth of college students seeking a disability label, usually learning disability (LD) and/or attention deficit/hyperactivity disorder (ADHD), in order to obtain special considerations in the admission process, supportive services, or other accommodations (e.g., course substitutions, extended time for exams, preferential seating, readers, transcribers). The authors have been involved in some referrals that were clearly appropriate, but also in several that were not. The legal-ethical professional issue here serves to make an investigative practitioner out of what was previously an advocate. That is, in both these areas, the client stands to gain something from being labeled that is contrary to the traditional notions of labeling as a necessary evil in order to receive services judged required for the child's or adult's educational well-being.

The issue in both these areas is not the legitimacy of the programs or the need for services. Rather, school psychologists, especially those working in secondary and post-secondary educational settings, may find themselves in somewhat adversarial roles with their clients, not unlike the role attorneys may play in defending a client they know to be guilty. The problems and dilemmas surrounding these cases are detailed in a paper on persons seeking accommodations for the Law School Admissions Test (LSAT, Ranseen, 1998). Reviewing 50 cases in which individual adults were diagnosed as ADD or ADHD for accommodations on the LSAT, he found that only 8% had any previous diagnosis during childhood or adolescence and 48% were diagnosed following *completion* of law school. The paper should be required reading for anyone involved with postsecondary assessments for accommodations. The paper is also worthy for its discussion of the problems of adult ADD and ADHD diagnosis. At the very least it will raise the level of consciousness for practitioners.

At this point, we offer no solutions to these dilemmas, but we do advise caution in both the training and practice of school psychologists to be alert to the issues surrounding practices with Section 504 and the Americans With Disabilities Act (ADA, Public Law 101-336, 1990). Many postsecondary institutions have adopted specific documentation requirements and procedures predicated on national guidelines from the Association on Higher Education and Disability (1997). The potential adversarial circumstances will probably spread to other practice areas as ethics and law continue to scrape like tectonic plates on the landscape of practice.

Funding

Another variable influencing school psychology practice is the source of funding for school psychological services. Few studies have attempted to connect the sources of funding with the types of services provided by school psychologists. Eberst (1984) found that the most common funding for school psychological services emanated from sources related to special education, then general education, and lastly from local monies. Summarizing her practice findings, Eberst concluded:

> The type of funding appears to have little effect on the role and function of school psychologists. The comments of the respondents suggested that school psychologists spend most of their time conducting individual psychoeducational assessments of handicapped children, writing reports, and serving on multidisciplinary and/or evaluation teams. These activities are mandated in most states, regardless of the primary source of funding used (p. 15).

It appears that perceptions of the school psychologist's role and function transcend the financial sources of their support. We believe the Eberst study supports our contention that administrator perceptions of needs and role expectations/demands are paramount in determining what school psychologists do on a daily basis. Funding itself does not appear to be a strong determinant but seems to help shape the perceptions and subsequent expectations for services. We include it, therefore, as among the sub-factors that relate to the first two direct determinants discussed earlier. It does not appear to be critical from the perspective of the practitioner since at least half of practitioners surveyed continue to report being uncertain about the source of funding for their positions (Curtis, Hunley, Sawyer, Walker, & Baker, 1999; Graden & Curtis, 1991).

In the past decade, Medicaid funding has been drawn upon by many states to reimburse services of school psychologists in school settings. A recent survey revealed that in 41 states mental health services provided in school systems were reimbursed by Medicaid. The most commonly reimbursed services included individual and group therapy and psychological evaluations. The credentials required of the service provider varied from state to state but it was clear that school-based school psychologists were often able to have their services reimbursed. The amount of statewide Medicaid funding expended to school systems varied from under 1 million to more than $83 million (Wrobel & Krieg, 1998). The extent of influence that Medicaid or other third-party reimbursement plans might have on school psychology practice is unclear.

A Comment on Canadian School Psychology

Canadian and U.S. history share many commonalties. Though European influences are noticeable, Canada's educational system and its practice of school psychology are similar in many respects to that of the United States. Whereas the U.S. system of education is developed around state and federal influence, that of Canada is developed around 10 independent provincial systems of elementary and secondary education and indirect federal influence; there is however, no national department of education. Regulatory influences are observed as well with provincial legislation analogous to the provisions of our Public Law 94-142 and its reauthorizations. Many parallels exist in the field of school psychology. Practice concerns such as role and function restrictions, supervision, or the doctoral issue, are also observed in Canadian literature and conferences. Provincial authorities regulate the practice of psychology and struggles between provincial psychology boards and education boards for the credentialing of educational (school) psychologists are often parallel to those observed in the United States. In several provinces, there are separate associations of psychologists and school psychologists (e.g., Alberta, British Columbia, Manitoba, Quebec), and they hold separate affiliations with the Canadian Psychological Association (CPA) and/or Canadian Association of School Psychologists (CASP).

Although it is beyond our capability, we believe that an adaptation of Figures 7.1 and 7.2, and Table 7.1 could be readily implemented to describe the professional regulation of school psychology in Canada. Thus we feel that with modest changes, the direct and indirect forces identified for professional regulation of school psychology in the United States can be applied to Canada as well. The rich cultural influences of its bilingual (English and French) and native heritage make the practice of Canadian school psychology as complex and challenging as that of practice in the United States (Fagan, 1987b). The importance of Canadian school psychology is reflected in our decision to include a chapter in this text (see Chapter 9). For additional information on Canadian school psychology see, Cole (1992), the NASP *Communiqué* (Vol. 12, No. 7, 1984; Vol. 27, No. 5, 1999), and the *Canadian Journal of School Psychology* (Vol. 6, No.1, 1990; Vol. 11, No. 2, 1995; Vol. 12, No. 2, 1996).

CONCLUSION

The factors controlling preparation, credentialing, and daily roles and functions are summarized in Table 7.1. The scheme of determinants in Table 7.1 represents the current thinking of the authors. We acknowledge that others might view the relative strength of the determinants differently. However, we doubt that others will view any of the determinants as unworthy of inclusion.

We have divided the controlling variables into those we consider direct and indirect for each area of regulation. Reviewing the variables involved in controlling preparation and credentialing for practice, we observe that the direct variables for preparation serve as the indirect variables for credentialing, and vice versa. The direct variables in each domain are largely independent and become the indirect variables in the other's domain. The credentialing of school psychologists is perhaps the most complex area of professional regulation.

In our opinion, the factors directly controlling practice are distinct from those for training and credentialing. At least in part, the distinction may explain the persistence of traditional school psychology practice even after many years of increased training and credentialing requirements.

It is clear from Figures 7.1 and 7.2 and Table 7.1 that two broad domains of influence exist in school psychology. Major changes in the education arena or in the psychology arena have subsequent impact on school psychology. Accreditation changes by APA or NCATE will influence standards for school psychology training; changes in certification or licensing agencies will influence credentialing standards. Legislation and litigation in education or psychology can influence the daily practice of school psychologists.

The influence of the determinants may vary as a function of school and non-school employment. Educational influences are expected to be more evident to one's employment conditions in school settings while psychological influences are expected to be more evident in non-school settings. Adjustments would need to be made in some of the practice determinants in order to apply them to non-school settings. Whether we consider school psychology to be trapped between, or adroitly straddling, the fields of education and psychology, the dual influences are dramatic. Despite the dual influences, school psychology has acquired the major symbols of professionalization as well as their attendant regulations.

TABLE 7.1 Sources of professional control

Preparation for Employment	Credentialing for Employment	Roles and Functions During Employment
Direct Influence		
APA accreditation standards	SDE licensing requirements	District demands and expectations
NCATE/NASP accreditation standards	SBEP licensing requirements	District perception of needs
SDE program approval requirements		Consumer response to services
Designation (National Register & ASPPB) criteria		Desired functions of school psychologist
		Competencies of school psychologist
Indirect Influence		
ASPA	NCATE/NASP accreditation standards	Orientation of the training program
CDSPP	APA accreditation standards	Credentialing requirements
SDE certification requirements	SDE program approval requirements	State laws and regulations
SBEP licensing requirements	Designation criteria	State and local professional associations
APA/NASP IOC	ASPPB position statements	NASP and APA position statements
APA position statements	APA position statements	Ethics
NASP position statements	NASP position statements	Legislation and litigation
State association positions	State association positions	
SDE rules and regulations	NASDTEC positions	
Division 16-APA positions	Division 16-APA positions	
Training program and faculty orientations	NCSP requirements	
	Training program and faculty orientations	

PRACTICAL EXERCISES

1. What is the accreditation status of your training program and that of other programs in your state?
2. Survey other students in your program to determine in what state(s) they intend to practice and whether they intend to work in school or non-school settings.
3. What are the practice and non-practice credentials of the faculty in your program and department?
4. Report to your class on the requirements of the ABSP and the National Certification System in school psychology.
5. What are the certification and licensure requirements in the state in which your training program is located?
6. What do practitioners in your area describe as the main determinants of their role and function?
7. Can you think of additional determinants and where they would fit into Table 7.1?
8. What do practitioners in your area describe as their main legal-ethical problems?
9. How are alleged ethical violations adjudicated by practitioners in your state?
10. What have been the results of state and federal monitoring visits to your local school district? Are the district and its psychological services considered to be in compliance with the provisions of the IDEA?

NOTE

1. Portions of this chapter appear in Fagan (1990a) and are reproduced here by permission of the National Association of School Psychologists; and in Fagan (1982) and reproduced with permission of the National Association of Vocational Education Special Needs Personnel.

Practica, Internships, and Job-Site Considerations

For those of you just beginning school psychology training, the prospects of internship sites and jobs may seem too remote even to consider at this time. Just getting through the current term —not to mention comprehensive exams, theses, and whatever other long-range academic obstacles lie in wait—may appear to be an impossible dream. Still, it is in your own best interest to start thinking about short-term and long-term professional goals early in training to motivate yourself when you are feeling overwhelmed and to prepare yourself appropriately to meet these professional goals.

This chapter examines a number of vital issues including practicum experiences, internship sites, first job sites, and career options beyond the first year. Within this last context, we describe some alternative job settings available to those with degrees and experience in school psychology.

FIELD EXPERIENCES: HISTORICAL BACKGROUND

The notion of field experience, including internships, as an essential part of practitioner training is nearly as old as the field of school psychology itself. Witmer provided practical demonstrations as part of his instruction to practitioners during the early years of the psychological clinic at the University of Pennsylvania. Morrow (1946) contended that the earliest formal internships were those offered at the Vineland Training School in New Jersey as early as 1908 and that these were essentially "school psychology internships." As indicated in Chapter 2, Norma Cutts was among the interns trained at Vineland. Training School publications of that era suggest the nature of the paid experience (Goddard, 1914). Wallin (1919) had called for such experience in the training of psychologists but few programs appear to have complied immediately.

Although practica in university clinics and community agencies were part of school psychology training and credentialing requirements by the mid-1930s (Fagan, 1999), the practice of requiring field experiences increased in popularity, and detailed proposals for a 1-year internship as part of doctoral training were put forth in 1945 (APA & AAAP, 1945). The first state department of education-sponsored internship program appears to have been the one initiated in Ohio in the 1950s (Bonham & Grover, 1961). The Thayer conference proceedings (Cutts, 1955) provide considerable discussion of practicum and internship conceptualizations, practices, and recommendations.

In 1963, a conference was held at George Peabody College for Teachers in Nashville, Tennessee to discuss the internship in school psychology. In the proceedings from the so-called Peabody Conference, Susan Gray (1963a, p. 1) noted that "since the internship is usually taken in an area geographically and administratively separate from the training institution, it deserves particular attention, for the inevitably wide variability in such non-university settings carries within it the danger of diffusion of purpose and of standards for training."

Although the Peabody conference was specifically aimed at doctoral-level internships, many of the ideas and principles established at that Conference remain in practice today. For example, the proceedings maintain that the internship should be part of the continuous training process leading to preparation in school psychology and that the internship should be a transitional phase between being a student and being a professional.

Another issue addressed at the Peabody conference and still highly relevant is that, ideally, the internship should offer a balance between "service" and "training." Interns should be expected to work hard for and provide service to their employers. On the other hand, the training aspects of the internship should not be neglected. Interns should not be considered merely inexpensive school psychologists. Rather the internship should be a year filled with new experiences, complete with ample opportunities to discuss issues, ask questions, observe procedures, acquire skills and knowledge, and try out a variety of professional roles and functions.

The widespread formalization of field experience including practicum and internship requirements is much more recent and is directly related to increased credentialing requirements by SDEs and licensing boards, reciprocally connected to increased standards of training especially by APA and NASP. Early SDE credentialing requirements often included a practicum and less often an internship. At the present time, all SDEs and licensing boards have some form of field experience requirement for credentialing (Curtis, Hunley, & Prus, 1998).

CURRENT PRACTICES IN FIELD EXPERIENCES

Practica

When discussing field experiences for students in school psychology training programs, we are actually talking about two different types or levels of professional preparation. A clear distinction should be made between field experiences completed in conjunction with academic requirements, often called practica, and field experiences that serve as the final step in training, known as internships. According to the *Standards for Training and Field Placement Programs in School Psychology* (NASP, 1994c), practica refer to those field experiences occurring prior to the internship that help training program faculty assess students' skills and determine students' readiness for the internship. Practica experiences are expected to correspond directly to the training program's training objectives in terms of content, supervision, and evaluation. Usually students are expected to complete specific assignments and grades are assigned based upon the quality of these completed assignments. Curtis et al. (1998) note that practica are usually focused on one particular skill (e.g., behavioral consultation) or on a limited range of skills (e.g., components of the assessment process).

Training programs vary dramatically in their practicum requirements. Thomas (1998) noted that master's-level training programs require a median number of 225 "clock hours" (i.e., actual hours spent) of practicum experience with a range of 40 to 1,200 hours. Specialist-level programs require a median number of 360 clock hours (range 25–1,278), whereas doctoral-level programs require a median number of 600 clock hours of practicum work (range = 30 - 2,000). Some training programs require practicum work in non-school settings (e.g., on-campus clinics) as well as school settings whereas other training programs require experience only in one type of setting.

Ideally, to our way of thinking, practicum experiences should be developmental or graduated. As students learn various professional techniques in their classes they begin to apply those techniques under close faculty supervision in working with actual clients. In this way it is hoped a strong relationship will be forged between academic training and practical skills. Students generally receive academic credit for their practicum experiences although the amount of credit varies from one training institution to another.

Practicum training might be thought of as an introduction to the practice of school psychology. Through practica, students gain an initial awareness of some of the rewards and also some of the frustrations inherent in being a human service professional. Students begin to notice that in addition to skills and training, professional success is also tied to interpersonal skills such as diplomacy, initiative, and cooperation. It is during the practica that students often gain firsthand knowledge of the complexity of many of the issues encountered by school psychologists (as discussed in previous chapters). They learn that in working with an individual child the school psychologist also must work with a family, a classroom, a school building, a school system, state and federal legislation and mandates, and professional guidelines. In addition, students learn firsthand the importance of conducting all of their work in a socially responsible and ethical manner.

A major difference between practica and internship experiences involves the role of the university in each of the settings. In practica, a university faculty member is generally the person directly responsible for supervising and evaluating the students' experiences. The faculty member arranges settings for the experiences, makes the assignments, and assigns the grades. Although a field-based person (e.g., school psychologist, school principal) may play an active role in ensuring that a practicum is a positive learning experience and may be involved in consulting with the faculty member regarding a given student's performance, it is the faculty member who is ultimately responsible for the experience.

Internships

The school-based internship experience in school psychology is a professional apprenticeship. Most commonly, for students in sixth-year or specialist-level training programs, the internship follows 2 years of graduate-level academic training including practicum and field experiences. For students in doctoral programs, the internship follows all required coursework but is still completed prior to receiving the doctoral degree. In either case, the internship is often the final requirement for the terminal degree. It is a halfway house providing the opportunity for a smooth transition between the academic environment and the full-time job of the practicing school psychologist. Although most, if not all, training programs provide practical opportunities for students to work in the schools while completing their coursework and developing their professional skills, these practicum requirements are not equivalent to a full-time, year-long supervised internship in the schools.

During the internship, the site supervisor has much more responsibility than do university personnel for the day-to-day supervision and evaluation of the intern's activities. The site supervisor and the intern work closely together in developing a comprehensive "internship plan" and in ensuring that items on the plan are accomplished and evaluated. University faculty members observe interns from a more distant perspective, visiting the intern occasionally during the year, hosting the intern's return visits to the university, and acting as consultants when questions or problems arise. Although the university supervisor usually assigns the final grade and gives official university approval for the intern, the site supervisor generally advises the university faculty member as to the intern's professional performance and recommends that the intern be approved or not be approved for credentialing. Readers should note that in field experiences, generally, three parties are involved: the student, the university supervisor, and the site supervisor.

Although all three parties play important roles, the degree of influence over the student tends to shift from the university supervisor to the site supervisor in the transition from practicum to internship.

In our experience, many interns report that they learn more during the internship year than throughout all of their years of undergraduate and graduate coursework and practicum experiences combined. Along this same line, many interns have reported to us that the knowledge they acquire in their graduate classes becomes clearer and more meaningful during the internship. One former student remarked that, much to her surprise, by the end of her internship she realized she had used information from every class she had taken in graduate school, including research and statistics!

Despite extensive practicum experiences, students going into the internship often feel unsure of their professional abilities. Even those who have excelled in their undergraduate and graduate studies may experience self-doubts. Moving from graduate student status to intern status can involve a number of stressors: moving away from a familiar environment, leaving friends and colleagues, meeting new people, starting a new job, and changing one's status from student to professional (Phillips, 1990b; Solway, 1985).

By the completion of the internship most students seem to develop not only enhanced professional skills but also enhanced self-confidence overall. Gray (1963a) stated that during the internship students learn about their own strengths and weaknesses — and how to accentuate their strengths while correcting or at least minimizing their weaknesses.

A formal discussion of current practices in internships might logically begin with a look at internship requirements. In the National Association of School Psychologists publication entitled *Standards for Training and Field Placement Programs in School Psychology* (1994, pp. 12-14), the following standards apply to the internship experience:

1. The internship experience is provided at or near the end of the formal training period.
2. The internship experience occurs on a full-time basis over a period of one academic year, or on a half-time basis over a period of two consecutive academic years.
3. The internship experience is designed according to a written plan that provides the student opportunities to gain experience in the delivery of a broad range of school psychological services. Services include, but are not limited to assessment for intervention, counseling, behavior management, and consultation.
4. The internship experience occurs in a setting appropriate to the specific training objectives of the program.

5. The internship experience is provided appropriate recognition through the awarding of academic credit.
6. The internship experience occurs under conditions of appropriate supervision. Field-based internship supervisors hold a valid credential as a school psychologist for that portion of the internship that is in a school setting. That portion of the internship which appropriately may be in a non-school setting requires supervision by an appropriately credentialed psychologist.
7. Field-based internship supervisors are responsible for no more than two interns at any given time. University internship supervisors are responsible for no more than 12 interns at any given time.
8. Field-based internship supervisors provide, on average, at least two hours per week of direct supervision for each intern.
9. The internship is based on a positive working relationship and represents a collaborative effort between the university program and field-based supervisors to provide an effective learning experience for the student. University internship supervisors provide at least one on-site contact per semester with each intern and supervisor.
10. The internship placement agency provides appropriate support for the internship experience including:
    a. A written contractual agreement specifying the period of appointment and the terms of compensation
    b. A schedule of appointment consistent with that of agency school psychologists (e.g., calendar, participation in in-service meetings, etc.)
    c. Provision for participation in continuing professional development activities
    d. Expense reimbursement consistent with policies pertaining to agency school psychologists
    e. An appropriate work environment including adequate supplies, materials, secretarial services, and office space
    f. Release time for internship supervisors
    g. A commitment to the internship as a training experience
11. The quality of the internship experience is systematically evaluated in a manner consistent with the specific training objectives of the program.
12. The internship experience is conducted in a manner consistent with the current legal-ethical standards of the profession.

Elsewhere in the *Standards* it is noted that internships for students in specialist programs should consist of at least 1,200 clock hours of experience including at least 600 clock hours in a school setting. Internships for students in doctoral programs should consist of at least 1,500 clock hours or experience including at least 750 clock hours in a school setting. Students in doctoral programs who have already completed a school-based internship as part of a specialist program may complete their pre-doctoral internships in non-school settings.

In addition to the NASP requirements for internships, individual states and training programs often have requirements of their own. The publication, *Credentialing Requirements for School Psychologists* (Curtis, Hunley, & Prus, 1998), in its discussion of field experiences contains the following description of the internship:

> An internship usually is a supervised culminating field experience that occurs after the completion of most or all coursework in a training program. Some states and accrediting bodies require that... internships consist of experience beyond that which is obtained in practica courses. Pre-degree field experience must have associated academic credit (e.g., semester hours or quarter hours) to qualify under certification or licensure regulations in some states (p. 10).

A set of questions relative to the internship experience required by your state and your training program is provided at the conclusion of this chapter. Guidelines from your state department of education as well as discussions with your training program faculty members should provide answers to these questions.

Other Internship Considerations

Let us now move to some of the less formal aspects of the internship year. Included in this section is information concerning deciding upon an internship site, applying for an internship, and choosing between sites. Additional information is provided relevant to what happens if something goes wrong during the internship.

Deciding Upon an Internship Site

Psychology is focused upon differences between individuals. When it comes to the consideration of internship and job sites, individual differences are readily apparent. All of us have our own priorities, values, and professional and personal likes and dislikes, strengths and weaknesses. We bring these characteristics and preferences with us as we embark on a search for the perfect internship or job site.

Many of these variables change over time depending upon life circumstances. If you are married, for example, you may need to think about employment opportunities for your spouse. If you have young children issues such as day care and the quality of the local schools may be important considerations. To guide you through this decision-making process, a set of questions to consider as you think about various internship sites is included below. Many prospective interns begin their search by focusing upon geographical, social, and financial factors or considerations.

Students should ask the following questions:

1. Are there internships available close to where I currently live?
2. Do I want to stay in the area where I currently live?
3. Can I afford to live in a particular area on an internship salary?
4. If not, can I live with my parents, other relatives, or friends for the duration of the internship?
5. What factors limit my mobility (e.g., family, romantic attachments)?
6. How do I feel about various locations in terms of climate, personal safety, cleanliness of environment, proximity to loved ones, educational opportunities, and so on?
7. How far am I willing to drive to work each day? What are the roads like on which I would be driving? How is the traffic? Is public transportation an option?
8. If I am married, is my spouse willing and/or able to relocate?
9. Are there opportunities for my spouse to find a job, take classes, work toward a degree, and/or make friends?
10. Does moving now make sense for my spouse and for me?
11. If I have children, how good are the local schools?
12. Is there high quality, reasonably-priced day care available?
13. Will there be a problem if I am the school psychologist in the school my children attend?
14. What kinds of opportunities for a social life will I have in a given location?
15. How is the overall cost of living (e.g., housing, taxes, food, health care) in the area?
16. Is housing available?
17. How large is the community?
18. What do I like to do in my spare time (i.e, hobbies, recreational activities, cultural events etc.)? Will I be able to pursue these activities in my new location?
19. If I move somewhere for an internship, what are the chances that a school psychologist's job would be open there during the following school year?

After considering possible locations in which you would like to work, your next step is to find out whether an internship placement is available somewhere around your preferred location. Generally such openings are publicized through a variety of channels: state school psychological associations, training programs, and state departments of education. Find out from your program faculty how internship positions are typically advertised in your area. In Illinois, for example, the annual convention of the Illinois School Psychologists Association held in early spring has a large room at the convention set up specifically for interviews of prospective interns by site supervisors and for interviews of job seekers by site administrators, often a chief school psychologist or a special education director. In Ohio, the Inter-University Council has internships allocated to it by the SDE and then distributes the internship slots according to program needs. The Illinois method allows for more freedom of mobility among prospective interns whereas the Ohio method allows for better regionalization of the interns along with their continued proximity to their training programs.

Applying for an Internship

When an internship becomes available, applicants are usually encouraged to submit resumes (often called "vitas" or "vitae"), academic transcripts, letters of recommendation, and other materials. Universities generally have placement offices designed to facilitate this process. Personnel in such offices maintain files for job applicants containing the information mentioned above. Such files are called "placement files" or "placement papers" and will be sent to prospective employers upon your request. The benefit of using the services of a placement office is that it saves the inconvenience of collecting and sending out the various required papers—particularly the letters of reference—each time you apply for a job. In addition to the ease of procedure initially, a placement office facilitates updating and maintenance of your file for future use. Placement offices also keep track of a limited number of job openings and listings of appropriate available jobs may be sent out periodically to those using their services. We strongly encourage you to register with your university placement offices.

School psychology faculty members may be invaluable sources of information as well. Ask your faculty members whether they would be willing to review your resume and offer suggestions for items to include and items to delete. Also it is advisable, if not mandatory, to ask *at least* one of your school psychology faculty members to serve as a reference. Only in rare cases of extreme personal conflict would a student be justified in not having such a recommendation. Whether or not a school psychology faculty member's name is listed as a reference, site supervisors frequently seek out trainers' opinions of the applicants in advance of making decisions.

The Internship Interview

Assuming that you survive the initial applicant screening process (i.e., you possess the basic credentials for the job), the next step in finding a school psychology internship is the interview. The format of such interviews varies considerably from place to place depending upon, among other factors, the educational agency's past experience with interns and the number of applications they receive. Some school districts invite all applicants to come for interviews on the same day. School personnel move the prospective interns through various stations of the interview process throughout the day and often make their decisions within a short period of time. Other educational agencies are much less structured. They may merely ask you to schedule an interview at a mutually convenient time.

At times the person or persons conducting the interview will have specific questions, such as, "What instruments would you use if you were asked to assess a developmentally delayed 3-year-old with a hearing impairment?" or "How would you handle an irate parent who disagrees with the results of your assessment?" Some interviewers ask difficult questions to determine how you react to stressful situations. (Merely reading the two questions mentioned above may have triggered a stressful reaction among some of you reading these words.) Other interviewers may simply tell you a bit about what the job would entail and then take you around to meet a few staff members.

Most interviews eventually arrive at the point where you are asked if *you* have questions. Although you probably will have a lot of questions about prospective internships, we would recommend *not* starting out immediately by asking about salary, fringe benefits, and the long-term job outlook. Instead, focus upon content issues first and leave the other questions until somewhat later in the interview. Depending upon the information already given, you might wish to start with more general questions about the community and school district and then move into more specific concerns. Try to focus upon the questions most important to you as you consider internship sites. It is important to ask some questions during an interview; a lack of questions might indicate a lack of interest in the position to the interviewer.

What follows are community and school-related questions:

1. What is the overall socio-economic level of the population?
2. What is the educational level of the people in this area? How committed is the community to education?
3. How many schools are in the district (or cooperative or education agency, etc.)?
4. How do students in the schools perform academically compared to state or national norms?
5. How big are the schools?
6. How are the schools divided in terms of grades?
7. What is the average class size?

8. Is there some sort of district-wide handbook?
9. Generally what are the rules regarding punishment and rewards?
10. What kinds of special education classes or other services are available?
11. How much inclusion is occurring, and how do the teachers respond to having children with disabilities in their classrooms?
12. What are some of the problems causing concern in the district (such as gangs, drugs, theft, violence, or cults)?
13. How safe are the schools?
14. What kind of turnover rate is there for teachers and other school personnel?
15. What is the financial status of the school district?
16. Is there a history of teacher strikes?
17. How enthusiastic are staff members about new ideas, new programs, and so forth?
18. How familiar are administrators, teachers, and other staff members with the various roles and functions of the school psychologist?
19. How involved is the community in school activities?
20. What kinds of resources are available nearby in terms of medical care, counseling, and so on for purposes of referral?

What follows are job description concerns:

1. How many months would I work?
2. How many schools would I be responsible for?
3. How far apart are these schools?
4. What resources and materials are available to me (e.g., up-to-date testing materials, secretarial services, Dictaphones)?
5. What type of computers are used in the office? Will I have access to the Internet and e-mail?
6. Where would my home office be?
7. Is there adequate space for me to work in the various schools?
8. How many other school psychologists are employed here?
9. Who will my supervisor be?
10. What is my supervisor's philosophy of school psychology?
11. About how much supervisory time would I receive?
12. Will I have the opportunity to work with more than one school psychologist?
13. Will my office be near the offices of other school psychologists?
14. How much turnover has there been among the school psychologists?
15. How well do the school psychologists get along with one another?
16. How many case studies would I be expected to complete?
17. How much responsibility would I have for these cases?
18. What is the approximate salary I would be offered?

19. What kinds of fringe benefits are available (e.g., medical insurance, dental insurance, sick days, retirement plan)?
20. If I do a good job during the internship what are the chances that there would be a permanent position open for me next year?

Obviously you would not want to ask all of the above questions during the interview. There is such a thing as overkill. On the other hand, you do want answers to most if not all of these questions before making a final decision about an internship site particularly if you are in the enviable position of choosing between two or more internship offers.

The Job Offer: The Principle of Supply and Demand

In recent years in school psychology there have been insufficient numbers of trained personnel to fill all of the available internships and jobs. Educational agencies need school psychologists to comply with federal and state legislation and most prospective interns with even a moderate degree of geographical mobility have had their choice of internship sites. After examining school psychology shortages for the 1989-1990 school year and factoring in such things as attrition (school psychologists who leave their positions temporarily or permanently), estimated number of school psychology graduates, and total number of school psychology practitioners, Connolly and Reschly (1990, p. 12) concluded the following:

1. There is a serious national shortage of practitioners.
2. There are vast state and regional differences (in supply and demand).
3. Many of the available graduates may not be able or willing to relocate in other regions.
4. The location of positions is not even across the rural, urban, and suburban settings.
5. Numbers of practitioners and student ratios vary significantly across states, within regions, and between regions.

In support of their conclusions, Connolly and Reschly indicated that 57% of the vacancies were in rural areas, 27% were in urban areas, and 16% were in suburban areas. Also, though the ratio of school psychologists to students was approximately one school psychologist for every 2,100 students nationally, in Connecticut the ratio was 1:617 whereas in Texas the ratio was 1:6,537.

Even with such shortages in mind, however, prospective interns seem always to worry about getting job offers. If you have a specific site in mind as a first choice, and if other prospective interns are interested in that site as well, you may wonder how to go about getting the internship site staff to choose you over your competition.

It is probably safe to say that few if any internship sites consider academic grade point average as the single most critical factor in the decision-making process. Letters of recommendation from your program faculty, however, are important. Two students from a single training program tend to have similar coursework and may obtain similar grades. If each has a letter of recommendation from the same faculty member, and if your letter is full of superlatives ("This is the best student I've ever had in my 30 years of experience") whereas the other student's letter is lukewarm ("This student tended to be slightly above average in his performance in classes and practica"), you probably would be offered the job first.

Impressions made during the interview are also important. If you are neatly dressed, speak well, arrive on time, ask appropriate questions, and appear polite yet friendly, you will generally have a better chance at being offered a job over someone who looks messy, mumbles, arrives late, has no questions, and appears rude and/or hostile. After all, the people who interview you realize that if you are hired they may come into contact with you on a daily basis on the job. They not only are looking for someone with academic credentials, but they also want someone with whom they think that they and others can get along.

We recommend to our students that they prepare a professional portfolio of material to take with them on their internship interviews. The portfolio can include a variety of information but should always contain a copy of your transcript, catalog descriptions of the courses you have completed, copies of sample psychological reports you have completed (with all identifying information deleted), notes from interventions and counseling sessions, and some information about your training program's philosophy and objectives. Some training programs may require that you maintain such portfolios. Even if your program does not require a portfolio, however, it is to your advantage if you compile all of the information into a convenient readable format. Material in the portfolio also provides a convenient means of pulling relevant materials together for post-internship job interviews or for those students who may wish to apply for additional graduate work after the internship. Students who have put the effort into compiling portfolios have frequently remarked that interviewers were impressed with these packets. Specific suggestions for information in a professional portfolio include the following:

1. A current vita or resumé
2. A brief (one typewritten page) statement of your philosophy of education/school psychology and your professional goals
3. A copy of your internship plan and any evaluations during the internship
4. Letters of reference
5. A list of your experiences in teaching, counseling, and intervention
6. A summary of your research project or thesis (or the proposal for the project if not complete)

7. A list of assessment instruments administered
8. A sample behavioral consultation plan
9. The number of actual hours you spent in the schools during practicum
10. One (or more) psychoeducational report that you consider your best work *with all identifying information removed.*
11. A summary of any group work you have done
12. A summary of any individual counseling you have done
13. A summary of your duties in any assistantship
14. Any certifications (teacher certifications, etc.)
15. Transcripts from all post-secondary coursework
16. Syllabi from all of your graduate classes and possibly photocopies of text covers and tables of contents (this will save you time when seeking certification or admission to other graduate programs in the future)
17. Any committees you have served on
18. Certificates from workshops/conferences you have attended
19. Photocopies of the catalog pages for the years you attended grad school (these typically contain course descriptions)
20. A copy of your program's graduate guidelines

Opportunities and Difficulties During the Internship Year.

Once you have been offered and have accepted an internship, what happens next? Usually you will sit down with your supervisor(s) early in the internship and develop an internship plan, which is a list of activities to be completed or competencies to be acquired by the end of the internship. Make certain you are aware of all state and training program requirements for the internship ahead of time so that you do not get caught at the end of your internship with one or more deficiencies. For example, if your state requires that at least 20 school days be spent with each of four populations (e.g., preschool, elementary school, secondary school, and low-incidence handicapped), you will need to set aside time to accomplish all of these. Similarly if your training program requires you to assess at least four preschoolers, consult with at least 10 teachers, and observe in all special education programs, you need to make certain that you accomplish and document these activities.

Aside from sharpening your existing skills, the internship should provide you with the opportunity to expand your repertoire of skills. If most of your field experience or practica work has involved children ages 5–12, make it a point during the internship to work with infants, preschoolers, and adolescents. Along the same lines, the internship should be a time for you to attend workshops, read up on professional topics with which you are unfamiliar, and discuss with your supervisor and with your colleagues various legal and ethical questions and concerns.

Undoubtedly many of these topics and questions were discussed at some point often in a hypothetical sense during your training. During the internship, however, when real rather than hypothetical situations occur, the answers to your professional, legal, and ethical questions take on an added importance and relevance.

Many interns report that their internships start off slowly. They are not quite certain what to do and their supervisors, especially those who have not supervised interns before, are not certain what to do with them. It is not uncommon for interns to spend much of the first month or so visiting local agencies, being introduced to personnel at their supervisor's schools, observing their supervisors performing a variety of tasks, attending workshops, and just generally becoming oriented to the site. Although such activities contribute to a certain amount of restlessness on the intern's part, the slow pace generally picks up after a month or 6 weeks and by the end of the year interns may look back with some regret at the good old days before they had calendars full of meetings, appointments, and other similar responsibilities.

Intern supervisors vary in the amount of supervision they are willing and able to provide. Some supervisors spend several weeks observing the intern's skills in assessment and consultation before allowing the intern to work independently. Other supervisors assume that, because an intern has earned the university's seal of approval, the intern's skills are adequate and close observation is not needed. Likewise, some supervisors will read and correct interns' psychoeducational reports all year. Others will read the first few reports, make suggestions, and feel sufficiently comfortable with the intern's report writing skills to read only the most difficult reports or those involving potentially delicate situations.

What if Something Goes Wrong During the Internship?

We have worked with students, interns, and internship supervisors long enough to know that although most internships progress smoothly, there are times when troubles arise. Such troubles can occur at any time during the internship and usually take one of the following forms.

Intern-supervisor conflicts. After going through the application, interview, and selection processes, interns and supervisors are usually fairly compatible with one another. Occasionally, however, as in any working relationship in which two individuals must work closely together, there are disagreements and conflicts. For example, an intern may want more supervision than the supervisor is providing, a supervisor may find that the intern does not meet what he or she considers the minimum level of competence in assessment or counseling, an intern may feel the supervisor is using out-of-date assessment techniques, or the supervisor may be overwhelmed with job demands and find the intern to be overly dependent or demanding.

When such conflicts arise, interns often confide in their fellow interns at other sites and/or the faculty from their training programs; supervisors may also call the university to complain or to consider their alternatives. Some of these conflicts may be worked out by mutual agreement or through common-sense arrangements (e.g., if the intern wants more supervision, voicing the concern to the supervisor might result in scheduling a 2-hour meeting at the same time each week or arranging to have lunch together twice a week). Other conflicts may not be as easy to resolve (e.g., sexual harassment or extreme philosophical differences) and only another supervisor or another site are feasible alternatives. As with most interpersonal conflicts, keeping communication lines open, considering alternatives, and seeking outside advice are all important avenues to pursue in attempting to work through such conflicts. Finally, the importance of the university "supervisor" as an advisor and a sounding board should not be underestimated.

Using computers, specifically e-mail, to promote communication between interns and university supervisors is a recent means of making sure more frequently that all is going well on the internship. With e-mail, interns from a training program may communicate with each other and with their trainers, asking questions, seeking advice, and making suggestions on a more immediate basis than is possible with the twice yearly visits by the trainer to the site. E-mail also prevents the so-called telephone tag that often occurs when busy people try to get in touch with each other by telephone. Current students may also be involved in these e-mail exchanges so that they have a better understanding of the day-to-day world of the intern.

Personal crises. Occasionally during the internship year, either the intern or the supervisor experiences a personal crisis that brings the internship to a standstill (e.g., a serious illness or the death of a family member). If the intern is unable to complete the year under such circumstances, arrangements generally can be made to postpone all or part of the internship until the following school year. Keep in mind that most universities have rules regarding the number of years in which all coursework and requirements must be completed.

If the intern supervisor is unable to fulfill his/her supervisory duties, other arrangements can usually be made as well. For example, in a district with several school psychologists, the intern may simply be assigned to another supervisor. In other cases, the intern may have to secure another internship placement for the duration of the experience. In all cases, training program faculty should be consulted and kept informed as circumstances change.

Intern impairment. Several articles have addressed the notion of trainee and/or intern impairment (Bernard, 1975; Boxley, Drew, & Rangel, 1986; Knoff & Prout, 1985; Lamb, Cochran, & Jackson, 1991). In their 1991 paper, Lamb et al. define impairment as something that interferes with the performance of professional duties. Such interference may take the following forms:

1. An inability or unwillingness to acquire and integrate professional standards into one's repertoire of professional behavior.
2. An inability to acquire professional skills and reach an accepted level of competency.
3. An inability to control personal stress, psychological dysfunction, or emotional reactions that may affect professional functioning (p. 292).

We include this information not to frighten students but rather to emphasize the continued importance of accountability and evaluation coupled with professional ethical responsibilities throughout school psychology training and practice. It is the responsibility of faculty members and of intern supervisors to monitor students' skills and progress closely and in a consistent and ongoing manner in order to ensure quality control within our profession. Recall from earlier discussions that NASP and APA have each developed ethical guidelines for professional behavior. Many state associations have their own ethical guidelines as well. Spend time throughout your training familiarizing yourself with these principles.

The Next Step

Following completion of the internship, most state departments of education have specific procedures that must be followed in order to obtain certification in school psychology (e.g., paperwork, state-mandated competency tests). At the conclusion of this chapter, a list of questions can be found regarding the certification requirements in your state. Be certain to familiarize yourself with these procedures in order to expedite the certification process (see Chapter 7).

YOUR PROFESSIONAL LIFE AFTER THE INTERNSHIP

After your internship plan has been completed to your supervisor's satisfaction, and after all other university and state-mandated requirements for certification have been met, it is time to consider the next step on your professional career ladder. We recommend giving serious consideration to short-term and long-term professional goals. In our experience, most new graduates of school psychology programs will want to find jobs initially as school psychologists and begin to practice the skills acquired over the past 3 or so years of training. Others, however, may decide to return to school for additional training either to gain skills in a particular area of school psychology (e.g., counseling, early childhood assessment and intervention, or neuropsychological assessment) or to prepare for other school psychology-related career options (e.g., school psychology faculty positions). Those individuals who for family and/or financial reasons are place bound may be anxious simply about finding any appropriate position within reasonable commuting distance.

For the majority, who will not be seeking additional training immediately upon the conclusion of the internship, moving from student status to professional status is often considered a major turning point in life. As with any such turning point there are privileges (e.g., no more assigned homework or readings) but there are also responsibilities (e.g., less supervision and more accountability for your actions). Many graduates of our programs have reported as interns and as certified school psychologists that they are amazed and even overwhelmed occasionally at the respect they are given by virtue of their professional positions. Of course, while such high esteem is flattering, it, too, carries with it an additional responsibility for ethical and mature practice.

Your job search will involve many of the same issues and questions posed in the section above regarding internships. Geographical, family, and financial factors will likely influence your job seeking. Such issues as job description, salary, and fringe benefits are generally more important in job seeking than in the search for an internship since the current search may lead to long-term employment in a particular setting. Nancy Sherer, the Human Resources Benefits Director at Western Illinois University, suggests asking the following questions with respect to fringe benefits in addition to visiting the individual in charge of Human Resources and reviewing any brochures available:

1. What group plans are available for health insurance, health maintenance organizations, long-term disability, life insurance, dental insurance, and vision insurance?
2. On what date would I be covered under these plans?
3. What is my cost for coverage under these plans?
4. What is the cost for my spouse and children to be covered?
5. Will I be covered through the summer months?
6. If I have a claim, what will my portion of the cost be?
7. What are the exclusions or limitations of the coverage?
8. If I am ill or injured, how much would I be required to pay in a year?
9. Am I restricted to certain health care providers?
10. Do I have any coverage if I go outside of these providers?
11. How are claims filed?
12. If I do not choose additional life insurance now, what would be required to add life insurance at a later date?
13. What retirement plans are available? What amount do I contribute? What amount is contributed by my employer?
14. If I leave, what amount of my retirement may I withdraw?

In addition to these questions you will need to know if the staff is unionized or not. If so, are you required to pay union dues whether or not you are a member? You might also wish to ask about sick days, personal days, family leave, and so forth. Those who have never held a full time professional position before will be amazed at and perhaps overwhelmed by the number of options available and the number of forms that need to be signed. (You may also be surprised at how little seems to be left in your paycheck after all of the deductions.)

We believe school psychologists looking for first positions should, if possible, work in close proximity to at least one experienced school psychologist. Ideally the first job provides the opportunity for the new school psychologist to find a professional mentor; that is, a more experienced colleague who will provide support and advice when difficulties arise and who will assist you in establishing your own professional role. Keep in mind also that the NASP credentialing standards call for 1 year of post-internship supervised experience before receiving a permanent credential through one's SDE or elsewhere. This signals the importance the profession places on close working relationships with other, more-experienced school psychologists early in one's professional career. Of course, part of the difficulty is that many school psychologists are in settings alone or with only one other practitioner. To combat this professional isolation, many new school psychologists also find it helpful to keep in touch with their graduate school faculty members, their internship supervisors, and/or their graduate student peers in order to form a network of professional support. The advent of e-mail has facilitated this process greatly. E-mail listservs, such as the one for NASP members, in which individuals can call upon a group of others for ideas and advice can provide quick consultations on particular issues. Recent discussions on the NASP listserv have involved what to do about a youngster with selective mutism, whether to indicate a specific program for a student in a psychological report, and a request for ideas about helping schools develop crisis intervention plans. Occasionally a school psychologist will share specific test scores and request that colleagues help with interpretation. Although e-mail does not take the place of face-to-face contact with a colleague, it may help ease feelings of professional isolation.

The First Job and Beyond

Although many school psychologists are content to practice their profession from the time they become certified until the time of their retirement, others may choose to branch out in different directions. For those who are employed as practicing school psychologists but who wish to stay current professionally and/or expand their professional horizons, there are various ways of accomplishing this. Continuing education, or continuing professional development (CPD), is one possibility. Currently mandated in order to maintain national certification (NCSP) status, CPD may take many forms such as attendance at professional conferences and workshops, independent readings, teleconferences, university coursework, and independent research efforts. Developing new skills, keeping up with professional developments, and trying out a variety of intervention techniques are all ways of maintaining a high level of interest and involvement in the field of school psychology.

Another avenue which some school psychologists pursue is that of active participation in professional organizations and associations. Organizations such as state school psychology associations and NASP welcome students, interns, and school psychologists who wish to become involved. There is always work to be done on the various organizational committees and subcommittees, anything and everything from addressing legal issues to planning and running the annual convention. Once you make some contacts with people in the organization, you may be surprised at the speed and enthusiasm with which committee chairs and officers encourage your involvement. Another way to get a foot in the door of professional associations is to contribute your time and talents to the newsletter. Look over recent issues of the newsletter to determine the types of articles printed as well as the name and address of the editor along with any specific procedures for manuscript submission. Write up and submit a summary of something that you have done, observed, read, or thought about that you think other school psychologists might find useful and/or interesting.

Job Stress and Burnout

Job stress and burnout among school psychologists have been under investigation recently (Huebner, 1992; Wise, 1985). In Chapter 3 we reported the results of several studies relevant to job satisfaction among practicing school psychologists (Conoley & Henning-Stout, 1990; Fagan, 1988b; Henning-Stout, 1992; Levinson et al., 1988; and Solly & Hohenshil, 1986). Such studies suggest that many factors relate to job satisfaction including age, affiliation with school psychology associations, gender, psychologist to student ratio, and quality of professional supervision.

Wise (1985) formulated a list of professional stressors, the *School Psychologists and Stress Inventory,* and asked a national sample of practicing school psychologists to rate the relative stressfulness of each of the stressors. Figure 8.1 presents the rankings of the relative stressfulness of events listed in the inventory.

Huebner (1992) administered the *School Psychologists and Stress Inventory* along with the *Maslach Burnout Inventory* or MBI (Maslach & Jackson, 1986) and a questionnaire regarding demographic data as well as job satisfaction. The MBI has three scales: Emotional Exhaustion (EE), Depersonalization (DP), and Personal Accomplishment (PA). Huebner's findings suggest that burnout is a serious problem for many school psychologists. In fact, more than one-third of his respondents met the criteria for emotional exhaustion; more than one-fourth met

FIGURE 8.1 Relative rankings of stressful events by 534 school psychologists

(1 = most stressful; 35 = least stressful)
1. Notification of unsatisfactory job performance
2. Not enough time to perform job adequately
3. Potential suicide cases
4. Working with uncooperative principals and other administrators
*5. Feeling caught between child's needs and administrative constraints (i.e., trying to fit a child into an existing program)
*5. Threat of a due process hearing
7. Lack of appropriate services for children
*8. Child abuse cases
*8. Incompetent and/or inflexible "superiors"
*8. A backlog of more than five reports to be written
*11. Working in physically dangerous situations (e.g., gang-ruled high schools)
*11. A backlog of more than 10 referrals
13. Pressure to complete a set number of cases (e.g., you must test at least 100 children a year)
14. Conferences or staffings with resistant teachers
15. Conferences or staffings with resistant parents
16. Teacher dissatisfaction with your recommendations
17. Report writing
18. Conducting in-service workshops
19. Keeping your district "legal" (i.e., in compliance with federal, state, and local regulations)
*20. Public speaking engagements (e.g., PTA)
*20. Insufficient recognition of your work
*20. Telling parents their child is handicapped
23. Lack of consensus in a staffing
24. Inadequate secretarial help
25. Being told that you have it easy by classroom teachers
*26. A change in the schools or districts which you serve
*26. Lack of contact with professional colleagues
*26. Screening bilingual children
*26. Conducting parent groups
30. Lack of availability of appropriate assessment materials
31. Impending teachers' strike in your district
32. Supervising an intern or school psychology graduate student
33. Keeping up with current professional literature
34. Carrying testing equipment around in unfavorable weather conditions
35. Spending time driving between schools

* Tie in rankings

the criteria for reduced personal accomplishment, and nearly 10% met the criteria for depersonalization. Huebner further reported that specific stressors seem to contribute to burnout among school psychologists. Stressors relating to lack of adequate support and/or resources (e.g., incompetent or inflexible supervisors, inadequate secretarial help, and lack of contact with colleagues) seemed to be the most important contributor to emotional exhaustion and depersonalization. Stressors related to time management (e.g., backlogs of referrals and reports), high risk to self and others (e.g., potential suicide cases or threat of a due process hearing), and interpersonal conflict (e.g., conferences with resistant teachers or working with uncooperative administrators) also contributed to emotional exhaustion.

A more recent study (Huebner & Mills, 1998) investigated the link between occupational stressors, burnout, and personality characteristics among school psychologists. Higher scores on the neuroticism scale related to higher degrees of emotional exhaustion and reduced personal accomplishment, and lower levels of depersonalization. Extraversion and conscientiousness were negatively correlated with emotional exhaustion and positively correlated with reduced personal accomplishment. Agreeableness was negatively correlated with emotional exhaustion and depersonalization.

How can school psychologists cope with the high degree of stress often encountered on the job? Huebner and Mills (1998) suggest that school psychologists pay attention to their own well-being as well as the well-being of their colleagues. Maslach (1976) suggests the use of professional time outs where alternative professional activities can be substituted for one's primary professional activity. For example, those school psychologists whose primary functions involve conducting assessments and planning interventions for children with disabilities may wish to become involved in other functions such as helping to develop a gifted program in a school, working with a group of parents of children with disabilities, participating in the district's preschool screening program, or talking to a high school psychology class about what a school psychologist does. Involvement in state school psychology committee and leadership activities and conference attendance are other coping strategies.

Huebner (1992) noted that strategies aimed at changing the organization itself might be especially effective for those school psychologists whose stressors are related to the organizational aspects of the school system. If there is a lack of appropriate testing materials or insufficient secretarial help, for example, efforts might be made to secure additional funding by documenting such needs for school administrators or by applying for state or federal grants.

Zins, Maher, Murphy, and Wess (1988) suggest the establishment of professional peer support groups as a strategy for dealing with stress and burnout. In addition to providing support for group members, such support groups may serve professionals by providing a network of colleagues to share ideas, obtain feedback, and discuss problems and issues. School psychologists often work in settings in which they are the only members of their profession in a given school building or even in one or more school districts. Peer support groups may alleviate some of the feelings of professional isolation created in such situations.

An additional strategy for coping with professional burnout is to consider changing jobs. A book entitled *Stay or Leave* (Gale & Gale, 1989, p. 13) regarding job selection generally (i.e., not specifically geared to helping professionals) cites five reasons why the majority of high performers move to new positions. The five include: "Limited personal growth opportunities; restrictions that inhibit their ability to do their best work; personality conflicts with superiors or coworkers; insufficient recognition or compensation; and economic realignments, mergers and acquisitions."

Although the language of some of these reasons sounds more appropriate for someone in the business world than for those of us in the helping professions, the underlying reasons that people in various settings move on to new jobs are fairly standard. While most school psychologists work in supportive settings with friendly colleagues, we do know of school psychologists who are unhappy with their jobs for a variety of reasons. Some school psychologists complain about the lack of opportunities for role expansion or personal growth. Such complaints generally include the following kinds of statements:

1. "I feel as though all I do is test."
2. "My supervisor told me if I want to do counseling that's fine, provided I still complete 120 case studies a year."
3. "I'd like to do more consultation but I'm snowed under with referrals and reevaluations."

Similar to these complaints are those relating to restrictions that limit one's work:

1. "I can't do counseling because the social worker counsels."
2. "My supervisor, who is not a school psychologist, thinks that all I can or should do is test."
3. "Most of the teachers I work with don't even want to hear the word 'inclusion,' they just want me to get children with difficulties out of their classrooms so they can teach those who can learn most easily."
4. "I feel over trained for the job I'm expected to perform."

Personality conflicts with superiors or co-workers can be among the most stressful occurrences in life. Often we spend nearly as much or more time with our co-workers than with our spouses or friends (and at least we get to choose our spouses and friends). Let's face it, there are people who for whatever reason get under your skin. Co-workers can have annoying personal habits (too much perfume or too little deodorant), they can talk too loudly or too much, interrupt you when you don't want to be interrupted, criticize notions that are dear to you, hoist work off onto you and not carry their fair share of the workload, try to tell you what you should be doing, and so on. Sometimes it seems as though there should be a parallel institution to divorce court for people who work together. Even though as psychologists we may believe that we can modify the behavior of even the most cantankerous co-worker, in fact we may fail, or we may give up and/or look for a new job before we fail.

As if difficult co-workers are not enough of a problem, difficult supervisors can make one's life a living hell. As stated previously, supervisors of school psychologists often are not trained as school psychologists. Supervisors may be assistant superintendents, directors of special education, pupil personnel directors, building principals, or individuals in a variety of other educational administrative positions. Some may have quite different ideas, philosophies, and priorities when dealing with children with difficulties and disabilities. The job of the school psychologist is often difficult enough without the complicating factor of defending your actions to an unsympathetic supervisor. In Wise's (1985) study of stressful events for school psychologists (Figure 8.1), 4 of the 10 most stressful events related to administration and supervision: notification of unsatisfactory job performance (#1), working with uncooperative principals and other administrators (#4), feeling caught between a child's needs and administrative constraints (#5), and, incompetent and/or inflexible superiors (#9). In Chapter 3, similar job stresses and dissatisfactions are identified.

The fifth reason for switching jobs, cited earlier, economic realignments, mergers, and acquisitions, may be the least relevant to school psychologists. Yet within school systems there are frequent realignments such as having school psychologists, school social workers, speech and communication therapists, and guidance counselors working out of a centralized office; changing a district from a group of neighborhood schools to a series of centers that serve all children in the district in one or more grades. Such realignments can cause much grumbling among school personnel, parents, and children particularly during transitional periods. Mergers, also called school consolidations, frequently occur in rural areas no longer able to support independent local schools for reasons of decreasing monies and/or populations. These consolidations are usually born of necessity rather than choice and, as with realignments, often foster heated emotions and difficult transitional periods.

When school psychologists decide to leave a job for the above reasons or for personal/familial/financial reasons, some thought is generally given to available alternatives or options. Generally these alternatives fall into one or more of the following categories:

1. Moving to another school psychologist position or expanding your options within the field
2. Going back to school
3. Moving into a related field
4. Moving into an unrelated field
5. Using school psychology-related skills in a non-school setting

Moving to another school psychologist position is much like finding an initial position. You learn of job openings, apply, interview, and if an offer is made, you weigh the pros and cons of the new job against whatever other options are available. It is probably safe to say that no job is perfect, but there are certainly factors that make one position more appealing than others to the job seeker. Opportunities for role expansion, reasonable supervision, congenial co-workers, or an improved physical environment may make a large difference in your level of job satisfaction. Professional advancement is another reason why professionals may choose a new position. Recently, members of the NASP listserv have raised questions regarding the possibility of telecommuting (in this case working out of one's home with the help of the computer) or part time work for those with young children at home. If office space is at a premium, it may be that school psychologists will be allowed or even encouraged to work with children and teachers in the schools while performing administrative duties such as report writing and record keeping at home. Such arrangements may encourage individuals to accept positions at greater distances with the understanding that they will not have to commute 5 days a week.

Going back to school in a school psychology-related field is discussed at length in Chapter 6. After working in the schools for several years, most of us become aware of things that we are interested in and wish that we knew more about. Students returning to school to pursue a doctoral degree may decide to specialize in such an area (e.g., neuropsychology, organizational development, or the psychology of reading). Other individuals may decide to return to school on a part-time or full-time basis to take coursework in educational administration or supervision. Such individuals often have career goals of becoming supervisors of other school psychologists or district administrators of special education or pupil personnel services. It is not unthinkable for school psychologists who have returned to school to obtain law or medical degrees instead of the more traditional doctorate in school psychology. Such individuals of our acquaintance usually specialize in areas related to school psychology (e.g., school law or pediatric medicine), and often they serve a valuable function by addressing issues that require both areas of expertise.

Many school psychologists decide at some point in their careers that they would like to have a larger impact on the school system itself by becoming school administrators or supervisors of school psychologists. The NASP *Communiqué* ran an article about five individuals who are now working in administration after working as school psychologists (Blagg et al., 1997). Most of these individuals had worked more than 10 years as school psychologists before making the switch. Other individuals may take positions with state departments of education, applying their school psychology training to issues of state-wide importance.

The paragraphs above are not intended to give readers a bleak picture of school psychology or to imply that every school psychologist eventually burns out and decides to pursue alternative educational and/or employment options. Rather we encourage readers to bear in mind that all of the so-called helping professions including school psychology have their rewards as well as their frustrations. In addition, the particular job setting in which you find yourself working will have its own unique strengths and weaknesses. Finally, society is mobile and most people change jobs and even careers at some point. To help cope with some of the frustrations and weaknesses there are several options you may consider (e.g., CPD, professional involvement, changing jobs, or obtaining additional education). Another option might include pursuing employment in an alternative setting as discussed below.

Roles for School Psychologists in Alternative Settings

If a school psychologist chooses not to work for a school system or is unable to find an acceptable position within the schools, what other options are open? Several alternative routes are available to the individual trained as a school psychologist. Factors such as your personality, the community in which you live, your proximity to various kinds of facilities and services, and so forth will guide your search for jobs.

Assume that you live in a city with a population of about 300,000. The city houses a large university with a medical school, a variety of mental health facilities, several moderate-sized businesses and industries, and a few psychologists functioning as private practitioners. You might first consider working as a school psychologist for the university as a school psychologist involved in higher education. The role in higher education most familiar to most students is that of the trainer of school psychologists. Individuals choosing such a position may be involved in varying degrees in graduate training while often also teaching undergraduate or graduate classes in related fields of psychology, education, special education, or guidance and counseling. Working as a university faculty member offers many advantages. In most universities, there is more flexibility than in the public schools with respect to how you spend your time. Except for meeting your classes, holding office hours and attending department or committee meetings, your time is your own. Of course, you are expected to accomplish certain activities (e.g., research publications and presentations, and professional and community service) if you hope to be retained, promoted, and tenured. In most cases, however, you do not have to conform to the 8:00 AM to 4:30 PM daily schedule of a school system. Those of us who have made the transition from the public schools into the university setting often are pleasantly surprised by the relatively small amount of paperwork required of most faculty members. The major drawback of university teaching, to our way of thinking, is the lack of opportunity and time to spend helping individual children directly. Faculty members may have more of an impact on the field of school psychology in general through their students and their research efforts but less of a direct impact on individual children. To compensate for this lack of contact with children many school psychology faculty members of our acquaintance supervise students in practica and internships, hire themselves out as consultants to nearby school districts, or maintain private practices on a part-time basis. Of course, to be hired as a tenure-track candidate for a school psychology faculty position at most universities, possession of the doctoral degree is usually required.

Another less familiar role for the school psychologist within the realm of higher education is that of applying school psychological roles and functions to the college-age student. Sandoval (1988) suggests several possibilities for the post-secondary school psychologist. Many of the students with whom school psychologists work in elementary and secondary schools choose to attend college. Often the same needs they had for special services prior to college remain with them. School psychologists may help to facilitate such students' transition to college by consulting with other faculty about classroom accommodations and acting as advocates for students with disabilities. In addition, there is often a need for such an individual to work with the admissions office in interpreting the school records of students with disabilities and, if needed, providing additional assessment services. Once accepted into a college, a student with disabilities may need additional support services such as group or individual counseling or assistance with vocational assessment and guidance, some or all of which could be provided by a school psychologist employed in a counseling center, health center, or center for students with disabilities. School psychologists employed by junior colleges or 4-year colleges and universities may also be involved in preventive activities (e.g., substance abuse), promotion of positive mental health, career planning, stress management (e.g., test anxiety), and crisis intervention activities (e.g., for victims of sexual assault). An additional alternative for the school psychologist seeking nontraditional employment might be a position with a medical school or with medical personnel in the area. Shellenberger (1988) suggests that school psychologists could be most beneficial to family physicians by acting as psychological, educational and research consultants. Although such a role may require additional training for the school psychologist, opportunities exist to work cooperatively with family physicians. Related to the field of medicine is the possibility for qualified personnel to work with social, psychological, behavioral, and educational development of chronically ill children. A school psychologist could act as a liaison between physicians, families, and schools in meeting the needs of children with such chronic conditions as asthma, juvenile diabetes, cancer, AIDS, and so on. One publication suggests that from 5% to 15% of school-age children in the United States suffer from chronic health conditions (Johnson, Lubker, & Fowler, 1988). Power, DuPaul, Shapiro, and Parrish (1998, p. 15) note that "the neighborhood school is the logical setting to base health programs, given that schools are highly accessible to families and already have a mechanism to coordinate the efforts of parents and professionals... Psychologists and other school-based professionals increasingly are viewed as serving an important role" in addressing a wide range of student health problems in the schools.

Along this same line, some school psychologists have found employment within residential and day treatment facilities. Mordock (1988) noted that school psychologists employed in such facilities might be involved in the traditional roles of assessment, intervention, consultation, education, and evaluation as well as the nontraditional roles of managerial and administrative related functions. Generally residential and day treatment facilities address the needs of children who are emotionally disturbed, developmentally delayed, and/or have been in trouble with law enforcement authorities. According to Morris and Morris (1989) a school psychologist might be part of a team of professionals involved in the diagnosis, program design, and program evaluation of children in such facilities. Many of these roles and functions are those for which school psychologists are well prepared and little additional formal training would be necessary.

Wodrich (1988) discussed the contribution that school psychologists might make to the practice of pediatric medicine. He noted that pediatricians today are often asked questions about school readiness, behavior problems, and learning problems in addition to the usual array of medical questions. School psychologists with training and experience in answering such questions could certainly make a contribution either indirectly by consulting with pediatricians or directly by working with the children, their families, and their schools. Among the promising ways for pediatricians and school psychologists to work cooperatively is in the assessment, diagnosis, and treatment of children with attention deficit hyperactivity disorder (ADHD) and other learning and developmental disabilities. Surely the treatment of such prevalent problems would benefit from a multidisciplinary approach to research as well as treatment.

An additional possibility for school psychologists seeking alternative settings involves practice in community mental health centers. Conoley (1989) suggested the role of community/family service provider as an appropriate role for school psychologists. Applying such a role to working within a community mental health center, the school psychologist could engage in family consultation, parent training, and family therapy. Such a person could use many of the assessment techniques and intervention strategies that are part of the usual repertoire of the school psychologist. Conoley emphasized the use of behavior change strategies and assessment of individuals and families as particularly relevant to community mental health practice. Moreover, there is a need for increased home-school collaboration for which the school psychologist is specially trained.

Davis (1988) addressed the training needs for those moving from school to community mental health center settings. He suggested that individuals trained with skills in assessment, therapy, and consultation would probably have the easiest time applying school psychology skills within mental health centers. Davis also mentioned that community mental health centers may offer more opportunities to become involved with preventive activities than those offered within traditional school settings.

Is there a role for someone trained as a school psychologist in private practice? Certainly many of the roles and functions practiced in the schools can be adapted to practice in the private sector (e.g., assessment of individual children, counseling, or the planning of behavior management strategies). Pryzwansky (1989) noted that as yet few school psychologists are involved in private practice on a full-time basis. In fact, he reported that in a study by Pion, Bramblett, and Wicherski (1987) only 5% of doctoral-level school psychologists were engaged in full-time private practice. The percentage of master's or specialist-level school psychologists in full-time private practice is also small.

Pryzwansky suggested that we may see an increase in the number and percentages of school psychologists in private practice in the future. He attributed this projected increase to several factors. First, if public education were ever faced with cutbacks in federal funds, particularly for students with disabilities, it might lead to widespread unemployment among school psychologists. Private practice is one option for such individuals. Second, an increase in professional programs leading to the Psy.D. degree might increase the number of school psychologists who would be eligible for SBEP licensure in various states.

Finally, there are some aspects of private practice that make it attractive. Most psychologists look at private practice as having higher income possibilities than practice within the schools. Your income in private practice is to a large extent controlled by how many hours you are willing to work, the fees you charge and are able to collect, and your ability to attract clients. Of course, you have the additional overhead expenses (e.g., office space, assessment instruments, and secretarial help) for which practitioners in the schools are not responsible. Aside from the financial rewards, private practice offers more professional independence. You are not bound by all of the rules and regulations of a local board of education and/or a school administration. You can set your own hours and establish your own procedures. You may even be able to specialize in a particular type of case (e.g., child custody cases or cases involving abuse and neglect) providing there are sufficient numbers of such cases to fill your case load.

The drawbacks to private practice include the notion that there is a large degree of financial risk taking involved, that you may not attract sufficient clients, and that your training in school psychology with its emphasis on working with children within the context of the school setting, the family, and the community is quite different from the private setting in which clients come to your office for your services and may not wish for you to be in contact with other agencies or individuals. Private practice is a business and must be run like a business. Although you are not accountable to a supervisor or a board of education, you are indeed accountable to your clients (as well as financially accountable to the Internal Revenue Service) and thus may be more vulnerable to client influences on diagnoses and interventions. In addition, activities such as going to conventions and participating in continuing professional development take you away from business, thus having a direct impact on your income. Restrictions by insurance companies as to the services they will pay for, also have a direct impact on your income.

Moving away from the more traditional service models, opportunities exist for individuals trained as school psychologists in business and industrial settings. Maher and Greenberg (1988) suggested that there are increasing needs for individuals interested in human resource development (HRD). Human resource development includes such areas as motivating employees, improving the quality of the work environment, and increasing the level of satisfaction that employees derive from their jobs. Maher and Greenberg note that school psychologists working in the area of HRD might be involved in identifying workers' needs and frustrations on the job and in designing programs to address these needs. One of the differences between the traditional roles of the school psychologist in the school setting and the nontraditional role of the school psychologist in business and industry centers around the age of the clients. To be better prepared for such a role, school psychologists would need training in human development and education across the life span (Harrison & McCloskey, 1989). Some of the specific activities suggested by Harrison and McCloskey for the school psychologist in business and industry include services for handicapped employees, general business service (including personnel assessment, personnel education and training, organizational interventions, and counseling), research, and publishing.

A Brief Note on Retirement Planning

Although the authors of this text are at the point in our lives and careers in which we are probably far more interested in retirement than most of the readers of the text, we did want to say a few words about the importance of planning for retirement as soon as you start working. Take it from us, the years go by quickly and before you know it you are at the point where you begin to wonder if you have the resources to enjoy a comfortable and relatively worry-free retirement. School districts and universities usually have some sort of state teachers retirement fund to which the employer and the employee each contribute a portion of the employee's salary. For example, the district and you may each be expected to contribute 7% of your salary toward retirement from the time you first start to work. If you wish to put away more than that amount or if you are working in private practice, you have the option of putting part of your salary into either a 401(k) or similar retirement plan or into some type of Individual Retirement Account (IRA). When you invest in these plans the money you invest is not taxed and is deducted on your income tax to lower your taxable income, but the money you withdraw from the IRA at time of retirement is taxed. These retirement plans work especially well if you are moderately sure that your retirement tax rate will be less than your tax rate right now. There is a new IRA, the Roth IRA, which was introduced in 1998. The Roth IRA is different than a conventional IRA in one way. The money you invest in the Roth IRA is taxed already (i.e., the money cannot be used to reduce your taxable income on your income tax), but the money you withdraw from the IRA at time of retirement is tax free. This IRA works especially well if your tax rate is higher at retirement than it is now. Depending on your age and your financial status, it may make sense to use a combination of the two IRAs. As with questions about insurance and other fringe benefits, specific questions about retirement planning should be addressed to the human services staff at your place of employment and/or a professional financial advisor.

CONCLUSION

This chapter has addressed some of the more practical aspects of internships, first jobs, long-range career planning, and alternative or nontraditional settings for school psychologists. As such, we have applied information from several previous chapters. It is our hope that by examining some of the more practical issues, and contemplating your own professional goals, your preparation and training in school psychology will become more meaningful.

PRACTICAL EXERCISES

The following questions should be completed by students on the basis of written and/or oral information from training program faculty and the state department of education.

1. Requirements
   a. Is an internship required in this state in order to become a certified school psychologist?
   b. What are the state requirements for field experience and/or internship?
   c. Must I complete my internship in this state if I want to be certified here?
   d. What happens if for a variety of reasons (e.g., health, personal crisis, incompatibility with supervisor) I do not complete the full internship?
   e. How is the internship graded and who does the grading?
   f. What if I do not pass? Can I complete another internship?
   g. Must I complete my internship in a public school setting?
   h. Do I need to take some sort of state or national certification test in addition to the internship in order to be certified as a school psychologist?
2. Practical considerations
   a. What kinds of supervision will I get from the university?
   b. What kinds of supervision should I expect from my site supervisor(s)?
   c. Are certain internship sites considered exemplary?
   d. Are certain internship sites considered unacceptable?
   e. How do exemplary internship sites differ from unacceptable sites?
   f. If I want to be employed in a certain state eventually would I be better off doing my internship there or waiting until after the internship to move?
   g. If I complete my internship here and then decide to move to another state, how easy will it be for me to find employment and to become certified?
   h. Should I complete an internship even if I want to get my doctorate and teach at a university?
   i. Can I wait and complete my internship in a few years or must I complete it at a particular time in the program?
   j. If I want to or need to stay in this immediate area, what kind of internship will I be able to find?
   k. How much do internships in this state typically pay? How is this salary determined?

School Psychology In Canada: Past, Present, and Future Perspectives[1]

Donald H. Saklofske, Ph.D., University of Saskatchewan
Riva Bartell, Ph.D., University of Manitoba
Jeffrey Derevensky, Ph.D., McGill University
S. Gerald Hann, Ed.D.,
  Nova Scotia Department of Education
Barbara Holmes, Ed.D., School District 36, Surrey
Henry L. Janzen, Ph.D., University of Alberta

This chapter provides an overview of school psychology in Canada. Following from a description of our historical roots, attention is directed to key topics that influence both the current and future status of school psychology. Particular attention is focused on issues related to training and preparation, credentialing and accreditation, roles and functions, professional associations, and publications for and by school psychologists. Finally, we close with a statement of the challenges that confront us in the twenty-first century.

HISTORY OF SCHOOL PSYCHOLOGY ACROSS CANADA: A SEARCH FOR ROOTS

School psychology in Canada, as in the United States, has struggled to evolve with a unique professional identity in a system where the interdisciplinary roles of educational psychologist, counselor and an array of specialists within special education have vied for discrete territory. Fagan (1996b, p. 84) noted that, "Various sources suggest that what constitutes school psychology services today emerged from earlier services provided by teachers, persons titled visiting teachers, guidance personnel, and others trained more specifically in educational and clinical psychology." In the following perspective, the course of school psychology is traced as an independent discipline despite the recognition that its unfolding has interacted with other professional designations along the way. At the outset, it must be recognized that it is difficult to describe the history as well as the present status of school psychology in Canada from a national standpoint or in a general way. Because the education of school children is under the separate jurisdiction of the provinces and because of our geography, multicultural composition, and small but unevenly distributed population, the history of school psychology makes for 10 somewhat unique scenarios (11 counting the Northwest Territories, Yukon, and Nunavut with fewer than .5% of our population of 30,482,862 as of April 1999).

BEFORE 1950

Although authors generally concur that the 1950s mark the origins of school psychology in Canada (Goodman, 1973; Janzen, 1976, 1980; Perkins, 1990; Saklofske & Grainger, 1990), the foundations of the profession appear to date from very early in this century. Janzen and Massey (1990) suggest that the earliest vestiges of psychological service personnel in schools were "attendance officers" who were recruited in Manitoba in the 1900s. Janzen (1976) further claims that war veterans who had been employed as attendance officers used post-World War II access to free education as an opportunity to train as school psychologists. The use of such terminology, however, is probably premature in the evolution of the profession as we understand it today. It is more likely that the training offered some psychological knowledge which could be applied in school settings, probably with an emphasis on guidance and counseling or testing.

Perkins (1990) identified psychological services in Ontario schools as early as 1919 when a Mental Health Service for Schools was established by the Toronto Department of Public Health. "The primary role of the Service was to identify 'mentally defective' children so that special auxiliary classes could be provided for them. . . . As it became clear that not all children with learning problems were handicapped intellectually, the staff of the Service began to work more closely with school personnel in order to identify and, if possible, intervene in the problems underlying school failure" (p. 33). Bartell (1990) traced the historical precursors of school psychology in Manitoba to the early 1920s with the hiring of a specialist in testing and educational measurement. By 1941, the Health Department of the City of Winnipeg and the Winnipeg School Board had consolidated services within the Child Guidance Clinic to serve the needs of school psychology, social work, speech therapy, public health nursing, and psychiatry.

1950s AND 1960s

In a report on *Psychology in Canadian Universities and Colleges,* MacLeod (1955) made reference to psychologists appearing in some Canadian schools. A series of articles in the *Canadian Psychologist* refers to psychologists working in schools but offers little elaboration (Dorken, 1958; Dorken, Walker, & Wake, 1960; Keating, 1962). Myers (1958), commenting on the Thayer and Boulder conferences held to address professional psychology in the United States, noted that, unfortunately, nothing similar had taken place in Canada.

By 1962, Bowers commented on the growing demand for trained psychologists in applied settings and hoped "that the staffs of university departments of psychology will keep the training of school psychologists 'continually under review'" (p. 52). In the same year, Stein (1964) undertook a study of the status and role of school psychologists across Canada. The definition he adopted to identify relevant personnel was "any individual who is considered to be employed by a school system to serve in the role of school psychologist or who is not employed directly by a school system but who serves extensively in the same capacity" (p.3). The results of his survey indicated that, "School psychological personnel have no specific university preparation or psychological experience. Teaching experience is common. All workers do have qualifications and experience that are related somewhat to school psychology" (Stein, 1964, p. 12). Nonetheless, he identified 95 school psychology practitioners across the 10 provinces: British Columbia (10), Alberta (13), Saskatchewan (6), Manitoba (16), Ontario (40), Québec (6), New Brunswick (1), Nova Scotia (3), Prince Edward Island (0), and Newfoundland (0). Comments drawn from the questionnaires attest to the ambivalent status of the profession at the time.

1. School psychologists are not recognized for grant purposes.
2. No record is kept of non-instructional personnel.
3. School psychologists should be screening agents, give therapy to less severely disturbed, make referrals to outside clinics for the severely disturbed, and act as liaison between the home and school clinic.
4. School psychology represents a new and unpalatable interpretation of the service that public education should be required to take.
5. Supply is less than the demand, otherwise we would have everyone qualified as a school psychologist (Stein, 1964, pp. 3-4).

Stein further reported on the current organization of school psychology services in four major Canadian cities. In Vancouver, school age children were referred to the Mental Hygiene Division of the Metropolitan Health Centre. Edmonton employed seven "visiting teachers" to do psychometric testing and offer remedial instruction. In Winnipeg, as previously noted, school psychologists functioned as a part of the integrated Child Guidance Clinic and focused on psychological diagnosis. The Toronto Child Adjustment Service employed 27 psychological personnel to work with students having personality difficulties, poor social adjustment, unsatisfactory school achievement, and behavior problems.

A few years later, McMurray (1967, p. 208) noted that "to this day no Canadian psychology departments have graduated students with a specific special-ty in school psychology." At that time, a Ph.D. school psychology component had just been introduced within the Division of Applied Psychology at the Ontario Institute for Studies in Education. By 1971, Arthur (1971) had documented three additional school psychology training programs in Canada: at the Universities in Edmonton, and Calgary, Alberta, and Montreal, Québec. Schmidt (1976) added the University of British Columbia to the list.

1970s AND 1980s

By the 1970s there was clearly considerable growth and development despite ongoing debate over title and role definition. School boards such as the public system in Calgary not only had more than a dozen school psychologists working in the system, but some had additional expertise in areas such as intellec-tual giftedness and neuropsychology. Furthermore, graduate students from the University of Calgary received extensive practicum opportunities and supervision from the Calgary Board of Education. Weininger (1971), writing from the Ontario Institute for Studies in Education, made a passionate plea against the prevalent tendency to see the school psychologist as an "omnipotent, computer-like Superman, all seeing, all knowing, and ever ready to function at maximum efficiency twenty-five hours a day" (p. 125). Schmidt (1976) bemoaned the paucity of school psychology training programs in Canada and the resultant dependency on American trained personnel. One aspect of his solution was to combat the distinction between psychology and educational psychology and to view the latter as an application of general psychology to a particular field, in this case, education. He claimed that the separation of disciplines created confusion and left too many educational psychologists with "identity problems" (p. 7).

Concurrent with debates over role and title (Holmes, 1986), the impetus for affiliation with professional organizations was evolving at both provincial and regional or national levels. During the late 1970s and early 1980s independent school psychology organizations or divisions within provincial psychology colleges appeared in many provinces. These are described in the 1990 *Special Issue-The State of the Art of School Psychology in Canada* (*Canadian Journal of School Psychology*, 6(1)) and summarized here:

---

1. British Columbia Association of School Psychologists (BCASP) - 1985
2. Alberta Association of School Psychologists (AASP) - 1981
3. Saskatchewan Educational Psychology Association (SEPA) - 1982
4. Manitoba Association of School Psychologists (MASP) - early 1980s
5. Ontario Association of Consultants, Counsellors, Psychometrists, and Psychotherapists (OACCPP) - 1978
6. Groupe d'intérêt en psychologie scolaire (GIPS) - 1988

During this period of growth at the provincial level, Canadian school psychologists maintained a loose affiliation with the National Association of School Psychologists (NASP). Representation consisted of one member of the Board of Directors (the Canadian/Mexican Director) and two delegates, representing each of eastern and western Canada. Don Dawson (1980, 1981, 1982) worked to chronicle the relationship with NASP and, together with Dr. Marjorie Perkins from Ontario, to urge Canadian involvement in that organization, particularly with the scheduling of the NASP Annual Convention in Toronto in March, 1982. In a paper entitled *The Future of School Psychology in Canada*, Dawson (1982) provided a rallying call for school psychologists seeking professional identity and predicted that "The next two decades will be a critical period for school psychology" (p. 8). At that date, he estimated growth in the profession to have reached over 1,000 school psychologists in Canada.

In 1985 the Canadian Association of School Psychologists (CASP) was established and incorporated under the Canada Corporation Act in 1989. It remains a collegial rather than regulatory association and affiliates with the provincial organizations. CASP now publishes the *Canadian Journal of School Psychology* and holds an annual convention in locations from coast to coast.

Fagan, speaking at the Canadian Journal of School Psychology Conference in April 1988, estimated that there were at that time 4,000 school psychologists in Canada (Fagan, 1989b). He noted the phenomenal growth of the profession in the U.S. since the late 1960s and predicted that commensurate growth would continue in Canada.

1990s

In a chapter published in the book, *Professional Psychology in Canada* (Dobson & Dobson, 1993), Saklofske and Janzen (1993) pointed out that:

School psychology in Canada has become much more obvious in only the past ten years. There are well-established university training programmes and a great amount of activity both provincially and nationally to develop profession-al school psychology associations. There is a growing body of Canadian research focusing on school and educational psychology that is being published in Canadian journals (p. 313).

In the same volume, Holmes (1993) noted that "it is worth reiterating that school psychology is now experiencing its adolescent growth spurt and the attendant maturation dilemmas of that developmental period. . . .To call it exciting is an understatement. Guessing the outcome in the next decade or two is impossible, except that it will be in the direction of continued expansion and change" (p. 143).

Despite the optimism evident earlier in this decade, the last few years have yielded some sobering experiences in school psychology. Realities of budget limitations and cut-backs in education, as well as the search for alternatives to lengthy psychoeducational testing as the process for identification of children eligible for government funding, have been felt in reductions in school psychology staffing at least in Ontario and British Columbia. The long-standing call for other than an assessment role for school psychologists, which originated as a cry for recognition of broader professional capabilities, may well now be the rallying point in a struggle for survival. In our analysis, school psychology at the end of the century is revisiting many of the issues fundamental to its evolution over the last five decades. Yet again, the profession is addressing its status, its interrelationships with other psychological and educational service professions, and its capability to survive within a uniquely structured service delivery model. As with earlier decades of prediction, the future is yet unfolding!

TRAINING AND QUALIFICATIONS OF SCHOOL PSYCHOLOGISTS

An Overview of the Issues

While school psychologists may be found working in school, educational (e.g., technical institutions, universities) and many other settings (e.g., private practice, corporations) in every province and territory in Canada (see Saklofske & Janzen, 1993), the level and kind of university training and entry-level qualifications for employment as a school psychologist vary considerably (Holmes, 1993; Saklofske 1996). A number of factors appear to underlie the diversity of training and preparation found among practicing school psychologists. These include the proximity to university school psychology programs, the variability in Canadian university programs, the influence of psychology regulatory boards on the practice of psychology, the current thinking of local school boards and provincial education departments regarding the value they place on psychological services (see *Canadian Journal of School Psychology*, *11*(2), 1995 for some responses to a proposed reduction of school psychologists in an Ontario Board of Education), geography, regional diversity, financial and budgetary issues, size of school districts, and relationships with other agencies who employ psychologists.

In 1994, The Mississauga Conference on Professional Psychology examined the "dramatically changed landscape" in which psychology now finds itself and the impact this has for the training and preparation of psychologists in Canada. Some of these changes include new markets and practice domains for psychological services, new training models, program accreditation and credentialing criteria and various factors external to the discipline and profession of psychology. From the conference section focusing on Core Curriculum and Specialization came the following recommended principles:

1. Specialties and subspecialties in professional psychology should be recognized.
2. A core curriculum reflecting psychology as a discipline should be included across all the specialized areas of professional psychology.
3. A core curriculum should be defined for each of the different specialties.
4. Organized educational opportunities for the development of proficiencies in the specialties should be encouraged to complement general practice.

Clinical psychology programs in Canada that have received APA/CPA accreditation (see *www.cpa.ca/accredlist.htm*) tend to follow and endorse the above principles as they relate to both program training standards and post-training requirements for credentialing. However, there is much less consistency in other professional specialty areas including school psychology. Until Canadian school psychology programs endorse specific accreditation standards, whether it be those developed by APA for doctoral level training or by NASP for school psychologists trained at the specialist level, or even standards that might be created in Canada by the Canadian Association of School Psychologists (CASP) or some other professional organization such as the Canadian Psychological Association (CPA), there will continue to be considerable variability in the kind and extent of training found across Canadian universities. This is more than just an issue of portability of academic and training credentials across the provinces. Rather school psychology is a mature practice area that requires greater clarity in descriptions of training. That does not suggest that all training programs must be identical. Even the standards set for APA-accredited clinical psychology programs may be achieved in different ways but common essential learning and knowledge, practicum experiences, and so forth are clearly specified.

So far, CASP and the universities have not worked in a collaborative manner to describe the essentials of training programs for preparing school psychologists. Neither has CASP nor any other organization with an interest in the training and practice of school psychologists (e.g., CPA Section of Psychologists in Education) openly championed any particular training recommendations or supported the adoption of a profile of training requirements or standards, following the lead of APA and NASP. The universities, except for

McGill University in Montreal, Québec, have not taken the lead in either attempting to meet APA/CPA accreditation standards for school psychology training programs or participating in the creation of such standards within the Canadian context. Even at a provincial level, the school psychology associations vary in their interactions with and presence within the provincial universities. However, CASP has recently created a committee which will be working throughout 1999-2000 to develop, in consultation and collaboration with the university trainers, a proposed set of standards for graduate level school psychology training programs.

School Psychology programs such as those found at the University of British Columbia in Vancouver, University of Alberta in Edmonton, and University of Saskatchewan in Saskatoon, have continued, to evolve and be guided, in part, by the recommendations and standards proposed by the Trainers of School Psychologists, the National Association of School Psychologists, the International School Psychology Association, and, to a large extent, by the thinking of both the provincial psychology and teacher associations. The APA accredited program now offered by McGill University is the first and only program in Canada to meet the training requirements specified by the APA for doctoral level training in school psychology. Of interest is that while the McGill University program is now directing attention to the preparation of Ph.D. level school psychologists, the current training required by the L'ordre des Psychologues du Québec (OPQ) is a master's level degree in psychology.

The Master's Versus Doctoral Debate

An issue that continues to be debated in each province revolves around the master's versus Ph.D. level of training for psychologists in general. Some provinces have set the training standard for registration at a Ph.D. level with either no or some specific exemptions (e.g., working in a public institution such as university or school setting); for others, a master's degree is the entry level qualification. While never losing sight that it is the provincial regulatory bodies that "certify" psychologists, it may be that we could find ourselves in Canada following a history similar to that of APA Division 16, and NASP.

As alluded to above, the master's versus Ph.D. debate regarding entry level qualifications is more of an issue in provinces where the psychology registration acts require a Ph.D. and where there are few or no exemptions from the act. The authors do not recall one advertisement for educational or school psychologists in Saskatchewan over a 20-year period that has ever required or even suggested the need for more than a master's degree. A national survey of Canadian school psychologists who were members of CASP was conducted in 1992 (Bartell, 1996). Results showed that 37.3% held a doctoral degree, 57.8% a master's degree and less than 5% a bachelor's degree or non-academic qualification. However, these results will vary considerably across the provinces. The majority of school psychologists trained at the master's level will be found practicing in provinces in which

1. The registration act either does not require a Ph.D. or psychologists working for a school board or department of education are exempt from such regulations.
2. Doctoral level training programs are either very small or non-existent within the field of psychology or specialty of school psychology.
3. It is more difficult to attract doctoral level trained school psychologists.
4. Budgetary decisions and even salary grids are more in line with the hiring of persons with non-doctoral level training.

A recent exchange of correspondence with colleagues across Canada, including British Columbia, Alberta, Manitoba, Québec, New Brunswick, and Newfoundland indicated that school psychologists practicing in most provinces were trained at a master's level. As a case in point, master's level school psychology practitioners in Saskatchewan are deemed by employers to have the necessary training according to past and recent job advertisements. Further, a survey conducted by the Saskatchewan Educational Psychology Association (SEPA) showed reasonably consistent agreement in the kinds of training that school psychologists consider necessary to prepare them for employment (Saklofske & Grainger, 1990). At the time of this survey, 92% of practicing school psychologists had master's degrees in contrast to the earned doctorate degree required for registration as a psychologist in Saskatchewan. The current exemptions from the act allow school boards to use the title school psychologist for those trained usually at the master's level.

To complicate matters, the Saskatchewan Special Education Policy Manual describes the qualifications of personnel who are eligible to assess students requiring special education support services. Regarding school psychologists, it was recommended that they be qualified also to teach these students and, if not, to be a part of a team that meets these requirements. While the focus is more on teaching, assessment, and special needs children, there is nothing else that would clarify the kind and extent of training required to provide these services. It would not be all that rare to find a person trained in special education or counseling but with some course work in assessment working as a psychologist in school settings. In contrast to many of the Canadian provinces, Ontario has many more psychologists with Ph.D. degrees working for school boards, especially in the large urban centers such as Toronto. While the Ontario Psychological Association has long required doctoral level training for certification (although there are now two levels of certification), a fairly large number of school psychologists has been trained in clinical and other applied psychology programs. Thus the primary focus of the university training programs completed by now-practicing school psychologists is not necessarily reflected in the name or level of their earned university degree.

University Training Programs

Graduate training programs in psychology and educational psychology departments at the master's and Ph.D. levels are found at many Canadian universities, which number around 90 institutions. A summary of Canadian graduate programs in professional psychology, at the master's and/or Ph.D. levels showed that 15 offered "educational psychology" programs and seven offered school psychology programs (Dobson & Dobson, 1993). It is sometimes not clear if a school psychology foundation or even specialty can be attained in the programs labeled or described as educational psychology. For example, the majority of school psychologists employed in Saskatchewan schools are graduates from either the Educational Psychology or the Education of Exceptional Children Departments (which were amalgamated in 1998) at the University of Saskatchewan. Yet until recent years, the Educational Psychology Department specialized mainly in the training of counselors, while the cognate department trained special education and resource teachers. This may, in part, underlie the reason for the title "educational psychologist" still being used in Saskatchewan schools. While a school psychology specialization has slowly been developed within the Educational Psychology Department over the past 10 years, "Ed. Psychs. and School Psychs." are still seen as synonymous. Even the professional association in this province is the only one in Canada that has *educational* in contrast to *school* psychology in its name (i.e., Saskatchewan Educational Psychology Association).

The different training and entry routes into school psychology positions are most cogently described by Bartell (1996). The training backgrounds of respondents, of whom 58% had earned master's degrees, to this national survey included: Educational Psychology (41.4%), Clinical Psychology (39.2%), Counseling (32.4%), School Psychology (31.2%), Child/Social Psychology (25.8%), Teacher Education (22.05%), Special Education (18.8%), School Administration (4.3%) and Other (17.7%). It should be noted that the percentages clearly indicated that respondents often labeled their training program under more than one category (e.g., educational psychology reflecting the department and counseling reflecting the more specialized program). Bartell concluded:

> Thus the diverse education and training backgrounds of this sample, which on the face of it could be viewed as enriching, reflect the national dilemma of a lack of consistent, unified, and coherent preparation for the practice of school psychology. Furthermore, the large variation in the requirements for certification and licensure for the practice of school psychology, as well as

the use of the title of school psychologists in Canada... militates against the coherence of the profession (pp. 88-89).

Frost (1983) expressed concerns about the professional identity confusion, in part, created by at least two different paths for entry into the practice of school psychology. While he recognized that school psychology is defined by its context, the school, it is a specialty area of psychology and therefore draws its knowledge and practices from the discipline of psychology. Frost stated:

> Some school psychologists... identify with education and forget psychology. They do this at their peril... Unless the school psychologist can successfully differentiate him/herself from these other professionals, then he/she will be absorbed by them. I would maintain that the only way a school psychologist can demonstrate individuality, and worth to the employing system, is to be a psychologist and convey to the clients information and services based on psychology in its various forms (p. 9).

In contrast to school psychology programs, the trend over the past years is for the clinical psychology programs to move toward both the doctoral level and APA/CPA accreditation. As credentialing standards shift toward the doctoral level, and the market place in hospitals, community agencies, and private practice now has this expectation, the clinical programs have responded in kind. There is a growing trend for clinical programs to either move students with undergraduate degrees directly into doctoral programs or at least not to view the master's degree as the terminal point in university preparation. This is not the trend to date in school psychology training where these university programs in Canada are housed in the colleges of education and particularly departments of educational psychology. These departments may also include programs in special education, school counseling, and other sub-specialty areas. School psychology is not considered a specialty or even full program major in some of these departments but rather is "inferred" through course work that will most often also include one or more courses on psychological and educational assessment. As well, educational psychology departments in many cases, are still focused on training to a master's degree level, so that the number of doctoral students graduating with a major in school psychology is, indeed, small.

This separation of, or distinction between, university departments of educational psychology and psychology, has resulted in quite different identities and views on training, except in those provinces where regulatory bodies play a key role in determining who can be called a psychologist. In these instances, graduates should be able to meet the training standards set by acts regulating psychologists, regardless of specialization. Of note is that there are no specialty designations included in the regulatory acts for psychologists in any of the Canadian provinces. Also where teacher education/certification is a requirement of employment, the criteria for entry into a graduate level school psychology program may again lean more toward a background in teacher training in contrast to psychology preparation, at the undergraduate level.

The university programs most often associated with training school psychologists tend to be found in western Canada. While the University of Calgary had a well-established program in school, clinical and community psychology during the 1970s and 1980s, under the direction of Dr. Barry Frost, it is the program at the University of Alberta coordinated in the main by Dr. Hank Janzen that is considered by many to be the major training program for school psychologists. Other school psychology programs are found at the University of British Columbia, the University of Saskatchewan, and the University of Manitoba. However, there is considerable contrasts among these programs. The University of Manitoba offers only a 2-year training program at the master's level, while at the University of British Columbia the master's program requires 3 consecutive years of full-time study and the Ph.D. degree requires an additional 2 years of full-time study, including an internship. The University of Saskatchewan has a master's degree program in school psychology, and a "special case" Ph.D. in school psychology is currently offered.

As one moves eastward into Ontario, there are a number of universities that offer master's and Ph.D. programs in clinical and other applied areas. In contrast to several of the doctoral programs in clinical psychology, there are no designated APA approved programs in school psychology in Ontario. The Ontario Institute of Studies in Education/University of Toronto offers both Ph.D. and Ed.D. degrees but also a Master of Arts in Child Study and Education. In fact, until about 25 years ago, this program provided the training for many psychologists who wished to work in the school systems in other parts of Canada. Until very recently, the programs offered by Québec universities concentrated "almost exclusively on a clinical approach to psychology... and are not sufficient for preparing these future professionals for the demands of working in the school environment" (Gagné, 1990, p. 44). One of the authors recalls a fairly recent meeting with several students from one of the Québec university graduate programs in school psychology where it was mentioned that the faculty were not trained in school psychology. In 1998, McGill University was awarded APA accreditation for its doctoral training program in school and applied child psychology. Graduate students at McGill in the past have been primarily from Montreal with the vast majority being bilingual and several being Francophone. As the program expanded, the number of unilingual English speaking students from outside Québec has grown and this has required more careful placements for practica and internship experiences. At this time, there is no direct relationship between the McGill University School Psychology program and either L'ordre des Psychologues du Québec (OPQ) or the Association Québecoise des Psychologues Scolaires (AQPS). While this new program certainly sets the standard for Canadian university training programs in school psychology (both because of the Ph.D. level and APA accreditation), it will be interesting to see how many other university programs follow this lead given the diversity of Canadian schools, varying provincial registration requirements (e.g., Ph.D. versus master's level entry) and market supply and demand.

The Atlantic provinces tend to train school psychologists in graduate programs offered by psychology and educational psychology departments but not within specialty programs designated as school psychology. For example, Memorial University focuses mainly on counseling in its education graduate program, although courses such as "assessing intelligence and learning" may be taken. It will be especially interesting to see the impact if the proposed change in provincial registration requirements from the master's to the Ph.D. level is proclaimed. If school boards are not exempt from this act, will Memorial University be expected to develop a doctoral program in school psychology, or will the province have to import school psychologists or even hire Ph.D. trained psychologists in clinical and other applied areas of psychology? The University of New Brunswick (UNB) does not offer a school psychology graduate program. Rather, the approximately 30 registered psychologists employed by the Anglophone school system received their master's level graduate training through the psychology department at UNB or elsewhere. One exception in eastern Canada is found at Mount St. Vincent University in Halifax that offers a Master of Arts in School Psychology. It is described as a clinical speciality for entry into the profession of school psychology. As outlined on its university webpage, "the program is designed to address the academic, research and professional practice requirement for certification as a psychologist in provinces/territories where master's level preparation is permitted." From the above description it can be seen that diversity in university training for school psychologists is the rule rather than the exception. However, certain programs are recognized for their school psychology emphasis and may eventually find it advantageous to follow the lead of McGill University in achieving APA accreditation. Until there is a commitment from university trainers, the national psychology (CPA, CASP) and provincial regulatory associations, provincial departments of education, and finally the school boards and districts that hire school psychologists, school psychology as a profession will continue to experience identity diffusion.

CREDENTIALING AND REGULATION OF SCHOOL PSYCHOLOGISTS IN CANADA

Barbara Holmes (1993) began her chapter on *Issues in Training and Credentialing in School Psychology* with the statement:

> Canadian readers of publications in school psychology are familiar with the dominance of American writers, American models, American issues and American developments in this professional area. The field has been so completely driven by the American experience that we in Canada have learned to predict our future on the basis of the American past gauging a 10- to 15-year interval between developments there and here. This experience of the predictive relationship is no less borne out today in training and credentialing issues than it has been in other aspects of professional development and practice (p. 123).

Before focusing specifically on school psychology in Canada, we shall describe the current situation regarding the regulation of psychology in general. The title "psychologist" may only be used by persons who hold certificates of registration from the provincial or territorial psychology regulatory boards. In Canada, only the Yukon Territories have not yet implemented a statute regulating psychology. Portability of credentials is not yet automatic in Canada, because of the differing registration criteria, and there is no speciality registration for psychologists in Canada. Rather, certification as a psychologist as defined in any province of Canada, permits one to be called a psychologist, although newer acts are moving toward the inclusion of "scope of practice" descriptions (McKee, 1996). While there are a number of APA accredited clinical psychology programs and others that specialize in the training of social psychologists, counselors and school psychologists, current certification acts are mainly focused on the use and protection of the title "psychologist." Until "scope-of-practice" and possible specialty designation legislation is endorsed in Canada, registered psychologists may describe their areas of practice and competencies such as child assessment, family counseling, and cognitive-behavioral treatment therapy. The CPA codes of ethics as well as the principles of professional conduct adopted by the regulatory bodies serve as the guides to practice.

Since the registration of psychologists occurs at the provincial, and territorial level, there is variability in the entry level qualifications (i.e., master's versus doctoral degree) and other criteria such as EPPP scores. Discussions have taken place over the years regarding the possibility of a national level certification that would allow for greater ease of practicing in more than one province (i.e., portability of credentialing/certification) but a consensus has not been achieved. The eligibility

	Academic Entry Requirements	Supervised Experience	Examinations	Exemptions
British Columbia	Doc. Or equivalent (Indep.)	1 year pre-doc.	EPPP 65% Oral	University, Government, Schools
Alberta	Master's (Indep.)	1 year (1,600 hrs) post-master's	EPPP 70% Oral	University, Government, Health Board, Schools
Saskatchewan	Doc. (Indep.) (Change to master's in 2000)	No experience requirements (likely to change in 2000)	EPPP 70% Oral	University, Government, Health Board, Schools
Yukon	No legislation governing practice of psychology			
Manitoba	Doc. (Indep.) Master's (P Assoc. Supervised)	Doc. (1 pre- and 1 post-year) Master's (4 years post plus 1 year on supervision register)	EPPP Doc.: 70% Mas.: 65% Oral	University, Government, Schools, Hospitals
Ontario	Doc. (Indep.) Master's (P.Assoc. Indep.)	Doc. (1 pre- and 1 post- year) Master's (4 years post plus 1 year on supervision register)	EPPP 70% Oral jurisprudence	University
Québec	Master's (Indep.)	none	no EPPP no oral, Ethics	none
Newfoundland	Master's (Indep.) (possible change to Ph.D.)	Doc. (1 pre- and 1 post-year) Master's (2 years post)	EPPP (pass score not set), no oral	University
Northwest Territories	Master's Degree in Psychology from a Canadian University	1 year (1,600 hours) while on an Intern's Registry. Previous supervised experience from another jurisdiction may be considered.	An exam "may" be required.	None
Nova Scotia	Master's (Indep.)	Doc. (1 pre-and 1 post-year) Master's (6 years post)	EPPP 70% Oral	None
Prince Edward Island	Doc. (Indep.) Master's (indep. In inst/agency only)	Doc. (1 pre and 1 post year) Master's (2 years post)	no EPPP Oral	University
New Brunswick	Master's (Indep.)	Doc. (1 pre and 1 post year) Master's (4 years post)	EPPP 65% Oral	University

criteria for certification as a psychologist in the 10 provinces and territories of Northern Canada have been summarized by the Canadian Psychological Association and appear in Table 9.1. Several provinces will soon be implementing changes in the entry level requirements for registration. For example, Newfoundland may be adopting the doctoral degree as the entry level for registration while training at the master's level will likely replace the Ph.D. entry level in Saskatchewan within the next year or two. Discussions are currently underway in Manitoba which appear to parallel those occurring in Saskatchewan.

Before returning to a discussion of types of certification of school psychologists and surrounding issues, it should be mentioned that the Canadian Register of Health Service Providers in Psychology (CRHSPP) was created in 1985 in an effort to provide a cross-Canada directory of registered psychologists. Its statement of purpose is summarized as:

> The Register has been organized as a non-profit corporation for the purpose of identifying health service providers in psychology meeting educational and training standards set by the Register consistent with standards of practice acceptable to the profession and also for the purpose of promoting professional standards of practice acceptable to the profession and also the purpose of promoting professional standards by encouraging continuing education and research (Canadian Register, 1999, p. 10).

Inclusion in the Register is based on the provincial registration standards, education and earned degrees, and supervised experience. While "areas of expertise/specialized health services" are listed for each registrant, this does not include specialty designations such as school psychology and supervised practice.

As mentioned before, registration as a psychologist is a provincial matter and the eligibility criteria vary as shown in Table 9.1. Unless there is an exemption within the psychologists act which allows other agencies such as school boards and education departments to hire and title individuals as school psychologists (e.g., in British Columbia, Alberta, Saskatchewan, and Manitoba as shown in Table 9.1), school psychologists must also be registered psychologists. Given this variability in the criteria for credentialing as a psychologist and the exemptions that occur in some provinces, not only are some interesting regional differences created but also some difficulties when a school psychologist applies for employment in another province with different registration criteria. Of course, new changes to the existing criteria for registration pose another potential problem, especially when the standards are being raised. For example, Newfoundland may soon implement the Ph.D. as the entry-level degree for certification. Although currently registered psychologists with M.A. or M.Ed. degrees may not be affected, individuals not attaining a doctoral level degree after the new act takes effect will no longer be eligible for employment as school psychologists if there are no exemptions in the act or arrangements for direct supervision of master's trained psychologists. Most of Newfoundland's practicing school psychologists, like those in so many other provinces, have master's level degrees. It will be interesting to see if the school districts are prepared to hire and pay Ph.D. psychologists or whether there will be a cutback in school psychology personnel both because of cost factors and also availability. The situation in Saskatchewan with the new act will see psychologists with M.A. or M.Ed. training who meet other criteria (e.g., passing the EPPP) now eligible for registration following a grandparenting period.

Variations across Canada suggest that the provincial and territorial education departments may also list criteria for the hiring and practice of school psychology. Thus while school psychologists in New Brunswick may be licensed at a master's degree level (plus supervised experience, passing both the EPPP and an ethics examination), they may not have any school-related experience or a teaching background. In contrast, most advertised positions in Saskatchewan require a teaching degree or certificate as well as graduate training in school psychology, even though this is not currently sufficient for registration as a psychologist. Because, at least for the time being in some provinces, criteria for the hiring of school psychologists may be imposed by the departments of education and even school districts, readers may wish to seek further information from the sources provided in Table 9.1.

Two interesting approaches to the regulation of school psychologists outside of the provincial psychology regulatory bodies have been implemented in Manitoba and British Columbia. School psychologists in Manitoba are hired by school divisions and the Child Guidance Clinic. In order to be hired as a school psychologist, it is first necessary to be certified with a clinician certificate by the Department of Education which has criteria based on training (e.g., master's degree). In turn, it is necessary to be certified as a school psychologist in order to be a full member of the Manitoba Association of School Psychologists (MASP). At the same time all of this occurs quite independent of the Manitoba Psychologists Association (PAM) which is the regulatory body and which currently requires a Ph.D. for certification. Should the new Psychologist's Act be proclaimed, the current exemptions and the clinical certificate will likely disappear as persons presently holding the title "psychologist" are grandparented. A major question at this time is whether Manitoba will follow the two-level model found in Ontario (i.e., psychologist and psychological associate) or maintain a one-level registration at the master's level. Another major issue revolves around defining scope of practice in the new act.

The British Columbia Psychological Association (BCPA) registers psychologists only at the Ph.D. level. In spite of considerable difficulty in the relationship between BCPA and the B.C. Association of School Psychologists (BCASP), the latter organization has independently set standards for school psychologists which have been widely accepted by employers of school psychologists. These standards of course only have application and validity in the public school setting because of the exemptions in the Psychologist's Act (which also includes colleges, universities and government institutions). Since the exemption clause to the Act is quite specific in defining the employment situation in which a person can be called a school psychologist, BCASP can exclude persons from membership if they are not employed in a school setting or publicly funded and operated education setting. The criteria for membership in BCASP include:

1. A minimum of a master's degree in educational psychology or equivalent with course work in individual assessment, measurement, statistics, educational interventions, and 400 hours of supervised school psychology practicum or an approved two-year field-based supervised practicum.
2. A criminal record search.
3. A Canadian citizenship or landed immigrant status.
4. Two professional references completing a question form.
5. Employment by a public school or other exempted agencies.
6. Successful completion of the Educational Testing Service NASP exam (passing mark is 670).
7. A non-refundable $50 certification fee.

It can be seen that there is considerable variability across Canada with respect to the registration of school psychologists and the regulation of school psychology practice. Further changes may be expected in at least several provinces over the next few years.

ROLES AND FUNCTIONS OF SCHOOL PSYCHOLOGISTS

The emergence of school psychology from its educational and psychological historical roots has helped shape the role and function of practicing Canadian school psychologists. The growth of school psychology and of training programs in school psychology during the past 30 years has been unparalleled. The past decade has witnessed slow but obvious changes to the traditional roles and models that define the practices of school psychologists. The present day role of Canadian school psychologists has emerged from the services that were initially provided by teachers, personnel referred to as "visiting teachers," guidance staff, and those trained in educational and clinical psychology (Fagan, 1996b). Evolution of school psychology in Canada began in the 1950s and by the early 1970s, most areas of Canada had professionals working in the role of school psychologist. Fagan (1996b) suggests that the creation of present day roles and functions of Canadian school psychologists was shaped by many different forces including such factors as: provincial and national education and psychology standards, school district demands, consumer response to the services provided, and the availability of training programs.

Geographically, culturally, and linguistically, Canada is a diverse country. Yet, independent of these essential factors, the primary role of school psychologists has been, and continues to be, focused on the problems faced by children, educators, and parents. Similar to the United States, the education of children is a provincial/territorial mandate, with each jurisdiction having its own Ministry of Education and respective Education Acts. Few, if any, federal initiatives other than direct funding to the respective provincial legislatures filters down to the schools. As a result, wide discrepancies in terms of job descriptions, funding, and priorities exist. Independent of jurisdictional diversity, the factors that continue to dictate the role of school psychologists are related primarily to the characteristics and needs of the school population. These factors include the number of psychologists employed in a particular district, the extent of their caseload, the psychologist-student ratio, an individual's training and professional orientation, rural versus urban work setting, the priorities established at local levels, and the overall "credibility" of the psychological team and the profession within each of the provinces (Saklofske & Janzen, 1993).

Nevertheless, surveys conducted by Dumont (1989) and Neudorf (1989), a special issue of the *Canadian Journal of School Psychology* (Vol. 6, No. 1, 1990) devoted to examining the status of school psychology in Canada, and preliminary data from a national 1997-1998 study (Kaufman & Smith, 1998) report considerable commonality in the practices of school psychologists. The more traditional role of school psychologists reflecting psychological and psychoeducational assessments, direct student service delivery models, and the development and implementation of clinical and educational prescriptive programs is still widely adhered to in Canada. However, the more traditional roles are being modified or disregarded in some jurisdictions. Alternative roles of consultation (Cole & Siegel, 1990; Sladeczek & Heath, 1997), program prevention and intervention (Cole, 1995), and parent and teacher training (Greenough, Schwean, & Saklofske, 1993; Philips, Schwean & Saklofske, 1997) are gaining in popularity. School psychologists practicing in Canada are realizing that alternative roles and functions may be more effective and appropriate in meeting the needs of students, parents, and teachers. Bartell (1995) recommends that school psychologists transform their roles and functions to meet the needs of their clients better. Canadian schools and families now, and in the future, require school psychologists to provide support in meeting the educational demands of a rapidly changing world. If Canadian school psychologists are to remain in control of their own destinies they must continue to evolve their roles and functions.

There remains a growing trend in several provinces, dependent upon training and licensing, for school psychologists to work in alternative settings such as hospital clinics, community service agencies, or in private practice. For some individuals, their professional functions may be quite diverse when compared to a psychologist employed by a school district. In other cases, school psychologists may be working in non-school settings, but providing services which are remarkably consistent with the practices of school psychologists in traditional school settings. As well, Canadian universities are expanding their training paradigm. One such example is the School/Applied Child Psychology program at McGill University. Housed within the Department of Educational and Counselling Psychology, this program emphasizes the training of school psychologists at the doctoral level in both the traditional school psychology role and in one which includes a wider community mental health paradigm. Undoubtedly, the diversified training of school psychologists will benefit the profession of psychology as a whole, as well as promote the specialty of school psychology. In the future, Canadian school psychologists with expertise in more than one practice setting will not only secure their own job prospects, but also promote an awareness of school psychology in settings other than schools.

Current Roles and Functions

Cole and Siegel (1990) described current and projected roles of Canadian school psychologists using a two-dimensional grid system. They described the goals of service delivery (primary, secondary, tertiary), and the various recipients of school psychological services (e.g., school system, teachers, parents, students). However, the professional roles of school psychologists was made ever so clear, when, in 1994, the Ontario Board of Trustees announced huge financial and service cutbacks and a subsequent proposed reduction of school psychologists. Depositions were submitted to the board and some of these were published in the *Canadian Journal of School Psychology* in 1995. The role of diagnostician as a primary function was mentioned in all of the presentations to the board. Carney (1995) stressed the proactive, early intervention and prevention programming functions carried out by school psychologists. He argued that social and emotional needs had to be met before students can focus on academic learning but also argued that community agencies do not provide the kinds of psychological services that directly address the learning issues. Beal and Service (1995) reinforced the major role of school psychologists in assessment and diagnosis but also described the provision of therapy to students with problems such as school phobia, anxiety disorders, depression, eating disorders, and attention difficulties. Hamovich (1995) added that school psychologists also provide crisis intervention and consultation to teachers and parents. The depositions were consistent in arguing that school psychologists play important roles in the life of a school system by offering a "wide range of services which include but are not limited to assessment, treatment, counseling, consultation, and program development (Beal & Service, 1995, p. 92). While understanding that the services provided by school psychologists across Canada will vary as a function of numerous factors, an examination of the types of roles and tasks performed will elucidate the diversity of their job description.

Psychological and Psychoeducational Assessments

Assessments by Canadian school psychologists vary depending upon the presenting problem and the reason for the referral (e.g., to develop a program for a particular child, for placement, or for retention decisions). These assessments will often include standardized instruments, some of which have been developed in Canada and others (e.g., WISC-III; Wechsler, 1996) which have Canadian norms (Saklofske, Hildebrand, Reynolds, & Wilson, 1998; Weiss, Saklofske, Prifitera, Chen, & Hildebrand, 1999) to assess intellectual, educational, social, emotional, personality and/or neuropsychological development (Saklofske & Janzen, 1990). More recently, other types of assessment procedures have been implemented and are gaining in popularity including curriculum-based instructional assessments, dynamic assessment, bilingual assessment, functional behavioral assessment, and continuous performance appraisals. Psychological assessments are not merely relegated to standardized tests but can also include interviews with parents and teachers, and observations of classroom behavior.

While placement, referral and retention decisions are often made on the basis of the findings, ultimately these assessments are designed to provide an in-depth understanding of the child's ability, achievement, and behavior. Specific recommendations for the child, teacher, and/or family will emanate from the assessment. Parent, child, and teacher meetings to discuss the findings, recommendations, and a plan of action are also part of the typical assessment process.

Direct Student Delivery Services

It is common practice for Canadian school psychologists to intervene directly with students and groups of students who encounter problems with their academic progress, or their intellectual, social, and/or emotional development. Depending on the school district, school psychologists may devote considerable time to direct service; however, district policies and caseloads sometimes limit the amount of time a school psychologist can devote to direct services. Given the wide diversity of potential problems, the list of the types of direct services is endless. Under most circumstances, school psychologists in Canada seldom provide direct remedial assistance for students. This type of activity is usually delegated to teachers, learning specialists, and special educators. However, school psychologists are sometimes instrumental in the development of individualized educational programs (IEP) and may be called upon to monitor a child's academic progress and the success of the implemented IEP. Other types of direct interventions may include working with children and adolescents on issues dealing with conflict resolution, divorce, social skill development, aggression, sexual abuse, and substance abuse. Canadian school psychologists frequently provide direct clinical services in the form of therapeutic intervention and counseling. In most cases, therapeutic support is short-term and students are referred to outside agencies for long-term treatment.

School psychologists play a key role in acting as referral agents to community services (Carney, 1995). They are also more often linked into a multi-disciplinary service delivery system for children and adolescents. Canada's system of socialized medicine allows for medical referrals to be made for all children, regardless of their socio-economic status. Collaboration between physicians, including psychiatrists, pediatricians, and neurologists is common practice for many Canadian school psychologists. Additional service to children is often supplemented by publicly funded professionals allied with the health and social sciences fields including physiotherapists, occupational therapists, social workers, and nurses. Government cutbacks and fiscal restraint has reduced the level of these services, but the principle of universality ensures medical treatment for all Canadians. This multi-disciplinary approach is extremely helpful in situations where children are experiencing considerable psychological and medical difficulties and require the assistance of many parties to guarantee their success at school.

Consultation

Consultation has become a major approach for providing school psychology services to children and adolescents. Although differences exist across models of consultation (e.g., Cole and Siegel, 1990; Zins, Kratochwill & Elliott, 1993), and these have been slow to develop and to be implemented in certain parts of Canada (see Sladeczek & Heath, 1997), the adoption of consultation models by many school psychologists and educators has far reaching implications. In addition to dealing with the child's presenting problem, consultation models assume an important educational component for teachers and parents such that their skill in analysis and resolution of problems will be increased. Successful behavioral consultants must have expertise both in coordinating and facilitating the problem-solving process and in modification of behavioral changes (Kratochwill, Elliott, & Carrington-Rotto, 1995).

Consultation not only represents a more cost-effective service, but it promotes several additional benefits which are not usually associated with more traditional school psychology roles (e.g., assessment). Consultation allows for greater collaboration between the student's home and school. While increased home and school collaboration has been shown to increase student achievement and learning (Christenson, Rounds, & Gorney, 1992), collaborative consultation is also more likely to be effective when treating students with behavioral disorders because it does not consider the child solely in the context of the school (Bartell, 1995). Canadian school psychologists continue to develop consultation skills, but this area of practice is still in its infancy. Greenough, Schwear, and Saklofske (1993) provided examples of collaborative consultation in more sparsely populated and remote regions of northern Saskatchewan where the population is predominantly Aboriginal. Remote regions of Canada pose unique social, cultural, economic, linguistic, and educational demands that require a very different approach to school psychology services and their delivery. Sladeczek and Heath (1997) reported that a literature search of Canadian consultation yielded only 24 articles between 1960 and 1997. In comparison, a similar search of literature in the United States by Gibson and Chard (1994) produced 1,643 studies. Gibson's and Chard's meta-analysis of those studies found considerable support for the effectiveness of the consultative process. Consultation by Canadian school psychologists has seen considerable progress in the past decade (Sladeczek and Heath,1997). The publication of *Effective Consultation in School Psychology* (Cole & Siegel, 1990) represents a significant step toward consultative methods which are being adopted by Canadian school psychologists. Continued application of consultation methods, supported by Canadian-based empirical research, will undoubtedly increase the prevalence of this important role for school psychologists.

Crisis Intervention and Crisis Team Management

Canadian school psychologists have become much more visible in the role of crisis intervention and crisis team management. Excessive school violence, displaced refugees, catastrophic accidents, and natural disasters require swift, immediate action and intervention. In many ways, the skills of the school psychologist must be relied upon to deal with community-based disasters (e.g., death of a student or teacher in a car accident) and post-traumatic stress disorder (PTSD). The unfortunate reality is that no school is immune or exempt from the kinds of crises that can significantly and negatively affect all members of a school community. As Jay (1989) states, even "successful" schools in prominent, affluent areas are at-risk for some type of crisis. Recent events of fatal school shootings in Canada and in the United States clearly demonstrate this sobering fact. Dealing with the consequences of school crises is one role of the school psychologist in Canada. Children exposed to school-based violence are at-risk for immediate psychological stress and for PTSD and may need direct or indirect crisis intervention. Another role of the school psychologist in crisis situations is to support school staff and assist in the overall coordination of the crisis response. Sadly enough, some Canadian children who develop PTSD may have experienced the initial trauma in another country. Canada, with its long history as a peace-keeping member of the United Nations, is considered a safe haven for many refugees from around the world. As such, many Canadian schools receive children who have witnessed or experienced tragic circumstances. Estimates indicate that approximately 31% of Canadian immigrant children have lived in some form of unstable and poor conditions

(Cole, 1998). Through crisis intervention students at risk for developing PTSD can be monitored and, if required, referred for mental health services by the school psychologist.

Prevention and intervention are also necessary components of any crisis intervention team (Poland, Pitcher, & Lazarus, 1995). Cole (1995) contends that primary intervention programs can target all students in a school and encourage pro-social behaviors and anti-violence beliefs. Further, secondary programs target at-risk students who are experiencing academic, social, and emotional, difficulties which could lead to violence. Tertiary prevention programs focus on students who have a history of difficulty and may require specialized programs such as anger management. In most jurisdictions in Canada, school psychologists occupy an important role in crisis intervention and crisis team management.

Program Development and Evaluation

The expanding role for Canadian school psychologists includes program development and/or the evaluation of existing programs. An emphasis on outcomes now requires school psychologists to occupy a more active role in program evaluation. An essential role to be played by school psychologists relies on their ability to design, implement and evaluate curriculum programs and social intervention programs (e.g., substance abuse, anti-violence, HIV/AIDS prevention, suicide prevention). Depending on caseloads and district policy, some Canadian school psychologists are more active than others in this role. Increased responsibilities in this area represent exciting opportunities for Canadian school psychologists by diversifying their roles and allowing them to implement empirically based programs which increase student learning and well-being (Greenspoon, 1998).

Parent Training

From a pedagogical perspective, educators have long sought to build partnerships between the schools and homes. Within rural communities schools often have assumed a leadership role in community events. Psychologists, in smaller towns, are well integrated within the community. The need for providing educational workshops on a multitude of issues is readily apparent. These workshops are well attended, and parenting courses designed to improve parenting skills and decrease child-rearing problems are thriving.

Some Projections on the Changing Roles of School Psychologists in Canada

The Canadian mosaic has been rapidly changing during the past decade. Canadian society is becoming more ethnically and culturally diverse. The need for psychological services in both official languages, French and English, has been increasing. The pressure to provide psychological services in French and in French immersion classes both inside and outside Québec and New Brunswick continues to grow. The demands to teach English as a second language for a large number of immigrants have increased dramatically. This influx of new Canadians is in addition to the large number of children of Aboriginal and First Nation ancestry. The increasing demands by parents and communities for opportunities for their children to learn in both official languages as well as preserving languages from a family's cultural heritage continues (e.g., Chinese, Cree). An emphasis on sensitivity to cross-cultural differences pervades our schools (Janzen, Patterson, & Patterson, 1993). This point may be most clearly made by referring to historical and contemporary changes in Québec associated with both religious and language issues. Unlike other provinces, historically, the public educational system in Québec was predicated upon religious lines. While there are a number of private schools and private religious schools (e.g., Jewish, Greek, Muslim) the majority of students within the province attend public, provincially supported schools. Throughout the province, two separate school systems were established; that is, Catholic and Protestant. The Catholic school system had a strong religious program of instruction as well as the traditional educational component. The Protestant school systems were created for all individuals who were not Catholic and had no religious program with the exception of a course in moral and religious education, which was not denominationally based. This is further complicated by the fact that the language of instruction could be either in French (which is the majority population) or English. While children throughout the province were Francophone, there remained a considerable number of English-speaking pupils. As a result, within many school boards, there was both an English and French speaking population such that there were Catholic French, Catholic-English, Protestant-French, and Protestant-English schools. Ironically, at one intersection in a large city such as Montreal, one could have four different elementary schools. Given a significant declining population and the desire by the provincial government to maintain its linguistic heritage, legislation was passed mandating that children whose mother tongue was not English were no longer eligible for an English education and were required to attend French schools. From a school psychology perspective, this necessitated psychological services to be provided in both French and English.

With a further decrease in the school population and a need to consolidate services in 1998, school boards were realigned based upon linguistic and geographical lines. However, it should also be noted that while the schools and school boards are now designated as either English or French, French is a required subject for all elementary and secondary school students. Equally important is that *French Immersion* classes (English children attending English schools but where the majority of the curriculum is presented in French) necessitate school psychologists to have a working knowledge of French, to be familiar with the curriculum, and frequently they are required to complete psychoeducational assessments using standardized French instruments (French versions of some widely used tests such as WISC-III, PPVT). Although psychological reports can be written in English, often parent meetings are held in French once again necessitating the school psychologist to be bilingual. Bilingualism is not necessarily a requirement, however it is extremely advantageous especially in the public school system. The need for bilingual proficiency in some private English schools is not as great.

It should be mentioned here that language issues have also had an impact on school psychology in New Brunswick. Two distinct and separate departments of education exist defined by language. There are 12 English and 6 Francophone school districts, and psychologists are hired to work in both settings. However, there is no crossover of psychologists and little collaboration between the departments and districts. Issues related to language, culture, and other social factors will continue to influence the roles and services assigned to, and provided by, school psychologists. It is hoped that psychological services in the schools will not be solely defined or restricted by language issues but that it will be the children (and teachers) and their needs that are the greatest determiners of the kind and extent of these services.

Slow to develop in many Canadian communities has been the involvement of the school psychologist as service provider to preschool children, and in early childhood programs, but also in adult education. Clearly, the comprehensive and effective implementation of early identification and prevention programs will require an increased involvement by school psychologists. Many adults are returning for further educational upgrading, and the school psychologist has an opportunity to participate at all levels of educational service delivery. It is now recognized that many incarcerated adolescents and adults have learning disabilities, AD/HD, and other conditions that may have contributed to school failure and early school leaving but which also must be confronted if rehabilitation programs are to be effective. School psychologists will also continue to play a significant role in special education services. While the course of special education in Canada remains on a pendulum (Canada has moved from the self-contained classroom to the mainstreamed classroom; see Schwean, Saklofske, Shatz, & Folk, 1996), greater requirements for consultation and parent education will continue to consume much of the school psychologist's time.

As we enter the twenty-first century the role of school psychologists in Canada is becoming more diverse. The role of psychological and psychoeducational assessments may not decrease. In fact, there is no good reason why it should since this is clearly an area of expertise that school psychologists bring to the educational setting. However, there will be a greater movement toward consultation, training, and program development. There will be an increasing necessity to provide services in both official languages, to be responsive to community and cultural groups, and to provide prevention services. There will be a need for greater numbers of school psychologists who can work closely with administrators, educators, and parents in a bilingual or multilingual environment. There will also be a need for more, not fewer, school-based psychologists. School psychologists will require the kind of training that will allow them to work both inside and outside the traditional school system. They must assume a leadership role in helping raise social policy issues and promote effective educational and psychological programs, which will promote student's educational, social, and emotional development.

PROFESSIONAL ASSOCIATIONS

School psychologists in Canada tend to identify more or less with the professions of psychology and education. This identification is partly influenced by the nature of their university training program. Those who initially completed B.Ed. degrees and who may have taught in schools for a time are more likely to maintain their connections with teacher associations. This link with the teaching profession is also related to the requirement, in some provinces and school districts, that school psychologists, counselors, and other support staff hold teacher certification in order to be hired to work in the schools. This also makes it considerably easier for school boards to link their psychology positions to teachers' salary grids, pension programs, and other benefit packages. However, issues of professional identity and affiliation have created a kind of schism in what should be a unified profession. For example, there appear to be many more school psychologists in practice than there are members of the school psychology associations either provincially or nationally. For example, there are approximately 30 school psychologists employed in the English speaking Department of Education in New Brunswick yet only 2 are CASP members. Similarly CASP has attracted only a very small percentage of practicing school psychologists into its membership even though it has been in existence since the mid 1980s.

Departments of Education

Table 9.2 lists the provincial and territorial departments and ministries responsible for education in Canada. Included are their phone numbers and websites so that interested readers may contact them for specific and up-to-date information relating to school psychology practice.

Provincial Psychology Associations

Those who have entered graduate programs in school psychology via undergraduate psychology degrees may have a greater affinity with provincial and national psychology organizations. Also the "bias" inherent in the various university programs will influence the development of one's professional identity as a school psychologist. In order to assist readers in gathering more and specific infor-

TABLE 9.2 Provincial and territorial departments and ministries responsible for education in Canada

Newfoundland
Department of Education
3rd Floor, Confederation Bldg, West Blk
Box 8700
St. John's NF A1B 4J6
Tel: (709) 729-5097
Fax: (709) 729-5896
http://public.gov.nf.ca/edu

Nova Scotia
Department of Education and Culture
Box 578
Halifax NS B3J 2S9
Tel: (902) 424-5605 or 424-5168
Fax: (902) 424-0511
http://www.ednet.ns.ca

Prince Edward Island
Department of Education
Box 2000
(Sullivan Bldg, 2nd and 3rd Fl, 16 Fitzroy St.)
Charlottetown PE C1A 7N8
Tel: (902) 368-4600
Fax: (902) 368-4663 or 368-4622
http://www.gov.pe.ca/educ

New Brunswick
Department of Education
P.O. Box 6000
C.P. 6000
Fredericton NB E3B 5H1
Tel: (506) 453-3678
Fax: (506) 453-3325
http://www.gov.nb.ca/education

Québec
Ministere de l'Education
Edifice Marie-Guyart
11e etage, 1035, rue de la Chevrotiere
Québec QC G1R 5A5
Tel: (418) 643-7095
Fax: (418) 646-6561
http://www.meq.gouv.qc.ca

Ontario
Ministry of Education and Training
Mowat Block
900 Bay Street
Toronto ON M7A 1L2
Tel: (416) 325-2929
Fax: (416) 325-2934
http://www.edu.gov.on.cal

Manitoba
Department of Education
Legislative Building
450 Broadway
Winnipeg MB R3C 0V8f
Tel: (204) 945-2211
Fax: (204) 945-8692
http://www.gov.mb.ca/educate/

Saskatchewan
Department of Education
Department of Post-Secondary Education and Skills Training
2220 College Avenue
Regina SK S4P 3V7
Tel: (306) 787-6030
Fax: (306) 787-2280
http://www.sasked.gov.sk.ca/

Alberta
Department of Education
West Tower, Devonian Building
11160 Jasper Avenue
Edmonton AB T5K 0L2
Tel: (403) 427-7219
Fax: (403) 427-0591
http://www.ednet.edc.gov.ab.ca

Alberta
Advanced Education and Career Development
7th Floor, Commerce Place
10155-102 Street
Edmonton AB T5J 4L5
Tel: (403) 422-4488
Fax: (403) 422-5126
http://www.aecd.gov.ab.cal

British Columbia
Ministry of Education
PO Box 9156, Stn. Prov. Govt
Victoria BC V8W 9H2
Tel: (250) 387-4611
Fax: (250) 356-3000
http://www.bced.gov.bc.ca

British Columbia
Ministry of Advanced Education,
Training and Technology
Tel: (250) 356-2771
Fax: (250) 356-3000
http://www.aett.gov.bc.ca/

Northwest Territories
Department of Education, Culture
and Employment
PO Box 1320
(4501-50 Avenue)
Yellowknife NT X1A 2L9
Tel: (867) 920-6240
Fax: (867) 873-0456

Yukon
Department of Education
PO Box 2703
Whitehorse, YT Y1A 2C6
Tel: (867) 667-5141
Fax: (867) 393-6339
http://www.gov.yk.ca/depts/education/

TABLE 9.3 Provincial and national psychology associations

**Association des psychologues
du Québec (APQ)**
1150, boul. St-Joseph Est, bureau 208
Montreal Québec H2J 1L5
Tel: 514-528-7498
Fax: 514-528-6020

Association of Newfoundland Psychologists
PO Box 13700, Station A
St. John's NF A1B 4G1
Tel: 709-739-5405

Association of Psychologists of Nova Scotia
PO Box 594, Station M
Halifax NS B3J 2R7
Tel: 902-422-9183
apns@ns.sympatico.ca

Association of Psychologists of the NWT
Box 1195
Yellowknife, NT X1A 2N8
Tel: 867-873-5371 and 867-873-8170
E-mail: *beach@tamarack.nt.ca*

British Columbia Psychological Association
1755 West Broadway, #202
Vancouver BC V6J 4S5
Tel: 604-730-0500 Toll-Free: 1-800-730-0522
Fax: 604-730-0502
E-mail: *bcpa@interchg.ubc.ca*

**College of Psychologists
of New Brunswick**
403 Regent St., Suite 211
Fredericton NB E3B 3X6
Tel: 506-459-1994
Fax: 506-459-3608
E-mail: *cpnb@nbnet.nb.ca*

L'ordre des Psychologues du Québec (OPQ)
Siege social de l'Ordre des psychologues
du Québec
1100, Avenue Beaumont, bureau 510
Mont-Royal Québec H3P 3H5
Tel: 514-737-6431
E-mail: *Sercomm@ordrepsy.qc.ca*

Manitoba Psychological Society Inc.
Box 151 RPO Corydon
Winnipeg MB R3M 3S7
Tel/Fax: 204-475-4531
E-mail: *mps@escaspe.ca*

Ontario Psychological Association
730 Yonge St. Suite 221
Toronto ON M4Y 2B7
Tel: 416-961-5552
Fax: 416-961-5516
E-mail: *opa@psych.on.ca*
http://www.psych.on.ca

**Prince Edward Island
Psychological Association**
Department of Psychology
University of PEI
Charlottetown PEI C1A 4P3
Tel: 902-566-0323
Fax: 902-628-4359

Psychologists Association of Alberta
Suite 520, Metropolitan Place
10303 Jasper Ave.
Edmonton AB T5J 3N6
Tel: 780-424-0294 Toll-Free: 1-888424-0294
Toll-Free Fax: 1-888-423-4048
Email: *paa@compusmart.ab.ca*
http://www.compusmart.ab.ca/paa

Psychological Association of Manitoba
59 Goulet St., Suite 307
Winnipeg MB R2H 0R5
Tel: 204-947-3698
Fax: 204-487-0784
E-mail: *pam@mts.net*

Psychological Society of Saskatchewan
c/o Child and Youth
1601 College Ave.
Regina SK S4P 3V7
Fax: 306-766-7888

Saskatchewan Psychological Association
Box 21064, 2105 8th St E
Saskatoon SK S7H 0T8
Tel: 306-343-1502

Canadian Psychological Association
151 rue Slater Street, Suite 205
Ottawa ON K1P 5H3
Tel: 613-237-2144 Toll-Free: 1-888-472-0657
Fax: 613-237-1674
http://www.cpa.ca/

TABLE 9.4 Numbers of member psychologists and school psychologists in Canada and each province/territory listed in provincial, CPA and CASP directories[3]

Province/Associations	Members[4]	CASP Membership[5]
NEWFOUNDLAND		
Newfoundland Bd of Examiners in Psych.	172	3
Association of Newfoundland Psychologists	97	
PRINCE EDWARD ISLAND		
Psychology Registration Bd of PEI	18	1
Psychological Association of PEI	25	
NOVA SCOTIA		
Nova Scotia Bd of Examiners of Psychology	297	9
Association of Psychologists of Nova Scotia	200	
NEW BRUNSWICK		
College of Psychologists of New Brunswick	286	2
(C.P.N.B. is both regulatory and fraternal)		
QUEBEC		
Ordre des Psychologues du Québec	5410	5
(OPQ is both regulatory and fraternal		
ONTARIO		
College of Psychologists of Ontario	1859	22
Ontario Psychological Association	1400	
MANITOBA		
Psychological Association of Manitoba	188	15
Manitoba Psychological Society	136	
SASKATCHEWAN		
Saskatchewan Psychological Association	96	34
Psychological Society of Saskatchewan	142	
ALBERTA		
College of Alberta Psychologists	1821	20
Psychological Association of Alberta	1820	
BRITISH COLUMBIA		
College of Psychologists of British Columbia	914	27
British Columbia Psychological Association	382	
NORTHWEST TERRITORIES		
Association of Psychologists of the NWT	9	–
CANADIAN PSYCHOLOGICAL ASSOCIATION[4]	**4218**	
CANADIAN ASSOCIATION OF SCHOOL PSYCHOLOGISTS[5]		**143**

mation about the provincial psychology associations, Table 9.3 lists the association name, address and phone, fax, or e-mail addresses.

Table 9.4 provides a current estimate of the number of psychologists who are members of provincial psychology associations and/or registered psychologists. The membership numbers for both CPA and CASP are also given as is the breakdown of CASP membership for each province.

Provincial School Psychology Associations

In those instances where school psychologists may not be eligible for registration because of Ph.D. or other requirements, they are much more likely either to form their own associations as occurred in western Canada or to maintain closer connections with provincial departments of education. Manitoba presents an interesting mosaic of professional connections. Though many school psychologists have joined the Manitoba Association of School Psychologists, some are registered psychologists with the Psychological Association of Manitoba but all are required to hold a clinicians certificate from the Department of Education. In those instances where school psychologists, at either the master's or Ph.D. level, are required to be registered as psychologists, as is the case in Ontario or New Brunswick, there is a stronger affinity with provincial psychology associations and a direct association with the regulatory colleges.

Possibly, it was because of this "split identity" but also because school psychology was increasingly being recognized as a specialty area in terms of training and practice, that school psychology associations began to appear during the 1980s. The increasing numbers of school psychologists employed by school systems produced the critical mass necessary for the creation of these new associations. The common purposes behind the formation of provincial school psychology associations was the need for a sense of professional identity, a communication network, continuing professional education, and a body that could lobby and advocate for a profession that tended to feel somewhat disconnected with psychology associations but also not fully connected with the teaching profession. The creation of school psychology associations was primarily a phenomenon of the early 1980s and especially conspicuous in western Canada where they still continue to thrive; that is, the British Columbia Association of School Psychologists (BCASP, 162 members), Alberta Association of School Psychologists (AASP, 72 members), Saskatchewan Educational Psychology Association (SEPA, 137 members), and the Manitoba Association of School Psychologists (MASP, 85 members). These numbers are approximate and based on current membership directories or estimates obtained from association members.

The greatest number of psychologists representing all specialty areas and working in all areas of health, social services, corrections, public and private corporations, private practice, and educational settings are found in Québec and

Ontario. In 1988, Québec school psychologists working primarily in the elementary schools formed an interest group called the Groupe d'intérêt en Psychologie Scolaire with the support of the provincial regulatory association. This specialty interest group is now known as the Association Québecoise des Psychologues Scolaires (AQPS) and has more than 400 members. In contrast, L'Ordre des Psychologues du Québec (OPQ) is the regulatory body with about 6,000 members of whom about 700 call themselves school psychologists. A master's degree in psychology is the requirement for registration as a psychologist in Québec, and all psychologists working in schools must be registered by the OPQ. In Ontario the interests of non-doctoral psychologists, including a number of psychologists employed by education boards, led to the creation of the Ontario Association of Consultants, Psychometrists, and Psychotherapists in 1978. However, changes in the Psychologists Act has given prominence to the Section of Psychologists in Education as a special interest group within the Ontario Psychological Association. This section has 166 members. In the Atlantic provinces, smaller and less formally structured school psychology associations have also been formed to provide continuing education and other professional needs (e.g., New Brunswick Association of Psychologists and Psychometrists in the Schools). However, many of Newfoundland's school psychologists, whether or not registered as psychologists within the Newfoundland Psychologists Association, have joined other associations such as the School Counsellors Association of Newfoundland. Since many of the school psychology associations are relatively small, the mailing addresses and contact persons (i.e., president, secretary) tend to change with annual elections. While a few are developing web pages (e.g., Québec, *www.aqps.gc.ca*), the most expedient way of contacting the provincial school psychology associations is through the provincial psychology associations (see Table 9.3).

National School Psychology Associations

In spite of the importance of provincial associations, Canadian school psychologists have demonstrated a strong desire to extend their professional network to include national and international associations. Canadian school psychologists were active in NASP prior to the formation of many of the provincial school psychology associations. For example, Sweet (1990) stated that "school psychologists in B.C. have always been active in professional organizations. In 1981 they constituted some 405 of the Canadian membership of the National Association of School Psychologists" (p. 1). NASP continues to be an attractive association for Canadian school psychologists (there are currently about 120 Canadian members of NASP) as does Division 16 for those who are members of APA. A smaller number of Canadians have also joined the International School Psychology Association.

While provincial school psychology associations were gathering momentum, the seeds for the Canadian Association of School Psychologists (CASP) were planted by Dr. Barry Frost in the early 1980s. Following the establishment of the four western provincial school psychology associations, an informal working group comprised of Dr. Carl Anserello (B.C.), Drs. Barry and Ruth Frost (Alberta), Dr. Don Saklofske (Saskatchewan), Retha Finch-Carriere (Manitoba), and Dr. Marjorie Perkins (Ontario) developed the framework for what became known as CASP in 1984. As an incorporated professional association representing school psychologists across Canada, the objectives of CASP included in their by-laws are:

1. To promote professional educational and social accountability among school psychologists across Canada.
2. To provide professional development for school psychologists nationwide.
3. To develop and promote national standards and ethical principles for school psychologists.
4. To represent the concerns and interests of school psychologists in a variety of settings.
5. To facilitate communication between and among professionals working in the area of school psychology.

CASP has three levels of membership and is affiliated with Canadian provincial school psychology associations, the International School Psychology Association, and the Canadian Psychological Association. CASP has developed standards for professional practice in school psychology as well as a code of ethics. CASP also publishes the *Canadian Journal of School Psychology* and, jointly with CPA, publishes a newsletter, and hosts an annual conference. Since 1990, the annual conferences have been held in partnership with one of the provincial school psychology associations with conferences held in all provinces with the exception of the Atlantic provinces. CASP has created a webpage (*www.stemnet.nf.ca/caspl*), and also formed a committee to explore program accreditation and school psychology credentialing. Table 9.4 notes the number of CASP members from each province. Of interest is that while Saskatchewan has relatively few registered psychologists, it has the largest membership in CASP. This is very much in contrast to the proportions shown for Québec and Ontario. Unfortunately, the impact of CASP has not been great in Atlantic Canada even though there are smaller numbers of school psychologists in these provinces.

The Canadian Psychological Association (CPA) is the national professional association and in most ways parallels the American Psychological Association. Some 4,000 members of CPA make this a relatively strong association although it is interesting to note that the provincial psychology group in Québec has more members than does CPA. At the same time, CPA has become an effective organization through the development of professional standards and codes of ethics, and through the promotion of training and educational opportunities for psychologists. As is the case with the APA, the CPA has created a number of special interest divisions. The Section on Psychologists in Education has a much broader membership than Division 16 of APA or CASP with a membership of approximately 96. Its mission statement (see *www.cpa.ca/psyedu.html*) includes:

> The CPA Section on Psychologists in Education includes members across Canada who are front-line school psychologists, psychologists in hospitals, agencies, and private practice addressing issues pertinent to education and mental health for infants to elderly; university academics in educational psychology and psychology departments who conduct applied research and/or act as clinical trainers; and graduate students from all above areas. Section goals included urging communication between members over this wide country so that common issues can be addressed between and among Provinces; indeed, so that issues can be confronted with support from CPA head Office in Ottawa. The section has merged its newsletter recently with CASP's to increase circulation and, thus, communication among Psychologists in Education in Canada.

A recent revision to the Section mission statement adds the following goals:

1. To promote communication among Canadian psychologists interested in education issues.
2. To facilitate the application of research outcomes in educational psychology to instructional settings.
3. To increase public awareness of the activities and contributions of Canadian psychology to the whole area of education.
4. To enhance the quality of education at all levels, from pre-school to university.

The membership of this section is probably slightly different from that found in the various provincial groups. For example, there are very few university trainers who are members of SEPA, and most members of BCASP are school-based practicing psychologists. The membership of the CPA Section includes university trainers as well as researchers, school psychologists in both direct practice and administrative roles, psychologists in both the public and private sector addressing issues relevant to both education and mental health, and graduate students in school psychology and more general educational psychology.

One very exciting example of the collaboration between the CPA Section and the CASP is the publication of the first two research-based booklets in the CANSTART series. Both booklets are authored by Dr. Marvin Simner from the University of Western Ontario, and are available from the CPA (*www.cpa.ca/publist.html*).

The first booklet, *Predicting and Preventing Early School Failure: Classroom Activities for the Preschool Child*, is now in its third printing, and the second booklet, *Promoting Reading Success: Phonological Awareness Activities for the Kindergarten Child*, has just gone into a second printing. This work has been extended to include the new outreach program initiated by CANSTART.

Last, a number of school psychologists who have come through teacher education and special education programs identify more with educational and teacher associations and tend to be more active in such organizations as the Canadian Council for Exceptional Children and the Canadian Society for the Study of Education as well as the provincial and national teachers' federations. Some school psychologists were trained primarily in counseling programs and therefore are more likely to maintain memberships in the Canadian Guidance and Counselling Association and its provincial counterparts. For example, in Newfoundland, school psychologists do not have a separate association. Because they are registered with the board of examiners of the Newfoundland Psychological Association, their professional identity is linked to that group. However school psychologists are also found in the membership of the School Counsellors Association of Newfoundland. Provincial counseling associations are quite separate from psychology and school psychology associations in western Canada.

Relationships Among Associations

Unfortunately the relationships between the various associations has not always been positive. The creation of provincial school psychology associations which are independent from the provincial psychology regulatory bodies has produced some direct conflicts. For example, even at this time, the relationship between the school psychology and the regulatory psychology associations in both Saskatchewan and Manitoba varies from chilly to hostile, given that both provinces are in the process of negotiating their respective Psychology Acts. This unfortunate tug-of-war, most often relating to the use of the title "psychologist" in the name of the provincial associations, was most conspicuous in British Columbia (Sweet, 1990; McKee, 1996). Sweet (1990) documents the series of events that led to the formation of the British Columbia Association of School Psychologists. After several years of injunctions, court hearings, legislative changes and the like, BCASP was granted the status of a registered society, independent of the BCPA and the B.C. Teacher's Federation. At the time of writing his article, Sweet clearly saw the need to explore the regulation of school psychologists:

> The profession remains largely fragmented, lacks an identity, and most serious of all, is unregulated; since the lifting of restrictions on the use of title within school districts, anyone can be hired by a district and called a

psychologist... we have moved from a situation replete with Type 1 errors, where bona fide school psychologists were denied title, to one which is fraught with the danger of Type 2 errors, the granting of title (and function) to unqualified persons. There is no doubt that a major task for the profession in the near future is to police its own ranks... to fail to do so would be to invite those who opposed the amendment to seek its revocation (p. 5).

In spite of the appearance and possibly the reality that our profession may be variously represented by or aligned with independent provincial school psychology associations (where they exist), provincial psychology regulatory associations, two national psychology associations, and provincial departments of education, a fairly recent event in Ontario provided a reassuring example of pulling together in support of school psychologists. Published in a special issue of the *Canadian Journal of School Psychology*, "Advocacy Issues and Events in School Psychology 1996," was a "collection of papers from deputations made on behalf of a number of psychological associations to a large Ontario school board in early 1995 when it threatened to reduce psychological services by two-thirds" (Carney & Cole, 1995, p. i-i). Several of the submissions were received from representatives of the Canadian Association of School Psychologists (Carney, 1995), Canadian Psychological Association (Beal & Service, 1995), Ontario Psychological Association (Hamovitch, 1995), and the Section on Psychology in Education of the Ontario Psychological Association (Jobin, 1995). Of great reassurance is that the initial recommendation to reduce significantly school psychologists and their services was modified and this board of education continues to be a provider of exemplary psychological services.

PUBLICATIONS BY AND FOR SCHOOL PSYCHOLOGISTS

The various publications for the exchange of information about research, and applied and professional issues are not only intended to serve the needs of the discipline and practice of psychology but are also regarded as a benchmark of maturity. A journal signals several messages to those who read it or merely see it on a shelf. It suggests that a discipline or speciality has a history and a future, has an identity and status, and both creates and disseminates knowledge as well as applications (Saklofske & Janzen, 1990). In contrast to the United States where there are several well-established school psychology journals and many others that publish research and applied papers of direct relevance to school psychologists, only a handful of psychology and education journals are published in Canada.

The major journal focusing on research and applied/practice issues of relevance to school psychologists is the *Canadian Journal of School Psychology*. The first issue of this journal appeared in 1985 and was published in British Columbia where school psychology was very much asserting its speciality status. There was clearly a need for a journal that published articles of relevance to school psychologists in Canada. It also provides a national forum for school psychology and other psychological and educational researchers and practitioners to publish the results of their investigations. Under the editorship of Dr. Gerald Koe, the journal provided a mix of refereed research papers but also articles which dealt with important professional issues. For example, the 1990 *Special Issue The State of the Art of School Psychology in Canada* was the first time that papers from across Canada were collected to portray school psychology training, practice, professional issues, and the like in each of the provinces and Yukon. In 1992, beginning with volume 8, the journal was turned over to and published by the Canadian Association of School Psychologists under the editorship of Dr. Hank Janzen and Dr. Don Saklofske. The editorial board was reconstituted to include many well-respected Canadian and American school psychology researchers, trainers, and practitioners. Over the next 6 years, several special issues of the journal were published (*Behavior Disorders of Children and Adolescents*, Vol. 9, No.1, 1993; *Advocacy Issues and Events in School Psychology*, Vol. 11, No. 2, 1995; *The Updated Wechsler Scales*, Vol. 12, No. 1, 1996; *Challenges and Issues for School Psychologists in the 21st Century*, Vol. 12, No. 2, 1996) along with regular issues featuring articles on topics ranging from assessment and consultation to program interventions and professional training issues. The journal is now under the editorship of Dr. Jeff Derevensky *(ino4@music.mcgill.ca)* and Dr. Marvin Simner *(simner@sscl.uwo.ra)*. Although the journal will continue to publish mainly refereed research and applied papers, new sections are now being included on research in progress, and test and book reviews in English and French (*saklofske@sask.usask.ca*). CJSP continues to be a well-respected journal in Canada and the USA.

The CPA publishes the *Canadian Journal of Behavioural Science* and *Canadian Psychology* which often include articles of relevance to school psychologists (e.g., ethics, assessment, intervention, consultation) and is published in either French or English. The CPA also publishes monographs (see *www.cpa.ca/publist.html*) that have been well received by school psychologists (e.g., CANSTART booklets). Other Canadian journals that are frequently read by school psychologists include the *Alberta Journal of Educational Research*, published at the University of Alberta, and the *McGill Journal of Education*, published at McGill University. Several special education journals are also published at the University of British Columbia, including the *Canadian Journal of Special Education*. There are a few more specialized journals such as the *Developmental Disabilities Bulletin*, published at the University of Alberta, that are found on the reading lists of school psychologists.

All of the provincial psychology and school psychology associations publish newsletters usually including a mix of business and professional announcements and short articles of an applied nature. Similarly the various specialty areas (e.g., clinical psychology) of the CPA publish newsletters. The CASP originally published a newsletter titled *Cognitions* which focused more on association issues and practical notes of interest, in contrast to the *CJSP*. The CASP newsletter recently merged with the CPA newsletter published by the Section on Psychologists in Education and this new joint publication *(Canadian Association of School Psychologists and Canadian Psychological Association Joint Newsletter)* now reaches a much wider audience than only school psychologists.

THE FUTURE OF SCHOOL PSYCHOLOGY IN CANADA

In contemplating a future course for school psychology in Canada, it is necessary and instructive to consider major influences and factors which have been shaping the evolution of the profession to date and the current challenges and opportunities for its future. The development of school psychological services in Canada has been uneven across its provinces and territories, influenced by unique contextual circumstances, such as a relatively small population spread over a vast territorial expanse, as well as by the vision of seminal individuals (see for example, Bartell, 1990, p. 26). Nevertheless, the commonalties in origins, models of service delivery and practices in Canada and the United States far exceed the differences. Fagan (1996b) attributes these commonalities to comparable social-political-educational circumstances in the United States and Canada which occasioned the development of psychological services to schools. To Fagan's list of common influences we need to add the institution of the school itself, in the generic sense, which as a universal phenomenon acts as another homogenizing influence (Bruner, Olver, & Greenfield, 1966). It will be argued here that the school, or schooling, as the locale for psychological services to children is the *raison d' être* and key to the future of the profession of school psychology.

It is important to recognize from the outset the overarching influences of historical forces on the evolution of school psychology in North America whose marks on the profession are still very much in evidence. An understanding and an appreciation of the impact of these forces on the evolution of school psychology will facilitate the discussion of its future. The beginnings of school psychology in Canada, much like those in the United States, date back to the early 1920s and are rooted in public recognition of the need to provide psychological services to children and adolescents in schools. Four important consequences for the development of school psychology as a specialty flowed from this early start.

First, external societal and consumer forces, such as school administrators, parents, and most significantly, legislative requirements and court decisions, determined to whom, by whom, which, how, and where psychological services were to be provided. Thus, the birth of the specialty of school psychology came primarily from without rather than from within the field of psychology, unlike, for example, the specialty of clinical psychology which developed around the same time. These external forces, valid and important as they were then, continue to drive, shape and exert control over the profession into the present and the future. To be clear, school psychology owes its very existence to these external forces whose influences were in many ways salutary to the broadening of its scope of practice and to bringing school psychologists into the mainstream of schools and schooling. For example, legislative requirements led to school psychologists' employment by school systems, and many school systems have involved school psychologists as members of their multidisciplinary school teams to provide consultation on assessment, interventions, and follow-up evaluations as well as to address specific psychoeducational issues (Cole, 1996). As a part of this expanded role, school psychologists have become involved as team members with various community agencies dealing, among others, with crisis situations, health, legal and policing issues. The point is that a significant, coherent and integrative conceptual stand by the profession will balance out the vagaries of external influences and put much necessary control in the hands of the profession.

Second, early psychological services were characterized by an individualized medical model and focused on "mental testing," identification and placement of individual school-age children with exceptionalities in need of special education. This historical fact served as the precursor for the close association of school psychology with special education and the testing function as well as the widespread identification of the school psychologist with a test kit by consumers and professionals alike. The traditional individual assessment function is, and will continue to be, an important and unique function of the role of school psychologists; however, increasingly, schools, families and communities are struggling with system-wide problems, such as violence, which call for a broader service model and consideration of the well-being of all school children.

Third, the diversity of psychological service providers contributed to a diffuse sense of professional identity which continues to plague school psychologists. The lack of national standards for the practice of school psychology and the fact that providers of school psychological services across provincial jurisdictions operate under different titles, such as educational psychologists, psycho-educational consultants—only the Province of Manitoba considers them officially "school psychologists"—illustrate this point. The lack of national standards for practice and credentialing of school psychologists in Canada inhibits the coming of age of the profession. As Pryzwansky (1993) observed, "Nothing defines a profession like its regulatory practices" (p. 220).

Fourth, the beginnings of the professionalization of school psychology in the 1950s and its emergence as a distinct specialty, recognized by the American Psychological Association (APA) and the Canadian Psychological Association (CPA), provided the nucleus for professional self-definition. It was only 15 years ago that the Canadian Association of School Psychologists (CASP) was founded. Through its *Canadian Journal of School Psychology* (CJSP) and annual national conferences, CASP has provided a much needed forum for sharing research findings and clinical reports and debating the roles and functions of school psychologists.

The view taken here is that the very nature of the evolution of the school psychology specialty bears within it both complex, dynamic challenges as well as creative opportunities. On the challenges side, school psychologists have depended on a multiplicity of external role definers, such as school boards, changing policies of provincial governments, legislation and the courts, parents and other consumer groups and social agencies, in terms of the definition of roles and functions of their own practice, budget allocations and increasing budget cuts and constraints, conflicting expectations, and close scrutiny for accountability. This puts an enormous strain on the practitioners in the field, and a serious responsibility on the profession to chart a course of action which will help school psychologists adapt as well as have an impact on the ever-changing contextual circumstances of their practice and to maximize their contribution to the well being, optimal growth and development of *all* school children, their schools, families and communities. The challenges are constantly increasing as a function of the growing complexities of our society and, more particularly, the transformation of the economy with its socio-economic and political ramifications, the technological and knowledge-based revolutions, and the growing ethno-cultural-linguistic diversity of the Canadian school population.

Within these dynamic complexities of contemporary schools, school psychologists are strategically positioned in relation to the hierarchy of school systems (Bartell, 1996). They occupy a boundary role in that they service individual schools but are employed by the school system. Thus, school psychologists could act as proactive school systems' psychologists and significantly influence the mainstream of schools and schooling. In reality, however, the modality of practice tends to be reactive to overwhelming service demands, which results in the underutilization of the unique expertise and potential of the psychologists and missed opportunities to influence the system. Almost two decades ago, Sewell (1981) cautioned the profession that it is "...an ill-conceived expectation that the practitioner's role can solve many of our professional dilemmas without asking practitioners to abandon their theoretical orientation and create non-traditional role models which are conceptually different from existing roles and expectations" (p. 232). Thus, the fundamental challenge and opportunity for the profession in general and in Canada in particular, is to articulate a proactive and comprehensive conceptual framework to guide psychological service delivery models and practice in a changing environment. Closely related to the need to change the modality of practice is the need to regulate the profession by establishing national standards for the training, practice, and credentialing of school psychologists.

What direction, then, could school psychology in Canada follow? We believe that "as long as school psychologists are not integral to schools they can be eased out of schools" (Bartell, 1996, p. 87). Without a vigorous, concentrated, proactive, and multi-pronged action the likelihood is that school psychologists will become marginalized, overworked, and increasingly stressed out or, alternatively, school psychological services will increasingly be contracted out or outsourced. On the other hand, school psychology will flourish if we change the ways in which we conceptualize, train and deliver school psychological services so that they best meet the needs of changing schools, families, and communities (Bartell, 1996). These best ways hinge on a view of the school psychologist as a systems psychologist; that is, the psychologist who services the school as a whole and its community. The hope is that moving the focus of the debate from professional self-identity to a proactive-systems focus on the urgent and emergent needs of schools, families and communities will facilitate a consensus of internal and external stakeholders of school psychology that system-based problems require system-based solutions. Clearly, this is not a simple road to travel. Who can bring about such changes from within? University trainers are responsible for the initial preparation of future school psychologists and, thus, can initiate the process and link new models of practice to modifications in their training programs. Simultaneously, field supervisors could influence their novice practitioners as part of their socialization into the profession and veteran professionals could join the change process through professional development activities, conference, journal, newsletter, and website dialogue.

The challenge of establishing common ground for the practice of school psychology in Canada is reasonably attainable in the foreseeable future. The initiative has already been taken by CASP and the following steps will set the stage for the ultimate goal of credentialing all practicing school psychologists in Canada:

1. Under the auspices of CASP, a national committee on national standards has already been at work for some time and a proposal for action approved (Bartell & Saklofske, 1998). A recent survey of CASP members provided support from the membership for the establishment of national standards for practice.

2. With the active support of university trainers, all training programs in Canada are being examined and compared with a view to the development of a set of guidelines for a core curriculum which will ensure training standards. It should be noted that all school psychology

programs in Canada at the master's as well as at the Ph.D. level are housed in faculties of education and typically in departments of educational psychology.

3. The next step in the process will involve mapping out a framework for a core curriculum with due consideration for the training guidelines of the APA, NASP, and the International School Psychologists Association (see Saklofske, 1996).

4. Subsequently, a dialogue involving university trainers, practitioners, and national and provincial psychology and specialty associations will have to take place (Dobson & Dobson, 1993; Saklofske, 1996).

5. A successful outcome of this process will provide a strong case for school psychology stakeholders and provincial governments across Canada to support and implement the credentialing of school psychologists in all jurisdictions.

NOTES

1. Each of the authors made a unique and substantial contribution to this chapter. We acknowledge the input from colleagues and school psychologists across Canada including Bill Benson, Peter Molloy, Serge Lacroix, and Sandy Stanton (British Columbia), Bev Vargo (Manitoba), Marvin Simner (Ontario), Tom Gardner (Québec), Juanita Mureika (New Brunswick), Freida Hjartarson and Ron Martin (Newfoundland). Thanks to Sharon Boechler for her clerical assistance. Preparation of this chapter was partly supported by the John Ranton McIntosh Research Grant awarded to the first author.

2. Adopted from Canadian Psychological Association Webpage (*www.cpa.ca/licensing.html*).

3. Adapted from Council of Provincial Associations of Psychologists

4. Based on 1998 membership numbers

5. Based on 1999 CASP membership directory

CHAPTER 10

International School Psychology

Thomas Oakland, University of Florida

When people first travel abroad, differences in language, religion, dress, food, clothing, attitudes, driving styles, and other features that help define a culture often become very apparent. However, as travelers become more familiar with this new culture, similarities between it and their native culture also become more apparent.

In a similar fashion, impressions that initially identify differences in how school psychologists are prepared and practice in other countries often change to include more mature beliefs that recognize both similarities and differences. As shown in this chapter, differences often reflect social, economic, and cultural conditions within a country. Despite these differences, considerable similarities exist in the more important areas that define the specialty of school psychology.

People who are flexible in their thinking and do not assume automatically that their ways are superior are likely to appreciate the richness offered through the specialty of school psychology when it is viewed internationally. The diversity found within school psychology internationally reflects its strengths and demonstrates its capacity to adapt to important local conditions. Moreover, the nature of school psychology in Canada and the United States can benefit from knowledge of the various methods employed by their international colleagues to meet the educational and psychological needs of students, parents, and teachers. Those who believe school psychology is an American tradition may be surprised to learn that many school psychology milestones occurred first in other countries. For example, school psychology emerged first in Europe, and the Venezuela Society of School Psychology was the world's first national society of school psychology, formed in 1968 (Oakland, Feldman, & Leon De Viloria, 1995).

This chapter describes some important and defining qualities of the international dimensions of school psychology and examines similarities and differences commonly found within this specialty of professional psychology. Issues that pertain directly to Canada and the United States are not emphasized. Topics include the history of school psychology, including eight contributions that had a material influence on forming, shaping, and defining international school psychology; school psychologists' demographic qualities; their roles and functions, preparation, and external and internal qualities that influence them. Three internationally approved standards are described in some detail. The chapter concludes by outlining possible futures for the profession at the international level.

HISTORY OF SCHOOL PSYCHOLOGY

Early Roots

School psychology's origins lie in the disciplines of philosophy and biology and later in psychology and education. A country's cultural and social conditions constitute the soil and nutrients that give birth to and sustain its school psychology practices (Oakland, 1993).

Significant social changes in Western Europe and the United States during the latter half of the nineteenth century gave rise to the origins of psychology and the need for applied psychologists in public education. For centuries, lifestyles generally were characterized by personalized, rural, family-centered environments dependent on agriculture and small family-run businesses. Members of the immediate and extended family generally took care of one another's needs.

Children were raised to follow in their parents' footsteps, boys to assume responsibility for the farm or small business and girls to marry, raise children, and assume other important domestic duties. Children were expected to work at an early age. Education generally was restricted to teaching basic reading and number facts, often within the home. Families required the services of few professionals, even physicians, as family members and close friends assumed responsibility for their common and special needs. Life generally was stable.

However, during the late 1800s, many lifestyles changed. People often were thrust into depersonalized, urban, industrially centered environments. Life changes associated with these conditions were exacerbated when families migrated to a new country. Boys no longer could follow in their fathers' vocational footsteps. Child labor laws restricted their work, thus creating time for, and in some locations requiring, at least an elementary education. Both boys and girls were to be educated. Education began to replace lineage and physical endurance as important pathways to personal success and social stability.

Emergence of Social and Educational Issues Within Schools

In school settings, problems exhibited by children that were overlooked in homes became evident. Some children learned slowly, others had sensory or physical problems, still others attended school irregularly, were unruly, or displayed other qualities different from their peers or that were unacceptable to teachers. Teachers needed assistance to help address such problems.

With increasing urbanization, other problems emerged that may have been overlooked or simply were not evident in smaller and more personalized settings, or if identified were attended to by families and friends. For example, more children were orphaned, were brought before the law for repeated misdemeanors or even felonies, ran away from home, or exhibited other social, emotional, or mental problems that suddenly warranted public attention. New public and private agencies and institutions were established to care for their needs, including juvenile courts, alms houses, settlement homes, and state-run institutions for the mentally retarded and emotionally disturbed.

Professionals with expertise in the social sciences were needed to assist agency personnel in accurately assessing children's needs, diagnosing their problems, and suggesting primary, secondary, and tertiary prevention methods to address their needs and those of society. The professions of psychology and social work emerged, in part, from these conditions.

Need for a Discipline of Psychology

Preparation of professionals in social science first requires the presence of a social science. One began to emerge in the middle of the 1800s following the pioneering efforts of psychologists in Western Europe and the United States. Efforts of some early pioneers are most evident. Wundt established the first laboratory of psychology in Leipzig, Germany in 1879. Galton later opened a laboratory in London and collected psychological data on a cross-section of Londoners. Itard and Sequin developed methods to work with children with developmental disabilities. Freud's work captured the attention of many influential persons, helped legitimize psychological theory and practice, and had a large influence on institutions, in particular social service agencies and courts. These and other pioneers who laid the foundation of psychology typically had degrees in biology or its companion profession, medicine. Many were influenced by Darwin's 1859 publication, *On the Origin of Species*, which advanced a coherent theory of organic evolution. (Readers are encouraged to consult Chapter 2 in this book for a discussion of historical features in greater detail.)

Four Common School Psychological Services Systems

School psychology emerged first within Western Europe and the United States. Four forms of school psychological services evolved in Western Europe during the first half of the twentieth century (Wall, 1955). Similar service delivery models existed in Canada and the United States. The various forms of service delivery reflect the dynamic nature of school psychology and its need to tailor services in light of a country's needs, resources, and other contextual conditions.

Under one system, school psychologists were assigned to one large school or a group of schools. They often were members of a team that also included a school social worker and a medical officer. Their object was to promote primary prevention programs, those that would prevent the occurrence of academic, social, emotional, and related problems. School psychologists typically were responsible for improving the mental health of the school community, improving teaching skills, and providing guidance and adjustment services to normal students.

A second system, found mainly in the United Kingdom, emphasized the coordination of services between the school and community. Services were attached to and required funding from local education agencies. Activities included the coordination of prevention, research, and guidance activities; provision of remedial interventions and psychotherapy; and diagnosis. The goals of this second system were to prevent the occurrence of problems or, once identified, to address them directly. Elementary, secondary, and technical school students were the intended beneficiaries of their services.

A third system relied principally on community-based child guidance clinics for the provision of services. These clinics typically were headed by psychiatrists who, together with psychologists and social workers, formed a team in order to assess and diagnose childhood disorders and recommend interventions that typically were implemented in schools, homes, and other institutions.

A fourth system, founded in the United Kingdom in 1893, emphasized research on issues important to child growth and development. Work by Binet in Paris and Galton in London exemplifies this movement.

Growth of School Psychology Between the Early 1900s and Mid-Century

A profession is expected to base its practices on well-defined theory, research, and technology developed by a mature discipline. During the first third of the twentieth century, many persons believed the emerging discipline of psychology lacked sufficient maturity and knowledge to warrant status as an emerging profession. School psychology grew little during this period.

The discipline and the profession of psychology, including school psychology, developed in parallel fashion. Each benefited from the other. For example, the early work by and others lead to the development of tests useful in the practice of school psychology through the assessment of achievement, intelligence, and other school-related qualities. The availability of tests also facilitated research on issues important to the emerging discipline of psychology, including its specialties in child development and educational psychology.

As noted in Chapter 2, the term "school psychologist" first appeared in print in 1910 when W. Stern, a German psychologist, suggested that assessment services provided by psychologists were needed in schools (Fagan & Delugach, 1984). Stern (1910) drew parallels between a school's need to employ physicians to attend to students' medical needs and a school's need to employ psychologists to attend to students' psychological needs, especially those who display abnormal characteristics. The term *school psychologist* first appeared in English the following year when Day (Stern, 1911) translated Stern's work. Other important international milestones are found in Table 10.1.

School psychology displayed few signs of evolving into a profession with international dimensions during the first half of the twentieth century. However, events associated with the recovery from World War II (WW II) had a major influence on its character and international dimensions. Some of the most important are summarized below.

INCREASED INTERNATIONAL PROFESSIONALISM

The growth and expansion of school psychology in Western Europe together with interests of international bodies in school psychology began to emerge following WW II. Eight important contributions that had a material influence on forming, shaping, and defining international school psychology include two United Nations Educational, Scientific, and Cultural Organization (UNESCO) conferences in Europe, the Thayer Conference in the United States, the foundation laid for international school psychology by Catterall, the International Year of the Child, the formation of the International School Psychology Association, and two international surveys of school psychology. Three later events also helped shape and define international school psychology: the approval of a definition of school psychology, guidelines for their academic and professional preparation, and an ethics code.

1948 UNESCO Conference

World War II had profound effects across all of Europe. Financial, industrial, and human resources had been severely depleted and were insufficient for rebuilding the infrastructure for a modern and civilized society. Furthermore, resources to provide educational and social services were needed and in short supply. In 1948, UNESCO convened an international conference of representatives from 43 nations to discuss methods that ministries of education could utilize to promote needed school psychological services (UNESCO, 1948). Three recommendations were offered: establish research institutes to improve the quality of teaching and school achievement, establish guidance programs based on sound psychological practices, and improve the preparation of large numbers of school psychologists.

TABLE 10.1	Milestones in international school psychology

1879	First psychology laboratory established in Germany by Wundt
1896	First psychological clinic established at the University of Pennsylvania by Lightner Witmer
1899	First school-based child study department established in Antwerp, Belgium
1905	A reliable measure of mental ability published by Binet
1910	First appearance of the term "school psychologist" in print by Stern
1948	UNESCO-sponsored international conference on school psychology
1954	Thayer Conference on school psychology in the United States
1956	UNESCO-sponsored European conference on school psychology
1968	Formation of the first national association of school psychology: Venezuelan Society of School Psychology
1972	Formation of the International School Psychology Committee (ISPC)
1975	First ISPC-sponsored international colloquium on school psychology
1979	International Year of the Child
1982	International School Psychology Association's constitution and bylaws adopted
1990	ISPA's Code of Ethics adopted
1996	ISPA's Definition of School Psychology adopted
1996	ISPA's International Guidelines for the Preparation of School Psychologists adopted

1956 UNESCO Conference

A second UNESCO conference 8 years later explored ways that the science of child study and educational psychology could be used more effectively in European schools. The conference report (Wall, 1956) reaffirmed the need to improve guidance services, educational methodology and teaching practices, and to increase the number of school psychologists. Improved services for children with handicapping conditions also were recommended.

The conference report emphasized the need for services that were pervasive and integrated into all important components of schooling, tailored to students from preschool through technical and vocational schools, assisted students in making transitions from school to work, provided counseling, assisted in teacher preparation, and utilized consultation. European countries that became leaders in school psychology (e.g., Denmark, France, Sweden, United Kingdom) took an active role in these meetings, and their services were influenced by these recommendations.

Thayer Conference

The Thayer Conference (Cutts, 1955), although held in the United States, also was to have an important influence on school psychology abroad, given the growing influence of the United States in international affairs. This conference was instrumental in defining the nature of school psychology within the United States, identifying two levels of preparation, delineating the primary functions of practice, and suggesting desired personal and professional qualities. Recommendations from the Thayer Conference have had far-reaching consequences on the practice of school psychology within the United States and have provided standards somewhat different from those found in Europe and against which comparisons could be made.

Foundation for International School Psychology

Calvin Catterall helped establish the foundation for international school psychology during the 1970s and early 1980s. He brought to light the international dimensions of school psychology through his correspondence, study tours, scholarship, and leadership in forming the International School Psychology Association (ISPA). A review of his personal correspondence reveals his exchange of letters with leaders of school psychology in many countries. He often traveled abroad to visit with them and had them as guests in his Columbus, Ohio home. Catterall organized study tours of school psychology services to most continents. Descriptions of school psychology services in 34 countries and three broader geographic regions in his books on international school psychology (Catterall, 1976, 1977, 1979a) were instrumental in introducing the international scope of the specialty to a larger number of school psychologists. Catterall also was a driving force behind the formation of ISPA.

Frances Mullen (Fagan & Wells, 1999) was another individual instrumental in laying the foundation for international school psychology. She believed American psychologists could benefit from knowledge of psychological practice in other countries. In 1972 she proposed and was instrumental in forming an international committee within APA's Division of School Psychology. The following year she and Catterall drew up a statement of purposes for the committee and distributed it to colleagues around the world. She later served as editor of *World-Go-Round*, the committee's newsletter.

International Year of the Child

The International Year of the Child, spearheaded by a 1979 United Nations declaration, highlighted the importance of reviewing children's psychological, social, and educational needs, the nature of existing services, and the provision of new programs consistent with each country's conditions, needs, and priorities. This international focus on children served as a magnet, drawing leaders of school psychology within their respective countries to a common table to discuss common issues and to work together to achieve common goals.

A 1979 meeting of the International School Psychology Committee at York, England, featured issues important to the International Year of the Child. This conference set the stage for the 1983 International Conference on the Psychological Abuse of Children and Youth, held in the United States. Materials and proceedings of this international conference are contained in the personal archives of Thomas Fagan at the University of Memphis. These two international meetings provided a successful test of school psychologists' ability and commitment to work constructively on important issues that transcend geographic boundaries.

Formation of the International School Psychology Association

Efforts to sustain professional activities require a viable professional association. The ISPA emerged from efforts by national leaders in school psychology within the United States (e.g., Catterall and Mullen) and in Europe (e.g., Anders Poulsen in Denmark) to promote professionalism in school psychology at an international level. The ISPA evolved from the International School Psychology Committee, first formed in 1972 within the American Psychological Association's Division of School Psychology and in 1973 within the National Association of School Psychologists (NASP). Calvin Catterall and Frances Mullen were most instrumental in these efforts. The ISPA's constitution and bylaws initially were approved in 1982.

The ISPA has four major objectives: to foster communication between psychologists in educational settings, to encourage the implementation of promising practices in school psychology, to raise the effectiveness of education, and to promote the maximum contribution of psychology to education. The ISPA sponsors yearly meetings, called annual colloquia, frequently in developing countries to help stimulate the growth of school psychology in a region. For example, recent annual meetings were held in Portugal in 1991, Turkey in 1992, Slovakia in 1993, Brazil in 1994, Hungary in 1996, Latvia in 1998, Switzerland/Germany in 1999, and New Hampshire (U.S.A.) in 2000. The ISPA began publishing its newsletter, *World Go Round*, in 1973. It has also sponsored a scholarly journal, *School Psychology International*, since 1979.

Membership of the ISPA in the year 2000 was approximately 1,000 and came from individuals in approximately 45 countries. Twenty-two national associations of school psychologists are affiliated with the ISPA. Members of the ISPA executive committee in 2000 resided in Brazil, the Slovak Republic, Denmark, Hungary, Israel, Turkey, and the United States. Thus, its membership and leadership come from many countries. Its international office is located at Hans Kundsens Plads 1A, 1.tv., 2100 Copenhagen 0, Denmark.

Two International Surveys

In the mid-1940s, UNESCO conducted a survey of 43 ministries of education to determine the availability of school psychology personnel and the nature of their services and to obtain information pertinent to salaries and professional preparation (UNESCO, 1948). Respondents indicated that work was provided mainly in three areas: detection of mentally retarded children, educational guidance, and prevocational guidance. Services generally were provided in larger cities and often through institutes, laboratories, and other centers providing educational consultation. Although many educators expressed an interest in the practice of school psychology, school psychology services typically were not available in schools. This 1948 survey provided information important to the previously described 1948 UNESCO report and conference.

UNESCO convened a second conference several years later to examine how the science of child study and educational psychology could be used more effectively in European schools. A regional study of European countries (Wall, 1956) reaffirmed the need to improve guidance practices, educational methodology, and teaching practices.

In 1990, Oakland conducted a second and more comprehensive international survey of school psychology in 54 countries (Oakland & Cunningham, 1992). Information from this survey provided a more current and expanded picture of school psychology internationally and formed the basis for developing a definition of school psychology together with guidelines for their academic and professional preparation. The following information is drawn from Oakland's survey.

STATUS OF SCHOOL PSYCHOLOGY INTERNATIONALLY

In 1990, an estimated 57,000 school psychologists worked in the 53 reporting countries other than the United States. Given the growth of school psychology within the last decade, this figure now is estimated to be at least 66,000. Thus, including the United States, there are approximately 90,000 school psychologists in the world. The average number of school psychologists is strongly associated with a country's gross national product (GNP), a measure of a country's wealth arising from its production of goods and services. Countries with a high GNP average about 2,000 school psychologists per country whereas those with a low GNP average about 300. Some countries with large populations had few school psychologists. The then-Soviet Union had about 1,000, and China had about 250. Some countries with small populations had fewer than 10 school psychologists.

Internationally, the average ratio of school psychologists to students is 1:11,000. However, ratios vary in relation to a country's GNP. The median ratios are 1:3,500 in high GNP nations and 1:26,000 in low GNP nations. China has the highest ratio of 1:680,000, given its student population of 170 million. This ratio is expected to improve, given current efforts by leaders in education and psychology to increase the number of school psychologists working in Chinese schools.

As noted elsewhere, the development of school psychology strongly reflects a country's domestic conditions. In most developing countries, fewer psychologists are prepared in clinical, counseling, and other areas of professional psychology, and the practice of psychology, including school psychology, is less specialized. Thus, there are fewer psychologists to provide clinical services. Services often are not found in rural areas. A school psychologist working in a developing country may be the only psychologist within a large geographic region who is professionally prepared to work with children. His or her practice will be broader (e.g., may include counseling services to children, youth, and families; vocational guidance; assessment; consultation; and systems intervention within the community and schools). In contrast, in most developed countries, the ratio between psychologists in private practice and the population is better, and the practice of psychology, including school psychology, is more specialized.

The 1990 survey found school psychologists typically were female (62%), within their 30s, and had been in the profession an average of 10 years. Median incomes differed considerably, with a high of $17,000 in high-GNP nations and a low of $3,000 in low-GNP nations. Those working in low-GNP nations generally are younger, have fewer years of service, and have an undergraduate degree in psychology as their highest degree.

Titles used to describe those who provide school psychological services differ. The most common titles are psychologists (used in 82% of the countries), school psychologists (in 73%), educational psychologist (in 67%, a commonly used title in countries associated with the British Commonwealth), or counselor (in 55%).

The preparation of school psychologists has a decisive influence on the nature of school psychology services (Wilson & Reschly, 1996). An understanding of the preparation of school psychologists internationally provides important insights as to the nature of their services internationally. Many countries offer both under-graduate and graduate school psychology programs. High GNP countries typically offered more programs at the master's level whereas low GNP countries typically have fewer master's programs and more undergraduate programs. Almost all students first obtain a 4-year undergraduate degree in psychology, and few major in education. Master's degrees typically require an additional 2 years of preparation. In 1990, doctoral-level programs to prepare school psychologists to work in schools were available only in the United States and Canada. Brazil now offers a doctoral program at the Pontifica Catholic University. Conflicts between doctoral and non-doctoral school psychologists generally are unknown outside of North America because almost no doctoral-level school psychologists work full-time in schools in other countries.

School psychology programs are subject to external review by professional associations in about one half of the reporting countries. Psychological associations provide these reviews in 39% of the countries and educational associations in 16%. Thus, when viewed internationally, the profession of psychology tends to have a stronger influence on the preparation of school psychologists than does education. The somewhat common request that all psychologists, including school psychologists, be members of the national psychological association also reflects school psychology's stronger ties with psychology than education. In contrast to school psychology programs in low GNP countries, those in high GNP countries are more likely to be subject to external reviews, especially by psychological associations.

Among the faculty who teach in school psychology programs internationally, 35% have doctoral degrees, 50% have master's degrees, while the degrees of the remaining 15% are unknown. Seventy percent teach full-time and 30% teach part-time. Faculty typically work 21 hours weekly at a university and an additional 5 hours in other locations. Most have two or more jobs. Twenty percent reportedly have scholarly reputations nationally and 2% have scholarly reputations internationally. Salaries received by faculty vary considerably. They are higher for those who have taught more years and who have worked in high GNP countries. Faculty salaries for those who have taught between 5 to 10 years averaged $33,000 in high GNP countries and $4,000 in low GNP countries.

THE INFLUENCE OF REGULATIONS

Some External Conditions that Influence School Psychology's Growth

The degree to which school psychology is regulated also reflects its development. Regulation includes various restraints imposed either externally (e.g., who may use the titles "psychologist" and "school psychologist") or internally (e.g., the presence of a professional association with high standards for membership and an association-sponsored ethics code). Regulations in school psychology are found principally in legal and ethical standards. Professional psychology, including school psychology, generally is stronger in countries that impose external and internal standards on service.

The influence of external regulations on practice within the 53 countries that participated in Oakland's 1990 survey, excluding the United States, was found to be considerable (Cunningham, 1994). The 53 countries cluster into one of six groups based on the degree of external regulations.

School psychology was unregulated in the eight countries that comprised cluster one (Burkina Faso, Papua New Guinea, Greece, Iran, Yemen, Niger, South Korea, and Ethiopia). Degrees of regulation increased incrementally for those that comprised clusters two (Ecuador, Egypt, Mexico, Japan, India, Sudan, Costa Rica, Chile, and Ghana), three (Austria, Dominican Republic, Italy, Kuwait, Lebanon, The Netherlands, People's Republic of China, Poland, Russia, Saudi Arabia, and Thailand), four (Australia, Brazil, Columbia, Germany, Hong Kong, Hungary, Iceland, Ireland, Nigeria, Spain, Czechoslovakia, Turkey, and Venezuela), and five (Canada, Finland, France, Norway, Scotland, South Africa, Sweden, Switzerland). School psychologists working in countries that comprise the sixth cluster had the highest degree of regulation (Denmark, England, Israel, and New Zealand).

The nature of services often was similar within each cluster and differed somewhat from those performed by school psychologists working in other clusters. For example, school psychologists working in cluster one focused more heavily on biologically based conditions (e.g., providing basic care to children with severe mental retardation). Those in clusters two and three devoted greater effort to socializing younger students and providing vocational guidance to older students. For example, the socialization of young children is a high priority to families in Central and South American countries. Furthermore, countries heavily influenced by socialism (e.g., Russia, China, Poland, Italy) utilized school psychologists to help promote socialist values. School psychologists working in countries that form clusters four and five typically conducted educational and psychological appraisals and worked on special education issues within public school settings. Those working in countries that form cluster six performed many of the activities found in clusters four and five; in addition, their work often emphasized systems interventions (e.g., consultation, organizational development, research, and evaluation).

The degree to which school psychology services are regulated is strongly associated with various other domestic conditions. For example, compared to countries in the lower clusters, countries in the higher clusters tend to be wealthier, have lower birth rates, more physicians per person, higher levels of education, and spend more federal tax revenues on housing, social security, and welfare.

In summary, school psychology is strongest in countries that are wealthier, devote a higher percentage of their tax revenue to elementary and second education, have and enforce universal education, have well-established regular education programs, offer well-established special education services, and have low drop-out rates. School psychology is weakest in those countries with weak elementary and secondary education systems and those in which educational programs in rural areas are inferior to those found in urban areas.

Some Internal Conditions that Influence School Psychology's Growth

Although various conditions outside of psychology and education strongly influence school psychology, various conditions within its control also influence its future. School psychology has considerable influence over the following conditions: formation of professional associations; recruitment and maintenance of professional membership; creation of its literature, standards, and certification and licensure provisions; models for and nature of professional preparation; professional and political relationships with others; and writing its history (Oakland & Cunningham, 1999).

While serving as a Fulbright Scholar in 1988, this author traveled through much of Brazil to meet directors of school psychology programs. Professional school psychology in Brazil then was at its infancy. Its interests were cared for through a national psychological association. However, as one can expect, the interests of school psychology did not constitute the highest priority for the national psychological association.

Recognizing this, two directors of school psychology programs, Dr. Solange Wechsler at the University of Brasilia and Dr. Raquel Guzzo at the Pontifica Catholic University in Campinas, united forces to help create the Brazilian Association of School and Educational Psychologists (ABRAPP). The Association's first national meeting, held in 1992, attracted more than 400 conference delegates. It then co-sponsored an international meeting of school psychologists in 1994 which attracted more than 800 delegates, the largest international meeting of school psychologists. The ABRAPP continues to recruit and maintain membership. It published the first scholarly journal in school psychology in Brazil in 1997 and has been instrumental in publishing books needed by school psychology programs. The ABRAPP's lobbying efforts to mandate school psychology services throughout Brazil were fulfilled when the President of Brazil signed a decree requiring these services. The ABRAPP continues its efforts to improve the quality of services to Brazilian children by encouraging Brazil's most able students to become school psychologists, by improving students' academic and professional preparation, and by creating other resources needed for effective service.

This is but one example of growth and development that can come from effective national leadership. The example illustrates, in part, the formation of a national school psychology association that went on to help write its history, recruit and maintain membership, create its literature, and work to improve preparation and professional standards. Through its efforts, school psychology has earned higher status among psychologists and officials in education and enjoys improved political relationships.

Availability of Test Use

Assessment is a universal enterprise (Oakland & Hambleton, 1995), and school psychologists are expected to be experts in assessment. The practices of school psychologists working in the United States and other industrialized nations are enhanced by the availability of various tests and other assessment methods to assist them in their work. However, the availability of tests is not universal. School psychologists in many countries have few if any locally developed standardized tests to use and must rely on tests developed elsewhere, including those that lack locally appropriate norms, reliability, and validity estimates.

An international survey of tests used with children and youth in 44 countries, not including the United States, identified 455 tests used somewhat frequently (Oakland & Hu, 1989; 1991; 1992; Hu & Oakland, 1991). Measures of intelligence, personality, and achievement were most readily available. About 50% of the tests were developed within other countries and imported for use. Foreign-developed tests tended to be used more commonly than locally developed tests within the 44 reporting countries. Validity studies were available on between 50 and 70% of the tests and reliability estimates on 50 to 60%. Local national norms were available on 80% of achievement tests and about 60% of intelligence and personality tests.

Test use is not uniform throughout the world. Highest test use occurs in highly industrialized nations; lowest test use occurs in the least developed countries. The Middle East and least developed nations typically rely on foreign developed tests.

The 10 most commonly used measures include, in descending order of use, (a) the Wechsler Intelligence Scales for Children, (b) Ravens Progressive Matrices, (c) Bender-Gestalt, (d) Rorschach, (e) Stanford-Binet, (f) Wechsler Adult Intelligence Scales, (g) Thematic Apperception Test (TAT), (h) Differential Aptitude Test, (i) Minnesota Multiphasic Personality Inventory, and (j) the Frostig Developmental Test of Visual Perception (Oakland & Hu, 1992). These tests assess a narrow range of abilities, and some are adult measures. Eight were developed in the United States. Tests maligned in the United States as being culturally biased often are used outside the United States. Such tests frequently lack adequate norms, validity, and reliability estimates for use in these countries. At least two tests, the TAT and Frostig, are known to have low reliability and are not used widely in the United States.

School psychologists and others who use tests report a critical need for both group and individual tests of achievement, intelligence, vocational interests and aptitudes, social development, and personality, as well as more moderate needs for entrance measures for primary, secondary, and tertiary schooling. Virtually all responding countries reported the need for tests that assess qualities important for those who are mentally retarded, blind, deaf, slower learners, emotionally and socially disturbed, physically impaired, and gifted. The need for measures to identify students with learning disabilities is most critical. Given an estimated 150 million children internationally (Oakland & Phillips, 1997), children with learning disabilities exceed those with all other mentally handicapping conditions combined and constitute the largest number of underserved or unserved students.

LAWS AND ETHICS THAT GUIDE PRACTICE

As previously noted, the nature of school psychology services tends to differ between countries, in part, due to the degree to which services and practices are regulated. The availability of laws governing professional entry as well as the nature and authorization of services generally signify more advanced stages in a profession's development. The demonstration of suitable ethical behaviors and the availability of an ethics code also signify advanced stages in a profession's development. Information on laws and ethics is reviewed below.

Laws Governing School Psychology

Countries differ considerably in the availability of laws that govern who may declare themselves to be school psychologists. In most countries persons without an academic degree may call themselves school psychologists. In developing countries school psychologists typically are required to have an undergraduate degree in psychology. They also may be required to hold membership in the national psychological association. In countries with higher professional standards such as Israel and many within Western Europe, a graduate degree, like a master's degree in education or psychology, commonly is required. No country requires a doctoral degree for entry into the profession.

The availability of laws that govern school psychology practice also differs. Most countries have no laws governing psychological or school psychological practice. In other countries, federal laws and statutes govern psychological services (e.g., Scandinavian countries) while state laws prevail in still others (e.g., Germany).

Laws that regulate school psychological services within special education exist only in the most highly developed countries and often are similar. For example, laws governing special education services often resemble those commonly found under the Individuals with Disabilities Education Act within the United States (e.g., Oakland, Cunningham, Poulsen, & Meazzini, 1991).

In some countries (e.g., Brazil), the federal government has delegated considerable control of professional psychology to its national psychological society. In these countries, all psychologists typically must be members of national psychological societies and abide by their rules and regulations.

Although a country may have laws that authorize the provision of school psychology services, the laws may not be enforced. For example, a head of state may decree all schools shall have one or more school psychologists. However, needed financial resources for and administrative implementation of this decree may be unavailable. There also may be insufficient numbers of qualified personnel to fully implement the laws.

Ethics Governing School Psychology

Advanced professions are expected to have self-imposed standards that reflect their moral and ethical values. These standards are offered in support of an implicit social contract between a profession and society. The contract provides considerable freedom for self-governance to a profession and in turn a profession places the interests of its clients and those of society above more self-serving interests of the profession and its members.

Professionals are expected to display suitable ethical behaviors. Ethics common to most professions include the following five features: non-malfeasance (i.e., to do no harm), beneficence (i.e., to help others derive benefit from one's services), autonomy (i.e., promoting client's freedom to think, choose, and act, albeit within legal boundaries), loyalty, and justice.

Professional associations typically are expected to assume leadership for the formation and enforcement of ethics codes. Ethics codes often have five purposes: to educate the profession and public as to suitable behaviors, to acknowledge the profession's obligation to provide services at a high level, to create enforceable standards of conduct, to create criteria important to certification and licensure, and to advocate for high levels of service when lower levels may be promulgated by others (e.g., when a school principal mandates conditions incompatible with professional ethics). Among an estimated 22 national associations of school psychology, few have developed ethics statements.

ISPA's LEADERSHIP IN DEVELOPING STANDARDS

Well-established professional associations can be expected to assume leadership for the development and enforcement of statements that help define the parameters of professional practice, the nature of professional preparation, and ethics codes. The ISPA leadership recognized that these essential provisions did not exist in most countries. Thus members developed and approved statements in these three areas to acknowledge the international nature of the profession and to assist national societies in their development. These statements are summarized below. The development and approval of these statements were facilitated by knowledge from a prior survey (Oakland & Cunningham, 1992) and other sources that similarities among school psychologists and the services they perform outnumber differences.

Definition of School Psychology and Provision of Services

The following draws heavily from *A Definition of School Psychology*, a position statement approved by the ISPA General Assembly in 1996 (Oakland & Cunningham, 1997).

School psychologists are prepared in a core curriculum that contains academic content in basic areas of psychology and education, professional content important to the practice of school psychology, and information relevant to work in culturally diverse settings. Professional content provides preparation in assessment, intervention, consultation, organizational and program development, supervision, and research. School psychologists acquire knowledge and experiences working in various settings in which services may be delivered, including schools, homes, clinics, agencies, hospitals, and other institutions. Practices may include individual, group, and organizational work in public and privately supported settings.

School psychologists are knowledgeable of various assessment models and methods. The primary goals of assessment are to describe a person's abilities and qualities accurately, determine the etiology of disorders, plan and evaluate interventions, and prevent the onset of disabling conditions.

School psychologists foster various forms of interventions intended to help promote development, to acquire and optimize personal, social, family, and community resources, and to minimize difficulties and disorders. Interventions involve school psychologists working directly with individuals, groups, and systems, or indirectly (e.g., through consultation and testing) with teachers, principals, and other educational personnel, parents and other family members, as well as other professionals and paraprofessionals. Interventions may be directed toward promoting well being and preventing the onset of problems (i.e., primary prevention), minimizing difficulties once they occur (i.e., secondary prevention), and stabilizing disabilities and working to ensure basic and needed services are provided to those who can be expected to manifest one or more disabling conditions over some years (i.e., tertiary prevention). Direct services include counseling and other forms of therapeutic services, teaching, tutoring, and other interventions in which a school psychologist works with one or more individuals in need of services. Indirect services include assessment and program planning, pre-service and in-service professional preparation, supervision, consultation, collaboration, research and evaluation, and other methods by which needed services are delivered by others with the assistance of school psychologists.

Consultation services typically recognize and emphasize the importance of using cooperative and collaborative methods to address problems. They encourage participation in ways to promote knowledge of psychology and education and their proper applications to enhance growth and development.

Organizational and program development services are provided to schools, school districts, agencies, as well as other organizations and administrative units at local, regional, national, and international levels. Services may include assessment and evaluation, interventions, coordination, program planning, curriculum and instructional development and evaluation, and consultation. Typical goals include promoting and strengthening the coordination, administration, planning, and evaluation of services within one unit or between two or more units responsible for serving infants, children, youth, or adults.

Supervision refers to professional services provided by those with advanced preparation and experience who are able to assume responsibility and accountability for the provision of school psychological services. The administrative unit responsible for providing school psychological services should be directed by a school psychologist who also is responsible for supervising the activities of school psychologists working within the unit.

School psychologists are committed to a service delivery model in which research and theory form a primary basis for practice. They can be expected to be knowledgeable of research relevant to practice and guide their services accordingly. In addition, school psychologists are expected to contribute to research and theory by engaging actively in research, evaluation, professional writing, and other scholarly activities intended to advance knowledge and its applications relevant to school psychology.

School psychologists are knowledgeable of, and provide services in ways consistent with, legislation, public policy, administrative rulings, and ethical principles and codes that govern services. School psychologists continue their professional development in ways that help insure that their practices are consistent with current knowledge, legislation, and codes of professional practice and conduct.

Academic and Professional Preparation of School Psychologists

ISPA leadership recognized that guidelines for the preparation of school psychologists also were needed in order to help insure quality control in school psychology programs and to reflect curricula found in countries with well-established programs. To be viable within a country, school psychology must reflect that country's domestic conditions. Thus the practices of school psychologists and preparation must reflect these differing domestic conditions.

As previously noted, a school psychologist in many countries obtains a degree and certificate to practice upon completing a 4- or 5-year degree, one equivalent in length to many undergraduate degrees in the United States or Canada. However, students graduating from these programs typically are required to take all their courses in psychology, school psychology, and education. They often have few electives. Their transcripts reflecting coursework in these three areas resemble those of many specialist-level trained school psychologists in the United States.

Despite national differences in academic degrees needed by school psychologists, the nature of their coursework and other qualities associated with their preparation are remarkably similar (Oakland & Cunningham, 1992; Cunningham, 1994; Cunningham & Oakland, 1998). Knowledge of these similarities enabled the formation of *International Guidelines for the Preparation of School Psychologists*. These *Guidelines* were approved by the ISPA General Assembly in 1996 (Cunningham & Oakland, 1998).

The preparation of school psychologists typically includes academic preparation and professional practice. Each is addressed below.

Core Academic Knowledge of Psychology

Students typically take courses in the following academic areas: developmental psychology, psychology of learning and cognition, educational psychology, personality psychology, social psychology, statistics and research design, experimental psychology, and biological psychology.

Assessment and Intervention Services

All school psychologists receive preparation in assessment and intervention. Preparation typically emphasizes intellectual, academic, emotional, and social assessment. In addition, programs prepare students for behavioral, affective, educational, and social-systems interventions. The primary prevention of academic and social problems is a common and important goal. The school psychologist's primary focus on children and youth within the context of classrooms, schools, families, communities, and other systems is universal.

Interpersonal Skills

Effective collaboration, consultation, and leadership require well-developed interpersonal skills. Trust and faith, qualities enhanced by well-developed interpersonal skills, form the foundation of all professional relationships. In addition, listening and communication skills, respect for the views and expertise of others, recognition of the assets and limitations of other professionals, and a mature understanding of issues and effective methods to address them comprise other interpersonal skills that influence a school psychologist's ability to work with others.

Professional Skills in Decision Making

Professional judgments require more than a cookbook approach to practice. Professional judgment should be based on decision making that considers important qualities that characterize the child and the contexts within which the child is being raised, is informed by research, and is motivated by problem-solving orientations that consider the viability of alternative courses of actions. The importance of developing and employing reflective problem-solving methods is emphasized.

Purposes of Statistical Methods and Research Design

Many programs in Canada and the United States prepare school psychologists to be scientists as well as practitioners. A goal of these programs is to prepare professionals who have solid knowledge of current theory and science, whose practices are based on research, and who themselves contribute to the literature. For such programs, courses in research design and statistics enhance students' roles as practitioners and scientists.

Although the preparation of school psychologists in some countries such as Israel and Denmark also have this scientific emphasis, most psychologists are prepared to be consumers of literature and to have solid knowledge of current theory and science. They are neither prepared nor expected to contribute to this literature. Such school psychology programs are more likely to require courses in quantitative and qualitative methods of assessment, descriptive and inferential statistics, together with research design that enable school psychologists to become reflective consumers of literature.

Most research in psychology is conducted by those with doctoral degrees. Since few school psychologists receive doctoral degrees, expectations that school psychologists will contribute to literature through scholarly activities are not common.

Knowledge of Legal and Ethical Basis for Services

Students in school psychology programs also receive information on the legal basis (e.g., laws, administrative rulings, regulations) governing practice if one exists in their country. As noted elsewhere, legal provisions often do not strongly influence the work of school psychologists.

Model School Psychology Curriculum

The Guidelines for the Preparation of School Psychologists (Cunningham & Oakland, 1998) describes a model curriculum for a school psychology program. Course work includes core courses in psychology, including developmental, educational, social, and personality psychology; learning and cognition; and measurement, research design, and statistics. Courses in educational foundations promote knowledge of education. Specialization in school psychology is promoted through such courses as professional issues in school psychology, educational and psychological assessment, consultation, exceptional children, school-based interventions, and organizational and program development. The model program also includes provisions for research activities together with supervised practica and internships.

Ethics Codes

Ethics codes are developed with the firm belief that professional conduct is expected to exemplify a profession's values. As previously noted, these typically include doing no harm; helping others derive benefit from professional services;

promoting a client's freedom to think, choose, and act; displaying loyalty; and promoting justice. Professionals are expected to transcend narrow personal, social, and cultural values and attitudes; adopt positions that benefit professional-client relationships; and act in ways consistent with the best interests of students, educators, parents, institutions, the community, and the profession. Most of these qualities are supported universally, permitting the approval of an ethics code by an international professional community.

The ISPA leadership recognized the need for an ethics code for school psychology. Its members approved a *Code of Ethics* in 1990 (Oakland, Goldman, and Bischoff, 1997), one that is similar to those published by the National Association of School Psychologists (1997a) and the American Psychological Association (1992). This ethics code addresses issues important to the following areas: professional responsibility, confidentiality, professional growth, professional limitations, professional relationships, assessment, and research. The following information draws extensively from this code.

Professional Responsibility

School psychologists familiarize themselves with the goals and philosophy of the school system, families, and other organizations within which they work, and work effectively within their organizational structure. They are knowledgeable of laws, administrative codes, and regulations. School psychologists should not allow personal prejudices or biases to interfere in their decision making nor should they engage in discriminatory procedures or practices based on one's social or economic background, race, disability, age, gender, sexual preference, religion, or national origin.

Confidentiality

School psychologists safeguard confidential student information. Confidential information is discussed only for professional purposes and only with persons clearly concerned with the case. Consent is obtained from parents or students before releasing confidential information.

Professional Growth

School psychologists recognize the need for and participate in continuing professional development. They maintain knowledge of current scientific and professional information.

Professional Limitations

School psychologists are aware of their professional limitations and offer only those services that are within their areas of professional competence.

Professional Relationships

The welfare of children and youth is of primary importance. School psychologists do not exploit their professional relationships for personal gain. They strive to develop harmonious and cooperative relationships with colleagues and school staff and attempt to resolve possible unethical practices of colleagues in a constructive manner.

Assessment

School psychologists typically administer tests according to published guidelines and interpret them in light of suitable norms, reliability, validity, and other well-established standards. They are accountable for the methods they use and are able to defend their use.

Research

School psychologists inform parents when their children are participating in research projects and ensure that students participating in research do not suffer any mental or physical distress from the procedures. They communicate research results to educators, parents, students, and other interested parties in ways that ensure their exactness and limitations.

When conducting cross-cultural research, school psychologists abide by the research ethics of the countries in which they are working. They demonstrate respect for the host culture and avoid actions that violate cultural expectations or reveal culturally biased perspectives. Investigators are knowledgeable of cross-cultural methodology and familiar with the cultural context of research settings.

FUTURE OF SCHOOL PSYCHOLOGY INTERNATIONALLY

The development of school psychology internationally is likely to remain uneven. School psychology is and can be expected to be strong and stable in fewer than 15 countries (e.g., those that comprise previously described clusters five and six). School psychology is emerging as a strong and stable profession in another 26 to 28 countries (e.g., those that comprise clusters three and four). School psychology is barely discernible in many other countries. For example, about 50% of the world's population of 5.6 billion reside in China, India, Indonesia, and Pakistan. Yet, the number of school psychologists found in these countries is so small that they could be seated easily in a large auditorium. Furthermore, some countries with large populations (e.g., China, Indonesia, Pakistan) lack programs for the preparation of school psychologists. Its status in many of the remaining countries is less clear (Oakland & Wechsler, 1988). Some are experiencing significant improvements (e.g., Greece) while others are in a state of decline (e.g., Venezuela).

Among the more than 200 countries in the world, information about school psychological practice is readily available on only 54. Thus, little is known about the status of school psychology in most countries. The growing recognition that education serves as an important pathway to a country's financial prosperity and social stability together with the growing prestige and importance of psychology suggest bright futures for school psychology.

Five External Qualities that Will Favorably Influence the Growth of School Psychology

The future of school psychology will be strongly influenced by five qualities external to psychology (Russell, 1984): a nation's economy, geography, language, interests and priorities, and cultural factors.

Economic Factors

Economic realities strongly influence psychology. As noted, psychology is stronger in nations with higher GNP that are industrialized in contrast to those dependent on agriculture or tourism. Moreover, within countries, psychology is stronger in urban areas, given their concentration of wealth, than in rural areas. Consequently, growth of school psychology is likely to be stronger in countries that are more prosperous; within them, growth will occur first in larger cities.

Geography

Geographic barriers between nations also influence the development of psychology. Psychology reaches countries most closely linked politically, geographically, and by transportation and communication. The birth and rapid growth of psychology in Germany, France, and England occurred, in part, because of their close links. In contrast, the growth of psychology in Arab countries has been slower. Thus, growth of school psychology is likely to be stronger in countries that have fewer geographic barriers (e.g., mountains, oceans) between them and countries in which psychology is strong.

Language

Language, an important component of communication, figures importantly in transporting psychology. German, French, and English historically constituted the international languages of scientific and professional practice. Psychology generally remains less developed in countries in which these languages are not widely used.

English has become the most prominent language of science and the professions. English-language countries, especially the United States, have numerous outstanding graduate and research programs from which school psychologists in almost all countries have benefited. Many world leaders have been educated in English-language countries, later returning home to assume leadership roles as professors and researchers, maintaining close contacts with their English-speaking colleagues, and relying on English-language scholarly publications for much of their continued professional development. Much of the theory and research that forms the basis for preparing school psychologists comes from the United States. Most scientific scholarship in psychology appears in English. All international conferences use English as their primary language. As a result, many graduate programs in psychology, including school psychology, now require their students to read English. Thus the growth of school psychology is likely to be stronger in countries that encourage its students to acquire facility with English.

National Needs and Priorities

National needs and priorities strongly influence the degree to which psychological services are initiated and sustained. School psychological services always emerge because national leaders and the public see value associated with the provision of these services. Services are initiated in response to national needs. Services are sustained if school psychological services are seen as providing continued value. For example, the goal of school psychology in socialist countries is to help promote social values in children. The goals of school psychology in the United States (e.g., to promote children as strong and independent citizens) also are consistent with its national priorities. The growth of school psychology is likely to be stronger when the profession is responding to important national needs and priorities.

Cultural Conditions

Cultural conditions also have a decisive influence on the emergence of and support for psychology. Psychology and its professional specialties emerge and remain strong when they are seen by others as providing technically sophisticated and relevant services within a context that respects cultural values and mores. Psychology has a decided western emphasis that limits its influence in many regions of the world (e.g., the Middle East, the Pacific Rim). The acceptance of the discipline and practice of psychology depends, in part, on the extent to which psychology expands to embrace conditions that are important to child growth and development together with educational, social, and cultural issues in non-western nations. As a result, the growth of school psychology will be stronger when its knowledge and theory go beyond its current dependency on Canadian, European, and United States sources.

Five Internal Qualities that Will Influence the Growth of School Psychology

Many of the five qualities described above are beyond the control of school psychology. However, other conditions over which school psychology has more control also can influence its future (Oakland & Saigh, 1989; Oakland, 1992; Oakland & Cunningham, 1999). Five are reviewed below.

Promote Professionalism

Professional associations representing school psychologists have been formed in fewer than 10% of countries. Professional associations are needed to help promote high standards for the preparation of school psychologists and the delivery of services. Leaders of professional associations serve as the profession's spokespersons, provide vision and direction, and work to ensure that needed services are supported during periods of economic, social, and political turmoil. The attainment of the remaining four conditions depends, in part, on the formation of strong and viable national associations of school psychology.

Codify the Scope and Functions of School Psychology

Statements prepared and endorsed by national professional associations that describe the scope and functions of service are needed. Such statements establish the boundaries of service and provide strong direction to academic and professional preparation.

Expand Professional Activities

As noted earlier, services in many countries are restricted to caring for the needs of the mentally retarded and providing assessments. Although these services are important, they constitute a limited range of possible services the profession can provide and clients need. Emphasis on primary prevention (Oakland, 1990; Wechsler & Oakland, 1990), interventions, consultation, organizational and program development, and supervision are needed to expand the nature of school psychological services and to demonstrate the profession's ability to meet national needs and priorities.

Improve Its Interface With Education

School psychology straddles two arenas: education and psychology. School psychologists often wonder to which they owe their primary allegiance. Internationally, most school psychologists work in and for schools. Their primary allegiance must be to education as it provides the context and financial compensation for their work. Those who work in the private sector may ally themselves more closely with psychology.

Educators often determine whether school psychologists become viable members of the education establishment. Moreover, the development of school psychology generally follows a discernible pattern. General education services from elementary through post-secondary levels typically are offered first, followed by special education services. Thereafter, school psychology services develop (Catterall, 1979b; Saigh & Oakland, 1989). Leaders in special education often serve as gatekeepers for school psychological services and strongly influence whether such services are provided. Their views are most critical when federal laws governing special education services are vague or absent.

Within most sub-Saharan African countries, with the exception of South Africa, the practice of school psychology is marginal, at best. Given a desire to better understand whether school psychology is likely to grow in this important region, directors and other leaders within special education in 12 eastern- and southern-African countries were surveyed to determine their views as to whether they would endorse the inclusion of school psychology services in their countries (Mpofu, Zindi, Oakland, & Peresuh, 1997). Respondents reported the availability, regulation, and utilization of school psychology services to be low. Visibility and utilization are higher when school psychology is recognized formally and regulated at a national level. The services of school psychologists prepared abroad were seen as less relevant and supportable to the services of those prepared in this region as the former often lack an understanding of the socio-cultural context of education.

Promote Scholarship and Technical Contributions

School psychology practices that reflect a country's socio-cultural conditions are needed. Scholarship on socio-cultural conditions is more readily available in developed countries and less readily available, although highly needed, in less developed countries (Oakland & Wechsler, 1990).

As previously noted, the need for nationally developed psychological and educational tests also is particularly critical to improving professional services (Hu & Oakland, 1991; Oakland & Hu, 1989, 1991, 1992; Oakland & Hambleton, 1995). Tests to assess children's achievement, intelligence, personality and temperament, and other qualities and to identify those with learning disabilities are greatly needed.

Some years ago school psychologists in New Zealand set about to expand scholarship and test availability in their country. They were instrumental in forming the New Zealand Council for Educational Research to assist in the promotion of scholarship and test development. Other models exist to assist countries and regions in promoting scholarship and technical contributions. These and other efforts to promote scholarship and technology on which school psychological services depend are needed in most regions.

CONCLUSION

Knowledge of school psychology's international dimensions enriches an understanding of the specialty. The practice of school psychology is found in most nations with advanced educational systems. The nature of school psychology services reflects a country's social, economic, and educational systems. Increases in the numbers of school psychology programs and school psychology practitioners as well as the scope of their services are expected. The ISPA has helped establish a professional infrastructure that enables school psychology to acquire higher levels of professionalism. The growth of school psychology internationally will depend heavily on school psychology's success in establishing viable national associations that can provide needed leadership at this important level.

C H A P T E R   1 1

Perspectives on the Future of School Psychology

The decade of the 1990s was replete with historical publications in psychology and school psychology. It was the decade in which we reached the centennials of the founding of the American Psychological Association in 1992 and the first psychological clinic in 1996, the 50th anniversary of Division 16 in 1995, and the 30th anniversary of NASP in 1999. Throughout this book we have reported the progress and accomplishments of school psychology in the areas of roles, practice, credentialing, training, accreditation, organizational, and professional development. From the ideas, technological developments, and practices of a few persons in the late nineteenth and early twentieth centuries, school psychological services have developed into a major specialty of professional psychology. Most, if not all, of the major symbols of professional development have been accomplished. What about school psychology's future?

In this final chapter we address the future of school psychology from several perspectives. First we look at futuristic perspectives written before 1970. We then discuss more recent viewpoints. Finally we provide our own viewpoints about the future. In so doing, we return to several of the questions in Chapter 1, and provide our predictions about the future. We then present some general recommendations and guidelines for entering the future. In response to critics who have called for dramatic and rapid change in contemporary school psychologists' roles and functions, we take a more cautious approach to change while predicting a future characterized by increasing diversity of roles, functions, and practice settings.

PRE-1970 VIEWPOINTS ON THE FUTURE

Enmeshed with generic clinical psychology in many locales, for all practical purposes, most of school psychology was without discussions of its own future for many years. Considering the unclear identity of school psychology before the 1940s, the lack of futuristic writing is not surprising. However, Hollingworth (1933) made the following predictions about what psychological services would be rendered in the next quarter-century (i.e., by 1958):

> Judging the future from the past, we venture to predict that this service will become a part of scholastic routine everywhere. It will become inconceivable that once upon a time the American people forcibly seized the children of the nation and subjected them from seven to fourteen or sixteen years of age indiscriminately to undifferentiated education, without knowledge of their abilities, their mental contents, or their emotional problems.

> By means of scientific psychological service education will become differentiated on the rational basis of individual differences in biological nature. The school will be fitted to the child. Suicide of pupils, in despair at failure, will be unknown. Truancy will become a thing of the past. The uneducable will be impersonally recognized as such. The gifted will be selected for the extraordinary opportunity which suits them by nature. Special talents and defects will be considered in school placements.

> It is surely inconceivable that the blind *wish* to believe all men created equal will finally prevail over demonstrated truth. Chaos will not be permitted to continue where order has been made possible.

> The more scientific (precise, disinterested, and verifiable) psychological service becomes, the more humanitarian does it automatically become. Without *impersonal* knowledge of the child, idealists do mainly "good deeds which are harmful." True idealism demands impersonal truth as a basis for action. In the field which we are considering, the pioneers have done their work of acquiring new knowledge, preparing themselves to use it, charting a departure, and showing the way to found education on a scientific knowledge of childhood. It is for the psychological service of the future to develop this work by continuing to discover and apply impersonal knowledge of the child's nature and deeds (p. 379).

Now, almost 70 years since her predictions, Hollingworth would probably be content with the current knowledge base of what was then generic clinical and applied psychology, but its limited application in education would be disconcerting. We believe she would be very disappointed with the nature of the educational order established and the persistent problems of student academic learning and emotional/behavioral disorders.

With the founding of Division 16 (APA), a separate identity for school psychology began to crystallize and authors looked more closely at the future prospects of the field. In her presidential address to Division 16, Bertha Luckey (1951) stated:

> The psychologist of the future should have a thorough grounding in clinical psychology, group tests, and other devices which furnish crude means of sifting the population, but the real contribution and real pressures of school psychologists will always be in the specialized fields that require more basic knowledge of human development and its variations. This includes special approaches to various subjects, and especially those tool subjects that must constantly be used in the educational situation, as reading, writing, arithmetic, etc. (p. 10).

The Thayer conference proceedings (Cutts, 1955) stressed recommendations and predictions for the future. These included (a) two levels of training and practice in the schools with the master's-level practitioner offering limited, supervised services (the two levels were also to be reflected in training, with accreditation available at both levels); (b) increased availability of part-time doctoral study for in-service psychological workers; and (c) SDE certification at two levels commensurate with training and accreditation. The proceedings also predicted a future with continued high demand for school psychologists. The conference was an agenda for Division 16-APA, which set about the business of accomplishing its recommendations. Although the two levels of school psychology never gained widespread acceptance, they can be observed in some states, and Division 16 was successful in producing certification guidelines, training guidelines for the doctoral and master's level, ABPP, and accreditation (Fagan, 1993).

In the 1960s, the growth of school psychology was reflected in a wave of books discussing roles and functions and the future of the field (see Appendix B). O'Shea (1960) painted the future with a broad brush declaring that "the day has long since past when any psychologist relies upon a 'one-shot' testing period" (p. 280). Her future school psychologist would be involved with what we now consider ecological assessment of the classroom, contributing to the decision-making process of school district affairs (e.g., curriculum planning, personnel policies), consultation and interventions with the school staff, working more effectively with parents, collaborating with non-school agencies, initiating psychotherapy in the school setting, creating more effective learning environments, advocating for the importance of the social sciences in an era dominated by a need for mathematicians and physical scientists, and contributing to knowledge through research. She even suggested that every school building in the larger cities should have a well-trained doctoral school psychologist, echoing a plea by Symonds many years before (Symonds, 1933). Rural areas might have a single psychologist supervising the work of lesser trained personnel in several districts.

Hirst (1963) predicted a strong need for school psychologists, substantial increases in the doctoral force over the next 20 years, the rising involvement of school psychologists in the diagnosis of learning disabilities, and greater involvement in counseling and psychotherapy as school psychologists acquired training in those areas. Hirst also predicted increased roles of in-service education, prevention, research, and program evaluation. Gray (1963a) advocated a broad future of applications of psychology to education, and the necessity of maintaining the scientist-professional model of training and practice.

Among the more comprehensive discussions was that of Magary (1967a). Blending others' preferences for the future with his own, Magary predicted the emergence of treatment-oriented roles and consultation, the school psychologist as a high school (and even elementary school) teacher of psychology, the legal-ethical problems facing school psychologists in private practice, the need for well-established training models and program growth, and improved internship and certification models. Although he praised the growth of school psychology, Magary felt there were already too many professional associations and journals and that consolidation was needed in the future. He stated that school psychologists needed to establish a stronger identity as pupil personnel services (PPS) workers and members of the school faculty rather than seek a separate identity just for themselves. Magary's desire for greater cooperative efforts and PPS teamwork has been only partially realized. It was true that school psychologists shared areas of knowledge and practice with school counselors and social workers, but the "hardening of the categories approach in pupil personnel services" deplored by Magary became a hallmark of each PPS area in the 1970s. School psychology's categorization was effectively augmented by the joint efforts of NASP (formed a few years after Magary's book appeared) and Division 16, in which Magary was very active. Magary's chapter is an excellent description of school psychology's overall professional development in the 1960s.

Finally, a little-known work by Gelinas and Gelinas (1968) depicted a very positive future for school psychologists from the standpoint of employment alternatives within the school system. They foresaw opportunities for advancement to administrative positions including those of director of psychological services, principal, assistant superintendent for pupil services, and superintendent. Their discussion of the advantages for women in choosing a future as a school psychologist is instructive about how much the status of women has changed since the 1960s (see Gelinas & Gelinas, 1968, "Family Life," pp. 111-112).

Authors of the 1960s overestimated the rise of doctoral training and doctoral credentialing and the breadth of functioning school psychologists would achieve. They were writing in an era of rapid growth in school psychology and failed to see the impact on role and function that emerging legislation for exceptional children would later have in the form of Public Law 94-142. The impact of NASP was also unforeseen. As a major advocate for non-doctoral school psychologists, NASP may have inadvertently impeded the rise of doctoral school psychology. We doubt the authors of the 1960s could have predicted either the growth of the field since 1970 or the persistence of its traditions.

POST-1970 VIEWPOINTS ON THE FUTURE

Bardon and Bennett (1974) suggested that the future would include better trained school psychologists able to offer a wider variety of services than the child-centered services of the past. One can see in their discussion of a "developmental-educational approach" the influence of earlier writers and the prototype of Bardon's later position on school psychologists being involved with a psychology of schooling (Bardon, 1983).

Another future perspective was provided by Tindall (1979), who expressed concern for the lack of role expansion which had been predicted by earlier writers. He foresaw serious conflicts over the APA-NASP differences in training and credentialing policies. He considered it probable that specializations would develop within school psychology and expressed the need for accountability via APA and NASP standards and ethics. Tindall felt that most of Magary's earlier predictions were not yet realized and that the field needed to avoid divisiveness that would draw school psychology away from the larger profession of psychology, leaving the school psychologist with a "meaningless title and a bag of techniques" (p. 22).

In the 1980s, Herron, Herron, and Handron (1984) expressed concern for continuing identity problems, doctoral-non-doctoral issues, the proliferation of training at the non-doctoral level, and decreasing job demand. They sensed a future based on the doctoral level in school psychology, with fewer but better training programs, limited job demand, expanded service settings, and more indirect service provision such as consultation. Another perspective viewed the future in terms of the content and process changes needed in school psychology (Reynolds et al., 1984). Blending traditional approaches and necessary changes, they called for reanalysis of assessment, diagnosis, and treatment, as well as the methods and vehicles for delivering services including the need for more follow-up services, and a reconsideration of the sources of power in service delivery. Their changes were conceptualized within the framework of reciprocal determinism, and they forecast the need for much broader applications of psychological science. For example, future assessment was described as much broader than traditional normative approaches applied to internal characteristics and would include behavioral and environmental assessment.

Bergan (1985) considered the major future scientific advances to be associated with cognitive psychology and developments in behavioral and path-referenced assessment. Drawing heavily from the discussions at the Spring Hill (Ysseldyke & Weinberg, 1981) and Olympia conferences (Brown, Cardon, Coulter, & Meyers, 1982), Bergan mentioned several professional developments including training specializations, expanded practice settings, increased legal influences on practice, greater accountability, and role expansion into other settings including the private practice sector. The Spring Hill and Olympia conferences were the most concentrated future discussions in school psychology since the Thayer conference. As at Thayer, many subjects were discussed and many plans for action considered, but recommendations far exceeded predictions for the future. The proceedings provide comprehensive descriptions of the issues and anxieties of the field in the early 1980s. The Olympia conference provided a process for considering the future at subsequent conferences held by numerous state school psychology associations.

The National School Psychology Inservice Training Network (1984) published its *School Psychology: Blueprint For Training And Practice*, which advocated broader roles for school psychologists primarily in school settings. In conjunction with greater inclusion of exceptional children in regular education, the recommended domains of school psychology leadership and function were class management, interpersonal communication and consultation, basic academic skills, basic life skills, affective/social skills, parental involvement, classroom organization and social structures, systems development and planning, personnel development, individual differences in development and learning, school-community relations, instruction, legal/ethical and professional issues, assessment, multicultural concerns, and research. The domains formed the basis for recommendations regarding future training. The *Blueprint* was revised in 1997 and is discussed below.

After an optimistic discussion of the field generally, Phillips (1990b) cautiously considered the future of school psychology:

> School psychology is at a turning point, and several possibilities exist for its future. Will school psychology be an occupation that continues to play a role limited largely to assessment and determinations of special education eligibility? Will school psychology become a two-tiered occupation, consisting of doctoral school psychologists increasingly engaged in a variety of nontraditional (and non-school) roles and non-doctoral school psychologists who continue to be engaged in the traditional assessment role? Or will school psychology become a specialty and profession that reaches for new roles, that raises the academic standards of training programs and the practical competence of its members,

thus engendering prestige, compensation, and working conditions good
enough to be recognized as a specialty and profession of first class? (p. 252)

Phillips' preferred future for school psychology is characterized by greater professionalization as a doctoral specialty of psychology, with an increased socio-cultural
orientation to behavior and learning. He cautions against school psychology
establishing its primary orientation with education instead of with psychology.

Woody, LaVoie, and Epps (1992) identify a future with continued need
for school psychological services with school-children and possibly with adults,
a broader role engaging the entire school population, a need for continuing education beyond training and credentialing, an increase of school psychologists in private practice, and increased feminization and concern for women's and minority
issues in training and practice.

Among the most recent perspectives on the future are those provided by
the revised *Blueprint for School Psychology* (Ysseldyke et al., 1997) and a chapter
by Oakland and Cunningham (1999). The *Blueprint* identifies several domains of
practice that can be tied to training in school psychology and form the basis of the
revision of the NASP training standards that go into effect in 2002. The 10
domains are: Data-based Decision Making and Accountability; Interpersonal
Communication, Collaboration, and Consultation; Effective Instruction and
Development of Cognitive/Academic Skills; Socialization and Development of
Life Competencies; Student Diversity in Development and Learning; School
Structure, Organization, and Climate; Prevention, Wellness Promotion, and Crisis
Intervention; Home/School/Community Collaboration; Research and Program
Evaluation; and Legal, Ethical Practice, and Professional Development.

Oakland and Cunningham describe models for understanding the future
of school psychology and then identify potential changes in terms of areas over
which school psychology has most, some, and little control. Most control would
be in guild areas such as membership, associations, literature and standards,
credentialing and preparation. Some control would be in areas such as school
finance, federal and state laws and regulations, school-based service provision,
expansion of services beyond the schools, the number of training programs and
practitioners, and public perceptions of the field. Little control is identified in
broader areas such as cultural, political, and social components of employment
settings, or knowledge produced from unrelated disciplines. They identify several
areas of future tension. Among these they foresee the historical unity of the field
in terms of training, services, and practice settings yielding to a growing plurality
of such aspects that threaten the solidarity and identity of school psychology.
They also foresee tension between the current lengthy training period of school
psychologists compared to other professionals and the need for extending
preparation to keep up with the growth of service needs; the need for more ser-

vices in an atmosphere of tight or diminishing financial resources; the possibility of other professionals taking their place as the increased demands on schools to provide unattainable services exceeds the skills of the available school psychologists; the need to shift emphasis from remediation to prevention; practitioner desires to expand services beyond special education to general education; and the tension from shifting from traditional to emerging assessment strategies. Overall they forecast a fairly stable future for school psychology and suggest that "a retrospective view of school psychology in 10 years is likely to find the number of significant changes to be far less than its consistencies over this period" (p. 51). Finally, a forthcoming miniseries in the *School Psychology Review* (Vol. 29, No. 4) will explore several aspects of school psychology in the twenty-first century (Fagan & Sheridan, 2000).

PESSIMISTIC VIEWPOINTS ON THE FUTURE

Since the 1960s, there have been several doomsday publications predicting that school psychology might not survive the future because of the following scenarios:

1. Our narrow conceptualization of psychology's contributions as clinical services (Lighthall, 1963).
2. Our failure to keep up with the changing needs of education and to become psychologists of schooling instead of school psychologists (White, 1968-1969).
3. Our lack of proper training and identity (Clair & Kiraly, 1971).
4. Our conflicting interests in being a child advocate and agent of change for the schools while a school employee (Silberberg & Silberberg, 1971).
5. Our lack of training in response to federal legislative mandates for the handicapped (Hayes & Clair, 1978).
6. The adverse impact of service provision through contracting (Hirsch, 1979).

Owing to the forces discussed in Chapter 7, school psychology, with broader roles but still entrenched in tradition, survived the pessimistic predictions. Perhaps the doomsday forecasts were meant only to serve as stimuli to draw a vital field in new directions. Now at the end of the twentieth century, we continue to observe a few dire predictions about the future of school psychology. A review of national and state association newsletters of the past decade yields several articles suggesting we need dramatically to change our ways of training and practice or we will not survive the future (see e.g., Batsche, 1992).

Collectively the discussions of our future have suggested a need for greater unification around a theoretical identity, expanded doctoral training and work force, role expansion, expansion of work settings, increased research, evaluation, accountability, and preparedness for changes in psychology and education. If there is a single theme throughout all of the future discussions since the Thayer conference, it is the desire and need to expand; that is, to expand in practitioner numbers, settings, and especially roles and functions. Other recent future discussions follow this theme and place it in the context of changes observed in psychology and education (Cobb, 1990; Jackson, 1990; Knoff, Curtis, & Batsche, 1997; Oakland & Cunningham, 1999; Phillips, 1990b; and Pryzwansky, 1990). Cobb (1992) and Conoley (1992) have suggested that school psychology may cease to be a specialty, becoming more generically a part of applied and professional psychology. As professional psychology specialties mature they would become more alike in what Phillips (1990b) called "interspecialty ecumenism," a process that could be augmented by changes in specialty recognition (DeMers, 1993). In these viewpoints, school psychology would be more closely aligned with the contributions of educational psychology and consultation models, pursuing prevention as well as intervention goals. The prevention perspective is also encouraged by Alpert (1985).

PERSONAL VIEWPOINTS ON THE FUTURE

So long as the context remains the same, it is generally accepted that the best predictor of future behavior is present behavior. If you want to know what the field of school psychology will look like 6 months or a few years from now, its present description is probably generalizable. This is so because we have a substantial database about the present, including the conditions under which school psychological services are perceived as needed, practiced, and regulated. But what about 10, 20, or 50 years from now? Predicting the future that far forward is very risky. A 1900 publication predicting "What may happen in the next hundred years" (Watkins, 1900) is remarkable for what it predicted and for what it failed to predict. Although Watkins predicted global use of telephones and televising of events, he incorrectly predicted that there would be no C, X, or Q in our alphabet and that we would practically exterminate mosquitoes, houseflies, and roaches. Although predicting the use of airplanes especially in war, he incorrectly predicted that cities would be free from noise because of subways and overhead roadways. He spoke of the use of medical inspectors in schools but not psychologists. Like others who have attempted to predict the future, we too are faced with the uncertainty of what lies ahead. We are always stuck with our present and former understanding of conditions from which to predict future conditions. If present conditions were unalterable, we could easily predict a long-term future for school psychology which would be much like the present. Some and perhaps many school psychologists, especially those promoting different roles and functions, would be distressed by such consistency. While the lack of significant change provides security by ensuring a future similar to the present, it also stagnates professional growth. We may fear the directions that education, psychology, and school psychology might take in the future, but meaningful change is important. However, change simply for the sake of change is no guarantee of improvement.

Our ability to predict future change depends on our success in identifying the professional regulatory forces (contexts) most likely to change, the direction of their change, and the relative impact such changes could have on accreditation, credentialing, and practice. Meaningful and lasting change in school psychologists' roles and/or functions must be preceded by change in several influential variables, especially those at the local employment level. However, we must be prepared to accept change in several areas of professional regulation in addition to those in which *we* have greater control. For example, we must be prepared for changes in certification standards or special education regulations, as well as in administrators' perceptions of our own competencies. Below we discuss several of these variables and the directions we think they will take.

Before presenting predictions and recommendations for the future, let us first draw some conclusions about the general accomplishments of the field. In achieving the symbols of professionalism, school psychology has successfully straddled the influences of education and psychology to carve out a sphere of influence which is interdependent with both areas. School psychology now has strong professional organizations, a large work force of trainers and practitioners, ethics, standards for training, credentialing, and practice, credentials for the school and non-school sectors, and its own literature. Issues of survival and identity are largely behind us. Now in a period of stability, we are contending with which future directions will have the most beneficial outcomes for the field. The present diversity of opinions about what we are and what we should be doing is considerably different than in the 1960s. Then, the issues were being debated among persons who were often not themselves trained or identified with school psychology; many came from strong clinical or educational psychology backgrounds. In the 1990s, the issues are being debated by the offspring of the thoroughbred years, full-fledged school psychologists in both training and credentialing. We have arrived at a point where we can argue among ourselves without fear of serious professional division.

Another difference is in the kind of future that should be considered. School psychology has gone through periods related to the emergence of services, to identity and survival, to growth and stability, and is now entering a period of maturity and revision. The major growth period of school psychology, at least in quantitative terms, is probably behind us. What lies ahead is substantial qualitative growth and only modest quantitative growth. For example, public education enrollments, including those of special education, will not change as dramatically as in the past 25 years, but the nature of schooling and how we provide special education could change in significant ways. Moreover, the number of training institutions will continue to stabilize while the nature of training will continue to change. Let us return to some of the questions discussed in Chapter 1, and provide some predictions for the future, say for the next 20 years.

How Many School Psychologists Will There Be?

Given the problems of supply and demand, the relatively stable number of training programs, the expectations for school enrollment growth, and the recommended and existing service ratios, the overall size of the work force will probably not exceed 30,000–35,000. Thus the 500% growth of the past three decades (5,000-25,000) is not likely to recur in the next few decades. Nevertheless, an increase to 30,000–35,000 would represent substantial growth in the number of school psychologists and afford continued expansion in settings and roles. Although such growth would improve the overall service ratio, it would be far short of the current NASP recommended ratio of 1:1,000 school children and a maximum of four schools served (NASP, 1997b). The NASP standards are currently under revision but the ratio recommendation will remain the same.

Related to the future quantity of school psychologists is the fact that school psychologists in the second wave of employment (1950-1970) are in a retirement phase that will extend over the next decade or two (Fagan, 1988b). We continue to question the ability of training programs to produce enough graduates to fulfill the needs for replacement and new positions. This is already seen in the shortages reported in some states and in difficulties that some training programs are having in finding faculty replacements. Thus, it is conceivable that the actual quantitative growth could be smaller than the range cited above.

Diversity Representation

The field of school psychology will continue to be disproportionately female. The ratio of females to males entering training and practice will continue to favor females. Up considerably from the 46% estimate of Smith (1984), females now comprise about 75% of the work force, and this could rise to as high as 80–85%. The phenomenon is part of a broader feminization of the entire field of psychology. What impact this will have on the field is unclear but it will unfold in the near future. We can expect to see a stronger presence of women in the organizational leadership (several women have served as NASP, Division 16, and state association presidents in recent years), the appointment of women to editorial positions (e.g., in 1996 the *School Psychology Review* became the first school psychology journal to publish under a female editor, Patti Harrison; *Psychology in the Schools* appointed LeAdelle Phelps as editor, effective March, 1999), and a steady increase in women among training program faculty (Thomas, 1998). To a large extent, the future of school psychology will be in the hands of its female leadership. The trend will be attended by considerable concern for gender issues such as differential treatment, salaries, and sexual harassment, and issues of domestic impact (e.g., balancing work and family, violence, abuse). Discussing the importance of affirmative action in employment, Woody et al. (1992) raise the specter that "the enthusiasm for righting past wrongs against females and minorities can be a breeding ground for reverse discrimination against males, especially if they are older and Caucasian" (p. 14). These authors do not support actions which would in effect allow two wrongs to make a right. Equally important issues are why males have chosen other fields and how we can attract more males into school psychology. We would not be surprised to see in the next decade student recruitment and employment notices encouraging males to apply.

The field will continue to have difficulties in seeking greater minority representation. Unless considerably more minority students enter undergraduate training in psychology and other fields from which training programs attract graduate students, it is unlikely that the present 6–7% minority representation will grow beyond 10%. The *School Psychology Review* (Vol. 21, No. 4, 1992) contains a series of articles related to multicultural issues in school psychology. Among the issues discussed were the lack of empirical knowledge on African-American and Hispanic students (Gopaul-McNicol, 1992), and the complex and variable nature of multicultural training in school psychology graduate programs (Rogers et al., 1992; see also Division 16 newsletter, *The School Psychologist*, Vol. 49, No. 4, 1995, and Vol. 50, No. 1, 1995). Certain training programs can be expected to make greater contributions in this area than most others. Training programs and practitioners need to be sensitive to multicultural issues and their impact on practice. Increased knowledge, experience, and sensitivity may be the most strident gains to be made in the near future. It is unlikely there will be a sufficient pool of minority undergraduates from which to draw in order for school psychology training programs to achieve proportional representation between practitioners and their clientele. A recent publication provides excellent practice recommendations to improve sensitivity to such concerns and more adequately to serve diverse student groups (Rogers et al., 1999).

In addition to gender and minority representation, the future will include more practitioners who themselves have disabilities. Some of this representation will come from increasing age of the practitioner pool, occasioned unfortunately by the likelihood of increasing ailments and disabilities. In addition we will see increased numbers of graduate trainees with disabilities and more emphasis in selected training programs on specializing with certain areas of disability. An example is the new advanced graduate certificate in school psychology and deafness at Rochester Institute of Technology initiated in 1999.

At What Levels Will School Psychologists Be Trained?

The most probable change will be in the degree emphases of colleges and universities. An increasing number of eligible institutions will establish doctoral programs, specialist-level programs will stabilize in number, and the traditional 1- or 2-year master's degree programs will continue to fade away. Less probable is a large increase in the number of institutions offering any programs. The current number of institutions offering training is between 200 and 230. We doubt that number will change much, and it is possible that budgetary problems, program duplication, and other factors will lead to a reduction in the number of program institutions. For example, if specialist level programs are forced to continue adding requirements to meet NCATE/NASP accreditation, it could become impractical for some institutions to continue offering programs. The number of doctoral programs will rise to about 100 and the pursuit of national accreditation will increase in importance. Unless NASP emerges as an ASPA recognized accreditor, APA will continue to gain strength as the most representative and desired accreditor at the doctoral level. Non-doctoral accreditation will continue to be managed by NCATE/NASP or possibly by NASP alone. The state partnership effort in NCATE will have an impact on how NASP standards are implemented locally. It is possible that NASP could join forces with APA in a joint accreditation agreement for doctoral programs.

The work force will soon achieve a level of 70% specialist and 30% doctorate. A more balanced doctoral-non-doctoral condition (i.e., 50%) is a few decades away. Specializations, primarily among the doctoral work force, will continue to increase. Whether at the specialist or doctoral level, we can only train people to do so much within the confines of existing programs. The specialist and doctoral standards of APA and NASP have already strained program curricula. As the needs of our clients expand or change, training programs can only accommodate them within narrow limits. Curriculum modifications are certainly possible, but there is little room for additional courses and experiences, and state regulations in higher education limit the number of hours a degree program can require. Some alleviation of the problem could occur if NASP were to approve separate accrediting standards for the doctoral and specialist levels. The forthcoming revision of the NASP training standards requires that doctoral programs demonstrate greater emphasis of several areas of the 1997 *Blueprint*. School psychologists will have to accept the inevitability of continued professional development (CPD) beyond basic entry-level training. Although the number of persons holding the NCSP has dropped in recent years, with perhaps 50% of school psychologists holding the NCSP, there is a strong likelihood of CPD activity to maintain this credential. If more states were to require the NCSP for credentialing, it would also ensure CPD activity.

The long-standing affiliation of school psychology training programs with 4-year institutions of higher education may weaken. The shift to a professional school model now very visible in clinical psychology could be in the future of school psychology as well (Pion, 1992). The shift could bring about greater sensitivity to practitioner issues, and much greater availability of doctoral program training for practicing school psychologists (Brown, 1989). The shift would not be without its risks. Training could drift away from the traditional scientist-practitioner model, creating a schism among trainers and practitioners alike. Such a shift would have its impact in SBEP licensing but probably be felt less in SDE licensing where the NCSP standards could provide the glue to hold NASP's training ideology together. However, NASP training standards undergo periodic review and/or revision, and a stronger practitioner orientation could emerge in the future. School psychology can learn from clinical psychology what the potential impact of the professional school model might be. This is more than merely an increase in the number of Psy.D. graduates from institutions unable to grant the Ed.D. or Ph.D. degree. Much of what has occurred in clinical psychology is a shift away from traditional academic institution roots to free-standing professional schools. This is beginning to occur in school psychology. Suggestions for retaining the scientist-practitioner model within a doctoral and non-doctoral training program future are provided by Knoff, Curtis, and Batsche (1997). They provide suggestions for program administration and content, as well as faculty and student characteristics.

Another potential change is the preparation of school psychologists with greater educational than psychological identity. While the distinctions between training programs within educational psychology or psychology departments may not be clear, there are differences. The rapid growth of training programs in the 1960s and 1970s and their accreditation has moved us more in the direction of education academic units than psychology units. Earlier orientations of trainers and programs may have been overly psychological (i.e., clinical), but we must strive to maintain an appropriate representation of both psychology and education, and an identity as psychologists. Education-based programs, even doctoral programs, are readily influenced by education college changes made in response to state or national reform efforts that are more directed toward instruction than psychological practice. School psychology trainers may argue that improving instruction is a laudable goal for all school psychologists; but such goals are more closely related to educational psychology than to the traditional and even contemporary practice of professional psychologists. The overlaps and differences signify the continuing influence of our Witmerian and Hallian roots, and the distinctions between what Bardon and others have referred to as school psychology in contrast to applied educational psychology (or a psychology of schooling). We will need to respect an increasing diversity in training program orientations as well as diversity in practitioner orientations and settings.

We do not foresee a time when school psychology programs will be offered entirely through distance learning technology. Although some course requirements may be met in this manner, the faculty-student interaction, which is such a necessary part of training (e.g., practica) will never be eliminated completely.

How Will Practitioners Be Credentialed for Practice?

Because all states have credentialing in some form for the school and non-school sectors, there is little room for quantitative growth in credentialing. The qualitative issues of the future revolve around the changing requirements for these credentials and their titles. We believe the school sector will continue to require non-doctoral training and the non-school sector will continue to move in the directions set by APA at the doctoral and postdoctoral levels. SDE credentialing will increasingly rely on the specialist degree and the NCSP for reciprocity. State boards of examiners in psychology will continue to license at the doctoral level in most states and requirements for postdoctoral training and/or additional years of supervised experience will be more widespread. Non-doctoral credentials for non-school practice will continue to be limited and fought by various forces. The doctoral degree will continue to be the choice primarily for practitioners desiring to be employed with the fewest professional and legal restrictions. For persons desiring full-time employment in school districts, the forecast is for continued high demand for non-doctoral practitioners in most states, though such persons will experience restricted, and often prohibited, non-school practice. If more SDEs relinquish their credentialing authority, we will observe more states experiencing problems retaining the title "school psychologist" and perhaps ending up with "specialist in school psychology." The long-term reciprocal impact of accreditation and credentialing, and wider recognition of the NCSP, will be greater state-to-state reciprocity in credentialing.

What Is the Employment Outlook?

School psychologists will continue to find public school districts and cooperative agreement districts as their most common employment settings. Nontraditional settings, including private practice, will continue to increase, perhaps to include 25% of the work force. Employment opportunities will be best for persons having specializations, and mobility, as well as for those interested in working in rural and developing areas, certain urban districts, many non-school settings, and in private practice. Moreover, there continues to be a growing shortage of school-based practitioners in several states as observed several years ago (Connolly & Reschly, 1990; National Association of State Consultants for School Psychological Services, 1987).

With substantial training program growth in the 1960s, many senior-level academic positions will be replaced in the near future. It is our experience that such positions are more likely to be replaced by junior-level positions (assistant professorships). In some instances, training programs that were managed by a single senior-level faculty member are being closed upon that person's retirement. This seems to be in reaction to tighter education budgets, lower student demand for training, duplication of programs among state institutions, and the cost of replacement and additional faculty to meet accreditation standards that did not exist when these programs were started. Nevertheless, we consider the outlook for academic positions to be favorable. Indeed, it appears that many training programs are having difficulty filling available faculty positions and perhaps a decreasing proportion of new doctorates are interested in such positions. Relatedly, we do not foresee a time when school districts will be willing or able to employ large numbers of doctoral-level school psychologists at appropriate salaries.

Training programs are encouraged to recruit more students in order to offset the supply-demand gap and avoid its potentially negative influences on the profession (Fagan, 1988b). Of course, we are not advocating a lowering of standards for admission or retention within programs. To offset the gap, universities will have to stretch existing resources and tight budgets, or provide additional resources such as faculty, student financial aid, and equipment. Related supply and demand issues include the need for minority recruitment possibly declining program enrollments, increasing female student representation, and continuing problems in rural service delivery. Opportunities in nontraditional settings and independent practice are discussed in *School Psychology Review* (Vol. 17, No. 3, 1988) and in D'Amato and Dean (1989).

Will the Service Ratio Improve?

The remarkable improvement of the service ratio of school psychologists to school-aged children in the past 30 years will not be matched in the next 20 years. Now hovering around 1:2,000 (improved from approximately 1:5,000 in 1970), ratio improvement could be hampered by increasing school enrollments, stability or possibly even decreases in training program enrollment, and expanded service settings available to graduates. The nationwide ratio will probably not improve beyond 1:1,500. Of course, many settings will have much better ratios and we expect the range of ratios to be reduced, such that few settings will exceed 1:4,000. As more school psychologists seek non-school and private practice employment, we may need to reconsider traditional calculation methods of the service ratio to include school and non-school practitioners, and perhaps all school-aged children in the community.

What Will Be the Most Common Services Provided?
Has Anything Really Changed?

School psychology has gradually evolved from very narrow testing roles and functions to much broader conceptualizations of assessment. Target behaviors have shifted from precisely measured reaction times and physical attributes to less precise but more instructionally related attributes of children and the learning environment, especially ability and school achievement. As a result, the instrumentation has changed from laboratory equipment to test kits for almost every conceivable psychoeducational ability and skill. Over the past decades, as regulations for special education became more widespread, the use of tests and thus examiners were also increasingly accepted. The shift in assessment technology to the testing of various traits influenced the special education eligibility paradigm of normative deviance (i.e., judging exceptionalities by comparisons to group averages on specific traits, behaviors, skills). A paradigm of nationally normative deviance for special education eligibility was widely established by 1930 and is still present. The tools of testing have improved as a result of greater attention to standardization, reliability, validity, and cultural sensitivity.

Could we have a future paradigm shift where eligibility is individually driven and where eligibility and placement are done irrespective of national norms? Perhaps, but it would not be a technological change; rather it would be an ideological change; the technology already exists. However, the notion that millions of parents and teachers, in 15,000 districts and more than 80,000 buildings are going to abandon normative assessment seems remote to us. We also doubt that test developers and corporations are going to abandon their normative pursuits quickly and easily. Further, how will special services for children be controlled and *funded* without normative criteria for eligibility that sets limits on behaviors and/or traits? There has not been, nor will there be, enough money in education to allow for a system where a child can be declared eligible for special services (involving state and federal funds) based only on the judgment of the local team members in the absence of normative data. Such might be an ideal situation, but we are heading into a future where tight educational funding and related accountability will continue to resist special education expansion. Further, to suggest that parents and educators in the future will not be interested in national normative comparisons is shortsighted. In fact, American education may be moving dangerously in the direction of increased normative assessment as it tries to cope with public criticism. We believe that a national curriculum with national standards based on nationally normed tests would lead to more children falling through the cracks in the inevitable difficulties of matching state and national curricular expectations to the instruction of all children.

Although school psychologists remain primarily in the assessment role, they are more aware of the role's limitations, employ instruments that are more technologically adequate and culturally sensitive, and have outcome data on traditional school psychology functions. We have also gone from a medical model of assessment focused heavily on what is wrong with the child, to concepts of ecological, family, and systems assessment. Thus to the question, *Has anything really changed?* the answer is "yes" and "no." Even though the practice of school psychology has consistencies across the twentieth century, several things have changed and the circumstances within which the field exists have changed as well. While we still observe the dominance of the assessment role, that role is much better understood, and has broadened to a variety of assessment models, settings, problems, and clients. A recent comparison study by Reschly (1998) found that while roles had shifted negligibly over the past decade, some shifts in assessment functions were observed. Interestingly, he found that nontraditional assessment functions appeared to consume as much practitioner time as traditional functions.

In Chapter 1, we took the position that the assessment role applies to almost all aspects of school psychology practice. We believe that school psychologists, regardless of practice settings, will continue to be identified with, and respected for, their expertise in assessment. Despite continued use of normative testing, a broadened and more sophisticated intervention-oriented assessment role is expected to continue emerging (Reschly, 1988). The future practitioner must continue to strive for assessment practices that lead to effective interventions in remediation, consultation, therapy, systems changes, and so forth. This need for an assessment-intervention link requires an ongoing examination of our approaches to assessment. The newer forms of assessment, shifting emphases from trait to state, from internal to observable behaviors, and from nationally normative to locally compared progress warrant serious consideration. We see future school psychologists providing measurable assessment-based interventions, with instructional as well as mental health utility.

Beware of Bandwagons

School psychologists should avoid being drawn into trendy practices and bandwagons that result in a frequently changing menu of service functions. We have seen trendy practices come and go in education and school psychology: the initial teaching alphabet (ITA), perceptual-motor and neurological interventions (e.g., Frostig, Doman-Delacato), or modality assessment and intervention (e.g., the ITPA). No doubt we are always in the midst of some bandwagon. We must also be wary of political bandwagons ushered in by well-intended but fleeting political movements. For example, aligning school psychology with the school reform bandwagon of America 2000 may have enhanced our visibility, but the National Educational Goals of America 2000 were more politically correct than attainable (Sullivan, 1999). Political movements quickly become old news when political forces change. We must concern ourselves with where school psychology will be when political movements change. Several experts have come forward in defense of our public system of education after a decade or more of political pressure for widespread reform (Bracey, 1991; Hodgkinson, 1991; Sandia Study Helps Focus Educational Improvement Agenda, 1992). Aligning school psychology's future with that of education may help to place the "school" in school psychology, but it risks diminishing our identity with psychology. America 2000 had only vague goals related to children with disabilities, and the importance of mental health services. School psychology should align itself with trends or movements that are clearly in the interests of children as well as consistent with the tenets and ethics of the profession itself. Working with others to ban corporal punishment is a positive example. In the assessment arena, we have yet to heed Trachtman's advice to avoid bandwagons, to understand the person as well as the interaction, and to appreciate the complementary nature of various assessment techniques (see Trachtman, 1981, pp. 149-150). Lambert (1981; 1998) offers additional insights about our tendency to be drawn toward bandwagons and to accept others' criticisms of school psychology practice and offers advice based on her career.

In the career of the practicing school psychologist, trends will come and go; wheels will be invented and reinvented. We have observed the special education labels change from disabled, to handicapped, and back to disabled. We can discern the lineage of minimal brain dysfunction, to hyperactivity, and attention deficit hyperactivity disorder. There is also lineage between Watsonian behaviorism and Skinnerian theory, Ellis' rational-emotive therapy and cognitive behavior modification, and from mainstreaming to the regular education initiative and inclusion. The recent "outcome-based education" seems to be a new form of individually guided education or mastery learning. Diagnostic teaching is trace-able to Witmer's use of the term in the early 1900s. The major tests of intelligence and achievement also have discernible historical lineage. In the past decade we have seen the resurgence of criterion-referenced assessment in apparently improved forms under the names "portfolio assessment," "authentic assessment," and "curriculum-based assessment." These buzz words may be little more than new expressions of the buzz word "accountability." The recent advocacy by NASP and other professional groups of intervention-linked assessment holds promise not because it is something new, but because the intervention role of the school psychologist is given priority. We are cautiously optimistic about the staying power of the newer assessment approaches, and hope that research will provide a means of judging their utility for the practice of school psychology. Undergirding this debate are some basic differences of opinion regarding the merits of traditional assessment with its process, trait, and aptitude orientations, and nontraditional assessment with its behavioral, situational and contextual, and outcome orientations. These differences have existed in the assessment literature for decades and are not likely to be resolved in the foreseeable future. We believe both orientations have contributions to make to practice and are complementary in nature.

Mental Health Orientation

We also foresee school psychologists increasing their mental health-related services. The schools have historically underserved the so-called emotionally disturbed (and socio-emotional or behavior disordered) children, but national-level studies have drawn greater attention to this category and have recommended the improvement of services to such children (Dwyer, 1991; National Center for Education in Maternal and Child Health, 1988). Movement significantly in the direction of mental health prevention and intervention will require specialized training as well as a shift in perception among school authorities toward viewing the school setting as an appropriate arena for promoting mental health. If widely accepted, schools could be conceptualized as centers for academic and personal-social learning. It is unlikely that most school psychologists could effectively manage both areas (academics and mental health) without considerable additional training and experience. More likely is the differential staffing of school psychologists by training, specializations, and interest and possibly a greater infusion of counseling and clinical psychologists, along with social workers and school counselors, into the mental health service area of education. Such practices have been promoted under the topics of school-linked and school-based comprehensive clinic models (Pfeiffer & Reddy, 1998; Tyson, 1999; Vance & Pumariega, 1999).

Be Cautious With Change

Can school psychologists survive the future operating within a traditional refer-test-report model? Certainly some can in settings where the controlling variables for role and function continue to expect or accept such narrow practice. However, we believe that school psychologists will need assessment that is linked to behavioral changes and instruction. Even though the dominant role of the school psychologist has been assessment, we have indicated that the role has broadened and will continue to do so. Most change will be in the direction of interventions and consultation (see e.g., *School Psychology Quarterly*, Vol. 13, No. 2, 1998; *School Psychology Review*, Vol. 26, No. 3, 1997). These roles are readily compatible with traditional roles, have long traditions in many places, are practiced to some extent by almost all school psychologists, and can be expanded within regular education or special education, whether or not the latter is categorical or non-categorical, segregated, or inclusive. Further, the technology of the newer methods (e.g., CBA) is familiar to many school psychologists and since it is not difficult to learn, it may open doors further for consultation with teachers and support personnel who would be engaged in implementation. The intervention-linked assessment approaches also fit well with the pre-referral assessment aspects of traditional service delivery.

However, as Gredler (1992) cautions, we cannot change to nontraditional roles and functions without addressing the need for traditional forms of assessment. Our history has been very closely related to that of special education. If school psychology practice moved in directions incongruent with educators' perceptions of school children's needs, the relationship could quickly dissolve.

When we are no longer perceived as useful to solving problems in ways which have outcomes for the schooling of children, we will cease to exist. Changes in the regulation of special education could also have implications for the continuation of this relationship. If the eligibility paradigm shifted to something that no longer required traditional assessment or any psychological services, many school psychology positions would be lost. We predict the persistence of the traditional roles (despite ongoing internal protest), because employers continue to perceive as important our roles as sorters and repairers even if they dislike some of the functions we perform or being required to have us perform them. There are job security risks in giving educators the impression that we no longer want to do the things we have done, and which they have asked us to do for more than a half-century. There are job security risks in encouraging the state and federal government no longer to conceptualize as important what we have historically done. Brandt (1992) describes some of the risks involved to children and psychologist employment opportunities that might occur as a result of abandoning assessment responsibilities. Of course, some would contend that there are risks in maintaining the status quo. We agree, but believe a more patient, calculated, and documented approach to change is warranted.

Association Development

The future direction of organizational expansion is uncertain. APA experienced enormous expansion through its divisional structure before the founding of the American Psychological Society (APS) and the American Association of Applied and Preventive Psychology (AAAPP). Many other psychology groups were also founded, including NASP. The continued expansion of associations representing specialized orientations and practices continues to fragment the field of psychology. Whether this leads to a reorganization of the psychology solar system or the establishment of new solar systems remains to be seen. Despite the presence of the AAAPP, the future of school psychology rests largely with Division 16 (APA) and NASP, and both seem to have secure futures (Fagan, 1993). As long as school psychologists retain an identity with psychology, Division 16 is safe in the arena of psychology. Even a merger of APA with APS and/or AAAPP would preserve that identity in some form. For its part, NASP's security is tied primarily to the continued employment of school psychologists in the public schools, and we see no reason to believe the schools will choose not to employ school psychologists. Thus NASP will continue to serve as school psychologists' most visible organizational representative. A merger of NASP and Division 16 (APA) is considered possible but remote. At the international level, the International School Psychology Association is without peer and should experience continued growth and importance in the future.

With every state having a state association for school psychologists, separate from the state psychological association in most instances, state school psychology associations' futures are as secure as that of school psychology in general. These separate state associations are not likely to merge into the state psychological associations. For the foreseeable future the major issues for state associations are their capacity to attract dedicated professionals into leadership roles, and to manage and represent the expanding training and practice of school psychology effectively. These concerns hold for the national associations as well. National and state association leadership will increasingly be female, and we discern a shift toward stronger practitioner (as opposed to trainer) representation in the highest offices. The growth of female representation in the field is now observed in leadership at all levels and in publications (Skinner, Robinson, Brown, & Cates, 1999). Female representation in the elected officerships of NASP and Division 16 have continued to be strong. Minority representation in leadership will likely not increase unless a means can be found for increasing minority recruitment and representation in the field generally. The NASP presidency of Deborah Crockett (1997-1998) marked the first time that an African-American held a national school psychology association presidency.

PRESCRIPTIONS FOR CHANGE

Many times in books such as this, glimpses of the future are provided without a concomitant list of suggestions to help readers arrive at the future relatively unscathed. While we do not claim to have all or even most of the answers, our experience has suggested that certain steps may facilitate school psychology's successful journey into the future.

Unifying Theoretical Orientation

We have had various unifying themes suggested over the past 30 years: Gray's (1963b) data-oriented problem solver; Reger's (1965) educational programmer; White's (1968-1969) psychology of schooling; Bardon's (1983) applied educational psychology; Elliott and Witt's (1986a) reciprocal determinism; and finally developmental, family and social systems approaches (e.g., Medway & Cafferty, 1992; Plas, 1986; Woody, LaVoie & Epps, 1992). All are useful viewpoints for some, but not necessarily for all, school psychologists. We are of the opinion that school psychology has achieved the major symbols of professionalization and does not need a unifying theory of practice to establish its professional identity further.

In response to the quest for a unifying theory of school psychology, we ask, *Why?* What is the unifying theory of counseling psychology, or clinical psychology? Few seem concerned that other specialties lack a unifying theory of practice, and we should not be overly concerned about this for school psychology. Is not school psychology rapidly becoming as diverse in settings, practices, and theoretical orientations as other specialties? Is there to be no place in school psychology for various theoretical viewpoints and orientations (e.g., behavioral, psychodynamic, developmental, psychoneurological, family systems, or organizational development)? We hope there will be room for considerable diversity. This is not to say that we advocate theoretical chaos or a laissez faire future. Rather we believe the strongest future for school psychology is one allowing for several types of school psychologists unified around a very broad theme which uses contributions of psychological science to education. This theme can embrace traditional and nontraditional assessment, consultation, counseling and psychotherapy, remedial interventions, curriculum development and evaluation, family system, school system, and community educational issues. Our unity should be provided by the focus on psychological applications to education, and not be limited to particular theoretical orientations, or the omission of certain roles and functions. There is room in our future for school psychologists of many orientations, traditional and nontraditional.

Dichotomies and Polarizations

Such an expansive future, in the context of our more restricted past, will intensify certain areas of conflict. We discern several dichotomies which could divide and polarize members of the profession: doctoral versus non-doctoral training and credentialing, the regular education initiative and inclusion versus more traditional special education, the school psychologist as consultant versus traditional service provider, professionals aligned with education versus those aligned with psychology, those aligned with academic learning versus those aligned with mental health, or school-based employees versus non-school-based employees. The reader can probably think of others. A challenge to future leadership is the task of effectively representing the increasing diversity of the field. Some splintering of the field into special interest groups of school psychologists is inevitable, and NASP's structure of interest groups is an effective management approach. If we fail to represent effectively the inevitable diversity, special interest groups may gravitate toward associations outside of NASP and Division 16. The first group to defect could be the school psychologists in the non-school sector, especially those in private practice.

Ideology-Reality Gaps

Every profession experiences tension between its ideologies and its realities. School psychology has training, credentialing, and practice standards from both APA and NASP which represent the current ideologies of the field; but it is widely recognized (more so in some locales than others) that our ideologies are ahead of the realities of training, credentialing, and practice. Many training programs are not in line with accreditation standards. Many states are out of line with credentialing standards. The practice ideologies saturating our literature are not widely observed. Our standards are ideologies or models to which we should aspire. They do not necessarily represent the norm of existing practices. An example of this is the NASP service ratio recommendation of 1:1,000 in the presence of NASP survey data indicating that the typical ratio is about 1:2,000.

It is important to have ideologies as guides to the future. However, when the ideology starts to be portrayed as the present reality, or what the present must soon become, we risk alienating practitioners and trainers for whom the ideology may currently be neither acceptable nor possible. For example, advocates of curriculum-based assessment have a very important message to deliver about the linkage of assessment to intervention. The message however, is couched in discussions that suggest normative-referenced assessment is obsolete (which it is not), that most school psychologists are heavily into the new approach (which they are not), and that those who are not into it, or about to get into it, are part of the problem in school psychology's future (which they are not). The message does not convey effectively the complementary nature of normative and criterion-referenced assessment, and the different purposes of each approach. While we concur with the importance of direct assessment that leads to intervention, we believe that the proponents are too zealously selling their ideology. The system of American education, or for that matter society in general, will not quickly abandon the notion of nationally normative deviancy as the basis for categorical eligibility; whether it be for mental retardation, learning disability, or behavioral disorder. We believe this "down with traditional practice" bandwagon represents an example of an ideology going too far astray of reality. Unless better advocated in the context of reality, it will suffer the fate that behavior analysis in education suffered in the 1970s (Baer & Bushell, 1981). Let it be clear, we are not advocating the status quo. The newer forms of assessment follow an important paradigm and have demonstrated their effectiveness (Ranes, 1992; Rosenfield & Kuralt, 1990; Shapiro, 1989; Shinn, 1989; Shinn, Nolet, & Knutson, 1990; see also special issues of *School Psychology Review*, Vol.15, No. 3, 1986, and Vol. 18, No. 3, 1989). Rather we are advocating that effective long-term change is more likely to occur when blended into the training and practice realities of the present. The ideology-reality gap represents a special case of the dichotomy-polarization problem. As such, too large a gap runs the same risk of splintering the field as the dichotomous tensions.

Professional Burnout

We must address and come to terms with the issue of professional burnout. Often it seems that the best, brightest, and most caring members of the profession are the most likely to become frustrated during their first few years on the job. Through local, state, regional, and national professional contacts, we need to form networks of school psychologists to provide collegial support and understanding. Many school psychologists, particularly those in rural areas, have few if any regular contacts with other school psychologists. Our organizations, publications, and telecommunications technology provide the vehicles for creating these networks.

Serving the Entire School Population

We should emphasize the broader use of our skills in serving the entire school population, not limiting our services to those who might qualify for special education vis-à-vis the categorical schemes of IDEA and its amendments. Children who are gifted and talented, children who are experiencing temporary difficulties because of stresses at home or at school, children who fall in the "low average range" on a variety of assessment instruments, all of these children should be regarded as being within the appropriate domain of the school psychologist. In the recent past, there has been renewed interest in the drawing together of regular and special education. A resurgence of remedial services, positioned between regular and special education, could provide the link for this relationship. Renewed interest in academic remedial services available to children in need in every elementary school building, or on an itinerant basis, could draw together the different ideologies about the delivery of special education and school psychological services.

Serving a Broader Age Range

We must also expand the age range of the clients we serve. In the past decade, interest has been growing in the "birth to kindergarten years" of children's lives and in the years 18–21. For the younger age range, our goals should include serving the needs of children already experiencing difficulties while preventing difficulties for children who are at risk because of congenital problems, family background, or socio-economic status. For the older age range, we must address the issues related to why students drop out of school. Perhaps an increased focus on vocational training including work-study programs is needed for many or even all students. This would of course include transition programs from school to community settings. Beyond secondary school, the notion of school psychologists working in junior colleges and in four-year institutions is a logical expansion of our services as well.

Concern for the General Welfare of Society

We must encourage our profession to continue its record of caring about social problems which bear directly upon the clients we serve. School psychologists should not limit their concern for children to the hours that children spend in school. The clientele of the future will not be limited to the 10% or so of the school population deemed in the past to be "exceptional" for purposes of schooling. The problems of homelessness, of abuse and neglect, of unemployment, of separation and divorce, of drug addiction, all of these problems are part of the reality for the children with whom we work. School psychologists will also be employed in settings with an increasingly multicultural population. The multicultural diversity of the schools will be most pronounced in urban settings. We must be concerned for both the academic progress of children and ensuring that their basic physical and psychological needs are met. We must work closely with other professionals and agencies to take an increasingly holistic approach in our work with children. This also means extending our activities into voluntary work beyond the time we spend in school. Increased social activism and especially involvment in governmental and professional relations on behalf of our state and national organizations are important.

Using Our Resources and Continuing Professional Development

To accomplish our goals, school psychologists need to use all available resources in creative ways. We may need to find ways to reduce or simplify paper work or to cut back on other time-consuming activities in order to find time to address more important concerns. We may need to employ an increasingly preventive approach in an attempt to deal with small problems before they escalate into major crises. We may need to look around us to see who we can enlist to help us in our efforts to help children. Retired persons, unemployed persons, college students, and even other students in our schools may need to be recruited to help prevent problems or to intervene in existing situations.

If we are to address these concerns, we must continue to emphasize the need for continued professional development for all school psychologists. Continuing education is important as a means of keeping up with new developments, improving our existing skills, acquiring new skills, and providing an opportunity to reflect on our own professional development and to increase awareness of what others are doing.

The international school psychology community is an increasingly visible resource. Advanced communication technologies and professional travel have made the worldwide practice of psychology far more accessible than in the past. Represented by the International School Psychology Association, the practices of other countries offer additional perspectives on many aspects of training and practice. Literature about school psychology in other countries dates at least to the 1940s (see Fagan et al., 1985). Discussions of Canadian and international school psychology appear in Chapters 9 and 10, respectively. The journal, *School Psychology International*, is an excellent source of current international information.

A Patient Approach to Change

U.S. education has adhered to a structure of schooling recognizable in the early twentieth century, and school psychology has served education within that structure, and also within a practice ideology assigned to it mainly by school administrators. For most of the twentieth century, school psychology grappled with concerns about restricted roles and functions with the ideal of nontraditional service provision only occasionally realized. Even contemporary school psychologists encounter resistance to service delivery alternatives. Although many are critical of our system of education, we must be mindful that the structure of contemporary U.S. education is but a century old, a long time for some practices but not so long for others. We believe that the delivery systems for education and school psychology may both be wearing thin and ready for change. However, because we see change emerging in the context of a century of compulsory schooling and psychological services, we believe that any change will have to occur in a gradual, planned, and contextual manner: an evolutionary process.

Although U.S. education may change, even dramatically so, in the next 20 years, it will do so in the context of continued state-level responsibility and regulation, the lobbying power of more than 2 million teachers, the physical facilities of more than 80,000 school buildings, and funding mechanisms which continue to be strained. The established educational system is not about to discharge its teachers and abandon its school buildings under the guise of school reform. We need to be patient with our future and recognize that maintaining the positive aspects of our progress is as important as changing other aspects.

Whatever future lies ahead, it will not come forth uniformly across the country. Like present conditions, the future will be characterized by uneven quantitative and qualitative development. This is related to the fact that the professional system of regulation (recall Figure 7.1) has no overarching authoritative agency which can effect uniform change throughout the system. Another factor is that all the regulatory agencies and influences are managed by people of varying competencies, who come and go. The quality of services statewide or district-wide can be seriously affected by individuals in key positions. Having high-quality services in the present does not guarantee that future services will be of such quality. Having accomplished certain goals in the present does not preclude their importance in the future. Professional issues and problems are not permanently solved. Because our work is people intensive we cannot solve a problem and move on to something else, ignoring the past. We are continuously forced to educate and reeducate key individuals about the services of school psychologists. This is especially so in an era of high turnover of educational administrators, organizational leadership, and societal change.

Accountability

An increase in our professional visibility may be predicated upon an increase in our professional accountability. Increased enumerative accountability allows us to provide an accurate picture of how we spend our time to those considering the profession. Increased process and outcome accountability efforts can bring about positive changes within the profession, thus enhancing our image in the eyes of the public. With an increase in our professional accountability, we can continue to document our value in all of our roles and functions. The school psychologist of the future must be concerned with accountability data not only to protect necessary services, but to demonstrate how some services are more necessary than others. Methods of accountability were discussed in Chapter 5 and also appear in Fairchild and Zins (1992). These efforts enhance the value of existing practitioners and the field itself to prospective students.

Roles Clarification

A clarification of the whole spectrum of our roles and functions is needed so that consumers (e.g., parents, teachers, students) will have a better understanding of what school psychologists can do. Although efforts at public relations by national and state organizations have increased greatly, we still need greater visibility. As trainers we frequently have prospective students ask, *What exactly does a school psychologist do?* If we hope to increase the number of students, especially minority students, we must promote the field of school psychology actively. We need a realistic and attractive description of the field, as well as adequate pay, benefits, and opportunities for advancement, which will attract top notch undergraduate students as well as high quality non-traditional students into our graduate training programs.

Another need in role clarification is to distinguish between the terms "role" and "function." We should refrain from interchanging these terms and consider more closely what are the roles of the school psychologist and their attendant functions. Roles are not the things we do but rather the service conceptualizations within which we perform our functions. The distinction helps us to understand that the traditional role of the school psychologist is often victimized by concerns that are really directed at its functions. For example, critics contend that we must abandon the traditional assessment role of intelligence testing, but intelligence testing is simply one function within a broader assessment role. What the critics actually mean, and we agree, is that school psychologists need to adjust the functions of the assessment role to include more instructionally relevant forms of testing or appraisal. Thus, critics sometimes victimize roles when they mean to victimize functions. We view the assessment role as central to most of the school psychologist's practice in traditional and nontraditional areas. Specializations such as neuropsychology, preschool, or vocational school psychology offer more modern functions to the traditional roles.

Historically two major roles have existed. Beyond the role of "child sorter" has been the role of "child repair person," providing direct and indirect interventions via functions such as remedial teaching, behavior modification, counseling and psychotherapy, and consultation, with individual children or in groups. Repairs included the home as well as the learning environment. In more recent decades, we have seen increasing numbers of school psychologists expand their role to the study of systemic problems; perhaps we could consider this an "engineering" role related to design, appraisal, consultation, advocacy, and systems change.

All roles of the school psychologist have engaged them in areas of schooling where problems were perceived to exist, and their alleviation was expected to have positive instructional and mental health outcomes for children. These are central aspects of the education industry to which school psychologists are attached.

The Importance of Technology

All roles and their attendant functions will be influenced by technological advancements, especially in communications, assessment instrumentation, and interventions that rely on increasing medical and pharmaceutical discoveries. Though far from accomplishment now, in the coming decade all practitioners will have personal computer applications or access thereto which will assist in their daily functions. While many of these advancements will not produce major changes in the school psychologist's roles and functions, they will facilitate their implementation and could free up time for expanded practices. The communications revolution of the late twentieth century has taken us from a highly regulated period of traditional devices such as telephones, television, and radios to an almost unmanageable means of communicating by the Internet, FAX, and cellular equipment. The changes will be fraught with many problems including maintaining confidentiality and scrutinizing innumerable sources on the internet for validity. The future will definitely be a buyer and user beware period.

Forthcoming breakthroughs in medical technology and research will necessitate close relationships between school psychologists and the medical community. The advancements in these areas may move us from a century where advancements mainly provided alleviation of conditions to a century where prevention and cure could prevail.

Tolerance for Diversity

As psychology itself has matured through centrifugal diversity, so too will school psychology. The field is expanding outward from center, away from its past of traditional roles, functions, and settings. Almost every conceivable type of school psychologist will exist in the coming decades. Roles and functions may be defined more by setting than in the past. The model of school psychologists working only in school settings has already changed. We have expanded from a small group of clinic-based psychologists to a diverse field of practitioners in every school district nationwide, and in other settings as well. In our conceptualization, school psychology's future would be adversely restricted by selecting a minimum number of ideologies or models for the future and alienating the growth of others.

School psychologists must also achieve a better grasp of their place in the employment context. School psychologists are associated with the education industry, among the largest industries in the nation. Most school psychologists have highly specific roles in the education industry despite the fact that some have other, perhaps even more preferred, roles. Critical appraisals of school psychologists as technicians versus professionals (e.g., Ysseldyke, 1986) imply that they should deny their traditional roles and functions in the system, and assume similar roles (e.g., as professionals instead of as technicians). The technician-professional comparison is similar to Phillips (1990b) discussion of employing mechanistic and probabilistic paradigms in practice. Although we agree that many of the problems addressed by school psychologists do not lend themselves to simple technical solutions, some do, and the needs may change over time. Phillips (1990b) stated, "School psychologists apply their knowledge and skills in different ways, in different settings, and at different times, in accordance with current ideas within school psychology in particular and psychology in general, and within the public schools in particular and education in general" (p. 22). Bardon and Bennett (1974) viewed school psychology in three stages, with the Stage III practitioner of the present having emerged from earlier times when Stages I (tester) and II (clinician making diagnoses and recommendations) were more necessary, desirable, or convenient. Ysseldyke's and Phillips' conceptualization of the school psychologist as a professional is akin to Bardon and Bennett's Stage III "psychologist with a variety of skills and knowledge who applies his knowledge broadly and in diverse ways to a specific setting—the school" (p. 20). The same conceptualization permeates the school psychology *Blueprint For Training And Practice* and its 1997 revision, which appear to be premised on the conceptualizations of Bardon, Ysseldyke and others (National School Psychology Inservice Training Network, 1984; Ysseldyke et al., 1997). We believe that for the foreseeable future there will continue to be school psychologists at various levels of role and function development. Such diversity has been typical of school psychology practice, and may form the basis for two or more levels of training, credentialing, and practice in the future.

Considering the magnitude of the education industry in which school psychologists are employed, some comparisons to positions in other service industries may be instructive. If school psychologists were in the law enforcement system, would they be police officers, supervisors, or chiefs of police? In the postal system, would they be letter carriers, inspectors, or postmasters? Would they be flight attendants, pilots, or air traffic controllers? School psychologists should understand their roles in the educational system and perform them well while working to improve the opportunities for some school psychologists to perform other roles in the system. We need recognition of this diversity instead of the constant clamor that we should *all* be doing something more glamorous. Surely, school psychologists in Illinois or Wisconsin did not lobby for the right to administrative certification so that *all school psychologists would* become administrators! They did so in order that *some school psychologists could* become administrators (and if they wanted to, they could count their school psychology experience toward the attainment of that certificate).

We also wish to raise the question, *What's wrong with the sorter and repairer roles of the school psychologist?* We are not necessarily sanctioning the traditional functions here, but rather the roles. Are there not thousands of school psychologists satisfied with these roles? If you review the role and function studies of the past 30 years, when asked what they would *ideally* have as their roles, school psychologists persistently indicate one-third or more of their time in traditional assessment, a higher proportion of time if you include preferences for traditional intervention roles. These surveys also reveal fairly high degrees of job satisfaction. If we abandoned traditional roles would we be serving the best interests of children or the education industry? The role and function critics refuse to recognize that every school psychologist cannot have a position analogous to a police chief, a postmaster, or an air traffic controller.

Several times each year our literature reports another study advocating the need for practitioners to provide particular services. If a list were prepared of the articles about the importance of certain roles and functions of the school psychologist, it would make even the most competent practitioner feel deficient. The fact is, practitioners cannot be all things to all people. We cannot all be experts in everything. In the future, most school psychologists will continue in the sorting and repairing roles but with new functions; many will also serve consultation roles, and some will serve research and evaluation or administrative roles. Is there not a need for various roles, and is there not room in the system for them all? If there is not, then the future of school psychology will be plagued with dissension and segmentation.

Roland Kaser (1993), a Swiss school psychologist, reviewed the worldwide complaint by school psychologists to be something different than what they have been. Kaser raises an ethical issue stating, "Psychologists commit themselves, according to the ethical code of their profession, to make all efforts to protect the emotional and physical well-being of the individual. Renunciation of problem-oriented, individual case work in favor of preventive work exclusively at the level of the school would be in violation of the basic ethical principles of the profession" (pp. 12-13). He raises several important issues including the absence of traditional services in the non-school sector to which schools might turn for help, the illusion that individual problems of children can be avoided through even the best preventive services, and that role development needs to be conceptualized in a career context where experience and continuing education facilitate the expansion of roles and functions. In his developmental model, four foci of activity (diagnosis, counseling and consultation, supervision, and directing teaching or research) emerge over time in one's career as a function of additional training and experience. Thus practitioner careers move in the direction from diagnostic child study activities to broader activities such as consultation and supervision. Kaser's analysis is a stark contrast to conceptualizations of role change which imply that we should drop what we are now doing, and that even entry-level practitioners should pursue consultant, supervisor, and administrator roles in the absence of traditional experience.

CLOSING THOUGHTS

The future of school psychology appears to be very favorable. School psychology, positioned between psychology and education, has survived a century of change and growth, and will continue to do so. Despite criticisms, there is no reason to sound the alarm. Instead, we suggest that we sound the alarm for reason! School psychology is an important but small ship on the sea of education. We comprise about one-half of 1% of public school employees. We are hardly the center of the education universe. To school administrators, our role and function problems must appear relatively minor on a Monday morning when the buses are not running on time, the air conditioning is out at some buildings, and the teachers are threatening to go on strike. As a source of professional influence, school psychologists can only hope to achieve a position where they can provide sage counsel to the forces which make the waves on the sea. Beyond such counsel, school psychologists must be prepared to sail their ship on the calmest or the stormiest of seas, and to continue service provision in many modes as advocates for children and for psychological applications to education. Perhaps the same could be said for our relative status within psychology. However, we perceive school psychology to have a stronger presence and status in psychology than in education.

We have looked at the future along several of the dimensions on which we have described our past and our present. School psychology has a rich past, an unprecedented present, and a very promising future under almost any scenario drawn for psychology and education. The United States is increasing in its diversity in many ways. We are more culturally diverse. We have increasing diversity in products and services. Our telecommunications are also more diverse; phones are used for traditional one-to-one communication as well as conferences, data transmission, and even entertainment; and television seems to have a channel for every conceivable constituency. School psychology must find the means to manage its own inevitable diversity. There must be room for those whose jobs depend on traditional assessment functions; those who consult; those who do curriculum-based assessment, therapy, in-service education, or junior college work; those who work in rural or urban areas, in schools, agencies or independent practice; and those who work with all ages of people engaged in schooling.

James Gibson, an experimental psychologist, once noted that the world, when viewed from the caboose of a forward moving train, seems to flow inward while from the locomotive the world seems to flow outward (Neisser, 1981).

Where we are positioned gives the impression of convergence or expansion even though looking at the same terrain. School psychology has always had to ride two trains at the same time: the train of psychology and that of education. Only recently has school psychology had a train of its own. At least on our own train, we need to view the future from the front. If there is no room for viewing the future as expanding, we will have a future that is little more than our past. If the field is fractionated in the next 20 years, it will be the result of trying to manage its future by ignoring its past.

> I do not know all the duties that the future will hold for the school psychologist but I will agree that it is a challenging array, never the same, with constantly new avenues of research opening up. There are large rewards in friendships and social contacts. The school psychologist is on the line of skirmish. There may be a lot of dust and noise, humor and pathos, but I guarantee it will never be a quiet or dull life (Luckey, 1951, p. 10).

School Psychology Data Sheet

ighNATIONAL LEVEL

National Association of School Psychologists (NASP)
    4340 East West Highway., Suite 402
    Bethesda, MD 20814-9457
    Phone: (301) 657-0270; FAX (301) 657-0275;
    Website: *www.nasponline.org*
Executive Director: _____
President: _____
Dates and Location of Next Convention: _____

Current Membership Total: _____
Annual Dues: Member: _____, Student: _____
Journal: *School Psychology Review*
Newsletter: *Communiqué*
NASP region in which your state is located? _____
Name of Your Regional Delegate Representative: _____
Name of your NASP State Delegate: _____
Current Number of NASP Members in your State: _____

American Psychological Association (APA)
    750 First St., NE
    Washington, DC 20002-4242
    (202) 336-5500
    Website: *www.apa.org*
Executive Director: _____
President: _____
Division 16 President: _____

Dates and Location of Next Convention: _____

_____

Current Membership Total: _____ (APA), _____ (Div. 16)

Annual Dues: Member: _____ (APA), _____ (Div. 16)

Student: _____ (APA), _____ (Div. 16)

Journals: *American Psychologist, School Psychology Quarterly*

Newsletters: *APA Monitor, The School Psychologist*

Estimated Number of School Psychologists in the U.S.: _____

Number of State Associations for School Psychologists: _____

STATE LEVEL

State School Psychology Association Data

Name: _____

Address: _____

_____

Phone: _____

Website: _____

President: _____

President-Elect: _____

Dates and Location of Next Convention: _____

_____

Name of Newsletter: _____

Number of Members: _____

Annual Dues: Member: _____ Student: _____

State Psychology Association Data

Name: _____

Address: _____

_____

Phone: _____

Website: _____

President: _____

President-Elect: _____

Dates and Location of Next Convention: _____

_____

Name of Newsletter: _____

Number of Members: _____

Annual Dues: Member: _____ Student: _____

State Department of Education

Name: _____

Address: _____

_____

Phone: _____

State Commissioner: _____

State Consultant for School Psychology: _____

State's Definition of School Psychologist: _____

_____

Other

Number of Practitioners in Your State: _____

Number of Practitioners in Your Local Community: _____

Number of Practitioners in Your Local District: _____

School Psychology Training Program Data For Your State

Names of Programs	*Available Degrees*
1. _____	_____
2. _____	_____
3. _____	_____
4. _____	_____
5. _____	_____
6. _____	_____
7. _____	_____
8. _____	_____

Credentialing Data For Your State

Name of Agency	*Credential Offered*
1. _____	_____
2. _____	_____
3. _____	_____

Primary Journals and Books on School Psychology

JOURNALS ON SCHOOL PSYCHOLOGY

Canadian Journal of School Psychology, McGill University, 3700 McTavish St., Montreal, Quebec, H3A 1Y2 Canada.

Journal of School Psychology, Pergamon Press, Inc., Elsevier Science, Inc., 655 Avenue of the Americas, New York, NY 10010.

Psychology in the Schools, John Wiley and Sons, Inc., 605 Third Ave., New York, NY 10158.

School Psychology International, Sage Publications Ltd., P.O. Box 5096, Thousand Oaks, CA 91359.

School Psychology Quarterly (formerly, *Professional School Psychology*), Guilford Press, 72 Spring St., New York, NY 10012.

School Psychology Review (formerly, *School Psychology Digest*), National Association of School Psychologists, 4340 East West Hwy., Suite 402, Bethesda, MD 20814-9457.

BOOKS ON SCHOOL PSYCHOLOGY

This list was prepared by using the following references: Fagan, Delugach, Mellon, & Schlitt (1985); Fagan, (1986b); French (1986); Whelan & Carlson (1986), and Kraus & Mclaughlin (1997).

Alpert, J. L., & Associates. (1982). *Psychological consultation in educational settings.* San Francisco: Jossey-Bass.

Attwell, A. A. (1972). *The school psychologist's handbook* (Rev. in 1976). Los Angeles: Western Psychological Services.

Bardon, J. I., & Bennett, V. C. (1974). *School psychology.* Englewood Cliffs, NJ: Prentice Hall.

Bergan, J. R. (Ed.) (1985). *School psychology in contemporary society: An introduction.* Columbus, OH: Charles E. Merrill.

Blanco, R. F., & Rosenfeld, J. G. (1978). *Case studies in clinical and school psychology.* Springfield, IL: Charles C. Thomas.

Brown, D., Pryzwansky, W. B., & Schulte, A. C. (1998). *Psychological consultation: Introduction to theory and practice.* Boston: Allyn and Bacon.

Catterall, C. D. (Ed.). (1976). *Psychology in the schools in international perspective: Vol. I.* Columbus, OH: Author (92 S. Dawson Ave., 43209).

Catterall, C. D. (Ed.). (1977). *Psychology in the schools in international perspective: Vol. II.* Columbus, OH: Author (92 S. Dawson Ave., 43209).

Catterall, C. D. (Ed.). (1979). *Psychology in the schools in international perspective: Vol. III.* Columbus, OH: Author (92 S. Dawson Ave., 43209).

Claiborn, W. L., & Cohen, R. (Eds.). (1973). *School intervention: Vol. 1* New York: Behavioral Publications. (Volume of a continuing series in community-clinical psychology.)

Cole, E., & Siegel, J. A. (Eds.). (1992). *Effective consultation in school psychology.* Toronto: Hogrefe & Huber.

Conoley, J. C., & Conoley, C. W. (1982). *School consultation: A guide to practice and training.* New York: Pergamon Press.

Conoley, J. C., & Conoley, C. W. (1992). *School consultation: Practice and training* (2nd ed.). New York: Macmillan.

Cull, J. G., & Golden, L. B. (Eds.). (1984). *Psychotherapeutic techniques in school psychology.* Springfield, IL: Charles C. Thomas.

Curtis, M. J., & Zins, J. E. (Eds.). (1981). *The theory and practice of school consultation.* Springfield, IL: Charles C. Thomas. (All but a few of the chapters are previously published articles in school psychology and related journals.)

Cutts, N. E. (Ed.). (1955). *School psychologists at mid-century.* Washington, DC: American Psychological Association.

D'Amato, R. C., & Dean, R. S. (Eds.). (1989). *The school psychologist in nontraditional settings: Integrating clients, services, and setting.* Hillsdale, NJ: Erlbaum.

Eiserer, P. E. (1963). *The school psychologist.* Washington, DC: Center for Applied Research in Education.

Elliott, S. N., & Witt. J. C. (Eds.). (1986). *The delivery of psychological services in schools: Concepts, processes, and issues.* Hillsdale, NJ: Erlbaum.

Erchul, W. P., & Martens, B. K. (1997). *School consultation: Conceptual and empirical bases of practice.* New York: Plenum.

Fagan, T. K., Delugach, F. J., Mellon, M., & Schlitt, P. (1986). *A bibliographic guide to the literature of professional school psychology 1890-1985.* Washington, DC: National Association of School Psychologists.

Fagan, T. K., & Warden. P. G. (Eds.). (1996). *Historical encyclopedia of school psychology.* Westport, CT: Greenwood.

Fagan, T. K., & Wise, P. S. (1994). *School psychology: Past, present, and future.* White Plains, NY: Longman.

Fagan, T. K., & Wise, P. S. (2000). *School psychology: Past, present, and future* (2nd ed.). Bethesda, MD: National Association of School Psychologists.

Fairchild, T. N. (Ed.). (1977). *Accountability for school psychologists: Selected readings.* Washington, DC: University Press of America. (A collection of articles published in school psychology journals and some non-published speeches, etc.)

Fein, L. G. (1974). *The changing school scene: Challenge to psychology.* New York: John Wiley.

Fine, M. J. (Ed.). (1989). *School psychology: Cutting edges in research and practice.* Washington, DC: National Education Association and the National Association of School Psychologists.

Fischer, L., & Sorenson, G. P. (1991). *School law for counselors, psychologists, and social workers.* New York: Longman.

Gelinas, P. J., & Gelinas, R. P. (1968). *A definitive study of your future in school psychology.* New York: Richards Rosen Press.

Gottsegen, M. G., & Gottsegen, G. B. (Eds.). (1960). *Professional school psychology: Vol. 1.* New York: Grune & Stratton.

Gottsegen, M. G., & Gottsegen, G. B. (Eds.). (1963). *Professional school psychology: Vol. 2.* New York: Grune & Stratton.

Gottsegen, G. B., & Gottsegen, M. G. (Eds.). (1969). *Professional school psychology: Vol. 3.* New York: Grune & Stratton.

Gray, S. W. (1963). *The psychologist in the schools.* New York: Holt-Rinehart & Winston.

Gredler, G. R. (Ed.). (1972). *Ethical and legal factors in the practice of school psychology: Proceedings of the First Annual Conference in School Psychology.* Philadelphia, PA: Temple University.

Gutkin, T. B., & Reynolds, C. R. (Eds.). (1990). *The handbook of school psychology* (2nd ed.). New York: John Wiley.

Herron, W. G., Green, M., Guild, M., Smith, A., & Kantor, R. E. (1970). *Contemporary school psychology.* Scranton, PA: Intext.

Herron, W. G., Herron, M. J., & Handron, J. (1984). *Contemporary school psychology: Handbook of practice, theory, and research.* Cranston, RI: Carroll Press.

Hildreth, G. H. (1930). *Psychological service for school problems.* Yonkers-On-Hudson, NY: World Book Co. (Perhaps the earliest book on school psychology that employs the term "school psychologist.")

Hirst, W. E. (1963). *Know your school psychologist.* New York: Grune & Stratton.

Holt, F. D., & Kicklighter, R. H. (Eds.). (1971). *Psychological services in the schools: Readings in preparation, organization and practice.* Dubuque, IA: Wm. C. Brown. (Mostly reprints from school psychology and related journals.)

Hynd, G. W. (Ed.). (1983). *The school psychologist: An introduction.* Syracuse, NY: Syracuse University Press.

International Bureau of Education. (1948). *School psychologists* (Publication No. 105). Paris: UNESCO.

Jackson, J. H., & Bernauer, M. (Eds). (1968). *The psychologist as a therapist.* Milwaukee, WI: Milwaukee Public Schools.

Jacob, S., & Hartshorne, T. (1991). *Ethics and law for school psychologists.* Brandon, VT: Clinical Psychology Publishing.

Jacob-Timm, S., & Hartshorne, T. S. (1994). *Ethics and law for school psychologists (2nd ed.)* Brandon, VT: Clinical Psychology Publishing Company

Jacob-Timm, S., & Hartshorne, T. S. (1998). *Ethics and law for school psychologists (3rd ed.)* New York: John Wiley.

Kratochwill, T. R. (Ed.). (1981). *Advances in school psychology: Vol. 1.* Hillsdale, NJ: Erlbaum.

Kratochwill, T. R. (Ed.). (1982). *Advances in school psychology: Vol. 2.* Hillsdale, NJ: Erlbaum.

Kratochwill, T.R. (Ed.). (1983). *Advances in school psychology: Vol. 3.* Hillsdale, NJ: Erlbaum.

Kratochwill, T. R. (Ed.). (1985). *Advances in school psychology: Vol. 4.* Hillsdale, NJ: Erlbaum.

Kratochwill, T. R. (Ed.). (1986). *Advances in school psychology: Vol. 5.* Hillsdale, NJ: Erlbaum.

Kratochwill, T. R. (Ed.). (1988). *Advances in school psychology: Vol. 6.* Hillsdale, NJ: Erlbaum.

Kratochwill, T. R. (Ed.). (1990). *Advances in school psychology: Vol. 7.* Hillsdale, NJ: Erlbaum.

Kratochwill, T. R., Elliott, S. N., & Gettinger, M. (Eds.). (1992). *Advances in school psychology: Vol. 8.* Hillsdale, NJ: Erlbaum.

Lawrence, M. M. (1971). *The mental health team in the schools.* New York: Behavioral Publications.

Magary, J. F. (Ed.). (1967). *School psychological services in theory and practice, a handbook.* Englewood Cliffs, NJ: Prentice Hall.

Maher, C.A., Illback, R. J., & Zins, J. E. (Eds). (1984). *Organizational psychology in the schools: A handbook for professionals.* Springfield, IL: Charles C. Thomas.

Marzolf, S. S. (1956). *Psychological diagnosis and counseling in the schools.* New York: Holt, Rinehart & Winston.

Medway, F. J., & Cafferty, T. P. (1992). *School psychology: A social psychological perspective.* Hillsdale, NJ: Erlbaum.

Meyers, J., Martin, R., & Hyman, I. (Eds.). (1977). *School consultation: Readings about preventive techniques for pupil personnel workers.* Springfield, IL: Charles C. Thomas.

Meyers, J., Parsons, R. D., & Martin, R. (1979). *Mental health consultation in the schools.* San Francisco: Jossey-Bass.

Miezitis, S., & Orme, M. (Eds.). (1977). *Innovation in school psychology.* Toronto: The Ontario Institute for Studies in Education.

Milofsky, C. (1989). *Testers and testing: The sociology of school psychology.* New Brunswick, NJ: Rutgers University Press.

Mok, P. P. (1962). *A view from within: American education at the crossroads of individualism.* New York: Carlton Press.

Nolen, P. A. (1983). *School psychologist's handbook: Writing the educational report.* Springfield, IL: Charles C. Thomas.

Phillips, B. N. (1990). *School psychology at a turning point: Ensuring a bright future for the profession.* San Francisco, CA: Jossey-Bass.

Phye, G. D., & Reschly, D. J. (Eds.). (1979). *School psychology perspectives and issues.* New York: Academic Press.

Plas, J. M. (1986). *Systems psychology in the schools.* New York, NY: Pergamon Press.

Reger, R. (1965). *School psychology.* Springfield, IL: Charles C. Thomas.

Reynolds, C. R., & Gutkin, T. B. (Eds.). (1982). *The handbook of school psychology.* New York: John Wiley.

Reynolds, C. R., & Gutkin, T. B. (Eds.). (1999). *Handbook of school psychology* (3rd ed.). New York: John Wiley.

Reynolds, C. R., Gutkin, T. B., Elliott, S. N., and Witt, J. C. (1984). *School psychology: Essentials of theory and practice.* New York: John Wiley.

Rosenbaum, D. S., & Toepfer, C. F. (1966). *Curriculum planning and school psychology: The coordinated approach.* Buffalo, NY: Hertillon Press.

Saigh, P., & Oakland, T. (Eds.). (1989). *International perspectives on psychology in the schools.* Hillsdale, NJ: Erlbaum.

Schmuck, R. A. & Miles, M. B. (Eds.). (1971). *Organization development in schools.* Palo Alto, CA: National Press Books.

Scholl, G. T. (Ed.). (1985). *The school psychologist and the exceptional child.* Reston, VA: Council For Exceptional Children.

Shapiro, E. S. (1987). *Behavioral assessment in school psychology.* Hillsdale, NJ: Erlbaum.

Spadafore, G. J. (Ed.). (1981). *School psychology: Issues and answers.* Muncie, IN: Accelerated Development, Inc. (The readings are previously published articles or presentations.)

Talley, R. C., Kubiszyn, T., Brassard, M., & Short, R. J. (Eds.). (1996). *Making psychologists in schools indispensable: Critical questions and emerging perspectives.* Washington, DC: American Psychological Association.

Thomas, A., & Grimes, J. (Eds.). (1985). *Best practices in school psychology.* Washington, DC: National Association of School Psychologists.

Thomas, A., & Grimes, J. (Eds.). (1990). *Best practices in school psychology: II.* Washington, DC: National Association of School Psychologists.

Thomas, A., & Grimes, J. (Eds.). (1995). *Best practices in school psychology: III.* Bethesda, MD: National Association of School Psychologists.

United Nations Educational, Scientific and Cultural Organisation. (1948). *School psychologists* (International Bureau of Education Publication No. 105). Geneva, Switzerland: Author.

Valett, R. E. (1963). *The practice of school psychology: Professional problems.* New York: John Wiley.

Wall, W. D. (Ed.). (1956). *Psychological services for schools.* New York: New York University Press.

Wallin, J. E. W. (1914). *The mental health of the school child (The psycho-educational clinic in relation to child welfare, Contributions to a new science of orthophrenics and orthosomatics).* New Haven: Yale University Press. (Some of the chapters were previously published but have been substantially revised.)

White, M. A., & Harris, M. W. (1961). *The school psychologist.* New York: Harper.

Woody, R. H., LaVoie, J. C., & Epps, S. (1992). *School psychology: A developmental and social systems approach.* Boston: Allyn and Bacon.

Ysseldyke, J. E. (Ed.). (1984). *School psychology: The state of the art.* Minneapolis, MN: University of Minnesota, National School Psychology Inservice Training Network.

American Psychological Association Ethical Principles of Psychologists and Code of Conduct

TABLE of CONTENTS

INTRODUCTION

PREAMBLE

GENERAL PRINCIPLES

ETHICAL STANDARDS

1. GENERAL STANDARDS

3.04 Media Presentations
3.05 Testimonials
3.06 In-Person Solicitation

4. THERAPY

4.01 Structuring the Relationship
4.02 Informed Consent to Therapy
4.03 Couple and Family Relationships
4.04 Providing Mental Health Services to Those Served by Others
4.05 Sexual Intimacies With Current Patients or Clients
4.06 Therapy With Former Sexual Partners
4.07 Sexual Intimacies With Former Therapy Patients
4.08 Interruption of Services
4.09 Terminating the Professional Relationship

5. PRIVACY AND CONFIDENTIALITY

5.01 Discussing the Limits of Confidentiality
5.02 Maintaining Confidentiality
5.03 Minimizing Intrusions on Privacy
5.04 Maintenance of Records
5.05 Disclosures
5.06 Consultations
5.07 Confidential Information in Databases
5.08 Use of Confidential Information for Didactic or Other Purposes
5.09 Preserving Records and Data
5.10 Ownership of Records and Data
5.11 Withholding Records for Nonpayment

6. TEACHING, TRAINING SUPERVISION, RESEARCH, AND PUBLISHING

6.01 Design of Education and Training Programs
6.02 Descriptions of Education and Training Programs
6.03 Accuracy and Objectivity in Teaching
6.04 Limitation on Teaching
6.05 Assessing Student and Supervisee Performance
6.06 Planning Research
6.07 Responsibility
6.08 Compliance With Law and Standards
6.09 Institutional Approval

6.10 Research Responsibilities
6.11 Informed Consent to Research
6.12 Dispensing With Informed Consent
6.13 Informed Consent in Research Filming or Recording
6.14 Offering Inducements for Research Participants
6.15 Deception in Research
6.16 Sharing and Utilizing Data
6.17 Minimizing Invasiveness
6.18 Providing Participants With Information About the Study
6.19 Honoring Commitments
6.20 Care and Use of Animals in Research
6.21 Reporting of Results
6.22 Plagiarism
6.23 Publication Credit
6.24 Duplicate Publication of Data
6.25 Sharing Data
6.26 Professional Reviewers

7. FORENSIC ACTIVITIES

7.01 Professionalism
7.02 Forensic Assessments
7.03 Clarification of Role
7.04 Truthfulness and Candor
7.05 Prior Relationships
7.06 Compliance With Law and Rules

8. RESOLVING ETHICAL ISSUES

8.01 Familiarity With Ethics Code
8.02 Confronting Ethical Issues
8.03 Conflicts Between Ethics and Organizational Demands
8.04 Informal Resolution of Ethical Violations
8.05 Reporting Ethical Violations
8.06 Cooperating With Ethics Committees
8.07 Improper Complaints

INTRODUCTION

The American Psychological Association's (APA's) Ethical Principles of Psychologists and Code of Conduct (hereinafter referred to as the Ethics Code) consists of an Introduction, a Preamble, six General Principles (A - F), and specific Ethical Standards. The Introduction discusses the intent, organization, procedural considerations, and scope of application of the Ethics Code. The Preamble and General Principles are *aspirational* goals to guide psychologists toward the highest ideals of psychology. Although the Preamble and General Principles are not themselves enforceable rules, they should be considered by psychologists in arriving at an ethical course of action and may be considered by ethics bodies in interpreting the Ethical Standards. The Ethical Standards set forth *enforceable* rules for conduct as psychologists. Most of the Ethical Standards are written broadly, in order to apply to psychologists in varied roles, although the application of an Ethical Standard may vary depending on the context. The Ethical Standards are not exhaustive. The fact that a given conduct is not specifically addressed by the Ethics Code does not mean that it is necessarily either ethical or unethical.

Membership in the APA commits members to adhere to the APA Ethics Code and to the rules and procedures used to implement it. Psychologists and students, whether or not they are APA members, should be aware that the Ethics Code may be applied to them by state psychology boards, courts, or other public bodies.

This Ethics Code applies only to psychologists' work-related activities, that is, activities that are part of the psychologists' scientific and professional functions or that are psychological in nature. It includes the clinical or counseling practice of psychology, research, teaching, supervision of trainees, development of assessment instruments, conducting assessments, educational counseling, organizational consulting, social intervention, administration, and other activities as well. These work-related activities can be distinguished from the purely private conduct of a psychologist, which ordinarily is not within the purview of the Ethics Code.

The Ethics Code is intended to provide standards of professional conduct that can be applied by the APA and by other bodies that choose to adopt them. Whether or not a psychologist has violated the Ethics Code does not by itself determine whether he or she is legally liable in a court action, whether a contract is enforceable, or whether other legal consequences occur. These results are based on legal rather than ethical rules. However, compliance with or violation of the Ethics Code may be admissible as evidence in some legal proceedings, depending on the circumstances.

In the process of making decisions regarding their professional behavior, psychologists must consider this Ethics Code, in addition to applicable laws and psychology board regulations. If the Ethics Code establishes a higher standard of conduct than is required by law, psychologists must meet the higher ethical standard. If the Ethics Code standard appears to conflict with the requirements of law, then psychologists make known their commitment to the Ethics Code and take steps to resolve the conflict in a responsible manner. If neither law nor the Ethics Code resolves an issue, psychologists should consider other professional materials (Note 1) and the dictates of their own conscience, as well as seek consultation with others within the field when this is practical.

The procedures for filing, investigating, and resolving complaints of unethical conduct are described in the current Rules and Procedures of the APA Ethics Committee. The actions that APA may take for violations of the Ethics Code include actions such as reprimand, censure, termination of APA membership, and referral of the matter to other bodies. Complainants who seek remedies such as monetary damages in alleging ethical violations by a psychologist must resort to private negotiation, administrative bodies, or the courts. Actions that violate the Ethics Code may lead to the imposition of sanctions on a psychologist by bodies other than APA, including state psychological associations, other professional groups, psychology boards, other state or federal agencies, and payors for health services. In addition to actions for violation of the Ethics Code, the APA Bylaws provide that APA may take action against a member after his or her conviction of a felony, expulsion or suspension from an affiliated state psychological association, or suspension or loss of licensure.

PREAMBLE

Psychologists work to develop a valid and reliable body of scientific knowledge based on research. They may apply that knowledge to human behavior in a variety of contexts. In doing so, they perform many roles, such as researcher, educator, diagnostician, therapist, supervisor, consultant, administrator, social interventionist, and expert witness. Their goal is to broaden knowledge of behavior and, where appropriate, to apply it pragmatically to improve the condition of both the individual and society. Psychologists respect the central importance of freedom of inquiry and expression in research, teaching, and publication. They also strive to help the public in developing informed judgments and choices concerning human behavior. This Ethics Code provides a common set of values upon which psychologists build their professional and scientific work.

This Code is intended to provide both the general principles and the decision rules to cover most situations encountered by psychologists. It has as its primary goal the welfare and protection of the individuals and groups with whom psychologists work. It is the individual responsibility of each psychologist to aspire to the highest possible standards of conduct. Psychologists respect and protect human and civil rights, and do not knowingly participate in or condone unfair discriminatory practices.

The development of a dynamic set of ethical standards for a psychologist's work-related conduct requires a personal commitment to a lifelong effort to act ethically; to encourage ethical behavior by students, supervisees, employees, and colleagues, as appropriate; and to consult with others, as needed, concerning ethical problems. Each psychologist supplements, but does not violate, the Ethics Code's values and rules on the basis of guidance drawn from personal values, culture, and experience.

GENERAL PRINCIPLES

Principle A: Competence

Psychologists strive to maintain high standards of competence in their work. They recognize the boundaries of their particular competencies and the limitations of their expertise. They provide only those services and use only those techniques for which they are qualified by education, training, or experience. Psychologists are cognizant of the fact that the competencies required in serving, teaching, and/or studying groups of people vary with the distinctive characteristics of those groups. In those areas in which recognized professional standards do not yet exist, psychologists exercise careful judgment and take appropriate precautions to protect the welfare of those with whom they work. They maintain knowledge of relevant scientific and professional information related to the services they render, and they recognize the need for ongoing education. Psychologists make appropriate use of scientific, professional, technical, and administrative resources.

Principle B: Integrity

Psychologists seek to promote integrity in the science, teaching, and practice of psychology. In these activities psychologists are honest, fair, and respectful of others. In describing or reporting their qualifications, services, products, fees, research, or teaching, they do not make statements that are false, misleading, or deceptive. Psychologists strive to be aware of their own belief systems, values, needs, and limitations and the effect of these on their work. To the extent feasible, they attempt to clarify for relevant parties the roles they are performing and to function appropriately in accordance with those roles. Psychologists avoid improper and potentially harmful dual relationships.

Principle C: Professional and Scientific Responsibility

Psychologists uphold professional standards of conduct, clarify their professional roles and obligations, accept appropriate responsibility for their behavior, and adapt their methods to the needs of different populations. Psychologists consult with, refer to, or cooperate with other professionals and institutions to the extent needed to serve the best interests of their patients, clients, or other recipients of their services. Psychologists' moral standards and conduct are personal matters to the same degree as is true for any other person, except as psychologists' conduct may compromise their professional responsibilities or reduce the public's trust in psychology and psychologists. Psychologists are concerned about the ethical compliance of their colleagues' scientific and professional conduct. When appropriate, they consult with colleagues in order to prevent or avoid unethical conduct.

Principle D: Respect for People's Rights and Dignity

Psychologists accord appropriate respect to the fundamental rights, dignity, and worth of all people. They respect the rights of individuals to privacy, confidentiality, self-determination, and autonomy, mindful that legal and other obligations may lead to inconsistency and conflict with the exercise of these rights. Psychologists are aware of cultural, individual, and role differences, including those due to age, gender, race, ethnicity, national origin, religion, sexual orientation, disability, language, and socioeconomic status. Psychologists try to eliminate the effect on their work of biases based on those factors, and they do not knowingly participate in or condone unfair discriminatory practices.

Principle E: Concern for Other's Welfare

Psychologists seek to contribute to the welfare of those with whom they interact professionally. In their professional actions, psychologists weigh the welfare and rights of their patients or clients, students, supervisees, human research participants, and other affected persons, and the welfare of animal subjects of research. When conflicts occur among psychologists' obligations or concerns, they attempt to resolve these conflicts and to perform their roles in a responsible fashion that avoids or minimizes harm. Psychologists are sensitive to real and ascribed differences in power between themselves and others, and they do not exploit or mislead other people during or after professional relationships.

Principle F: Social Responsibility

Psychologists are aware of their professional and scientific responsibilities to the community and the society in which they work and live. They apply and make public their knowledge of psychology in order to contribute to human welfare. Psychologists are concerned about and work to mitigate the causes of human suffering. When undertaking research, they strive to advance human welfare and the science of psychology. Psychologists try to avoid misuse of their work. Psychologists comply with the law and encourage the development of law and social policy that serve the interests of their patients and clients and the public. They are encouraged to contribute a portion of their professional time for little or no personal advantage.

ETHICAL STANDARDS

1. GENERAL STANDARDS

These General Standards are potentially applicable to the professional and scientific activities of all psychologists.

1.01 Applicability of the Ethics Code

The activity of a psychologist subject to the Ethics Code may be reviewed under these Ethical Standards only if the activity is part of his or her work-related functions or the activity is psychological in nature. Personal activities having no connection to or effect on psychological roles are not subject to the Ethics Code.

1.02 Relationship of Ethics and Law

If psychologists' ethical responsibilities conflict with law, psychologists make known their commitment to the Ethics Code and take steps to resolve the conflict in a responsible manner.

1.03 Professional and Scientific Relationship

Psychologists provide diagnostic, therapeutic, teaching, research, supervisory, consultative, or other psychological services only in the context of a defined professional or scientific relationship or role. (See also Standards 2.01, Evaluation, Diagnosis, and Interventions in Professional Context, and 7.02, Forensic Assessments.)

1.04 Boundaries of Competence

(a) Psychologists provide services, teach, and conduct research only within the boundaries of their competence, based on their education, training, supervised experience, or appropriate professional experience.

(b) Psychologists provide services, teach, or conduct research in new areas or involving new techniques only after first undertaking appropriate study, training, supervision, and/or consultation from persons who are competent in those areas or techniques.

(c) In those emerging areas in which generally recognized standards for preparatory training do not yet exist, psychologists nevertheless take reasonable steps to ensure the competence of their work and to protect patients, clients, students, research participants, and others from harm.

1.05 Maintaining Expertise

Psychologists who engage in assessment, therapy, teaching, research, organizational consulting, or other professional activities maintain a reasonable level of awareness of current scientific and professional information in their fields of activity, and undertake ongoing efforts to maintain competence in the skills they use.

1.06 Basis for Scientific and Professional Judgments

Psychologists rely on scientifically and professionally derived knowledge when making scientific or professional judgments or when engaging in scholarly or professional endeavors.

1.07 Describing the Nature and Results of Psychological Services

(a) When psychologists provide assessment, evaluation, treatment, counseling, supervision, teaching, consultation, research, or other psychological services to an individual, a group, or an organization,they provide, using language that is reasonably understandable to the recipient of those services, appropriate information beforehand about the nature of such services and appropriate information later about results and conclusions. (See also Standard 2.09, Explaining Assessment Results.)

(b) If psychologists will be precluded by law or by organizational roles from providing such information to particular individuals or groups, they so inform those individuals or groups at the outset of the service.

1.08 Human Differences

Where differences of age, gender, race, ethnicity, national origin, religion, sexual orientation, disability, language, or socioeconomic status significantly affect psychologists' work concerning particular individuals or groups, psychologists obtain the training, experience, consultation, or supervision necessary to ensure the competence of their services, or they make appropriate referrals.

1.09 Respecting Others

In their work-related activities, psychologists respect the rights of others to hold values, attitudes, and opinions that differ from their own.

1.10 Nondiscrimination

In their work-related activities, psychologists do not engage in unfair discrimination based on age, gender, race, ethnicity, national origin, religion, sexual orientation, disability, socioeconomic status, or any basis proscribed by law.

1.11 Sexual Harassment

(a) Psychologists do not engage in sexual harassment. Sexual harassment is sexual solicitation, physical advances, or verbal or nonverbal conduct that is sexual in nature, that occurs in connection with the psychologist's activities or roles as a psychologist, and that either: (1) is unwelcome, is offensive, or creates a hostile workplace environment, and the psychologist knows or is told this; or (2) is sufficiently severe or intense to be abusive to a reasonable person in the context. Sexual harassment can consist of a single intense or severe act or of multiple persistent or pervasive acts.

(b) Psychologists accord sexual-harassment complainants and respondents dignity and respect. Psychologists do not participate in denying a person academic admittance or advancement, employment, tenure, or promotion, based solely upon their having made, or their being the subject of, sexual harassment charges. This does not preclude taking action based upon the outcome of such proceedings or consideration of other appropriate information.

1.12 Other Harassment

Psychologists do not knowingly engage in behavior that is harassing or demeaning to persons with whom they interact in their work based on factors such as those persons' age, gender, race, ethnicity, national origin, religion, sexual orientation, disability, language, or socioeconomic status.

1.13 Personal Problems and Conflicts

(a) Psychologists recognize that their personal problems and conflicts may interfere with their effectiveness. Accordingly, they refrain from under taking an activity when they know or should know that their personal problems are likely to lead to harm to a patient, client, colleague, student, research participant, or other person to whom they may owe a professional or scientific obligation.

(b) In addition, psychologists have an obligation to be alert to signs of, and to obtain assistance for, their personal problems at an early stage, in order to prevent significantly impaired performance.

(c) When psychologists become aware of personal problems that may interfere with their performing work-related duties adequately, they take appropriate measures, such as obtaining professional consultation or assistance, and determine whether they should limit, suspend, or terminate their work-related duties.

1.14 Avoiding Harm

Psychologists take reasonable steps to avoid harming their patients or clients, research participants, students, and others with whom they work, and to minimize harm where it is foreseeable and unavoidable.

1.15 Misuse of Psychologists' Influence

Because psychologists' scientific and professional judgments and actions may affect the lives of others, they are alert to and guard against personal, financial, social, organizational, or political factors that might lead to misuse of their influence.

1.16 Misuse of Psychologists' Work

(a) Psychologists do not participate in activities in which it appears likely that their skills or data will be misused by others, unless corrective mechanisms are available. (See also Standard 7.04, Truthfulness and Candor.)

(b) If psychologists learn of misuse or misrepresentation of their work, they take reasonable steps to correct or minimize the misuse or misrepresentation.

1.17 Multiple Relationships

(a) In many communities and situations, it may not be feasible or reasonable for psychologists to avoid social or other nonprofessional contacts with persons such as patients, clients, students, supervisees, or research participants. Psychologists must always be sensitive to the potential harmful effects of other contacts on their work and on those persons with whom they deal. A psychologist refrains from entering into or promising another personal, scientific, professional, financial, or other relationship with such persons if it appears likely that such a relationship reasonably might impair the psychologist's objectivity or otherwise interfere with the psychologist's effectively performing his or her functions as a psychologist, or might harm or exploit the other party.

(b) Likewise, whenever feasible, a psychologist refrains from taking on professional or scientific obligations when pre-existing relationships would create a risk of such harm.

(c) If a psychologist finds that, due to unforeseen factors, a potentially harmful multiple relationship has arisen, the psychologist attempts to resolve it with due regard for the best interests of the affected person and maximal compliance with the Ethics Code.

1.18 Barter (With Patients or Clients)

Psychologists ordinarily refrain from accepting goods, services, or other nonmonetary remuneration from patients or clients in return for psychological services because such arrangements create inherent potential for conflicts, exploitation, and distortion of the professional relationship. A psychologist may participate in bartering only if (1) it is not clinically contraindicated, and (2) the relationship is not exploitative. (See also Standards 1.17, Multiple Relationships, and 1.25, Fees and Financial Arrangements.)

1.19 Exploitative Relationships

(a) Psychologists do not exploit persons over whom they have supervisory, evaluative, or other authority such as students, supervisees, employees, research participants, and clients or patients. (See also Standards 4.05 - 4.07 regarding sexual involvement with clients or patients.)

(b) Psychologists do not engage in sexual relationships with students or supervisees in training over whom the psychologist has evaluative or direct authority, because such relationships are so likely to impair judgment or be exploitative.

1.20 Consultations and Referrals

(a) Psychologists arrange for appropriate consultations and referrals based principally on the best interests of their patients or clients, with appropriate consent, and subject to other relevant considerations, including applicable law and contractual obligations. (See also Standards 5.01, Discussing the Limits of Confidentiality, and 5.06, Consultations.)

(b) When indicated and professionally appropriate, psychologists cooperate with other professionals in order to serve their patients or clients effectively and appropriately.

(c) Psychologists' referral practices are consistent with law.

1.21 Third-Party Requests for Services

(a) When a psychologist agrees to provide services to a person or entity at the request of a third party, the psychologist clarifies to the extent feasible, at the outset of the service, the nature of the relationship with each party. This clarification includes the role of the psychologist (such as therapist, organizational consultant, diagnostician, or expert witness), the probable uses of the services provided or the information obtained, and the fact that there may be limits to confidentiality.

(b) If there is a foreseeable risk of the psychologist's being called upon to perform conflicting roles because of the involvement of a third party, the psychologist clarifies the nature and direction of his or her responsibilities, keeps all parties appropriately informed as matters develop, and resolves the situation in accordance with this Ethics Code.

1.22 Delegation to and Supervision of Subordinates

(a) Psychologists delegate to their employees, supervisees, and research assistants only those responsibilities that such persons can reasonably be expected to perform competently, on the basis of their education, training, or experience, either independently or with the level of supervision being provided.

(b) Psychologists provide proper training and supervision to their employees or supervisees and take reasonable steps to see that such persons perform services responsibly, competently, and ethically.

(c) If institutional policies, procedures, or practices prevent fulfillment of this obligation, psychologists attempt to modify their role or to correct the situation to the extent feasible.

1.23 Documentation of Professional and Scientific Work

(a) Psychologists appropriately document their professional and scientific work in order to facilitate provision of services later by them or by other professionals, to ensure accountability, and to meet other requirements of institutions or the law.

(b) When psychologists have reason to believe that records of their professional services will be used in legal proceedings involving recipients of or participants in their work, they have a responsibility to create and maintain documentation in the kind of detail and quality that would be consistent with reasonable scrutiny in an adjudicative forum. (See also Standard 7.01, Professionalism, under Forensic Activities.)

1.24 Records and Data

Psychologists create, maintain, disseminate, store, retain, and dispose of records and data relating to their research, practice, and other work in accordance with law and in a manner that permits compliance with the requirements of this Ethics Code. (See also Standard 5.04, Maintenance of Records.)

1.25 Fees and Financial Arrangements

(a) As early as is feasible in a professional or scientific relationship, the psychologist and the patient, client, or other appropriate recipient of psychological services reach an agreement specifying the compensation and the billing arrangements.

(b) Psychologists do not exploit recipients of services or payors with respect to fees.

(c) Psychologists' fee practices are consistent with law.

(d) Psychologists do not misrepresent their fees.

(e) If limitations to services can be anticipated because of limitations in financing, this is discussed with the patient, client, or other appropriate recipient of services as early as is feasible. (See also Standard 4.08, Interruption of Services.)

(f) If the patient, client, or other recipient of services does not pay for services as agreed, and if the psychologist wishes to use collection agencies or legal measures to collect the fees, the psychologist first informs the person that such measures will be taken and provides that person an opportunity to make prompt payment. (See also Standard 5.11, Withholding Records for Nonpayment.)

1.26 Accuracy in Reports to Payors and Funding Sources

In their reports to payors for services or sources of research funding, psychologists accurately state the nature of the research or service provided, the fees or charges, and where applicable, the identity of the provider, the findings, and the diagnosis. (See also Standard 5.05, Disclosures.)

1.27 Referrals and Fees

When a psychologist pays, receives payment from, or divides fees with another professional other than in an employer - employee relationship, the payment to each is based on the services (clinical, consultative, administrative, or other) provided and is not based on the referral itself.

2. EVALUATION, ASSESSMENT, OR INTERVENTION

2.01 Evaluation, Diagnosis, and Interventions in Professional Context

(a) Psychologists perform evaluations, diagnostic services, or interventions only within the context of a defined professional relationship. (See also Standards 1.03, Professional and Scientific Relationship.)

(b) Psychologists' assessments, recommendations, reports, and psychological diagnostic or evaluative statements are based on information and techniques (including personal interviews of the individual when appropriate) sufficient to provide appropriate substantiation for their findings. (See also Standard 7.02, Forensic Assessments.)

2.02 Competence and Appropriate Use of Assessments and Interventions

(a) Psychologists who develop, administer, score, interpret, or use psychological assessment techniques, interviews, tests, or instruments do so in a manner and for purposes that are appropriate in light of the research on or evidence of the usefulness and proper application of the techniques.

(b) Psychologists refrain from misuse of assessment techniques, interventions, results, and interpretations and take reasonable steps to prevent others from misusing the information these techniques provide. This includes refraining from releasing raw test results or raw data to persons, other than to patients or clients as appropriate, who are not qualified to use such information. (See also Standards 1.02, Relationship of Ethics and Law, and 1.04, Boundaries of Competence.)

2.03 Test Construction

Psychologists who develop and conduct research with tests and other assessment techniques use scientific procedures and current professional knowledge for test design, standardization, validation, reduction or elimination of bias, and recommendations for use.

2.04 Use of Assessment in General and With Special Populations.

(a) Psychologists who perform interventions or administer, score, interpret, or use assessment techniques are familiar with the reliability, validation, and related standardization or outcome studies of, and proper applications and uses of, the techniques they use.

(b) Psychologists recognize limits to the certainty with which diagnoses, judgments, or predictions can be made about individuals.

(c) Psychologists attempt to identify situations in which particular interventions or assessment techniques or norms may not be applicable or may require adjustment in administration or interpretation because of factors such as individuals' gender, age, race, ethnicity, national origin, religion, sexual orientation, disability, language, or socioeconomic status.

2.05 Interpreting Assessment Results

When interpreting assessment results, including automated interpretations, psychologists take into account the various test factors and characteristics of the person being assessed that might affect psychologists' judgments or reduce the accuracy of their interpretations. They indicate any significant reservations they have about the accuracy or limitations of their interpretations.

2.06 Unqualified Persons

Psychologists do not promote the use of psychological assessment techniques by unqualified persons. (See also Standard 1.22, Delegation to and Supervision of Subordinates.)

2.07 Obsolete Tests and Outdated Test Results

(a) Psychologists do not base their assessment or intervention decisions or recommendations on data or test results that are outdated for the current purpose.

(b) Similarly, psychologists do not base such decisions or recommendations on tests and measures that are obsolete and not useful for the current purpose.

2.08 Test Scoring and Interpretation Services

(a) Psychologists who offer assessment or scoring procedures to other professionals accurately describe the purpose, norms, validity, reliability, and applications of the procedures and any special qualifications applicable to their use.

(b) Psychologists select scoring and interpretation services (including automated services) on the basis of evidence of the validity of the program and procedures as well as on other appropriate considerations.

(c) Psychologists retain appropriate responsibility for the appropriate application, interpretation, and use of assessment instruments, whether they score and interpret such tests themselves or use automated or other services.

2.09 Explaining Assessment Results

Unless the nature of the relationship is clearly explained to the person being assessed in advance and precludes provision of an explanation of results (such as in some organizational consulting, pre-employment or security screenings, and forensic evaluations), psychologists ensure that an explanation of the results is provided using language that is reasonably understandable to the person assessed or to another legally authorized person on behalf of the client. Regardless of whether the scoring and interpretation are done by the psychologist, by assistants, or by automated or other outside services, psychologists take reasonable steps to ensure that appropriate explanations of results are given.

2.10 Maintaining Test Security

Psychologists make reasonable efforts to maintain the integrity and security of tests and other assessment techniques consistent with law, contractual obligations, and in a manner that permits compliance with the requirements of this Ethics Code. (See also Standard 1.02, Relationship of Ethics and Law.)

3. ADVERTISING AND OTHER PUBLIC STATEMENTS

3.01 Definition of Public Statements

Psychologists comply with this Ethics Code in public statements relating to their professional services, products, or publications or to the field of psychology. Public statements include but are not limited to paid or unpaid advertising, brochures, printed matter, directory listings, personal resumes or curriculum vitae, interviews or comments for use in media, statements in legal proceedings, lectures and public oral presentations, and published materials.

3.02 Statements by Others

(a) Psychologists who engage others to create or place public statements that promote their professional practice, products, or activities retain professional responsibility for such statements.

(b) In addition, psychologists make reasonable efforts to prevent others whom they do not control (such as employers, publishers, sponsors, organizational clients, and representatives of the print or broadcast media) from making deceptive statements concerning psychologists' practice or professional or scientific activities.

(c) If psychologists learn of deceptive statements about their work made by others, psychologists make reasonable efforts to correct such statements.

(d) Psychologists do not compensate employees of press, radio, television, or other communication media in return for publicity in a news item.

(e) A paid advertisement relating to the psychologist's activities must be identified as such, unless it is already apparent from the context.

3.03 Avoidance of False or Deceptive Statements

(a) Psychologists do not make public statements that are false, deceptive, misleading, or fraudulent, either because of what they state, convey, or suggest or because of what they omit, concerning their research, practice, or other work activities or those of persons or organizations with which they are affiliated. As examples (and not in limitation) of this standard, psychologists do not make false or deceptive statements concerning (1) their training, experience, or competence; (2) their academic degrees; (3) their credentials; (4) their institutional or association affiliations; (5) their services; (6) the scientific or clinical basis for, or results or degree of success of, their services; (7) their fees; or (8) their publications or research findings. (See also Standards 6.15, Deception in Research, and 6.18, Providing Participants With Information About the Study.)

(b) Psychologists claim as credentials for their psychological work, only degrees that (1) were earned from a regionally accredited educational institution or (2) were the basis for psychology licensure by the state in which they practice.

3.04 Media Presentations

When psychologists provide advice or comment by means of public lectures, demonstrations, radio or television programs, prerecorded tapes, printed articles, mailed material, or other media, they take reasonable precautions to ensure that (1) the statements are based on appropriate psychological literature and practice, (2) the statements are otherwise consistent with this Ethics Code, and (3) the recipients of the information are not encouraged to infer that a relationship has been established with them personally.

3.05 Testimonials

Psychologists do not solicit testimonials from current psychotherapy clients or patients or other persons who because of their particular circumstances are vulnerable to undue influence.

3.06 In-Person Solicitation

Psychologists do not engage, directly or through agents, in uninvited in-person solicitation of business from actual or potential psychotherapy patients or clients or other persons who because of their particular circumstances are vulnerable to undue influence. However, this does not preclude attempting to implement appropriate collateral contacts with significant others for the purpose of benefiting an already engaged therapy patient.

4. THERAPY

4.01 Structuring the Relationship

(a) Psychologists discuss with clients or patients as early as is feasible in the therapeutic relationship appropriate issues, such as the nature and anticipated course of therapy, fees, and confidentiality. (See also Standards 1.25, Fees and Financial Arrangements, and 5.01, Discussing the Limits of Confidentiality.)

(b) When the psychologist's work with clients or patients will be supervised, the above discussion includes that fact, and the name of the supervisor, when the supervisor has legal responsibility for the case.

(c) When the therapist is a student intern, the client or patient is informed of that fact.

(d) Psychologists make reasonable efforts to answer patients' questions and to avoid apparent misunderstandings about therapy. Whenever possible, psychologists provide oral and/or written information, using language that is reasonably understandable to the patient or client.

4.02 Informed Consent to Therapy

(a) Psychologists obtain appropriate informed consent to therapy or related procedures, using language that is reasonably understandable to participants. The content of informed consent will vary depending on many circumstances; however, informed consent generally implies that the person (1) has the capacity to consent, (2) has been informed of significant information concerning the procedure, (3) has freely and without undue influence expressed consent, and (4) consent has been appropriately documented.

(b) When persons are legally incapable of giving informed consent, psychologists obtain informed permission from a legally authorized person, if such substitute consent is permitted by law.

(c) In addition, psychologists (1) inform those persons who are legally incapable of giving informed consent about the proposed interventions in a manner commensurate with the persons' psychological capacities, (2) seek their assent to those interventions, and (3) consider such persons' preferences and best interests.

4.03 Couple and Family Relationships

(a) When a psychologist agrees to provide services to several persons who have a relationship (such as husband and wife or parents and children), the psychologist attempts to clarify at the outset (1) which of the individuals are patients or clients and (2) the relationship the psychologist will have with each person. This clarification includes the role of the psychologist and the probable uses of the services provided or the information obtained. (See also Standard 5.01, Discussing the Limits of Confidentiality.)

(b) As soon as it becomes apparent that the psychologist may be called on to perform potentially conflicting roles (such as marital counselor to husband and wife, and then witness for one party in a divorce proceeding), the psychologist attempts to clarify and adjust, or withdraw from, roles appropriately. (See also Standard 7.03, Clarification of Role, under Forensic Activities.)

4.04 Providing Mental Health Services to Those Served by Others

In deciding whether to offer or provide services to those already receiving mental health services elsewhere, psychologists carefully consider the treatment issues and the potential patient's or client's welfare. The psychologist discusses these issues with the patient or client, or another legally authorized person on behalf of the client, in order to minimize the risk of confusion and conflict, consults with the other service providers when appropriate, and proceeds with caution and sensitivity to the therapeutic issues.

4.05 Sexual Intimacies With Current Patients or Clients

Psychologists do not engage in sexual intimacies with current patients or clients.

4.06 Therapy With Former Sexual Partners

Psychologists do not accept as therapy patients or clients persons with whom they have engaged in sexual intimacies.

4.07 Sexual Intimacies With Former Therapy Patients

(a) Psychologists do not engage in sexual intimacies with a former therapy patient or client for at least two years after cessation or termination of professional services.

(b) Because sexual intimacies with a former therapy patient or client are so frequently harmful to the patient or client, and because such intimacies undermine public confidence in the psychology profession and thereby deter the public's use of needed services, psychologists do not engage in sexual intimacies with former therapy patients and clients even after a two-year interval except in the most unusual circumstances. The psychologist who engages in such activity after the two years following cessation or termination of treatment bears the burden of demonstrating that there has been no exploitation, in light of all relevant factors, including (1) the amount of time that has passed since therapy terminated, (2) the nature and duration of the therapy, (3) the circumstances of termination, (4) the patient's or client's personal history, (5) the patient's or client's current mental status, (6) the likelihood of adverse impact on the patient or client and others, and (7) any statements or actions made by the therapist during the course of therapy suggesting or inviting the possibility of a post-termination sexual or romantic relationship with the patient or client. (See also Standard 1.17, Multiple Relationships.)

4.08 Interruption of Services

(a) Psychologists make reasonable efforts to plan for facilitating care in the event that psychological services are interrupted by factors such as the psychologist's illness, death, unavailability, or relocation or by the client's relocation or financial limitations. (See also Standard 5.09, Preserving Records and Data.)

(b) When entering into employment or contractual relationships, psychologists provide for orderly and appropriate resolution of responsibility for patient or client care in the event that the employment or contractual relationship ends, with paramount consideration given to the welfare of the patient or client.

4.09 Terminating the Professional Relationship

(a) Psychologists do not abandon patients or clients. (See also Standard 1.25e, under Fees and Financial Arrangements.)

(b) Psychologists terminate a professional relationship when it becomes reasonably clear that the patient or client no longer needs the service, is not benefiting, or is being harmed by continued service.

(c) Prior to termination for whatever reason, except where precluded by the patient's or client's conduct, the psychologist discusses the patient's or client's views and needs, provides appropriate pretermination counseling, suggests alternative service providers as appropriate, and takes other reasonable steps to facilitate transfer of responsibility to another provider if the patient or client needs one immediately.

5. PRIVACY AND CONFIDENTIALITY

These Standards are potentially applicable to the professional and scientific activities of all psychologists.

5.01 Discussing the Limits of Confidentiality

(a) Psychologists discuss with persons and organizations with whom they establish a scientific or professional relationship (including, to the extent feasible, minors and their legal representatives) (1) the relevant limitations on confidentiality, including limitations where applicable in group, marital, and family therapy or in organizational consulting, and (2) the foreseeable uses of the information generated through their services.

(b) Unless it is not feasible or is contraindicated, the discussion of confidentiality occurs at the outset of the relationship and thereafter as new circumstances may warrant.

(c) Permission for electronic recording of interviews is secured from clients and patients.

5.02 Maintaining Confidentiality

Psychologists have a primary obligation and take reasonable precautions to respect the confidentiality rights of those with whom they work or consult, recognizing that confidentiality may be established by law, institutional rules, or professional or scientific relationships. (See also Standard 6.26, Professional Reviewers.)

5.03 Minimizing Intrusions on Privacy

(a) In order to minimize intrusions on privacy, psychologists include in written and oral reports, consultations, and the like, only information germane to the purpose for which the communication is made.

(b) Psychologists discuss confidential information obtained in clinical or consulting relationships, or evaluative data concerning patients, individual or organizational clients, students, research participants, supervisees, and employees, only for appropriate scientific or professional purposes and only with persons clearly concerned with such matters.

5.04 Maintenance of Records

Psychologists maintain appropriate confidentiality in creating, storing, accessing, transferring, and disposing of records under their control, whether these are written, automated, or in any other medium. Psychologists maintain and dispose of records in accordance with law and in a manner that permits compliance with the requirements of this Ethics Code.

5.05 Disclosures

(a) Psychologists disclose confidential information without the consent of the individual only as mandated by law, or where permitted by law for a valid purpose, such as (1) to provide needed professional services to the patient or the individual or organizational client, (2) to obtain appropriate professional consultations, (3) to protect the patient or client or others from harm, or (4) to obtain payment for services, in which instance disclosure is limited to the minimum that is necessary to achieve the purpose.

(b) Psychologists also may disclose confidential information with the appropriate consent of the patient or the individual or organizational client (or of another legally authorized person on behalf of the patient or client), unless prohibited by law.

5.06 Consultations

When consulting with colleagues, (1) psychologists do not share confidential information that reasonably could lead to the identification of a patient, client, research participant, or other person or organization with whom they have a confidential relationship unless they have obtained the prior consent of the person or organization or the disclosure cannot be avoided, and (2) they share information only to the extent necessary to achieve the purposes of the consultation. (See also Standard 5.02, Maintaining Confidentiality.)

5.07 Confidential Information in Databases.

(a) If confidential information concerning recipients of psychological services is to be entered into databases or systems of records available to persons whose access has not been consented to by the recipient, then psychologists use coding or other techniques to avoid the inclusion of personal identifiers.

(b) If a research protocol approved by an institutional review board or similar body requires the inclusion of personal identifiers, such identifiers are deleted before the information is made accessible to persons other than those of whom the subject was advised.

(c) If such deletion is not feasible, then before psychologists transfer such data to others or review such data collected by others, they take reasonable steps to determine that appropriate consent of personally identifiable individuals has been obtained.

5.08 Use of Confidential Information for Didactic or Other Purposes

(a) Psychologists do not disclose in their writings, lectures, or other public media, confidential, personally identifiable information concerning their patients, individual or organizational clients, students, research participants, or other recipients of their services that they obtained during the course of their work, unless the person or organization has consented in writing or unless there is other ethical or legal authorization for doing so.

(b) Ordinarily, in such scientific and professional presentations, psychologists disguise confidential information concerning such persons or organizations so that they are not individually identifiable to others and so that discussions do not cause harm to subjects who might identify themselves.

5.09 Preserving Records and Data

A psychologist makes plans in advance so that confidentiality of records and data is protected in the event of the psychologist's death, incapacity, or withdrawal from the position or practice.

5.10 Ownership of Records and Data

Recognizing that ownership of records and data is governed by legal principles, psychologists take reasonable and lawful steps so that records and data remain available to the extent needed to serve the best interests of patients, individual or organizational clients, research participants, or appropriate others.

5.11 Withholding Records for Nonpayment

Psychologists may not withhold records under their control that are requested and imminently needed for a patient's or client's treatment solely because payment has not been received, except as otherwise provided by law.

6. TEACHING, TRAINING SUPERVISION, RESEARCH, AND PUBLISHING

6.01 Design of Education and Training Program

Psychologists who are responsible for education and training programs seek to ensure that the programs are competently designed, provide the proper experiences, and meet the requirements for licensure, certification, or other goals for which claims are made by the program.

6.02 Descriptions of Education and Training Programs

(a) Psychologists responsible for education and training programs seek to ensure that there is a current and accurate description of the program content, training goals and objectives, and requirements that must be met for satisfactory completion of the program. This information must be made readily available to all interested parties.

(b) Psychologists seek to ensure that statements concerning their course outlines are accurate and not misleading, particularly regarding the subject matter to be covered, bases for evaluating progress, and the nature of course experiences. (See also Standard 3.03, Avoidance of False or Deceptive Statements.)

(c) To the degree to which they exercise control, psychologists responsible for announcements, catalogs, brochures, or advertisements describing workshops, seminars, or other non-degree- granting educational programs ensure that they accurately describe the audience for which the program is intended, the educational objectives, the presenters, and the fees involved.

6.03 Accuracy and Objectivity in Teaching

(a) When engaged in teaching or training, psychologists present psychological information accurately and with a reasonable degree of objectivity.

(b) When engaged in teaching or training, psychologists recognize the power they hold over students or supervisees and therefore make reasonable efforts to avoid engaging in conduct that is personally demeaning to students or supervisees. (See also Standards 1.09, Respecting Others, and 1.12, Other Harassment.)

6.04 Limitation on Teaching

Psychologists do not teach the use of techniques or procedures that require specialized training, licensure, or expertise, including but not limited to hypnosis, biofeedback, and projective techniques, to individuals who lack the prerequisite training, legal scope of practice, or expertise.

6.05 Assessing Student and Supervisee Performance

(a) In academic and supervisory relationships, psychologists establish an appropriate process for providing feedback to students and supervisees.

(b) Psychologists evaluate students and supervisees on the basis of their actual performance on relevant and established program requirements.

6.06 Planning Research

(a) Psychologists design, conduct, and report research in accordance with recognized standards of scientific competence and ethical research.

(b) Psychologists plan their research so as to minimize the possibility that results will be misleading.

(c) In planning research, psychologists consider its ethical acceptability under the Ethics Code. If an ethical issue is unclear, psychologists seek to resolve the issue through consultation with institutional review boards, animal care and use committees, peer consultations, or other proper mechanisms.

(d) Psychologists take reasonable steps to implement appropriate protections for the rights and welfare of human participants, other persons affected by the research, and the welfare of animal subjects.

6.07 Responsibility

(a) Psychologists conduct research competently and with due concern for the dignity and welfare of the participants.

(b) Psychologists are responsible for the ethical conduct of research conducted by them or by others under their supervision or control.

(c) Researchers and assistants are permitted to perform only those tasks for which they are appropriately trained and prepared.

(d) As part of the process of development and implementation of research projects, psychologists consult those with expertise concerning any special population under investigation or most likely to be affected.

6.08 Compliance With Law and Standards.

Psychologists plan and conduct research in a manner consistent with federal and state law and regulations, as well as professional standards governing the conduct of research, and particularly those standards governing research with human participants and animal subjects.

6.09 Institutional Approval

Psychologists obtain from host institutions or organizations appropriate approval prior to conducting research, and they provide accurate information about their research proposals. They conduct the research in accordance with the approved research protocol.

6.10 Research Responsibilities

Prior to conducting research (except research involving only anonymous surveys, naturalistic observations, or similar research), psychologists enter into an agreement with participants that clarifies the nature of the research and the responsibilities of each party.

6.11 Informed Consent to Research

(a) Psychologists use language that is reasonably understandable to research participants in obtaining their appropriate informed consent (except as provided in Standard 6.12, Dispensing with Informed Consent). Such informed consent is appropriately documented.

(b) Using language that is reasonably understandable to participants, psychologists inform participants of the nature of the research; they inform participants that they are free to participate or to decline to participate or to withdraw from the research; they explain the foreseeable consequences of declining or withdrawing; they inform participants of significant factors that may be expected to influence their willingness to participate (such as risks, discomfort, adverse effects, or limitations on confidentiality, except as provided in Standard 6.15, Deception in Research); and they explain other aspects about which the prospective participants inquire.

(c) When psychologists conduct research with individuals such as students or subordinates, psychologists take special care to protect the prospective participants from adverse consequences of declining or withdrawing from participation.

(d) When research participation is a course requirement or opportunity for extra credit, the prospective participant is given the choice of equitable alternative activities.

(e) For persons who are legally incapable of giving informed consent, psychologists nevertheless (1) provide an appropriate explanation, (2) obtain the participant's assent, and (3) obtain appropriate permission from a legally authorized person, if such substitute consent is permitted by law.

6.12 Dispensing With Informed Consent

Before determining that planned research (such as research involving only anonymous questionnaires, naturalistic observations, or certain kinds of archival research) does not require the informed consent of research participants, psychologists consider applicable regulations and institutional review board requirements, and they consult with colleagues as appropriate.

6.13 Informed Consent in Research Filming or Recording

Psychologists obtain informed consent from research participants prior to filming or recording them in any form, unless the research involves simply naturalistic observations in public places and it is not anticipated that the recording will be used in a manner that could cause personal identification or harm.

6.14 Offering Inducements for Research Participants

(a) In offering professional services as an inducement to obtain research participants, psychologists make clear the nature of the services, as well as the risks, obligations, and limitations. (See also Standard 1.18, Barter [With Patients or Clients].)

(b) Psychologists do not offer excessive or inappropriate financial or other inducements to obtain research participants, particularly when it might tend to coerce participation.

6.15 Deception in Research

(a) Psychologists do not conduct a study involving deception unless they have determined that the use of deceptive techniques is justified by the study's prospective scientific, educational, or applied value and that equally effective alternative procedures that do not use deception are not feasible.

(b) Psychologists never deceive research participants about significant aspects that would affect their willingness to participate, such as physical risks, discomfort, or unpleasant emotional experiences.

(c) Any other deception that is an integral feature of the design and conduct of an experiment must be explained to participants as early as is feasible, preferably at the conclusion of their participation, but no later than at the conclusion of the research. (See also Standard 6.18, Providing Participants With Information About the Study.)

6.16 Sharing and Utilizing Data

Psychologists inform research participants of their anticipated sharing or further use of personally identifiable research data and of the possibility of unanticipated future uses.

6.17 Minimizing Invasiveness

In conducting research, psychologists interfere with the participants or milieu from which data are collected only in a manner that is warranted by an appropriate research design and that is consistent with psychologists' roles as scientific investigators.

6.18 Providing Participants With Information About the Study

(a) Psychologists provide a prompt opportunity for participants to obtain appropriate information about the nature, results, and conclusions of the research, and psychologists attempt to correct any misconceptions that participants may have.

(b) If scientific or humane values justify delaying or withholding this information, psychologists take reasonable measures to reduce the risk of harm.

6.19 Honoring Commitments

Psychologists take reasonable measures to honor all commitments they have made to research participants.

6.20 Care and Use of Animals in Research

(a) Psychologists who conduct research involving animals treat them humanely.

(b) Psychologists acquire, care for, use, and dispose of animals in compliance with current federal, state, and local laws and regulations, and with professional standards.

(c) Psychologists trained in research methods and experienced in the care of laboratory animals supervise all procedures involving animals and are responsible for ensuring appropriate consideration of their comfort, health, and humane treatment.

(d) Psychologists ensure that all individuals using animals under their supervision have received instruction in research methods and in the care, maintenance, and handling of the species being used, to the extent appropriate to their role.

(e) Responsibilities and activities of individuals assisting in a research project are consistent with their respective competencies.

(f) Psychologists make reasonable efforts to minimize the discomfort, infection, illness, and pain of animal subjects.

(g) A procedure subjecting animals to pain, stress, or privation is used only when an alternative procedure is unavailable and the goal is justified by its prospective scientific, educational, or applied value.

(h) Surgical procedures are performed under appropriate anesthesia; techniques to avoid infection and minimize pain are followed during and after surgery.

(i) When it is appropriate that the animal's life be terminated, it is done rapidly, with an effort to minimize pain, and in accordance with accepted procedures.

6.21 Reporting of Results

(a) Psychologists do not fabricate data or falsify results in their publications.

(b) If psychologists discover significant errors in their published data, they take reasonable steps to correct such errors in a correction, retraction, erratum, or other appropriate publication means.

6.22 Plagiarism

Psychologists do not present substantial portions or elements of another's work or data as their own, even if the other work or data source is cited occasionally.

6.23 Publication Credit

(a) Psychologists take responsibility and credit, including authorship credit, only for work they have actually performed or to which they have contributed.

(b) Principal authorship and other publication credits accurately reflect the relative scientific or professional contributions of the individuals involved, regardless of their relative status. Mere possession of an institutional position, such as Department Chair, does not justify authorship credit. Minor contributions to the research or to the writing for publications are appropriately acknowledged, such as in footnotes or in an introductory statement.

(c) A student is usually listed as principal author on any multiple-authored article that is substantially based on the student's dissertation or thesis.

6.24 Duplicate Publication of Data

Psychologists do not publish, as original data, data that have been previously published. This does not preclude republishing data when they are accompanied by proper acknowledgment.

6.25 Sharing Data

After research results are published, psychologists do not withhold the data on which their conclusions are based from other competent professionals who seek to verify the substantive claims through reanalysis and who intend to use such data only for that purpose, provided that the confidentiality of the participants can be protected and unless legal rights concerning proprietary data preclude their release.

6.26 Professional Reviewers

Psychologists who review material submitted for publication, grant, or other research proposal review respect the confidentiality of and the proprietary rights in such information of those who submitted it.

7. FORENSIC ACTIVITIES

7.01 Professionalism

Psychologists who perform forensic functions, such as assessments, interviews, consultations, reports, or expert testimony, must comply with all other provisions of this Ethics Code to the extent that they apply to such activities. In addition, psychologists base their forensic work on appropriate knowledge of and competence in the areas underlying such work, including specialized knowledge concerning special populations. (See also Standards 1.06, Basis for Scientific and Professional Judgments; 1.08, Human Differences; 1.15, Misuse of Psychologists' Influence; and 1.23, Documentation of Professional and Scientific Work.)

7.02 Forensic Assessments

(a) Psychologists' forensic assessments, recommendations, and reports are based on information and techniques (including personal interviews of the individual, when appropriate) sufficient to provide appropriate substantiation for their findings. (See also Standards 1.03, Professional and Scientific Relationship; 1.23, Documentation of Professional and Scientific Work; 2.01, Evaluation, Diagnosis, and Interventions in Professional Context; and 2.05, Interpreting Assessment Results.)

(b) Except as noted in (c), below, psychologists provide written or oral forensic reports or testimony of the psychological characteristics of an individual only after they have conducted an examination of the individual adequate to support their statements or conclusions.

(c) When, despite reasonable efforts, such an examination is not feasible, psychologists clarify the impact of their limited information on the reliability and validity of their reports and testimony, and they appropriately limit the nature and extent of their conclusions or recommendations.

7.03 Clarification of Role

In most circumstances, psychologists avoid performing multiple and potentially conflicting roles in forensic matters. When psychologists may be called on to serve in more than one role in a legal proceeding - for example, as consultant or expert for one party or for the court and as a fact witness - they clarify role expectations and the extent of confidentiality in advance to the extent feasible, and thereafter as changes occur, in order to avoid compromising their professional judgment and objectivity and in order to avoid misleading others regarding their role.

7.04 Truthfulness and Candor

(a) In forensic testimony and reports, psychologists testify truthfully, honestly, and candidly and, consistent with applicable legal procedures, describe fairly the bases for their testimony and conclusions.

(b) Whenever necessary to avoid misleading, psychologists acknowledge the limits of their data or conclusions.

7.05 Prior Relationships

A prior professional relationship with a party does not preclude psychologists from testifying as fact witnesses or from testifying to their services to the extent permitted by applicable law. Psychologists appropriately take into account ways in which the prior relationship might affect their professional objectivity or opinions and disclose the potential conflict to the relevant parties.

7.06 Compliance With Law and Rules

In performing forensic roles, psychologists are reasonably familiar with the rules governing their roles. Psychologists are aware of the occasionally competing demands placed upon them by these principles and the requirements of the court system, and attempt to resolve these conflicts by making known their commitment to this Ethics Code and taking steps to resolve the conflict in a responsible manner. (See also Standard 1.02, Relationship of Ethics and Law.)

8. RESOLVING ETHICAL ISSUES

8.01 Familiarity With Ethics Code

Psychologists have an obligation to be familiar with this Ethics Code, other applicable ethics codes, and their application to psychologists' work. Lack of awareness or misunderstanding of an ethical standard is not itself a defense to a charge of unethical conduct.

8.02 Confronting Ethical Issues

When a psychologist is uncertain whether a particular situation or course of action would violate this Ethics Code, the psychologist ordinarily consults with other psychologists knowledgeable about ethical issues, with state or national psychology ethics committees, or with other appropriate authorities in order to choose a proper response.

8.03 Conflicts Between Ethics and Organizational Demands

If the demands of an organization with which psychologists are affiliated conflict with this Ethics Code, psychologists clarify the nature of the conflict, make known their commitment to the Ethics Code, and to the extent feasible, seek to resolve the conflict in a way that permits the fullest adherence to the Ethics Code.

8.04 Informal Resolution of Ethical Violations

When psychologists believe that there may have been an ethical violation by another psychologist, they attempt to resolve the issue by bringing it to the attention of that individual if an informal resolution appears appropriate and the intervention does not violate any confidentiality rights that may be involved.

8.05 Reporting Ethical Violations

If an apparent ethical violation is not appropriate for informal resolution under Standard 8.04 or is not resolved properly in that fashion, psychologists take further action appropriate to the situation, unless such action conflicts with confidentiality rights in ways that cannot be resolved. Such action might include referral to state or national committees on professional ethics or to state licensing boards.

8.06 Cooperating With Ethics Committees

Psychologists cooperate in ethics investigations, proceedings, and resulting requirements of the APA or any affiliated state psychological association to which they belong. In doing so, they make reasonable efforts to resolve any issues as to confidentiality. Failure to cooperate is itself an ethics violation.

8.07 Improper Complaints
Psychologists do not file or encourage the filing of ethics complaints that are frivolous and are intended to harm the respondent rather than to protect the public.

HISTORY AND EFFECTIVE DATE.

This version of the APA Ethics Code was adopted by the American Psychological Association's Council of Representatives during its meeting, August 13 and 16, 1992, and is effective beginning December 1, 1992. Inquiries concerning the substance or interpretation of the APA Ethics Code should be addressed to the Director, Office of Ethics, American Psychological Association, 750 First Street, NE, Washington, DC 20002-4242.

This Code will be used to adjudicate complaints brought concerning alleged conduct occurring after the effective date. Complaints regarding conduct occurring prior to the effective date will be adjudicated on the basis of the version of the Code that was in effect at the time the conduct occurred, except that no provisions repealed in June 1989, will be enforced even if an earlier version contains the provision. The Ethics Code will undergo continuing review and study for future revisions; comments on the Code may be sent to the above address. The APA has previously published its Ethical Standards as follows:

American Psychological Association. (1953). *Ethical standards of psychologists. Washington, DC: Author.*

American Psychological Association. (1958). Standards of ethical behavior for psychologists. *American Psychologist, 13,* 268- 271.

American Psychological Association. (1963). Ethical standards of psychologists. *American Psychologist, 18,* 56-60.

American Psychological Association. (1968). Ethical standards of psychologists. *American Psychologist, 23,* 357-361.

American Psychological Association. (1977, March). Ethical standards of psychologists. *APA Monitor,* 22-23.

American Psychological Association. (1979). *Ethical standards of psychologists.* Washington, DC: Author.

American Psychological Association. (1981). Ethical principles of psychologists. *American Psychologist, 36,* 633-638.

American Psychological Association. (1990). Ethical principles of psychologists (Amended June 2, 1989). *American Psychologist, 45,* 390-395.

Request copies of the APA's *Ethical Principles of Psychologists and Code of Conduct* from the APA Order Department, 750 First Street, NE, Washington, DC 20002-4242, or phone (202) 336-5510.

NOTE 1:

Professional materials that are most helpful in this regard are guidelines and standards that have been adopted or endorsed by professional psychological organizations. Such guidelines and standards, whether adopted by the American Psychological Association (APA) or its Divisions, are not enforceable as such by this Ethics Code, but are of educative value to psychologists, courts, and professional bodies. Such materials include, but are not limited to, the APA's General Guidelines for Providers of Psychological Services (1987), Specialty Guidelines for the Delivery of Services by Clinical Psychologists, Counseling Psychologists, Industrial/Organizational Psychologists, and School Psychologists (1981), Guidelines for Computer Based Tests and Interpretations (1987), Standards for Educational and Psychological Testing (1985), Ethical Principles in the Conduct of Research With Human Participants (1982), Guidelines for Ethical Conduct in the Care and Use of Animals (1986), Guidelines for Providers of Psychological Services to Ethnic, Linguistic, and Culturally Diverse Populations (1990), and Publication Manual of the American Psychological Association (3rd ed., 1983). Materials not adopted by APA as a whole include the APA Division 41 (Forensic Psychology)/American Psychology-Law Society's Specialty Guidelines for Forensic Psychologists (1991).

A P P E N D I X   D

National Association of School Psychologists
The Principles for Professional Ethics

The contents of this booklet are standards documents that were approved by the Delegate Assembly of the Association on July 15, 2000, in Durham, New Hampshire.

This document was prepared by the Professional Standards Revision Committee.

Additional copies are available from:
NASP Publications
4340 East West Highway
Suite 402
Bethesda, Maryland 20814

Or can be found on the NASP website: www.nasponline.org

I. INTRODUCTION

The formal principles that elucidate the proper conduct of a professional school psychologist are known as *Ethics*. By virtue of joining the Association, each NASP member agrees to abide by the *Ethics*, acting in a manner that shows respect for human dignity and assuring a high quality of professional service. Although ethical behavior is an individual responsibility, it is in the interest of an association to adopt and enforce a code of ethics. If done properly, members will be guided toward appropriate behavior, and public confidence in the profession will be enhanced. Additionally, a code of ethics should provide due process procedures to protect members from potential abuse of the code. The NASP *Principles for Professional Ethics* have been written to accomplish these goals.

The principles in this manual are based on the assumptions that 1) school psychologists will act as advocates for their students/clients, and 2) at the very least, school psychologists will do no harm. These assumptions necessitate that school psychologists "speak up" for the needs and rights of their students/clients even at times when it may be difficult to do so. School psychologists also are constrained to provide only those services for which they have acquired an acknowledged level of experience, training, and competency. Beyond these basic premises, judgment is required to apply the ethical principles to the fluid and expanding interactions between school and community.

There are many different sources of advice for the proper way to behave; local policies, state laws, federal laws, credentialing standards, professional association position statements, and books that recommend "Best Practices" are just a few. Given one's employment situation and the array of recommendations, events may develop in which the ethical course of action is unclear.

The Association will seek to enforce the Ethical Principles with its members. NASP's *Guidelines for the Provision of School Psychological Services* are typically not enforced, although all members should work toward achieving the hallmarks of quality services delivery that are described therein. Similarly, "position statements" and "best practices" documents are not adjudicated. The guidance of the *Ethical Principles* is intentionally broad to make it more enduring than other documents that reflect short-term opinions about specific actions shaped by local events, popular trends, or recent developments in the field. The member must use judgment to infer the situation-specific rule from the general ethical principle. The lack of a specific reference to a particular action does not indicate permission or provide a defense against a charge of unethical practice. (For example, the document frequently refers to a school psychologist's relationships with a hypothetical "student/client." Because school psychologists work in a wide variety of settings, there is no single term that neatly identifies the "other" individual in the professional relationship. Therefore, one should apply *Ethical Principles* in all professional situations, realizing that one is not released from responsibility simply because another individual is not strictly a "student" or a "client.")

The principles in this manual are organized into several sections as a result of editorial judgment. Therefore, principles discussed in one section may also apply to other sections. Every school psychologist, regardless of position (e.g., practitioner, researcher, university trainer, supervisor, state or federal consultant, administrator of psychological services) or setting (e.g., public or private school, community agency, hospital, university, private practice) should reflect upon the theme represented in each ethical principle to determine its application to her or his individual situation. For example, although a given principle may specifically discuss responsibilities toward "clients," the intent is that the standards would also apply to supervisees, trainees, and research participants. At times, the *Ethics* may require a higher standard of behavior than the prevailing policies and pertinent laws. Under such conditions, members should adhere to the *Ethics*. Ethical behavior may occasionally be forbidden by policy or law, in which case members are expected to declare their dilemma and work to bring the discrepant regulations into compliance with the *Ethics*. To obtain additional assistance in applying these principles to a particular setting, a school psychologist should consult with experienced school psychologists and seek advice from the National Association of School Psychologists or the state school psychology association.

Throughout the *Principles for Professional Ethics*, it is assumed that, depending on the role and setting of the school psychologist, the client could include children, parents, teachers and other school personnel, other professionals, trainees, or supervisees.

Procedural guidelines for filing an ethical complaint and the adjudication of ethical complaints are available from the NASP office or website (*www.nasponline.org*).

II. PROFESSIONAL COMPETENCY

A. GENERAL

1. School psychologists recognize the strengths and limitations of their training and experience, engaging only in practices for which they are qualified. They enlist the assistance of other specialists in supervisory, consultative, or referral roles as appropriate in providing services. They must continually obtain additional training and education to provide the best possible services to children, families, schools, communities, trainees, and supervisees.
2. Competence levels, education, training, and experience are declared and accurately represented to clients in a professional manner.

3. School psychologists do not use affiliations with persons, associations, or institutions to imply a level of professional competence that exceeds that which has actually been achieved.

4. School psychologists engage in continuing professional development. They remain current regarding developments in research, training, and professional practices that benefit children, families, and schools.

5. School psychologists refrain from any activity in which their personal problems or conflicts may interfere with professional effectiveness. Competent assistance is sought to alleviate conflicts in professional relationships.

6. School psychologists know the *Principles for Professional Ethics* and thoughtfully apply them to situations within their employment setting or practice. Ignorance or misapplication of an ethical principle is not a reasonable defense against a charge of unethical behavior.

III. PROFESSIONAL RELATIONSHIPS

A. GENERAL

1. School psychologists are committed to the application of their professional expertise for the purpose of promoting improvement in the quality of life for children, their families, and the school community. This objective is pursued in ways that protect the dignity and rights of those involved. School psychologists accept responsibility for the appropriateness of their professional practices.

2. School psychologists respect all persons and are sensitive to physical, mental, emotional, political, economic, social, cultural, ethnic and racial characteristics, gender, sexual orientation, and religion.

3. School psychologists in all settings maintain professional relationships with children, parents, and the school community. Consequently, parents and children are to be fully informed about all relevant aspects of school psychological services in advance. The explanation should take into account language and cultural differences, cognitive capabilities, developmental level, and age so that it may be understood by the child, parent, or guardian.

4. School psychologists attempt to resolve situations in which there are divided or conflicting interests in a manner that is mutually beneficial and protects the rights of all parties involved.

5. School psychologists are responsible for the direction and nature of their personal loyalties or objectives. When these commitments may influence a professional relationship, school psychologists inform all concerned

persons of relevant issues in advance, including, when applicable, their direct supervisor for consideration of reassignment of responsibilities.

6. School psychologists do not exploit clients through professional relationships or condone these actions in their colleagues. No individuals, including children, clients, employees, colleagues, trainees, parents, supervisees, and research participants, will be exposed to deliberate comments, gestures, or physical contacts of a sexual nature. School psychologists do not harass or demean others based on personal characteristics. School psychologists do not engage in sexual relationships with their students, supervisees, trainees, or past or present clients.

7. Dual relationships with clients are avoided. Namely, personal and business relations with clients may cloud one's judgment. School psychologists are aware of these situations and avoid them whenever possible.

8. School psychologists attempt to resolve suspected detrimental or unethical practices on an informal level. If informal efforts are not productive, the appropriate professional organization is contacted for assistance, and procedures established for questioning ethical practice are followed:

   a. The filing of an ethical complaint is a serious matter. It is intended to improve the behavior of a colleague that is harmful to the profession and/or the public. Therefore, school psychologists make every effort to discuss the ethical principles with other professionals who may be in violation.

   b. School psychologists enter into the complaint process thoughtfully and with concern for the well-being of all parties involved. They do not file or encourage the filing of an ethics complaint that is frivolous or motivated by revenge.

   c. Some situations may be particularly difficult to analyze from an ethical perspective. School psychologists consult ethical standards from related fields and seek assistance from knowledgeable, experienced school psychologists and relevant state/national associations to ascertain an appropriate course of action.

   d. School psychologists document specific instances of suspected ethical violations (i.e., date, time, relevant details) as well as attempts to resolve these violations.

9. School psychologists respect the confidentiality of information obtained during their professional work. Information is revealed only with the informed consent of the child, or the child's parent or legal guardian, except in those situations in which failure to release information would result in clear danger to the child or others. Obsolete confidential information will be shredded or otherwise destroyed before placement in recycling bins or trash receptacles.

10. School psychologists discuss confidential information only for professional purposes and only with persons who have a legitimate need to know.
11. School psychologists inform children and other clients of the limits of confidentiality at the outset of establishing a professional relationship.

B. STUDENTS

1. School psychologists understand the intimate nature of consultation, assessment, and direct service. They engage only in professional practices that maintain the dignity and integrity of children and other clients.
2. School psychologists explain important aspects of their professional relationships in a clear, understandable manner that is appropriate to the child's or other client's age and ability to understand. The explanation includes the reason why services were requested, who will receive information about the services provided, and the possible outcomes.
3. When a child initiates services, school psychologists understand their obligation to respect the rights of a child to initiate, participate in, or discontinue services voluntarily (See III-C-2 for further clarification). When another party initiates services, the school psychologist will make every effort to secure voluntary participation of the child.
4. Recommendations for program changes or additional services will be discussed with appropriate individuals, including any alternatives that may be available.

C. PARENTS, LEGAL GUARDIANS, AND APPOINTED SURROGATES

1. School psychologists explain all services to parents in a clear, understandable manner. They strive to propose a set of options that takes into account the values and capabilities of each parent. Service provision by interns, practicum students, or other trainees should be explained and agreed to in advance.
2. School psychologists recognize the importance of parental support and seek to obtain that support by assuring that there is direct parent contact prior to seeing the child on an ongoing basis. (Emergencies and "drop-in" self-referrals will require parental notification as soon as possible. The age and circumstances under which children may seek services without parental consent varies greatly; be certain to comply with III-D-5.) School pyschologists secure continuing parental involvement by a frank and prompt reporting to the parent of findings and progress that conforms to the limits of previously determined confidentiality.

3. School psychologists encourage and promote parental participation in designing services provided to their children. When appropriate, this includes linking interventions between the school and the home, tailoring parental involvement to the skills of the family, and helping parents gain the skills needed to help their children.
4. School psychologists respect the wishes of parents who object to school psychological services and attempt to guide parents to alternative community resources.
5. School psychologists discuss with parents the recommendations and plans for assisting their children. The discussion includes alternatives associated with each set of plans, which show respect for the ethnic/cultural values of the family. The parents are informed of sources of help available at school and in the community.
6. School psychologists discuss the rights of parents and children regarding creation, modification, storage, and disposal of confidential materials that will result from the provision of school psychological services.

D. COMMUNITY

1. School psychologists also are citizens, thereby accepting the same responsibilities and duties as any member of society. They are free to pursue individual interests, except to the degree that those interests compromise professional responsibilities.
2. School psychologists may act as individual citizens to bring about social change in a lawful manner. Individual actions should not be presented as, or suggestive of, representing the field of school psychology or the Association.
3. As employees or employers, in public or independent practice domains, school psychologists do not engage in or condone practices that discriminate against children, other clients, or employees (if applicable) based on race, disability, age, gender, sexual orientation, religion, national origin, economic status, or native language.
4. School psychologists avoid any action that could violate or diminish the civil and legal rights of children and other clients.
5. School psychologists adhere to federal, state, and local laws and ordinances governing their practice and advocacy efforts. If regulations conflict with ethical guidelines, school psychologists seek to resolve such conflict through positive, respected, and legal channels, including advocacy efforts involving public policy.

E. OTHER PROFESSIONALS

1. To best meet the needs of children and other clients, school psychologists cooperate with other professional disciplines in relationships based on mutual respect.

2. School psychologists recognize the competence of other professionals. They encourage and support the use of all resources to best serve the interests of children and other clients.

3. School psychologists should strive to explain their field and their professional competencies, including roles, assignments, and working relationships to other professionals.

4. School psychologists cooperate and coordinate with other professionals and agencies with the rights and needs of children and other clients in mind. If a child or other client is receiving similar services from another professional, school psychologists promote coordination of services.

5. The child or other client is referred to another professional for services when a condition or need is identified which is outside the professional competencies or scope of the school psychologist.

6. When transferring the intervention responsibility for a child or other client to another professional, school psychologists ensure that all relevant and appropriate individuals, including the child/client when appropriate, are notified of the change and reasons for the change.

7. When school psychologists suspect the existence of detrimental or unethical practices by a member of another profession, informal contact is made with that person to express the concern. If the situation cannot be resolved in this manner, the appropriate professional organization is contacted for assistance in determining the procedures established by that profession for examining the practices in question.

8. School psychologists who employ, supervise, or train other professionals, accept the obligation to provide continuing professional development. They also provide appropriate working conditions, fair and timely evaluation, and constructive consultation.

F. SCHOOL PSYCHOLOGIST TRAINEES AND INTERNS

1. School psychologists who supervise interns are responsible for all professional practices of the supervisees. They assure children and other clients and the profession that the intern is adequately supervised as designated by the practice guidelines and training standards for school psychologists.

2. School psychologists who conduct or administer training programs provide trainees and prospective trainees with accurate information regarding

program sponsorships/endorsements/accreditation, goals/objectives, training processes and requirements, and likely outcomes and benefits.

3. School psychologists who are faculty members in colleges or universities or who supervise clinical or field placements apply these ethical principles in all work with school psychology trainees. In addition, they promote the ethical practice of trainees by providing specific and comprehensive instruction, feedback, and mentoring.

4. School psychology faculty members and clinical or field supervisors uphold recognized standards of the profession by providing training related to high quality, responsible, and research-based school psychology services. They provide accurate and objective information in their teaching and training activities; identify any limitations in information; and acknowledge disconfirming data, alternative hypotheses, and explanations.

5. School psychology faculty members and clinical or field supervisors develop and use evaluation practices for trainees that are objective, accurate, and fair.

IV. PROFESSIONAL PRACTICES—GENERAL PRINCIPLES

A. ADVOCACY

1. School psychologists typically serve multiple clients including children, parents, and systems. When the school psychologist is confronted with conflicts between client groups, the primary client is considered to be the child. When the child is not the primary client, the individual or group of individuals who sought the assistance of the school psychologist is the primary client.

2. School psychologists consider children and other clients to be their primary responsibility, acting as advocates for their rights and welfare. If conflicts of interest between clients are present, the school psychologist supports conclusions that are in the best interest of the child. When choosing a course of action, school psychologists take into account the rights of each individual involved and the duties of school personnel.

3. School psychologists' concerns for protecting the rights and welfare of children are communicated to the school administration and staff as the top priority in determining services.

4. School psychologists understand the public policy process to assist them in their efforts to advocate for children, parents, and systems.

B. SERVICE DELIVERY

1. School psychologists are knowledgeable of the organization, philosophy, goals, objectives, and methodologies of the setting in which they are employed.

2. School psychologists recognize that an understanding of the goals, processes, and legal requirements of their particular workplace is essential for effective functioning within that setting.
3. School psychologists attempt to become integral members of the client service systems to which they are assigned. They establish clear roles for themselves within that system.
4. School psychologists who provide services to several different groups may encounter situations in which loyalties are conflicted. As much as possible, the stance of the school psychologist is made known in advance to all parties to prevent misunderstandings.
5. School psychologists promote changes in their employing agencies and community service systems that will benefit their clients.

C. ASSESSMENT AND INTERVENTION

1. School psychologists maintain the highest standard for educational and psychological assessment and direct and indirect interventions.
    a. In conducting psychological, educational, or behavioral evaluations or in providing therapy, counseling, or consultation services, due consideration is given to individual integrity and individual differences.
    b. School psychologists respect differences in age, gender, sexual orientation, and socioeconomic, cultural, and ethnic backgrounds. They select and use appropriate assessment or treatment procedures, techniques, and strategies. Decision-making related to assessment and subsequent interventions is primarily data-based.
2. School psychologists are knowledgeable about the validity and reliability of their instruments and techniques, choosing those that have up-to-date standardization data and are applicable and appropriate for the benefit of the child.
3. School psychologists use multiple assessment methods such as observations, background information, and information from other professionals, to reach comprehensive conclusions.
4. School psychologists use assessment techniques, counseling and therapy procedures, consultation techniques, and other direct and indirect service methods that the profession considers to be responsible, research-based practice.
5. School psychologists do not condone the use of psychological or educational assessment techniques, or the misuse of the information these techniques provide, by unqualified persons in any way, including teaching, sponsorship, or supervision.
6. School psychologists develop interventions that are appropriate to the presenting problems and are consistent with data collected. They modify

or terminate the treatment plan when the data indicate the plan is not achieving the desired goals.

7. School psychologists use current assessment and intervention strategies that assist in the promotion of mental health in the children they serve.

D. REPORTING DATA AND CONFERENCE RESULTS

1. School psychologists ascertain that information about children and other clients reaches only authorized persons.
   a. School psychologists adequately interpret information so that the recipient can better help the child or other clients.
   b. School psychologists assist agency recipients to establish procedures to properly safeguard confidential material.
2. School psychologists communicate findings and recommendations in language readily understood by the intended recipient. These communications describe potential consequences associated with the proposals.
3. School psychologists prepare written reports in such form and style that the recipient of the report will be able to assist the child or other clients. Reports should emphasize recommendations and interpretations; unedited computer-generated reports, pre-printed "check-off" or "fill-in-the-blank" reports, and reports that present only test scores or global statements regarding eligibility for special education without specific recommendations for intervention are seldom useful. Reports should include an appraisal of the degree of confidence that could be assigned to the information. Alterations of previously released reports should be done only by the original author.
4. School psychologists review all of their written documents for accuracy, signing them only when correct. Interns and practicum students are clearly identified as such, and their work is co-signed by the supervising school psychologist. In situations in which more than one professional participated in the data collection and reporting process, school psychologists assure that sources of data are clearly identified in the written report.
5. School psychologists comply with all laws, regulations, and policies pertaining to the adequate storage and disposal of records to maintain appropriate confidentiality of information.

E. USE OF MATERIALS AND TECHNOLOGY

1. School psychologists maintain test security, preventing the release of underlying principles and specific content that would undermine the

use of the device. School psychologists are responsible for the security requirements specific to each instrument used.

2. School psychologists obtain written prior consent or they remove identifying data presented in public lectures or publications.

3. School psychologists do not promote or encourage inappropriate use of computer-generated test analyses or reports. In accordance with this principle, a school psychologist would not offer an unedited computer report as his or her own writing or use a computer-scoring system for tests in which he or she has no training. They select scoring and interpretation services on the basis of accuracy and professional alignment with the underlying decision rules.

4. School psychologists maintain full responsibility for any technological services used. All ethical and legal principles regarding confidentiality, privacy, and responsibility for decisions apply to the school psychologist and cannot be transferred to equipment, software companies, or data-processing departments.

5. Technological devices should be used to improve the quality of client services. School psychologists will resist applications of technology that ultimately reduce the quality of service.

6. To ensure confidentiality, student/client records are not transmitted electronically without a guarantee of privacy. In line with this principle, a receiving FAX machine must be in a secure location and operated by employees cleared to work with confidential files, and e-mail messages must be encrypted or else stripped of all information that identifies the student/client.

7. School psychologists do not accept any form of remuneration in exchange for data from their client data base without informed consent.

F. RESEARCH, PUBLICATION, AND PRESENTATION

1. When designing and implementing research in schools, school psychologists choose topics and employ research methodology, subject selection techniques, data-gathering methods, and analysis and reporting techniques that are grounded in sound research practice. School psychologists clearly identify their level of training and graduate degree on all communications to research participants.

2. Prior to initiating research, school psychologists working in agencies without review committees should have at least one other colleague, preferably a school psychologist, review the proposed methods.

3. School psychologists follow all legal procedures when conducting research, including following procedures related to informed consent, confidentiality, privacy, protection from harm or risks, voluntary participation,

and disclosure of results to participants. School psychologists demonstrate respect for the rights of and well-being of research participants.

4. In publishing reports of their research, school psychologists provide discussion of limitations of their data and acknowledge existence of disconfirming data, as well as alternate hypotheses and explanations of their findings.

5. School psychologists take particular care with information presented through various impersonal media (e.g., radio, television, public lectures, popular press articles, promotional materials.). Recipients should be informed that the information does not result from or substitute for a professional consultation. The information should be based on research and experience within the school psychologist's recognized sphere of competence. The statements should be consistent with these ethical principles and should not mistakenly represent the field of school psychology or the Association.

6. School psychologists uphold copyright laws in their publications and presentations and obtain permission from authors and copyright holders to reproduce other publications or materials. School psychologists recognize that federal law protects the rights of copyright holders of published works and authors of non-published materials.

7. When publishing or presenting research or other work, school psychologists do not plagiarize the works or ideas of others and acknowledge sources and assign credit to those whose ideas are reflected.

8. School psychologists do not publish or present fabricated or falsified data or results in their publications and presentations.

9. School psychologists make available data or other information upon which conclusions and claims reported in publications and presentations are based, provided that the data are needed to address a legitimate concern or need and that the confidentiality and other rights of all research participants are protected.

10. If errors are discovered after the publication or presentation of research and other information, school psychologists make efforts to correct errors by publishing errata, retractions, or corrections.

11. School psychologists accurately reflect the contributions of authors and other individuals in publications and presentations. Authorship credit and the order in which authors are listed are based on the relative contributions of the individual authors. Authorship credit is given only to individuals who have made substantial professional contributions to the research, publication, or presentation.

12. School psychologists only publish data or other information that make original contributions to the professional literature. School psychologists do not publish the same findings in two or more publications and

do not duplicate significant portions of their own previous publications without permission of copyright holders.

13. School psychologists who participate in reviews of manuscripts, proposals, and other materials for considertion for publication and presentation respect the confidentiality and proprietary rights of the authors. School psychologists who review professional materials limit their use of the materials to the activities relevant to the purposes of the professional review. School psychologists who review professional materials do not communicate the identity of the author, quote from the materials, or duplicate or circulate copies of the materials without the author's permission.

V. PROFESSIONAL PRACTICE SETTINGS—INDEPENDENT PRACTICE

A. RELATIONSHIP WITH EMPLOYERS

1. Some school psychologists are employed in a variety of settings, organizational structures, and sectors and, as such, may create a conflict of interest. School psychologists operating in these different settings recognize the importance of ethical standards and the separation of roles and take full responsibility for protecting and completely informing the consumer of all potential concerns.

2. School psychologists dually employed in independent practice and in a school district may not accept any form of remuneration from clients who are entitled to the same service provided by the school district employing the school psychologist. This includes children who attend the non-public schools within the school psychologist's district.

3. School psychologists in independent practice have an obligation to inform parents of any school psychological services available to them at no cost from the public or private schools prior to delivering such services for remuneration.

4. School psychologists working in both independent practice and employed by school districts conduct all independent practice outside of the hours of contracted public employment.

5. School psychologists engaged in independent practice do not use tests, materials, equipment, facilities, secretarial assistance, or other services belonging to the public sector employer unless approved in advance by the employer.

B. SERVICE DELIVERY

1. School psychologists conclude a financial agreement in advance of service delivery.
   a. School psychologists ensure to the best of their ability that the client clearly understands the agreement.
   b. School psychologists neither give nor receive any remuneration for referring children and other clients for professional services.
2. School psychologists in independent practice adhere to the conditions of a contract until service thereunder has been performed, the contract has been terminated by mutual consent, or the contract has otherwise been legally terminated.
3. School psychologists in independent practice prevent misunderstandings resulting from their recommendations, advice, or information. Most often, direct consultation between the school psychologist in private practice and the school psychologist responsible for the student in the public sector will resolve minor differences of opinion without unnecessarily confusing the parents, yet keep the best interests of the student or client in mind.
4. Personal diagnosis and therapy are not given by means of public lectures, newspaper columns, magazine articles, radio and television programs, or mail. Any information shared through mass media activities is general in nature and is openly declared to be so.

C. ANNOUNCEMENTS/ADVERTISING

1. Appropriate announcement of services, advertising, and public media statements may be necessary for school psychologists in independent practice. Accurate representations of training, experience, services provided, and affiliation are done in a restrained manner. Public statements must be based on sound and accepted theory, research, and practice.
2. Listings in telephone directories are limited to the following: name/names, highest relevant degree, state certification/licensure status, national certification status, address, telephone number, brief identification of major areas of practice, office hours, appropriate fee information, foreign languages spoken, policy regarding third-party payments, and license number.
3. Announcements of services by school psychologists in independent practice are made in a formal, professional manner using the guidelines of V-C-2. Clear statements of purposes with unequivocal descriptions of the experiences to be provided are given. Education, training, and experience of all staff members are appropriately specified.

4. School psychologists in independent practice may use brochures in the announcement of services. The brochures may be sent to other professionals, schools, business firms, governmental agencies, and other similar organizations.
5. Announcements and advertisements of the availability of publications, products, and services for sale are professional and factual.
6. School psychologists in independent practice do not directly solicit clients for individual diagnosis, therapy, and for the provision of other school psychological services.
7. School psychologists do not compensate in any manner a representative of the press, radio, or television in return for personal professional publicity in a news item.

References

Accredited doctoral programs in professional psychology: 1998. (1998). *American Psychologist, 53*(12), 1324-1335.

Accredited internship and postdoctoral programs for training in psychology: 1998. (1998). *American Psychologist, 53*(12), 1304-1323.

Agin, T. (1979). The school psychologist and collective bargaining: The brokerage of influence and professional concerns. *School Psychology Digest, 8,* 187-192.

Akron, Ohio, Public Schools. (1991). *Recommendations manual.* Akron, OH: Akron Public Schools, Psychological Services Staff.

Albayrak-Kaymak, D., & Dolek, N. (1997). New challenges facing school psychologists in Turkey. *World-Go-Round* (Newsletter of the International Association of School Psychologists), *24*(5), 4.

Albee, G. W. (1998). Fifty years of clinical psychology: Selling our soul to the devil. *Applied and Preventive Psychology, 7,* 189-194.

Algozzine, B., Christenson, S., & Ysseldyke, J. E. (1982). Probabilities associated with the referral to placement process. *Teacher Education and Special Education, 5,* 19-23.

Allen, W. (1993). Comprehensive contracted services: Assets to the field of school psychology. *Communiqué, 22*(1), 3-4.

Allensworth, D., Lawson, E., Nicholson, L., & Wyche, J. (Eds.). (1997). *Schools and health: Our nation's investment.* Washington, DC: National Academy Press.

Alpert, J. L. (1985). Change within a profession: Change, future, prevention, and school psychology. *American Psychologist, 40,* 1112-1121.

American Association of State Colleges and Universities. (n.d.). *The specialist degree.* Washington, DC: Author. (circa. 1968).

American Counseling Association. (1995). *ACA code of ethics and standards of practice.* Alexandria, VA: Author.

American Psychiatric Association. (1994). *Diagnostic and statistical manual of mental disorders* (4th ed.) Washington, DC: Author.

American Psychological Association. (1953). *Ethical standards of psychologists.* Washington, DC: Author.

American Psychological Association. (1981). Specialty guidelines for the delivery of services by school psychologists. In APA, *Specialty guidelines for the delivery of services* (pp. 33-44). Washington, DC: Author. See also *American Psychologist, 36,* 640-681.

American Psychological Association. (1985). *Standards for educational and psychological testing.* Washington, DC: Author.

American Psychological Association. (1986). *Guidelines for computer-based tests and interpretations.* Washington, DC: Author.

American Psychological Association. (1987a). Model act for state licensure of psychologists. *American Psychologist, 42,* 696-703.

American Psychological Association. (1987b). *General guidelines for providers of psychological services.* Washington, DC: Author.

American Psychological Association. (1989). *Ethical principles of psychologists.* Washington, DC: Author.

American Psychological Association. (1992). *Ethical principles of psychologists and code of conduct.* Washington, DC: Author. See also *American Psychologist, 47,* 1597-1611.

American Psychological Association. (1995). *Guidelines for engaging in the contractual provision of psychological services in schools.* Washington, DC: Author.

American Psychological Association. (1996). *Psychology/careers for the twenty-first century.* Washington, DC: Author.

American Psychological Association, Committee on Employment and Human Resources. (1986). The changing face of American psychology. *American Psychologist, 41,* 1311-1327.

American Psychological Association, Committee on Psychological Tests and Assessment. (1996a). *Statement on the disclosure of tests data.* Washington, DC: Author.

American Psychological Association, Office of Program Consultation and Accreditation, Education Directorate. (1996b). *Guidelines and principles for accreditation of programs in professional psychology: Vol. 1; Accreditation operating procedures of the Committee on Accreditation: Vol. 2.* Washington, DC: Author.

American Psychological Association. (1998, May). *Surviving and thriving in academia: A guide for women and ethnic minorities.* Washington, DC: Author.

American Psychological Association and American Association for Applied Psychology Committee on Graduate and Professional Training. (1945). Subcommittee report on graduate internship training in psychology. *Journal of Consulting Psychology, 9,* 243-266.

Anastasi, A. (1992, August). *A century of psychological testing: Origins, problems, and progress.* Paper presented at the annual meeting of the American Psychological Association, Washington, DC.

Anderson, W. T., Hohenshil, T. H., & Brown, D. T. (1984). Job satisfaction among practicing school psychologists: A national study. *School Psychology Review, 13,* 225-230.

Andrews, T. J., Wisniewski, J. J., & Mulick, J.A. (1997). Variables influencing teachers' decisions to refer children for school psychological assessment services. *Psychology in the Schools, 34,* 239-244.

Archival description of the specialty. (1998). *CDSPP Press* (Newsletter of the Council of Directors of School Psychology Programs), *17*(1), 8.

Arthur, A. Z. (1971). Applied training programmes of psychology in Canada: A survey. *The Canadian Psychologist, 12,* 46-65.

Association of Psychology Postdoctoral and Internship Centers. (1997). *APPIC directory of internship and postdoctoral programs in professional psychology 1997-1998.* Washington, DC: Author.

Association of State and Provincial Psychology Boards. (1998). *ASPPB model act for licensing psychologists.* Montgomery, AL: Author.

Association on Higher Education and Disability. (1997). *Guidelines for documentation of a learning disability in adolescents and adults.* Columbus, OH: Author. (Contact: AHEAD, P.O. Box 21192, Columbus, OH 43221-0192.)

Baer, D. M., & Bushell, D. (1981). The future of behavior analysis in the schools? Consider its recent past, and then ask a different question. *School Psychology Review, 10,* 259-270.

Bahr, M. W. (1996). Are school psychologists reform-minded? *Psychology in the Schools, 33,* 295-307.

Barbarin, O. A. (1992). Family functioning and school adjustment: Family systems perspectives. In F. J. Medway and T. P. Cafferty (Eds.), *School psychology: A social psychological perspective* (pp. 137-163). Hillsdale, NJ: Erlbaum.

Bardon, J. I. (1979). How best to establish the identity of professional school psychology. *School Psychology Digest, 8,* 162-167.

Bardon, J. I. (1983). Psychology applied to education: A specialty in search of an identity. *American Psychologist, 38,* 185-196.

Bardon, J. I. (1986). Psychology and schooling: The interrelationships among persons, processes, and products. In S. N. Elliott & J. C. Witt (Eds.), *The delivery of psychological services in schools: Concepts, processes, and issues* (pp. 53-79). Hillsdale, NJ: Lawrence Erlbaum.

Bardon, J. I. (1987). The translation of research into practice in school psychology. *School Psychology Review, 16,* 317-328.

Bardon, J. I., & Bennett, V. C. (1974). *School psychology.* Englewood Cliffs, NJ: Prentice Hall.

Barona, A., & Garcia, E. E. (Eds.). (1990). *Children at risk: Poverty, minority status, and other issues in educational equity.* Washington, DC: National Association of School Psychologists.

Bartell, R. (1990). School psychology in Canada: The state of the art in Manitoba. *Canadian Journal of School Psychology, 6,* 23-31.

Bartell, R. (1995). Historical perspective on the role and practice of school psychology. *Canadian Journal of School Psychology, 11* (2), 133-137.

Bartell, R. (1996). The argument for a paradigm shift or what's in a name? *Canadian Journal of School Psychology, 12,* 86-90.

Bartell, R., & Saklofske, D. (1998). *Proposal for national standards for Canadian school psychologists.* A draft paper adopted by the Canadian Association of School Psychologists.

Batsche, G. M. (1992). Training in school psychology: Future oriented or mired in the past? *Communiqué, 20*(7), 2.

Batsche, G. M. (1996). National certification in school psychology. In T. K. Fagan & P. G. Warden (Eds.), *Historical encyclopedia of school psychology* (pp. 223-225). Westport, CT: Greenwood Press.

Batsche, G. M., Knoff, H. M., & Peterson, D. W. (1989). Trends in credentialing and practice standards. *School Psychology Review, 18,* 193-202.

Batts, J., & Grossman, F. (1997). Frequently asked questions (FAQs): Ethics and standards. *Communiqué, 25*(6), 16.

Beal, A. L. & Service, J. (1995). Submission to an Ontario Board of Education concerning proposed reduction in psychological services. *Canadian Journal of School Psychology, 11*(2), 90-92.

Bender, R. H. (1991). If you can count it, you can improve it: Total quality transformation tools sculpt better handle on system. *The School Administrator, 9* (48), 24-26, 35.

Benjamin, L. T., & Shields, S. A. (1990). Leta Stetter Hollingworth (1886-1939). In A. N. O'Connell & N. F. Russo (Eds.), *Women in psychology: A bio-bibliographic sourcebook* (pp. 173-183). Westport, CT: Greenwood.

Benson, A. J. (1985). School psychology service configurations: A regional approach. *School Psychology Review, 14,* 421-428.

Bent, R. J., Packard, R. E., & Goldberg, R. W. (1999). The American Board of Professional Psychology, 1947 to 1997: A historical perspective. *Professional Psychology: Research and Practice, 30,* 65-73.

Bergan, J. R. (1985). The future of school psychology. In J. R. Bergan (Ed.), *School psychology in contemporary society: An introduction* (pp. 421-437). Columbus, OH: Charles E. Merrill.

Bernard, J. L. (1975). Due process in dropping the unsuitable clinical student. *Professional Psychology, 6,* 275-278.

Berne, E. (1964). *Games people play: The psychology of human relationships.* New York: Grove.

Bersoff, D. N. (1981). Testing and the law. *American Psychologist, 36*, 1047-1056.

Bersoff, D. N. (1982a). Larry P. and PASE: Judicial report cards on the validity of individual intelligence tests. In T. Kratochwill (Ed.), *Advances in school psychology: Vol. 2* (pp. 61-95). Hillsdale, NJ: Erlbaum.

Bersoff, D. N. (1982b). The legal regulation of school psychology. In C. R. Reynolds & T. B. Gutkin (Eds.), *The handbook of school psychology* (pp. 1043-1074). New York: John Wiley.

Beutler, L. E., & Fisher, D. (1994). Combined specialty training in counseling, clinical, and school psychology: An idea whose time has returned. *Professional Psychology: Research and Practice, 25*, 62-69.

Bevan, W. (1981). On coming of age among the professions. *School Psychology Review, 10*(2), 127-137.

Biddle, B. J. (1997). Foolishness, dangerous nonsense, and real correlates of state differences in achievement. *Phi Delta Kappan, 79*(1), 9-13.

Blagg, D., Durbin, K., Kelly, C., McHugh, C., & Safranski, S. (1997). School psychologists as administrators: Five journeys. *Communiqué, 25*(8), 14-15.

Bogie, M. A. (1997, October). *Shopping the market: Finding the malpractice insurance policy that fits your needs.* Amityville, NY: The American Professional Agency.

Bonham, S. J., & Grover, E. C. (1961). *The history and development of school psychology in Ohio.* Columbus: Ohio Department of Education.

Bontrager, T., & Wilczenski, F. L. (1997). School psychology practice in an era of educational reform. *Communiqué, 25*(8) 28-29.

Bowers, J. E. (1962). Wanted: trained psychologists for employment in school systems. *The Canadian Psychologist, 3*, 51-52.

Boxley, R., Drew, C., & Rangel, D. (1986). Clinical trainee impairment in APA approved internship programs. *The Clinical Psychologist, 39*, 49-52.

Bracey, G. W. (1991). Why can't they be like we were? *Phi Delta Kappan, 73*, 104-117.

Brandt, J. (1992). Response to Hall and Slate: Maine may offer important lessons. *Communiqué, 21*(4), 20.

Brandt, J. E. (1996). Prereferral assessment. In T. K. Fagan & P. G. Warden (Eds.) *Historical encyclopedia of school psychology.* Westport, CT: Greenwood.

Bronfenbrenner, U. (1979). *The ecology of human development.* Cambridge, MA: Harvard University Press.

Brooks, B., & Seigel, P. (1996). *The scared child: Helping kids overcome traumatic events.* New York: John Wiley.

Brotemarkle, R. A. (Ed.). (1931). *Clinical psychology: Studies in honor of Lightner Witmer to commemorate the thirty-fifth anniversary of the founding of the first psychological clinic.* Philadelphia: University of Pennsylvania Press.

Brown, D. T. (1989). The evolution of entry-level training in school psychology: Are we now approaching the doctoral level? *School Psychology Review, 18*, 11-15.

Brown, D. T., Cardon, B. W., Coulter, W. A., & Meyers, J. (Eds.). (1982). The Olympia proceedings [Special issue]. *School Psychology Review, 11*(2).

Brown, M. B., Hohenshil, T. H., & Brown, D. T. (1998). Job satisfaction of school psychologists in the United States. *School Psychology International, 19*(1), 79-89.

Brown, D. T., & Lindstrom, J. P. (1977). *Directory of school psychology training programs in the United States and Canada.* Washington, DC: National Association of School Psychologists.

Brown, D. T., & Minke, K. M. (1984). *Directory of school psychology training programs.* Washington, DC: National Association of School Psychologists.

Brown, D. T., & Minke, K. M. (1986). School psychology graduate training: A comprehensive analysis. *American Psychologist, 41,* 1328-1338.

Brown, M. B., Swigart, M. L., Bolen, L. M., Hall, C. W., & Webster, R. T. (1998). Doctoral and nondoctoral practicing school psychologists: Are there differences? *Psychology in the Schools, 35*(4), 347-354.

Bruner, J. S., Oliver, R. R., & Greenfield, P. M. (1966). *Studies in cognitive growth.* New York: John Wiley.

Butler, A. S., & Maher, C. A. (1981). Conflict and special service teams: Perspectives and suggestions for school psychologists. *Journal of School Psychology, 19,* 62-70.

Byrd, B., Goldsworthy, S., & Robertson, B. (1999, January 24). Education needs more than band-aids. *The Commercial Appeal* (Memphis), pp. B3-B4.

California Association of School Psychologists. (1991). CASP position paper. The role of assessment in California schools: Ensuring student success. *CASP Today, 4*(August), 7.

Canadian Association of School Psychologists. (n.d.). *Standards for professional practice in school psychology.* Winnipeg: Author.

Canadian Psychological Association. (1991*). Canadian code of ethics for psychologists (Rev. ed.).* Ottawa: Author.

Canadian Register of Health Service Providers. (1999). *1999 directory.* Ottawa: Author.

Canter, A. (1990a). Issues related to third-party reimbursement. *Communiqué, 19*(3), 14.

Canter, A. (1990b). Policy needed for handling parents' requests for protocols. *Communiqué, 19*(2), 2.

Canter, A. (1991a). Alternative sources of funding may be mixed blessing. *Communiqué, 19*(6), 16.

Canter, A. S. (1991b). Effective psychological services for all students: A data based model of service delivery. In G. Stoner, M. R. Shinn, & H. M. Walker (Eds.), *Interventions of achievement and behavior problems* (pp. 49-78). Washington, DC: National Association of School Psychologists.

Canter, A. S., & Carroll, S. A. (Eds.). (1998). *Helping children at home and school: Handouts from your school psychologist.* Bethesda, MD: National Association of School Psychologists.

Canter, A., & Crandall, A. (Eds.). (1994). *Professional advocacy resource manual: Preserving school-based positions.* Washington, DC: National Association of School Psychologists.

Caplan, G. (1970). *The theory and practice of mental health consultation.* New York: Basic Books.

Cardon, B., Kuriloff, P., & Phillips, B. N. (Eds.). (1975). Law and the school psychologist: Challenge and opportunity [Special issue]. *Journal of School Psychology, 13*(4).

Carlson, H. S. (1978). The AASPB story. *American Psychologist, 33,* 486-495.

Carlson, J. F., & Martin, S. P. (1997, April). *Responsible use of computer-based test interpretation and report generation software: Implications for practice.* Paper presented at the annual meeting of the National Association of School Psychologists, Anaheim, CA.

Carlson, C. I., & Sincavage, J. M. (1987). Family-oriented school psychology practice: Results of a national survey of NASP members. *School Psychology Review, 16,* 519-526.

Carney, P. (1995). Submission to an Ontario Board of Education from the Canadian Association of School Psychologists. *Canadian Journal of School Psychology,* 11(2), 89.

Carney, P., & Cole, E. (1995). Editorial: Advocacy issues and events in school psychology. *Canadian Journal of School Psychology, 11*(2), i-i.

Cattell, J. McK. (1890). Mental tests and measurement. *Mind, 15,* 373-380.

Catterall, C. D. (1967). *Strategies for prescriptive interventions.* Santa Clara, CA: Santa Clara Unified School District.

Catterall, C. (Ed.). (1976). *Psychology in the schools in international perspectives: Vol. 1.* Columbus, OH: Author.

Catterall, C. (Ed.). (1977). *Psychology in the schools in international perspectives: Vol. 2.* Columbus, OH: Author.

Catterall, C. (Ed.). (1979a). *Psychology in the schools in international perspectives: Vol. 3.* Columbus, OH: Author.

Catterall, C. (1979b). State of the art. In C. Catterall (Ed.), *Psychology in the schools in international perspective: Vol. 3* (pp. 193-219). Columbus, OH: Author. (Now available from International School Psychology Association.)

CDSPP Doctoral Level Internship Guidelines. (1998). *CDSPP Press* (Newsletter of the Council of Directors of School Psychology Programs), *16*(2), 7-8.

Centra, J. A., & Potter, D. A. (1980). School and teacher effects: An interrelational model. *Review of Educational Research, 50,* 273-291.

Chernay, G. (n.d.). *Accreditation and the role of the Council on Postsecondary Accreditation.* Washington, DC: Council on Postsecondary Accreditation.

Christenson, S. L., & Conoley, J. C. (Eds.). (1992). *Home-school collaboration: Enhancing children's academic and social competence.* Washington, DC: National Association of School Psychologists.

Christenson, S.L., Rounds, T., & Gorney, D. (1992). Family factors and student achievement: An avenue to student's success. *School Psychology Quarterly, 7,* 178-206.

Cincinnati Public Schools, Board of Education. (1912). *83rd annual report of the board of education.* Cincinnati, OH: Author.

City of Chicago, Board of Education. (1941). *Bureau of Child Study and the Chicago adjustment service plan.* Chicago: Author.

City of New York, Board of Education. (1938). *Bureau of Child Guidance five year report 1932-1937.* New York: Author.

Clair, T. N., & Kiraly, J. (1971). Can school psychology survive in the 70's? *Professional Psychology, 2,* 383-388.

Clay, R. A. (1996, June). New state laws jeopardize fate of school psychology. *APA Monitor, 27*(6), 25.

Clinchy, E. (1998). The educationally challenged American school district. *Phi Delta Kappan, 80*(4), 272-277.

Cobb, C. T. (1990). School psychology in the 1980s and 1990s: A context for change and definition. In T. B. Gutkin & C. R. Reynolds (Eds.), *The hand book of school psychology* (pp. 21-31). New York: John Wiley.

Cobb, C. T. (1992, August). *Will there be a school psychology symposium at the 150th APA convention?* Paper presented at the annual meeting of the American Psychological Association, Washington, DC.

Cohen, R. D. (1985). Child-saving and progressivism, 1885-1915. In J. M. Hawes & N. R. Hiner (Eds.), *American childhood: A research guide and historical handbook* (pp. 273-309). Westport, CT: Greenwood.

Cohen, R. J., Swerdlik, M. E., & Phillips, S. M. (1996). *Psychological testing and assessment: An introduction to tests and measurement* (3rd ed.). Mountain View, CA: Mayfield.

Cole, E. (1992). Characteristics of students referred to school teams: Implications for preventive psychological services. *Canadian Journal of School Psychology, 8,* 23-36.

Cole, E. (1995). Responding to school violence: Understanding today and tomorrow. *Canadian Journal of School Psychology, 11*(2), 108-116.

Cole, E. (1996). An integrative perspective on school psychology. *Canadian J Journal of School Psychology, 6,* 115-121.

Cole, E. (1998). Immigrant and refugee children: Challenges for education and mental health services. *Canadian Journal of School Psychology, 14* (1), 36-50.

Cole, E., & Siegel, J. A. (Eds.). (1990). *Effective consultation in school psychology.* Toronto: Hogrefe & Huber.

Connolly, L. M., & Reschly, D. (1990). The school psychology crisis of the 1990s. *Communiqué, 19*(3), 1–12.

Conoley, J. C. (1989). The school psychologist as a community/family service provider. In R. C. D'Amato & R. S. Dean (Eds.), *The school psychologist in nontraditional settings: Integrating clients, services, and settings* (pp. 33-65). Hillsdale, NJ: Erlbaum.

Conoley, J. C. (1992, August). *2042: A prospective look at school psychology.* Paper presented at the annual meeting of the American Psychological Association, Washington, DC.

Conoley, J. C., & Conoley, C. W. (1992). *School consultation: Practice and training* (2nd ed.). New York: Macmillan.

Conoley, J. C., & Gutkin, T. B. (1986). Educating school psychologists for the real world. *School Psychology Review, 15*, 457-465.

Conoley, J. C., & Henning-Stout, M. (1990). Gender issues and school psychology. In T. R. Kratochwill (Ed.), *Advances in school psychology: Vol. 7* (pp. 7-31). Hillsdale, NJ: Erlbaum.

Constable, R., McDonald, S., & Flynn, J. P. (Eds.). (1999). *School social work: Practice, policy & research perspectives* (4th ed.). Chicago: Lyceum Books.

Cook, S. W. (1958). The psychologist of the future: Scientist, professional, or both, *American Psychologist, 13*, 635-644.

Cornwall, A. (1990). Social validation of psycho-educational assessment reports. *Journal of Learning Disabilities, 23*, 413-416.

Cravens, H. (1985). Child-saving in the age of professionalism, 1915-1930. In J. M. Hawes & N. R. Hiner (Eds.), *American childhood. A research guide and historical handbook* (pp. 415-488). Westport, CT: Greenwood.

Cravens, H. (1987). Applied science and public policy: The Ohio Bureau of Juvenile Research and the problem of juvenile delinquency 1913-1930. In M. M. Sokal (Ed.), *Psychological testing and American society 1890-1930* (pp. 158-194). New Brunswick, NJ: Rutgers University Press.

Cremin, L. A. (1988). *American education: The metropolitan experience 1876-1980.* New York: Harper & Row.

Crespi, T. D. (1998). Considerations for clinical supervision. *The Texas School Psychologist, 15*(2), 14-15.

Crespi, T. D., & Fischetti, B. A. (1997). Counseling licensure: An emerging credential for health care professionals. *Communiqué, 25*(5), 17-18.

Crossland, C. L., Fox, B, J., & Baker, R. (1982). Differential perceptions of role responsibilities among professionals in the public school. *Exceptional Children, 48*, 536-537.

Cubberley, E. P. (1909). *Changing conceptions of education.* Cambridge, MA: Riverside Press.

Cubberley, E. P. (Ed.). (1920). *Readings in the history of education.* Boston: Riverside Press.

Culbertson, F. (1975). Average students' needs and perceptions of school psychologists. *Psychology in the Schools, 12*, 191-196.

Cummings, J. A., Huebner, E. S., & McLeskey, J. (1985). Issues in the preservice preparation of school psychologists for rural settings. *School Psychology Review, 14*, 429-437.

Cunningham, J. (1994). *A contextual investigation of the international development of psychology in the schools.* Unpublished doctoral dissertation, University of Texas at Austin.

Cunningham, J., & Oakland, T. (1998). International School Psychology Association Guidelines for the Preparation of School Psychologists. *School Psychology International, 19*, 19-30.

Curtis, M. J., & Batsche, G. M. (1991). Meeting the needs of children and families: Opportunities and challenges for school psychology training programs. *School Psychology Review, 20,* 565-577.

Curtis, M., Batsche, G., & Tanous, J. (1996). Nondoctoral school psychology threatened: The Texas experience. *Communiqué, 24*(8), 1, 6-8.

Curtis, M., Graden, J., & Reschly, D. (1992). *School psychology as a profession: Demographics, professional practices, and job satisfaction.* Symposium conducted at the annual meeting of the National Association of School Psychologists, Nashville, TN.

Curtis, M. J., Hunley, S. A., & Prus, J. R. (Eds.). (1998). *Credentialing requirements for school psychologists.* Bethesda, MD: National Association of School Psychologists.

Curtis, M. J., Hunley, S. A., Walker, K. J., & Baker, A. C. (1999). Demographic characteristics and professional practices in school psychology. *School Psychology Review, 28,* 104-116.

Curtis, M. J., & Meyers, J. (1985). Best practices in school-based consultation: Guidelines for effective practice. In A. Thomas & J. Grimes (Eds.), *Best practices in school psychology* (pp. 79-94). Kent, OH: National Association of School Psychologists.

Curtis, M. J., & Zins, J. E. (1986). The organization and structuring of psychological services within educational settings. In S. N. Elliott & J. C. Witt (Eds.), *The delivery of psychological services in schools: Concepts, processes, and issues* (pp. 109-138). Hillsdale, NJ: Erlbaum.

Curtis, M. J., & Zins, J. E. (1989). Trends in training and accreditation. *School Psychology Review, 18,* 182-192.

Cutts, N. E. (Ed.). (1955). *School psychologists at mid-century.* Washington, DC: American Psychological Association.

Daley, C. E., Nagle, R. J., & Onwuegbuzie, A. J. (1998, April). *Ethics training in school psychology in the United States.* Paper presented at the annual meeting of the National Association of School Psychologists, Orlando, FL.

D'Amato, R. C., & Dean, R. S. (Eds.). (1989). *The school psychologist in nontraditional settings: Integrating clients, services, and settings.* Hillsdale, NJ: Erlbaum.

Dana, R. H., & May, W. T. (Eds.). (1987). *Internship training in professional psychology.* Washington, DC: Hemisphere.

Davis, J. M. (1988). The school psychologist in a community mental health center. *School Psychology Review, 17,* 435-439.

Dawson, D. (1980). Editorial. *The Alberta School Psychologist, 1*(2), 1.

Dawson, D. (1981, August). Editorial. *NASP Canada/Mexico Newsletter, 1,* 4-6.

Dawson, D. (1982, January). The future of school psychology in Canada. *NASP Canada/Mexico Newsletter, 2,* 4-8.

Dawson, P., Mendez, P., & Hyman, A. (1994,). Average school psychologist's salary tops $43,000. *Communiqué, 23*(1), 1, 6.

DeMers, S. T. (1993). The changing face of specialization in psychology. *The School Psychologist, 47*(l), 3, 8.

Deno, E. (1970). Special education as developmental capital. *Exceptional Children, 37,* 229-237.

Devore, J., & Fagan, T. (1979). Availability of professional non-teaching pupil services in rural and urban Tennessee school districts. *Educational Quest, 23*(1), 9-12.

Diana v. *California State Board of Education* (F. Supp. N.D. Cal. 1970).

DiVerde-Nushawg, N., & Walls, G. B. (1998). The implication of pager use for the therapeutic relationship in independent practice. *Professional Psychology: Research and Practice, 29,* 368-372.

Dobson, K., & Dobson, D. (Eds.). (1993). *Professional psychology in Canada.* Toronto: Hogrefe & Huber.

Dorken, H. (1958). The functions of psychologists in mental health services. *The Canadian Psychologist, 7,* 89-95.

Dorken, H., Walker, C. B., & Wake, F. R. (1960). A 15-year review of Canadian trained psychologists. *The Canadian Psychologist, 1,* 123-130.

Duis, S., Rothlisberg, B., & Hargrove, L. (1995). *Collaborative consultation: Are both school psychologists and teachers equally trained?* Paper presented at the annual meeting of the Council for Exceptional Children, Indianapolis, IN.

Dumont, F. (1989). School psychology in Canada: Views on its status. In P. Saigh & T. Oakland (Eds.), *International perspectives on psychology in the schools* (pp. 211-222). Hillsdale, NJ: Erlbaum.

Dunn, L. M. (1973). An overview. In L. M. Dunn (Ed.), *Exceptional children in the schools: Special education in transition* (pp. 1-62). New York: Holt, Rinchart & Winston.

Dwyer, K. (1991). Children with emotional and behavioral disorders: An under-served population. *Communiqué, 20*(1), 21.

Dwyer, K., Osher, D., & Warger, C. (1998). *Early warning, timely response: A guide to safe schools.* Washington, DC: U.S. Department of Education, Special Education and Rehabilitative Services.

Eberst, N. D. (1984). *Sources of funding of school psychologists.* Washington, DC: National Association of School Psychologists.

Elias, C. L. (1999). The school psychologist as expert witness: Strategies and issues in the courtroom. *School Psychology Review, 28,* 44-59.

Elliott, S. N., & Witt, J. C. (Eds.). (1986a). *The delivery of psychological services in schools: Concepts, processes, and issues.* Hillsdale, NJ: Erlbaum.

Elliott, S. N., & Witt, J. C. (1986b). Fundamental questions and dimensions of psychological service delivery in schools. In S. N. Elliott & J. C. Witt (Eds.), *The delivery of psychological services in schools: Concepts, processes, and issues* (pp. 1-26). Hillsdale, NJ: Erlbaum.

Elliott, S. N., Witt, J. C., & Kratochwill, T. R. (1991). Selecting, implementing, and evaluating classroom interventions. In G. Stoner, M. R. Shinn, & & H. M. Walker (Eds.), *Interventions for achievement and behavior problems* (pp. 99-135). Silver Spring, MD: National Association of School Psychologists.

Engin, A. W. (1983). National organizations: Professional identity. In G. W. Hynd (Ed.), *The school psychologist: An introduction* (pp. 27-44). Syracuse, NY: Syracuse University Press.

Engin, A. W., & Johnson, R. (1983). School psychology training and practice: The NASP perspective. In T. R. Kratochwill (Ed.), *Advances in school psychology: Vol. 3* (pp. 21-44). Hillsdale, NJ: Erlbaum.

English, H. B. (1938). Organization of the American Association of Applied Psychologists. *Journal of Consulting Psychology, 2,* 7-16.

English, H. B., & English, A. C. (1958). *A comprehensive dictionary of psychological and psychoanalytic terms: A guide to usage.* New York: Longmans, Green.

Erchul, W. P., & Raven, B. H. (1997). Social power in school consultation: A contemporary view of French and Raven's bases of power model. *Journal of School Psychology, 35*(2), 137-171.

Erchul, W. P., Scott, S. S., Dombalis, A. O., & Schulte, A. C. (1989). Characteristics and perceptions of beginning doctoral students in school psychology. *Professional School Psychology, 4*(2), 103-111.

Ethics Committee issues statement on services by telephone, teleconferencing and internet. (1998, January). *APA Monitor, 29*(1), 38.

Examination for License as Psychologist (announcement). (1925, December 29). Department of Education, The City of New York, Office of the Board of Examiners.

Fagan, T. K. (1985). Sources for the delivery of school psychological services during 1890-1930. *School Psychology Review, 14,* 378-382.

Fagan, T. K. (1986a). The evolving literature of school psychology. *School Psychology Review, 15,* 430-440.

Fagan, T. K. (1986b). The historical origins and growth of programs to prepare school psychologists in the United States. *Journal of School Psychology, 24,* 9-22.

Fagan, T. K. (1986c). School psychology's dilemma: Reappraising solutions and directing attention to the future. *American Psychologist, 41,* 851-861. See also *School Psychology Review, 16*(l).

Fagan, T. K. (1987a). Gesell: The first school psychologist. Part II. Practice and significance. *School Psychology Review, 16,* 399-409.

Fagan, T. K. (1987b). *Trends in the development of United States school psychology with implications for Canadian school psychology.* Paper presented at the first annual meeting of the Canadian Association of School Psychologists, Winnipeg.

Fagan, T. K. (1988a). The first school psychologist in Oklahoma. *Communiqué, 17*(3), 19.

Fagan, T. K. (1988b). The historical improvement of the school psychology service ratio: Implications for future employment. *School Psychology Review, 17,* 447-458.

Fagan, T. K. (1989a). Obituary: Norma Estelle Cutts. *American Psychologist, 44,* 1236.

Fagan, T. K. (1989b). School psychology: Where next. *Canadian Journal of School Psychology, 5,* 1-7.

Fagan, T. K. (1990a). Best practices in the training of school psychologists: Considerations for trainers, prospective entry-level and advanced students. In A. Thomas & J. Grimes (Eds.), *Best practices in school psychology: II* (pp. 723-741). Washington, DC: National Association of School Psychologists.

Fagan, T. K. (1990b). Contributions of Leta Hollingworth to school psychology. *Roeper Review, 12*(3), 157-161.

Fagan, T. K. (1990c). Research on the history of school psychology: Recent developments, significance, resources, and future directions. In T. R. Kratochwill (Ed.), *Advances in school psychology: Vol. 7* (pp. 151-182). Hillsdale, NJ: Erlbaum.

Fagan, T. K. (1992). Compulsory schooling, child study, clinical psychology, and special education: Origins of school psychology. *American Psychologist, 47*, 236-243.

Fagan, T. K. (1993). Separate but equal: School psychology's search for organizational identity. *Journal of School Psychology, 31*, 3-90.

Fagan, T. K. (1994). A critical appraisal of the NASP's first 25 years. *School Psychology Review, 23*(4), 604-618.

Fagan, T. K. (1995). Trends in the history of school psychology in the United States. In A. Thomas, & J. Grimes (Eds.), *Best practices in school psychology: III,* (pp. 59-67). Washington, DC: National Association of School Psychologists.

Fagan, T. K. (1996a). A history of Division 16 (School Psychology): Running twice as fast. In D. A. Dewsbury (Ed.), *Unification through division: Histories of the divisions of the American Psychological Association: Vol. 1* (pp. 101-135). Washington, DC: American Psychological Association.

Fagan, T. K. (1996b). Historical perspective on the role and practice of school psychology. *Canadian Journal of School Psychology, 6*(1), 83-85.

Fagan, T. K. (1997). Culminating experiences in NASP approved non-doctoral school psychology training programs. *Trainers' Forum, 16*(1). Insert.

Fagan, T. K. (1999). Training school psychologists before there were school psychologist training programs: A history 1890-1930. In C. R. Reynolds & T. B. Gutkin (Eds.), *The handbook of school psychology* (pp. 2-33). New York: John Wiley.

Fagan, T. K., & Delugach, F. J. (1984). Literary origins of the term "school psychologist." *School Psychology Review, 13*, 216-220.

Fagan, T. K., Delugach, F. J., Mellon, M., & Schlitt, P. (1985). *A bibliographic guide to the literature of professional school psychology 1890-1985.* Washington, DC: National Association of School Psychologists.

Fagan, T. K., Gorin, S., & Tharinger, D. (2000). National Association of School Psychologists and the Division of School Psychology, APA: Now and beyond. *School Psychology Review, 29*(4), in press.

Fagan, T. K., Hensley, L. T., & Delugach, F. J. (1986). The evolution of organizations for school psychologists in the United States. *School Psychology Review, 15*, 127-135.

Fagan, T. K., & Schicke, M. C. (1994). The service ratio in large school districts: Historical and contemporary perspectives. *Journal of School Psychology, 32,* 305-312.

Fagan, T. K., & Sheridan, S. M. (Guest Eds.). (2000). Miniseries: School psychology in the 21st century. *School Psychology Review, 29*(4), in press.

Fagan, T. K. & Warden, P. G. (Eds.) (1996). *Historical encyclopedia of school psychology.* Westport, CT: Greenwood.

Fagan, T. K., & Wells, P. D. (1999). Frances Mullen: Her life and contributions to school psychology. *School Psychology International, 20,* 91-102.

Fagan, T. K., & Wells, P. D. (2000). History and status of school psychology accreditation in the United States. *School Psychology Review, 29,* 28-58.

Fagan. T., K., & Wise, P. S. (1994). *School psychology: Past, present, and future.* White Plains, NY: Longman.

Fairchild, T. N, (1975). Accountability: Practical suggestions for school psychologists. *Journal of School Psychology, 13,* 149-159.

Fairchild, T. N., & Seeley, T. J. (1996). Evaluation of school psychological services: A case illustration. *Psychology in the Schools, 33,* 46-55.

Fairchild, T. N., & Zins, J. E. (1992). Accountability practices of school psychologists: 1991 national survey. *School Psychology Review, 21,* 617-627,

Fairchild, T. N., Zins, J. E., & Grimes, J. (1983). *Improving school psychology through accountability* (filmstrip and manual). Washington, DC: National Association of School Psychologists.

Farling, W. H., & Hoedt, K. C. (1971). *National survey of school psychologists.* Washington, DC: National Association of School Psychologists.

Featherstone, H. (1980). *A difference in the family: Living with a disabled child.* New York. Penguin.

Ferguson, D. G. (1963). *Pupil personnel services.* New York: Center for Applied Research in Education.

Field, A. J. (1976). Educational expansion in mid-nineteenth-century Massachusetts: Human capital formation or structural reinforcement? *Harvard Educational Review, 46,* 521-552.

Fine, M. J. (Ed.). (1991). *Collaboration with parents of exceptional children.* Brandon, VT: Clinical Psychology Publishing.

Fireoved, R., & Cancelleri, R. (1985). What training programs need to emphasize: Notes from the field. *Trainers' Forum, 5*(1), 4-5.

Fischer, L., & Sorenson, G. P. (1991). *School law for counselors, psychologists, and social workers.* New York: Longman.

Fischetti, B. A., & Crespi, T. D. (1997). Clinical supervision: School psychology at a crossroad. *Communiqué, 25*(6), 18.

Fischetti, B. A., & Crespi, T. D. (1999). Clinical supervision for school psychologists: National practices, trends, and future implications. *School Psychology International, 20*(3), 278-288.

Fish, M. C., & Massey, R. (1991). Systems in school psychology practice: A preliminary investigation. *Journal of School Psychology, 29,* 361-366.

Fly, B. J., van Bark, W. P., Weinman, L., Kitchener, K. S., & Lang, P. R. (1997). Ethical transgressions of psychology graduate students: Critical incidents with implications for training. *Professional Psychology: Research and Practice, 28*, 492-495.

Forrest v. *Ambach*, 436 N.Y.S. 2d 119 (1980); 463 N.Y.S. 2d 84 (1983).

Fournier, C. J., & Perry, J. D. (1998). The report of the U.S. Commission on Child and Family Welfare: Implications for psychologists working with children and families. *Children's Services: Social Policy, Research, and Practice, 2*, 45-56.

Fowler, E., & Harrison, P. L. (1995). Best practices in continuing professional development for school psychologists. In A. Thomas & J. Grimes (Eds.), *Best practices in school psychology: III* (pp. 81-89). Bethesda, MD: National Association of School Psychologists.

Fox, R. E., Barclay, A. G., & Rodgers, D. A. (1982). The foundations of professional psychology. *American Psychologist, 37*, 306-312.

Frank, G. (1984). The Boulder Model: History, rationale, and critique. *Professional Psychology: Research and Practice, 15*, 417-435.

French, J. L. (1984). On the conception, birth, and early development of school psychology: With special reference to Pennsylvania. *American Psychologist, 3 9*, 976-987.

French, J. L. (1986). Books in school psychology: The first forty years. *Professional School Psychology, 1*, 267-277.

French, J. L. (1988). Grandmothers I wish I knew: Contributions of women to the history of school psychology. *Professional School Psychology, 3*, 51-68.

French, J. L. (1990). History of school psychology. In T. B. Gutkin & C. R. Reynolds (Eds.), *Handbook of school psychology* (pp. 3-20). New York: John Wiley.

Frisby, C. L. (1998). Formal communication within school psychology: A 1990-1994 journal citation analysis. *School Psychology Review, 27*(2), 304-316.

Frost, B. (1983). Invited address. Paper presented at the meeting of the Psychologists Association of Alberta, Calgary, Alberta, Canada.

Fry, M. A. (1986). The connections among educational and psychological research and the practice of school psychology. In S. N. Elliott & J. C. Witt (Eds.), *The delivery of psychological services in schools: Concepts, processes and issues* (pp. 305-327). Hillsdale, NJ: Erlbaum.

Gagne, N. (1990). The situation of Québec school psychology services in 1989. *The Canadian Journal of School Psychology, 6*(1), 39-45.

Gale, B., & Gale, L. (1989). *Stay or leave.* New York: Harper & Row.

Gallagher, J. J. (Ed.). (1980). *Parents and families of handicapped children.* [Special issue] *New Directions for Exceptional Children.* San Francisco: Jossey-Bass.

Gallagher, J. J., & Vietze, P. M. (Eds.). (1986). *Families of handicapped persons: Research, programs, and policy issues.* Baltimore, MD: Brookes.

Gargiulo, R. M. (1985). *Working with parents of exceptional children: A guide for professionals.* Boston: Houghton Mifflin.

Gelinas, P. J., & Gelinas, R. P. (1968). *A definitive study of your future in school psychology.* New York: Richards Rosen Press.

Gerken, K. C. (1981). The paraprofessional and the school psychologist: Can this be an effective team? *School Psychology Review, 10,* 470-479.

Gerner, M. (1981). The necessity of a teacher background for school psychologists. *Professional Psychology, 12,* 216-223.

Gerner, M. (1983). When face validity is only skin deep: Teaching experience and school psychology. *Communiqué, 11*(8), 2.

Gerner, M., & Genshaft, J. (1981). *Selecting a school psychology training program,* Washington, DC: National Association of School Psychologists.

Gibson, G., & Chard, K.M. (1994). Quantifying the effects of community mental health consultation interventions. *Consulting Psychology Journal: Practice and Research, 46* (4), 13-25.

Gickling, E. E., & Rosenfield, S. (1995). Best practices in curriculum-based assessment. In A. Thomas and J. Grimes (Eds.), *Best Practices in School Psychology: III* (pp. 587-595). Washington, D. C.: National Association of School Psychologists.

Glasser, W. (1990). *The quality school: Managing schools without coercion.* New York: Harper & Row.

Goddard, H. H. (1914). *The research department: What it is, what it is doing, what it hopes to do.* Vineland, NJ: The Training School.

Goh, D. S. (1977). Graduate training in school psychology. *Journal of School Psychology, 15,* 207-218.

Goldstein, A. P., Harootunian, B., & Conoley, J. C. (1994). *Student aggression: Prevention, management, and replacement training.* New York: Guilford.

Goldwasser, E., Meyers, J., Christenson, S., & Graden, J. (1983). The impact of P.L. 94-142 on the practice of school psychology: A national survey, *Psychology in the Schools, 20,* 153-165.

Goodman, M. (1973). Psychological services to schools: Meeting educational needs of tomorrow. *The Canadian Psychologist, 14,* 249-255.

Gopaul-McNicol, S. (1992). Guest editor's comments: Understanding and meeting the psychological and educational needs of African-American and Spanish-speaking students. *School Psychology Review, 21,* 529-531.

Gopaul-McNicol, S. A. (1997). A theoretical framework for training monolingual school psychologists to work with multilingual/multicultural children: An exploration of the major competencies. *Psychology in the Schools, 34,* 17-29.

Goslin, D. A. (1965). *The school in contemporary society.* Glenview, IL: Scott, Foresman.

Goslin, D. A. (1969). *Guidelines for the collection, maintenance and dissemination of pupil records.* Troy, NY: Russell Sage Foundation.

Graden, J. L. (1989). Redefining "prereferral" intervention as intervention assistance: Collaboration between general and special education. *Exceptional Children, 56,* 227-231.

Graden, J. L., Casey, A., & Bonstrom, O. (1985). Implementing a prereferral intervention system. Part II: The data. *Exceptional Children, 51,* 487-496.

Graden, J. L., Casey, A., & Christenson, S. L. (1985). Implementing a prereferral intervention system. Part I: The model. *Exceptional Children, 51,* 377-384.

Graden, J., & Curtis, M. (1991). *A demographic profile of school psychology: A report to the Delegate Assembly of the National Association of School psychologists.* Washington, DC: National Association of School Psychologists.

Gray. S. (1963a). *The internship in school psychology: Proceedings of the Peabody Conference, March 21-22, 1963.* Nashville, TN: George Peabody College for Teachers, Department of Psychology.

Gray, S. W. (1963b). *The psychologist in the schools.* New York: Holt, Rinehart & Winston.

Gredler, G. R. (Ed.). (1972). *Ethical and legal factors in the practice of school psychology: Proceedings of the First Annual Conference in School Psychology.* Philadelphia: Temple University Press.

Gredler, G. R. (1992). Review of E. Cole & J. A. Siegel (Eds.), *Effective consultation in school psychology. Psychology in the Schools, 29,* 192-195.

Greenspoon, P.J. (1998). *Toward an integration of subjective well-being and psychopathology.* Unpublished doctoral dissertation, University of Saskatchewan.

Greenough, P., Schwean, V. L., & Saklofske, D. H. (1993). School psychology services in northern Saskatchewan: A collaborative-consultation model. *Canadian Journal of Special Education, 9,* 1-12.

Grossman, F. (1992). Ethical dilemma: What do you do when your boss asks you to do something you're not trained for? *Communiqué, 24*(4), 18.

Guadalupe Organization, Inc. v. *Tempe Elementary School District No. 3,* Civ. No. 71-435 (D. Ariz. 1972).

Gutkin, T. B., & Curtis, M. J. (1990). School-based consultation: Theory, techniques, and research. In T. B. Gutkin & C. R. Reynolds (Eds.), *Handbook of school psychology* (pp. 577-611). New York: John Wiley.

Gutkin, T. B., & Curtis, M. J. (1999). School-based consultation theory and practice: The art and science of indirect service delivery. In C. R. Reynolds & T. B. Gutkin (Eds.), *The handbook of school psychology* (3rd ed.) (pp. 598-637). New York: John Wiley.

Gutkin, *T. B.,* & Reynolds, C. R. (Eds.). (1990). *The handbook of school psychology.* New York: John Wiley.

Hagemeier, C., Bischoff, L., Jacobs, J. & Osmon, W. (1998, April). *Role perceptions of the school psychologist by school personnel.* Poster session presented at the annual meeting of the National Association of School Psychologists.

Hagin, R. A. (1993). Contributions of women in school psychology: The Thayer report and thereafter. *Journal of School Psychology, 31,* 123-141.

Hall, G. S. (1911). *Educational Problems* (2 vols.). New York: D. Appleton.

Hamovich, G. (1995). Submission to the chair and members of the Education and Finance Committee of an Ontario Board of Education. *Canadian Journal of School Psychology, 11*(2), 96-98.

Happe, D. (1990). Best practices in identifying community resources. In A. Thomas & J. Grimes (Eds.), *Best practices in school psychology: II* (pp. 1009-1047). Kent, OH: National Association of School Psychologists.

Harrington, R. G. (1985). Best practices in facilitating organizational change in the schools. In A. Thomas & J. Grimes (Eds.), *Best practices in school psychology* (pp. 193-206). Kent, OH: National Association of School Psychologists.

Harris, J. D., Gray, B. A., Rees-McGee, S., Carroll, J. L., & Zaremba, E. T. (1987). Referrals to school psychologists: A national survey. *Journal of School Psychology, 25*, 343-354.

Harrison, P. L., & McCloskey, G. (1989). School psychology applied to business. In R. C. D'Amato & R. S. Dean (Eds.), *The school psychologist in nontraditional settings. Integrating clients, services, and settings* (pp. 107-137). Hillsdale, NJ: Erlbaum.

Hart, S. (1991). From property to person status: Historical perspective on children's rights. *American Psychologist, 46*, 53-59.

Hatch, N. O. (1988). Introduction: The professions in a democratic culture. In N. O. Hatch (Ed.), *The professions in American history* (pp. 1- 13). Notre Dame, IN: University of Notre Dame Press.

Havey, M. (1999). School psychologists' involvement in special education due process hearings. *Psychology in the Schools, 36*, 117-123.

Hayes, M. E., & Clair, T. N. (1978). School psychology: Why is the profession dying? *Psychology in the Schools, 15,* 518-521.

Henning-Stout, M. (1992). *Practitioners describe the gender climates of their workplaces: Graduates of an M.S. program.* Paper presented at the annual meeting of the National Association of School Psychologists, Nashville, TN.

Hermann, D. L., & Kush, J. C. (1995, Spring). Survey of projective assessment training practices in school psychology graduate programs. *Insight* (Newsletter of the Association of School Psychologists of Pennsylvania), *15* (3), 15-16.

Herron, W. G., Herron, M. J., & Handron, J. (1984). *Contemporary school psychology: Handbook of practice, theory, and research.* Cranston, RI: Carroll Press.

Hershey, J. M., Kopplin, D. A., & Cornell, J. E. (1991). Doctors of psychology: Their career experiences and attitudes toward degree and training. *Professional Psychology: Research and Practice, 22*, 351-356.

Hildreth, G. H. (1930). *Psychological service for school problems.* Yonkers-on-Hudson, NY: World Book Co.

Hintze, J. M., & Shapiro, E. S. (1995). Best practices in the systematic observation of classroom behavior. In A. Thomas and J. Grimes (Eds.), *Best Practices in School Psychology III* (pp. 651-660). Washington, DC: National Association of School Psychologists.

Hirsch, B. Z. (1979). Is school psychology doomed? *The School Psychologist* (Division 16 APA newsletter), *33*(4), 1.

Hirst, W. E. (1963). *Know your school psychologist.* New York: Grune & Stratton.

Hobson v. Hansen, 269 F. Supp. 401, 514 (D.D.C. 1967), *aff'd. sub nom*, *Smuck* v. *Hobson*, 408 F.2d 175 (D.C. Cir. 1969).

Hodgkinson, H. (1991). Reform versus reality. *Phi Delta Kappan, 73*, 8-16.

Hogan, D. B. (1983). The effectiveness of licensing: History, evidence, and recommendations. *Law and Human Behavior, 7*(2-3), 117-138.

Hollingworth, L. S. (1918). Tentative suggestions for the certification of practicing psychologists. *Journal of Applied Psychology, 2*, 280-284.

Hollingworth, L. S. (1933). Psychological service for public schools. *Teachers College Record, 34*, 368-379.

Holmes, B. J. (1986, December). *Task force on school psychology report.* Paper submitted to the B. C. Psychological Association, Vancouver, BC.

Holmes, B. (1993). Issues in training and credentialing in school psychology. In K. S. Dobson & D. J. G. Dobson (Eds.), *Professional Psychology in Canada* (pp. 123-146). Toronto: Hogrefe & Huber.

Hu, S., & Oakland, T. (1991). Global and regional perspective on testing children and youth: An international survey. *International Journal of Psychology, 26*(3), 329-344.

Huebner, E. S. (1992). Burnout among school psychologists: An exploratory investigation into its nature, extent, and correlates. *School Psychology Quarterly, 7*, 129-136.

Huebner, E. S., & Hahn, B. M. (1990). Best practices in coordinating multidisciplinary teams. In A. Thomas & J. Grimes (Eds.), *Best practices in school psychology: II* (pp. 193-206). Washington, DC: National Association of School Psychologists.

Huebner, E. S., & Mills, L. B. (1998). A prospective study of personality characteristics, occupational stressors, and burnout among school psychology practitioners. *Journal of School Psychology, 36*, 103-120.

Hughes, J. N. (1979). Consistency of administrators' and psychologists' actual and ideal perceptions of school psychologists' activities. *Psychology in the Schools, 16*, 234-239.

Hughes, J. N. (1986). Ethical issues in school consultation. *School Psychology Review, 15*, 489-499.

Hughes, J. N. (1996). Guilty as charged: Division 16 represents the specialty of doctoral school psychology. *Communiqué, 25*(1), 8, 10.

Hummel, D. L., & Humes, D. W. (1984). *Pupil services: Development, coordination, and administration.* New York: Macmillan.

Hunley, S. A, & Curtis, M. J. (1998). The changing face of school psychology: Demographic trends, 1990-1995. *Communiqué, 27*(1), 16.

Hutt, R. B. W. (1923). The school psychologist. *The Psychological Clinic, 15*, 48-51.

Hyman, I., Bilker, S., Freidman, M., Marino, M., & Roessner, P. (1973, October). Preliminary report of national survey of school psychologists. *The School Psychologist* (Division of School Psychology newsletter), *28* (1), 3.

Hyman, I., Flynn, A., Kowalcyk, R., & Marcus, M. (1998, April). *The status of school psychology trainers with regard to licensing and ABPP.* Paper presented at at the meeting of Trainers of School Psychologists, Orlando, FL.

Hyman, I., Friel, P., & Parsons, R. (1975). Summary of a national survey on collective bargaining, salaries, and professional problems of school psychologists. *Communiqué, 4*(3), 1-2.

Hynd, G. W., Cannon, S. B., & Haussmann, S. E. (1983). The exceptional child. In G. W. Hynd (Ed.), *The school psychologist: An introduction* (pp. 121-144). Syracuse, NY: Syracuse University Press.

Illback, R, J, (1992). Organizational influences on the practice of psychology in the schools. In F. J. Medway & T. P. Cafferty (Eds.), *School psychology: A social psychological perspective* (pp. 165-191). Hillsdale, NJ: Erlbaum.

Illback, R. J., Zins, J. E., & Maher, C. A. (1999). Program planning and evaluation: Principles, procedures, and planned change. In C. R. Reynolds & T. B. Gutkin (Eds.) *The handbook of school psychology* (3rd ed.) (pp. 907-932), New York: John Wiley.

Iowa School Psychologists Association (1983, June 25). *Provision of school psychological services in the private sector.* Mimeo.

Itkin, W. (1966). The school psychologist and his training. *Psychology in the Schools, 3,* 348-354.

Jackson, J. H. (1990). School psychology after the 1980s: Envisioning a possible future. In T. B. Gutkin & C. R. Reynolds (Eds.), *The handbook of school psychology* (pp. 40-50). New York: John Wiley.

Jackson, J. H. (1992). Trials, tribulations, and triumphs of minorities in psychology: Reflections at century's end. *Professional Psychology: Research and Practice, 23,* 80-86.

Jacob-Timm, S. (1999). Ethically challenging situations encountered by school psychologists. *Psychology in the Schools, 36,* 205-217.

Jacob-Timm, S., & Hartshorne, T. (1998). *Ethics and law for school psychologists.* New York: John Wiley.

Jacobsen, R. L. (1980, June 16). The great accreditation debate: What role for the government? *The Chronicle of Higher Education, 20*(16), 1.

Jann, R. J. (1991). Research indicates employers pressure members to act unethically. *Communiqué, 20*(4), 11-12.

Janzen, H. L. (1976). Psychology in the schools in English speaking Canada. In C. D. Catterall (Ed.), *Psychology in the schools in international perspective: Vol. 1* (pp. 163-183). Columbus, OH: Author.

Janzen, H. L. (1980, June). Psychological services to schools: Meeting educational and psychological needs of tomorrow. *The Alberta School Psychologist, 1,* 1.

Janzen, H. L., & Massey, D. S. (1990). The state of the art of school psychology in Alberta. *Canadian Journal of School Psychology, 6*(1), 9-13.

Janzen, H., Patterson, J., & Patterson, D. (1993). The future of psychology in the schools. *Canadian Journal of School Psychology, 9*(2), 174-180.

Jay, B. (1989, January). Managing a crisis in the schools. *National Association of Secondary School Principals Bulletin,* 14-17.

Jobin, H. (1995). Deputation to the Trustees of an Ontario Board of Education. *Canadian Journal of School Psychology. 11*(2), 99-100.

Johnson, P. M., Lubker, B. B., & Fowler, M. G. (1988). Teacher needs assessment for the educational management of children with chronic illnesses. *Journal of School Health, 58*, 232-235.

Johnson, D. B., Malone, P. J., & Hightower, A. D. (1997). Barriers to primary prevention efforts in the schools: Are we the biggest obstacle to the transfer of knowledge? *Applied and Preventive Psychology, 6*, 81-90.

Joint Committee on Internships for the Council of Directors of School psychology Programs; Division of School Psychology, APA; and National Association of School Psychologists. (1999). *Directory of internships for doctoral students in school psychology.* Available from Dr. Joseph French, 227 CEDAR Bldg., Pennsylvania State University, University Park, PA 16802.

Jordan, K. F., & Lyons, T. S. (1992). *Financing public education in an era of change.* Bloomington, IN: Phi Delta Kappa.

Kaminer, Y. (1994). *Adolescent substance abuse.* New York: Plenum.

Kaplan, M. S., & Kaplan, H. E. (1985). School psychology: Its educational and societal connections. *Journal of School Psychology, 23*, 319-325.

Kaser, R. (1993). A change in focus ... without losing sight of the child. *School Psychology International, 14*, 5-19.

Kaufman, F., & Smith, T. (1998, June). *The roles and function of Canadian psychological service providers.* Poster session presented at the annual meeting of the Canadian Psychological Association, Edmonton, Alberta, Canada.

Keating, A. C. (1962). A counselling psychologist in an Ontario junior high school. *Canadian Psychologist, 3*, 14-17.

Kehle, T. J., Clark, E., & Jenson, W. R. (1993). The development of testing as applied to school psychology. *Journal of School Psychology, 31*, 143-161.

Keilin, W. G. (1998). Internship selection 30 years later: An overview of the APPIC matching program. *Professional Psychology: Research and Practice, 29*(6), 599-603.

Keith-Spiegel, P., & Koocher, G. P. (1985). *Ethics in psychology.* Hillsdale, NJ: Erlbaum.

Kimball, P., & Bansilal, S. (1998, December). School psychologists and due process hearings. *VASP Bulletin, 26*(3), 5-7.

King, C. R. (1993). *Children's health in America: A history.* New York: Twayne.

Knapp, S. J., Vandecreek, L., & Zirkel, P. A. (1985). Legal research techniques: What the psychologist needs to know. *Professional Psychology: Research and Practice, 16*, 363-372.

Knoff, H. M. (1986). *Graduate training in school psychology: A national survey of professional coursework.* Washington, DC: National Association of School Psychologists.

Knoff, H. M., Curtis, M. J., & Batsche, G. M. (1997). The future of school psychology: Perspectives on effective training. *School Psychology Review, 26*, 93-103.

Knoff, H. M., McKenna, A. F., & Riser, K. (1991). Toward a consultant effectiveness scale: Investigating the characteristics of effective consultants. *School Psychology Review, 20*, 81-96.

Knoff, H., & Prout, H. (1985). Terminating students from professional psychology programs: Criteria, procedures, and legal issues. *Professional Psychology: Research and Practice, 16,* 789-797.

Korman, M. (1974). National Conference on Levels and Patterns of Professional Training in Psychology. *American Psychologist, 29,* 441-449.

Kraus, T., & Mcloughlin, C. S. (1997). An essential library in school psychology. *School Psychology International, 18,* 343-349.

Kratochwill, T., Elliot, S., & Carrington-Rotto, P. (1995). School-based behavioral consultation. In A. Thomas & J. Grimes (Eds.), *Best practices in school psychology: III* (pp. 519-538). Washington, DC: National Association of School Psychologists.

Kubiszyn, T., Brown, R., Landau, S., DeMers, S., & Reynolds, C. (1992, August). *APA Division-16 Task Force preliminary report: Psychopharmacology in the schools.* Washington, DC: American Psychological Association, Division 16.

Lacayo, N., Sherwood, G., & Morris, J. (1981). Daily activities of school psychologists: A national survey. *Psychology in the Schools, 18,* 184-190.

Lamb, D. H., Cochran, D. J., & Jackson, V. R. (1991). Training and organizational issues associated with identifying and responding to intern impairment. *Professional Psychology: Research and Practice, 22,* 291-296.

Lambert, N. M. (1981). School psychology training for the decades ahead or rivers, streams and creeks: Currents and tributaries to the sea. *School Psychology Review, 10,* 194-205.

Lambert, N. M. (1993). Historical perspective on school psychology as a scientist-practitioner specialization in school psychology. *Journal of School Psychology, 31,* 163-193.

Lambert, N. M. (1998). *School psychology: The whole is more than the sum of its parts.* Paper presented at the annual meeting of the National Association of School Psychologists, Orlando, FL.

Larry P. v. Riles, 343 F. Supp. 1306 (N.D. Cal. 1972); *aff'd.,* 502 F. 2d 963 (9th Cir. 191/ 4); 495 F. Supp. 926 (N.D. Cal. 1979); *aff'd.,* 793 F.2d 969 (9th Cir. 1984).

Levinson, E. M., Fetchkan, R., & Hohenshil, T. H. (1988). Job satisfaction among practicing school psychologists revisited. *School Psychology Review, 17,* 101-112.

Lichtenstein, R., & Fischetti, B. A. (1998). How long does a psychoeducational evaluation take? An urban Connecticut study. *Professional Psychology: Research and Practice, 29,* 144-148.

Lighthall, F. F. (1963). School psychology: An alien guild. *Elementary School Journal, 63,* 361-374.

Little, S. G. (1997). Graduate education of the top contributors to the school psychology literature: 1987-1995. *School Psychology International, 18,* 15-27.

Luckey, B. M. (1951, May). Duties of the school psychologist: Past, present, and future. *Division of School Psychologists Newsletter,* 4-10.

Luellen, W., & Avant, J. (1998, July). First annual student services intern conference. *FASP Newsletter, 24*(3), 31-32.

Lund, A. R., Reschly, D. J., & Connolly Martin, L. M. (1998). School psychology personnel needs: Correlates of current patterns and historical trends. *School Psychology Review, 27*(1), 106-120.

Magary, J. F. (1966). A school psychologist is... *Psychology in the Schools, 3*, 340-341.

Magary, J. F. (1967a). Emerging viewpoints in school psychological services. In J. F. Magary (Ed.), *School psychological services in theory and practice: A hand book* (pp. 671-755). Englewood Cliffs, NJ: Prentice Hall.

Magary, J. F. (Ed.). (1967b). *School psychological services in theory and practice: A handbook.* Englewood Cliffs, NJ: Prentice Hall.

Maher, C. A., & Greenberg, R. E. (1988). The school psychologist in business and industry. *School Psychology Review, 17*, 440-446.

Maher, C. A., Illback, R. J., & Zins, J. E. (Eds.). (1984). *Organizational psychology in the schools: A handbook for Practitioners.* Springfield, IL: Charles C. Thomas.

Maher, C. A., & Zins, J. E. (1987). *Psychoeducational interventions in the schools: Methods and procedures for enhancing student competence.* New York: Pergamon.

Maier, H. W. (1969). *Three theories of child development.* New York: Harper & Row.

Manderscheid, R. W., & Sonnenschein, M. A. (1996). *Mental health, United States, 1996.* Rockville, MD: U.S. Department of Health and Human Services. *Marshall et al.* v. *Georgia.* U.S. District Court for the Southern District of Georgia, CV482-233, June 28, 1984; Aff'd (11th cir. no. 84-8771, October 29, 1985).

Martens, B. K., & Keller, H. R. (1987). Training school psychologists in the scientific tradition. *School Psychology Review, 16*, 329-337.

Martens, E. H. (1939). *Clinical organization for child guidance within the schools.* (Office of Education Bulletin No. 15). Washington, DC: Government Printing Office.

Martin, R. (1978). Expert and referent power: A framework for understanding and maximizing consultation effectiveness. *Journal of School Psychology, 16*, 49-55.

Martin, R. P. (1983). Consultation in the schools. In G. Hynd (Ed.), *The school psychologist: An introduction* (pp. 269-292). Syracuse, NY: Syracuse University Press.

Martin, S. (1999). Revision of ethics code calls for stronger former client sex rule. *APA Monitor, 30*(7), 44.

Maslach, C. (1976, September). Burned-out. *Human Behavior,* 16-22.

Maslach, C. M., & Jackson, S. E. (1986). *Maslach Burnout Inventory* (2nd ed.). Palo Alto, CA: Consulting Psychologist Press.

Mattie T. v. *Holladay* (D.C. 75 31 S, N.D. Miss. 1979).

May, J. V. (1976). *Professionals and clients: A constitutional struggle.* Beverly Hills, CA: Sage.

MacLeod, R. B. (1955). *Psychology in Canadian universities and colleges.* Ottawa: Canadian Social Science Research Council.

McCarney, S. B., Wunderlich, K. C., & Bauer, A. M. (1993). *The pre-referral intervention manual* (2nd ed.). Columbia, MO: Hawthorne Educational Services.

McDaid, J. L., & Reifman, A. (1996, November).What school psychologists do: Time study of psychologists' services in San Diego. *Communiqué, 25*(3), 8, 10.

McGuire, P. A. (1998). The freedom to move from state to state. *APA Monitor, 29*(8), 27.

McKee, W. T. (1996). Legislation, certification, and licensing of school psychologists. *Canadian Journal of School Psychology, 12*(2), 103-114.

McKinley, D. L., & Hayes, M. (1987). Moving ahead in professional psychology. *The Counseling Psychologist, 15*, 261-266.

Mcloughlin, C. S., Leless, D. B., & Thomas, A. (1998). The school psychologist in Ohio: Additional results from OSPA's 1997 omnibus survey. *The Ohio School Psychologist, 43* (3), 3–5.

McLaughlin, M., Vogt, M. E., Anderson, J. A., DuMez, J., Peter, M. G., Hunter, A. (1998). *Portfolio models across the teaching profession.* Norwood, MA: Christopher-Gordon.

McManus, J. L. (1986). Student paraprofessionals in school psychology: Practices and possibilities. *School Psychology Review, 15*, 9-23.

McMaster, M. D., Reschly, D. J., & Peters, J M. (1989). *Directory of school psychology graduate programs.* Washington, DC: National Association of School Psychologists.

McMinn, M. R., Buchanan, T., Ellens, B. M., & Ryan, M. K. (1999). Technology, professional practice, and ethics: Survey findings and implications. *Professional Psychology: Research and Practice, 30*, 165-172.

McMurray, J. G. (1967). Two decades of school psychology: Past and future. *Canadian Psychologist, 8*, 207-217.

McReynolds, P. (1997). *Lightner Witmer: His life and times.* Washington, DC: American Psychological Association.

Medway, F. J. (1996) Turning imperfection into perfection: Some advice for making psychology indispensable in the schools. In R. C. Talley, T. Kubiszyn, M. Brassard, & R. J. Short (Eds.), *Making psychologists in schools indispensable: Critical questions & emerging perspectives* (pp. 111-116). Washington, DC: American Psychological Association.

Medway, F. J., & Cafferty, T. P. (1992). *School psychology: A social psychological perspective.* Hillsdale, NJ: Erlbaum.

Meyers, J., Alpert, J. L., & Fleisher, B. D. (1983). *Training in consultation: Perspectives from mental health, behavioral and organizational consultation.* Springfield, IL: Charles C. Thomas.

Miller, C. D., Witt, J. C., & Finley, J. L. (1981). School psychologists' perceptions of their work: Satisfactions and dissatisfactions in the United States. *School Psychology International, 2*(2), 1-3.

Millman, J. (Ed.). (1981). *Handbook of teacher evaluation.* Beverly Hills, CA: Sage.

Mills v. Board of Education of the District of Columbia, 348 F. Supp. 866 (1972); *contempt proceedings,* EHLE 551:643 (D.D.C. 1980).

Minke, K. M., & Brown, D. T. (1996). Preparing psychologists to work with children: A comparison of curricula in child-clinical and school psychology programs. *Professional Psychology: Research and Practice, 27,* 631-634.

Monroe. V. (1979). Roles and status of school psychology. In G. Phye & D. Reschly (Eds.), *School psychology: Perspectives and issues* (pp. 25-47). New York: Academic Press.

Moore, M. T., Strang, E. W., Schwartz, M., & Braddock, M. (1988). *Patterns in special education service delivery and cost.* Washington, DC: Decision Resources Corporation.

Mordock, J. B. (1988). The school psychologist working in residential and day treatment centers. *School Psychology Review, 17,* 421-428.

Morgan, E. M. (1998). *A complete guide to the advanced study in and profession of school psychology.* Delaware, OH: Author.

Morris, R. J., & Morris, Y. P. (1989). School psychology in residential treatment facilities. In R. C. D'Amato & R. S. Dean (Eds.), *The school psychologist in nontraditional settings: Integrating clients, services, and settings* (pp. 159-183). Hillsdale, NJ: Erlbaum.

Morrow, W. R. (1946). The development of psychological internship training. *Journal of Consulting Psychology, 10,* 165-183.

Moss, J. A., & Wilson, M. S. (1998). School psychology services preferred by principals. *CASP Today, 48*(1), 15-17.

Mpofu, E., Zindi, F., Oakland, T., & Peresuh, M. (1997). School psychology practices in East and Southern Africa: Special educators' perspectives. *The Journal of Special Education, 31,* 387-402.

Mullen, F. A. (1967). The role of the school psychologist in the urban school system. In J. F. Magary (Ed.), *School psychological services in theory and practice: A handbook* (pp. 30-67). Englewood Cliifs, NJ: Prentice Hall.

Mullen, F. A. (1981). School psychology in the USA: Reminiscences of its origin. *Journal of School Psychology, 19,* 103-119.

Murray, B. (1995). APA recognizes areas of expertise in practice. *APA Monitor, 26*(4), 45.

Murray, B. (1998, December). The authorship dilemma: Who gets credit for what? *APA Monitor, 29*(12), 1.

Myers, R. (1958). Professional psychology in Canada. *Canadian Psychologist, 7,* 27-36.

Nagle, R. J., & Medway, F. J. (Guest Eds.). (1982). Psychological services in the high school. *School Psychology Review, 11,* 357-416.

Napoli, D. S. (1981). *Architects of adjustment: The history of the psychological profession in the United States.* Port Washington, NY: Kennikat.

NASP adopts position on testing and strikes. (1973). *Communiqué, 1*(3), 1.

National Association of School Psychologists. (1972). *Guidelines for training programs in school psychology.* Washington, DC: Author.

National Association of School Psychologists. (1973). *Competency continuum for school psychologists and support personnel.* Washington, DC: Author.

National Association of School Psychologists. (1974). *Principles for professional ethics.* Washington, DC: Author.

National Association of School Psychologists. (1984a). *Principles for professional ethics.* Washington, DC: Author.

National Association of School Psychologists. (1984b). *Standards for the provision of school psychological services.* Washington, DC: Author.

National Association of School Psychologists. (1989). *Membership directory.* Washington, DC: Author.

National Association of School Psychologists. (1992). *Principles for professional ethics.* Washington, DC: Author.

National Association of School Psychologists. (1994a). *Standards for credentialing of school psychologists.* Bethesda, MD: Author.

National Association of School Psychologists. (1994b). *NCATE-approved curriculum guidelines: Masters, post-masters, specialist, and doctoral programs in school psychology.* Washington, DC: Author.

National Association of School Psychologists. (1994c). *Standards for training and field placement programs in school psychology.* Washington, DC: Author.

National Association of School Psychologists. (1997a). *Principles for professional ethics.* Bethesda, MD: Author.

National Association of School Psychologists. (1997b). *Standards for the provision of school psychological services.* Bethesda, MD: Author.

National Association of School Psychologists, Multicultural Affairs Committee. (1998). *Directory of bilingual school psychologists.* Bethesda, MD: Author.

National Association of State Consultants for School Psychological Services. (1987, August). Committee report on personnel shortages in school psychology. Available from NASP, Bethesda, MD.

National Center for Education in Maternal and Child Health. (1988). *The financing of mental health services for children and adolescents.* Washington, DC: Author.

National Council for Accreditation of Teacher Education. (1997). *Standards, procedures and policies for the accreditation of professional education units.* Washington, DC: Author.

National Learning Corporation. (1997). *School psychology teaching area examination.* Syosset, NY: Author.

National School Psychology Inservice Training Network. (1984). *School psychology. A blueprint for training and practice.* Minneapolis, MN: Author.

Neisser, U. (1981). Obituary: James J. Gibson (1904-1979). *American Psychologist, 36,* 214-215.

Nelson, W. W. (1998). The naked truth about school reform in Minnesota. *Phi Delta Kappan, 79,* 679-684.

Nelson, J. R., Peterson, L., & Strader, H. (1997). The use of school psychological services by charter schools. *Communiqué, 26*(1), 12.

Neudorf, J. (1989). *The role and tasks of educational psychologists in Saskatchewan.* Unpublished master's thesis, University of Regina, Saskatchewan, Canada.

New York State Association for Applied Psychology, Special Committee on School psychologists. (1943). Report on the functions, training and employment opportunities of school psychologists. *Journal of Consulting Psychology, 7,* 230-243.

Newland, T. E. (1980). Psychological assessment of exceptional children and youth. In W. M. Cruickshank (Ed.), *Psychology of exceptional children and youth* (pp. 74-135). Englewood Cliffs, NJ: Prentice Hall. (See also Chapter 2 in Salvia J., & Ysseldyke, J. E. (1991). *Assessment.* Boston: Houghton Mifflin.)

Oakland, T. (1990). Psicologia escolar no Brazil: Passado, presente, e futuro [School psychology in Brazil: Past, present, and future]. *Psicologia: Tedria e Pesquisa, 5*(2), 191-201.

Oakland, T. (1992). Formulating priorities for international school psychology toward the turn of the twentieth century. *School Psychology International, 13,* 171-177.

Oakland, T. (1993). A brief history of international school psychology. *Journal of School Psychology, 31,* 109-122.

Oakland, T. D., & Cunningham, J. L. (1992). A survey of school psychology in developed and developing countries. *School Psychology International, 13,* 99-129.

Oakland, T., & Cunningham, J. (1997). International School Psychology Association definition of school psychology. *School Psychology International, 18,* 195-200.

Oakland, T., & Cunningham, J. (1999). The futures of school psychology: Conceptual models for its development and examples of their applications. In C. R. Reynolds & T. B. Gutkin (Eds.), *The handbook of school psychology* (pp. 34-53), New York: John Wiley.

Oakland, T., Cunningham, J., Poulsen, A., & Meazzini, P. (1991). An examination of policies governing the normalization of handicapped pupils in Denmark, Italy, and the United States. *International Journal of Special Education, 6* (2), 386-402.

Oakland, T., Feldman, N., & Leon De Viloria, C. (1995). School psychology in Venezuela: Three decades of progress and futures of great potential, *School Psychology International, 16,* 29-42.

Oakland, T., Goldman, S., & Bischoff, H. (1997). Code of Ethics of the International School Psychology Association. *School Psychology International, 18,* 291-298.

Oakland, T., & Hambleton, R. (Eds.). (1995) *International perspectives on assessment of academic achievement.* Norwell, MA: Kluwer.

Oakland, T., & Hu, S. (1989). Psychology in the schools of four Asian countries. *Psychologia, 32,* 71-80.

Oakland, T., & Hu, S. (1991). Professionals who administer tests with children and youth: An international survey. *Journal of Psychoeducational Assessment, 9*(2), 108-120.

Oakland, T., & Hu, S. (1992). The top ten tests used with children and youth worldwide. *Bulletin of the International Test Commission, 5,* 99-120.

Oakland, T. & Phillips, B. (1997). *Addressing the needs of children with learning disabilities: Advocacy by the International School Psychology Association.* Paper presented to UNESCO's Committee on the Rights of the Child, Geneva, Switzerland

Oakland, T., & Saigh, P. (1989). Psychology in the schools: An introduction to international perspectives. In Saigh, P., & Oakland, T. (Eds.). *International perspectives on psychology in the schools* (pp. 1-22). Hillsdale, NJ: Erlbaum.

Oakland, T., & Wechsler, S. (1988). School psychology in five South American countries: A 1989 perspective. *Revista Interamericana de Psicologia/Interamerican Journal of Psychology, 22,* 41-55.

Oakland, T., & Wechsler, S. (1990). School psychology in Brazil: An examination of its research infrastructure. *School Psychology International, 11,* 287-293.

Ochoa, S. H., Rivera, B., & Ford, L. (1997). An investigation of school psychology training pertaining to bilingual psycho-educational assessment of primarily Hispanic students: Twenty-five years after *Diana* v. *California. Journal of School Psychology, 35,* 329-349.

Orlosky, D. E., McCleary, L. E., Shapiro, A., & Webb, L. D. (1984). *Educational administration today.* Columbus, OH: Charles E. Merrill.

O'Shea, H. E. (1960). The future of school psychology. In M. G. Gottsegen & G. B. Gottsegen (Eds.), *Professional school psychology* (pp. 275-283). New York: Grune & Stratton.

Our Voice. (1983). *47*(8), 1 (Official publication of the International Union of Life Insurance Agents, Milwaukee, WI).

Ownby, R. (1991). *Psychological reports: A guide to report writing in professional psychology* (2nd ed.). Brandon, VT: Clinical Psychology Publishing.

P.A.R.C. [Pennsylvania Association for Retarded Citizens] v. *Commonwealth of Pennsylvania,* 334 F. Supp. 1257 (1971), 343 F. Supp. 279 (1972).

P.A.S.E. [Parents in Action in Special Education] v. *Hannon,* 506 F. Supp. 831 (N.D. Ill. 1980).

Per your request...school psychologist to student ratios. (1995, Winter). *CASP Today* (Newsletter of the California Association of School Psychologists), *45*(2), 4.

Perkins, M. (1990). School psychology in Ontario. *Canadian Journal of School Psychology, 6*(1), 34-38.

Pesce v. *J. Sterling Morton High School District,* 651 F. Supp. 152 (N.D. Ill. 1986).

Petersen, D. R. (1976). Is psychology a profession? *American Psychologist, 38,* 572-581.

Peterson, R. L., Peterson, D. R., Abrams, J. C., & Stricker, G. (1997). The National Council of Schools and Programs of Professional Psychology educational model. *Professional Psychology: Research and Practice, 28,* 373-386.

Peterson, K. A., Waldron, D. J., & Paulson, S. E. (1998). *Teachers' perceptions of school psychologists' existing and potential roles.* Paper presented at the annual meeting of the National Association of School Psychologists, Orlando, FL.

Petition for reaffirmation of the specialty of school psychology. (1997, March 5). Washington, DC: American Psychological Association. See also, Archival Description of the Specialty: School Psychology (1998), *CDSPP Press, 17*(1), pp. 8-10.

Pfeiffer, S. I. (1980). The school-based interprofessional team: Recurring problems and some possible solutions. *Journal of School Psychology, 18,* 388-394.

Pfeiffer, S. I., & Marmo, P. (1981). The status of training in school psychology and trends toward the future. *Journal of School Psychology, 19,* 211-216.

Pfeiffer, S. I., & Reddy, L. A. (1998). School-based mental health programs in the United States: Present status and a blueprint for the future. *School Psychology Review, 27*(1), 84-96.

Pfeiffer, S. I., & Reddy, L. A. (Eds.). (1999). Inclusion practices with special needs students: theory, research, and application. *Special Services in the Schools. 15* (1-2), whole issue

Phelps, L. (1998, November). CRSPPP and recognition of school psychology as a specialty. *CDSPP Press* (Newsletter of the Council of Directors of School Psychology Programs), *17*(1), 7-10 (includes archival description of the specialty).

Philips, D., Schwean, V. L., & Saklofske, D.H. (1997). Treatment effects of a school-based cognitive-behavioral program for aggressive children. *Canadian Journal of School Psychology, 13*(1), 60-67.

Phillips, B. (1985). Education and training. In J. R. Bergan (Ed.), *School psychology in contemporary society: An introduction* (pp. 92-115). Columbus, OH: Charles E. Merrill.

Phillips, B. N. (1990a). Law, psychology, and education. In T. R. Kratochwill (Ed.), *Advances in school psychology: Vol. 7* (pp. 79-130). Hillsdale, NJ: Erlbaum.

Phillips, B. N. (1990b). *School psychology at a turning point: Ensuring a bright future for the profession.* San Francisco: Jossey-Bass.

Phillips, B. N. (1993). Trainers of School Psychologists and Council of Directors of School Psychology Programs: A new chapter in the history of school psychology. *Journal of School Psychology, 31,* 91-108.

Phillips, B. N. (1999). Strengthening the links between science and practice: Reading, evaluating, and applying research in school psychology. In C. R. Reynolds and T. B. Gutkin (Eds.), *The Handbook of School Psychology* (3rd ed.) (pp. 56-77). New York: John Wiley.

Phillips, V., & McCullough, L. (1990). Consultation-based programming: Instituting the collaborative ethic in schools. *Exceptional Children, 56,* 291-304.

Pickover, B., Barbrack, C., & Glat, M. (1982). Preventive and educative programs within the high school. *School Psychology Review, 11,* 399-408.

Pion, G. M. (1992, April). *Professional psychology's human resources: Scientists, practitioners, scientist-practitioners, or none of the above?* Paper presented at the 1992 Accreditation Summit, American Psychological Society, Chicago, IL.

Pion, G. M., Bramblett, J. P., & Wicherski, M. (1987). *Preliminary report: 1985 doctorate employment survey.* Washington, DC: American Psychological Association.

Pipho, C. (1999, February). The profit side of education. *Phi Delta Kappan, 80*(6), 421-422.

Pitcher, G. D., & Poland, S. (1992). *Crisis intervention in the schools.* New York: Guilford.

Plas, J. M. (1986). *Systems psychology in the schools.* New York: Pergamon.

Plas, J. M., & Williams, B. (1985). Best practices in working with community agencies. In A. Thomas & J. Grimes (Eds.), *Best practices in school psychology (pp.* 331-340). Kent, OH: National Association of School Psychologists.

Poland, S., Pitcher, G., & Lazarus, P. (1995). Crisis intervention. In A. Thomas & J. Grimes (Eds.), *Best practices in school psychology: III* (pp. 445-458). Washington, DC: National Association of School Psychologists.

Pope, K. S., & Vetter, V. A. (1992). Ethical dilemmas encountered by members of the American Psychological Association. *American Psychologist, 47,* 397-411.

Power, T. J., DuPaul, G. J., Shapiro, E. S., & Parrish, J. M. (1998). Role of the school-based professional in health-related services. In. L. Phelps (Ed.), *Health-related disorders in children and adolescents* (pp. 15-26). Washington, DC: American Psychological Association.

Prasse, D. P. (1988). Licensing, school psychology, and independent private practice. In T. R. Kratochwill (Ed.), *Advances in school psychology: Vol. 6* (pp. 49-80). Hillsdale, NJ: Erlbaum.

Prasse, D. (1995). Best practices in school psychology and the law. In A. Thomas & J. Grimes (Eds.), *Best practices in school psychology: III* (pp. 41-50). Bethesda, MD: National Association of School Psychologists.

Prout, H. T., Meyers, J., & Greggo, S. P. (1989). *The acceptability of PsyD graduates in the academic job market.* Unpublished. (Available from the authors at ED 233, SUNY Albany, Albany, NY 12222).

Pryzwansky, W. B. (1982). School psychology training and practice: The APA perspective. In T. R. Kratochwill (Ed.), *Advances in school psychology: Vol. 2* (pp. 19-39). Hillsdale, NJ: Erlbaum.

Pryzwansky, W. B. (1989). Private practice as an alternative setting for school psychologists. In R. C. D'Amato & R. S. Dean (Eds.), *The school psychologist in nontraditional settings: Integrating clients, services, and settings* (pp. 76-85). Hillsdale, NJ: Erlbaum.

Pryzwansky, W. B. (1990). School psychology in the next decade: A period of some difficult decisions. In T. B. Gutkin & C. R. Reynolds (Eds.), *The handbook of school psychology* (pp. 32-40). New York: John Wiley.

Pryzwansky, W. B. (1993). The regulation of school psychology: A historical perspective on certification, licensure, and accreditation. *Journal of School Psychology, 31,* 219-235.

Pryzwansky, W. (1998). Task Force on Post-Doctoral Education and Training in School Psychology purpose statement. *CDSPP Press* (Newsletter of the Council of Directors of School Psychology Programs), *16*(2), 9-11.

Pryzwansky, W. (1999). Accreditation and credentialing systems in school psychology. In C. R. Reynolds & T. B. Gutkin (Eds.), *The handbook of school psychology* (pp. 1145-1158). New York: John Wiley.

Pryzwansky, W. B., & Wendt, R. N. (1987). *Psychology as a profession: Foundations of practice.* New York: Pergamon.

Public Law (P.L.) 93-380. Family Educational Rights and Privacy Act of 1974. (20 U.S.C. and 34 C.F.R.).

Public Law (P.L.) 94-142. Education for All Handicapped Children Act of 1975. (20 U.S.C. and 34 C.F.R.).

Public Law (P.L.) 99-457. Education of the Handicapped Amendments of 1986. (20 U.S.C. 1470).

Public Law (P.L.) 101-476. Individuals with Disabilities Education Act, 1990. (104 Stat. 1103).

Public Law 101-336. Americans With Disabilities Act of 1990. 42 U.S.C.A.: 12101 et seq. (West 1993).

Public Law (P. L.) 105-17, Individuals with Disabilities Education Act, 1997.

Raimy, V. C. (Ed.). (1950). *Training in clinical psychology.* New York: Prentice Hall.

Kanes, R. G. (1992). District-wide implementation of curriculum based measurement: First year outcomes. *CASP Today* (Newsletter of the California Association of School Psychologists), *51*(4), 7.

Ranseen, J. D. (1998). Lawyers with ADHD: The special test accommodation controversy. *Professional Psychology: Research and Practice, 29,* 450-459.

Reeder, G. D., Maccow, G. C., Shaw, S. R., Swerdlik, M. E., Horton, C. B., & Foster, P. (1997). School psychologists and full-service schools: Partnerships with medical, mental health, and social services. *School Psychology Review, 26*(4), 603-621.

Reger, R. (1965). *School psychology.* Springfield, IL: Charles C. Thomas.

Reinhardt, J., & Martin, M. (1991). Ethics forum. *Communiqué, 20*(2), 10-11.

Reschly, D. J. (1979). Nonbiased assessment. In G. D. Phye & D. J. Reschly (Eds.), *School psychology: Perspectives and issues* (pp. 215-256). New York: Academic Press.

Reschly, D. J. (1983). Legal issues in psychoeducational assessment. In G. W. Hynd (Ed.), *The school psychologist: An introduction* (pp. 67-93). Syracuse, NY: Syracuse University Press.

Reschly, D. J. (1988). Special education reform: School psychology revolution. *School Psychology Review, 17,* 459-475.

Reschly, D. J. (1998, August). *School psychology practice: Is there change?* Paper presented at the annual meeting of the American Psychological Association, San Francisco, CA.

Reschly, D. J., & Bersoff, D. N. (1999). Law and school psychology. In C. R. Reynolds & T. B. Gutkin (Eds.), *The handbook of school psychology* (pp. 1077-1112), New York: John Wiley.

Reschly, D. J., & Connolly, L. M. (1990). Comparisons of school psychologists in the city and country: Is there a "rural" school psychology? *School Psychology Review, 19,* 534-549.

Reschly, D. J., Kicklighter, R. H., & McKee, P. (1988a). Recent placement litigation: Part 1. Regular education grouping: Comparison of *Marshall* (1984, 1985) and *Hobson* (1967, 1969). *School Psychology Review, 17,* 9-2 1.

Reschly, D. J., Kicklighter, R. H., & McKee, P. (1988b). Recent placement litigation: Part 2. Minority EMR over-representation: Comparison of *Larry P.* (1979, 1984, 1986) with *Marshall* (1984, 1985) and *S-1* (1986). *School Psychology Review, 17,* 22-38.

Reschly, D. J., Kicklighter, R. H., & McKee, P. (1988c). Recent placement litigation: Part 3. Analysis of differences in *Larry P., Marshall,* and *S-1* and implications for future practices. *School Psychology Review, 17,* 39-50.

Reschly, D. J., & McMaster-Beyer, M. (1991). Influences of degree level, institutional orientation, college affiliation, and accreditation status on school psychology graduate education. *Professional Psychology: Research and Practice, 22,* 368-374.

Reschly, D. J., & Wilson, M. S. (1992). *School psychology faculty and practitioners: 1986 to 1991 trends in demographic characteristics, roles, satisfaction, and system reform.* (Unedited manuscript for Reschly and Wilson, 1995).

Reschly, D. J., & Wilson, M. S. (1995). School psychology practitioners and faculty: 1986 to 1991-92 trends in demographics, roles, satisfaction, and system reform. *School Psychology Review, 24,* 62-80.

Reschly, D. J., & Wilson, M. S. (1997). Characteristics of school psychology graduate education: Implications for the entry-level discussion and doctoral-level specialty definition. *School Psychology Review, 26*(1), 74-92.

Reynolds, C. R., & Gutkin, T. B. (Eds.). (1982). *The handbook of school psychology.* New York: John Wiley.

Reynolds, C. R., & Gutkin, T. B. (Eds.). (1999). *Handbook of school psychology* (3rd ed.). New York: John Wiley.

Reynolds, C. R., Gutkin, T. B., Elliott, S. N., & Witt, J. C. (1984). *School psychology: Essentials of theory and practice.* New York: John Wiley.

Roberts, R. D. (1970). Perceptions of actual and desired role functions of school psychologists by psychologists and teachers. *Psychology in the Schools, 7,* 175-178.

Roberts, R. D., & Solomons, G. (1970). Perceptions of the duties and functions of the school psychologist. *American Psychologist, 25,* 544-549.

Rogers, M. R., Ingraham, C. L., Bursztyn, A., Cajigas-Segrede, N., Esquivel, G., Hess, R., Nahari, S. G., & Lopez, E. C. (1999). Providing psychological services to racially, ethnically, culturally, and linguistically diverse individuals in the schools: Recommendations for practice. *School Psychology International,* 20, 243-264.

Rogers, M. R., Ponterotto, J. G., Conoley, J. C., & Wiese, M. J. (1992). Multicultural training in school psychology: A national survey. *School Psychology Review,* 21, 603-616.

Romans, J. S. C., Boswell, D. L., Carlozzi, A. F., & Ferguson, D. B. (1995). Training and supervision practices in clinical, counseling, and school psychology programs. *Professional Psychology: Research & Practice, 26,* 407-412.

Rosebrook, W. M. (1942). Psychological service for schools on a regional basis. *Journal of Consulting Psychology, 6,* 196-200,

Rosenberg, R. (1982). *Beyond separate spheres: Intellectual roots of modern feminism.* New Haven, CT: Yale University Press.

Rosenberg, S. L. (1995). Maintaining an independent practice. In A. Thomas & J. Grimes (Eds.), *Best practices in school psychology: III* (pp. 145-152). Washington, DC: National Association of School Psychologists.

Rosenberg, S. L., & McNamara, K. M. (1988). *Independent practice of school psychology: Annotated bibliography and reference list.* Washington, DC: National Association of School Psychologists.

Rosenfeld, J. G., & Blanco, R. F. (1974). Incompetence in school psychology: The case of "Dr. Gestalt." *Psychology in the Schools, 11,* 263-269.

Rosenfield, S. (1996). The school psychologist as citizen of the learning community. In R. C. Talley, T. Kubiszyn, M. Brassard, & R. J. Short (Eds.) *Making psychologists in schools indispensable: Critical questions & emerging perspectives* (pp. 83-88). Washington, DC: American Psychological Association.

Rosenfield, S., & Gravois, T. (1999). Working with teams in the school. In C. R. Reynolds & T. B. Gutkin (Eds.), *The handbook of school psychology* (pp. 1025-1040), New York: John Wiley.

Rosenfield, S., & Kuralt, S. K. (1990). Best practices in curriculum-based assessment. In A. Thomas & J. Grimes (Eds.), *Best practices in school psychology: II* (pp. 275-286). Washington, DC: National Association of School Psychologists.

Ross, D. (1972). *G. Stanley Hall: The psychologist as prophet.* Chicago, IL: University of Chicago Press.

Ross, M. J., Holzman, L. A., Handal, P. J., & Gilner, F. H. (1991). Performance on the Examination for the Professional Practice of Psychology as a function of specialty, degree, administrative housing, and accreditation status. *Professional Psychology: Research and Practice, 22,* 347-350.

Ross, R. P. (1995). Best practices in implementing intervention assistance teams. In A. Thomas & J. Grimes (Eds.) *Best practices in school psychology: III* (pp. 227-237). Washington, DC: National Association of School Psychologists.

Ross-Reynolds, G. (1990). Best practices in report writing. In A. Thomas & J. Grimes (Eds.) *Best practices in school psychology: II* (pp. 621-633).

Washington, DC: National Association of School Psychologists.

Russell, R. (1984). Psychology in its world context. *American Psychologist, 39,* 1027-1025.

Saigh, P., & Oakland, T. (Eds.). (1989). *International perspectives on psychology in the schools.* Hillsdale, NJ: Erlbaum.

Saklofske, D. H. (1996). Moving toward a core curriculum for training school psychologists. *Canadian Journal of School Psychology, 12,* 91-96.

Saklofske, D. H., & Grainger, J. (1990). School psychology in Saskatchewan. *Canadian Journal of School Psychology, 6*(1), 15-21.

Saklofske, D. H., Hildebrand, D. K., Reynolds, C.R., & Wilson, V. L. (1998). Substituting Symbol Search for Coding on the WISC-III: Canadian normative tables for Performance and Full Scale IQ scores. *Canadian Journal of Behavioural Science, 20*(2) 57-68.

Saklofske, D. H., & Janzen, H. L. (1990). School-based assessment research in Canada. *McGill Journal of Education, 25*(1), 5-23.

Saklofske, D. H. & Janzen, H. L. (1993). Contemporary issues in school psychology. In K. S. Dobson & D. J. G. Dobson (Eds.), *Professional Psychology in Canada* (pp.313-350). Toronto: Hogrefe & Huber.

Sales, B. D., Krauss, D. A., Sacken, D. M., & Overcast, T. D. (1999). The legal rights of students. In C. R. Reynolds & T. B. Gutkin (Eds.), *The handbook of school psychology* (pp. 1113-1144), New York: John Wiley.

Salvia, J., & Ysseldyke, J. E. (2001). *Assessment (*8th ed.). Boston: Houghton-Mifflin.

Sanders, C. (1992). Update: School psychologist employment rights. *Intervention* (Newsletter of the Arizona Association of School Psychologists), *24*(2), 4-5.

Sandia study helps focus educational improvement agenda. (1992). *Wyoming School Psychology Association Newsletter, 11*(3), 1, 4-5, 7.

Sandoval, J. (1988). The school psychologist in higher education. *School Psychology Review, 17,* 391-396.

Sandoval, J. (1993). The history of interventions in school psychology. *Journal of School Psychology, 31,* 195-217.

Sarason, S. B. (1971). *The culture of the school and the problem of change.* Boston: Allyn & Bacon.

Sattler, J. M. (1992). *Assessment of children* (3rd ed.). San Diego, California: Author.

Sattler, J. M. (1998). *Clinical and forensic interviewing of children and families: Guidelines for the mental health, education, pediatric, and child maltreatment fields.* San Diego: Author.

Schmidt, W. H. O. (1976, November). The training of educational psychologists in Canada. *CSSE News,* 4-8.

Schmuck, R. A., & Miles, M. B. (1971). *Organization development in schools.* Palo Alto, CA: National Press Books.

Schudson, M. (1980). Review of, M. S. Larson, The rise of professionalism: A sociological analysis. *Theory and Society, 9,* 215-229.

Schwarz, J. (1986). *Radical feminists of heterodoxy: Greenwich Village 1912-1940.* Norwich, VT: New Victoria.

Schwean, V. L., Saklofske, D. H., Shatz, E., & Folk, G. (1996). Achieving supportive integration for children with behavioral disorders in Canada: Multiple paths to realization. *Canadian Journal of Special Education, 11*(1), 35-50.

Seligman, M. (Ed.). (1991). *The family with a handicapped child.* Boston: Allyn & Bacon.

Seligman, M., & Darling, R. B. (1997). *Ordinary families, special children.* New York: Guilford.

Sewell, T. E. (1981). Shaping the future of school psychology: Another perspective. *School Psychology Review, 10,* 232-242.

Shapiro, E. S. (1989). *Academic skills problems: Direct assessment and intervention.* New York: Guilford.

Shaw, S. R., & Swerdlik, M. E. (1995). Best practices in facilitating team functioning. In A. Thomas and J. Grimes (Eds.), *Best Practices in School Psychology: III* (pp. 153-159). Washington, DC: National Association of School Psychologists.

Shellenberger, S. (1988). Family medicine: The school psychologist's influence. *School Psychology Review, 17,* 405-410.

Shinn, M. R. (Ed.). (1989). *Curriculum-based measurement: Assessing special children.* New York: Guilford.

Shinn, M. R. (Ed.). (1995). Curriculum-based measurement and its use in a problem-solving model. In A. Thomas and J. Grimes (Eds.), *Best Practices in School Psychology: III* (pp. 547-567). Washington, DC: National Association of School Psychologists.

Shinn, M. R., Nolet, V., & Knutson, N. (1990). Best practices in curriculum-based measurement. In A. Thomas & J. Grimes (Eds.), *Best practices in school psychology: II* (pp. 287-307). Washington, DC: National Association of School Psychologists.

Siegel, A. W., & White, S. H. (1982). The child study movement: Early growth and development of the symbolized child. In H. W. Reese & L. Lipsitt (Eds.), *Advances in child development and behavior: Vol. 17* (pp. 233-285). New York: Academic Press.

Silberberg, N. E., & Silberberg, M. C. (1971). Should schools have psychologists? *Journal of School Psychology, 9,* 321-328.

Skinner, C. H., Robinson, S. L., Brown, C. S., & Cates, G. L. (1999). Female publication patterns in *Schools Psychology Review, Journal of School Psychology,* and *School Psychology Quarterly* from 1985-1994. *School Psychology Review, 28,* 76-83.

Sladeczek, I., & Heath, N. (1997). Consultation in Canada. *Canadian Journal of School Psychology, 13*(2), 1-14.

Slater, R. (1980). The organizational origins of public school psychology. *Educational Studies, 2, 1-11.*

Sleek, S. (1998, December). Psychology's cultural competence, once "simplistic," now broadening. *APA Monitor, 29*(12), 1.

Smith, D. K. (1984). Practicing school psychologists: Their characteristics, activities, and populations served. *Professional Psychology: Research and Practice, 15*, 798-810.

Smith, D. K., Clifford, E. S., Hesley, J., & Leifgren, M. (1992). *The school psychologist of 1991: A survey of practitioners.* Paper presented at the annual meeting of the National Association of School Psychologists, Nashville, TN.

Smith, D. K., & Mealy, N. S. (1988). *Changes in school psychology practice: A five-year update.* Paper presented at the annual meeting of the American Psychological Association, Atlanta, GA.

Smith, F. (1997). Comparisons of state associations. *The Louisiana School Psychologist, 8*(5), 3-4.

Snyder, T. D., Hoffman, C. M., & Geddes, C. M. (1997). *Digest of educational statistics 1997.* Washington, DC: United States Department of Education, Office of Educational Research and Improvement.

Social Security Administration. (1998). *Social security: A guide to SSI for groups and organizations.* Washington, DC: Author.

Sokal, M. M. (1982). The Committee on the Certification of Consulting Psychologists: A failure of applied psychology in the 1920's. In C. J. Adkins & B. A. Winstead (Eds.), *History of applied psychology: Department of Psychology Colloquium Series II* (pp. 71-90). Norfolk, VA: Old Dominion University, Department of Psychology, Center for Applied Psychological Studies.

Solly, D. C., & Hohenshil, T. H. (1986). Job satisfaction among school psychologists in a primarily rural state. *School Psychology Review, 15*, 119-126.

Solway, K. S. (1985). Transition from graduate school to internship: A potential crisis. *Professional Psychology: Research and Practice, 16*, 50-54.

Sorenson, J. L., Masson, C. L., Clark, W. W., & Morin, S. F. (1998). Providing public testimony: A guide for psychologists. *Professional Psychology: Research and Practice, 29*, 588-593.

Spring, J. (1989). *American education: An introduction to social and political aspects.* New York: Longman.

Stanhope, V. (1995). Congress targets children's SSI benefits. *Communiqué, 23*(7), 3.

Steil, D. A. (1994). Post secondary school psychology: Come on in, the water's fine. *Communiqué, 22*(8), 28-30.

Stein, H. L. (1964). *The status and role of school psychologists in Canada.* Unpublished.

Stern, W. D. (1910). Ubernormale kind. *Der Saemann Monatschrift Fuer Paedagogische Reform.* Jahrg, s. 97-72 U.S. 160-167.

Stern, W. (1911). The supernormal child: II. *Journal of Educational Psychology, 2,* 181-190.

Stern, W. (1914). *The psychological methods of testing intelligence.* Baltimore, MD: Warwick & York.

Stewart, K. J. (1986). Disentangling the complexities of clientage. In S. N. Elliott & J. C. Witt (Eds.), *The delivery of psychological services in schools: Concepts, processes,* and *issues* (pp. 81-107). Hillsdale, NJ: Erlbaum.

Stoner, G., & Green, S. K. (1992). Reconsidering the scientist-practitioner model for school psychology practice. *School Psychology Review, 21,* 155-166.

Strein, W. (1996a). Administrative Supervision. In T. K. Fagan & P. J. Warden (Eds.), *Historical encyclopedia of school psychology* (pp. 12-13). Westport, CT: Greenwood.

Strein, W. (1996b). Professional Supervision. In T. K. Fagan & P. J. Warden (Eds.), *Historical encyclopedia of school psychology* (pp. 297-298). Westport, CT: Greenwood.

Stringfield, S. (Guest Ed.). (1991). Looking to the future of Chapter 1. *Phi Delta Kappan, 72,* 576-60-7.

Stumme, J. M. (1995). Best practices in serving as an expert witness. In A. Thomas & J. Grimes (Eds.), *Best practices in school psychology:III* (pp. 179-190). Bethesda, MD: National Association of School Psychologists.

Sullivan, L. (1999). Progress: The National Education Goals. *Communiqué, 27*(6), 12.

Sutkiewicz, F. (1997, May). Ethical issues involved with computer use: How to avoid the pitfalls. *The Wisconsin School Psychologist, 96*(3), 1, 6-7.

Sweet, T. (1990). School psychology in British Columbia: The state of the art. *Canadian Journal of School Psychology, 6*(1), 1-8.

Swenson, E. V. (1998, Winter). Applications of the APA ethics code to the training of school psychologists in the classroom. *Trainers' Forum, 16*(2), 12-15.

Symonds, P. M. (1933). Every school should have a psychologist. *School and Society, 38*(976), 321-329.

Symonds, P. M. (Ed.). (1942). [Special issue]. *Journal of Consulting Psychology, 6*(4).

Tallent, N. (1993). *Psychological report writing* (4th ed.). Englewood Cliffs, NJ: Prentice Hall.

Talley, R. C., Kubiszyn, T., Brassard, M., & Short, R. J. (Eds.). (1996). *Making psychologists in schools indispensable: Critical questions and emerging perspectives.* Washington, DC: American Psychological Association.

Tarasoff v. *Regents of California,* 529 P.2d 553 (1974); 551 P.2d 334 (1976).

Task Force on Psychology in the Schools. (1993). *Delivery of comprehensive school psychological services: An educator's guide.* Washington, DC: American Psychological Association.

Telzrow, C. F. (1999). IDEA amendments of 1997: Promise or pitfall for special education reform? *Journal of School Psychology, 37,* 7-28.

Tennessee Department of Education, Division of Special Programs. (1993). *Special education student evaluation manual (Rev.).* Nashville, TN: Author.

Tenure...Questions & Answers. (1997, Spring). *CASP Today* (Newsletter of the California Association of School Psychologists), *46*(3), 12.

Terman, L. M. (1916). *The measurement of intelligence: An explanation of and complete guide for the use of the Stanford revision and extension of the Binet-Simon Intelligence Scale.* Boston: Houghton Mifflin.

Tharinger, D. J. (1996). Psychologists in the schools: Routes to becoming indispensable. In R. C. Talley, T. Kubiszyn, M. Brassard, & R. J. Short (Eds.), *Making psychologists in schools indispensable: Critical questions and emerging perspectives* (pp. 105-110). Washington, DC: American Psychological Association.

Thomas, A. (Ed.). (1998). *Directory of school psychology graduate programs.* Bethesda, MD: National Association of School Psychologists.

Thomas, A. (1999a). School psychology 2000: A national database. *Communiqué, 28*(1), 26.

Thomas, A. (1999b). School psychology 2000. *Communiqué, 28*(2), 28.

Thomas, A., & Grimes, J. (Eds.). (1985). *Best practices in school psychology.* Washington, DC: National Association of School Psychologists.

Thomas, A., & Grimes, J. (Eds.). (1990). *Best practices in school psychology II.* Washington, DC: National Association of School Psychologists.

Thomas, A., & Grimes, J. (Eds.). (1995). *Best practices in school psychology III.* Bethesda, MD: National Association of School Psychologists.

Thomas, A., & Pinciotti, D. (1992). *Administrators' satisfaction with school psychologists: Implications for practice.* Paper presented at the annual meeting of the National Association of School Psychologists, Nashville, TN.

Thomas, A., & Witte, R. (1996). A study of gender differences among school psychologists. *Psychology in the Schools, 33,* 351-359.

Thorndike, E. L. (1912). *Education: A first book.* New York: Macmillan.

Tindall, R. H. (1964). Trends in the development of psychological services in the schools. *Journal of School Psychology, 3,* 1-12.

Tindall, R. H. (1979). School psychology: The development of a profession. In G. D. Phye & D. J. Reschly (Eds.), *School psychology: Perspectives and issues* (pp. 3-24). New York: Academic Press.

Tracy, M. (1998). Be aware of malpractice risks when using electronic devices. *The National Psychologist, 7*(1), 17.

Trachtman, G. M. (1981). On such a full sea. *School Psychology Review, 10,* 138-181.

Trachtman, G. M. (1996). Indispensability: The holy grail. In R. C. Talley, T. Kubiszyn, M. Brassard, & R. J. Short (Eds.), *Making psychologists in schools indispensable: Critical questions & emerging perspectives* (pp. 9-13). Washington, DC: American Psychological Association.

Tyack, D. B. (1976). Ways of seeing: An essay on the history of compulsory schooling. *Harvard Educational Review, 46,* 355-389.

Tyson, H. (1999). Kappan special report: A load off the teachers' backs: Coordinated school health programs. *Phi Delta Kappan, 80*(5), K1-K8.

UNESCO (1948). *School psychologists.* Paper presented at the XI International Congress on Public Education by UNESCO and I.B.E. *Publication No. 105.* Geneva: International Bureau of Education.

United States Department of Education. (1998, August). *Early warning, timely response: A guide to safe schools.* Washington, DC: Author.

Valesky, T. C., Forsythe, G., & Hall, M. L. (1992). *Principal perceptions of school-based decision making in Tennessee schools. (Policy Practice Brief,* No. 9201). Memphis, TN: Memphis State University, Center for Research in Educational Policy.

Valett, R. E. (1963). *The practice of school psychology: Professional problems.* New York: John Wiley.

Valett, R. E. (1967). *The remediation of learning disabilities: A handbook of psychoeducational resource programs.* Palo Alto, CA: Fearon.

Vance, H. R., & Pumariega, A. J. (Guest eds.) (1999). School-based mental health services [Special issue]. *Psychology in the Schools, 36*(5).

Van Sickle, J. H., Witmer, L., & Ayres, L. P. (1911). *Provision for exceptional children in the public schools.* (U.S. Bureau of Education Bulletin No. 14). Washington, DC: Government Printing Office.

van Strein, P. J. (1998). Early applied psychology between essentialism and pragmatism: The dynamics of theory, tools, and clients. *History of Psychology, 1,* 205-234.

Veatch, B. A. (1978). *Historical and demographic influences in the development of a situation specific model of school psychological services.* Cincinnati, OH: University of Cincinnati, DAI, v39 (09), Sec. A, 5423.

Waguespack, A., Stewart, W. T., & Dupre, C. (1992). *Consulting with teachers about interventions: How much do teachers remember?* Paper presented at the annual meeting of the National Association of School Psychologists, Nashville, TN.

Waldron, N. L., McLeskey, J., Skiba, R. J., Jancaus, J., & Schulmeyer, C. (1998). High and low referring teachers: Two types of teachers-as-tests? *School Psychology International, 19,* 31-41.

Wall, W. (1955). School psychological services in Europe. In N. E. Cutts (Ed.), *School psychologists at mid-century: A report of the Thayer conference* (pp. 183-194). Washington DC: American Psychological Association.

Wall, W. (1956). *Psychological services for schools.* New York: University Press for UNESCO Institute of Education.

Wallin, J. E. W. (1914). *The mental health of the school child.* New Haven, CT: Yale University Press.

Wallin, J. E. W. (1919). The field of the clinical psychologist and the kind of training needed by the psychological examiner. *School and Society, 9,* 463-470.

Wallin, J. E. W. (1920). The problems confronting a psycho-educational clinic in a large municipality. *Mental Hygiene, 4,* 103-136.

Wallin, J. E. W., & Ferguson, D. G. (1967). The development of school psycho logical services. In J. F. Magary (Ed.), *School psychological services in theory and practice: A handbook* (pp. 1-29). Englewood Cliffs, NJ: Prentice Hall.

Walter, R. (1925). The functions of a school psychologist. *American Education, 29,* 167-170.

Watkins, J. E. (1900, December). What may happen in the next hundred years. *The Ladies Home Journal.* For a popular analysis of this, see Roberts, R. (1993–1994). 20th century predictions: What came true, what didn't—and why. *The Elks Magazine, 72*(6), 30-41.

Watkins, C. E., Tipton, R. M., Manus, M., & Hunton-Shoup, J. (1991). Role relevance and role engagement in contemporary school psychology. *Professional Psychology: Research and Practice, 22,* 328-332.

Wechsler, D. (1996). *WISC-III Manual Canadian Supplement.* Toronto: The Psychological Corporation

Wechsler, S., & Oakland, T. (1990). Preventive strategies for promoting the education of low income Brazilian children: Implications for school psychologists from other Third World nations. *School Psychology International, 11,* 83-90.

Weininger, O. (1971). The school psychologist as chameleon. *Canadian Counsellor, 5*(2), 125-134.

Weiss, L. G., Saklofske, D. H., Prifitera, A. Chen, H. Y., & Hildebrand, D. K. (1999). The calculation of the WISC-III General Ability Index using Canadian norms. *Canadian Journal of School Psychology, 14*(2), 1-10.

Wells, P. D., & Fagan, T. K. (1999). APA accreditation of school psychology training programs: Does it lead to superior outcomes for graduates? Submitted.

Whelan, T., & Carlson, C. (1986). Books in school psychology: 1970 to the present. *Professional School Psychology, 1,* 279-289.

Whipple, G. M. (1914). *Manual of mental and physical tests: Part 1: Simpler processes.* Baltimore, MD: Warwick & York.

Whipple, G. M. (1915). *Manual of mental and physical tests: Part 2: Complex processes.* Baltimore, MD: Warwick & York.

White, M. A. (1968-1969). Will school psychology exist? *Journal of School Psychology, 7*(2), 53-57.

Wilczenski, F. L., Phelps, L., & Lawler, M. (1992). Publishing guidelines for school psychologists. *Communiqué, 21*(4), 14.

Will, M. (1989, January). *The role of school psychology in providing services to all children.* Washington, DC: U.S. Department of Education, Office of Special Programs and Rehabilitative Services.

Williams, K. J., & Williams, G. M. (1992). Applications of social psychology to school employee evaluation and appraisal. In F. J. Medway & T. P. Cafferty (Eds.), *School psychology: A social psychological perspective* (pp. 333-354). Hillsdale, NJ: Erlbaum.

Wilson, M. S., & Reschly, D. J. (1995). Gender and school psychology: Issues, questions, and answers. *School Psychology Review, 24*(1), 45-61

Wilson, M., & Reschly, D. (1996). Assessment in school psychology training and practice. *School Psychology Review, 25,* 9-23.

Wise, P. S. (1985). School psychologists' ratings of stressful events. *Journal of School Psychology, 23*, 31-41.

Wise, P. S. (1986). *Better parent conferences: A manual for school psychologists.* Washington, DC: National Association of School Psychologists.

Wise, P. S. (1995). Communicating with parents. In A. Thomas and J. Grimes (Eds.), *Best Practices in School Psychology: III* (pp. 279-287). Bethesda, MD: National Association of School Psychologists.

Wise, P. S. Smead, V. S., & Huebner, E. S. (1987). Crisis intervention: Involvement and training needs of school psychology personnel. *Journal of School Psychology, 25*, 185-187.

Wishy, B. (1968). *The child and the republic: The dawn of modern American child nurture.* Philadelphia: University of Pennsylvania Press.

Witmer, L. (1897). The organization of practical work in psychology. *Psychological Review, 4*, 116-117.

Witmer, L. (1907). Clinical psychology. *The Psychological Clinic, 1*(1), 1-9.

Witt, J. C., & Elliott, S. N. (1985). Acceptability of classroom intervention strategies. In T. R. Kratochwill (Ed.), *Advances in school psychology: Vol. 4* (pp. 251-288). Hillsdale, NJ: Erlbaum.

Wodrich, D. L. (1988). School psychological practice in a department of pediatrics. *School Psychology Review, 17,* 411-415.

Wonderly, D. M., & Mcloughlin, C. (1984). Contractual services: A viable alternative. *School Psychology International, 5*(2), 107-113.

Woody, R. H. (1998). Copyright law in school psychology training. *Trainers' Forum, 16*(3), 1, 4-7.

Woody, R. H., & Davenport, J. (1998). The *Blueprint I* revisited: Training and practice in school psychology. *Psychology in the Schools, 35*(1), 49-55.

Woody, R. H., LaVoie, J. C., & Epps, S. (1992). *School psychology: A developmental and social systems approach.* Boston: Allyn & Bacon.

Wrobel, G., & Krieg, F. (1998, September). Health care report. *NASP Executive Committee Minutes.* Washington, DC: National Association of School Psychologists.

Yoshida, R. K., Fenton, K. S., Maxwell, J. P., & Kaufman, M. J. (1978). Group decision making in the planning team process: Myth or reality? *Journal of School Psychology, 16*, 237-244.

Ysseldyke, J. E. (1986). Current practice in school psychology. In S. N. Elliott & J. C. Witt (Eds.), *The delivery of psychological services in schools: Concepts, processes, and issues* (pp. 2—51). Hillsdale, NJ: Erlbaum.

Ysseldyke, J. E., & Christenson, S. L. (1988). Linking assessment to intervention. In J. L. Graden, J. E. Zins, & M. J. Curtis (Eds.), *Alternative educational delivery Systems: Enhancing instructional options for all students* (pp. 91-109). Washington, DC: National Association of School Psychologists.

Ysseldyke, J., Dawson, P., Lehr, C., Reschly, D., Reynolds, M., & Telzrow, C. (1997). *School psychology: A blueprint for training and practice II.* Bethesda, MD: National Association of School Psychologists.

Ysseldyke, J., & Elliott, J. (1999). Effective instructional practices: Implications for assessing educational environments. In C. R. Reynolds and T. B.

Gutkin (Eds.), *The handbook of school psychology* (3rd ed.) (pp. 497-518). New York: John Wiley.

Ysseldyke, J. E., & Weinberg, R. A. (Eds.). (1981). The future of psychology in the schools: Proceedings of the Spring Hill Symposium [Special issue]. *School Psychology Review, 10*(2).

Zelizer, V. A. (1985). *Pricing the priceless child: The changing social value of children.* New York: Basic Books.

Zins, J. (1982). *Accountability for school psychologists: Developing trends.* Washington, DC: National Association of School Psychologists.

Zins. J. E. (1990). Best practices in developing accountability procedures. In A. Thomas & J. Grimes (Eds.), *Best practices in school psychology II* (pp. 323-337). Washington, DC: National Association of School Psychologists.

Zins, J. E., Curtis, M. J., Graden, J. L., & Ponti, C. R. (1988). *Helping students succeed in the regular classroom: A guide for developing intervention assistance programs.* San Francisco: Jossey-Bass.

Zins, J. E., & Erchul, W. P. (1995). School consultation. In A. Thomas & J. Grimes (Eds.), *Best practices in school psychology III* (pp. 609-623). Washington, DC: National Association of School Psychologists.

Zins, J. E., & Halsell, A. (1986). Status of ethnic minority group members in school psychology training programs. *School Psychology Review, 15,* 76-83.

Zins, J., Kratochwill, T., & Elliott, S. (Eds.). (1993). *Handbook of consultation services for children.* San Francisco: Jossey-Bass.

Zins, J. E., Maher, C. A., Murphy, J. J., & Wess, B. P. (1988). The peer support group: A means to facilitate professional development. *School Psychology Review, 17,* 138-146.

Zins, J. E., & Ponti, C. R. (1990). Best practices in school-based consultation. In A. Thomas & J. Grimes (Eds.), *Best practices in school psychology II* (pp. 673-693). Washington, DC: National Association of School Psychologists.

Zirkel, P. A. (1992). Confident about confidences? *Phi Delta Kappan, 73,* 732-734.

Index

Language: 303, 337338, 355, 377-378, 434, 436-437,
442-443, 445, 452, 464, 467, 471, 475
Larry P. v. Riles (1972, 1974, 1979, 1984): 55, 115,
274
Latchkey kids: 114
Latvia: 362
Learning disabilities: 56, 148, 174, 189, 338, 369,
380, 386
Least restrictive environment: 32, 63, 90, 272-273
Legal issues: 300
Legislation: 13, 55-56, 71, 74, 77, 94, 101, 117, 132,
230, 232, 255, 259, 262, 271-273, 277-279,
284, 292, 326-327, 337, 352, 372, 387
Length of contract: 18
Letters of recommendation: 160, 249, 253, 289, 293
Liability insurance: 19, 58, 271-272
Liaison role: 104, 145, 308, 315
Licensure: 323, 367, 370, 432, 444, 450, 475
Literature (school psychology): 6, 13-14, 17, 20, 24-
25, 38-39, 48-49, 61-62, 65, 108, 116, 146,
149-151, 165, 168, 180, 225, 271, 275,
277, 367, 374, 389, 392, 406, 408, 423,
444, 473
Litigation: 55, 63, 77, 229, 232, 255, 262, 268, 271-
272, 274, 278-279
L'ordre des Psychologues du Quebec (OPQ): 320,
325, 341, 344
Luckey, B.,: 40, 385, 415

Magary, J.: 4, 53, 62, 161, 187, 386-387, 424
Mainstreaming: 32, 63, 90-91, 273, 401
Manitoba: 277, 314-315, 321, 327-329, 340-342,
343, 345, 347, 351, 354
Manitoba Association of School Psychologists
(MASP): 317, 343
Marital status: 109
Marshall v. Georgia (1984, 1985): 116
Maslach Burnout Inventory: 300
Massachusetts: 29, 45, 224
Mattie T. v. Holladay (1979): 274
Maxfield, F.: 185
McGill University: 216, 313, 320, 324-325, 332,
349, 421
Medicine and medical settings: 31, 50, 59, 216, 305,
308, 334, 357
Memorial University: 325
Memphis city schools: 83-86, 94
Mental health: 2, 32, 52, 69, 71, 73, 83-87, 105,
139, 141, 148, 151, 186, 260, 307, 309,
332, 336, 346, 402, 411, 446, 471
centers: 7-8, 45, 52, 85, 98-99, 102, 211-212
consultation: 2, 12, 246, 271, 425
service for schools: 27, 36, 104, 185, 358, 426
Mental retardation: 31, 79, 366, 406
Merrill, M.: 44, 46
Mills v. Board of Education for the District of Columbia
(1972, 1980): 274
Minority representation in school psychology: 188
Mississaugua Conference: 319
Mount St. Vincent University: 216, 325
Mullen, F.: 24, 45, 160, 361-362
Multidisciplinary teams (staffings): 103-104
Multifactored assessment: 125

National Association of School Psychologists (NASP):
190, 227, 232, 235, 280, 285, 317, 320,
344, 362, 375, 417, 421, 423, 461, 463
Communiqué: 17, 61, 135, 144, 224-225, 267,
271, 273, 278, 305, 417
Directory of Graduate Training Programs: 9
membership of: 13-14
*Standards for Provision of School
Psychological Services:* 260, 266, 462
*Standards for Training and Field Placement
Programs in School Psychology:* 283, 285
National Association of State Consultants for School
Psychological Services: 60, 225, 397
National Council for Accreditation of Teacher
Education (NCATE): 54, 60, 206, 223, 231, 235
National Education Association (NEA): 94, 423
National Organization for Victim Assistance (NOVA):
144
National School Psychology Certification System
(NCS): 221
National School Psychology Examination: 26, 61, 252
National School Psychology Inservice Training
Network: 57, 108, 388, 412
Neuropsychology: 9, 410
New Brunswick: 315, 321, 325, 329, 336, 338-340,
342-343, 354, 425
New York City: 25, 40, 45, 48, 214
Public Schools: 43
New York State: 47, 184, 186
New York University: 25, 42, 184-185, 214, 426
New Zealand: 366, 380
Newfoundland: 212, 315, 321, 327-329, 340, 342,
344, 347, 354
Newland, T. E.: 21, 185
Nonschool practice: 41, 50, 57, 60, 211, 219, 245-
248, 253, 397
Normative deviance: 399
Northwest Territories (Canada): 314, 327, 340, 342
Nova Scotia: 212, 313, 315, 327, 340, 342

Occupational therapists: 344
Office of Special Education and Rehabilitative
Services (OSERS): 64
Ohio: 25-26, 35, 134, 213, 257, 282, 289, 361
Ohio School Psychologists Association: 25
Ohio State University: 16, 42, 45, 214
Olympia conference: 338
Ontario: 425
Ontario Association of Consultants, Counsellors,
Psychometrists, and Psychotherapists
(OACCPP): 317
Ontario Institute for Studies in Education: 316, 425
Organizational consultation: 6, 65, 141, 144-145,
151, 172
Organizational development: 10, 47, 53, 145, 151,
201, 217, 305, 366, 405
Outcome data: 160, 172, 174-176, 179-180,
242, 399

P.A.R.C. v. Commonwealth of Pennsylvania
(1971, 1972): 274
P.A.S.E. v. Hannon (1980): 115, 274
Paraprofessionals: 114, 175, 225, 227, 250, 371
Parent conferences: 171-172